FAIRNESS
—— VERSUS ——
WELFARE

FAIRNESS

—— VERSUS ——

WELFARE

LOUIS KAPLOW

STEVEN SHAVELL

HARVARD UNIVERSITY PRESS

Cambridge, Massachusetts, and London, England

First Harvard University Press paperback edition, 2006

Library of Congress Cataloging-in-Publication Data
Kaplow, Louis.
Fairness versus welfare / Louis Kaplow and Steven Shavell.
p. cm.
Includes bibliographical references and index.
ISBN-13 978-0-674-00622-5 (cloth)
ISBN-10 0-674-00622-4 (cloth)
ISBN-13 978-0-674-02364-2 (pbk.)
ISBN-10 0-674-02364-1 (pbk.)
1. Fairness. 2. Ethics. 3. Justice. 4. Social policy. 5. Law and ecomomics.
I. Shavell, Steven, 1946– II. Title

K247.K37 2002
340'.11—dc21   2001051527

To my wife, Jody Forchheimer,
and to my children, Irene and Leah

LOUIS KAPLOW

□

To my children, Amy and Robert

STEVEN SHAVELL

SUMMARY OF CONTENTS

CONTENTS

PART TWO ☐ ANALYSIS

PART THREE □ EXTENSIONS

PROLOGUE

In this book, we ask what criteria ought to guide social decisionmaking. Our thesis is that social decisions should be based *exclusively* on their effects on the welfare of individuals—and, accordingly, should not depend on notions of fairness, justice, or cognate concepts.

This thesis runs counter to conventional wisdom and much academic evaluation of social policy, conflicts directly with the views of most twentieth-century moral philosophers, and may well grate against the reader's intuition. For example, most individuals would accord at least some weight to the idea that punishment should fit the crime, even when the fitting punishment is not the most effective way to reduce criminal activity. And most people would favor providing a level playing field for competitors in the marketplace because fairness to participants demands it, even when it might not be most conducive to productivity.

Let us describe how we—two economists (one also a lawyer) on a law school faculty—came to develop our thesis. Our training as economists as well as our natural inclinations lead us to evaluate policies based on what ultimately matters to people, that is, on how policies affect individuals' well-being. But we have encountered particularly acute criticism of this approach in the legal academy, where invocations of fairness and justice are the norm. As a consequence, we have been thinking about and responding to the criticism since we joined the law faculty in the early 1980s. In 1995, we decided to embark on a systematic investigation of the conflict between fairness-based analysis and that grounded in an exclusive concern for individuals' well-being.

Although our initial focus in our work was on normative legal analysis, it was apparent to us from the outset that our subject is not limited to the law but rather concerns the most general questions of social policymaking and moral philosophy. Moreover, in the basic legal settings that we examine, the relevant notions of fairness are considered mainly by moral philosophers. In fact, the settings that we investigate span a number of the most basic subjects addressed in moral philosophy: What is A's obligation to B when A wrongfully injures B? When are individuals obligated to keep promises, and what duty do promisors owe to promisees when they do not? What protections should individuals receive when the state's apparatus is used to resolve disputes? When and to what extent should the state impose punishment? These questions have engaged philosophers from Aristotle to Hume and Kant, to Ross and Hare and Rawls.

In light of the foregoing, we were led to broaden and deepen our normative analysis. What we have produced, although it is framed in legal settings, is an expansive inquiry into the principles that should guide public policy. The reader might naturally wonder what makes our analysis of this subject distinctive. We believe that our book makes three types of contributions.

First, we offer a number of arguments indicating that the conflict between notions of fairness and welfare is much sharper than has been appreciated. One of our conclusions in this regard is particularly striking: Under any method of evaluating social policy that accords positive weight to a notion of fairness, there must exist situations in which *all* individuals will be made worse off. To illustrate, consider a principle of fairness under which victims have the right to obtain compensation from their injurers. Suppose that all individuals are identically situated in the sense that each is just as likely to gain as a victim (receiving compensation) as he is to lose as an injurer (paying compensation). Now, viewing the matter prospectively, before individuals know whether they will turn out to be victims or injurers, it is clearly possible that upholding the right to compensation will make everyone worse off if implementing the compensation requirement is costly. In the early stages of our research, we constructed a variety of such examples showing that endorsement of particular notions of fairness will sometimes make everyone worse off. These results, which we found somewhat surprising, led us to inquire about their generality. We subsequently developed two formal arguments, presented in this book as well as in separate articles, establishing that virtually any method of evaluation that gives weight to notions of fairness will sometimes lead to choices that make all persons worse off. (The foregoing argument and others that we offer do not apply to many principles concerning the distribution of income or well-being, which are often advanced under the rubric of fairness and justice, because they are in fact embraced by a welfare-based approach.)

This conclusion has strong implications. Most individuals—including many of the philosophers we have queried—would not readily endorse a principle of fairness if doing so implies (as it does) that it may be deemed socially good to make everyone worse off. It is, after all, difficult to understand the point of a notion of fairness if every person to whom one presumably seeks to be fair may be made worse off as a result. For the many who ground moral principles in individuals' freedom and autonomy, the foregoing is especially troublesome because it is hard to argue that all individuals, if given the opportunity, would freely choose to make themselves worse off. Furthermore, as we explain, one of the arguments underlying our conclusion poses an important challenge to those who adhere to the Golden Rule, Kant's categorical imperative, or the requirement that ethical principles be acceptable to parties situated behind a veil of ignorance.

Second, we undertake a thorough and systematic analysis of a number of notions of fairness in a variety of important, paradigmatic contexts, including, as noted, those in which one person wrongfully harms another, in which persons promise to perform contracts, in which procedures are provided for legal redress, and in which the state imposes punishment. By focusing on such basic cases, by making our analysis concrete, and by examining in detail the conditions under which implications of fairness and welfare are aligned and when they conflict, we believe that we are able to achieve a significantly better understanding of fairness-based evaluation than has been presented elsewhere. In particular, we consider at length whether the commonly proffered rationales for the notions, or others that we might imagine, can withstand scrutiny when the full ramifications of fairness principles are made clear. An additional benefit of our investigation is that very different notions of fairness are explored in parallel. Because most of our arguments apply to each of them, it appears that we have identified generic deficiencies in notions of fairness rather than merely ad hoc shortcomings of this or that notion.

Third, we consider a number of ways in which the broad appeal that many notions of fairness possess can be reconciled with our thesis that they should not be accorded independent weight in the evaluation of social policy. Most importantly, we examine the nature and origins of our moral instincts and intuitions, which provide the implicit or explicit grounding for many arguments of twentieth-century philosophers. This discussion, it should be emphasized, is descriptive and scientific in nature, not a matter of ethical theory. The subject of the origin of our moral feelings, though largely ignored in modern philosophical literature, has received substantial attention in the past from such prominent philosophers as Hume, Mill, and Sidgwick, and was explored by Darwin as well. Drawing upon these thinkers as well as modern scholars in social, cognitive, and natural sciences, we offer a synthetic, welfare-based account of the origin of notions of fairness. Specifically, we suggest that these notions, which may be inculcated or innate, have emerged because of their functional value in governing our behavior in everyday social interactions; individuals' belief in notions of fairness reduces their inclination to engage in harmful behavior and otherwise leads them to act in ways that promote human welfare.

To the extent that the welfare-based explanation for our moral instincts and intuitions is valid, it makes no sense—indeed, it would be paradoxical—to impute significance to the notions of fairness that embody them when doing so comes at the expense of human welfare. Moreover, there is an often-overlooked distinction in contexts that helps to explain why seemingly appealing notions of fairness would sometimes lead us astray in designing social policy: The underlying moral intuitions and instincts arose for the purpose of regulating behavior in informal interactions in everyday life, whereas the realm of policymaking often differs from that of everyday life in important ways that we delineate.

We hope that this book will be of interest to a wide spectrum of readers. Because our exploration of notions of fairness and welfare addresses the normative foundation of public policy, it should be relevant to the work of social scientists, policy analysts, and others who are interested in the criteria that should govern social decisions. The book should be of particular interest to moral philosophers because we take issue with many of them in a fundamental way. We have attempted to consider their writing in depth, as our notes and list of references should make evident, and we relate our thesis to a wide range of basic topics in moral philosophy, including the relevance of two-level moral theories, the doctrine of double effect, the meaning of well-being, the problem of objectionable preferences, and the permissibility of ever punishing the innocent.

ACKNOWLEDGMENTS

We have accumulated many debts in the course of our work on this book. First, we wish to acknowledge the numerous colleagues, both at our own institution and elsewhere, who offered us comments, references, and constructive criticism. With apologies to those we may have omitted, they were: Larry Alexander, Patrick Atiyah, Randy Barnett, Brian Barry, Lucian Bebchuk, Eric Bilsky, David Charny, Jules Coleman, Robert Cooter, David Cope, Michele Cotton, David Dolinko, Robert Ellickson, Richard Fallon, Daniel Farber, George Fletcher, Barbara Fried, Jesse Fried, Daniel Friedmann, Gerald Frug, Nuno Garoupa, Jeffrey Gordon, Keith Hylton, Howell Jackson, Christine Jolls, Avery Katz, Gregory Keating, Mark Kelman, Lewis Kornhauser, Mark Lemley, Richard McAdams, Daniel Meltzer, Thomas Miceli, Liam Murphy, Richard Musgrave, Jeffrey O'Connell, Jeremy Paul, Eric Posner, Richard Posner, Eric Rasmusen, Judith Resnik, Andrei Shleifer, Kenneth Simons, William Stuntz, Cass Sunstein, Jeremy Waldron, Alvin Warren, Alan Wertheimer, Lucie White, and Benjamin Ziporsky. We also wish to express our appreciation for the efforts of university press reviewers (one of whom, we learned through correspondence, was Jonathan Baron) for unusually extensive and insightful comments, some covering the entire manuscript, including many of the notes.

In addition, we presented most of the chapters, often at an early stage, at academic seminars or conferences. We are grateful to the organizers of these events and to participants, who were generous with their time and criticism; these experiences were instrumental in guiding our further research and revision. Hosting organizations and institutions were: the American Association of Law Schools (annual meeting), the American Law and

Economics Association (annual meetings), Boston University, University of California at Berkeley, University of California at Los Angeles, University of Chicago, Columbia University, the European Association of Law and Economics (annual meeting), Fordham University, George Mason University, Georgetown University, Harvard University, University of Michigan, National Bureau of Economic Research, New York University, Northwestern University, University of Pennsylvania, University of Southern California, Stanford University, University of Toronto, Vanderbilt University, University of Virginia, and Yale University.

As will be apparent to the reader, despite our extensive personal efforts to engage the literature in the various fields relevant to our project, we could not possibly have completed our work without the help of many talented research assistants. Again with apologies to any whom we have overlooked, they were: Scott Angstreich, Sarah Apsel, Alison Aubry, David Bailey, Monika Bickert, Jonathan Chan, Susan Chen, Thomas Cheng, Jonathan Cohn, Kurt Dudas, Josh Feltman, Ted Folkman, Adam Forchheimer, Edward Greim, Sean Griffith, Matthew Hellman, Bert Huang, Benjamin Keith, Clint Keller, Alon Klement, Kahyeong Lee, Allon Lifshitz, Heather Mahar, Jason Mendro, Steven Mitby, Michael Nunnelley, David Olson, J. J. Prescott, Jeffrey Rowes, Holger Spamann, Eric Stock, Neill Tseng, Serrin Turner, and Josh Wolson.

Our undertaking could not have been successful without a range of additional support. In this regard, we wish to acknowledge the personal encouragement of our dean and friend, Robert Clark, over the many years that we have worked on our manuscript. Of the secretaries, library staff, and others at the law school who have contributed to our efforts, we especially wish to recognize Regina Roberts and Elizabeth Sponheim. In the later stages of the work, we also were fortunate to benefit from the extensive and expert editorial assistance of Matthew Seccombe, Laura Sigman, and student editors of the *Harvard Law Review,* where a version of the manuscript was published in volume 114 (2001). In addition, we appreciate the contributions of Michael Aronson as well as the editorial and production staff of the Harvard University Press. For financial support, we are grateful to the John M. Olin Center for Law, Economics, and Business at Harvard Law School as well as for Harvard Law School's general research funds.

FAIRNESS

— VERSUS —

WELFARE

PART ONE

FRAMEWORK

CHAPTER I

---☐---

Introduction

This book is concerned with the principles that should guide society in its evaluation of legal policy. We consider two fundamental approaches to such normative evaluation, one based on how legal rules affect individuals' welfare and the other grounded in notions of fairness.

To illustrate these approaches, consider a proposal to replace tort liability for automobile accidents with a regime of insurance supplemented by heightened enforcement of traffic laws. Suppose that investigation showed that everyone would expect to be better off under the proposal because it would improve the comprehensiveness of victim compensation and reduce overall administrative costs, without increasing the number of accidents.[1] Under the welfare-based normative approach, the proposal would be deemed socially desirable. Under the fairness-oriented normative approach, however, the proposal might be problematic. Specifically, denying a victim the opportunity to sue a negligent injurer once an accident has happened would be regarded as unfair under the principle of corrective justice or under the view that the injurer violated the victim's right to bodily integrity.[2]

Our central claim is that the welfare-based normative approach should be exclusively employed in evaluating legal rules. That is, legal rules should be selected entirely with respect to their effects on the well-being of individu-

---

1. We do not adopt any particular view about the effects that the proposal actually would have. For further discussion and references to the literature on related tort reforms, see section III.F.

2. See subsection III.B.1.

als in society. This position implies that notions of fairness like corrective justice should receive no independent weight in the assessment of legal rules. (Thus, if the tort reform proposal would have the effects that we hypothesized, it would be considered socially desirable.) After stating the reasons that lead us to our basic conclusion, we amplify and illustrate our analysis through systematic examination of a number of clearly specified, paradigmatic situations in major areas of law. As will become evident from our consideration of legal problems and from an appreciation of the inclusiveness of our approach, the thesis that we advance is not an extreme one, although it will be seen to have important implications for the analysis of legal policy.[3]

We begin in chapter II by discussing the method of policy assessment that depends solely on individuals' well-being, which economists refer to as welfare economics. The welfare economic conception of individuals' well-being is a comprehensive one. It recognizes not only individuals' levels of material comfort, but also their degree of aesthetic fulfillment, their feelings for others, and anything else that they might value, however intangible.[4] The welfare economic notion of individuals' well-being incorporates compensatory goals, because the prospect of compensation raises the well-being of potential victims of harm if they are risk averse and uninsured. Moreover, the economic notion of social welfare is one that is concerned explicitly with the distribution of income.[5] Welfare economics thus accommodates all factors that are relevant to individuals' well-being and to its distribution. Conversely, welfare economics omits any factor that does not affect any indi-

---

3. Our thesis is entirely normative in nature; it is a claim about how legal policy analysis should be performed, not a (positive) claim about how such analysis actually is undertaken or about the content of existing legal doctrine.

4. Furthermore, we will address the manner in which issues concerning possible differences between individuals' preferences and their true well-being can be taken into account under the framework of welfare economics. See section VIII.B, discussing imperfect information, changes in preferences, objectionable preferences, and related matters.

5. The reasons that welfare economics incorporates distributive concerns are sketched in subsection II.A.3. Some readers may find a tension between our critique of notions of fairness and our endorsement of distributive concerns, which are often articulated under the rubric of fairness. As we explain later in this introduction and elaborate in subsection II.B.1, our critique is limited to notions of fairness that give weight to factors unrelated to individuals' well-being, whereas many principles of equity in distribution do not depend on such factors, but rather depend exclusively on well-being. For further elaboration, see subsections II.A.2 and II.A.3. Accordingly, for purposes of this book, we define as notions of fairness only those notions that give weight to factors that are independent of well-being.

vidual's well-being. Therefore, advocating the exclusive use of welfare economics, as we do, is equivalent to adopting the moral position that the design of the legal system should depend solely on concerns for human welfare.

The normative framework of welfare economics, as just described, differs from what many view as the normative economic approach. Under a common understanding of normative economic analysis, legal rules are assessed by reference to wealth maximization or efficiency, criteria that many construe as omitting important aspects of individuals' well-being and as ignoring distributive concerns. We defend not this popular conception of the normative economic approach,[6] but rather the encompassing framework of welfare economics.

After explaining the nature of the welfare economic approach, we consider methods of evaluating legal rules based on notions of fairness, taken in this book to embrace justice, rights, and cognate concepts.[7] Such evaluation characteristically involves the examination of particular features of situations to determine what legal rule is most fitting according to a given principle of fairness. Thus, as in our illustration, if an accident has occurred, an analyst might ask whether imposing liability on the injurer would comport with a concept of corrective justice in light of various aspects of the injurer's act.[8]

In this book, we focus on analysts' use of notions of fairness for reasons that are not reducible to concerns about individuals' well-being. That is, we emphasize analysts' adoption of notions of fairness as *independent* evaluative

---

6. The degree to which the popular conception accurately characterizes actual work in normative economic analysis of law is an issue that we do not directly consider in this book, although our discussion in subsection II.A.3 sheds some light on it.

7. Although "fairness," "justice," "rights," and similar terms are often used in different senses, it will not be necessary to distinguish among them for our purposes. See note 48 in chapter II.

8. As we elaborate in subsection II.B.1, most notions of fairness are, as moral philosophers would term them, nonconsequentialist in character. That is, the notions determine which legal rule is best based not on the consequences of adopting the rule for a class of acts, but rather based directly on what are deemed to be relevant characteristics of the acts in question. Welfare economics, by contrast, is consequentialist in nature, because welfare economic assessments of legal rules depend (entirely) on the effects of the rules. Welfare economics, it should be noted, is a particular species of consequentialism, for it is based (exclusively) on a particular set of consequences, namely, those that bear on individuals' well-being. (Furthermore, we note that utilitarianism, although sometimes used broadly to refer to welfarism, more classically denotes a particular form of welfarism, wherein distributive judgments are based on the principle that the sum of individuals' well-being should be maximized. For elaboration on the relationship between distributive judgments and welfare economics, see subsections II.A.2 and II.A.3.)

principles—principles employed to assess the desirability of legal rules without regard to the effects of the rules on individuals' well-being.[9] An analyst who accords independent significance to corrective justice would deem it important to impose liability on certain injurers because they acted wrongfully, without reference to whether liability might deter harmful acts or otherwise advance individuals' well-being.

Before proceeding, we wish to clarify two aspects of our definition of notions of fairness. First, many analysts who view notions of fairness as independent evaluative principles would also accord weight to individuals' well-being when assessing legal policy. For example, such analysts would deem imposing liability on injurers who acted wrongfully to be valuable in itself, but they would also consider relevant any effect of rules of liability on individuals' well-being; one possibility is that fairness and welfare would be traded off in some manner. We include such mixed forms of evaluation in our definition of notions of fairness, and we will be concerned with these notions when they lead one to choose policies different from those that one would choose if exclusive regard were given to individuals' well-being. Second, some analysts employ principles that they describe as involving fairness but that, on examination, relate solely to individuals' well-being; thus, these principles are encompassed by welfare economics. For purposes of this book, we define notions of fairness to exclude such principles. We have no fundamental dispute with those who agree with the substance of our position but choose to express their views using different language; we obviously are concerned not with terminology but rather with the substance of evaluative principles. In particular, we care about whether a principle depends exclusively on individuals' well-being or instead accords weight to other factors, as all of the notions of fairness that we examine in this book appear to do.[10]

Following the discussion of the nature of the two normative approaches, we address the central question of which ought to be employed. Should the

---

9. As should be clear from our discussions of particular notions of fairness in chapters III–VI, the dominant use of notions of fairness in legal policy analysis appears to be as independent evaluative principles. Other uses of notions of fairness—which are related to individuals' well-being (as possible tastes individuals might have or as proxy principles used to identify welfare-promoting policies)—will be noted later in this introduction.

10. We do, however, have practical concerns about terminology. As we discuss in subsection VII.B.2 and suggest elsewhere, we believe that the quality of policy analysis will tend to be improved if analysts are explicit about their objectives. The language of fairness (and that of justice and rights) can be problematic in this regard because such language has many meanings, some of which turn out to be opposed to individuals' well-being.

evaluation of legal policy be guided by welfare economics or by principles of fairness? In answering this question, the first element of our analysis is an explanation of why pursuing notions of fairness may reduce individuals' well-being—and always does so when ideas of fairness lead one to choose a different legal rule from that prescribed by welfare economics. The second aspect of our analysis is an attempt to determine whether there are sound reasons to promote notions of fairness at the expense of individuals' well-being; after reflection on the situations examined and on the relevant literature, we are unable to find reasons that seem satisfactory.[11]

In chapters III–VI, we develop these two themes by examining fundamental legal problems in the areas of torts, contracts, legal procedure, and law enforcement. In each situation that we consider, we initially ascertain how pertinent legal rules affect parties' behavior.[12] We next identify which legal rules are best according to welfare economics and which are best according to the principles of fairness that seem naturally relevant, including many principles discussed by commentators.[13] We then turn our attention in each case to the two primary arguments that underlie our thesis that legal policy assessment should be premised on welfare economics rather than on notions of fairness.

Our first argument, that advancing notions of fairness reduces individuals' well-being, is in fact tautological on a general level. By definition, welfare economic analysis is concerned with individuals' well-being, whereas fairness-based analysis (to the extent that it differs from welfare economic analysis) is concerned with adherence to certain stipulated principles that do not depend on individuals' well-being. Thus, promoting notions of fairness may well involve a reduction in individuals' well-being.

Nevertheless, the conclusion that pursuing notions of fairness is necessarily at the expense of individuals' well-being is not usually emphasized, and often is not even explicitly acknowledged, by analysts who employ notions of fairness to evaluate legal policy. Likewise, although the existence of a tension

11. We discuss the relationship between our book and Posner's recent criticisms of the application of academic moral philosophy (much of which is concerned with notions of fairness) to the law in note 87 in chapter II.

12. In doing so, we find it convenient to use the standard, stylized assumption of rational, maximizing actors that economists employ. But our conclusions about welfare economics and fairness-based analysis do not depend on this assumption. For further elaboration, see subsection VIII.D.5.

13. We consider the writing of legal commentators who examine principles of fairness in particular legal contexts because this scholarship is of direct relevance to our arguments. In some fields, the law-oriented literature on fairness draws heavily upon related philosophical work, to which we also refer, sometimes extensively.

between pursuit of notions of fairness and concern for individuals' well-being is sometimes noted in general philosophical literature, the true extent of the opposition is rarely addressed. In other words, the basic conflict between notions of fairness and individuals' well-being is not one that is well appreciated. By presenting the reader with a range of important legal contexts, in each of which individuals' well-being is shown to be reduced if the relevant fairness principles are given evaluative importance, we hope that the problematic implications of fairness-based legal policy analysis will come to be better understood.

The foregoing difficulty with fairness-based analysis is especially striking in a number of paradigmatic situations in which we demonstrate that promoting notions of fairness would make *everyone* worse off.[14] Suppose, for example, that all individuals would fare better under strict liability than under the negligence rule.[15] If the negligence rule were nevertheless adopted because an onlooking analyst deemed it to be more fair, all individuals would be made worse off than they would be under strict liability, the rule that would be favored under welfare economics. The point that giving weight to fairness in the choice of legal rules may harm all persons should be deeply troubling to analysts who suggest that notions of fairness ought to serve as independent evaluative principles.

The second part of our general argument involves, as noted, a consideration of whether there exist sound rationales that can justify pursuing notions of fairness at the expense of individuals' well-being. Of course, we cannot disprove the existence of such rationales through deductive reasoning.[16] We can, however, attempt to identify plausible justifications for notions of fairness by examining the literature that advances them and by reflecting on the situations that we analyze. When we do so, we discover very little basis for the use of notions of fairness as independent evaluative principles. Indeed, some writing on notions of fairness takes the principles to be self-evident and thus not needing any explicit justification. Other writing

---

14. In each area that we examine, we show that it is possible that pursuit of the standard notions of fairness may make everyone worse off. Indeed, as we discuss in subsection II.C.1, this possibility is general: It arises with respect to *any* notion of fairness.

15. See, for example, subsection III.C.1(c), describing a case in which individuals are injurers and victims equally often and strict liability involves lower legal costs than the negligence rule but has the same behavioral effects.

16. Nevertheless, our preceding point does seem to rule out certain types of rationales that may be offered for notions of fairness. This claim can be appreciated by posing the question: To whom is one being fair? That basic question cannot be answered unproblematically for any notion of fairness because, as we show, pursuing a notion of fairness will sometimes make everyone worse off.

suggests that notions of fairness are valid because they are in accord with our instincts or intuitions. However, it is unclear as a logical matter how such an alignment provides an affirmative warrant for giving independent weight to notions of fairness. Moreover, the origins of our moral instincts and intuitions may reside substantially in their tendency to advance individuals' well-being; if so, it would not make sense to employ them to support notions of fairness in cases in which the notions are opposed to individuals' well-being.[17]

Other features of claims about notions of fairness raise difficulties. For example, many analysts of criminal law endorse notions of retributive justice, under which wrongful acts are supposed to be punished to a fitting extent by the state. Yet the most common justifications offered for retributive justice refer to the need to restore some sort of moral balance in the world. As we elaborate, this line of reasoning seems to rely more on a conclusory metaphor than on implications derived from argument in the usual sense. Retributive theorists assert as well that punishment should follow automatically from the commission of a wrongful act, but they fail to offer a theory of which acts are wrongful, and they also would agree that many acts that all acknowledge to be wrongful (such as lying) should not ordinarily be punished by the state. Thus, it is often difficult even to identify the content of leading notions of fairness. In addition, many notions of fairness lead the analyst to adopt an ex post perspective (asking, for example, what punishment is appropriate given that a crime has been committed and the criminal has been apprehended and convicted). Use of the ex post perspective tends to diminish the importance of outcomes that did not occur but might have, even when those other outcomes were more likely (most criminals go scot-free), and also leads us to ignore the effect of the legal rules under consideration on individuals' behavior (whether crimes are committed). Such an incomplete view is unlikely to lead to sound policy choices. In addition, it often implies that the rule deemed more fair may result in more unfair outcomes or in a greater incidence of the behavior whose wrongfulness underlies the motivation of the theory (it is, after all, wrongs that give rise to the need for retribution). We find that similar difficulties exist with regard to a wide range of notions of fairness in a variety of legal settings.

For the foregoing reasons, we believe that analysts who accord independent weight to notions of fairness bear a substantial burden of explanation.

---

17. We will suggest that our moral instincts and intuitions are an aspect of the apparatus of social norms, as we discuss later in this introduction and in section II.D, and as we elaborate in each legal context that we consider, especially in our analysis of theories of retributive justice in section VI.D.

They must provide the reasons why a society should willingly make its members—possibly all of them—worse off in order to advance a particular conception of fairness.[18]

The main claim of our book raises the question of why notions of fairness are so widely employed and respected if they are, as we argue, inappropriate in normative legal analysis. An important part of our suggested answer
is that principles of fairness are appealing because they often correspond to
internalized social norms (which, as will become clear, must be distinguished
from principles that are appropriate to employ in legal policy assessment).[19]
Internalized social norms—such as keeping promises and holding wrongdoers accountable for their actions—are maxims that people want to obey
because the maxims have been inculcated in them or are inborn. These social
norms appear attractive to us not only because they are internalized, but
also because they possess instrumental social value: They guide individuals'
decisions and curb opportunistic behavior in everyday life. Indeed, social
norms are often instilled in us or have otherwise evolved precisely because
they promote well-being. In light of their internalized character and instrumental value, it is not surprising that, when individuals engage in legal policy
analysis, they attach importance to social norms and, accordingly, to notions
of fairness that seem to embody such norms.

We examine the implications of the correspondence between social
norms and notions of fairness initially in section II.D and then in chapter
VII, where we directly consider the relevance of our analysis to the work of
legal academics and other legal policy analysts. We also apply this analysis
in each of the particular legal contexts that we study.[20] We emphasize that
it would be a logical error to take the appeal of notions of fairness, which
we suggest is based on their roots in social norms, as a justification for ac-

---

18. As our discussion of the relevant literature reveals, some analysts do not really purport
to provide an explicit, affirmative warrant for notions of fairness. Rather, they seem concerned
with matters of definition or with what are really positive inquiries, such as investigations of
what principles are implicit in prevailing legal doctrines or in common intuitions. To the
extent that some literature on notions of fairness is not concerned with normative analysis,
our criticism obviously is inapplicable. (It appears, however, that many other commentators
rely on such work to support normative positions.)

19. We also explore additional explanations for the appeal of notions of fairness. One,
noted later in this introduction, concerns the tendency of notions of fairness to serve as proxy
devices for identifying policies that advance individuals' well-being. See also subsection
II.B.2(c), suggesting that the ex post perspective of notions of fairness helps to explain their
attractiveness, and subsection VII.B.1, offering explanations for why legal policy analysts are
inclined to employ notions of fairness.

20. See section III.E, subsections IV.C.2(g), V.A.6, V.B.3(f), and section VI.D.

cording the notions independent weight in assessing legal policy.[21] That the analyst, as an individual, has in a sense been programmed to conduct his or her life in accord with social norms is not a legitimate reason for the analyst to elevate such norms to the status of independent evaluative principles for use in a qualitatively different context, the design of legal rules. Moreover, that internalized social norms appear to exist largely to promote our well-being reinforces our conclusion that it is a mistake for the analyst to treat such norms as if they were independent evaluative principles, to be pursued at the expense of our well-being.[22]

Although our thesis is that legal policy analysts should rely exclusively on welfare economics, the important role of internalized social norms suggests that the situation of legal decisionmakers, notably legislators, regulators, and judges, is more complicated than that of legal policy analysts, who are mainly academics. The reason is that legal decisionmakers must translate the advice of the analysts into policies for which the decisionmakers are generally accountable to ordinary citizens—and citizens, in turn, may be more familiar with notions of fairness.

Our discussion of internalized social norms has an additional implication, one that may result in the norms having some importance for the choice of legal rules within the framework of welfare economics, but this point must be carefully interpreted. Specifically, if individuals have internalized a social norm that is related to a notion of fairness, they may have a taste for fairness, in the sense that they may feel better off or worse off depending on whether their conception of fairness is reflected in legal rules or in the actual operation of the legal system.[23] For example, people might feel upset if wrongdoers escape punishment, quite apart from any view people might have about the effect of punishment on the crime rate. Now, any factor that influences individuals' well-being is relevant under welfare economics, and a taste for fairness is no different in this respect from a taste

21. We wish to state clearly, however, that our argument in no way suggests that social norms are inappropriate in everyday life—the context in which they arose—or that efforts by educational and other institutions to inculcate or improve social norms are undesirable.

22. When the origin of an internalized social norm has a different explanation—for example, a norm may have arisen to advance one group's self-interest at another's expense, see note 92 in chapter II—the argument that there is no foundation for viewing the norm as an appropriate criterion for legal policy assessment is straightforward.

23. See note 10 in chapter II, noting the relationship between tastes for fairness and the expressive function of law. Additionally, legal rules themselves may affect individuals' preferences for ideas of fairness. See subsection II.D.2. We discuss how welfare economics addresses the more general phenomenon that legal rules may affect preferences in subsections VIII.B.2 and VIII.B.3.

for a tangible good or for anything else. Observe, though, that the welfare economic significance of a notion of fairness depends directly on the strength of individuals' actual tastes for it and is thus an entirely empirical issue.[24] The status of a concept of fairness under welfare economics is therefore quite distinct from that of an independent evaluative principle as envisioned by most moral philosophers and legal academics.

There is another respect in which notions of fairness may be relevant under welfare economics: They may serve as proxy devices to aid in identifying legal policies that tend to advance individuals' well-being. For instance, corrective justice requires that injurers who act wrongfully be held liable for the harm they cause, but imposing such liability may also deter harm, which would raise individuals' well-being. Indeed, given that notions of fairness often correspond to social norms that themselves serve to enhance welfare, it is not surprising that pursuing notions of fairness often promotes individuals' well-being (regardless of whether this is an analyst's intention in employing such notions). As a result, there will be some alignment between the policies favored under the two methods of assessment, which reduces the overall tension between the two approaches and helps to explain why notions of fairness have appeal—or, at a minimum, why they do not appear problematic on their face. This overlap between the two approaches will, of course, be incomplete. Because a concept of fairness is only a proxy method for identifying policies that foster the well-being of individuals, an analyst who focuses on fairness principles instead of engaging in explicit welfare economic analysis could well be led astray, as we will suggest may have happened in many areas of legal policy.[25] Also, we observe that there is an important conceptual difference between an analyst's employing a notion of fairness for the sole purpose of attempting to determine which policies enhance individuals' well-being, in which case there would be no conflict between the analyst's ultimate goals and those of welfare economics, and the analyst's using notions of fairness as independent evaluative principles, to be upheld even at the expense of individuals' well-being.

We round out our analysis in chapter VIII, where we offer a series of observations about the breadth and soundness of welfare economics and address common criticisms of normative law and economics. In the course of our discussion, we consider, among other issues, the relationship between

24. We comment on ways to measure such tastes and on factors bearing on the likelihood that they are empirically important in subsection VIII.B.4.

25. For example, the analyst who is led to impose liability on wrongful injurers may err by overlooking alternative regimes that better deter or by failing to see that the reduction in harm is not worth the costs of achieving it.

individuals' preferences and their true well-being, concerns about inequality and bad luck, and how welfare economics can incorporate various legal institutional considerations.[26] We offer final remarks in chapter IX, where we outline a number of challenges that must be met for there to be a prima facie case for according weight to notions of fairness.[27]

26. More specifically, with regard to preferences and well-being, we discuss problems of imperfect information, the possible influence of the law on individuals' preferences, whether objectionable preferences should be trumped, and preferences for fairness per se. Concerning inequality and bad luck, we examine differences between the ex ante and the ex post views in identifying winners and losers, and inequality in the treatment that legal rules afford. (Inequality in the distribution of income is considered in subsection II.A.3.) With respect to legal institutional considerations, we address the accuracy of the legal process, the problem of controlling government officials' behavior, the legitimacy of legal institutions, and the costs of legal administration. We also analyze various concerns about the application of the economic approach, namely, those involving the valuation of life, omission of soft variables, possible costs of permitting market trade, indeterminacy of economic analysis, and problems of predicting the behavior of individuals who may not be rational, self-interested maximizers of their own well-being.

27. Individuals who wish to be selective in their reading of this book should not omit chapter II, on the nature of welfare economics and of notions of fairness; they should also read at least one of chapters III–VI, in which we develop our argument in different areas of law, and chapter VII, in which we draw out the implications of our analysis for legal academics and government decisionmakers.

———■———

Welfare Economics and Notions of Fairness

In section A of this chapter, we discuss the basic nature of welfare economics, and, in section B, we describe the fundamental difference between normative evaluation that employs notions of fairness and evaluation that is based on welfare economics. In section C, we provide an overview of our critique of the use of notions of fairness in the assessment of legal policy. Finally, in section D, we comment on the correspondence between notions of fairness and social norms of everyday life, and we consider how this correspondence helps to explain the appeal that notions of fairness possess. As we noted above, however, and as we explain in this section, the reasons that notions of fairness have some attraction do not justify the use of the notions as independent principles in evaluating legal rules.

A. Welfare Economics

In economic analysis that is designed to evaluate social policy, two steps are necessarily involved. The first is to determine the effects of the policy, that is, to undertake positive analysis, for the effects of the policy will enter into its assessment. To evaluate a legal rule concerning driving behavior, for example, one must ascertain the rule's influence on accident frequency. In chapters III–VI, where we consider various legal rules in a range of legal contexts, we begin in each instance by engaging in such positive analysis.

The second step is to evaluate the effects of the policy in order to determine its social desirability, that is, to engage in normative analysis. This step involves the framework of welfare economics and is our focus in the present section and throughout the book.[1] The hallmark of welfare economics is that policies are assessed exclusively in terms of their effects on the well-being of individuals. Accordingly, whatever is relevant to individuals' well-being is relevant under welfare economics, and whatever is unrelated to individuals' well-being is excluded from consideration under welfare economics. Because of the central importance of the concept of well-being to welfare economics and to understanding how analysis under that approach differs from analysis based on notions of fairness, we devote subsection 1 to an elaboration of the idea of well-being. There we emphasize that well-being is to be understood expansively, to include everything that is of concern to an individual.

To complete the assessment of a policy under welfare economics, it is necessary to aggregate the information about each individual's well-being to form an overall social judgment. We discuss this aspect of welfare economics in subsection 2. Because under welfare economics the evaluation of a policy depends on how it influences individuals' well-being and on nothing else, the ultimate judgment about a policy under welfare economics is clear in cases in which all individuals are made better off or all are made worse off by the policy. When, however, some individuals gain and others lose under a policy—that is, when the policy affects the distribution of income and well-being—the welfare economic approach requires one to make a distributive judgment, a point that we elaborate in subsection 3. But the assessment under welfare economics is still based exclusively on how the policy affects individuals' well-being.

Before proceeding with our discussion of the nature of welfare economics, let us consider further the example from our introduction to illustrate more concretely how welfare economic analysis of legal policy is conducted. Suppose that an analyst wishes to compare a regime of negligence-based liability for automobile accidents with a pure no-fault insurance regime.[2] Initially, the analyst would engage in positive analysis, which involves identifying differences in the effects of the regimes; under welfare economics, the relevant differences are those that pertain to individuals' well-being. Thus, the analyst would examine the influence of liability on driving behavior, taking into account that liability creates incentives to drive safely, that these incentives are mitigated

---

1. Welfare economics is the field of economics concerned with normative evaluation. For examinations of the normative foundations of welfare economics and the form of the social welfare function (which we discuss in notes 15 and 22), see Arrow (1951), Harsanyi (1977, chapter 4), and Sen (1982). For references on applied welfare economics, see Boadway and Bruce (1984), Little and Mirrlees (1974), Mueller (1989, chapter 19), Ng (1979, 2000), and Drèze and Stern (1987).

2. For further discussion and references, see section III.F.

by drivers' ownership of liability insurance, and other factors. Also, the analyst would consider that important incentives to drive safely exist even under a no-fault regime, namely, drivers' concerns about injury to themselves and about traffic laws. In addition, the analyst would identify the effects of the two regimes on the financial risks that individuals bear. Under the negligence regime, victims of automobile accidents would receive compensation through the legal system when they suffered harm due to negligence, and the extent of compensation would depend on injuring drivers' assets and liability insurance coverage; of course, victims might also possess their own first-party insurance coverage. Under a no-fault regime, all victims would be compensated through first-party insurance coverage.[3] Furthermore, the analyst would compare the aggregate administrative costs under the two regimes, that is, litigation costs plus private insurance costs under the negligence regime versus insurance costs under the no-fault regime.

After identifying the various effects of the two regimes on individuals' well-being,[4] the analyst employing welfare economics would combine them to make an overall evaluation of the regimes. For example, if individuals tend to be alike—to drive for similar amounts of time, to pose and be subject to essentially equal accident risks—the analyst would simply determine the net of all of the costs and benefits of each system and choose the one producing the greatest net benefit per person. If, however, individuals differ in relevant respects, the analyst would have to consider distributive issues as well. Suppose, for example, that adopting a no-fault regime would produce large gains for the middle class and the wealthy and result in small losses to the poor, and that the analyst viewed this distributive effect negatively. Then the analyst would favor the no-fault regime only if the adverse effect on distribution were modest relative to its other benefits, or if there were some other way (notably, through income taxes and transfer programs) to compensate the poor. Under welfare economics, the analyst would consider these and other factors relevant to individuals' well-being, but the analyst would not take into account factors that do not bear on individuals' well-being, notably, whether liability under the negligence rule is required by corrective justice or other notions of fairness that some would accord independent significance.[5]

---

3. The analyst would also consider risks borne by injurers under the two regimes; liability risks would be nonexistent under the no-fault regime but positive (although mitigated by liability insurance) under the negligence regime.

4. We do not mean to suggest that the preceding list is exhaustive; the point is that *any* effect of a regime on individuals' well-being would be included and weighted according to its magnitude.

5. To clarify, notions of fairness would not enter the welfare economic analysis as independent evaluative principles. But as we discuss in subsection 1, a notion of fairness would

1. Individuals' Well-Being

Under welfare economics, normative evaluations are based on the well-being of individuals. Economists often use the term "utility" to refer to the well-being of an individual, and, when there is uncertainty about future events, economists use an ex ante measurement of well-being, "expected utility."[6]

The notion of well-being used in welfare economics is comprehensive in nature. It incorporates in a positive way everything that an individual might value—goods and services that the individual can consume, social and environmental amenities, personally held notions of fulfillment, sympathetic feelings for others, and so forth. Similarly, an individual's well-being reflects in a negative way harms to his or her person and property, costs and inconveniences, and anything else that the individual might find distasteful. Well-being is not restricted to hedonistic and materialistic enjoyment or to any other named class of pleasures and pains.[7] The only limit on what is included

---

be given weight under welfare economics as a taste if individuals actually derive pleasure from satisfying the notion of fairness—in the sense that their well-being is higher when the law or outcomes under it reflect the notion of fairness. In this instance, satisfaction of the notion of fairness would constitute a component of well-being, rather than a principle that is traded off against well-being.

6. More precisely, the primitive element for analysis of an individual's well-being is that individual's ordering of possible outcomes. The analyst assigns numerical tags—utility indexes—to the outcomes to reflect the ordering: That is, if one outcome is preferred to another, the preferred outcome is assigned a higher utility. Thus, if outcome A is preferred to B, which in turn is preferred to C, A might be assigned utility of 10, B assigned utility of 8, and C assigned utility of 5; equivalently, A might be assigned utility of 100, B utility of 18, and C utility of 16. Any assignment of utility numbers such that the utility of A is highest and that of C lowest would represent the individual's preference ordering equally well. The point is that utility numbers need not be interpreted as objective, measurable quantities, but rather should be understood as constructed, auxiliary numbers selected by the analyst to represent the underlying rank-ordering of the individual. When uncertainty is involved, the theory of how utility represents preferences is more refined. But the underlying idea that utility numbers are chosen by the analyst remains the same. See Raiffa (1968, 86–89) and Savage (1972, chapter 5). We note that the utility index needs to be specified further when one aggregates individuals' well-being to compute social welfare. See note 15.

7. See, for example, Becker (1993, 386); and Little (1985, 1187 n.2), who refers to the "oft-refuted accusation that economists ignore the psyche" in objecting to the use of the term "material welfare" as an apt description of Pigou's early twentieth-century economic writings. We observe that the early utilitarians, many of whom espoused hedonism and its variants, did not in fact hold narrow views of well-being, despite conventional wisdom to the contrary. See, for example, Bentham ([1781] 1988, 33), listing, at the outset of a chapter on the kinds of pains and pleasures, some "simple pleasures," which include, in addition to pleasures of the senses and wealth, the pleasures of skill, amity, a good name, piety, benevolence, imagina-

in well-being is to be found in the minds of individuals themselves, not in the minds of analysts.[8]

We note that the concept of well-being, which covers situations involving uncertainty, incorporates the value of protection against risk. Accordingly, well-being is generally increased by the availability of insurance and

---

tion, and association. Mill criticized the view that utilitarianism is limited to certain categories of pleasure. See Mill ([1861]1998, 54–57). (Interestingly, he pointed out that the Greek philosopher Epicurus, who addressed such issues, was mischaracterized as having a narrow view of pleasure. Ibid. (56).) In fact, Mill appears to have endorsed higher intellectual pleasures as superior to more basic pleasures of the senses (although there is some dispute among modern scholars as to whether Mill held this position as a matter of principle, in seeming conflict with his other arguments, or purely as an empirical matter). Compare Sidgwick (1907, 402): "The term Pleasure is not commonly used so as to include clearly *all* kinds of consciousness which we desire to retain or reproduce: in ordinary usage it suggests too prominently the coarser and commoner kinds of such feelings; and it is difficult even for those who are trying to use it scientifically to free their minds altogether from the associations of ordinary usage. . . ."

8. Some philosophers, such as Scanlon, have expressed skepticism about the concept of well-being. See, for example, Scanlon (1998). Many such arguments, however, do not seem pertinent to the concept as we have defined it in the text. For example, some doubts reflect the view that well-being is not understood in a sufficiently expansive manner, whereas we impose no restrictions on what may be included. Other doubts involve resistance to the idea of interpreting well-being as an objective concept specified by an analyst, rather than according to what the individuals under consideration really care about, but the former is not how we define well-being. We consider some common objections concerning the make-up of individuals' preferences in section VIII.B. (Different reservations reflect the view that individuals' well-being as they experience it should not be the basis for normative analysis; these reservations do relate to the substantive argument of our book.)

Let us also comment briefly on the relationship between our conception of individuals' well-being and the views of modern political theorists and legal academics advancing what are referred to as "communitarian" or "republican" theories of individuals and the role of the state. See, for example, Arendt (1963); MacIntyre (1984); Pocock (1975); Sandel (1982); Taylor (1989); Walzer (1983); Fallon (1989), expressing skepticism about republican theories in a survey that focuses on constitutional law scholarship; and Gardbaum (1992), emphasizing, in a survey of political theorists and legal scholars, the lack of a necessary connection between their descriptive claims about the nature of individuals and their normative claims. The literature advances a descriptive claim, which is that individuals' desires are importantly influenced by the communities in which they live. This view does not bear on our definition of well-being or on our analysis, both of which are independent of the origins of well-being. Thus, we might imagine that individuals' desires are in part inherited; in part influenced by family; in part determined by interactions with others, including the community at large; in part shaped by legal rules and institutions (see subsection VIII.B.2); and so forth. Some such theorists also advance normative claims that do conflict with our argument. Notably, some insist that community participation should be encouraged for its own sake (rather than for instrumental reasons ultimately related to the promotion of individuals' well-being, such as that

other means of compensation, including legal redress for injury. In the language of economics, individuals generally are risk averse and thus are made better off by insurance, or implicit insurance, against financial risk.[9]

---

individuals would find participation rewarding, that it would lead them to behave better toward each other, or that it would improve the quality of laws or the functioning of government) or that particular conceptions of the good (independent of individuals' actual well-being) should be promoted. A theme of our analysis is that it is difficult to defend such notions, because they imply that members of society should pursue a course of action that, when it conflicts with a welfare-based approach, can only be detrimental to their well-being. See also subsection VIII.B.4, addressing the idea that an analyst's notion of the good should be substituted for individuals' actual well-being.

9. The assumption that an individual is risk averse is equivalent to the assumption that an individual's utility increases with income but at a decreasing rate—that is, the marginal utility of income decreases with the level of income. The assumption means that an additional dollar produces less of an increase in utility the more income one already has, which will tend to be true because individuals are inclined to allocate scarce dollars first to those goods and services that they value most highly.

Risk-averse individuals will, for example, refuse an even-odds bet for $1,000 because the utility gain if they win $1,000 is less than the utility loss if they lose $1,000. By similar reasoning, subjecting individuals to the risk of an uncompensated, uninsured loss (say, a 10% chance of losing $10,000) will reduce their utility more than would subjecting them to a certain loss with the same expected value ($1,000). This trait implies that individuals will tend to find the purchase of insurance attractive. In essence, insurance involves the transfer of income from situations in which income is relatively high (and thus the marginal utility from income is relatively low) to situations in which income is low (and thus the marginal utility from income is relatively high); such a transfer increases expected utility.

To elaborate on the reason that risk-averse individuals are made better off by insurance, suppose that I have an income of $50,000 but am subject to a 50% risk of losing $20,000 tomorrow. Assume further that my marginal utility per dollar is higher when my income is low—say, it is 4 per dollar when my income is $30,000 (that is, $50,000–$20,000) and only 2 per dollar when my income is $50,000. To keep the analysis simple, let us now consider my decision to enter into the following simple contract with an insurance company: I pay them $1 today and they agree to pay me $2 tomorrow if I indeed lose $20,000. This contract will increase my expected utility. To see that this is true, consider the two possibilities: If I do lose the $20,000, I have paid my $1 insurance premium but receive a $2 payment from the insurance company, so my net income is $30,001, $1 higher than without the insurance. If I do not lose the $20,000, I have paid my premium of $1, so my income is $49,999. In sum, I have a 50% chance of gaining $1 when I am relatively poor—which increases my utility by 4—and a 50% chance of losing $1 when I am relatively rich—which decreases my utility by only 2. The resulting effect on my expected utility is a gain of 1: (50% × 4) + (50% × −2) = 1. This gain indicates how insurance increases expected utility. (The logic of the example suggests that I would prefer to purchase complete insurance, paying a premium of $10,000 for a payment of $20,000 in the event of loss, giving me a certain income of $40,000. As long as my coverage is not yet complete, the utility gain from additional coverage, when I am relatively worse off, will exceed the utility loss from paying the premium in the event that no loss occurs, when I am better off.)

We further note a particular source of well-being that has special relevance to our book, namely, the possibility that individuals have a taste for a notion of fairness, just as they may have a taste for art, nature, or fine wine. For example, an individual might derive pleasure from knowing that vicious criminals receive their just deserts (independent of the anticipated effects of punishment on the incidence of crime) or that legal rules reflect a favored conception of fairness.[10] In such cases, satisfying the principle of fairness enhances the individual's well-being, just as would satisfying his preference for wine. (Our discussion of social norms in section D will help to explain why individuals may in fact have tastes regarding notions of fairness.[11])

One should sharply distinguish the preceding observation—about how tastes for notions of fairness, when they exist, are a component of individuals' well-being and thus are relevant under welfare economics—from the views about notions of fairness that we criticize in this book. Under those views, notions of fairness are held to be direct bases for legal policy assessment and to possess importance independent of whether individuals have tastes for the notions (in the sense that satisfaction of such tastes affects their well-being). Under welfare economics, by contrast, the relevance to policy analysis of a notion of fairness depends solely on how much, if at all, individuals' well-being is affected by their tastes for fairness. As a consequence, the welfare economic importance of fairness depends on what individuals' tastes happen to be and thus involves a question that is entirely empirical in character; philosophers' or policy analysts' views of which notions of fairness should be

10. The latter possibility is related to the idea that individuals might be displeased if the law failed to "express" their beliefs. See, for example, Sunstein (1996a). See also Adler (2000, 1364–74), surveying writings on expressive theories.

11. In particular, our discussion suggests that individuals are inculcated with fairness norms such that they feel virtuous when they act fairly and remorseful when they act unfairly, and that they are motivated to take actions in response to the unfair behavior of others. Such feelings and motivations tend to constitute, or be associated with, tastes for notions of fairness, which in turn may be satisfied to a greater or lesser degree by a particular legal rule. See note 117. Mill states that:

> [V]irtue [is something that was] originally a means, and which if it were not a means to anything else, would be and remain indifferent, but which by association with what it is a means to, comes to be desired for itself, and that too with the utmost intensity. . . . What was once desired as an instrument for the attainment of happiness, has come to be desired for its own sake. In being desired for its own sake it is, however, desired as *part* of happiness. (Mill [1861] 1998, 83)

Certain eighteenth-century moral philosophers address the relationship between notions of fairness and individuals' moral sense, which is understood as akin to tastes in some respects. See Hutcheson ([1725–1755] 1994) and Hume ([1751] 1998).

endorsed by members of an enlightened society are irrelevant.[12] It is our understanding, however, that legal academics, policy analysts, philosophers, and others who invoke notions of fairness when assessing legal policy do not view their arguments and concerns as involving individuals' actual tastes (although they may well believe in some instances that many people are in agreement with them, or they may wish to convince others to adopt their beliefs).[13]

12. Compare Baron (1993, 144): "Public decisions are made for the public, and the emotions of the decision makers are trivial by comparison. Technically, the decision makers are part of the public, so their emotions might be included, but these emotions are trivial in the scheme of things."; and Mirrlees (1982, 71 n.13): "But I want government ministers to try to maximise utility, even if their personal sense of achievement is gravely compromised, their crazy industrial dreams unfulfilled: the ministers' utility deserves no significant weight in our assessments of utility in comparison to the millions who may suffer."

13. For example, in the literature on retributive justice, commentators insist that their conception of fairness is distinct from individuals' tastes. See subsection VI.D.2. Usually, however, the philosophical and legal academic literature on notions of fairness does not explicitly address the relationship, if any, between such notions and individuals' tastes. Yet it is clear from the arguments given in the literature that the writers' endorsement of notions of fairness is not based on the notions' importance as tastes. In addition, this writing essentially lacks empirical content, whereas it would necessarily be substantially empirical if it were concerned with fairness as a taste. Moreover, the literature sometimes advances notions of fairness that are opposed to the popular will, as, for instance, when the popular will supports less protection of criminal defendants. See, for example, Husak (1995, 154): "[C]ritical morality is distinct from the conventional mores of communities. Public opinion polls consistently reveal that many citizens are prepared to sacrifice rights in order to help reduce crime. Only the application of a critical morality can justify the protection of rights against the apparent willingness of many citizens to relinquish them." Also, even those who invoke public opinion to support their views do not suggest that the weight given to notions of fairness should be determined entirely by the strength of individuals' desire for more fairness in preference, say, to more fine wine. Finally, we note that some positions of philosophers are clearly distinguished from popular views:

> But it is quite absurd to want to comply with popularity in the first investigation, on which all correctness of basic principles depends. Not only can this procedure never lay claim to the very rare merit of a true *philosophic popularity,* since there is no art in being commonly understandable if one thereby renounces any well-grounded insight; it also produces a disgusting hodge-podge of patchwork observations and half-rationalized principles, in which shallow pates revel because it is something useful for everyday chitchat, but the insightful . . . avert their eyes. . . . (Kant [1785] 1997, 21–22)

The suggestion that what are presented as moral views really involve individuals' tastes tends to be put forward by critics, not by fairness proponents describing their own views. See, for example, R. Posner (1998, 1644), giving an example, and ibid. (1645), suggesting that "many moral claims are just the gift wrapping of theoretically ungrounded (and ungroundable) preferences or aversions."

Rather, they believe that notions of fairness should serve as independent principles to be used in assessing legal policy. Hence, the role of notions of fairness under welfare economics—solely as a taste that individuals might have—is quite different from the role of notions of fairness that we will be criticizing.

Before continuing, we observe that we will usually assume that individuals comprehend fully how various situations affect their well-being and that there is no basis for anyone to question their conception of what is good for them. Therefore, when we say that an individual is better off, there will be no doubt about what we mean. We focus on instances in which well-being is unambiguous because our purpose is to address whether legal policy analysis should consider solely effects on individuals' well-being—however that notion is best understood or measured—or also (or instead) should consider factors that are independent of individuals' well-being. We note, however, that our assumption that well-being is unambiguous is one of convenience; if individuals do not understand how situations affect their well-being, our argument may be applied to individuals' actual well-being—what they would prefer if they correctly understood how they would be affected—rather than to individuals' well-being as reflected in their mistaken preferences.[14] In any event, questions about which legal policies actually promote

---

14. For elaboration, see section VIII.B. We also note that much of our more formal argument has an even broader application. Namely, if an analyst thought that a concept of well-being that was qualitatively different from the welfare economic one (say, an objective view of the good life) was normatively compelling, important parts of our analysis would still hold. In particular, there would be no change in the logic of our argument that giving any weight to a notion of fairness that is independent of well-being always raises the possibility that everyone would be made worse off; everyone being made worse off would be interpreted by reference to the analyst's own conception of individuals' well-being. Of course, the foregoing observation could easily be taken too far—for example, by defining each individual's well-being as equivalent to the degree to which a policy satisfies some notion of fairness that is not conventionally understood to have anything to do with individuals' well-being. Such language usage would obscure important differences in normative positions.

In addition, although many who adhere to conceptions of well-being that differ from the welfare economic one should find much of our analysis convincing, other aspects of our argument favor the welfare economic conception because it is rooted in the actual well-being of individuals. To be sure, many analysts seem to define individuals' well-being not as something that has any relationship to individuals' actual preferences or feelings, however well informed, but rather as some conception that the analyst holds dear. We find such usage (like the aforementioned usage that would collapse all notions of fairness into well-being) confusing and misleading, both because well-being seems to refer to an actual rather than an external and conceptual state of existence and because referring to well-being as that of an individual suggests that the actual individual in question, rather than an analyst, is the direct object of concern. See subsection VIII.B.4. On different conceptions of well-being, see generally Griffin (1986), Ng (2000, chapter 4), Nussbaum and Sen (1993), and Sumner (1996).

individuals' well-being are logically distinct from whether and to what extent well-being should be the focus of policy assessment in the first place.

2. Social Welfare and Individuals' Well-Being

Under the rubric of welfare economics, the conception of social welfare is based on individuals' well-being. Specifically, social welfare is postulated to be an increasing function of individuals' well-being and to depend on no other factors.[15] It is also generally supposed that each individual's well-being

15. The notion of social welfare may be expressed formally. Suppose that there are n individuals, and let the well-being or utility of the first individual be denoted U_1, that of the second U_2, and so forth. Also, let x stand for an exhaustive description of a situation, interpreted as a state of the world that would prevail under a regime. Then social welfare, $W(x)$, can be written as

$$W(x) = F(U_1(x), U_2(x), \ldots, U_n(x)).$$

If x and x' are two situations, $W(x) > W(x')$ is interpreted to mean that situation x is socially preferred to situation x'. As noted in the text, it is also assumed that $W(x)$ increases if individuals' utilities (U_1, U_2, etc.) increase. It should be emphasized that social welfare, $W(x)$, is influenced by x *only* insofar as x affects the utilities of individuals; it is solely the utilities of individuals that determine social welfare. We note that economists often call W an individualistic social welfare function because social welfare depends on each individual's well-being and on nothing else. When we refer to a social welfare function in this book, we mean an individualistic social welfare function unless otherwise indicated.

A number of observations about social welfare functions should be made.

(1) As discussed in the text that follows, a social welfare function can be *any* increasing function of individuals' utilities. In the utilitarian case, for example, the function F is the sum $U_1 + U_2 + \ldots + U_n$. Any other function that is increasing in individuals' utilities, such as the product $U_1 \times U_2 \times \ldots \times U_n$, is also a possible social welfare function.

(2) Implicit in any social welfare function is a comparison of, and a way of trading off, different individuals' utilities. One can conceive of the construction of a social welfare function as a two-step process. First, an analyst makes interpersonal comparisons of utility (which technically involves choosing particular numerical representations for individuals' utility functions, see note 6). Second, the analyst chooses the function F that aggregates the measures of individuals' utilities. (This construction helps to explain why the arbitrariness of individual utility indexes discussed in note 6 does not render a social welfare function incoherent: If a different utility index for some individual is selected, the analyst can modify the function F accordingly.) Making interpersonal comparisons of utility relates to the connection between social welfare functions and judgments about income distribution, see subsection 3, for such judgments involve assessments of who is better and worse off, or of how one individual's gains compare to another individual's losses. Although we do not suggest that there is an uncontroversial, verifiable way to compare individuals' utilities, it is necessary to make some sort of interpersonal comparisons to address distributive issues, and there do exist coherent approaches to the task. For discussions of interpersonal comparisons by economists, philosophers, and others, see, for example, Baron (1993, chapter 5), Hare (1981, chapter 7), Little

affects social welfare in a symmetric manner, which is to say that the idea of social welfare incorporates a basic notion of equal concern for all individuals.[16]

In several different respects, the approach of welfare economics involves value judgments.[17] First, value judgments underlie the assumptions that social welfare depends on individuals' well-being, that this dependence is posi-

---

(1957, chapter 4), Sen (1973, 9–15), and Harsanyi (1955, 317–320; 1982, 39, 49–52). See also Hammond (1991), and note 20, discussing Robbins's views. The most direct application of this aspect of welfare economics occurs in economists' work on optimal income taxation. See note 31.

(3) As with individuals' utility indexes, see note 6, the particular number assigned to welfare (W) is not important; all that matters is the ranking of different regimes (with the appropriate adjustment for the case of uncertainty).

(4) We have stated that social welfare is taken to be independent of everything except individuals' utilities. It is, of course, possible to state a more general notion of social welfare, which can depend on literally anything, and some general formulations presented by economists allow for that possibility. We do not adopt this broader definition of social welfare when discussing welfare economics for the simple reason that our book focuses on the difference between assessment that is limited to effects on individuals' well-being (the individualistic social welfare function) and assessment that is not so limited, which largely falls under the rubric of fairness and related terms. (Only in our formal definition of notions of fairness in note 52 do we make use of the broader formulation.)

16. With respect to the social welfare function defined in note 15, the condition of equal concern (or, equivalently, equal treatment) is the stipulation that the value of W does not depend on which individual has which utility level. This assumption rules out a function that favors a specific individual at the expense of others. Formally, the equal treatment requirement is usually expressed as a symmetry or anonymity condition. For example, it is assumed that a situation in which Jill has utility of 5 and Bill has utility of 10 must be viewed as no better and no worse than one in which it is Jill who has utility of 10 and Bill utility of 5. This equality requirement does not, however, rule out attention to differences in income, ability, opportunity, need, and the like, as all these factors affect well-being and thus the level of utility. See subsection 3, discussing income distribution.

The reader may find our description of this notion of equal concern to be similar to that of many moral philosophers. See, for example, Hare (1997, 26), discussing how Kant's categorical imperative amounts to giving everyone equal weight, which involves treating everyone impartially. Among popular contemporary philosophers familiar to legal academics, Dworkin's views may be best known. See, for example, R. Dworkin (1977, 180–83, 272–78). Dworkin does not, however, define the concept of equal concern precisely, and, given his version of the notion, he may see it as having different implications from those described here.

17. Some critics of normative economic analysis of law have protested that it purports to provide objective answers to policy questions, in the sense that the answers are somehow not dependent on value judgments. See, for example, Horwitz (1980). This view, however, is not an accurate characterization of welfare economics, as we now explain.

tive, and that factors unrelated to individuals' well-being are irrelevant. In other words, to adopt welfare economics is to adopt the moral position that one should be concerned, positively and exclusively, with individuals' well-being. Moreover, because analysts generally assume that each individual's well-being affects social welfare in a symmetric manner, welfare economics is understood to include, as we said, a requirement that individuals count equally in an important sense.[18]

Second, a method of aggregation is of necessity an element of welfare economics, and value judgments are involved in aggregating different individuals' well-being into a single measure of social welfare.[19] The choice of a method of aggregation involves the adoption of a view concerning matters of

18. We note that this value judgment about equal treatment (the defense of which is not a subject of this book) rules out not only schemes of evaluation that show favoritism toward particular individuals or groups, but also certain libertarian or entitlement-based principles, namely, those stipulating that it matters which individuals achieve particular levels of well-being. (As we explain in note 16, this equality requirement implies that social welfare is unaffected by switching the levels of well-being of two individuals.) The standard welfare economic framework is also inconsistent with many libertarian approaches because, although the latter are understood to require that particular rights be honored regardless of the consequences, under welfare economics only information about the effect of legal rules (including those that embody particular rights) on individuals' well-being may be considered in assessing those rules. It is well known, however, that libertarian rights can be rationalized on instrumental grounds rather than interpreted as ends in themselves, regardless of how their enforcement affects the well-being of the individuals whose rights are enforced. See, for example, subsections V.C.2 and VIII.A.2, discussing the instrumental value of rights in protecting against government abuse of power, thereby promoting individuals' well-being. See also note 48, discussing the relationship between concepts of fairness, justice, and rights. See generally Sidgwick (1907, 274–78), offering a classic statement of the incoherence of a system of rights based on the idea of freedom as an end in itself.

19. In addition to providing a method of aggregating individuals' utilities, a complete account of social welfare would address questions about membership in the group of individuals whose utilities are to be aggregated—whether it includes all individuals in a nation, or in the world, or in some other group; whether it includes only the present generation or also future ones; and whether it includes only humans or, for example, all sentient beings. (The social welfare function in note 15 simply assumes that there is a given society with n members but does not assume that they constitute any particular type of group.) We note that these questions also must be addressed under other systems of evaluation. For example, if individual autonomy is to be honored, one must specify which individuals are entitled to such consideration. These topics, like the proper distribution of income, are beyond the scope of our inquiry, the purpose of which is to focus on the difference between evaluative principles that are denominated solely in terms of well-being and principles that are based in whole or in part on other factors—a distinction that is qualitatively similar regardless of how these other questions are answered.

distribution (as we explore further in subsection 3).[20] Various methods of aggregation are possible. For example, under the utilitarian approach, social welfare is taken to be the sum of individuals' utilities. Alternatively, the well-being of worse-off individuals might be given additional weight, as under the approach associated with John Rawls, wherein social welfare corresponds to the utility of the worst-off individuals.[21] In this book, we do not defend any specific way of aggregating individuals' well-being; that is, we do not endorse any particular view about the proper distribution of well-being or income.[22] Rather, we argue, in essence, that legal policy analysis should be guided by reference to *some* coherent way of aggregating individuals' well-being, in contrast to the view that policy analysis should be guided by notions of fairness and thus, at least in part, without regard to individuals' well-being.[23]

20. Let us briefly explain the relationship between this issue of aggregation and the previously mentioned point that individuals are to be treated symmetrically under welfare economics. The latter requirement means that, in comparing two policies, it does not matter which particular individuals are the winners and which are the losers; all that matters in comparing the two policies is how many individuals are at each level of well-being under each policy. But when there are both winners and losers, one cannot reach a final decision about which policy is best without making a judgment about whether the gains to the winners are more important than the losses to the losers.

The comparison of gains to winners and losses to losers is generally understood to involve interpersonal comparisons of well-being, as we discuss in note 15. In this regard, many have cited Robbins (1932, 138–143) as rejecting the view that such comparisons are possible. Interestingly, Robbins himself had long viewed this attribution as incorrect. See, for example, Robbins (1935, vii–x), and Robbins (1938), emphasizing his claims that the common stipulation that different individuals have equal capacities for satisfaction involves a value judgment rather than a scientifically verifiable hypothesis, and that the need for making value judgments when formulating policy recommendations should be understood not as a deficiency but rather as an inevitability. See also Little (1985, 1187), arguing that statements about the relative needs or happiness of persons can be more or less scientific, but conclusions about policy assessment derived from such statements are normative.

21. See Rawls (1971, 75–83). We observe, however, that maximizing the utility of the least-well-off individuals is not what Rawls actually favors; his real concern is with the distribution of what he calls "primary goods" rather than individuals' well-being. See Rawls (1971, 90–95; 1982). For further discussion, see note 27.

22. Among the more fully elaborated arguments concerning the aggregation of individuals' well-being into a single measure of social welfare are Harsanyi's justifications for utilitarianism. See Harsanyi (1953, 1955, 1975). For supportive views of (modern) philosophers, see, for example, Hare (1981) and Smart (1973). For differing views, see, for example, Sen (1979) and Williams (1973). See generally Sen and Williams (1982), a collection of essays by leading proponents of differing views.

23. Throughout this book, we refer to welfare economics as employing measures of social welfare that depend only on individuals' well-being. What we mean by this expression is that, *once a social welfare function is chosen* (that is, once a judgment about aggregation is made,

To some readers, there may appear to be a tension between our accepting the legitimacy of distributive judgments within welfare economics and our criticizing notions of fairness, particularly since many views about distribution are expressed using the language of fairness. In fact, however, there is no tension because of the manner in which we define notions of fairness for purposes of this inquiry and because of the substance of our criticism. As we elaborate in section B and throughout the book, our definition of notions of fairness includes all principles—but only those principles—that give weight to factors that are independent of individuals' well-being. And, as we elaborate in the next subsection, distribution can play an important role even under a system of evaluation that is concerned exclusively with individuals' well-being. Moreover, the criticisms of notions of fairness that we offer are not criticisms of the language that analysts use or of the need to make value judgments in assessing legal policy; rather, they are specific criticisms of giving weight to factors that are independent of individuals' well-being. Hence, our analysis does not affect distributive judgments that are confined to individuals' well-being.[24]

3. Comments on Social Welfare and the Distribution of Income

In this subsection, we elaborate on how questions about the distribution of income[25] fit within the framework of welfare economics, especially because

---

see note 15), any two policies can be compared using only information about how each policy affects individuals' well-being. We note that there is some potential for confusion about our statement that social welfare depends only on well-being because of the very fact that one needs a method of aggregating information about individuals' well-being in order to make an overall assessment. In this sense, the evaluations under welfare economics do not depend purely on the data (facts) about individuals' well-being (as is familiar from the point that one cannot get an "ought" from an "is"). Our contrast with notions of fairness, however, concerns the data themselves. Under a notion of fairness, some information other than that about each individual's well-being is given weight in a judgment about policy choice; that is, it is possible for two policies to result in identical levels of well-being for each individual yet for the judgment to differ. Under welfare economics, by contrast, the only information about a policy that is relevant is information about how it affects each individual's well-being.

24. However, as we suggest in note 27, some distributive principles that have been advanced do depart from consideration of individuals' well-being. Our criticism does implicate such principles.

25. We discuss the distribution of income rather than the distribution of well-being because much analysis of distributive issues refers to the distribution of income and because many redistributive policies operate through individuals' incomes. As should be apparent from our discussion, however, welfare economics also incorporates distributive issues involving well-being that may arise independently of income differences (such as when individuals have

the relevance of income distribution under welfare economics contrasts sharply with the popular view that income distribution is unimportant under normative economic analysis of law.[26]

Our main point is that many basic concerns about the overall distribution of income are encompassed by the welfare economic approach.[27] This

---

different physical capacities). For convenience, however, we do not generally refer as well to the distribution of well-being even when such language might be more accurate.

26. See, for example, Hanson and Hart (1996, 330), observing that "[p]erhaps the most common criticism of law and economics is that it overlooks or, worse, displaces questions of distribution or equity" and asserting that "[e]conomists respond in part by observing that distributional questions taken by themselves fall outside the reach of economic science"; and Tribe (1985, 594): "This disregard of the *distributional* dimension of any given problem is characteristic of the entire law-and-economics school of thought. . . ." There are a number of explanations for the common belief that income distribution is unimportant in normative economic analysis of law. First, some law and economics scholars have stated (incorrectly, in our view) that distribution ought not matter in principle. Second, much law and economic analysis omits distributional considerations, and many legal academics do not seem to appreciate that, even if one thinks that income distribution is important, there are often good reasons for leaving it aside in one's analysis (as we discuss in the text to follow). Third, because the framework of welfare economics has not been well presented in the legal academic literature, we believe that there is a lack of familiarity with the welfare economic approach and the reasons that the distribution of income is important under that approach.

We also note that one implication of the fact that welfare economics incorporates consideration of the distribution of income is that the familiar objection concerning the potential conceptual indeterminacy of the Kaldor-Hicks efficiency test is inapposite. See subsection VIII.D.4(b).

27. However, not all criteria for assessing the proper distribution of income are admissible under welfare economics. In particular, arguments favoring equality, not by reference to individuals' well-being, but based upon some standard independent of well-being, are outside the scope of welfare economics and therefore are among the notions of fairness that are subject to our critique. For example, John Rawls is concerned with the distribution of primary goods rather than the distribution of well-being. See note 21, and Rawls (1980, 526–27), stating that primary goods "are *not* to be understood as general means essential for achieving whatever final ends a comprehensive empirical or historical survey might show people usually or normally to have in common" (emphasis added), and explaining that his position revises suggestions in *A Theory of Justice*, in which the list of primary goods might have seemed to depend purely on psychological, statistical, or historical facts about people, rather than on a conception of the person that is fixed prior to examining general social facts. In similar spirit, Amartya Sen considers individuals' "capabilities" rather than their actual well-being as conventionally understood. See, for example, Sen (1985).

These alternative formulations often have implications similar to those of a social welfare function based upon individuals' well-being. When they do not, however, we find them unpersuasive for reasons analogous to the criticisms of notions of fairness that we offer in this book. Specifically, when the analyst decides which goods are primary or which capabilities are to count, and what importance each is to have, and then weights them differently from how the

can be seen by reflecting on the implications of the fact that social welfare depends on individuals' well-being. First, the distribution of income will matter to social welfare because a dollar of income often will raise the utility of some individuals more than that of others. Notably, redistributing income from the rich to the poor will tend to raise social welfare, assuming that the marginal utility of income is greater for the poor than for the rich.[28] Second, the distribution of income may matter to social welfare because it affects the distribution of well-being, and, under the welfare economic approach, social welfare may depend directly on how equally well-being is distributed among individuals. For example, as previously noted, more weight might be placed on the well-being of less-well-off individuals, in which case social welfare would tend to be higher if income were redistributed from the better

---

actual individuals in society weight them—which is precisely when this formulation has different implications from those of welfare economics—individuals will be made worse off. The reason is that they will be given less of those things that they value more than the analyst does and more of those things that they value less than the analyst does. Indeed, such alternative approaches sometimes would favor regimes under which everyone is worse off. This claim is easiest to see in the case in which all individuals have the same preferences and the analyst's formulation does not correspond to individuals' preferences, which is to say, whenever the analyst's approach differs from welfare economics. (The claim is a direct implication of the proof in Kaplow and Shavell (2001).) This analysis suggests that these alternative formulations can be viewed as a species of paternalism, see subsection VIII.B.1, but a sort that is not ultimately based on raising individuals' actual well-being. See, for example, Baron (1993, 152–54), suggesting that the importance of particular goods and capabilities can be explained with regard to their effects on individuals' well-being and noting that proponents may find such explanations inadequate, but asking: "[W]hat alternative kind of justification can be provided [?] . . . What reason would anyone have to endorse a norm for satisfying desires that people do not have . . . at the expense of desires that people have in fact?"; and Sumner (1996, 42–80), criticizing "objective" theories of welfare, including Rawls's and Sen's formulations, because they are detached from what actually matters to individuals.

28. In the case of a utilitarian social welfare function, for example, redistributing a dollar from an individual with lower marginal utility of income to one with higher marginal utility of income will, all else being equal, raise social welfare: Because the utility of the former individual will fall less than the utility of the latter individual will rise, total utility will be greater. (With regard to many other social welfare functions, individuals' marginal utility will similarly tend to be relevant but may not be decisive because of the next factor identified in the text.) A familiar implication of the diminishing marginal utility of income is that, under a utilitarian social welfare function, complete equality will be optimal if all individuals' utility functions are the same and there are no incentive effects associated with redistribution. And as Lerner has shown, if utility functions differ but the state cannot determine who has which utility function, it still follows that an equal distribution is optimal. See Lerner (1944, 28–34). See also Sen (1973, 83–87), showing that an equal distribution also maximizes any standard social welfare function in these circumstances.

off to the worse off (independently of whether the marginal utility of income for the worse off were greater than that for the better off).[29] Third, the distribution of income may matter to social welfare because some individuals' well-being may depend directly on the distribution of income, as when individuals feel sympathy toward those who are less fortunate.[30] We also note that, in accord with the foregoing, there is a substantial body of work by economists on matters concerning income distribution.[31]

The significance of the distribution of income under welfare economics raises the question of why much normative economic analysis of social policy and, in particular, of law does not address distributive concerns directly. To a degree, this omission may reflect some analysts' lack of concern about the distribution of income.[32] However, we now wish to explain why ignoring

29. That is, under such a social welfare function, it is possible for social welfare to be higher when two individuals' levels of well-being are more nearly equal, even if the sum total of their well-being is the same. In contrast, under the utilitarian social welfare function, only the total utility matters, not the distribution of utility (although recall that the distribution of *income* does matter, see note 28). There is a debate about whether and to what extent social welfare should be taken to depend on the distribution of individuals' well-being (see sources cited in note 22), but this is a debate within the framework of welfare economics. That is, the debate is about how social welfare depends on individuals' well-being, not whether it should. However the debate is resolved, note that social welfare depends only on individuals' well-being; information on aspects of a situation other than their effects on well-being is irrelevant in assessing social welfare. See note 23.

30. To illustrate, suppose that parents care about the welfare of their children and that many children turn out to be poor. Then a government program that helps poor children contributes to social welfare in two ways: directly, by increasing the well-being of the poor children, and indirectly, by increasing the well-being of the parents of poor children, who have higher utility because their children are better off. Similar logic applies to the case in which the well-being of the wealthy depends on the plight of the poor or that in which the poor envy the rich. See, for example, Duesenberry (1949, 101), Hochman and Rodgers (1969), and Boskin and Sheshinski (1978).

31. Many economists writing in the field of public economics study the distributive effects of taxation and other government policy. Indeed, two recent recipients of the Nobel prize in economics, Vickrey and Mirrlees, have done so. See, for example, Vickrey (1947) and Mirrlees (1971). See also Royal Swedish Academy of Sciences (1996), announcing the award to Vickrey and Mirrlees and highlighting their contributions regarding redistributive taxation, among other subjects. In particular, the subject of optimal income taxation is concerned with how to design the tax system (and, in extensions of the basic model, other aspects of government policy) to maximize social welfare, understood in just the manner described here. See, for example, Mirrlees (1971) and Tuomala (1990).

32. That is, some of those who undertake research in normative law and economics do not understand their efforts to be grounded in welfare economics, as we describe it. On this point, see our discussion of wealth maximization later in this subsection.

distributive effects in legal policy analysis is often the most sensible course even though the distribution of income is generally viewed to be important, as it is under welfare economics.

First, when undertaking any kind of analysis, it is often useful to focus on certain factors in order best to understand their effects, leaving other considerations aside. Thus, as a matter of analytical convenience, economists may choose to study stylized models in which individuals' well-being and social welfare are determined in a simple manner, and, in particular, one in which the distribution of income does not affect social welfare.[33] For example, in a model of accidents, we might consider a hypothetical world where individuals' well-being and social welfare depend only on a simple aggregate, such as total accident losses plus prevention costs plus legal administrative costs.[34] Such a model and social goal would be useful to examine if the purpose were to understand accident prevention and incentives. Use of the model would hardly mean that the analyst actually considered the distribution of income (or other factors, such as risk-bearing costs) to be irrelevant to the determination of true social welfare.[35]

33. Economists are often criticized for using stylized models and for making restrictive assumptions, but such criticism reflects a misunderstanding of scientific method. Stylized models are helpful for understanding problems, and the statement of assumptions makes explicit the domain of one's analysis. Economists' use of assumptions actually is similar to legal academics' and philosophers' use of "hypotheticals," the stipulated facts of which constrain one to analyze the implications of given assumptions in an orderly fashion.

34. In the stylized model, losses and costs might be expressed in terms of only one good, and the well-being of each individual might be taken to equal the quantity of that good that he has. Relatedly, a common aspect of the economic approach is to express all costs and benefits in terms of a common denominator. In law and economics writing, this denominator is usually money. However, as the text to follow indicates, this approach does not entail embracing "wealth maximization" as the ultimate principle. See also subsection VIII.D.1, on valuing life, pain and suffering, and other nonpecuniary factors. We note that any logically consistent and complete system for evaluating legal rules is, in fact, equivalent to expressing everything, including factors sometimes viewed as incommensurable, in terms of a common denominator. See note 52, presenting a formal statement of assessment based on fairness, and note 114 in chapter VIII, further discussing the issue of incommensurability.

35. For example, in our own work, we sometimes analyze models in which only incentives are at issue, while at other times we undertake analysis in which income distribution is important. Other analysts may choose to specialize completely; for example, some public finance economists and legal academics who study the tax system focus primarily on matters pertaining to the distribution of income. Academic writing is properly viewed as a large, cooperative enterprise, within which each work seeks to make a contribution without necessarily being concerned with all aspects of the enterprise. In this context, specialization makes sense. See also subsection VII.B.2, discussing the proper approach to policy research by legal academics.

We recognize that some economic analysts of law, like other analysts, too readily make

Second, many legal rules probably have little effect on the distribution of income.[36] For example, in contractual settings, price adjustments will often negate the distributive effects of rules (if a seller is adversely affected by a rule, he will raise his price). In important tort domains, such as automobile accidents, injurers and victims will, on average, tend to have similar incomes; hence, the distributive effects of the choice of legal rules will be small. Likewise, in many areas of corporate law, most investors will be on each side of a type of transaction (approximately) equally often, so any distributive effects of rules that are favorable to one type of party will tend to cancel out in the balance. If legal rules are likely to have little distributive effect, it will do little harm to ignore this effect in the analysis.

Third, when legal rules do have distributive effects, the effects usually should not be counted as favoring or disfavoring the rules because distributional objectives can often be best accomplished directly, using the income tax and transfer (welfare) programs.[37] One reason economists have tended to favor these direct means of redistribution is that they reach all individuals

---

policy recommendations based upon incomplete analysis. This is a problem to be avoided, but it does not bear on the value of making explicit simplifying assumptions for the purpose of advancing the understanding of complex problems.

36. Some critics, see, for example, Ackerman (1971) and Kennedy (1982, 1987), have gone to great lengths to show that it is possible—not necessarily likely—that *some* redistribution can be accomplished in particular legal settings. But such illustrations do not establish a general ability to achieve substantial redistribution in any systematic manner through use of the sorts of legal rules generally analyzed.

37. Even though the normative economic approach is often faulted for slighting distributive concerns, critics usually do not acknowledge the central role of the income tax and transfer system in influencing the distribution of income; nor do they address the arguments for relying exclusively upon the tax and transfer system to achieve distributive objectives. See, for example, Hanson and Hart (1996, 330), noting that omission of distribution is the most common objection to law and economics analysis and asserting that economists often claim that distribution is outside the discipline, but not mentioning taxation, or the analysis of it as a distributive tool by economists or other law and economics scholars. Indeed, even writers in law and economics advance arguments that implicitly assume that taxes are not available for redistributive purposes. See, for example, Arlen (1992), arguing that legal rules should reflect parties' wealth, discussed in Kaplow and Shavell (1994b, 676 n.14). For a discussion of exceptions, see note 38.

Although the evaluation of legal rules generally should not depend upon distributive consequences, policymakers (particularly legislators, who design the tax and transfer system) need to be aware of any significant distributive effects of legal rules overall, so that these can be taken into account in designing distribution policy. (However, there may be no need separately to identify the redistributive effects of legal rules, especially of particular rules, because general data on the distribution of income and measures of the standard of living will tend to capture the aggregate of distributive effects from all sources.)

and are based explicitly on income. In contrast, particular legal rules affect only relatively small fractions of the population and ordinarily constitute relatively crude means of redistribution. For example, a pro-plaintiff tort rule will affect only people involved in accidents, and the resulting redistribution will be haphazard because whether and to what extent plaintiffs are poorer than defendants will vary greatly from context to context. In addition, the income tax and transfer programs tend to involve less distortion and inefficiency than does redistribution through legal rules. The reason is that redistribution through legal rules entails both the inefficiency of redistribution generally (due to adverse effects on work incentives) and the additional cost involved in adopting less efficient legal rules.[38]

38. See, for example, Hylland and Zeckhauser (1979), Shavell (1981), Ng (1984), and Kaplow and Shavell (1994b).

The limited work in legal academia that directly addresses the possibility of redistribution through taxation rather than through legal rules does not reflect an understanding of the generally greater efficiency of redistribution through taxation. See, for example, Kennedy (1982, 613), stating that inefficiencies from compulsory terms and from redistribution through taxation "involve exactly the same kinds of waste," leaving a difficult empirical question as to which is preferable; and Kronman (1980a, 508), arguing that, because taxation as well as contractual regulation has efficiency costs, determining the preferable means of redistribution raises an empirical question that "must be resolved on a case-by-case basis, in the light of detailed information about the circumstances likely to influence the effectiveness of each method of redistribution."

Some recent literature has questioned the relative inefficiency of skewing legal rules to redistribute income. One critique emphasizes subtle qualifications to the argument about the relative inefficiency of distorting legal rules, qualifications that—as we suggested in Kaplow and Shavell (1994b, 680–81)—are tangential to the view that legal rules should favor the poor and that do not seem likely to be of much practical importance. See Sanchirico (2000). But see Kaplow and Shavell (2000b). Another qualification that we noted concerns whether individuals accurately perceive the redistributive impact of legal rules, rather than over- or underestimate it. See Kaplow and Shavell (1994b, 671 n.5). Jolls suggests that underestimation is likely. See Jolls (1998). We are skeptical of this suggestion. That individuals with assets routinely buy liability insurance is inconsistent with many of the arguments presented, which take the position that individuals perceive risky tort liability as less costly than having to pay the expected value of liability with certainty. Also, the view that individuals keep different "mental accounts" (here, for earnings and losses incurred as a result of tort judgments) could imply either overestimation or underestimation (and the commonly noted phenomenon of loss aversion suggests that it is the tort losses that would receive more rather than less weight in individuals' decisionmaking). Jolls discusses both of these points, see Jolls (1998, 1666–67, 1672), but she does not find them as plausible as we do. In the end, we agree with Jolls that questions of individuals' reactions to legal rules ultimately are empirical matters. In any event, whether one attaches importance to either of these critiques is immaterial for present purposes because, as we explain in the text, distributive concerns are relevant under welfare economics and should be addressed in whatever manner turns out to be best.

It therefore appears that there are sound reasons for much normative economic analysis of law not to take explicit account of the distribution of income.[39] As we have stressed, these reasons derive from judgments about the best ways to organize analysis and to accomplish distributive objectives, not from a belief that distributive concerns lack normative importance. If these reasons are inapplicable in a particular setting, a proper welfare economic analysis will take distributional concerns into account.

The foregoing analysis helps to illuminate the view that the appropriate social goal is "wealth maximization": maximizing the total dollar value of, or willingness to pay for, social resources. Many legal academics seem to be under the impression that wealth maximization is *the* economic measure of social welfare.[40] This belief is perhaps not surprising, both because wealth maximization possesses some intuitive appeal and because it is the goal that Posner advanced two decades ago in the most sustained attempt by a legal scholar to defend a normative law and economics approach.[41] However,

39. A separate argument concerns differences among legal institutions; in particular, some would favor judges' choosing legal rules on distributive grounds because legislatures may not engage in the optimal degree of redistribution, due to the balance of political forces. We do not address here matters of accountability and other questions involving the proper division of labor in this regard, but we do offer two observations that are usually overlooked by those who advocate that courts actively engage in redistribution. First, on average and in the long run, it is not clear that judges, who are elected or are appointed by elected officials, have significantly different distributive preferences from legislators'. Hence, judicial redistribution that deviates from the legislative plan, if successful, would not over the long run produce a different distributive outcome, but it would result in inefficiencies both in periods in which judges redistributed more than the legislature would on its own and in periods in which they redistributed less. Second, legislatures can directly overturn court decisions (outside the constitutional context, which does not substantially regulate the extent of redistribution), and, in any event, legislatures set income taxes and transfer programs freely. Furthermore, many legal rules fall partially or wholly within the legislative domain to begin with. Hence, it seems unlikely that judges could succeed in implementing a regime that was significantly more or less redistributive than the one favored by the legislature.

40. See note 26.

41. The most important articles are R. Posner (1979, 1980a), both of which are reprinted and revised in R. Posner (1981b, chapters 3–4). Since Posner wrote these articles, his views have evolved. See R. Posner (1990, 374–87; 1995a, chapter 19), adopting a pragmatic view of wealth maximization as instrumental rather than as foundational; R. Posner (1995b, 99–100), stating "I concede the incompleteness of 'wealth' [because] the concept of wealth is dependent on the assignment of property rights and . . . on the distribution of wealth across persons," but defending the pragmatic use of wealth maximization by judges in formulating tort doctrine; and R. Posner (1998, 1999), advancing a pragmatic approach and criticizing moral philosophy, while not addressing wealth maximization directly. (For discussion of Posner's views as reflected in the latter two references, see note 87.) *(continued)*

wealth—and thus wealth maximization—is not a well-defined concept; to compute wealth, one must know the prices of different goods and services, yet there is no natural set of prices to use.[42] More importantly, and more obviously, even if we possessed an unambiguous way of computing wealth, wealth still would not constitute a measure of social welfare under welfare economics because wealth is not defined in terms of individuals' well-being. As we have explained, a measure of social welfare under welfare economics must be a function of individuals' well-being. (This observation also reconciles the fact that total wealth is independent of its distribution with the point that distributive concerns may be an important determinant of social welfare under welfare economics.)

As a practical matter, though, the defects in the conceptual and normative foundations of wealth maximization do not imply that analysis based

---

Posner now describes attempts to make economics a source of moral guidance as "doomed efforts." R. Posner (1998, 1670). "I speak from experience." Ibid. (1670 n.62), describing Dworkin's article, cited below, as a powerful critique of his original paper on the subject. Relatedly, the primary debate in the legal academic world about the normative economic approach focuses on Posner's writing that advocates wealth maximization. See, for example, Baker (1975), R. Dworkin (1980), Kronman (1980b), R. Posner (1980d, 1981c), and Symposium on Efficiency As a Legal Concern (1980).

It is ironic, to say the least, that many people believe that the social goal of wealth maximization represents the standard economic view, when in fact, as we will explain, it does not, and when the thrust of many of the criticisms of wealth maximization—notably, the exclusion of distributional considerations—comports with the normative framework of welfare economics. Indeed, many economists who participated in the wealth maximization debate criticized Posner's position on distributional grounds. See, for example, Symposium on Efficiency As a Legal Concern (1980). See also Polinsky (1974, 1679–80), arguing that redistribution is relevant in the economic framework. Neither Posner nor his critics (nor any other legal academic writing supportive or critical of normative law and economics of which we are aware) directly take up the merits of welfare economics in a comprehensive manner.

42. One reason that there is no single, natural set of prices is that prevailing prices depend upon the distribution of wealth. (For example, if there is more inequality of wealth, there may be more demand for luxury goods, resulting in higher prices for such goods, and less demand for goods favored by the poor, lowering their prices.) In addition, prices are influenced by legal rules. (For example, products subject to stricter safety requirements will tend to sell at higher prices.) Moreover, the absence of a natural set of prices is not a problem that can be resolved by a simple price index adjustment, similar to adjustments for pure inflation, because relative prices differ. See generally Arrow (1958), discussing conceptual issues in measuring price, and ibid. (77), stating that "[t]here seems no recourse but to recognize frankly that a standard of living [the cost of which a consumer price index is designed to measure] is not any fixed basket of goods, but a subjective level of satisfaction"—which, we note, is a notion that wealth maximization eschews by focusing on wealth rather than well-being. For a sketch of the development of Posner's views on wealth maximization and how they relate to the problem of defining wealth, see Kornhauser (1998).

on wealth maximization will usually be misguided. As we have mentioned, it may be analytically useful to study models in which social welfare equals some simple wealth-like aggregate.[43] In addition, maximization of wealth (defined, perhaps, with respect to current prices) may in fact reasonably approximate maximization of social welfare in many contexts. Thus, under welfare economics, although wealth is not in itself deemed to be valuable, analysis that assesses policies based on their aggregate impact on wealth will often prove useful. (We observe that the preceding point about wealth applies as well to "efficiency." Efficiency is also a concept that captures aggregate effects of policies on individuals' well-being, and invocations of efficiency should thus be understood to entail a concern for individuals' well-being rather than obeisance to some technical or accounting notion.[44] Moreover, that efficiency does not reflect a concern for the distribution of income indicates that efficiency, like wealth, is only a proxy measure of social welfare, and one that is incomplete in an important respect.)

Finally, to avoid possible confusion, we offer a comment on the meaning of the term "distribution." In this book, we use the term to refer to concerns about the overall allocation of income or wealth—that is, about economic equality and inequality—of the sort we outline at the beginning of this subsection. However, concerns about who should prevail in a particular legal dispute are also often described as distributive. In such contexts, the word

43. Although there is no natural set of prices to use in measuring wealth, this problem may be overcome when undertaking such partial analysis by taking prices as given, or, as in some models, by implicitly stipulating that there is a single good (which thus becomes the common denominator for measuring, say, accident, prevention, and administrative costs). See note 34.

44. Schelling offers a similar observation:

> Unfortunately, economists use the term "efficiency[,]" [which] sounds more like engineering than human satisfaction, and if I tell you that it is not "efficient" to put the best runway lights at the poorer airport you are likely to think you know exactly what I mean and not like it, perhaps also not liking me. If I tell you that "not efficient" merely means that I can think of something better—something potentially better from the points of view of all parties concerned—you can at least be excused for wondering why I use "efficient" in such an unaccustomed way. The only explanation I can think of is that economists talk mainly to each other. (Schelling 1981, 52)

Regrettably, legal academics often understand efficiency as a technical concept, divorced from its roots in individuals' well-being, so that they see pursuing the economic goal of efficiency as unrelated to concerns for human welfare. See, for example, Schwartz (1997, 1802): "[W]hile deterrence can be seen as a way of achieving the somewhat austere goal of economic efficiency, deterrence *also* has deep roots in a humane and compassionate view of the law's functions." (emphasis added); and ibid. (1831): "But if accident prevention is an economic goal, it is *also* a generous, warm-hearted, compassionate, and humane goal. As such, it is a goal that can be and is in fact supported by a broad range of scholars." (Emphasis added.)

"distributive" refers to the allocation of a particular loss between the disputing parties (rather than to the degree of inequality in the distribution of income in the society), and the appropriate allocation is understood to be determined by notions of fairness such as corrective justice (rather than by a conception of the appropriate distribution of income in society as a whole).[45] Welfare economics is not concerned with distribution in this situational sense per se, although, as will become apparent in chapters III–VI, the division of losses between parties to disputes may often affect individuals' well-being in a number of respects.[46]

4. Concluding Remark

Our portrayal of welfare economics probably differs from the understanding that many legal academics (and others) have of the normative basis of law and economics, particularly with regard to the conception of individuals' well-being and the relevance of the distribution of income. In part, this divergence in views may exist because the welfare economic framework developed by economists has not been adequately presented in legal academic discourse.[47] In any event, we hope that our providing a fuller description of welfare economics will lead to a better appreciation of its appeal. We also hope that the foregoing discussion will clarify the contrast between welfare economics and policy assessment based on notions of fairness.

B. Notions of Fairness

1. The Basic Nature of Notions of Fairness

Notions of fairness—which we take in this book to include ideas of justice, rights, and related concepts—provide justification and language for legal

---

45. For further discussion of this issue and the related literature in the accident context, including comments on the difficulty many corrective justice proponents have had in distinguishing these notions of distribution, see section III.B.

46. For example, the prospect of payment or compensation may affect incentives, individuals' well-being when they are risk averse, and the overall distribution of income. But, setting aside these and any other ways that lawsuits may affect individuals' well-being, the bare fact that money may change hands in a lawsuit in certain circumstances, thereby changing how a loss is divided between the two parties, is of no consequence under welfare economics.

47. Some have suggested that much existing policy-oriented law and economics work does not follow the welfare economic approach as we describe it. We think that there is less truth to this point than meets the eye (see, for example, our comments in subsection 3, about the role of income distribution in the analysis of legal rules under welfare economics), but we do not seek to evaluate the existing body of work here.

policy decisions.[48] For example, under corrective justice, an individual who wrongfully injures another must compensate him, a requirement that has implications for the design of tort law.[49] Under the promise-keeping principle, individuals must keep promises, and by extension they must perform their contracts.[50] Under retributive justice, punishment should be in proportion to the gravity of wrongful acts, and thus criminal sanctions should fit the crimes committed.[51]

Although it does not seem possible to adduce a general definition of notions of fairness because they are so many and varied, we can identify a feature that is common to all notions of fairness that concern us in this book and that is central to our argument. *Notions of fairness have the property that evaluations relying on them are not based exclusively—and sometimes are not dependent at all—on how legal policies affect individuals' well-being.*[52] Indeed,

---

48. Most arguments that invoke one of these terms can be expressed using other related terms. For example, the notion that it is "unfair" for one who is injured to be denied compensation from the wrongdoer may also be described as a form of "injustice" or as a violation of a "right" to compensation. Although some writers distinguish among these terms, we find it convenient to use a single term—we have chosen "fairness"—to refer to any principle that does not depend solely on the well-being of individuals, as this section explains. Hence, our arguments concerning fairness-based analysis are broadly applicable to analyses based on justice or rights. Compare Hare (1981, chapter 9), stating that arguments drawing on "justice" and "rights" have the same character as those generally invoking our intuitive moral principles, on which see note 108, and thus have no real independent role in critical moral thinking. See generally note 12 in chapter VII, discussing the notion that the "right" is prior to the "good." We note, however, that welfare economics encompasses many of the concerns underlying invocations of "justice" and "rights," as we illustrate in chapters III–VI and discuss more generally in chapter VIII. See, for example, subsection A.3 (distribution of income), subsection VIII.A.2 (protection against abuse of power), and subsection VIII.C.2 (equal treatment). Indeed, defenders of rights often support them in ways that suggest an instrumental concern with promoting individuals' well-being. See, for example, Fallon (1989, 1697): "Most versions [of liberalism] insist that individual human beings are ultimate subjects of moral value, that they are capable of being oppressed by other human beings and by government, and that a society, in order to be just, must therefore recognize a system of individual rights and enforce those rights evenhandedly." See also ibid. (1698): "Most of us no longer believe that the good of the public could be anything other than some function of the good for individuals. . . ." Of course, the idea that rights may be important on consequentialist grounds, relating to the promotion of individuals' well-being, has long been familiar. See, for example, Mill (1859).

49. See subsection III.B.1.

50. See subsection IV.B.1.

51. See subsection VI.B.1.

52. What we mean by a notion of fairness can be expressed using the apparatus of welfare economics, as set out in note 15. There, we defined social welfare, $W(x)$, as a function that depended exclusively on individuals' utility functions, denoted $U_i(x)$, and thus welfare did

some analysis based on notions of fairness is entirely nonconsequentialist, in that it does not depend on any effects of legal rules. In such cases, it follows automatically that fairness-based analysis is independent of the effects of legal rules on individuals' well-being.[53] More commonly, analysts who accord

---

not depend directly on the situation x itself (that is, independently of how x might affect individuals' utilities). In contrast, a method of policy assessment that gives weight to a notion of fairness corresponds to a function $Z(x)$ that differs from (that is, cannot be expressed in the form of) the $W(x)$ function previously defined. Consider

$$Z(x) = F(U_1(x), U_2(x), \ldots, U_n(x), x).$$

Here, $Z(x)$ may depend not only on each individual's utility, but also directly on x, which includes all characteristics of the situation that will prevail under a legal regime. Thus, it is possible that a characteristic of the situation that affects no one's utility nevertheless affects $Z(x)$. Moreover, it may be that a characteristic that affects individuals' utilities influences $Z(x)$, but in a different manner. For example, a principle that says punishment should be proportional to the harm caused by an act depends on factors that do matter to people: Punishment matters to those punished and, because of deterrence, to others; and harm matters to victims. But under the principle in question, punishment is not assessed solely with regard to how it affects individuals' well-being—the $U_i(x)$—as was the case with the $W(x)$ function.

Some readers may be skeptical about whether a notion of fairness can be expressed in such formal terms. It should be understood, however, that this formulation simply involves a manner of communication. As we explained with regard to the social welfare function used in welfare economics, see note 15, the only essential point is that, whatever the principle of evaluation, it provides an ordering of all potentially relevant situations (legal regimes), denoted here for convenience by the variable x. Now, any numerical value can be assigned to any situation (regime), as long as the analyst assigns a higher number to regimes viewed more favorably than others, so that $Z(x) > Z(x')$ may then be interpreted to mean that situation x is socially preferred to situation x'. Thus, the main assumptions entailed in expressing a notion of fairness as a function, $Z(x)$, are that the notion indicates a preference among various regimes and that the notion is followed in a consistent manner.

53. Sidgwick describes "intuitional" ethics—in his taxonomy, the alternative to egoism and utilitarianism—as

> the view of ethics which regards as the practically ultimate end of moral actions their conformity to certain rules or dictates of Duty unconditionally prescribed. . . . Writers who maintain that we have "intuitive knowledge" of the rightness of actions usually mean that this rightness is ascertained by simply "looking at" the actions themselves, without considering their ulterior consequences. (Sidgwick 1907, 96)

See, for example, ibid. (98); Davis (1991), surveying and criticizing deontological, that is, nonconsequentialist, theories of contemporary philosophers; and Fletcher (1972, 540–41): "Whether the victim is [entitled to recover under the proposed theory] depends exclusively on the nature of the victim's activity when he was injured and on the risk created by the defendant. The social costs and utility of the risk are irrelevant, as is the impact of the judgment on socially desirable forms of behavior." We will not usually distinguish between notions of fairness that do not depend on any consequences and those that do depend on consequences but not on individuals' well-being. (It is, of course, logically possible to have consequentialist

weight to certain notions of fairness also take into account the consequences of legal rules; nevertheless, such analysts do not base their assessment of legal rules exclusively on the effects of the rules on individuals' well-being.

To illustrate this basic feature of notions of fairness, let us elaborate on the classical principle of corrective justice, which requires a person who wrongfully harms another to compensate the victim.[54] (For convenience, we will consider a pure version of the principle, under which the evaluation of a legal rule depends entirely on the extent to which it satisfies the principle and not on anything else, notably, the effects of a legal rule on individuals' well-being.) Application of this principle of fairness relies on a description of the circumstances of an adverse event: A person's conduct is examined to see if it was wrongful and caused harm—and, if so, the principle requires that person to pay compensation to the victim. By definition, then, the fair treatment of individuals depends on the situational character of an event. The determination of whether treatment is fair does not depend—as it would under welfare economics—on how that treatment will influence individuals' behavior and, in turn, on how such behavior will affect individuals' well-being.

Of course, requiring fair treatment will, in reality, have consequences. If wrongful, harmful conduct is penalized, we would expect there to be less of it, with attendant effects on individuals' well-being. (For example, holding

---

principles that are independent of welfare. For example, one could seek to reduce the number of wrongful acts—without regard for the cost of doing so or for how much individuals would benefit—because one deems wrongful acts to be evil per se.) Because our claim is that consequences for individuals' well-being are what should count in evaluation, not consequences unrelated to their well-being, we do not see a consequentialist fairness principle that is unrelated to well-being as better than a nonconsequentialist principle. In any event, as we discuss in chapters III–VI, most non-welfarist notions of fairness seem to be nonconsequentialist.

We also observe that, although many advance notions of fairness that are avowedly nonconsequentialist, their stance is in some respects hard to interpret because of the difficulty in defining which acts are to be considered morally relevant without reference to their actual or expected consequences, particularly given the focus under many moral theories on what individuals "will" to occur, that is, what they voluntarily choose to cause. (For example, to define which acts constitute murder, one would have to refer to acts having expected consequences that include the death of another person.)

> It must be observed, too, that it is difficult to draw the line between an act and its consequences: as the effects consequent on each of our volitions form a continuous series of indefinite extension, and we seem to be conscious of causing all these effects, so far as at the moment of volition we foresee them to be probable. However, we find that in the common notions of different kinds of actions, a line is actually drawn between the results included in the notion and regarded as forming part of the act, and those considered as its consequences. (Sidgwick 1907, 96–97)

54. See section III.B, discussing the literature on corrective justice.

negligent drivers liable will tend to reduce accidents, increase resources de-voted to precautions, result in expenditures on litigation, and provide com-pensation to some risk-averse victims.) But assessing such effects is not part of an analysis based on the notion of fairness that we have posited, because such normative analysis is avowedly independent of how the pursuit of fairness will influence the well-being of individuals. (Thus, the negligence rule may be favored even if there is little reduction in accidents, litigation costs are large, and compensated victims are already insured and thus bear no risk.) It follows from this characterization of fairness-based normative analysis and our prior description of welfare economics that the two approaches are potentially in conflict: Welfare economics is concerned exclusively with effects on individu-als' well-being, whereas notions of fairness like the principle of corrective jus-tice that we have been discussing are not at all concerned with such effects.

Our example involved a pure principle of fairness, under which legal rules are evaluated with no regard for individuals' well-being. Although anal-ysis based on such notions of fairness is embraced by some legal academics and by strictly deontological philosophers (notably, Kant[55]), a different

---

55. Kant states that morality is a quality of the will, and he asserts that

[a] good will is not good because of what it effects or accomplishes, because of its fitness to attain some proposed end, but only because of its volition, that is, it is good in itself and, regarded for itself, is to be valued incomparably higher than all that could merely be brought about by it. . . . (Kant [1785] 1997, 8)

See ibid. (10): "[T]he true vocation of reason must be to produce a will that is good, not perhaps *as a means* to other purposes, but *good in itself*. . . ."

We note that, despite Kant's clear statements in his *Groundwork of the Metaphysics of Morals* ([1785] 1997) and the conventional understanding of his body of work, which is that he is a purely deontological philosopher who entirely rejects alternatives such as utilitarianism, Kant scholars have identified important inconsistencies in Kant's writing that raise some ques-tions about the conventional interpretation:

As Kant himself points out in reply to criticisms by Christian Garve . . . , he never asserted, and nothing he says implies, that happiness is not of the utmost importance [citing a 1793 Kant essay]. The unconditional character of morality means that the desire for your own happiness must not stop you from doing what is right; it does not mean that morality is the only good and important thing. Happiness is conditionally valuable, but when its condition is met, it is a genuine good. The moral law commits us to the realization of the good things that rational beings place value on. A world in which good people are miserable is morally defective. (Korsgaard 1996, 28)

Jeffrie Murphy (1987) has found similar inconsistencies in Kant's treatment of the purposes of punishment, as we discuss in note 17 in chapter VI.

Another aspect of Kant's writing that makes it hard to understand him as a consistent deontologist is his belief that duties to others should be assessed in a way that resembles the method of welfare economics. See, for example, Korsgaard (1996, 349), observing that "Kant

stance is typical, as we said. In particular, it is our impression that most analysts of legal policy who attach importance to notions of fairness hold mixed normative views. That is, not only do they give weight to notions of fairness, but they also place weight, and perhaps significant weight, on how legal policies affect individuals' well-being—either because they understand individuals' well-being to be encompassed by some notions of fairness, or because they consider both fairness and individuals' well-being in reaching a final judgment. For example, a fairness-minded analyst might believe the negligence rule to be more fair than strict liability, if all else is equal, but might ultimately favor strict liability if the negligence rule turns out to be too expensive to administer.[56]

---

agrees that we have a duty to promote the happiness of others," and that, in examining this duty, Kant believed that " '[w]hat they count as belonging to their happiness is left up to them to decide'" (quoting Kant ([1797] 1983)); and Sidgwick (1907, 386): "And we find that when [Kant] comes to consider the ends at which virtuous action is aimed, the only really ultimate end which he lays down is the object of Rational Benevolence as commonly conceived—the happiness of other men." See also O'Neill (1989, 6), noting that Kant added to the second edition of his *Critique of Pure Reason* a motto, taken from Bacon, that included the statement that "they should be confident that I seek to support not some sect or doctrine but the basis of human greatness and well-being."

In addition to such statements, which seem to take a positive view of a consequentialist, welfare-based approach, Kant also makes consequentialist arguments to illustrate or support his seemingly deontological maxims. Thus, when he attempts to deduce requirements of morality from the categorical imperative,

> he fails, almost grotesquely, to show that there would be any contradiction, any logical (not to say physical) impossibility, in the adoption by all rational beings of the most outrageously immoral rules of conduct. All he shows is that the *consequences* of their universal adoption would be such as no one would choose to incur. (Mill [1861] 1998, 51–52)

See ibid. (97), observing that Kant's insistence that a principle be capable of adoption as a law by all rational beings cannot possibly rule out utter selfishness, so that giving meaning to Kant's principle requires that we understand rational beings as having a purpose of providing benefit to their collective interest. See generally Hare (1997, chapter 8, entitled "Could Kant Have Been a Utilitarian?").

56. As the preceding text suggests, such an outcome might be rationalized in one of two ways. First, the applicable notion of fairness may itself be understood as including a concern for individuals' well-being, in which case the fairness of making injurers compensate victims may be deemed to depend upon the cost of administering such compensation—perhaps because administrative costs must be borne by innocent victims, innocent taxpayers, or injurers who, although culpable, may be viewed as excessively punished if they bear a total cost larger than the harm they caused. Second, the notion of fairness may be independent of well-being but still not be decisive when well-being is affected. Thus, one might posit that the negligence rule is more fair but nevertheless favor strict liability because its cost savings exceed the extent of any unfairness associated with using it. Fairness-minded analysts are usually unclear about

We emphasize, however, that we take notions of fairness to be principles used in normative analysis such that at least some weight is given to factors that are independent of individuals' well-being. One could certainly define notions of fairness more broadly, to include as well principles that are equivalent to those of welfare economics. (And certain notions of fairness familiar to some readers may well have this feature, which is to say that these notions give exclusive weight to how legal rules affect individuals' well-being.) Moreover, as we discuss at many points below, notions of fairness are sometimes invoked not as evaluative principles in their own right, but rather as rules of thumb or proxy principles that may help identify legal rules that increase individuals' well-being. (For example, if wrongful acts are usually harmful acts, a practice of penalizing those who commit wrongful acts will tend to deter harmful activity.) But many notions of fairness are not ordinarily understood in this way, and our criticism of the use of notions of fairness obviously does not extend either to welfare economics or to the possibility that notions of fairness may serve as proxy principles for enhancing welfare rather than as independent evaluative criteria.[57]

Thus, to reiterate what we state at the outset of this subsection, *we employ the terminology of "notions of fairness" to refer only to principles that accord weight to factors that are independent of individuals' well-being.* Relatedly, we direct our criticism of fairness-based analysis precisely at those circumstances in which the legal rules that are chosen when weight is given to notions of fairness differ from the legal rules that would be selected under welfare economics.[58] That is, we define notions of fairness as we do—to include all principles that give weight to factors independent of individuals' well-being but only such principles—because the substance of our argument depends precisely on this characteristic.[59] Moreover, as we show throughout chapters III–VI, the leading notions of fairness that are used in legal policy analysis in a wide range of fields of law indeed have just this feature: Analysis

---

how they might incorporate consequences, particularly for individuals' well-being, into their analysis, but how a mixed view might be formulated is not relevant for our purposes.

57. However, our discussion in subsection VII.B.2 and elsewhere suggests that there is value in policy analysts' being clear and explicit about their objectives; in this respect, the language of fairness can be problematic even if it is used to express a welfare-economic-equivalent notion because fairness has many different meanings, some of which stand apart from, and are opposed to, individuals' well-being.

58. The reader should recall from subsection A.3 that many notions of fairness that are concerned with the distribution of income are principles that are concerned exclusively with individuals' well-being and thus can be seen as encompassed by welfare economics.

59. We remind the reader of our discussion in subsection A.2, which explains how our critique of notions of fairness is easily reconciled with our view that considerations of income distribution are admissible under welfare economics.

based on such notions does give weight to factors independent of individuals' well-being and, as a consequence, does result in different prescriptions from those of welfare economics.

2. Further Comments on Notions of Fairness

We now describe some problematic aspects of the meaning, nonconsequentialist nature, and ex post character of many notions of fairness. These difficulties, however, are independent of our main criticisms of the use of notions of fairness and accordingly are set aside in much of the book.

(a) Meaning. It is frequently difficult to ascertain what analysts mean when they discuss the fairness of legal rules. Analysts often use words like "fairness" without defining them. (For example, when discussing tort law, analysts may simply remark that a rule or result is "fair" or "unfair," leaving the reader to guess what that signifies.[60]) Moreover, when analysts do provide some elabo-

60. Compare Sidgwick (1907, 264): "[T]here is no case where the difficulty is greater, or the result more disputed, than when we try to define Justice."; ibid. (342–43), observing that moral notions are often left as "vague generalities," that we cannot make them definite without losing their broad acceptance, and that there may be alternative interpretations or no way to make them definite; ibid. (375), stating that a view of justice holds that "we ought to give every man his own," but that we cannot define "his own" except as equal to "that which it is right he should have," rendering the formulation tautological; and ibid. (392), explaining that the notion that morality depends on the "General Good," which consists in virtue, which depends on common morality, the prescriptions of which depend on a notion of the "General Good," is a further example of the circularity of moral theories. Bentham, commenting on the state of contemporary jurisprudence, expresses similar concerns:

> Had the science of architecture no fixed nomenclature belonging to it—were there no settled names for distinguishing the different sorts of buildings, nor the different parts of the same building from each other—what would it be? It would be what the science of legislation, considered with respect to its *form*, remains at present.
>
> Were there no architects who could distinguish a dwelling-house from a barn, or a side-wall from a ceiling, what would architects be? They would be what all legislators are at present. (Bentham [1781] 1988, 335)

This failure to provide definitions is not confined to analysts. It appears that judges, although they frequently invoke notions of fairness, often do not move beyond vague generalities:

> The most striking characteristic of fairness/rightness reasoning is the extent to which generalized, bottom-line assertions of fairness dominated [in the products liability opinions surveyed]. Nearly three-quarters of the decisions containing opinions relying upon fairness included general assertions—specific fairness reasons appeared in less than half of the fairness-based decisions. . . . This recurring pattern of reliance upon

ration of their concepts, their explanations are often incomplete in important respects. (They might, for instance, refer to corrective justice but fail to articulate what constitutes a wrong, even though wrongdoing is a main condition for requiring compensation under corrective justice.) Additionally, many analysts do not supply a basis for determining the scope of application of notions of fairness. (Corrective justice on its face is applicable to many areas of law but is invoked mainly in tort. Should we view corrective justice as applicable to contract law too, or is there an unstated limitation on its domain?) Relatedly, analysts rarely explain how they resolve the conflicts that arise among the different notions of fairness that may apply in a situation. (If one principle of justice requires the use of strict liability in order to compensate the innocent victim and another requires use of the negligence rule to avoid punishing nonculpable actors, what metaprinciple determines which rule should govern?[61])

Although in principle these deficiencies concerning meaning and scope might be remedied, they generally have not been, and we are left with considerable uncertainty about what fairness-based analysis actually entails, even in very basic settings.[62] We address this problem as best we can in the specific

---

vague assertions suggests that the judges grasped the concept of fairness intuitively, but found it somewhat difficult to explain analytically. (Henderson 1991, 1590–92)

61. As Mill observes:

Not only have different nations and individuals different notions of justice, but, in the mind of one and the same individual, justice is not some one rule, principle, or maxim, but many, which do not always coincide in their dictates, and in choosing between which, he is guided either by some extraneous standard or by his own personal predilections. (Mill [1861] 1998, 99)

See, for example, ibid. (100): "Each [principle] is triumphant so long as he is not compelled to take into consideration any other maxims of justice than the one he has selected, but as soon as their several maxims are brought face to face, each disputant seems to have exactly as much to say for himself as the others."; Sidgwick (1907, 271), observing that one "cannot get any new principle for settling any conflict that may present itself among such duties, by asking 'what Justice requires of us'"; and ibid. (350), stating that we have not been furnished "with a single definite principle, but with a whole swarm of principles, which are unfortunately liable to come into conflict with each other; and of which even those that when singly contemplated have the air of being self-evident truths, do not certainly carry with them any intuitively ascertainable definition of their mutual boundaries and relations." See also Hardin (1986, 67): "[C]onflicts between rights are fundamentally problematic for a rights theory that begins with rights and that therefore has no prior principle from which to resolve the conflict." Most of the particular examples offered in this paragraph in the text will be discussed in section III.B, especially in the footnotes, where we address the views of corrective justice proponents in some detail.

62. Compare Hare (1997, 31), discussing the impossibility of identifying which cases are covered by a moral principle without first identifying what it is about certain acts or consequences that makes them "wrong" in the first place.

legal contexts that we study in chapters III–VI. In each instance, we examine pertinent notions of fairness that are identified in the academic literature on the legal subject under consideration or that seem to be applicable even if not articulated in scholarly writing. When we are uncertain about which legal rule should be understood as most fair under a given notion of fairness, we simply consider each of the relevant possibilities.

(b) *Nonconsequentialist Character*. Adherence to nonconsequentialist notions of fairness seems to raise a basic tension with what one would imagine to be analysts' underlying motivation for caring about fairness. Namely, if consequences are ignored, the amount of fairness or unfairness is also ignored. To illustrate, a principle of fairness may favor a legal rule that prevents sellers from disadvantaging buyers in some way, even though the rule will result in buyers being hurt even more, taking into account that they will pay for the protection through higher prices. One would then have to ask whether such a result is really fairer to buyers. Or consider the notion of retributive justice that calls for punishment that fits the wrongful act. It is possible that a higher level of punishment would reduce or eliminate the occurrence of wrongs. Presuming that the theory's demand for punishment is motivated by the evil associated with wrongdoing (that is, wrongful acts are themselves unfair), it should be troubling that insistence on fair punishment may result in avoidable wrongdoing.[63] (Also, any unfairness associated with imposing a higher punishment is arguably mitigated by the fact that the higher punishment might rarely if ever have to be imposed.) We suspect that such conflicts have not been recognized because analysts focus on particular notions of fairness that, on their own terms, have a nonconsequentialist character. As a result, analysts are not inclined to pay attention to the effects of legal rules even when such effects concern the incidence of unfairness itself. (The following subsection offers a related reason that this difficulty with many notions of fairness has largely been ignored.)

63. We observe that these points constitute a criticism of notions of fairness on the assumption that fairness-minded analysts would deem more of the injustice with which their notions of fairness are concerned to be a bad thing. But in strict logic, an analyst could say, for example, that the injury to buyers through market price adjustments is the fault of the market rather than of the legal rule that set the market forces in motion. Or one could say that punishment and evil acts go hand in hand, but the extent of evil is of no concern to society—in other words, evil is something that, in itself, is a matter of indifference, even though it is a thing that, for some reason, provides a justification for punishing those who bring it about. Because the actual rationale for most notions of fairness is not well articulated in the literature, it is difficult to know whether the consequentialist internal critique sketched in the text would in fact be viewed as troubling by scholars who promote notions of fairness, particularly deontological philosophers. Nevertheless, we suspect that many others would view our observations as relevant.

(c) Ex Post Character. We find that most notions of fairness reflect an ex post perspective on the situations under examination, in contrast to the inclusive approach of welfare economics.[64] In this subsection, we briefly explain this point and suggest that it both lends support to our main arguments, which we sketch in section C, and helps reconcile the widespread appeal of notions of fairness with their shortcomings as independent evaluative principles.[65] (In subsection VIII.C.1, we elaborate on the normative arguments against the ex post perspective entailed by many notions of fairness.)

As we discuss in subsection 1, above, notions of fairness typically are used to reach conclusions based upon situational characteristics of events. Furthermore, it is often true—particularly in legal contexts—that an important, indeed central aspect of the events under examination is what in fact has happened.[66] That is, the assessments are usually made from an ex post perspective. Thus, when asking what rule is just as between an injurer and a victim in the accident context, it is generally assumed that an accident has in fact happened. In examining remedies for breach of contract, the focus is on those cases in which there is actually a breach. When determining what punishment is just for a convicted criminal, the discussion takes for granted that the criminal has been captured. In this respect, fairness-oriented analysts tend to focus on particular outcomes. Moreover, these outcomes are often relatively unlikely ones, given the acts in question. (Most instances of negligence do not cause accidents; for many types of crime, most criminals are not caught.[67])

---

64. To avoid providing repetitive cross-references here, we simply note that pertinent discussions appear in subsections III.C.1(f), III.D.1(e), III.D.1(f), III.E.3, III.E.4, IV.C.2(e), IV.C.2(f), V.A.5(c), V.B.3(e), V.B.6(b), VI.C.1(e)(iii), VI.C.2, and VI.D.3, and in note 111 in chapter III.

65. Compare Easterbrook (1984), identifying judges' tendency to take an ex post perspective, from which fairness arguments are more likely to be made.

66. There is an irony here: On one hand, as discussed in subsections B.1 and B.2(b), most notions of fairness are understood to be nonconsequentialist, whereas on the other hand, their application is very much dependent upon the consequences—often fortuitous ones—of individuals' acts. Some proponents of fairness-based analysis would, however, take issue with principles that depend on the consequences of acts rather than on the acts themselves, as understood from the point of view of the actor at the moment he decides to commit the act; accordingly, some of the analysis in the text would be inapplicable. See, for example, note 111 in chapter III, discussing an argument about the relevance of "moral luck" to the principle of corrective justice. In any event, most notions of fairness are nonconsequentialist (as the term is conventionally understood) in that, when choosing a legal rule to govern particular outcomes, fairness-oriented analysts do not consider relevant how the rules under consideration would affect what outcomes are likely to occur.

67. Even many intentional acts, such as certain breaches of contract, are probabilistic in nature—and often quite unlikely—when viewed ex ante. Thus, it may be that virtually every-

In addition to directing attention to particular, and often unlikely, outcomes, analysis based on notions of fairness frequently ignores important aspects of ex ante behavior that may well be responsible for the ultimate results. Individuals select what level of care to take, which affects the likelihood of accidents; they decide whether to enter into contracts (and at what price) and whether to breach; and they choose whether to commit criminal acts. Each of these decisions, moreover, may plausibly be influenced by what legal rule actors anticipate will be applied ex post, and it is these legal rules that notions of fairness are being used to select.[68]

Thus, in important respects, many notions of fairness focus on particular consequences and thereby ignore or undervalue other plausibly relevant aspects of the situation under examination. In this sense, the judgments reached under such notions of fairness are based on incomplete characterizations of situations. (There is, of course, no error in logic to the extent that the excluded considerations are deemed irrelevant; we argue later, however, that upon analysis it is difficult to sustain the view that such basic features of individuals' behavior and possible outcomes are morally irrelevant.) In contrast, welfare economics takes into account any effect of a legal rule that is pertinent to anyone's well-being. Accordingly, ex ante behavior, all of its possible outcomes, and the potential effects of legal rules thereon are central features that are examined under welfare economic analysis.

A priori, a welfare economic approach to policy assessment would seem superior to one based on notions of fairness to the extent that the former reflects a complete consideration of factors that plausibly seem relevant and the latter does not. Moreover, in our subsequent analysis of particular notions of fairness in specific legal contexts, we find that the two approaches often lead to different policy prescriptions precisely in those cases in which the ex post perspective implicit in fairness-based analysis omits an important consideration that welfare economic analysis captures. For example, notions of fairness pertaining to remedies for breach of contract seem to lead us astray in part because they do not take into account that remedies that seem fair ex post will tend to lead parties to adjust other contract terms (such as the contract price) ex ante in a manner that nullifies or even reverses the apparent effect of the seemingly fair legal rule, or to change parties' decisions whether to enter contracts or to commit breaches in the first place. When fair levels

---

one would breach a contract if a particular contingency arose, but, at the time a contract is originally made, that contingency is remote, whereas contingencies under which promisors will in fact perform are overwhelmingly more likely.

68. That many notions of fairness implicitly ignore how the rules in question affect whether wrongs occur in the first instance is noted in subsection B.2(b).

of punishment are set, standard application of the proportionality principle under theories of retributive justice tends to be problematic precisely in those cases in which the probability of apprehension is low. In such cases, penalties that seem unfairly high ex post (that is, applied to those few criminals who are captured) may actually be moderate or low in an expected sense, which is relevant to whether potential criminals will in fact choose to commit crimes and, arguably, to whether sanctions should be viewed as unfairly high.

Thus, when notions of fairness and welfare economics favor different legal policies, we argue in many contexts that the prescriptions of welfare economics are more compelling because they reflect a more complete and accurate assessment of what legal rules actually do. Of course, a form of analysis that accounts for a broader range of effects of legal rules and that determines their effects more accurately is superior only if the actual effects of legal rules are deemed relevant in the first instance. And as we have discussed, many—or all—effects of legal rules are considered to be irrelevant under many notions of fairness, especially those notions advanced by deontological moral philosophers. Our analysis, however, raises questions about whether this view can plausibly be defended once its implications are fully understood.

Finally, we observe that the ex post perspective of many notions of fairness helps explain their broad appeal. When policy analysts or members of the public at large consider what rule seems fair in a given situation, we tend to focus (as just described) on what has actually happened, for that is what we see in the case before us. We do not tend to focus on what did *not* happen (even when that may have been, ex ante, a much more likely outcome), and we do not directly observe the ex ante choice situation and how behavior may differ in the future as a consequence of the legal rule that we choose to apply to the situation at hand.

This tendency to focus on what is salient—and in particular, on what has actually happened—is related to familiar and prevalent cognitive biases.[69] Because the application of many notions of fairness seems to fit the pattern of certain types of errors in mental processing, cognitive psychology would seem to offer a partial explanation for the apparent attractiveness of fairness-based analysis.[70] As a normative matter, however, if the appeal of notions of fairness, when they conflict with welfare economics, derives from what

---

69. See generally Nisbett and Ross (1980) (survey); Baron and Hershey (1988), explaining how the particular outcomes of initial decisions influence assessments of the quality of those decisions; Fischhoff (1975), presenting experimental evidence of hindsight bias; and Tversky and Kahneman (1973), identifying the tendency of subjects to evaluate the probability of events based on the information that is most available or salient.

70. Baron has recently pursued this line of argument. See, for example, Baron (1993, 1998).

amount to mistakes in judgment, there is no basis for giving the notions weight as independent evaluative principles, to be pursued at the expense of individuals' well-being.

(d) *Concluding Remark.* We examine the foregoing problems in the contexts that we consider in chapters III–VI, but we do not make them the focus of our critique because they are not inherent in the idea of giving weight to notions of fairness. Leading notions of fairness, as articulated over the centuries and today, may have uncertain meaning and application, but perhaps more elaborate or rather different versions of the notions could be developed and a system for resolving conflicts among them could be created. Moreover, if they accounted for the consequences of legal rules and reflected a perspective that incorporated all plausibly relevant factors, such modified notions of fairness might not be subject to the difficulties that we have identified.[71] Nevertheless, the apparent existence of serious yet largely unrecognized internal deficiencies in many prominent notions of fairness suggests that, despite their distinguished lineage, these notions have not received sufficiently rigorous scrutiny. Furthermore, these sorts of problems in themselves raise questions about the plausibility of justifications for the notions (which, as we note in subsection C.2, are not generally supplied).

More importantly, even if the problems discussed in this subsection were overcome, there would remain the central point that we identify in subsection 1: Under notions of fairness, legal rules would still be evaluated based on factors that are independent of individuals' well-being. This property of notions of fairness is the focus of our critique, to which we now turn.

---

71. Fairness proponents have not, however, attempted to put forth notions of fairness that meet the sorts of objections that we have just noted. Indeed, the thrust of many arguments (especially those of philosophers) advancing notions of fairness has been anticonsequentialist and ex post in character, so substituting theories that are consequentialist and that adopt a more inclusive ex ante perspective would conflict with the spirit of the proponents' enterprise. Moreover, if one made the necessary modifications, one would then have notions of fairness that are much closer to the objectives of welfare economics: To apply them, one would have to trace the effects of legal rules and, in the end, trade off competing effects. The primary remaining possible distinction would be that fairness-based analysis would give different weight to the effects than would welfare economics. For example, under welfare economics, the value of deterring a wrong depends on the amount of harm thereby avoided, where harm is measured by the negative effects of the wrong on individuals' well-being. For a notion of fairness not to collapse into welfare economics, it would need to specify a different methodology for assigning weights to wrongful acts—that is, the weights would have to be independent of how the acts affect individuals' well-being.

C. Overview of Our Argument

1. The Argument for Welfare Economics and against Notions of Fairness

Our argument for basing the evaluation of legal rules entirely on welfare economics, giving no weight to notions of fairness, derives from the fundamental characteristic of fairness-based assessment: Such assessment does not depend exclusively on the effects of legal rules on individuals' well-being. As a consequence, satisfying notions of fairness can make individuals worse off, that is, reduce social welfare. Furthermore, individuals will be made worse off overall whenever consideration of fairness leads to the choice of a regime different from that which would be adopted under welfare economics because, by definition, the two approaches conflict when a regime with greater overall well-being is rejected on grounds of fairness.[72]

This point takes on special force when, as we show in important situations, fairness-based analysis leads to the choice of legal rules that reduce the well-being of *every* individual.[73] In particular, in symmetric contexts—those in which all individuals are identically situated (for example, an accident setting in which all are equally likely to be injurers or victims)—it is *always* the case that everyone will be worse off when a notion of fairness leads to the choice of a different legal rule from that chosen under welfare economics. The explanation for this result is straightforward. Because everyone is identically situated, whenever welfare economics leads to the choice of one rule over another, it must be that everyone is better off under the preferred rule. Hence, whenever a notion of fairness leads one to choose a different rule from that favored under welfare economics, everyone is necessarily worse off as a result.[74]

Indeed, the possibility that pursuing a notion of fairness may make everyone worse off is always present (whether or not the notion applies in

---

72. The thrust of our argument is similar to that of consequentialist philosophers (often, it turns out, utilitarians) who criticize nonconsequentialists (deontologists):

> [A]ny system of deontological ethics . . . is open to a persuasive type of objection which may well be found convincing by some of those people who have the welfare of humanity at heart. . . . [T]here must be some possible cases in which the dictates of the system clash with those of human welfare, indeed in which the deontological principles prescribe actions which lead to avoidable human misery. (Smart 1973, 5)

73. As we discuss in note 14, this argument is applicable even if one adopts a conception of well-being different from the welfare economic conception described in subsection A.1.

74. See Kaplow and Shavell (1999). The argument drawing on the symmetric case is developed in detail in the tort context in subsections III.C.1 and III.D.1.

symmetric contexts): It can be demonstrated that consistently adhering to any notion of fairness will sometimes entail favoring regimes under which every person is made worse off.[75] And it is not possible to circumvent this

75. For a formal proof of our claim (which does not make use of symmetric settings), see Kaplow and Shavell (2001). Rather than sketch the proof here, we present a heuristic explanation, applicable to asymmetric cases, that we think better conveys the relevant intuition.

(1) Consider rules X and Y, and suppose that rule X is deemed better under welfare economics but rule Y is deemed better under a notion of fairness. The welfare economic assessment means that, under the analyst's choice of the social welfare function, which embodies a distributive judgment, the overall situation under X is superior. See subsections A.2 and A.3.

(2) Now, construct a regime X' with the following characteristics: The overall level of social welfare and the extent of fairness are each the same as under rule X, but the distribution of well-being is the same as under rule Y—that is, the ratio of any two individuals' well-being is the same. (How do we identify such a regime? Consider all conceivable regimes with the same distribution of well-being as under rule Y and the same degree of fairness as under rule X. Now, in some such regimes, everyone will be better off than under rule X, so social welfare will be higher in such regimes than under rule X; and, in others, everyone will be worse off than under rule X. Since we can imagine all regimes in between, we can consider one in particular, which we are calling X', in which social welfare is the same as under rule X.)

(3) Next, compare situations X and X'. Even though the distributions are different, by construction (step 2) the overall level of social welfare is the same under the two regimes (and also, by construction, the extent of fairness is the same). If, for example, equality is greater under X' than under X, we would suppose that average incomes are lower under X'. The point is that, *whatever distributive judgment the analyst thinks appropriate*, it will be true by definition that, if one undertakes the above construction, the proper evaluation will rate X and X' equally, for social welfare (as defined under welfare economics) and the level of fairness are each the same in both situations.

(4) Finally, compare situations X' and Y. We know that the level of social welfare is higher under X' than under Y. (This is because we began, in step 1, with a case in which social welfare was higher under X than under Y, and, in step 2, we constructed X' such that it has the same level of social welfare as X; hence, social welfare under X' must be greater than under Y.) But because, in step 2, we constructed X' to have the same distribution as Y, it must necessarily be the case that everyone is better off under X' than under Y. (If total social welfare is greater under X' than under Y and the distribution of well-being is the same under both, it must be that every individual has a higher level of well-being under X'.)

This demonstration establishes that, if one insists on giving weight to a notion of fairness in an asymmetric case, then, whenever one chooses a rule different from one chosen under welfare economics, one expressly rejects a regime (here, X) that is equivalent—taking into account the combination of efficiency and distribution, and also holding fairness constant—to another regime (here, X') under which everyone would be better off than under the regime (here, Y) favored by the notion of fairness. In sum, even though in the asymmetric case the fairness-preferred rule may not itself make everyone worse off than under the alternative favored by welfare economics, choosing such a rule entails—if one is logically consistent—

problem by modifying notions of fairness in any plausible manner.[76] That any notion of fairness will sometimes make everyone worse off raises a sharp question: To whom is one being fair?

---

expressing a normative preference in another (constructed) situation for a rule under which everyone would be worse off. (We observe that the heuristic argument presented in this footnote differs from our formal proof and makes stronger implicit assumptions. The only substantial assumption required for our proof is that notions of fairness are, in mathematical parlance, continuous in a particular sense: The fairness assessment cannot change infinitely at the margin in response to a small, finite change in the level of some consumption good. For example, it cannot be that the notion of fairness under consideration gives more weight to, say, the population having one more peanut than it gives to an arbitrarily large degree of unfairness.)

We observe that, in the economics literature on social choice theory, a result exists that is a special case of the one that appears in the above-cited reference. Sen shows that following a particular notion of fairness—under which a stated domain of individuals' activity may not be regulated, even if that activity may affect the well-being of others—can lead to violation of the Pareto principle (that is, the principle that social choices should never make everyone worse off). See Sen (1970). The logic of his proof, in essence, is that allowing individuals to create externalities may make everyone worse off. Our argument, by contrast, applies to all notions of fairness, most of which do not have the feature that generated Sen's result.

We also note that Sen interprets the conflict he adduces as raising questions about the underlying appeal of the Pareto principle. We do not, however, find his interpretation plausible. Sen's condition (which he calls "liberalism" and which he and others have subsequently described as an implication of a form of libertarianism) might seem merely to protect a sphere of individuals' activity. Yet in fact, his condition is tantamount to a prohibition on individuals' voluntary waiver of their "rights" in the specified sphere (in exchange for some concession from others), and this implicit prohibition is the source of the conflict with the Pareto principle that Sen identifies. Thus, this conflict actually has its roots in a limitation on individuals' rights. Moreover, protecting a sphere of individuals' activity—commonly implemented by granting certain rights against government action—is familiarly justified on grounds of promoting individuals' well-being, because this sort of restriction on the government, while making some welfare-improving policies unavailable, produces an even greater expected gain by reducing the potential for the government's abuse of power. See, for example, Hardin (1986, 69–73) and subsection VIII.A.2. Sen's subsequent responses to these and other reactions to his argument seem to us to shift ground in a manner that eliminates the conflict he originally identified. In a later article, for example, Sen suggests that a contract by which parties mutually waive their rights may not work for a number of reasons: It may not be enforceable; enforcement may involve other adverse costs; and individuals may not in fact wish to enter into such a contract, because they prefer minding their own business. See Sen (1992, 144–46). In each instance, however, Sen no longer rejects in principle the state in which each party's rights are overridden and both parties are better off. Instead, such a state is deemed to be infeasible or for various reasons is not understood to make the parties better off after all. See also subsection VIII.B.3, addressing whether other-regarding preferences should be ignored in determining what is socially desirable.

76. This conclusion follows immediately from our proof that any notion of fairness conflicts with the Pareto principle, see Kaplow and Shavell (2001), because any modified notion

We observe that the foregoing conclusion is important in assessing the soundness of a notion of fairness regardless of whether pursuing the notion will in fact make everyone worse off in the particular setting under consider-

---

of fairness—if it has not been altered so as to require an exclusively welfare economic assessment—is still, formally, a notion of fairness; hence, our proof remains applicable to any modified notion. (In a recent article, Chang suggests that certain notions of fairness—not ones that we examine in chapters III–VI—could be modified so as to avoid conflicts with the Pareto principle. See Chang (2000a). As we explain in our reply, however, his attempt to circumvent the conflict requires abandoning basic notions of logical consistency; moreover, even then, his attempt is unsuccessful. See Kaplow and Shavell (2000a). But see Chang (2000b).)

We also note that, even if one could somehow modify some principle of fairness to avoid the objection that it may lead to choices under which the well-being of all individuals is reduced, one would have to ask whether the original motivation for the notion of fairness (whatever it might be) applies to the modified principle with sufficient force to justify its adoption. For example, if we view some act as intrinsically evil under a notion of fairness, but the notion becomes modified so that we give this evil no weight when such acts make everyone better off (but not when, say, they make almost everyone better off but a single person is ever-so-slightly worse off), a serious question arises whether we can still maintain the view that the act is intrinsically evil. See note 55 in chapter III, discussing the issue in the torts context. Compare Sidgwick (1907, 341–43), raising the question, in the context of discussing the need to modify moral principles to avoid conflicts, whether "the correctly qualified proposition will present itself with the same self-evidence as the simpler but inadequate one; and whether we have not mistaken for an ultimate and independent axiom one that is really derivative and subordinate."

Focusing on the symmetric case and on how it differs from asymmetric cases sheds further light on the inevitability of the conflict with the Pareto principle. First, as already explained in the text, any notion of fairness—however modified—will *always* make everyone worse off in the symmetric case whenever it favors a different regime from that favored under welfare economics. Second, as we elaborate in the tort context, the only important difference between symmetric and asymmetric cases is that the choice of legal rules may affect the distribution of income in the latter case. See subsection III.C.2(e). But, as explained in subsections A.2 and A.3, welfare economics already encompasses concerns about the distribution of income (or, more broadly, the distribution of well-being). That is, our definition of notions of fairness, which refers to all evaluative principles that differ from welfare economics, refers to notions based on matters other than concerns about income distribution. Hence, the only pertinent difference between the symmetric and asymmetric cases seems to be a factor (income distribution) that is separate from the concern of all notions of fairness that we consider. To sum up the argument, if notions of fairness are deemed to be flawed in the symmetric case because they can only make everyone worse off, and if asymmetric cases (that is to say, all other cases) do not differ from the symmetric case in a manner that is normatively relevant to the notions, then it follows that the notions are flawed in all cases. (This claim is related to the preceding point in this footnote because, in essence, the present argument is that, whatever the underlying basis for the notion of fairness is, it does not vary between symmetric cases, in which conflicts with the Pareto principle always arise, and asymmetric cases, in which such conflicts often do not arise.)

ation or how often that would be so.[77] We emphasize this observation because of the common belief among policy analysts that the Pareto principle—which holds that one should always favor a policy under which everyone is better off—has little relevance in making policy decisions because it will rarely be true that one legal rule will literally make everyone better off than does another rule. Our argument is that, although adherence to the Pareto principle may not directly determine policy *choices* in most real situations, it nevertheless has powerful implications for what *criteria* for making policy choices one can plausibly employ. That is, if one adheres to the view that it cannot be normatively good to make everyone worse off, then logical consistency requires that one can give no weight in normative analysis to notions of fairness because doing so entails the contrary proposition that sometimes it is normatively desirable to adopt a policy that makes everyone worse off. To restate the point, demonstrating that a theory, in some part of its intended domain of application, contradicts a principle to which one subscribes, shows the theory to be unacceptable.[78]

77. The arguments in the text that follows were first developed in Kaplow and Shavell (1999). For further elaboration in the tort context, see subsection III.C.1(e)(iii).

78. The importance of logical consistency in moral theory is often emphasized by philosophers. See, for example, Hare (1963, 93); ibid. (100–02), criticizing those who attempt to escape from the demands of consistency by refusing to make moral judgments in certain cases that prove problematic for their theory; Hare (1997, 22): "Logic does not forbid the adoption of different moral standards by different people; it simply prohibits a single person from adopting inconsistent standards at the same time. . . ."; Sidgwick (1907, 6): "[A] fundamental postulate of Ethics [is] that so far as two methods conflict, one or [the] other of them must be modified or rejected."; and ibid. (341), emphasizing the need for consistency and noting that "we frequently find ethical writers treating this point very lightly." See also Rawls (1980, 546), offering the following prescription when examining basic matters of justice: "[I]t is sensible to lay aside certain difficult complications. If we can work out a theory that covers the fundamental case, we can try to extend it to other cases later. Plainly a theory that fails for the fundamental case is of no use at all."

To many, the need for consistency will be evident, yet it is worth elaborating briefly. The application of a theory in a particular context can depend on any number of factors that are recognized under the theory. Thus, under welfare economics, if the amount of harm caused under a given regime or its administrative costs were to differ, the assessment might well change because, under the terms of the theory, assessments depend on individuals' well-being and these factors affect well-being. It does not follow, however, that it would be acceptable for an adherent of welfare economics to offer a different assessment after a change in a factor that did not influence well-being, for to do so would, essentially by definition, entail a rejection of welfare economics (which itself rules out the relevance of any such factor). Similarly, if one believed that a principle of fairness was absolute, and if that principle were nonconsequentialist (and thus necessarily independent of the effects of regimes on individuals' well-being), one could not favor a different regime from that dictated by the principle in order to avoid

We also wish to observe that the previously discussed symmetric case—in which notions of fairness make everyone worse off whenever their prescriptions differ from those of welfare economics—arguably has special significance under a number of broadly endorsed principles of normative analysis. In particular, we suggest that, upon examination, the Golden Rule, Kant's categorical imperative, and the construct of a veil of ignorance can each be seen to imply the requirement that all normative principles be tested in a symmetric setting. The reason is that normative analysis is understood to proceed from a disinterested perspective, which can be made explicit by imagining that one is equally likely to be in any possible role, that one will occupy each and every role, or some equivalent assumption—and it is precisely symmetric settings that have this property.[79] Thus, our argument

---

the problem that in some cases following the principle would lead to everyone being worse off. To do so would be to adopt a different principle. Compare note 55 in chapter III, discussing the issue in the tort context.

Nor can one avoid the problem that we describe in the text by adopting less absolute views of fairness, including commonly held mixed views that give weight to effects on individuals' well-being as well as to notions of fairness. On one hand, such mixed views can surely be consistent. On the other hand, we show at many points that such mixed views may in fact favor regimes under which everyone is worse off (and that this proposition is true whenever any weight, however little, is given to notions of fairness). Indeed, the discussion in the text of the symmetric case, indicating how any notion of fairness makes everyone worse off whenever it differs from welfare economics in that setting, is fully applicable to mixed views that give *any* weight to a notion of fairness. See also note 50 in chapter III, illustrating how, in the reciprocal case in the tort context, giving any weight to any notion of fairness will sometimes lead one to favor a legal rule under which everyone is worse off. And, as explained in note 76, our proof that all notions of fairness sometimes make everyone worse off applies to any modification of the notions (as long as any weight to fairness remains), and hence to any mixed view.

79. To understand why principles like the categorical imperative essentially require an assumption of symmetry, let us consider an example. Suppose that there are strong people and weak people. A strong person would be happy to live by the principle that "might makes right" because such a rule would be to his advantage. Furthermore, in the absence of a symmetry assumption, the categorical imperative does not interfere with his adopting this principle because, if it were adopted as a general rule for society, he would still benefit from it, because he is strong. In order for the categorical imperative to rule out principles like "might makes right," which are little more than statements of self-interest, it is necessary to imagine either that everyone is identical (neither strong nor weak) or that each of us is in each position (strong and weak) for a commonly specified period of time. This is precisely what is assumed to be true when one examines symmetric settings. See, for example, Hare (1963, 93–95); Hare (1997, 130–35), discussing Kant's categorical imperative; Korsgaard (1996, 100–01), stating that Kant's model of immoral conduct is built on the sort of case in which the problem is the temptation to make oneself an exception; and Sidgwick (1907, 389), criticizing Kant by observing: "[S]till a strong man, after balancing the chances of life, may easily think that he and such as he have more to gain, on the whole, by the general adoption of the egoistic

that following notions of fairness always makes everyone worse off in symmetric settings (whenever there is a conflict with the prescriptions of welfare economics) poses an unrecognized but real challenge to those who find compelling the types of moral theories just described and (as many do) also advance notions of fairness. It would seem either that such analysts must systematically favor notions that always make everyone worse off in the type of setting that they believe should be used to test moral concepts, or that they must abandon their notions of fairness in favor of welfare economics.[80]

The conclusion that in some circumstances all individuals will be made worse off as a consequence of pursuing any notion of fairness reveals that fairness-based analysis stands in opposition to human welfare at the most basic level. Now, as we state in the introduction, it is true that it is virtually a tautology to assert that fairness-based evaluation entails some sort of reduction in individuals' well-being, for notions of fairness are principles of evaluation that give weight to factors unrelated to individuals' well-being. Nevertheless, we do not believe that the full import of fairness-based analysis for human welfare is appreciated. Indeed, policy-oriented legal academic literature that uses notions of fairness as criteria for assessing legal rules rarely confronts or even acknowledges the existence of the conflict between giving weight to notions of fairness and advancing individuals' well-being. In order for the conflict to be better appreciated, we examine a range of important legal settings and discuss in specific terms how prominent notions of fairness lead to outcomes under which individuals are worse off. This constitutes the first step of our argument in chapters III–VI.

---

maxim. . . ." See also Sidgwick (1907, 380), noting that formulas like the Golden Rule are incomplete because "there may be differences in the circumstances—and even in the natures—of two individuals, A and B, which would make it wrong for A to treat B in the way in which it is right for B to treat A"; and Rawls (1980, 529): "[T]he background setup of the original position . . . situates [the parties] symmetrically [so that persons are not] advantaged or disadvantaged by the contingencies of their social position, the distribution of natural abilities, or by luck and historical accident over the course of their lives." For further discussion, see subsection VIII.C.1.

80. See notes 86 and 94 in chapter VIII, noting a range of philosophers, including many regularly cited in support of notions of fairness, who endorse such principles for testing moral concepts. We hardly mean to suggest that most proponents of these moral constructs endorse welfare economics, for most in fact do not. Rather, we are arguing that if one begins from the sparest form of the choice settings that those proponents endorse and recognizes our argument that in such settings all deviations from the prescriptions of welfare economics make everyone worse off, then a strong case indeed exists for concluding that their preferred frameworks, upon analysis, support welfare economics.

2. On the Rationale for Notions of Fairness

The second aspect of our critique of fairness-based analysis concerns the rationale for notions of fairness. We have just stated that furthering notions of fairness, whenever they favor policies different from those endorsed under welfare economics, leads to reductions in individuals' well-being. Moreover, we presume that legal policy analysts and policymakers care about individuals' well-being. Hence, it is especially important to explore what the rationale for notions of fairness might be.

Thus, in the various settings that we examine in chapters III–VI, we ask what society might be thought to gain—in what sense a better state of affairs might be said to exist—by pursuing commonly advanced notions of fairness at the expense of individuals' well-being. In this inquiry, we consider the legal academic and philosophical literature endorsing the particular notions of fairness that are put forward in each setting and attempt to identify the motivation for advancing notions of fairness at the cost of individuals' well-being. We also reflect on the essential features of the paradigmatic legal situations that we analyze and endeavor to determine why what is viewed as the fairer outcome might seem attractive.

We find that little explicit justification for notions of fairness—even those developed by prominent writers over the years—has in fact been offered.[81] Relatedly, many theorists seem to rely heavily on conclusory metaphors, such as the idea espoused by some retributivists that punishment is justified in order to restore a sort of moral balance in the world.[82] This shortcoming, we believe, helps to explain the previously identified problems of determining the meaning of notions of fairness and of resolving internal tensions:[83] When a principle's underlying rationale is unknown, we should

81. Hume comments on arguments in his time as follows:

> No, say you, the morality consists in the relation of actions to the rule of right. . . . What then is this rule of right? In what does it consist? How is it determined? By reason, you say, which examines the moral relations of actions. So that moral relations are determined by the comparison of actions to a rule. And that rule is determined by considering the moral relations of objects. Is not this fine reasoning? (Hume [1781] 1998, 159)

82. See, for example, subsection VI.B.1. Compare Munzer (1979, 426–27), arguing that Fried "makes no effort to state either line of argument" that his theory requires, that he offers "tantalizing suggestions [that] are not arguments," and that it is questionable whether "any reason [that is not circular can] be given within Fried's theory" for his central claim.

83. See subsection B.2.

not be surprised that it will be difficult to ascertain whether and how various factors affect its proper application.

Moreover, the motivations that we are able to identify (from the literature or from reflection on relevant situations) do not really provide good reasons for viewing notions of fairness as independent evaluative principles, even from the apparent perspective of those who favor giving weight to these concepts. In some instances, there seems to be little relationship between the purposes offered (or those that might be imagined) to support the notions of fairness and the actual implications of the notions for the choice of legal rules. For example, in some basic settings, the only effect of choosing punishment in accordance with retributive justice (aside from raising the costs of the legal system and increasing the number of innocent victims of crime) is to preserve the profitability of crime to some potential criminals—who themselves are viewed as wrongdoers according to retributive theory.[84] Or, pursuing the principle of corrective justice, under which wrongdoers must compensate victims for harm done independently of whether requiring such payments reduces individuals' well-being, has as its only other feature that in certain settings it favors some types of individuals over others based solely on characteristics determined by chance elements that seem morally arbitrary from any plausible perspective.[85]

An additional problem with the defenses offered for notions of fairness concerns the source of the underlying arguments. Sometimes, proponents of principles of fairness support the principles by reference to their consistency with existing legal doctrine. Such a claim, however, relies on positive analysis that by its very nature cannot provide a normative justification for the use of the principles for purposes of evaluation, including assessment of the very legal rules that were examined when identifying the principles of fairness.[86] Also, fairness proponents often appeal to intuitions or instincts. Yet, as we discuss at length (beginning in section D), this source of insight is an unreliable grounding in the context we are examining; the intuitions and instincts themselves usually have a basis in promoting individuals' well-being (rather than in some independent, conflicting purpose); and reliance on these sources is self-defeating because an important purpose of explicit normative analysis of legal policy is to identify when our intuitions or in-

---

84. See subsection VI.C.1(e).

85. See subsections III.D.1(f)(ii) and III.E.3.

86. It has been suggested that this difficulty arose with jurisprudential work in the distant past. See Bentham ([1781] 1988, 329 n.1), referring to the inconsistent focus of the work of Grotius, Pufendorf, and Burlamaqui with regard to distinguishing "is" from "ought" and other matters.

stincts may lead us astray. Finally, some fairness arguments seem implicitly to be motivated by the circumstances of a specific group of people (such as victims of wrongful acts). But as we state above, pursuing a notion of fairness can make literally everyone worse off, necessarily including anyone whose plight might have motivated the notion of fairness in the first place. In this respect, it may not be surprising that, upon reflection, it is difficult to identify rationales for notions of fairness: Most moral theories seem concerned in some way with individuals, whereas, by definition, notions of fairness are concerned with factors that are unrelated to and thus (when they differ from welfare economics) opposed to individuals' well-being.

Our contention that the rationales that seem to underlie notions of fairness do not justify treating these notions as independent evaluative principles is not, of course, one that can be established through logical deduction, for logic alone cannot tell us what our first principles of evaluation should be. Nevertheless, we believe that our specific discussions in chapters III–VI show that the deficiencies just described are indeed present and that, upon reflection, notions of fairness are difficult to defend. We also suggest that the problems identified in subsection B.2 concerning the meaning and internal coherence of notions of fairness raise serious questions about the possible bases for most notions of fairness, which should make it less surprising that careful scrutiny reveals the notions to be untenable.[87]

---

87. We should comment on the relationship between our critique of notions of fairness as evaluative principles and Richard Posner's recent criticism of moral philosophy. See R. Posner (1998) (1997 Holmes Lecture), and R. Posner (1999) (book expanding on Holmes Lectures). A substantial part of Posner's discussion displays a different focus from ours; his is an examination of whether the writing and argument of academic moral philosophers influences individuals' views of common morality. See, for example, R. Posner (1998, 1639–42). In this respect, his argument is positive rather than normative. See, for example, ibid. (1647), stating that he is not presenting "normative theories about the content of our moral obligations[, that is, theories] of how we *should* behave." We, however, are interested in normative theory—in particular, in whether legal policy analysts should employ welfare economics in evaluating legal rules. (For further discussion of how questions of common morality—that is, how ordinary individuals should behave toward others, see, for example, ibid. (1639)— differ from the moral question of how legal policy should be assessed, see subsection D.2, especially note 121.)

In addition, Posner advances the thesis that judges should ignore what he describes as academic moral philosophy and instead embrace pragmatism. Despite his disclaimer of interest in normative theory, this claim about how cases ought to be decided—and accordingly how at least some legal rules should be chosen—is by its nature a normative one, in the domain of moral philosophy. Although this part of Posner's argument, unlike the first, is related to our undertaking, we have some difficulty comparing his position with ours, because he does not examine in depth the moral basis for pragmatism and he does not clearly identify

Our two conclusions, about how the pursuit of notions of fairness makes individuals worse off and about the lack of affirmative warrant for using notions of fairness as evaluative principles, raise the question of why legal policy analysts (including ourselves), policymakers, and philosophers, among others, find these notions so appealing. We devote significant attention to this question throughout this book and offer a number of related answers (including one, concerning the ex post character of notions of fairness, that we already discussed in subsection B.2(c)).[88] An important part of the explanation, we believe, is suggested by the analysis in the next section.

D. Notions of Fairness and Social Norms

We submit that there is often a correspondence—indeed, sometimes an identity—between notions of fairness that are used as independent principles for the evaluation of legal rules and various social norms that guide ordinary individuals in their everyday lives. Moreover, we suggest that this

---

the purpose of a pragmatic inquiry. Nevertheless, he does consider a number of illustrations and in doing so makes frequent reference to welfare-related factors. See, for example, R. Posner (1998, 1696), referring to such social goals as peace and prosperity, and ibid. (1703–04), referring to adverse effects of racial segregation, such as impaired self-esteem and educational success, and concluding that the shared morality underlying *Brown* was a belief that "a government should have a reason for inflicting suffering on human beings." In addition, although he criticizes a wide range of academics who advance moral views applicable to the assessment of law, he almost never mentions utilitarians, welfare economists, or, more generally, consequentialists, suggesting that their views are not in substantial conflict with his own. See, for example, ibid. (1638–39), listing a large number of legal academics and philosophers who are representative of those whom he intends to criticize. More affirmatively, Posner clearly endorses consequentialism, see, for example, R. Posner (1999, 227), viewing "pragmatism as a disposition to ground policy judgments on facts and consequences," and he also indicates that he is "guided mainly by the kind of vague utilitarianism, or 'soft core' classical liberalism, that one associates with John Stuart Mill, especially the Mill of *On Liberty*." Ibid. (xii). There are, however, some instances in which he distances himself from such views, but for reasons that are unclear. See, for example, R. Posner (1998, 1697), emphasizing that one would not have to be a utilitarian to endorse certain criminal justice policies, yet identifying the real purposes of the stated policies as deterrence, prevention of criminal behavior, and, in another case, reduction in unauthorized violence. See also note 41, discussing Posner's earlier writing that advances wealth maximization as the proper basis for normative evaluation.

88. Another important reason that notions of fairness may be attractive is that they sometimes serve as proxy devices for advancing individuals' well-being (as we illustrate throughout chapters III–VI). For additional reasons for the appeal of notions of fairness to legal academics in particular, see subsection VII.B.1.

relationship between notions of fairness and social norms helps to reconcile the attraction that notions of fairness possess with our argument that such notions should not be given independent weight in the assessment of legal rules. Our discussion draws on a long tradition of work in the social sciences, evolutionary biology, and philosophy, including early contributions of Hume, Mill, Sidgwick, and Darwin,[89] and many of our conclusions concerning implications for understanding fairness arguments relate to themes developed in the more recent work of Baron and Hare.[90] In subsection 1, we examine the functions that social norms serve, and, in subsection 2, we consider the implications of the relationship between social norms and notions of fairness for our analysis.

1. The Nature of Social Norms

Ordinary individuals routinely draw on social norms in determining how they should behave in their daily lives—in interactions with friends, relatives, business associates, and the like—and social norms serve as principles in educating and governing children. These norms include such principles as telling the truth, keeping promises, not harming others, and being held accountable when one does cause harm.

Many notions of fairness employed to assess legal rules correspond to these social norms. For example, the promise-keeping theory of contract law may be identified with the social norm that individuals should keep their promises. The notions of corrective justice in tort and retributive justice in criminal law seem to be closely related to social norms about not harming others and being held responsible when one does so. Moreover, these notions of fairness contain limits on what sanctions are appropriate (the punishment should fit the crime rather than be excessive) that are similar to limits embodied in social norms (adverse reactions to wrongs should be proportionate, to avoid becoming wrongs themselves). As we discuss more fully in chapters III–VI, each notion of fairness employed by legal analysts that we consider indeed corresponds to an identifiable social norm.[91]

89. See, for example, Hume ([1751] 1998); Mill ([1861] 1998, chapter 5), the longest chapter in *Utilitarianism*, entitled "On the Connexion between Justice and Utility"; ibid. (68–71); Sidgwick (1907); and Darwin ([1874] 1998, chapters 4–5), chapter 5 entitled "On the Development of the Intellectual and Moral Faculties During Primeval and Civilized Times." See also Bentham ([1781] 1988, 309–33), section entitled "Limits between private Ethics and the Art of Legislation."

90. See, for example, Baron (1993) and Hare (1981).

91. As will become clear in subsection 2, it is important to distinguish carefully between social norms—which *describe* the principles that in fact serve to regulate interaction in every-

Having stated that there seems to be a relationship between notions of fairness and social norms, we now sketch what appears to be the role of social norms in regulating individuals' behavior in the informal situations that they confront in everyday life. Once we describe this function of social norms, we will be able to discuss how it bears on our understanding of notions of fairness used in legal policy analysis.

Social norms tend to be valuable regulators of everyday conduct for two reasons.[92] First, the presence of internalized social norms—against lying, larceny, or littering, for example—reduces the incidence of selfish, undesirable behavior. Individuals will have a motive to follow social norms if those who violate them experience feelings of guilt and encounter social disapproval, whereas those who comply with the norms feel virtuous and receive praise from others. That is, when a principle is embodied in an internalized social norm, there exists a system of internal rewards and punishments and related external (yet extralegal) rewards and punishments—in the form of social approval and disapproval—that serves to induce individuals to behave in accord with the principle.[93] If, instead, individuals were unconstrained by

---

day life—and notions of fairness—which are used to *prescribe* what legal rules should govern. We note that confusion can arise in part because, as we explain in the text to follow, individuals in everyday life regard social norms as prescriptive.

92. Of course, it is not always the case that social norms will promote individuals' well-being in the manner we describe in the text. Some social norms may have once advanced welfare but become counterproductive over time, although the norms are resistant to change. See, for example, Akerlof (1980), Campbell (1987, 175), R. Posner and Rasmusen (1999, 377–79), and Rubin (1982, 162, 172–73). See also Wilson (1980, 278), stating that current moral codes are essentially similar to those prevalent when humans lived in hunter-gatherer societies. Some social norms might have been in error from the outset. Some might promote welfare, but not to an optimal extent, perhaps reflecting compromises between individuals' self-interest and overall social welfare. See, for example, Vanderschraaf (1999). And some might advance one group's interest at the expense of another's (for example, solidarity among thieves helps them but harms society as a whole). See, for example, Axelrod (1986, 103–04) and R. Posner (1997, 366). See also Sidgwick (1907, 168–69), noting the tendency of moral codes to arise within groups, such as trades and professions, that may conflict with the general public good, and McAdams (1995), describing norms that promote intragroup status-seeking to the detriment of other groups. See generally Elster (1989, 99), offering reasons to question whether norms promote individual or common interests, and E. Posner (1996a), discussing various respects in which group norms may be inefficient.

93. See, for example, Hume ([1751] 1998, 149): "And by such universal principles [virtue and vice] are the particular sentiments of self-love frequently controuled and limited."; ibid. (150): "Other passions, though perhaps originally stronger, yet being selfish and private, are often overpowered by [the force of benevolent concern underlying moral sentiments], and yield the dominion of our breast to those social and public principles."; Sidgwick (1907, 29): "[T]he fear of moral censure and its consequences supplies a normally useful constraint on

social norms, their selfish tendencies would more often lead them to act opportunistically, such as by lying when they might gain thereby, stealing when they are stronger than their victim, or littering at their convenience. Thus, social norms can play an important role in channeling individuals' behavior in a socially desirable manner.[94]

---

the will of any individual."; ibid. (166–75), emphasizing the need for internal sanctions to help align self-interest with the social interest; ibid. (440), stating that inculcating justice as part of common morality has the effect of "checking malevolent or otherwise injurious impulses"; Pettit (1990); R. Posner (1998, 1663–64); and Trivers (1971, 50), suggesting an evolutionary basis for feelings of guilt. Strongly internalized social norms are obviously important if individuals are to feel guilty or virtuous depending on how they act. Strongly internalized norms also support external rewards and punishments because the individuals who bestow them must be internally motivated to do so (or themselves face rewards and punishments from others, and so forth). See Pettit (1990), emphasizing internal motivations, based on individuals' attitudes favoring compliance with norms and their desires to be regarded positively by others, and suggesting that others' attitudes automatically provide rewards and punishments, essentially at no cost to those who hold the positive or negative attitudes toward others. See also Smith ([1790] 1976, 116): "Nature, when she formed man for society, endowed him with an original desire to please, and an original aversion to offend his brethren. She taught him to feel pleasure in their favourable, and pain in their unfavourable regard. She rendered their approbation most flattering and most agreeable to him for its own sake; and their disapprobation most mortifying and most offensive." The social process by which good behavior is rewarded and bad behavior is punished, thereby promoting adherence to social norms, is not limited to the human species. See, for example, Waal (1982, 205–07).

94. In addition to the sources cited in notes 89 and 90, see, for example, Becker (1996, chapter 11), Ellickson (1991, chapters 10–11, 16), Ellickson (1989, 45–46), suggesting how society might induce individuals to behave cooperatively rather than selfishly, Frank (1988), Campbell (1975), Hirshleifer (1987), Pettit (1990), and R. Posner (1997).

For convenience, we will generally write in the text as though social norms are inculcated, but our analysis also applies when social norms have an evolutionary aspect (in the biological sense). On the sociobiology of norms of behavior, see Daly and Wilson (1988), Darwin ([1874] 1998, chapter 5), Campbell (1975, 1109–13), Hirshleifer (1977, 28), Rubin (1982), and Trivers (1971, 45–54). As Wilson observes:

[T]he hypothalamus and limbic system of the brain . . . flood our consciousness with all the emotions—hate, love, guilt, fear, and others—that are consulted by ethical philosophers who wish to intuit the standards of good and evil. What, we are then compelled to ask, made the hypothalamus and limbic system? They evolved by natural selection. That simple biological statement must be pursued to explain ethics and ethical philosophers, if not epistemology and epistemologists, at all depths. (Wilson 1980, 3)

See also R. Alexander (1987), arguing that philosophers misunderstand morality because they do not appreciate the evolutionary basis of moral behavior, notably, altruism as purportedly distinguished from selfishness; Daly and Wilson (1988, 254): "When we consult our sense of what is right or just—and all philosophers, however analytic, concede that moral arguments

If social norms are to be effective in countering opportunistic inclinations in the way just described, it seems that, given the nature of human psychology, they must operate as rather broad, superior principles that are generally not subject to case-by-case analysis and exception. Feelings of guilt or outrage, for example, seem likely to be more powerful if they are spontaneous reactions rather than products of dispassionate consideration and calculation. Moreover, if social norms called on individuals to make complex, situation-specific judgments, individuals' ability to rationalize and their tendency to misperceive events in a manner that aligns with their self-interest might dilute the norms' effectiveness. The type of "man who can say to himself without questioning or hesitation, 'Thou shalt not commit adultery' or 'Never, never tell a lie' is more likely, in the course of his life, to do what is optimific than one who is prepared to question these principles, in the sense of 'contemplate breaking them', on any but rather extraordinary occa-

---

ultimately rest on irreducible apprehensions of right and wrong—then we are consulting moral/emotional/cognitive mechanisms of the human mind. These mental mechanisms must surely have been shaped, like any other organized species-typical attributes of body or mind, by a history of selection."; Singer (1981), arguing that moral intuitions are ultimately rooted in biology and that the core elements of altruism and reciprocity are products of evolution, although when supplemented by reason they may be developed into a more universal ethical theory; Wilson (1993), arguing that innate moral sentiments, having biological as well as social origins, are an important and fairly immutable aspect of human nature that is rooted in humans' innate sociability, their desire for attachment and affiliation; and Mackie (1982b, 8): "[W]e can find a biological explanation for the tendency to feel nonmoral resentment of injuries and gratitude for benefits, and a sociological explanation for the development, out of these, of their moral counterparts."

Literature in many fields has in recent decades devoted increasing attention to the evolution of norms, although without necessarily emphasizing a biological foundation for the norms. See generally Binmore (1998), arguing that evolution and socialization produce social norms that coordinate behavior and are self-enforcing; Ben-Ner and Putterman (1998); Frank (1988), discussing respects in which sentiments restraining opportunistic behavior may be inherited rather than socially inculcated; Hayek (1973, 72–76), suggesting that rules to regulate antisocial behavior evolved even before the development of language in which to articulate them; Ullmann-Margalit (1977), suggesting a functional explanation for the emergence of social norms; Axelrod (1986), discussing the evolution of norms that regulate conflict; Bicchieri (1990), arguing that social norms of cooperation are an example of spontaneous orderings that emerge through evolutionary processes; Campbell (1975, 1104–09), presenting theories of social evolution; Gibbard (1982a), arguing that our sense of justice is an evolutionarily stable strategy for dealing with bargaining problems; Mackie (1982a), emphasizing the evolutionary, in contrast to consciously chosen, character of norms of common morality; and Vanderschraaf (1999), discussing how the social norms that evolve need not be optimal and tend to reflect compromises between self-interest and overall social welfare.

sions."[95] Finally, to the extent that the social norms to which we adhere are instilled in us when we are very young,[96] it is particularly important that the application of the norms not allow the individuals subject to them substantial discretion and room for judgment in determining when they apply.[97]

95. Hare (1973a, 10). See Becker (1996, 17), arguing that cooperation is more easily sustained when individual behavior is habitual; Brandt (1979, chapters 9, 11); Sidgwick (1907, 7–8): "[C]ommon moral opinion certainly regards the duty or virtue of Prudence as only a part—and not the most important part—of duty or virtue in general. Common moral opinion recognises and inculcates other fundamental rules—for example, those of Justice, Good Faith, Veracity—which, in its ordinary judgments on particular cases, it is inclined to treat as binding without qualification. . . ."; Baron (1994b, 32–33) (Baron's responses to comments on Baron (1994a)): "In some cases, people may behave better if they blindly obey the rules they are taught. A person who knows that the rule against lying is only a means to the best consequences might be too tempted to justify his harmful lying in that way."; Campbell (1975, 1123): "Human urban social complexity is a product of social evolution and has had to counter with inhibitory moral norms the biological selfishness which genetic competition has continually selected."; Hare (1982, 23, 31–38); ibid. (32): "[T]hese are not rules of thumb, but principles which [those who are inculcated with them] will not be able to break without the greatest repugnance, and whose breach by others will arouse in them the highest indignation."; Trivers (1971, 48–50), advancing the thesis that emotions evolved to reinforce reciprocal altruism by overcoming individuals' incentives to cheat, which would disrupt long-run relationships and their benefits; and Weisbrod (1977, 994). Compare R. Posner (1998, 1692): "A person who somehow managed to become perfectly reflective about his behavior would be a kind of monster; speaking for myself, I would prefer to be surrounded by ordinary, morally unreflective people. . . ." Legal academics have begun to pay more attention to social norms that guide behavior through feelings of shame and the prospect of other social sanctions as well as through the force of habit. See, for example, Ellickson (1991), E. Posner (1996b, 2000), McAdams (1997), R. Posner (1997), and Sunstein (1996b). See also Symposium: Law, Economics, and Norms (1996).

96. Under the competing theory that some social norms are innate, see note 94, our conclusion also follows.

97. See, for example, Baron (1993, 11–12) and Sartorius (1972, 208–210). Indeed, many social norms instilled in children have as a primary objective creating an immunity to arguments from others, whether strangers or peers, who might readily lead the children astray if they are willing to listen rather than insist on the principle that they have been taught. Compare R. Posner (1997, 366), stating that parents and teachers "try to drum norms into a child's head, where they may become habits that the child will feel uncomfortable breaking even after he grows up." The idea that social norms become second nature has long been noted.

> The views [about injustice that are] the most familiar to us are apt, for that very reason, to escape us; and what we have very frequently performed from certain motives, we are apt likewise to continue mechanically, without recalling, on every occasion, the reflections, which first determined us. The convenience, or rather necessity, which leads to justice is so universal, and every where points so much to the same rules, that the habit takes place in all societies. . . . (Hume [1751] 1998, 97)

(continued)

A second reason that social norms can be valuable is that they may serve as useful proxy principles, heuristics, or rules of thumb that promote individuals' welfare. Such use of norms is valuable because most decisions that individuals make are of such small consequence that refined consideration of possible actions would be a waste of effort.[98] In addition, it would be very costly, if not infeasible for many individuals to acquire the analytical skills and knowledge necessary to behave otherwise.[99] Relatedly, if decisions were made on a case-by-case basis, individuals would inevitably make some errors, particularly in certain settings, such as when a decision would produce immediate, tangible benefits or costs. Adhering to rules—such as always saving a given portion of one's paycheck or never having more than two drinks—may well reduce the rate of errors even though the rules themselves do not always prescribe the behavior that is truly best under the circumstances.[100] (We note that these sorts of benefits from following norms may complement the preceding function of curbing opportunistic behavior toward others: For example, never telling a lie may usually be ideal even from a selfish perspective because possible retaliation, loss of reputation, and so forth may make lying unlikely to be profitable in the long run.[101]) Like the

---

Some scholars have also suggested that society will resist changes in social norms. See, for example, Wilson (1980, 286): "To counteract selfish behavior and the 'dissolving power' of high intelligence, each society must codify itself. . . . Reform meets repression, because to the extent that the rules have been sanctified and mythologized, the majority of the people regard them as beyond question, and disagreement is defined as blasphemy."; and Akerlof (1980), stating that those who do not follow social norms are subject to reputational sanctions.

98. See, for example, Brandt (1979, 272), Ng (1979, 10), and Smart (1973, 42–43).

99. A potential cost of this lack of expertise is that citizens, in their capacity as voters, may have difficulty in making intelligent choices, a problem we examine in section VII.C. We also note that many individuals should and do have a nontrivial understanding of economic affairs because it is necessary for personal financial management and for many occupations, although the explicit normative framework of welfare economics generally is unfamiliar.

100. See, for example, Baron (1998, 17): "When we make decisions quickly, when we have a strong self-interest, when our information is compelling but unreliable, and perhaps in other cases, we must take into account the possibility of error as part of our judgment. We must override the judgment we would make without taking error into account, exactly because that judgment is likely to lead us away from the best consequences."; Frank (1988, chapter 4); Singer (1981, 161–62); Sartorius (1972, 211–13); and Smart (1973, 43).

101. Hume observes:

Honesty, fidelity, truth, are praised for their immediate tendency to promote the interests of society; but after those virtues are once established upon this foundation, they are also considered as advantageous to the person himself, and as the source of that trust and confidence, which can alone give a man any consideration in life. (Hume [1751] 1998, 122–23)

first function of social norms, curbing opportunistic behavior toward others, this benefit from following norms is obtained only if individuals are inclined to follow the norms rather automatically; reflective analysis of whether norms should be followed in each particular case would be self-defeating in light of the norms' purposes.[102] It is also necessary that the norms be simple and general in application.[103]

2. Implications for the Role of Notions of Fairness in Legal Policy Analysis

We now explore some implications of the foregoing characteristics of social norms for understanding the role of notions of fairness in legal policy analy-

---

102. This point is obvious when the benefit of a norm involves economizing on decisionmaking costs in the first place. It also holds true with respect to other rationales. See, for example, Hare (1981, 38), noting individuals' tendency to give in to temptation or to act imprudently when under stress, unless they have a strong intuitive motivation to follow certain principles.

103. If the norms are complex, context-specific calculation will be required. As Hare observes, there are additional reasons that norms cannot be too complex:

> The maxims themselves cannot be of unlimited specificity, for good practical reasons—above all the reason that they have to be built into our characters, and for this purpose a certain degree of generality is requisite. . . . [The maxims] have to be *fairly* general, just because to be useful they have to apply to many situations which resemble one another in important respects, and have to be a suitable guide for moral education, which cannot cope with principles of infinite specificity. (Hare 1986, 219–220)

See, for example, Brandt (1979, 201–02, 287), identifying limits on complexity and suggesting that there exist few opportunities for correction because of reliance on conditioning, and Hare (1973a, 14–16; 1981, 35–36). This point about the generality of social norms relates as well to the first purpose of such norms, curbing opportunistic behavior. If substantial reflection is required to apply the norms, individuals may be led to see that their own self-interest calls for precisely the actions that the norms were meant to curtail. There exist additional considerations that limit the sophistication of many social norms. For example, many norms must be taught to young children. Furthermore, because social approval and disapprobation are important in the enforcement of social norms, there needs to be general agreement on the norms' application, often in the presence of limited information; this need tends to limit the range of factors that can be included in any norm and the complexity of interaction among the factors that are admitted.

It is possible, of course, that subtle, more complex norms might, through sufficiently frequent experience (or human evolution), become habitual. It is unlikely, however, that these norms' complexity will be directly relevant to pertinent legal problems. For example, even if there were a highly refined social norm concerning when one should be permitted to break a lunch engagement, it would not follow that the same norm would be a good guide for determining which breaches of construction contracts or financial covenants should be excused.

sis. Our first point is that because analysts (such as ourselves) are members of society, and usually well-socialized members at that, one would naturally expect analysts to find social norms personally appealing.[104] This point can be appreciated by recalling some of the features of social norms that we have just described. These norms exercise substantial influence on our behavior and on our perceptions of others' behavior; we all undoubtedly have strong feelings about what is and is not proper. Moreover, our views about the application of social norms in various contexts tend to be resistant to scrutiny; we are inclined to believe in social norms even when we are presented with competing arguments, whether generated in our own minds or by others.[105] Finally, as indicated in various footnotes, social norms may well have an evolutionary basis, in which case their attractiveness is instinctive and likely to be resistant to challenge.

Given these features of social norms, consider how we are likely to react when confronted with various situations in our role as legal policy analysts, particularly when those situations seem analogous to ones in which prevailing social norms are applicable. It would be surprising if we were not influenced—often strongly—by the pull of social norms. When this point is combined with the observation that most notions of fairness that are employed in assessing legal rules in fact correspond to social norms that regulate everyday behavior, we have at least a partial explanation for the evident appeal of notions of fairness in normative legal analysis.[106]

104. Compare Sidgwick (1907, xii) (preface to second edition): "The morality that I examine in Book iii. is my own morality as much as it is any man's: it is, as I say, the 'Morality of Common Sense,' which I only attempt to represent in so far as I share it. . . ."

105. See, for example, Baron (1994a, 7): "[O]ur commitments to these rules [of everyday morality] are especially tenacious."; and ibid.: "The application [of such principles] may be unreflective. The principle has become a fundamental intuition, beyond question." As Calabresi observes:

> Moral attitudes develop and decay slowly. They become encrusted with significance that is often quite foreign to the situation that engendered them. The longer the history of a moral attitude toward an act, the more likely it is that the attitude will have become separated from its cause and the more difficult it will be to change the attitude even if the cause is no longer valid. All this is just a way of saying that, almost by definition, "moral" status has a strength of its own apart from the original source of the status. (Calabresi 1970, 296)

106. Furthermore, an element of the mechanism by which some social norms operate involves some individuals sanctioning others, such as by expressing disapproval when others speak or act in ways that seem to violate the norms. To the extent that analysis under welfare economics appears in tension with social norms, therefore, one would expect an automatic negative response to welfare economic analysis. We comment further on this phenomenon in subsection VII.B.1.

Second, this source of the appeal of notions of fairness—that they are associated with social norms to which we have an attachment—does not carry any implication that they should receive weight as evaluative principles when choosing legal rules. Quite the contrary is the case. In particular, we have suggested that the underlying function of social norms—to reduce opportunistic behavior toward others and to help us best advance our interests—is to further the well-being of individuals in society, and that may well be the primary reason that we seek to instill the norms.[107] If, then, the raison d'être for social norms is to promote individuals' well-being, it would be a non sequitur to elevate social norms into independent evaluative principles that are to be given weight at the expense of individuals' well-being. If we were self-conscious about the role of social norms and the origins of our

107. In addressing social norms concerning justice, Hume begins his discussion by stating:

> That justice is useful to society, and consequently that *part* of its merit, at least, must arise from that consideration, it would be a superfluous undertaking to prove. That public utility is the *sole* origin of justice, and that reflections on the beneficial consequences of this virtue are the *sole* foundation of its merit; this proposition, being more curious and important, will better deserve our examination and enquiry. (Hume [1751] 1998, 83)

After thus introducing his chapter on "Justice," he proceeds to show why public utility is in fact the sole basis for social norms involving justice. See Sidgwick (1907, book 4, chapter 3), noting and elaborating on Hume's argument, and ibid. (466): "Common-Sense morality is really only adapted for ordinary men in ordinary circumstances—although it may still be expedient that these ordinary persons should regard it as absolutely and universally prescribed, since any other view of it may dangerously weaken its hold over their minds." See also R. Posner (1998, 1662): "[W]hat is codified [in a society's moral code] is what is useful rather than what idealists might think is good."

We note that our argument in this paragraph holds even if norms have a genetic basis and arise through self-selection or if they arise through socialization but without anyone consciously and purposively instilling the norms, because surviving norms tend to be those that promote welfare. See, for example, Daly and Wilson (1988, 254): "Rather than representing the denial of self-interest, our moral sensibilities must be intelligible as a means to the end of fitness in the social environments in which we evolved." An important qualification, however, is that evolutionary selection (and, in certain settings, social selection) tends to promote species survival, which obviously is an important aspect of well-being but may diverge from overall well-being in the sense that we use here, see subsection A.1. In such cases, it is overall well-being that is relevant for purposes of normative analysis. For further references on the evolution of social norms, see note 94.

In cases in which a social norm is detrimental, see note 92, the argument for treating the norm as if it were an independent evaluative principle is obviously even weaker than our discussion in the text suggests.

instincts and intuitions about them, we would not be led to attach independent weight to notions of fairness for the purpose of assessing legal policy.[108]

108. Unless we believe our instincts and intuitions to have been implanted through an
infallible (perhaps divine) mechanism, we must inquire into their possible origins and functions in order to assess what weight, if any, we should give them as evaluative principles, no
matter how attractive they may appear to us. Furthermore, it is not valid simply to ask whether
our instincts and intuitions retain appeal when we stipulate, hypothetically, that any welfare-
promoting functions they might serve are to be ignored, because the force of instincts and
intuitions in our minds derives from our prior experiences or evolution. A range of scholars
have explored grounds for skepticism about the sorts of moral intuitions that we have been
discussing. See, for example, Baron (1998, 152): "[I]t is unclear just how our intuition came
to reflect what is right. What is the causal connection between something being morally right
and our intuition that it is right? It is easier to understand our intuitions as arising from
overgeneralizations of learned principles, or from the emotions that evolution gave us. . . .";
Baron (1994a), arguing that cognitive heuristics and biases like those known to influence many
nonmoral judgments similarly characterize moral intuitions that depart from consequentialism; Baron (1995, 36): "But, to someone who has been reading the literature on the psychology of heuristics and biases, [moral intuitions are] unlikely to tell one much about the correct
moral solution to these cases [that are typically presented by philosophers] or others."; ibid.
(39): "Given that these heuristics exist and that at least some of them are clearly erroneous,
how can we be sure that our moral intuitions are not in the same category?"; ibid., explaining
that we cannot rely on the fact that everyone strongly holds a moral intuition, for some
decisionmaking heuristics are similarly strongly held yet are known to be wrong; Brandt (1979,
236): "[T]here are good reasons for not appealing to intuitions as a test of moral truth: the
diversity of intuitions around the world, and our knowledge that our intuitions are what they
are because of the cultural tradition within which we stand."; Griffin (1986, 2): "[I]t is only
in moral philosophy that [intuitions] have risen so far above their epistemological station[].
In mathematics, the natural sciences, and other branches of philosophy, finding a conclusion
intuitively repugnant does not close an argument; it is a reason to start looking for a good
argument."; Hare (1982, 35): "Such are the intuitionists, to whom their good ingrained principles seem to be sources of unquestionable knowledge. Others of a more enquiring bent will
ask why they should accept these intuitions. . . ."; Hare (1973a, 16), suggesting that intuitionism seems attractive because our norms have been inculcated in such a manner that violation
creates a sense of guilt; Harsanyi (1995, 330–31), arguing that moral intuitions are an unreliable guide in ethics, that there is no reason to believe that individuals have direct access to
moral truths, and that intuitions vary across individuals and societies in a manner suggesting
that they are a product of their social environment; Ng (2000, 52): "No one can deny that
the initial evolution/development of morality must be purely instrumental (in enhancing either our welfare or our surviving and propagation fitness) as there existed no morality to
begin with. We then learned and taught our children and students to value moral principles,
etc. first as a way to increase the degree of adherence to these principles and hence our welfare.
Eventually, some, if not most, people came to value these principles in themselves by learning
and probably also by instinct."; Ng (1981b, 529–30), explaining that, although it is advantageous to adopt rules of ordinary conduct that are usually correct, and although these rules
may come to be valued for their own sake, these truths are not inconsistent with the belief that
a direct focus on social welfare should guide policy; Sidgwick (1907, 211): "[T]he psychological

Third, and related, it seems evident that using social norms as a guide for the design of legal rules will sometimes lead us astray, although this will

---

question, as to the *existence* of such [intuitive] moral judgments [must be] carefully distinguished from the ethical question as to their *validity*[;] . . . these questions are sometimes confounded. . . ."; ibid., suggesting that intuitions may be in error "just as many apparent perceptions through the organ of vision are found to be partially illusory and misleading"; ibid. (212), suggesting the need for "an inquiry into the antecedents of the apparent intuition, which may suggest to the reflective mind sources of error to which a superficial view of it is liable"; ibid. (393), acknowledging the importance of developing a moral character but denying that its elements "are the constitutents of Ultimate Good," and arguing that "the opposite is implied" because a good disposition is "clearly not valuable in itself but for the acts and feelings in which it takes effect, or for the ulterior consequences of these"; Singer (1981, 110): "[T]he idea of moral laws existing independently of the interests and preferences of living beings is implausible, once we have more straightforward explanations of the origins of ethics."; Smart (1973, 68): "It is undeniable that we do have anti-utilitarian moral feelings in particular cases, but perhaps they should be discounted as far as possible, as due to our moral conditioning in childhood."; and note 94, quoting Wilson. See generally Bentham ([1781] 1988, 17 n.1), describing appeals to intuition, under such names as "moral sense," "common sense," and "understandings," as involving no more than the speaker's relating his likes and dislikes; Hare (1997, chapter 5), criticizing intuitionism on the ground that it collapses into relativism and hence cannot be a proper ethical theory; and Westermarck (1932, chapter 2), criticizing philosophers who believe that what are really moral intuitions are instead some sort of objective moral truth. For further discussion, see note 121, which distinguishes between intuitions as social norms that guide behavior in everyday life and the critical analysis necessary to assess such intuitions, and subsection VI.C.4(b) and note 112 in chapter VI, which address the misleading nature of intuition about punishment of the innocent when applied to contexts different from those from which the intuition derives.

Despite a variety of criticisms of intuitionism from a range of scholars over a substantial period of time, many philosophers continue to rely on intuitions and devote little or no discussion to the arguments that cast doubt on their relevance to moral analysis. There are a few exceptions, but even then they do not address most of the reasons that have been given against the use of intuitions. See, for example, Urmson (1975), defending intuitionism by arguing, in essence, that anti-intuitionist theories are inconsistent with our intuitions, and not addressing any of the arguments that have been suggested to explain our intuitions in a manner that makes intuitionist moral philosophy untenable. Crisp describes the history and current failings of philosophical treatment of this subject as follows:

> [There is a need for] much deeper reflection than is common at present on the origin of our moral beliefs. There was a movement towards this in the latter half of the nineteenth century, in which Mill's chapter 5 played an important part, but it was unfortunately derailed by the confident intuitionism of G. E. Moore (1873–1958), W.D. Ross (1877–1971), and others. Despite the problems with Mill's account of the relation between utilitarianism and justice, his attempt to explain the peculiar phenomenon of morality was an important move in the right direction. (Crisp 1998, 32)

It is useful to distinguish the direct use of particular intuitions or instincts about the fairness of particular acts or rules from the systematic study of a wide range of such intuitions for the

not, of course, always be the case. Favorable outcomes may arise precisely because social norms tend to be conducive to individuals' well-being in the informal setting of everyday life. This tendency suggests that using the norms as guides to policy will sometimes lead us to choose legal rules that promote well-being. After all, the problems regulated by the formal legal system have much in common with—and are sometimes the same as—the problems that make certain social norms useful in everyday life. (We note that the propensity of notions of fairness to favor modes of behavior and, sometimes, legal rules that advance individuals' well-being may also help to explain the broad appeal of such notions.)

---

purposes of critically assessing them and thereby attempting to identify what principle or principles underlie them. The former sort of activity, which is used by many legal academics and philosophers in attempts to determine which legal rules are fair, is subject to the range of criticisms discussed in this section and in the sources just cited. See also Brandt (1979, 16–23), stating that "it is puzzling why an intuition—a normative conviction—should be supposed to be a test of anything"; Hare (1971, chapter 7); Hare (1981, v): "Philosophers . . . have lacked any clear idea of what constitutes a good argument on practical questions. Often they are content with appeals to their own and others' intuitions or prejudices; and since it is these prejudices which fuelled the violence in the first place, this is not going to help."; ibid. (7), referring to other modern moral philosophers "who appeal at every turn to their own and (they hope) their readers' moral intuitions" rather than engage in rational analysis; ibid. (12), arguing that the "'equilibrium'" that philosophers who rely on moral intuition reach "is one between the forces which might have been generated by prejudice, and no amount of reflection can make that a solid basis for morality," and noting that "two mutually inconsistent systems [can] be defended in this way[, which only shows] that their advocates [have] grown up in different moral environments"; Mill ([1861] 1998, 87): "That a feeling is bestowed on us by Nature, does not necessarily legitimate all its promptings. The feeling of justice might be a peculiar instinct, and might yet require, like our other instincts, to be controlled and enlightened by a higher reason."; and Smart (1973, 56), arguing that the foundation of ethical principles is insecure when it is based on "our particular feelings, which may be subtly distorted by analogies with similar looking (but in reality totally different) types of case, and by all sorts of hangovers from traditional and uncritical ethical thinking."

In the enterprise involving the systematic, critical study of our moral intuitions, our myriad and sometimes conflicting intuitions and instincts are not themselves seen as constituting a set of ultimate, independent evaluative principles but instead are taken as data to be scrutinized in order to identify their sources and shared elements. This approach is the one advanced by some of the theorists identified at the outset of this section, especially Hume and Sidgwick. See, for example, Sidgwick (1907, 216): "[T]hroughout these chapters I am not trying to prove or disprove Intuitionism, but merely by reflection on the common morality which I and my reader share, and to which appeal is so often made in moral disputes, to obtain as explicit, exact, and coherent a statement as possible of its fundamental rules." Our argument that leading notions of fairness across many fields of law correspond to social norms that themselves seem to have the common function of promoting individuals' well-being supports the conclusion reached by others, such as Hume and Sidgwick, that in-depth examination of everyday notions of morality identifies the promotion of welfare as their common core.

Nevertheless, social norms will not systematically provide reliable guides for legal policymaking.[109] An important reason is that the analogy between everyday life and the formal legal system is highly imperfect. The problems confronted in the two settings are not always the same. Moreover, even when the problems are the same, the contexts are not. The legal system generally employs different sanctions (damage awards, injunctions, fines, and imprisonment) from those used in informal social regulation (guilt and ostracism), and the availability of different remedies may well affect what should be deemed a violation.[110] In addition, the information available to the formal legal system and the administrative costs of operating it often differ substantially from their analogues in everyday interactions. In general, one should keep in mind that the legal system exists in large part because informal social regulation cannot successfully control certain forms of undesirable behavior, whereas the formal legal system, presumably because it differs in relevant respects, is up to the task.[111] Thus, one should not expect social norms suited

109. In addition to the points discussed in the text, social norms may be inappropriate guides because they do not maximize welfare even in the realm for which they were designed. See note 92. Baron offers a further reason that social norms about morality are unreliable:

We tend to see our intuitions [including moral intuitions] as the product of some natural force that, in some sense, understands more than we do. . . . I shall argue, however, that many of these intuitions arise in a much simpler way. They are the application of principles that *are* often consistent with bringing about good consequences but that are applied in cases where they do not do this. They are, in the language of psychology, overgeneralized. (Baron 1998, 5)

110. Because the different remedies involve different social costs of imposition and differ in their effectiveness, the conditions determining when and how they should be employed may well be different.

111. See, for example, R. Posner and Rasmusen (1999, 380–82), discussing when social norms, government action, or some combination of the two should be used to control behavior. The existence of crimes that are *malum prohibitum*—acts deemed to be evil because their prohibition is determined to be socially beneficial, even though they are not customarily regarded as evil—indicates one respect in which the formal legal system operates differently from social norms. More broadly, government action is considered appropriate in many areas even though social norms may not require action; for example, no strong affirmative duty to come to the assistance of others, especially strangers, is generally thought to exist, but this is not thought to be an argument against government provision of lifeguards or subsidies to medical research. Another indication of the contrast between the two settings is that, with the emergence of a modern legal system, there arose the social norm of not taking the law into one's own hands—a social norm that itself emphasizes the distinction between the two spheres and reserves certain action for the government.

It is also true that many actions that are viewed as wrong under prevailing social norms (ranging from deceit to rude behavior, and covering many acts within the family), and thus

to the realm of decisionmaking in ordinary life to be appropriate in the appreciably different domain of policy analysis designed to guide the formulation of legal rules.

Other characteristics of social norms imply that they are inadequate as guides for legal policy analysis. We have said that social norms must be relatively simple because they must be imparted to children and applied without sustained analysis.[112] Accordingly, these norms will sometimes lead individuals governed by them to behave in a less-than-ideal manner.[113] For the very same reason, social norms are unreliable guides for policy evaluation.[114] In addition, our discussion suggests that social norms tend to resist modification; in contrast, social problems, as well as the range of feasible solutions to them, have changed increasingly rapidly in recent history.[115]

----

proper sources of feelings of guilt and causes for ostracism, are not considered proper subjects of government regulation. In sum, the fact that a type of act violates or is required by a social norm is neither necessary nor sufficient to justify corresponding action by the government. See also note 121, discussing the distinction between the ideal content of social norms and the proper criteria for assessing such norms or for evaluating government policy, and note 24 in chapter VI, discussing how most commentators seem to reject the assumption of retributive theorists that society should punish individuals if and only if they commit wrongful acts.

112. See, for example, note 103. Simple norms not only aid actors who are deciding how to behave in the first place, but also help onlookers who must be able to assess whether actors have complied with norms in determining, for example, whether to express disapproval. See generally Pettit (1990, 743–44), emphasizing that, for social norms to be self-enforcing, others need to be in a position to know whether the norms have been violated.

113. See, for example, Rakowski (1991, 30), and sources cited in note 103.

114. Compare Atiyah (1981, 137), arguing that traditional moral notions about promise-keeping are less rich and flexible than the tools of the law; that morality is "created more slowly, less consciously, and perhaps less precisely" than is the law; and that morality is more likely than the law to overshoot by encouraging too much respect for the rule that promises be kept; and Hare (1981, 59–60), explaining that the prima facie principles, including rights, used in moral education and character formation necessarily must be simple and general and thus, when we are engaging in critical moral thinking, we must be able to override them in order to avoid incorrect decisions.

115. To the extent that social norms have a biological foundation, their evolution will be extremely slow relative to the current pace of change in the relevant environment. See, for example, Cosmides, Tooby, and Barkow (1992, 5–6), advancing the thesis that normal parts of contemporary life "are all the novel products of the last few thousand years," explaining that "our ancestors spent the last two million years as Pleistocene hunter-gatherers" and that "[t]hese relative spans are important because they establish which set of environments and conditions defined the adaptive problems the mind was shaped to cope with," and stating that "behavior generated by mechanisms that are adaptations to an ancient way of life will not necessarily be adaptive in the modern world"; Symons (1992), criticizing social scientists who fail to recognize that human psychology is based on adaptations that survived in the Pleistocene environment, which began over a million years ago, and suggesting that, accordingly, the resulting traits may

There is another important difference between the situations of everyday life, in which norms must be easily taught to children and readily applied without much thought, and the setting of legal policy analysis: The latter involves a collective enterprise undertaken by groups of researchers over a span of years or decades. Moreover, one of its chief aims is to determine when our simple intuitions about which legal rules are best turn out to be correct and when they are, upon examination, discovered to be mistaken. It would defeat the purpose of legal policy analysis if these intuitions, based on internalized social norms, provided the basis for our conclusions, displacing (indeed, being invoked as grounds for criticizing) explicit analysis of the actual effects of legal rules on individuals' well-being. Social norms did not arise for the purpose of guiding formal policy analysis. Just as norms that guide individuals in the use of electrical appliances (say, never open the back of an appliance while it is plugged in) may be the wrong norms—counterproductive ones—for engineers who design such devices, so other social norms for individual behavior may be ill-suited to the architects who design legal institutions.

In sum, we would expect that notions of fairness, which correspond to social norms, will sometimes serve as helpful proxy tools for identifying legal rules that raise individuals' well-being, but we would also predict that there often will be an important divergence between rules that promote fairness and those that advance well-being. When there is a divergence, analysts should follow welfare economics rather than fairness-based analysis. That the notions of fairness are rooted in social norms does not in itself imply that the notions have independent importance as evaluative principles; indeed, an understanding of social norms suggests the opposite.

We now turn to a fourth set of implications of the correspondence between notions of fairness and social norms—one concerning how notions

---

well be maladaptive in various settings in the modern world, which differ in important ways; and ibid. (138): "The brain/mind mechanisms that constitute human nature were shaped by selection over vast periods of time in environments different in many important respects from our own, and it is to these ancient environments that human nature is adapted."

Similarly, social norms, once inculcated, resist change and are often passed on to future generations without substantial reflection. See, for example, R. Posner (1998, 1666): "And think of how we acquire our moral views. We acquire them mostly in childhood, when moral instruction that appeals to reason takes a back seat to parental example, experience, and religion. Once engrained in us, a morality is difficult to change." Compare Gibbard (1982b, 73), suggesting that common morality will substantially but not completely promote well-being because of distortions in the process by which it evolves, and quoting Sidgwick for the view that deviations may involve exaggeration of something useful, extension by mistaken analogy, or survival of an element once but no longer useful.

'ness may in fact be relevant under the welfare economic framework , ...ugh not as independent evaluative principles). As we discuss in subsection A.1,[116] individuals may have tastes for a notion of fairness, and, to that extent, a welfare economic analysis of legal rules takes their tastes into account. An implication of the preceding examination of social norms is that individuals plausibly do have tastes for notions of fairness. The reason is that feelings of guilt about behaving wrongly or negative feelings about others' violations of social norms—and corresponding positive feelings about proper behavior—that lead us to behave in accordance with social norms are, in essence, tastes.[117]

Our choice of legal rules should not only reflect our tastes for notions of fairness, but also take into account the possible effects of such rules on our tastes for these notions themselves. In some instances, legal rules are thought to have symbolic, educative effects, such as may have been created by Supreme Court rulings on desegregation and by various civil rights statutes.[118] In these cases, the effect of legal rules on social norms would, by definition, be one of the effects of the legal rules; if the social norms, in turn, influence individuals' well-being, as they might, the effects would therefore be relevant under welfare economics.[119] (We explore this point further in subsections VIII.B.2 and VIII.B.3.)

116. For further discussion, including attention to the possibility that tastes regarding legal rules may rest on confusion, see subsection VIII.B.4.

117. Consider, for example, the norm that one should keep one's promises. In order for individuals to feel guilty about breaking promises or to feel annoyed enough at others who break promises to undertake some retaliatory effort, they must find breaking promises distasteful. Indeed, feeling guilty or annoyed about something and finding it distasteful are essentially two ways of describing a single phenomenon. Accordingly, because social norms usually require feelings of guilt, virtue, and the like in order to function, tastes often accompany social norms. (We qualify this point because certain norms can be self-enforcing; for example, many individuals may refuse to interact with those known to break promises purely out of self-interest, because promise-breakers have proved themselves to be unreliable. Even in such cases, however, some individuals would consistently keep their promises, rather than break them opportunistically, because they are inclined to feel guilty about breaking promises—that is, they have a taste for keeping promises.)

118. See note 39 in chapter VIII. To consider a more ordinary example, one might imagine that allowing a particular defense in cases of breach of contract (perhaps one that was desirable, but that for counterintuitive reasons would not generally be appreciated by the public at large) would somewhat undermine the social norm that promises be kept, which might adversely affect contracting in other realms (including informal realms in which legal redress is unavailable).

119. It is useful to distinguish between two channels through which legal rules, by changing social norms, might affect individuals' well-being. First, when the law changes a social norm, which in turn affects behavior, the resulting difference in behavior typically affects

Finally, we wish to emphasize that nothing in our argument suggests that social norms—many corresponding to notions of fairness—are inappropriate in regulating everyday life. Indeed, we have emphasized the value of social norms in promoting individuals' well-being. Thus, the welfare economic approach views social norms (at least, welfare-promoting ones) positively, and the approach is entirely consistent with a social policy of inculcating ethical codes of behavior.[120]

Because we embrace welfare economics and reject giving weight to notions of fairness only when they are taken as independent principles to be used in assessing legal policy, it should be clear that our critique in this book is directed toward legal academics and other policy analysts, not toward ordinary individuals in their everyday lives.[121] The main problem, as we see

---

individuals' well-being. Second, as we noted in the preceding paragraph in the text, social norms tend to correspond to tastes, so changes in social norms will tend to involve changes in tastes; when individuals' tastes change, the effect of any given set of actions on their well-being may also change. To illustrate these points using the example in the text concerning civil rights laws, individuals might behave differently from the way they did previously, even in contexts not directly regulated by the civil rights laws, and they might come to value given experiences—namely, interactions with individuals of other races—differently.

120. Compare Sidgwick (1907, 475): "The Utilitarian must repudiate altogether that temper of rebellion against the established morality. . . . He must, of course, also repudiate as superstitious that awe of it as an absolute or Divine Code which Intuitional moralists inculcate."

121. Let us comment on the relationship between the position we develop in the text and that usually adopted in moral philosophy. To begin with, we note that much writing about notions of fairness by philosophers (Kant being a good example) focuses on the problem of how individuals should behave in everyday life—that is, on the proper content of social norms. See, for example, Korsgaard (1996, xi): "The basic task of moral philosophy, for Kant, is to answer the question 'What should I do?'"; and Williams (1981). Most philosophers who discuss the promise-keeping notion, for instance, refer to individuals' moral duty to keep their promises and do not consider the rules of contract law. See subsection IV.B.1. Compare Smith ([1790] 1976, 330–35), distinguishing the duty to keep promises from the proper requirements of contract law and criticizing writers on jurisprudence for confusing the two distinct realms, and ibid. (341), observing that ancient moralists, such as Cicero and Aristotle, did not distinguish principles that should guide law from other virtues.

Moral philosophers' focus on everyday morality raises the question of what force such writing has for policy analysis. To be sure, moral philosophers do not usually disclaim the relevance of their writing to social policy; ordinarily, they do not mention this context. Thus, it is possible that, if these philosophers had specifically considered the often qualitatively different problem of designing rules for the formal legal system, they would have reached different conclusions. Nevertheless, these same philosophers do sometimes examine subjects that directly involve legal policy. For example, writing on retributive justice concerns punishment imposed by the state for the commission of crimes. See section VI.B. Retributive theorists generally do not acknowledge the difference between the two contexts and thus are not led to examine whether the mode of analysis that arguably is appropriate in one context should

it (and further elaborate in section VII.B), is that legal policy analysts—
being members of society and thus under the influence of internalized social

---

be used unaltered in the other. In particular, most moral philosophers do not seriously consider the possibility that our moral intuitions have their origins in social norms and, accordingly, should be viewed as lacking independent force in the context of policy evaluation. See,
for example, subsection VI.D.2, discussing social norms and principles of retributive justice.
See also note 108, offering reasons to believe that intuitions are unreliable guides in moral
analysis, and subsection VI.C.4 and note 112 in chapter VI, suggesting the unreliability of
intuitions under retributive theory concerning the punishment of the innocent.

It has also been emphasized by certain writers that, within the domain of rules of common morality designed to regulate everyday life, it is important to make a distinction analogous to the one we emphasize in the text—a distinction between the proper behavior of
individuals subject to the rules (social norms) and the sort of analysis that should be employed
when designing the rules. See, for example, Hare (1981), Baron (1994a), Harrod (1936), and
Rawls (1955). The analogue to policy analysts and government decisionmakers would be, for
example, individuals who formulate educational policy or promulgate religious creeds. See,
for example, Baron (1994a, 9–10) and Campbell (1975).

This distinction between levels of moral thought has a long lineage. See Hare (1981, 25),
tracing such two-level analysis to Aristotle and Plato, as well as to classical utilitarians. It
formed a centerpiece of Mill's critique of his contemporaries, many of whom espoused views
and advanced arguments quite similar to those of moral philosophers in the twentieth century.
See Mill ([1861] 1998, 68–71, 87–107). See also Urmson (1953, 33), referring in large part
to philosophers' treatment of this aspect of Mill's book and stating: "But even more perplexing
is the almost universal misconstruction placed upon Mill's ethical doctrines; for his *Utilitarianism* is a work which every undergraduate is set to read and which one would therefore expect
Mill's critics to have read at least once. But this, apparently, is not so." The distinction between
common morality and moral theory was also an important theme in Sidgwick (1907). See
ibid. (361): "[Common morality] may still be perfectly adequate to give practical guidance
to common people in common circumstances: but the attempt to elevate it into a system of
Intuitional Ethics brings its inevitable imperfections into prominence without helping us to
remove them."; and Gibbard (1982b), discussing Sidgwick's view that the morality of common
sense differs from that applicable to critical analysis of public policy or true morality. Most
recently, Hare has advanced this two-level view in a substantial body of philosophical work.
See, for example, Hare (1981, chapters 2–3, 8) and Hare (1982). He writes:

> Are moral philosophers up to no good, then, when they persuade us to ques-
> tion these [moral] principles [that guide individuals]? I have already implicitly pro-
> vided their defence against this attack when I said that the schooling which results
> in the adoption of the principles has to be well thought out. . . . [T]he guardians
> at least will have to do some thinking. . . . (Hare 1973a, 12)

Baron, a psychologist, has also elaborated these ideas. See, for example, Baron (1993, 1994a).
To emphasize the relevant distinctions, Baron uses the term "descriptive" to refer to the content of existing moral rules that individuals in fact employ, "normative" to identify the ultimate
principle for evaluation, and "prescriptive" to describe the enterprise of developing better
practical rules for individuals to employ in everyday life. With regard to the last category, he

norms—naturally find appealing those legal rules and institutions that seem fair, without appreciating the extent to which those feelings may be independent of whether particular legal regimes actually enhance the well-being of members of society. It is this tendency that we argue should be resisted. That is, even though notions of fairness are indispensable in guiding much of ordinary life and even though the notions may serve as proxy devices that help to identify policies that promote welfare, appeals to notions of fairness do not provide a proper basis for evaluating legal policies. After all, the very purpose of academic discourse—and a central obligation of those designing and reforming the legal system—is to go beyond the relatively reflexive responses of ordinary individuals, so that we can identify when our instincts and intuitions about what is the best policy lead us astray. Just as medical science may inform us that certain physical intrusions (surgical incisions) can save our lives rather than lead to our demise and that some cravings and accepted customs (many dietary habits) once believed to be healthful are detrimental, so legal policy analysts should see their function as undertaking the most careful, explicit examination possible to determine which legal rules in fact promote individuals' well-being.

It should be noted that the foregoing discussion does not directly address the important but distinct question concerning the proper use of notions of fairness by judges and other governmental decisionmakers, who occupy a position somewhere between policy analysts and the citizenry: They receive expert advice from the former but are accountable to the latter. The role, if any, of notions of fairness in their decisionmaking is examined in section VII.C, after we present our critique of notions of fairness as ultimate ends for legal policymaking.

---

takes into account that simply teaching individuals always to do what is normatively correct may not be feasible and may not result in individuals' actual decisions being as desirable as when they are guided by certain subsidiary rules. See also Austin ([1832] 1995, lectures 2–4); Goodin (1995), emphasizing that many objections to utilitarianism as a guide to individuals' decisions in ordinary life do not apply to utilitarianism as a guide to public decisionmaking; Singer (1981, chapter 6), emphasizing the need for rules for everyday life that are based on, although less demanding than, the proper first principles of ethics; and Sartorius (1972), explaining that many criticisms of utilitarianism misunderstand that different assessments are appropriate for actors occupying different roles. Despite the noted similarities, there is an important difference between the contexts of critically analyzing legal rules and of scrutinizing rules of common morality. Legal rules may often be desirable even if they cannot successfully be inculcated in citizens at large—because official sanctions may suffice to produce intended outcomes—whereas norms for everyday behavior can succeed only if they are broadly internalized.

PART TWO

ANALYSIS

CHAPTER III

—————☐—————

Torts

In this chapter, we follow the general plan that we describe above. In section A, we discuss how welfare economics applies to tort law, focusing as we do throughout this chapter on unintentional torts.[1] In section B, we outline the major notions of fairness bearing on the subject of tort law.

Then we consider basic, paradigmatic situations in which harms can occur. In each context, we evaluate different legal rules using welfare economics and notions of fairness and argue that evaluation should be based purely on individuals' well-being. Much of our analysis focuses on the case in which there is no uncertainty about whether harm will occur. This case, which we take up in section C, is simpler to examine, yet it involves most of the issues pertinent to a comparison of welfare economics and fairness-based legal policy analysis. In section D, we address the case in which harm is uncertain.

In section E, we consider the relationship between notions of fairness and social norms that guide individuals in everyday life, and we analyze the implications of this relationship for the relevance of notions of fairness to legal policy analysis. We believe that this inquiry will help to reconcile the widespread appeal of notions of fairness with our argument that they should not be given independent weight in evaluating rules of tort law. Finally, in section F, we examine the extent to which pursuing notions of fairness has led society astray in determining tort policy.

---

1. Our discussion encompasses accidents as well as nuisance claims. Intentional torts may raise some of the issues that we discuss here in addition to those that we examine in chapter VI, addressing criminal punishment.

A. Welfare Economics and Tort Law

Under welfare economics, the effects of tort law are relevant to the extent that they influence individuals' well-being. One manner in which tort liability may affect well-being is through the incentives it creates for potential injurers to take care or otherwise to adjust their behavior to reduce harm and thereby decrease their chances of having to pay damages.[2] Of course, the effect of liability on behavior will depend on a number of factors, including other incentives to avoid accidents that potential injurers may have (such as to prevent harm to themselves or to escape the sanctions of traffic laws or other safety regulations) and the fact that liability insurance coverage may dilute the incentive effect of tort law.

Second, tort law may affect individuals' well-being through its allocation of the risk of accident losses. In particular, the prospect of compensation will be valuable to risk-averse victims, but it will impose risk-bearing costs on risk-averse injurers. The importance of these effects of tort liability will depend on the extent to which parties have insurance—first-party insurance for victims (health, disability, and life insurance and coverage for property losses) and liability insurance for injurers.

Third, tort law affects individuals' well-being on account of its administrative costs. Parties incur legal fees and other expenses, in addition to devoting time to litigation, and the public bears costs in supporting the court system.

Finally, in some instances tort liability affects the distribution of income, such as when injurers and victims are largely distinct groups with different levels of income. As we explain in subsection II.A.3, such effects are also relevant under welfare economics (although, as we note, distributive issues may often best be addressed directly, through tax and transfer schemes).[3]

B. Notions of Fairness and Tort Law

In this section, we begin by stating the fundamental conceptions of fairness that seem most relevant in the context of torts. Then we discuss the body

---

2. Tort rules may also influence potential victims' behavior, an important effect but not one that we will address here.

3. Obviously, our list of ways in which tort law affects well-being is not exhaustive. For example, as we discuss in subsection E.2, it is possible that individuals have a taste for certain notions of fairness, in which case one or another tort rule might affect their well-being by satisfying or violating this taste. In that subsection we also consider tort law's possible influence on social norms concerning conduct that harms others, which would also be relevant under welfare economics.

of literature addressing corrective justice, the particular conception of fairness that has been most developed by tort law scholars.

1. Notions of Fairness

One notion of fairness is concerned with making the injurer pay for the harm he has occasioned. We find it convenient to refer to such a notion of fairness as one involving punishment, whether the motivation for the notion pertains to retribution, the desire to rectify the outcome created by the injurer's action (for example, for certain acts that are particularly dangerous even if not wrongful in some sense, it may be believed that an injurer should be responsible for any harm caused), or some other reason.[4] Of course, this idea can be modified in a number of respects, the most important being the notion that the injurer should pay for harm only if he was at fault, that is, if his behavior was negligent.[5]

---

4. We examine related notions of fairness that are applied in assessing law enforcement policy, particularly with regard to the criminal law, in chapter VI.

5. See, for example, M'Alister v. Stevenson, 1932 A.C. 562, 580 (appeal taken from Scot.): "The liability for negligence . . . is no doubt based upon a general public sentiment of moral wrongdoing for which the offender must pay."; and Calabresi (1970, 301): "It . . . strikes us as unfair if acts that we deem wrong and immoral go unpunished, quite apart from any issue of compensation of the possible victims of such acts. Such sentiments [as well as those pertaining to compensation] are often said to be the principal mainstays of the fault system." See also Keeton et al. (1984, 21–23), noting a tendency in modern tort law to identify liability with immoral conduct, some sort of moral delinquency on the part of an individual, though strict liability that is not premised on such shortcomings is increasingly recognized. Additionally, whether a notion of fairness requires that the injurer pay (or that the victim be compensated, as we discuss in the next paragraph) may depend on the victim's conduct, on whether the injurer's action was a "but for" cause or the proximate cause of the harm, and on other factors. For expositional simplicity, we will ignore these refinements.

Keating advances a notion of fairness that is meant to address the question of how the standard of care under the negligence rule should be set (remedying what he finds to be an important gap in Fletcher's reciprocity-based theory, discussed in subsection C.1(e)(ii) and note 56). See Keating (1996). He describes his approach as one motivated by social contract theory, as developed by John Rawls and other modern writers. He seeks to determine who should be found negligent by balancing two conflicting liberties: injurers' interest in freedom of action and victims' interest in security. Although we do not focus on the question of how negligence should be determined, our analysis in fact applies to any aspect of tort rules and any notion of fairness and hence to Keating's proposed approach. For example, one of his main prescriptions—that the negligence rule should require more than merely cost-justified precautions in an important class of cases, see ibid. (352–60)—clearly would make everyone worse off in the reciprocal setting (which we show in section C to be true when notions of fairness are applied to the choice among strict liability, the negligence rule, and no liability). We find the motivation for Keating's position to be obscure in important respects. Notably, the tradeoff of conflicting

Another notion of fairness concerns compensation—the idea that the victim should be made whole. This conception too can be modified by taking into account aspects of the injurer's (and the victim's) behavior, for example, by limiting the right to compensation to actions involving fault or the imposition of an unusually high degree of risk.[6]

In addition to notions of fairness that might independently call for punishment or compensation, another fairness principle might demand both

---

liberties would merely be different language for the tradeoff of conflicting effects on well-being if the importance of liberty to an individual were determined by the amount by which the individual values it. This leads us to infer that Keating has something else in mind, yet he presents no concrete alternative. Moreover, the resulting deviation from individuals as the source of value would seem to conflict with his claim that individuals' autonomy and liberty are the underlying bases for his argument. Relatedly, he offers an example in which he claims that the law should reject the fully informed waiver of liability by individuals—which would clearly make both parties to the posited transaction worse off—in the name of autonomy, freedom, and liberty. See ibid. (348–49). This discussion further contributes to the difficulty in determining what Keating means by these three terms, because they are conventionally interpreted as requiring that voluntary choices be honored, not trumped. See also ibid. (384), stating, in his conclusion, that his social contract theory places special emphasis on liberty interests that are particularly important in the realm of accident law because "their adequate protection is more central to our well-being than the optimal satisfaction of our preferences is," suggesting that he views individuals' preferences as somehow excluding those things that individuals feel are most important. (We also should note that, although Keating describes his theory as one based on reciprocity, it is rather different from Fletcher's. Most of the factors that Keating argues should affect how the negligence rule is set do not depend on whether risk is reciprocally imposed. That Keating does not view nonreciprocity as an important or necessary condition for liability is even more explicit in Keating (1997).)

6. See, for example, Calabresi (1970, 301), stating that "[i]t strikes critic and community as unfair if a person injured by someone who has violated a moral code is not compensated," and suggesting that this sentiment is often alleged to be an important underpinning of the fault system; Keeton et al. (1984, 20), suggesting that the need for compensation is an important factor influencing tort law and provides one of the justifications for liability; Speiser, Krause, and Gans (1983, 1:12), noting "broad judicial utterances to the effect that, 'The primary purpose of tort law is that of compensating plaintiffs for the injuries they have suffered wrongfully at the hands of others.'"; R. Posner (1972, 30), stating that implicit in the orthodox view of legal scholars "is that the dominant purpose of civil liability for accidents is to compensate the victim"; Sugarman (1985, 591): "Over the past few decades, it has become increasingly popular to view victim compensation as the central purpose of tort law."; and Seavey (1931, 211–12): "Tort liability . . . exists chiefly to compensate an individual, as nearly as may be, for loss caused by the defendant's conduct, either by making the financial position of the plaintiff as good as it was before, or would have been if the defendant had not acted, by giving him balm for his wounded pride or damaged body or by doing both." See also Carroll et al. (1991, viii), stating that defenders of traditional tort liability rely on basic common law principles, namely, that "[a]n injured party is entitled to compensation for all his losses," and that critics of the system do not dispute those principles.

that the injurer pay and that this payment go to the victim.[7] Under this view, the relationship between injurer and victim, both when harm is inflicted and when compensation is paid, is critical.[8] This position is usually advanced under the rubric of "corrective justice."[9]

7. In fact, under conventional tort law, the victim is compensated if and only if the injurer pays, so the notions of punishment and compensation are linked. If each type of fairness notion independently required liability in a particular instance, the two sorts of notions would be consistent; it is possible, of course, that one notion would call for compensation but another (such as one limiting punishment to individuals at fault) would not (notably, in cases of nonnegligent injury). Under corrective justice, such a conflict by definition cannot arise.

8. It would seem that such a principle would not be satisfied by a system of fines paid to the state, to punish injurers, combined with a social insurance fund that compensated accident victims. See, for example, Wright (1992, 704): "The departure from corrective justice occurs only when someone is involuntarily required to discharge the duty of another, or when the duty is initially placed on someone other than the party who should bear the duty as a matter of corrective justice, as occurs in compulsory no-fault compensation schemes." See also R. Posner (1981a, 198), suggesting that no-fault plans would violate corrective justice. But see ibid. (202–03), suggesting that under Posner's own view, which stipulates that corrective justice entails the pursuit of economic objectives, no-fault plans would not violate corrective justice if the plans were desirable. When some corrective justice theorists comment on alternatives to the tort system, they suggest that corrective justice may simply be inapposite. See, for example, Coleman (1995, 30), claiming that in New Zealand, where accident costs are compensated by the state, "there is no practice of corrective justice"—which implies that corrective justice may be moot in comparing the tort system to a no-fault compensation alternative; Perry (1992b, 513), suggesting that substituting compulsory no-fault insurance for the tort system might not violate any fundamental moral rights; and Weinrib (1989a, 412): "[I]n representing only the special morality of tort law, [corrective justice] provides no reason for preferring tort law to its competitors." Such a stance is consistent with the interpretation, discussed in the text to follow, that such theorists are primarily interested in giving a positive account of the tort system rather than advancing an independent evaluative principle. If corrective justice is taken to be an evaluative principle, however, this view seems untenable, as we discuss in note 12.

9. See, for example, Coleman (1995, 27): "[I]n every account of corrective justice, there is presumed to be a relationship between the parties that makes the claims of corrective justice appropriate to them—and not to others."; R. Posner (1981a, 190), stating that the connection between the injury to the victim and wrongdoing of the injurer is central to Aristotle's conception of corrective justice; Weinrib (1992, 411, 417, 424); and Weinrib (1994, 280–82), emphasizing the interdependence of the two opposing parties in Aristotle's notion of corrective justice, which distinguishes it from distributive justice. The notion of corrective justice, according to some interpretations, can be understood as embodying a libertarian view of liability wherein those who cause injuries are morally obligated to compensate their victims, who have an entitlement to be free from injuries caused by others. See, for example, Epstein (1973), offering such a theory, Epstein (1974), elaborating such a theory, and Perry (1997), describing and criticizing such theories. We note that not everyone who has claimed to advance notions of corrective justice has always held this view about the linkage between injurer and victim. See Coleman (1995, 27), referring to his former "annulment thesis."

We also observe that the notion of fairness discussed in recent decades in the corrective

Our discussion of notions of fairness is directed to conceptions that require either punishment or compensation independently, or both linked together, and most of our arguments are applicable to any of these conceptions. We usually speak of simple notions that merely call for punishment or for compensation in a particular situation, but we do this as a convenience, recognizing that notions of fairness may be more complex.[10]

Another dimension along which the positions of fairness proponents vary is the extent to which they would also give weight to the effects of legal rules on individuals' well-being. Most fairness-minded analysts appear to hold mixed views: rather than maintaining that a notion of fairness should be absolute, they would accept a less-than-perfectly-fair rule if the cost of implementing their preferred notion of fairness were excessive.[11] Accordingly, when we examine and criticize notions of fairness, our discussion should be understood to apply to analysts' views only insofar as they would give weight to their preferred notions of fairness.

---

justice literature has long been prevalent. See, for example, Calabresi (1970, 297): "For centuries society has seemed to accept the notion that justice required a one-to-one relationship between the party that injures and the party that is injured. . . ." But see ibid. (298 n.7), referring to a study suggesting the existence of a general feeling that victims should be attended to but indicating that the belief is not linked to a requirement that it be injurers who pay.

10. See note 5. Allowing for a different or more fact-dependent notion of fairness would change which rule is dictated by the notion in some circumstances. Our main criticism below, however, applies as long as the fairness concept does not always favor the rule that best promotes individuals' well-being. Moreover, our observations that notions of fairness appear moot in reciprocal contexts (without risk or with risk plus insurance) and arbitrary in nonreciprocal contexts do not seem to depend on the particular notion of fairness that is under examination.

11. See, for example, Calabresi (1970, 24–26), stating that "the principal goals of any system of accident law [are first,] it must be just or fair; second, it must reduce the costs of accidents," and presenting the view of justice as a constraint. Some analysts, however, suggest that notions of fairness should trump all considerations of individuals' well-being. See, for example, Benson (1992, 573–74), explaining the irrelevance of the objection that his theory accords no "independent significance to a person's interest in having things or to his or her needs and well-being," because "the moral significance of using things cannot lie in its relevance to human purposes, whether as part of a conception of the good or as a means to its attainment"; Fletcher (1972, 540–41), describing his favored paradigm of reciprocity as giving no weight to social costs or the impact of outcomes on socially desirable forms of behavior; Fletcher (1993, 1667): "Were it true that justice and utility were simply values to be traded off one against the other, the claims of justice would be vapid."; and Owen (1989, 725–26). See also Keating (1996), advancing a notion of fairness based on individuals' liberties—freedom of action and security— which are lexically prior to welfare, but sometimes suggesting that certain reductions in welfare are nevertheless relevant because they tend to reduce freedom of action. As we discuss in the next footnote, however, it is unclear to what extent Fletcher's view is meant to be descriptive rather than normative (whereas Owen clearly is advancing a normative claim).

2. Comments on the Literature

Before beginning our inquiry, we wish to offer some preliminary observations about fairness claims that involve corrective justice, because these claims have received the most sustained attention from tort law scholars, including Coleman, Perry, and Weinrib. Initially, we note that most authors who advance notions of corrective justice are making positive—that is, descriptive—arguments; in particular, they suggest that corrective justice is the principle that is most consistent with common law tort doctrine.[12] To this extent, their claims

12. "Most legal theorists who have been interested in corrective justice have been interested in it insofar as it might figure in an account, explanation or interpretation of various legal practices, especially tort law. . . ." Coleman (1995, 18). See ibid. (15), referring to his own book as arguing that "the core of tort law embodies [his] conception of corrective justice"; Coleman (1992a, 427), stating that the purpose of his article is to "develop the underlying moral principle involved in tort law"; R. Posner (1981a, 206 n.59), suggesting that it is "unclear to what extent Aristotle[, who invented the category of corrective justice,] thought he was doing more than describing legal concepts that happened to be prevalent in his society"; Schwartz (1997, 1801), indicating that "the combination of deterrence and justice can provide a better or fuller explanation for these [tort] doctrines"; ibid. (1802), noting a surge of "interest in theories interpreting tort law as an expression of what Aristotle called corrective justice"; Weinrib (1995, 1): "In this book I address a single question: How are we to understand private law?"; Weinrib (1989a, 404): "Tort law is to be considered . . . as a repository of non-instrumental judgments about action."; and Weinrib (1989b). See also Keating (1996, 313), advancing what he refers to as a social contract conception of fairness, which his article attempts to show "coheres with tort doctrine and practice better than the economic conception," and ibid. (382), summarizing his theses in positive terms in his conclusion.

Fletcher's argument presents a mixed case. See Fletcher (1972, 537–38), referring to tort law as "a unique repository of intuitions of corrective justice" and suggesting a positive claim, but stating that the questions involved are normative. See also ibid. (540), referring to what judges "should" do but, immediately thereafter, asking whether the doctrine "provide[s] a medium" for one or another purpose; ibid. (542), referring to the principle "expressed" in various situations governed by a range of tort doctrines and claiming that the cases follow his theory; ibid. (543), stating that the "task is to demonstrate the pervasive reliance of the common law on the paradigm of reciprocity," which is the notion of fairness he advances; ibid. (549–50), arguing that common law tort rules "express" his principle of fairness; and Fletcher (1983, 63), noting that most efforts to identify principles of tort law "suffer from a basic ambiguity" regarding whether they are positive or normative approaches, and claiming that, although ideally one might have a purely positive or normative theory, "the tension between the two . . . seems inescapable." Wright's argument is another mixed case. See Wright (1992, 629): "The only plausible approach, descriptively and normatively, is [one] which begins with our actual legal practices, attempts to discern the fundamental principles of morality and justice that underlie those practices, and then uses those fundamental principles to critique and shape our practices. . . ." Epstein seems to have fluctuated between normative and positive views. Compare Epstein (1973, 151), introducing the article that first lays out his theory by

about corrective justice have no direct relevance to our undertaking because our thesis is entirely normative, being concerned with the proper manner of assessing legal policy. (Indeed, we do not assert that the law fully reflects the prescriptions of welfare economics, and we argue, in section F, that the law is influenced by notions of fairness, perhaps including corrective justice.)

In spite of the descriptive focus of much writing on corrective justice, it appears that those theorists who claim that corrective justice best explains tort law also believe that corrective justice is normatively compelling.[13] In addition, we suspect that many analysts who are generally aware of the cor-

---

stating that his "task is to develop a normative theory of torts," with Epstein (1974, 165), introducing the article that extends his original theory by stating that his "task [is] to show how the tort law can be viewed usefully as a system of corrective justice appropriate for the redress of private harms . . . ; it is the implicit assumption upon which the common law approach to the law of torts has rested throughout most of its long history."

A clear exception to the generally descriptive thrust in the literature is Rakowski, who offers a normative account of corrective justice. See Rakowski (1991, chapters 10–11). His approach differs importantly in that he sees corrective justice as ultimately grounded in distributive justice, a view most others strongly resist. Under our classification, however, many notions of just distribution are concerned only with individuals' well-being and thus are encompassed by welfare economics, so there would be no inherent conflict with such a version of corrective justice. See subsections II.A.2 and II.A.3.

We also note that some corrective justice scholars who address alternatives to the tort system suggest that corrective justice has no bearing on whether the tort system should be replaced. See note 8. This view is coherent only if corrective justice is advanced as an entirely descriptive account of tort law. If the notions of fairness found in tort law are important evaluative principles, then abandonment of the tort system must be seen as involving serious injustice because it ensures that the principles would be wholly violated in every case in which there would have been liability.

13. Coleman observes that "legal theorists who invoke the concept of corrective justice mean to treat it as a substantive moral ideal." Coleman (1995, 20). "No doubt, in defending or rejecting tort practice as satisfying or failing to measure up to the demands of corrective justice, tort theorists typically mean to be expressing their pleasure or disfavor with current legal arrangements." Ibid. (20 n.7). (We cannot help but note the strong tension between this characterization and Coleman's claim quoted at the outset of note 12.) See also Schroeder (1995, 348 n.1): "Implicit and explicit references to the moral basis of corrective justice are common in the literature."; and Weinrib (1989a, 404): "[M]ost tort scholars would acknowledge that their subject has a moral dimension that economic analysis fails to illuminate." Consider as well the sources cited in the preceding footnote that expressly mix positive and normative approaches or have an exclusively normative approach. See also Keating (1996, 325), arguing that his social contract conception of the negligence rule is favored on "both normative and interpretive grounds."

We observe that an argument that a notion of fairness has normative appeal may be relevant to a positive argument in that it may be more plausible that judges have followed a specified principle if it seems appealing. However, in section E, we explain why notions of fairness may have appeal even though they do not constitute independent evaluative principles.

rective justice literature understand it as offering a normative vision that competes with one based exclusively on how legal rules affect individuals' well-being (and with other fairness-based theories). Accordingly, we now examine the literature's concept of corrective justice.

The most important point is that, at a fundamental level, corrective justice is not a complete, substantive notion of justice but instead refers to a category of principles of a particular logical type. Specifically, most corrective justice claims have the form: "If A wrongfully injures B, A must pay B for the loss B suffers as a consequence of A's act."[14]

In this regard, we emphasize that corrective justice is incomplete in that one must look elsewhere for a substantive theory of what counts as wrongful injury,[15] a point that most scholars state explicitly or acknowledge implic-

14. See, for example, Coleman (1995, 15): "[C]orrective justice is the principle that those who are responsible for the wrongful losses of others have a duty to repair them. . . ."; and Perry (1996, 74): "In general, corrective justice requires A to compensate B for loss caused by A's conduct (in a fault-based theory, by A's *faulty* conduct)."

15. In addition to determining what counts as a wrong, there is also the question of the nature and magnitude of correction that is appropriate given that a wrong has occurred. Most corrective justice proponents seem to agree that damages should simply equal the magnitude of the loss. There is some incompleteness here as.well, for when losses are nonmonetary but compensation is monetary, some translation must be made. Compare subsection VI.B.2, discussing the issue of the magnitude of punishment imposed by the state. One obvious answer is to set compensation equal to the amount of money that restores the victim to the level of utility enjoyed before harm occurred, but this answer (which roughly characterizes existing tort law) may or may not be right, depending on the underlying justification for the notion of fairness. More generally, some have questioned the basic principle that correction should in some sense equal the magnitude of the loss. See, for example, note 111, quoting Schroeder.

Indeed, even though corrective justice proponents trace their theories to Aristotle, their general prescriptions may not be consistent with Aristotle's statement about what corrective justice requires: "[C]orrective justice will be the intermediate between loss and gain. . . . Now the judge restores equality; it is as though there were a line divided into unequal parts, and he took away that by which the greater segment exceeds the half, and added it to the smaller segment." Aristotle (1980, book V, chapter 4). See ibid., using the subtitle "In What Sense [Justice] Is a Mean" for the relevant portion of book V, where "mean" is given a mathematical interpretation. When the injurer's gain is slight relative to a victim's loss (as in many automobile accident cases in which the victim's injury is severe but the injurer's benefit from failing to take care was negligible), this view would seem to require that the injurer pay half of the loss to the victim, because this result, "intermediate between loss and gain," restores equality between the two parties with respect to the particular event. Wright offers another view. He argues that Aristotle, who states that "the term 'gain' [is] not a term appropriate to certain cases, e.g. to the person who inflicts a wound" (ibid., book V, chapter 4), must have meant to impute a notional gain to the injurer, because then Aristotle's principle of the mean produces the fully compensatory result. See Wright (1992, 692–95). See also Weinrib (1994), seeking to interpret Aristotle in a manner consistent with contemporary theories of corrective

itly.[16] Thus, consistent with the prevailing formal definition of corrective justice, one could deem all injury caused by A's voluntary acts as wrongful,

---

justice. It seems to us that the difficulty of confidently knowing what Aristotle meant with regard to the standard tort case, combined with the very fact that he did not address it directly in expounding his notion of corrective justice, raises problems for modern tort scholars' reliance on him. Furthermore, Aristotle's direct discussion of corrective justice spans only a few pages and focuses on the meaning of the concept rather than on the question of why corrective justice should be regarded as having normative significance.

16. See, for example, Coleman (1992b, 353): "I have not yet defended either the condition [that gives rise to a claim of corrective justice] or the principle that justifies it. . . . All this remains to be worked out on another occasion. . . ."; Coleman (1995, 18 n.4), stating that his book provides only a "conceptual account of wrongfulness" and that only now is he beginning to provide a normative account; ibid. (18 n.5): "In fact, I do not here defend my conception of corrective justice. Rather, I take up the more basic question of how we ought to think about defending or exploring a particular conception of corrective justice."; Coleman (1992a, 444): "Nothing I have said here [addressed what] conception of wrong and wrongdoing is implicated in the mixed conception of corrective justice. . . ."; Perry (1992b, 450): "There are a number of quite different accounts of corrective justice thus understood, but it has proven surprisingly difficult to specify the circumstances under which correlative rights and obligations of reparation arise and to say why they are justified."; ibid. (490), stating, with regard to Honoré's theory, that "if a social decision to impose outcome-responsibility were possible we would be entitled to ask whether it was justified, and this would require us to offer moral reasons for accepting a supposedly premoral concept"; R. Posner (1981a, 193), observing that Aristotle's notion of corrective justice is a formal category and that the theory "does not tell us who is a wrongdoer or who has vested rights"; ibid. (206): "Aristotle did not explain *why* he thought there was a duty of corrective justice; he merely explained what that duty was."; Weinrib (1992, 411), stating that Aristotle's categories of corrective and distributive justice are formal ones, not substantive prescriptions; Weinrib (1994, 289): "Corrective justice presupposes some reason (or set of reasons) for regarding certain acts as wrongful and for rectifying their consequences."; and Weinrib (1983, 40): "Corrective justice in itself is devoid of a specific content, which, accordingly, must be sought elsewhere."

The theory's incompleteness is also implicit in many elaborations of the meaning of corrective justice. See, for example, Coleman (1992b, 331): "[W]rongful losses can result from *wrongdoing*. Drawing upon the previous distinctions, we might say that wrongdoing consists in the unjustifiable or otherwise impermissible injuring of others' legitimate interests. Wrongdoing is unjustifiable harming." (A theory of what is unjustifiable or otherwise impermissible or what is a legitimate interest is not provided.); Rakowski (1991, 230–31), discussing a representative example of an individual who has purchased a right to clean water or land free from noxious fumes, in which context it is suggested that, if no antinuisance right existed, this would not be what they in fact had purchased, and using the example to show that there is nothing internal to the theory that specifies what rights should be deemed to have existed when entitlements were initially acquired; Epstein (1979, 52): "[T]he ownership question remains insistent, and it can be answered only with recourse to treaties, statutes, ordinances, custom, and grants. No general theory of tort law, however powerful or profound, can tell us who owns what at the outset."; and Perry (1992b, 510), elaborating his own theory in suggesting

following certain libertarian approaches; alternatively, one could stipulate that wrongful acts are those acts by *A* that injure *B* and are inefficient.[17] That is, practically any substantive principle, including the one we advocate, could be embedded in corrective justice.[18] Because the corrective justice literature neither specifies nor defends alternative normative visions, it does not contain arguments that might challenge our case for relying solely on welfare economics for legal policy analysis.[19] (Instead, much of the literature on cor-

---

that "at a certain point outcome-responsibility for the harm a given action has produced should, so far as a publicly acknowledged obligation of reparation is concerned, be treated like culpable fault," but acknowledging that "[t]he conclusion that there is such a point, together with the *ex post* determination of when it has been reached, are not matters capable of rational demonstration within the confines of the distributive argument, nor are they claimed to be." See also Owen (1993, 434–36), suggesting that corrective justice models may "dazzle the intellect" but do not "help determine whether a harmful act was also 'wrongful,'" thereby leaving the models without a substantive core that could help resolve fundamental questions; Schroeder (1995, 349): "Notwithstanding the common repetition of the claim of moral justification for the duty to compensate, articulating the moral principle that underwrites this claim has proven extraordinarily elusive. . . . [T]he most readily apparent methods for moral assessment . . . reveal no principles that justify such duty, and several that are actually inconsistent with it."; and ibid., (355): "[A]ny moral explanation for the duty to compensate [under existing tort law, which limits attention to the injurer and victim,] must justify that practice, not simply adopt it."

The point in the text raises the question why corrective justice is believed to be such an important normative concept. If corrective justice only tells us that "whenever our other theory requires that *A* should pay *B*, it will violate corrective justice if we do not make *A* pay *B*," the notion of corrective justice seems redundant of that other theory. Corrective justice would seem to be able to play an independent role only if there exists a general category of wrongful acts that is determined independently of the context to which corrective justice applies. Yet most of us believe that there are many types of wrongs that individuals might commit that would not call for compensation.

17. Compare Coleman (1995, 29), noting that the identity of the cheapest cost avoider could, in principle, be used to define responsibility; and R. Posner (1981a, 201): "Once the concept of corrective justice is given its correct Aristotelian meaning, it becomes possible to show that it is not only compatible with, but required by, the economic theory of law."

18. If one deems acts to be wrongful based entirely on whether or not subjecting them to liability would raise social welfare, corrective justice's requirements would be equivalent to the prescriptions of welfare economics.

19. We address this literature when presenting our critique of notions of fairness. See subsections C.1(e)(ii) and C.2(e). The most important points about the literature are that it fails to offer an affirmative reason to give weight to corrective justice and it does not address the theory's problematic implications. Compare subsection VI.B.2, examining retributive justice and similarly finding that a leading notion of fairness seems to depend on another substantive theory to indicate which acts are wrongful and to what extent, and that the necessary theory is neither specified nor defended.

rective justice has addressed taxonomic questions concerning the distinction
between corrective justice and distributive, retributive, or other notions of
justice[20]—questions that are not important for our purposes.)

The failure of the corrective justice literature to offer a substantive theory
that determines what injuries are wrongful further implies that we cannot
know what criterion to use to determine which legal rule promotes fairness
in a given context.[21] For example, even if liability is to be limited to cases

20. See, for example, Coleman (1995, 27–28), dismissing his own prior notion, Perry's,
and Dworkin's because they lack the necessary elements of a proper theory of corrective justice;
Perry (1992a), criticizing Coleman's previous theory as a distributive theory rather than one
about corrective justice; Perry (1992b), criticizing most views of corrective justice for failing
to provide an account that is both coherent and independent of distributive justice; R. Posner
(1981a), dismissing others' theories because they do not strictly adhere to a proper definition
of corrective justice; Simons (1990, 121), arguing that Schroeder's position fits more with
retributive justice than with corrective justice; Weinrib (1994), offering a definition of gains
and losses that reconciles tort practice with Aristotle's notion of corrective justice; and Wright
(1992, 702–08), discussing how his view of Aristotle's notion distinguishes corrective and
retributive justice.

This debate about the true meaning of corrective justice has arisen, we suspect, because
of the notion's special standing as one of Aristotle's basic categories of justice. See, for example,
Fletcher (1993, 1667), criticizing Coleman for his apparent indifference "to the Aristotelian
tradition, without which the claims of corrective and distributive justice would hardly carry
the prestige they do in our thinking about law"; R. Posner (1981a), assessing the validity of
a broad range of theories of corrective justice primarily on the basis of their conformity to
Aristotle's original definition; and Weinrib (1994), attempting to reconcile prevailing understandings of corrective justice with Aristotle's. We note, however, that writers who draw on
Aristotle do not consider his statement of the purpose of the legal system that appears in the
first section of his book on justice:

> Now the laws in their enactments on all subjects aim at the common advantage
> either of all or of the best or of those who hold power, or something of the sort;
> so that in one sense we call those acts just that tend to produce and preserve hap-
> piness and its components for the political society. (Aristotle 1980, book V, chap-
> ter 1)

Nor do most such writers refer to Aristotle's actual definition of corrective justice, which
arguably calls for dividing a loss between the injurer and the victim rather than having the
injurer make the victim whole. See note 15, quoting and further discussing Aristotle's statement of what corrective justice requires.

21. See Simons (1990, 126): "[T]he concept of corrective justice is sufficiently vague—
some might say vacuous—that it might justify eliminating, not only any causation requirement, but also any of the requirements of traditional tort law."; and note 16, quoting Perry
on the difficulty of determining when corrective justice theory applies, and further addressing the theory's incompleteness. As an example, Fletcher favors strict liability for nonreciprocal acts and negligence for reciprocal ones, but since many acts are partially reciprocal and,

involving fault, we still must determine what behavior is to be regarded as faulty. Individuals could be considered to be at fault only when they intentionally mean to cause harm (close to a regime of no liability for accidents), whenever their voluntary action causes harm (akin to strict liability), whenever the cost-benefit (Learned Hand) negligence test is violated, or in any other set of circumstances. Hence, even if we know that a theory favors fault-based liability, we need to know the substantive theory that is to be used to define fault.[22] It is also difficult to determine the relevance of other factors relating to corrective justice's demand that compensation be paid, such as whether existing theories apply only to persons or also to firms and other entities, and whether parties' having insurance renders corrective justice moot or otherwise affects its applicability.[23]

Theories of corrective justice also fail to indicate the value of providing corrective justice relative to that of meeting other possible objectives.[24] First, we do not know what level of social resources proponents would be willing to devote to achieve a higher degree of corrective justice. Achieving corrective justice will, of course, be costly, both because it is expensive to operate the tort system and because greater expenditures can be made on each case in order to reduce the likelihood of legal error (which would result in a denial of corrective justice).[25] For example, if legal costs are $1,000 per case, should corrective justice be provided when wrongful conduct (such as carelessly bumping someone on the sidewalk) causes a trivial harm? Or only when the harm is great? And, if so, how great?

---

moreover, the extent of an act's reciprocity depends on how broadly one groups acts, there is usually no way to know which rule his approach favors. (He briefly acknowledges this problem. See Fletcher (1972, 572): "It is easy to assert that risks of owning a dog offset those of barbecuing in one's backyard, but what if the matter should be disputed?") One could apply a theory of corrective justice if one added, for example, a requirement that all acts in a given class are subject to the negligence rule, whereas those acts in another class are subject to strict liability. But to this extent, the theory would consist of little more than the two lists of acts.

22. Some corrective justice theorists do provide an indication of what legal rules they believe corrective justice requires; notably, many favor something like the existing negligence rule. The problem in such cases lies in understanding the basis for such views when the substantive theory of wrongfulness necessary to provide content to corrective justice remains unspecified.

23. See subsections C.1(f) and D.1(f).

24. We identify analogous respects in which theories of retributive justice lack completeness in subsection VI.B.2.

25. We address these sorts of issues (although not in a manner limited to corrective justice or the tort setting) in our discussion of legal procedure in chapter V.

Second, we do not know whether and how the number of instances of injustice matters under these theories, and thus we cannot determine what legal rule is most just. To illustrate, suppose that a seemingly unjust tort rule results in greater deterrence of wrongful acts. Moreover, assume (realistically) that when wrongful acts are not deterred, some of them never result in a lawsuit (due to the victim's inability to prove the injurer's identity or to finance a lawsuit) and some of those that do result in suits lead to erroneous verdicts. In this situation, the supposedly more just rule, by failing to deter as many wrongful acts, may result in more instances in which corrective justice is not achieved than a seemingly unjust rule.[26] Corrective justice theorists do not indicate whether it is the expected consequences of the rule or the way the rule is hoped to function that matters.

Third, when legal rules result in different levels of deterrence, the resulting difference in the number of wrongful acts might itself be thought relevant under a theory of corrective justice. After all, the theory calls for correction of acts that are deemed wrongful in some sense; hence, purely as a matter of justice, it would seem to be a better world if wrongful acts never occurred than if they occurred and each was corrected perfectly. (To test this notion, compare a world in which a supposedly unjust tort rule exists and deters all wrongful acts with a world in which a supposedly just rule operates with the result that a large fraction of the population falls victim to serious wrongdoing, but in which every instance of wrongdoing is corrected as the theory requires.) If a corrective justice proponent, therefore, is concerned not only with correcting wrongs but with the extent to which wrongs occur in the first instance, we would need to know how to trade off these objectives.[27]

A complete theory of corrective justice—indeed, of any notion of fairness applicable to tort law—would have to be capable of providing answers to these sorts of questions. Yet the literature on corrective justice does not generally address them; nor can we infer how they should be answered from statements of the theories that merely demand the correction of wrongs. Thus, the notions of fairness that we examine do not really allow us to determine which rule is the fairest. Although this shortcoming is not the focus of our critique, it seems that the serious incompleteness of theories of fair-

26. Furthermore, even if the supposedly more just rule does not result in greater injustice, the bare fact that reduced deterrence leads to many instances in which corrective justice is not achieved seems relevant.

27. That notions of fairness in tort law might best be understood as concerned with deterrence is a theme emphasized in Schwartz (1997).

ness in tort law reflects a failure to provide sound underlying justifications. If motivations were articulated, we would probably have a better idea of what these theories of fairness require.

We might imagine that the foregoing notions of fairness could be greatly extended and refined or that other notions could be offered that would allow one to assess fully the fairness of legal rules.[28] Our position, which we develop in the sections to follow, is that however such theories might be articulated, they should not guide legal policy analysis. We primarily examine simple notions of fairness—such as those favoring the imposition of liability for all harmful acts or only for negligent acts causing harm—but, as we explain, our main arguments are applicable to any evaluative principle whose prescriptions differ from those of welfare economics.

C. Welfare Economics versus Fairness in Paradigmatic Accident Situations

We now consider an extremely simple model of accidents in which potential[29] injurers undertake an activity that may cause harm to potential victims. We assume that injurers act in a manner that will cause harm with certainty unless they take precautions to prevent it. (The case in which harm is uncertain is the subject of section D.) Victims play no contributory role in accidents.[30] We first analyze the situation in which harm is perfectly reciprocal—that is, when those who are injurers in some instances are victims in other instances (such as when drivers can strike pedestrians, but the same individuals sometimes drive and sometimes walk). Then we consider a

---

28. We observe that if the theories were elaborated sufficiently to address all of the questions identified in the text, they would have a *structure* more similar to that of welfare economics, in that they would make explicit trade-offs involving such factors as deterrence and administrative costs. It does not follow, however, that a complete theory of fairness would be a welfare economic theory, because various factors (such as the measure of the social undesirability of a wrongful act) could be weighed differently from how they would be under welfare economics. Under welfare economics, for example, the importance of deterring wrongful acts depends in the first instance on how much individuals are harmed by the acts; under a notion of fairness, the importance could depend on something else.

29. Hereinafter, we usually dispense with the qualifier "potential" in order to simplify the exposition.

30. We also set aside problems of causation, injurers' activity levels, and other complicating factors.

wholly nonreciprocal situation, in which injurers and victims are separate groups.[31]

1. Reciprocal Accidents

(a) Description. In this basic case, we assume that individuals find themselves in the role of injurer and of victim exactly one time each. As mentioned, we might imagine that people sometimes drive cars and could cause injury to pedestrians, and other times walk and might be struck; or we might think that people sometimes burn leaves and that their smoke injures their neighbors, whereas other times it is their neighbors who burn leaves and whose smoke injures them. The activity of injurers will cause certain harm of $100[32] to victims unless injurers take a precaution; we assume the cost of the precaution to be $25 in some cases and $150 in others.

We consider three types of legal regimes. Under the rule of strict liability, an injurer must pay for the harm of $100 whenever he causes it. Under the negligence rule, the injurer must pay for the $100 harm only when he failed to take the precaution and the cost of the precaution is less than the harm it would prevent; thus, failure to take the precaution would result in liability for negligence if the precaution costs $25, but there would be no liability if the precaution costs $150.[33] The third regime we consider is one of no liabil-

31. We emphasize these extremes for the sake of clarity. Realistically, partial reciprocity is common, in which case the analyses of the two polar cases should be combined.

32. We follow the convention of placing a dollar value on harm even though the harm could be nonmonetary. In the language of welfare economics, as presented in subsection II.A.1, the relevant unit of measurement refers to individuals' well-being or utility. As we explain there, see note 6 in chapter II, the numbers assigned by a utility function are of no intrinsic significance, but merely represent individuals' rankings of various circumstances. Whether, for example, a nonmonetary harm is considered more or less important than an expenditure on prevention depends simply on whether individuals would prefer to make the expenditure to prevent the harm to themselves. Both utility measures and corresponding dollar amounts are the implicit valuations of individuals reflected in the choices they make. (A dollar valuation simply indicates the precaution cost above which individuals would rather suffer the harm and below which they would prefer to undertake the precaution. It has often been observed that, without placing *some* monetary value on an injury in this manner, one cannot say whether it is sensible to spend $1, $100, or $1 billion to avoid it.) In the present, reciprocal case, each person suffers the injury once and potentially undertakes the precaution once. As a result, the question can in fact be viewed as whether an individual would find the precaution worthwhile if it had the effect of preventing injury to himself. For further discussion of issues involving valuation, see subsection VIII.D.1.

33. That is, we follow the standard economic interpretation of the negligence rule, under which failure to take a precaution is negligent if and only if the cost of the precaution (here, $25) is less than the magnitude of the harm that would be avoided ($100).

ity, meaning simply that victims bear their losses regardless of injurers' behavior. Finally, we assume that the regimes of strict liability and of negligence may entail some costs associated with use of the legal system,[34] and we suppose that either of the two rules could be the cheaper one.[35]

(b) Effects of the Legal Rules. What are the effects of each of the three rules? That is, do potential injurers take the precaution, and if harm occurs, who pays for it?[36]

Under strict liability, injurers[37] will clearly find it in their interest to take the precaution if its cost is $25, because this cost is less than the $100 harm that would otherwise occur and for which they would otherwise be liable. Injurers will not undertake the precaution when its cost is $150, because this cost exceeds the $100 harm for which they would otherwise be responsible.[38] In the case in which the precaution is not taken because it costs $150, and accordingly harm does occur, injurers pay for the harm. The parties will also bear legal costs.[39]

34. We do not explicitly consider bargaining and settlement and for simplicity assume that liability results in the payment of damages. The reader can imagine this outcome to be the result of a settlement. An explicit model of bargaining, with the possibilities of settlement and litigation, could be considered, but doing so would not alter our main conclusions.

35. The negligence rule might be more expensive than strict liability because an inquiry into negligence needs to be made in court, whereas under strict liability it does not. However, the negligence rule might be cheaper than strict liability because, under the negligence rule, there will tend to be fewer cases, for if an injurer is not negligent and causes harm, there will not be a case (assuming that the victim realizes that the injurer was not negligent), whereas there will be under strict liability.

36. In answering these questions, we make the familiar assumptions that individuals act rationally in pursuit of their self-interest and that bargaining between potential injurers and victims before accidents occur is impossible. When these assumptions do not hold, see, for example, subsection VIII.D.5, the analysis of the legal rules would be different, but the contrasts that we offer between notions of fairness and welfare economics would be similar.

37. In the reciprocal case, injurers and victims are the same people. We nevertheless find it convenient to refer to individuals as injurers when referring to them in the role of injurers— here, when they decide what precautions to take.

38. More generally, the injurer will take the precaution whenever its cost is less than the harm prevented. This statement abstracts from the effects of litigation costs on parties' behavior. For example, if a victim's legal costs exceeded his losses, he would not have an incentive to bring suit, and thus injurers would not be led to take precautions. Here, however, we will assume for simplicity that legal costs will not be large enough for this event to occur. Were we to analyze the effects of administrative costs on the incentive to sue, and related issues, it would not affect the thrust of our conclusions. We return to this issue in chapter V.

39. We do not elaborate on which party bears what portion of the legal costs. Although the allocation of legal costs may affect behavior, see note 38, and may be directly relevant

Under the negligence rule, injurers will act in the same way as under strict liability. If the precaution cost is $25, injurers will take the precaution rather than bear liability of $100 for their negligence; and if the cost is $150, they will not take care because they will not be liable. In the latter case, harm occurs and victims bear the harm. Again, the parties will bear legal costs under the negligence rule.[40]

Under the regime of no liability, injurers do not take the precaution regardless of its cost, harm always occurs, and victims bear it.

(c) Choice of Legal Rules Using Welfare Economics. As a moment's reflection should make evident, in this perfectly reciprocal context, *every individual will be identically affected by any legal rule,* for each individual is once an injurer and once a victim. Thus, each individual will suffer a loss equal to total per capita social costs—the sum of any harm he suffers as a victim, plus any expenditures he makes on precautions as an injurer, plus any legal costs he incurs in each instance. (Any amount of damages that he will pay as an injurer he will receive as a victim, so that actual damages payments do not directly affect individuals' well-being, although they do so indirectly by influencing behavior.) Hence, all individuals will be best off under the rule that minimizes total social costs, and this rule will therefore be the best rule under any social welfare criterion of the sort we present in section II.A.

Let us now briefly explain why *any* of the three regimes could be the superior one. In essence, if the precaution is cheap (costs $25) and is thus worth inducing, a rule of liability will be desirable if legal costs are not too large.[41] Whether strict liability or the negligence rule will be better depends

---

to the fairness of various legal rules (including rules for allocating legal costs), taking such complications into account would not fundamentally alter our analysis of the difference between notions of fairness and welfare economics. Moreover, because we are examining a reciprocal setting, the allocation of legal costs will not in the end have any distributive effect.

40. Under a perfectly functioning negligence rule with perfectly informed parties, there are no administrative costs (because no one ever is negligent and there are no lawsuits since victims know that injurers were not negligent and that a tribunal would never mistakenly find them negligent). Although, to ease our exposition, we do not explicitly include the many realistic factors that result in the negligence rule being costly in practice, the reader can imagine that some such factors are present in the background.

41. If the legal costs of the cheaper liability rule exceeded $75, then the total cost of imposing liability (which includes the precaution cost of $25) would exceed $100, the amount of harm prevented; hence, a rule of no liability would be better. (In fact, if harm is effectively deterred, in a perfectly functioning legal regime there would be no lawsuits and thus no legal costs. The legal cost figures we are using are meant to refer to per capita legal costs that might nevertheless arise, say, due to suits brought by victims of some sort of harm who mistakenly think that the injurer is liable. See note 40.)

on which rule involves lower legal costs. If, however, the precaution costs $150, individuals will be worse off if they are induced to take care, and they will not in fact be led to do so under either strict liability or the negligence rule. Accordingly, a rule of no liability will be best because it produces the same outcome as the other liability rules with regard to behavior and harm, but no legal costs are borne.

To amplify, suppose that the cost of the precaution is $25 and legal costs are lower under strict liability than under the negligence rule; say, they are $5 under strict liability and $10 under the negligence rule.[42] Then strict liability would be the best rule. Under such a regime, total costs borne by each individual (who is once an injurer and once a victim) are $30: injurers are led to spend $25 on the precaution, and injurers and victims absorb $5 in legal expenses.[43] Under the negligence rule, total costs borne by each individual are $35, for similar reasons. And in the absence of liability, total costs are $100 because injurers do not take the precaution and each individual therefore suffers harm. Conversely, if legal costs are reversed, so that they are only $5 under the negligence rule and $10 under strict liability, then the negligence rule would be the superior rule. Finally, if the cost of the precaution is $150, then a rule of no liability would be best. Under that regime, each individual will of course bear a cost of $100. Under strict liability, the injurer will not take the precaution, but legal costs, say of $5, will be borne, so total costs will be $105; likewise, under the negligence rule, total costs will be $110.[44]

(d) *Choice of Legal Rules Using Notions of Fairness.* The comparison of the rules using notions of fairness is immediate. Strict liability will be best if the principle of fairness calls for punishment whenever someone causes harm, or if it calls for the compensation of all victims. Negligence will be the superior rule if the principle of punishment to which one subscribes is punishment for

42. One reason that legal costs may be expended even though no harm actually occurs is that, when harm does occur due to another cause, a victim may spend some funds on litigation, but after some initial effort by both sides, the injurer may be able to demonstrate to the victim that he was not the cause of the victim's losses. See note 40.

43. Note that in his role as an injurer, the typical individual will spend $25 plus some fraction of the legal costs, say $2.50, and in his role as victim, he will spend the remaining fraction of the legal costs, say the other $2.50. Thus, he will spend a total of $30. See also note 39, discussing the irrelevance of the allocation of legal costs between the parties in the present setting.

44. It is theoretically possible that there would never be a lawsuit under the negligence rule because no one would ever be negligent, but as a practical matter this will not usually be true. See notes 40 and 42.

fault; this will also satisfy the principle of fair compensation if that principle is a modified one that demands compensation only if the injurer was at fault. Otherwise, the negligence rule will not satisfy the compensation requirement, but strict liability will, creating a conflict between strict liability and the negligence rule that will have to be resolved by some other principle.[45] Under notions of corrective justice, the injurer's responsibility is explicitly linked to the victim's entitlement to compensation, so there will be no conflict; the question simply will be which rule most comports with corrective justice. The most common view favors the negligence rule, although some believe that corrective justice requires imposing strict liability.[46]

(e) Why the Choice of Legal Rules Should Be Based Only on Individuals' Well-Being. (i) The Argument for Welfare Economics and against Notions of Fairness. In this subsection, we explain that fairness-based evaluation of tort rules is problematic because adherence to any notion of fairness can only make everyone worse off. To be more precise, each individual's well-being will be reduced whenever the liability rule chosen using a notion of fairness differs from that chosen under welfare economics—that is, whenever the notion of fairness is given sufficient weight to be decisive.[47] This conclusion about notions of fairness follows immediately from the observations made in the preceding two subsections. In subsection (c), we explain that, in the present reciprocal context, all individuals would rank the legal rules the same way; thus, the legal rule favored by welfare economics is always one under which everyone is better off than under any other rule. It follows, therefore, that any deviation from the choice dictated by welfare economics must make everyone worse off.

In this regard, we note that notions of fairness may well require choosing rules different from those favored by welfare economics. As we note in subsection (d), the notions of fairness that we consider favor a particular rule, either the negligence rule or strict liability, without regard to either the cost

45. We also note that some notions of fairness may favor strict liability in certain cases—such as when an injurer's activity is unusually dangerous—and the negligence rule in others.

46. Much of the corrective justice literature has been concerned with determining the circumstances (if any) under which nonnegligent injurers should compensate victims. As we indicate in the text to follow, our critique applies to any resolution of this issue.

47. In other cases, the pursuit of fairness rather than welfare economics will be inconsequential. We ignore, here and throughout, notions of fairness (we might suppose mixed views, which also give weight to individuals' well-being) that never have enough weight to be decisive. We also disregard notions of fairness that are decisive only in the case in which two rules are precisely tied under welfare economics. In both instances, the importance of fairness is so trivial that, under its own terms, no effort should ever be expended to determine the notion's basis or applicability.

of precautions or legal expenses—two factors that play an important role in determining which rule makes everyone better off or worse off. For example, a notion of fairness that demands unconditional punishment or unconditional compensation would favor strict liability, and this will be so even when the negligence rule involves lower legal costs and results in the same behavior as under strict liability.[48] Similarly, a regime of no liability, one that does not satisfy the notions of fairness that we consider,[49] will be best for all individuals when liability does not influence precautions and is costly to administer.

We pause to emphasize that our general argument that pursuing notions of fairness can only make everyone worse off—and sometimes will do so—does not depend on the particular notions of fairness that we chose to examine. In the present context of reciprocal accidents, our analysis indicates that *any* notion of fairness would be subject to our criticism: employing welfare economics always entails choosing the rule under which everyone is better off than under each of the alternatives; hence, any deviation from the attempt to enhance individuals' well-being—in whatever setting—entails the result that everyone must be worse off. This conclusion is true whether the notion of fairness rests on a need for compensation, a demand for punishment, a desire to realize corrective justice, or any other basis. Moreover, this conclusion is true for any mixed view, under which weight is given both to a notion of fairness and to individuals' well-being; as long as any weight is given to a notion of fairness, one will sometimes be led to choose a different legal rule from that under welfare economics, and in every such instance, all individuals will be made worse off.[50]

48. Likewise, a notion of fairness that opposes punishment in the absence of fault will favor the negligence rule even when strict liability saves legal costs and induces the same behavior.

49. As a possible exception, see the discussion in note 8 of the applicability of the notion of corrective justice to the comparison between tort liability and no-fault regimes.

50. To elaborate, suppose initially that the total cost borne by each individual under the negligence rule is 105, that the total under strict liability is 110, and that the weight given by an analyst to fairness in favor of the negligence rule is 3. Thus, the advantage of the negligence rule in terms of individuals' well-being is 5 and in terms of fairness is 3, so the analyst who gives weight to a notion of fairness would prefer the negligence rule. Now, suppose that the administrative costs of the negligence rule are gradually increased. There will come a point after which well-being under the negligence rule will be below that under strict liability. For example, suppose that the administrative costs are raised to a level at which each individual's total costs under the negligence rule are 112. Then everyone is better off under strict liability—individuals' well-being is higher by 112–110, or 2—but the analyst who gives weight to a notion of fairness would still choose the negligence rule because fairness is given a weight of

Unless one's basic moral view disregards the well-being of all individu-als,[51] there must be something of substantial importance that is promoted by the pursuit of a notion of fairness for it to warrant overriding the well-being of everyone. As we now discuss, however, we find it very difficult to identify what that could be. A reason for this difficulty, we believe, is that there cannot be anyone to whom one is being fair when every human object of one's efforts to be fair is made worse off.[52]

(ii) Comments on the Literature. How would fairness advocates address this very basic and fundamental criticism? The short answer is that their re-sponse cannot readily be ascertained. Most writers who invoke notions of fair-ness take its value for granted, and none to our knowledge have directly con-fronted the potential conflict between their favored notions of fairness and everyone's well-being.

Some writers, notably corrective justice theorists, have presented elabo-rate conceptions of fairness. As we explain in subsection B.2, however, these theories usually are not developed in a manner that allows one to know how they would apply in many instances of interest or to understand the basis for believing that they have normative force.

In addition, most corrective justice theorists give little or no attention to the reciprocal case that we examine in this subsection. Yet it seems to us that any satisfactory normative theory must ultimately address this basic, paradigmatic situation.[53] More importantly, it does not appear to have been

---

3, which exceeds the benefit of strict liability in terms of individuals' well-being. (We note that this argument holds even if the weight given to fairness is very small. If, say, the weight is only 1, administrative costs under the negligence rule could be raised somewhat less than in the prior case, to the point at which each individual's total costs under the negligence rule are 110.5. Thus, again, the analyst who gives some weight to a notion of fairness would choose the negligence rule even though everyone is better off under strict liability.)

This argument in a more general form—that any notion of fairness, mixed or not, that departs from welfare economic analysis at all in any symmetric setting will sometimes favor a regime under which everyone is worse off—is developed in Kaplow and Shavell (1999).

51. Fletcher and some others appear to hold an absolute view wherein considerations of fairness trump any concern for individuals' well-being. See note 11.

52. See subsection II.C.2. Similarly, from the perspective of "justice," one can ask in what respect people would be the victims of an injustice on account of subjecting them to a rule under which they are better off rather than worse off. Or if one were to invoke "rights," one must consider whether a rule should be seen as violating rights when individuals whose rights are supposedly violated would unanimously prefer to forfeit those rights in order to benefit from the regime under which their well-being is greater.

53. We are somewhat surprised by the inattention to the reciprocal case. First, Fletcher's writing, discussed in the text that follows, brings this case into the spotlight. Second, the

recognized that applying any notion of fairness in the reciprocal case entails making everyone worse off in every instance in which the principle leads to a result different from that under welfare economics.[54] That any normative theory involving a notion of fairness has this implication in the simple, reciprocal case suggests that the theory suffers from a fundamental problem, not one of the sort that might be avoided merely by making minor adjustments.[55]

Fletcher's writing differs from that of most other tort theorists in that he pays special attention to the reciprocal context. He does not, however, address the basic defect that we identify. Rather, he advances a notion of fairness under which the preferred legal rule depends on whether or not the reciprocal case prevails: in the reciprocal case, his notion of fairness favors the negligence rule; in the nonreciprocal case, it favors strict liability.[56] A

---

reciprocal case is both a foundational one and one that has special importance under many leading approaches to moral theory (as we discuss in subsection (iii)).

54. Because, as we explain in subsection B.2, much of the work on corrective justice is presented as descriptive theory, the fact that the posited notions of fairness favor clearly undesirable rules in basic situations is not necessarily a defect, although one might have doubts about whether such defective principles accurately represent the consensus views of common law judges.

55. It will not do, for example, to argue that the theory remains valid and compelling generally, subject to some special exception for the reciprocal case, when the central determinants of the applicability of the theory have nothing to do with whether the reciprocal context applies. To explore this point further, suppose that some notion of fairness is expressly qualified such that it is ignored in cases in which everyone would be made worse off. Then, if the facts changed slightly so that a single individual, instead of being one cent worse off, is one cent better off, the preferred legal rule would change—now following the dictates of fairness principles rather than the prescription of welfare economics—even if everyone else is still much worse off. It is difficult to imagine the basis for such a principle that would trump substantial welfare losses in one case but not in the other. For additional discussion of the need for consistency in the application of normative principles, see subsection II.C.1 and subsection (iii).

Although we believe the present argument to be sufficient to displace most notions of fairness, we explain in subsection 2, why these notions are similarly defective in the nonreciprocal context. We note that our present objection would not necessarily be decisive against a theory that on its own terms applies different principles to the case of nonreciprocal harm. (As it turns out, the only theory in the literature that does so—Fletcher's—is nevertheless subject to our critique, as we discuss in the text to follow.)

56. See Fletcher (1972). To be more specific, nonreciprocity is both a necessary and a sufficient condition for liability under his approach. His support for the negligence rule in the reciprocal case, rather than a rule of no liability, stems from his belief that the actor's negligence makes the otherwise reciprocal situation nonreciprocal. It seems to us, however, that his preference for the negligence rule in the reciprocal case does not follow from his premise. If one adopted a rule of no liability in a perfectly reciprocal situation, everyone would be negligent—in our example, each person would cause one negligent instance of harm and

similar view about the relevance of reciprocity to determining when there should be liability is reflected in some of the factors in and commentary on the rule in the *Restatement of Torts* for determining which activities should be deemed abnormally dangerous and thus subject to strict liability rather than the negligence rule[57] (although the basis for the *Restatement*'s position is not as clear as the rationale for Fletcher's[58]).

These views about the relevance of reciprocity, not surprisingly, are problematic for the very reason we have been discussing. Namely, in the reciprocal case, the notion of fairness under discussion leads one to choose a legal rule without regard to its effects on individuals' well-being; hence, there will be cases in which the notion of fairness leads one to favor different legal rules from those chosen under welfare economics, and in all such cases

---

would suffer negligently caused harm once—meaning that the situation would involve perfect reciprocity. Thus, a rule of no liability would not appear to violate Fletcher's principle, which requires only that liability be assigned for nonreciprocally imposed risks. (We note, moreover, that unless the legal costs of liability are high relative to the benefits of precaution, this rule of no liability will make everyone worse off.) Compare Keating (1996, 314–17), identifying a similar incompleteness in Fletcher's view.

57. One factor explicitly refers to whether "the activity is not a matter of common usage," and another factor is interpreted in the commentary to negate strict liability "when the community is largely devoted to the dangerous enterprise and its prosperity largely depends upon it." *Restatement of the Law Second: Torts* (1977, §520(d), (f) and comment k). The "common usage" factor in subsection (d) seems to invoke directly the idea of reciprocity. The dependence of the community referred to in subsection (f) and the commentary on that factor seem to suggest situations in which there may not be literal reciprocity in that everyone engages in the same activity, but rather a more general reciprocity in that the community tends to share many of the risks and benefits (such as when most residents do not own oil wells but many are thus employed). As a result, oil wells may be abnormally dangerous and thus subject to strict liability in Kansas and Indiana but not in Texas and Oklahoma, where oil drilling is common and the risk due to it is, in a sense, reciprocal. Ibid. (§520(f) and comment k).

58. The comments on section 520 are not explicit about the purposes that underlie the elements of the definition of abnormally dangerous activities. The commentary to section 519, however, which is the section that provides for strict liability for abnormally dangerous activities as defined in section 520, describes the purpose as follows:

It is founded upon a policy of the law that imposes upon anyone who for his own purposes creates an abnormal risk of harm to his neighbors, the responsibility of relieving against that harm when it does in fact occur. The defendant's enterprise, in other words, is required to pay its way by compensating for the harm it causes, because of its special, abnormal and dangerous character. (Ibid., §519 comment d)

everyone will be worse off. In fact, this particular notion of fairness is sometimes more problematic than our foregoing discussion suggests, as can be
seen by examining the *Restatement*'s example involving oil rigs that are
otherwise abnormally dangerous.[59] The approach of Fletcher and the *Restatement* favors the negligence rule when everyone has oil rigs, even if strict
liability would result in a substantial, cost-effective reduction in serious accidents, to everyone's benefit.[60] Examined in its entirety, their position is perverse: it favors strict liability, the rule that effectively reduces harm, when
there is only one oil rig causing injuries, but endorses the negligence rule,
which is inferior in terms of reducing harm, when there are hundreds of oil
rigs, each causing equally serious damage.[61] In sum, those who have focused

59. This is not the only illustration. For example, the commentary to section 520(d),
ibid. (§520 comment i), indicates that containing water may be abnormally dangerous, but
not when everyone does it in household pipes or when every barnyard has a water tank, and
the commentary to section 520(f), ibid. (§520 comment k), notes as a further example that
reservoirs for livestock or irrigation ditches are not to be considered abnormally dangerous
in dry regions, where they are commonly used.

60. As we discuss in subsection (c), a rule of strict liability may make everyone better
off in the reciprocal context, in which case following the Fletcher/*Restatement* approach would
make everyone worse off. (Likewise, in the nonreciprocal context, the negligence rule may be
better, contrary to the Fletcher/*Restatement* prescription.) In the present illustration, the main
reason that strict liability may be more effective than the negligence rule is due to a factor
that we do not consider in our simple example in the text: namely, the level of activity—
how many miles a person drives, the number of oil rigs or the amount of time they are in
operation, and so forth. Activity levels are affected by strict liability, but might not be under
a negligence determination. See Shavell (1980b). It is especially important to control the activity level when the risk associated with that activity is high. (Our present discussion abstracts
from administrative costs—as does the treatment of the subject in the *Restatement* and by
most commentators. This omission has the potential to mislead, as emphasized in our previous
analysis.)

61. Indeed, it is not even clear that nonreciprocity is positively correlated with the desirability of imposing strict liability rather than negligence. Blasting is an unavoidably risky activity that most people do not undertake; hence, it is a nonreciprocal risk that under the Fletcher/
Restatement view seems appropriately subject to strict liability. However, countless (presumably most) nonreciprocal activities are not especially dangerous, and thus there is no particular
reason to impose strict liability. Conversely, some common activities give rise to approximately
reciprocal risks but are dangerous and thus may be properly subjected to strict liability. Moreover, with regard to the *Restatement of Torts*, there is no basis for defending the factors that
refer to reciprocity on the ground that they serve as indicators of dangerousness, because
factors (a) and (b) in section 520, see *Restatement of the Law Second: Torts* (1977, §520(a),
(b)), explicitly consider the degree of risk and extent of harm. Rather, the factors based on
reciprocity are offered as grounds for rejecting strict liability even when dangerousness is
established. See ibid. (comment i): "Certain activities, notwithstanding their recognizable danger, are so generally carried on as to be regarded as customary."; and ibid.: "The usual dangers

on the reciprocal case have no more confronted the fundamental defect in notions of fairness than those who have not.

(iii) The Significance of the Possibility That All Individuals May Be Made Worse Off under Any Notion of Fairness. We have shown that giving weight to any notion of fairness may make all individuals worse off and in fact does so in the present (reciprocal) setting whenever such a notion favors a different legal rule from that chosen under welfare economics. Because perfectly reciprocal settings generally do not exist in the world, the reader may question the significance of our demonstration. Nevertheless, there are a number of reasons (some of which we discuss in subsection II.C.1) that this conflict between notions of fairness and the well-being of all individuals is of great importance for those who accept the proposition that it is problematic to favor making everyone worse off.

First, as a matter of logical consistency, if a normative theory conflicts with a principle one endorses—in a basic setting that is within the theory's domain—the theory is thereby shown to be defective. Some normative theories, to be sure, have limited domains: a theory about when one should keep promises does not apply when there is an automobile accident (before which, one presumes, no promise about the bearing of losses had been made between the injurer and the victim). But the present situation is different, for theories of corrective justice and other notions of fairness in tort do apply to cases in which an injurer wrongfully harms a victim; indeed, this is the setting that the theories discussed here are designed to address. Moreover, even if perfectly reciprocal settings may not often arise in practice, the question of whether there is perfect, partial, or no reciprocity does not itself bear on whether the normative foundations of the notions of fairness under consideration are applicable.[62] If one endorses such a notion of fairness, therefore, one has endorsed in principle the idea that

---

resulting from an activity that is one of common usage are not regarded as abnormal, even though a serious risk of harm cannot be eliminated by all reasonable care."

62. This statement must be qualified because the underlying justifications for corrective justice theories have not been satisfactorily articulated, as we discuss in subsection B.2. It appears, however, that all such theories (with the exception of Fletcher's) require compensation for wrongful losses, and the concept of wrong seems to depend on the character of the injurer's act and not on various other factors, including the frequency with which the parties or others like them might come into contact, whether as potential injurers or potential victims. Outside of corrective justice theory per se, common notions of fairness involving, say, the idea that an injurer should be punished, similarly seem to depend on some notion of what an injurer is and which types of acts causing injury should be covered (for example, all acts, only voluntary acts, or only negligent acts).

it may well be good (produce a more just state of the world) to make every-one worse off in certain situations. If such a view cannot be defended,[63] then a normative theory that necessarily implies such a view is indefensible as well.[64]

Second, under many prevalent approaches to moral theory, normative principles must be tested in symmetric settings like the reciprocal context on which we have focused thus far. In particular, the Golden Rule, Kant's categorical imperative, and the construct of the veil of ignorance each command the moral analyst to treat problems as if they involved a purely reciprocal situation. For example, to treat others as one would have others treat oneself is indeed what happens when one contemplates adopting a rule in the reciprocal setting, for the way one will be induced to treat the other is in fact how the other will end up treating oneself.[65] Thus, for those commentators who accept these frameworks for moral assessment, a group that seems to include many who advance notions of fairness in the tort context,[66] our demonstration that any notion of fairness—whenever it fa-

63. Some might defend such a view by arguing that in certain contexts individuals may not understand what is best for themselves. But, as we explain in subsection II.A.1, we are focusing on cases in which individuals do not suffer from any infirmities. The point is simply that the logic of our demonstration here holds fully when individuals are perfectly informed and in all other respects are capable of making good decisions for themselves. For a discussion of how welfare economics addresses this issue and other complications concerning individuals' preferences, see section VIII.B.

64. See subsection II.C.1, elaborating the point generally, and note 55, discussing the point further in the tort context. Moreover, as we emphasize in subsection (i) and in note 50, as long as any weight is given to any notion of fairness, one will sometimes be led to choose a legal rule that makes everyone worse off. Thus, our point applies not merely to the particular notions of fairness that have been elaborated by theorists thus far, but to any notion that might be offered, if it departs from welfare economics.

65. For elaboration on the connection between these moral frameworks and symmetric settings for analysis, see subsection II.C.1, especially note 79 in chapter II, and subsection VIII.C.1. Some legal theorists have advanced related views in assessing the morality of risk-creating behavior. See, for example, Fried (1970, 183): "The general theorem advanced in this section [regarding the imposition of risks on others] is built on the proposition that the justifications for imposing this risk on others are analogous to those governing the rationality of imposing the risk on oneself."; and ibid. (204), stating that the relevant moral criterion involves asking what a rational person who did not know his particular circumstances would "agree to as included within morality."

66. Some fairness proponents in fact make explicit reference to such moral approaches in defending their normative views. See, for example, Keating (1996, 312 and n.2) and Weinrib (1983, 49–50). We note, however, that Keating is difficult to interpret in this regard because, despite his explicit endorsement of the Golden Rule and the idea of asking whether individuals could view an act as legitimate if they traded places with those burdened by their act and

vors rules different from those chosen under welfare economics—always makes everyone worse off in the symmetric setting should be particularly troubling.

Third, apart from the importance of our analysis of the reciprocal case from the perspectives of logical consistency and leading frameworks for testing moral principles, the reciprocal case has direct practical importance in the tort context. There is a real sense in which we play both the role of victim and that of injurer in our everyday activities. Not only, as we said in the example, do some people both drive and walk, but they also do myriad other things that expose themselves to or create the possibility of harm. It is true that a given person's exposure to risk, at least over a short interval, will usually exceed or be exceeded by the risk that he generates, but for many people there may over time be a rough equality of imposition of and exposure to risk. Moreover, various indirect payment flows contribute to the extent of reciprocity: when firms must compensate individual victims, many in the victim class pay through higher product prices or lower returns on their investments, and when injurers' insurance companies pay more, individuals' insurance premiums will be higher. Thus, there is a very real possibility that attending to a notion of fairness, thereby ignoring or devaluing what really affects individuals' well-being, would make most individuals worse off,[67] including the substantial majority of those who are the purported beneficiaries of the fairness notion—that is, the individuals, such as uncompensated victims, to whom one wants to be fair.[68]

---

thus bore its adverse effects themselves, he subsequently rejects as a test for reasonable risk imposition whether one would impose the risk on oneself. See Keating (1996, 323–25). He justifies this rejection by noting that others' ends may differ, but it would seem that proper application of the relevant tests would take this factor into account, such as by asking whether one would impose the risk on oneself if the resulting harm would hurt oneself as much as it would hurt the person who actually would be harmed. See note 79 in chapter II, discussing the relationship between tests like the categorical imperative and consideration of the symmetric case.

For general endorsements of such moral approaches, see the sources cited in note 94 in chapter VIII.

67. In making this statement, we, as we do elsewhere, take a prospective (ex ante) view, which we believe to be appropriate in this context. See subsection VIII.C.1, defending the ex ante perspective. See also note 86 in chapter VIII, explaining that our analysis does not, for the most part, require adopting an ex ante perspective.

68. Moreover, as we note below, even when harm is imposed in a somewhat nonreciprocal manner, all individuals could be made worse off as a consequence of pursuing a notion of fairness. See note 89. We are not, however, arguing that always choosing rules based solely on how they affect individuals' well-being rather than using some other criterion would

(f) *The Apparent Mootness of Concerns for Fairness.* Fairness considerations appear to be substantially moot in the present context for several reasons.[69] First and foremost, when harm is imposed reciprocally and legal rules
are applied consistently, a required payment from one individual to another will
be precisely offset by a return payment.[70] Specifically, suppose that a principle of
fairness demands that the injurer pay $100 for harm done. Because this same
individual will also receive $100 in his role as victim, the effect of the legal rule
on an injurer's wealth position is nil; the object of punishing the individual is
nullified at the end of the day. Similarly, if a principle of fairness holds that a
victim should receive $100 in compensation, this requirement will have no net
effect on the victim, for in his position as injurer he will have to surrender this
$100.

The explanation for how it is possible for analysts to invoke principles
of fairness that are intended to punish or to compensate, when in fact
they do neither, is that the fairness principles under consideration concern
only a particular harmful event, not the broader circumstances of individuals.[71] Given this narrow focus, one could argue, for example, that the goal
of punishment is served when someone who deserves to be punished pays
$100 even though it is known that, in the next millisecond, the person will
receive a rebate of $100 under the very same rule that punished him in

---

result in a Pareto improvement—in which case everyone would be better off. First, welfare
economics is explicitly concerned with distribution, and some economic policy is consciously redistributive, notably tax and transfer programs that redistribute wealth from the
rich to the poor. Second, even with regard to other rules, one would expect some individuals
to be repeated beneficiaries or repeated losers under one approach or another. Rather, our
point is that, because of substantial reciprocity, the systematic pursuit of notions of fairness
may well make most individuals worse off, including those to whom one was seeking to be
fair.

69. The latter two reasons that we note—the widespread use of insurance and the large
role of organizational defendants—have been mentioned by others. See, for example, R.
Posner (1972, 31–32), noting that, in his historical sample of tort cases, most negligence
defendants were firms held vicariously responsible for the negligence of their employees, a
result that is "hard to square with a moral approach" to the determination of liability; R.
Rabin (1996, 2273); and Sugarman (1985, 609–11).

70. In the nonreciprocal context, this problem arises when different nonreciprocal risks
are aggregated if those risks are offsetting. If mootness is to be avoided there, the pertinent
fairness theory must explain why certain risks should be viewed independently rather than
in combination. See also note 21, discussing this difficulty in Fletcher's theory.

71. See, for example, Weinrib (1989a, 408): "[E]ach harm done and suffered is the core
of a single transaction that relates *this* doer to *this* sufferer, and each such transaction is a
discrete unit of normative significance."; and ibid. (409): "[E]quality must operate within each
transaction."

the first place. We do not, however, find this view plausible[72] and are un-aware of any defense of this position in the literature.[73] Moreover, the fact that notions of fairness may well be moot in the reciprocal context is of practical as well as conceptual importance because there is a substantial degree of reciprocity in the realm of torts, as we discuss in subsection (e)(iii).

Second, both injurers and victims are often insured.[74] (The reason, of course, is that accidents are often probabilistic and individuals are typically risk averse; we explore the case in which harm is uncertain in section D.) Injurers are not obviously punished when it is their insurance company that pays tort damages, and victims are not really compensated if their receipt of damage payments merely reimburses their insurer under a subrogation

72. In subsection E.3 we do consider at some length the notion that being an injurer or victim per se might be relevant, although it is implicit in that discussion that distinctions between injurers and victims seem meaningful only when they are different groups of people.

Another reason that a notion of fairness might not be moot in the reciprocal context relates to the possibility that the notion is not really an independent evaluative principle, but rather serves as a proxy device for identifying effects relevant to individuals' well-being. Thus, if the purpose of punishment is to deter, it matters that both individuals rather than neither are punished. (The prospect of both being punished may be necessary to give each a proper incentive, but if neither would be punished and they knew this in advance, neither would have an incentive to behave properly.) Likewise, having a legal rule that punishes wrongful conduct might be important symbolically, in that it may reinforce social norms about proper behavior in activities that may injure others, or may enhance the legitimacy of the law by bringing it into line with social norms. In such cases, the fact that in some settings a legal rule may have no direct effect might be unimportant. (Moreover, granting an exception for such cases, or for others in which the legal rule was not necessary or desirable, could upset these symbolic functions if citizens do not appreciate the reasons for granting the exceptions and instead see them as sending a message that certain wrongful conduct should not be viewed as wrongful.)

73. As we note in subsection (e)(ii), analysts interested in notions of fairness do not seem to pay much attention to the reciprocal setting despite its foundational character (and Fletcher's emphasis on it in his early work). Fletcher's views seem to differ from those of most fairness theorists; his opposition to liability in the fully reciprocal context seems motivated by the notion that the freedom to impose risk on others serves as implicit compensation for being exposed to a similar risk. (One might have thought this would lead him to be indifferent among liability rules—or to choose among them on other grounds, such as their effects on accident rates and the level of legal costs incurred—rather than to prefer no liability. See note 56; compare Epstein (1973, 165 n.42): "Even if two risks were reciprocal, it does not follow that neither party should have [a right to recover damages] when injured.")

74. See section F.

arrangement.[75] In practice, therefore, to the extent that one or both parties have insurance, fairness seems moot on this ground as well.[76]

75. Typically, policies are written so that the insured is paid right away, and any duplicative amount collected in a tort suit goes to the insurer under a subrogation arrangement. See generally Appleman and Appleman (1972, vol. 6A, §§4051–4052), describing insurers' legal right to subrogation and the effect of policy provisions. The most plausible reason for the prevalence of subrogation is that it is in individuals' interests to have such insurance policies. The purpose of insurance is to insure, not to buy a lottery ticket with a potential payoff that exceeds the extent of any loss. That is, insurance is meant to reduce exposure to risk, not to increase it. Subrogation avoids the outcome in which people collect more than their losses and allows them to purchase policies more cheaply because, when insurers anticipate that they will collect tort judgments, they will charge lower premiums. See Shavell (1987, 235–40).

76. It is not inherent in notions of fairness that the effect of insurance be ignored, but fairness arguments and theories are often developed under the implicit assumption that insurance does not exist. Interestingly, a number of corrective justice theorists mention no-fault insurance alternatives to tort liability, see sources cited in note 8, without commenting on the prevalence of insurance under the existing tort regime, which makes the two systems much more similar in operation than commentators' discussions suggest. An exception is Wright, who believes that compulsory no-fault systems violate corrective justice, but that injurers' contracting for insurers to take over what would otherwise be their own obligations is consistent with corrective justice. See Wright (1992, 703–04), presenting this argument, but not addressing the apparent contradiction between his acceptance of voluntary insurance and his reliance on Aristotle's notion of corrective justice, which Wright interprets, see ibid. (692–95), as requiring the injurer, after causing a loss, to have his position reduced by the amount of the victim's loss.

We observe that, even when injurers have full coverage through liability insurance, punishment is not always fully eliminated. First, in the nonreciprocal case, potential injurers subject, say, to strict liability rather than the negligence rule, will pay higher premiums and victims will pay lower premiums. See note 112. (In the reciprocal context, however, different legal rules, abstracting from legal costs and incentive effects, serve merely to relabel whether payments are attributed to liability or first-party insurance policies of each individual.) Of course, if a notion of fairness requires punishment for actual harm done, as seems to be commonly suggested, such ex ante premium payments in an amount reflecting expected harm—which exceeds actual harm in the many instances in which harm does not occur and falls short (possibly far short) of actual harm when it does occur—would do little to promote fairness. Second, insured injurers may suffer reputational losses in addition to having to pay for harm. Even when such reputational losses occur, we suspect that much of the loss results from the publicity surrounding the act of injury rather than from the existence of a legal award. For most ordinary accidents, one supposes that often there is no reputational effect and that, if one exists, it results from learning that an individual caused an accident and not from the existence or size of the insurance company's unreported out-of-court payment (keeping in mind that most cases are settled).

We note that insurance is also relevant to an assessment of the effect of tort liability on individuals' well-being. In particular, liability insurance may attenuate the deterrent effect

Third, to the extent that notions of fairness demand punishment of individuals whose behavior is blameworthy, fairness will often be moot, or at least substantially attenuated, when the tort defendant is a firm.[77] The reason is that there may be little, if any, relationship between the culpable party and those who bear the costs of tort liability.[78] In the case of punitive damages, for example, the firm cannot procure reimbursement from the culpable employee. The most the firm may be able to do to the responsible individual is to fire him, and the prospect of ordinary damages may be sufficient to

---

of liability, in which case a welfare economic analysis may be favorable to a no-fault regime, as we discuss in section F. We note that deterrence is not always attenuated. To the extent that premiums reflect activity levels, that deductibles and co-insurance requirements are employed, that future premiums depend on past accident experience, or that insurers can observe parties' behavior (such as when fire insurance companies inspect insureds' premises), insured individuals will continue to have incentives to avoid accidents. Also, as in our example in subsection D.1, when incentive considerations are important, individuals may choose to take care so as to avoid most risk of causing injury and forgo insurance. See also note 98, discussing further the problem of moral hazard. For an analysis of how permitting individuals to purchase liability insurance tends to promote all individuals' well-being, see Shavell (1982a, 2000).

77. We refer to "firms" for convenience; our point actually pertains to organizational defendants more generally (although, instead of shareholders, the relevant individuals might be taxpayers for a governmental defendant, or some other group). See also R. Rabin (1996, 2273), indicating that organizational defendants predominate in many classes of tort cases.

78. When defendants are firms, economic arguments concerned with deterrence are influenced as well. Two points are worth noting. First, a proper economic analysis would take such effects into account, and this problem has indeed been a subject of investigation. See, for example, Kraakman (1984). Second, there is some basis for a presumption that firms should be treated analogously to individual injurers. When liability for harm is imposed on a firm, the firm has an incentive to take cost-effective measures to reduce the harm, such as adopting particular technologies, engaging in research, supervising employees more carefully, and charging higher product prices (that reflect the full social cost of what is produced), thereby reducing demand for the product. Exactly what mix of activities the firm will undertake may be hard to predict. Indeed, this very fact provides a justification for simply imposing liability and letting the firm's decisionmakers choose how to respond, rather than resorting to direct regulation of every decision the firm makes that pertains to the risk it creates. By contrast, there is no basis for an analogous presumption with regard to notions of fairness. The firm's response to liability is designed to maximize profits, which, when harm is fully internalized, tends to correspond to welfare maximization. The firm has no particular incentive (and sometimes no ability) to seek out individuals who, according to some postulated moral theory, have the requisite responsibility and to impose the punishment that the moral theory would demand. The text to follow offers illustrations of some of the possible deviations that might arise.

induce the firm to do so.[79] Additional liability might be borne by dispersed shareholders with no direct involvement in the incident.[80] With respect to products liability, customers (those whom we might seek to compensate[81]) are the ones most likely to bear the burden of heightened liability requirements, through price increases.[82] Thus, in many settings, fairness notions concerned with punishing injurers, even if valid, do not really seem to be addressed in a meaningful way through tort liability. We also note that fairness arguments

79. Often, the firm may not even have this opportunity. The responsible individuals are sometimes no longer employed by the firm when liability is imposed; they may have quit, retired, or died. Also, because in firms many people work together and make joint decisions, there often simply does not exist a single individual or a small group of people who are deserving of punishment in the sense intended by various fairness notions. Moreover, when there are culpable individuals, they can often conceal their behavior by hiding behind others. See, for example, Polinsky and Shavell (1998, 950–51).

It might nevertheless be argued that the firm should be punished because those higher up—or even the shareholders—are as culpable for not having prevented wrongful behavior as is the employee who acted egregiously. Frequently, however, an employee's irresponsible behavior may reflect bad luck for the corporation, or the inevitable mistakes that occur in the screening or monitoring of employees. It may also reflect the inability of a corporation to punish employee misbehavior with sufficient severity (which might suggest a need for criminal prosecution of the employee, but does not imply that the firm should be punished when it did not have available to it a sufficient threat to deter the employee's misbehavior). We surely want corporations to prevent egregious (and nonegregious, but nonetheless dangerous) actions. We do not, however, want corporations to spend exorbitant amounts of money to make such actions impossible—say, by hiring ten employees to monitor each employee who might cause harm, ten overseers for each monitor, and so forth. Nor do we want valuable products removed from the market because the firms that produce them cannot control their employees perfectly.

80. See, for example, Polinsky and Shavell (1998, 951–52). Polinsky and Shavell also discuss other respects in which notions of punishment seem attenuated when defendants are firms.

81. The situation is quite different when the victims are not the customers themselves, but instead are independent third parties (for example, pedestrians hit by rocks sent flying by poorly designed lawn mowers). Invocations of fairness by courts and commentators, however, do not usually note this important distinction, which has been emphasized in the economic analysis of products liability. See, for example, Polinsky and Shavell (1998, 934–36).

82. Indeed, in the case of certain harm (say, a product that, in the absence of liability, would have a price of $100 and will cause certain damage of $10), the prospect of liability would directly offset the compensatory effect (because the firm, knowing it would now have to pay $10 back to each customer, would raise its price to $110). Compare this situation to our more general discussion of the effect of contract provisions in section IV.C. (When harm is probabilistic, there is still no transfer on average between firms and customers, but there is in essence a provision of insurance. For a discussion of the provision of insurance through tort liability, see subsection D.1(f).)

favoring compensation may be attenuated when *victims* are firms because the usual motivations for compensation may thus be inapplicable.[83]

2. Nonreciprocal Accidents

(a) Description. We now assume that potential injurers and victims comprise two different groups of individuals.[84] The two different groups might be drivers and pedestrians, if we now make the assumption that drivers only drive and pedestrians only walk (no one does both). In all other respects, we suppose the situation to be as it was in our discussion of reciprocal accidents.

(b) Effects of the Legal Rules. The behavior of injurers under the different legal regimes will be as described before. The only difference is that, because the injurers and victims are distinct groups, the well-being of members of each group may differ, and, accordingly, the two groups will often have different preferences about legal rules. For example, victims will prefer strict liability to a rule of no liability because under strict liability they will be compensated for any harm that occurs, whereas injurers will prefer a rule of no liability.

(c) Choice of Legal Rules Using Welfare Economics. When the objective is enhancing individuals' well-being, the well-being of both injurers and victims will be relevant. Because these are two distinct groups of individuals, one of which may gain and the other of which may lose when a particular legal rule is chosen rather than another, the application of the welfare economic approach is not as straightforward as in the reciprocal case, where the choice of legal rules affects all individuals in the same manner.

As an initial matter, one can ask which rule produces the lowest per capita costs. If potential injurers and victims initially have similar levels of wealth, and the effects of the rules do not significantly change their levels of wealth, the lowest cost rule will usually be the one that produces the highest level of social welfare.[85]

---

83. The reasons that notions of fairness tend to be attenuated when victims are firms are similar to those applicable when injurers are firms. The incidence of uncompensated harm and of compensation tends to be dispersed. In addition, there often will be ex ante compensation through market prices (such as when the amount of capital invested in an industry subject to harm that is not compensated by the tort system is less than it otherwise would be, with the result that investors receive the normal rate of return in any event).

84. As noted at the outset of this section, we confine our analysis to the purely reciprocal case and, now, to the purely nonreciprocal case. For the many actual situations that are a mixture of the two, the analyses of the cases can be combined accordingly.

85. If, however, a legal rule has a substantial effect on parties' relative wealth, distributive reasons might favor one rule over another. For example, if losses were very large and income

But if, for example, victims are poor and injurers are rich, costs borne by victims may well be weighted more heavily than costs borne by injurers. In that event, strict liability may be preferable to the negligence rule because of the distributive effect.[86] Now, this distributive effect might favor the same rule as that which minimizes aggregate costs, in which case the rule would be best from the perspective of welfare economics. Alternatively, the negligence rule might be preferable to strict liability on grounds of minimizing total costs, say, because the negligence rule results in fewer lawsuits and thus involves lower administrative expenses.

In cases in which total costs are lower under one rule but the other is preferable on distributive grounds, either rule might turn out to be best, depending on the relative magnitudes of the two competing effects and how they are to be aggregated.[87] In particular, it is possible for strict liability to be superior even though the negligence rule produces lower total costs.

In sum, the welfare economic framework will, as always, result in choices among legal rules that depend on the rules' effects on individuals' well-being, which in the present context can be thought of as involving the combination of the rules' effects on total costs and on distribution. (In the reciprocal case, regardless of whether parties were equally wealthy, distributive effects do not have to be considered because there can never be such effects: any distributive gain when an individual is, say, an injurer would be forfeited when the same individual is in the role of victim.)

(d) Choice of Legal Rules Using Notions of Fairness. The evaluation of the fairness of the legal rules remains the same as before.[88] In particular, notions of fairness requiring that injurers be punished or that victims be compensated

---

was initially about equal, a rule that resulted in the loss being shared between the two parties might be optimal from a distributive perspective.

86. To simplify our exposition, we artificially confine the analysis to tort rules, ignoring that redistribution may be accomplished more efficiently through the income tax and transfer system. See subsection II.A.3 and note 38 in chapter II. In this book, we are not concerned with whether legal rules or the tax system should be used to promote distributive objectives. Rather, our claim is only that normative analysis of legal rules should be confined to individuals' well-being (a proposition that is consistent with a concern for the distribution of income), to the exclusion of notions of fairness (to the extent that the notions do not merely serve as a proxy principle for the welfare economic conception of social welfare, including concerns about the general distribution of income).

87. See subsections II.A.2 and II.A.3.

88. Only a fairness principle that explicitly depended on whether the situation was reciprocal would imply a different outcome. The analysis to follow is equally applicable to such a principle. See also pages 107–10 and notes 55 and 61, criticizing such theories.

favor strict liability, and notions that condition punishment or compensation upon the injurers' fault favor the negligence rule.

(e) Why the Choice of Legal Rules Should Be Based Only on Individuals' Well-Being. As we explain in subsection 1(e)(iii), most notions of fairness apply to the reciprocal case on their own terms, in which event their basic failure in that context demonstrates an essential deficiency in the notions. Moreover, we noted that many normative frameworks explicitly dictate that the correct rule in a nonreciprocal case is that which is appropriate in the reciprocal case. Nevertheless, we find it useful to examine separately the conflict between welfare economics and notions of fairness in the nonreciprocal case.

Because legal rules have distributive effects in the nonreciprocal case, it is no longer true that all individuals are worse off any time a notion of fairness leads to the choice of a rule different from that which best promotes individuals' well-being.[89] We do not believe, however, that the absence of unanimous dissent fundamentally affects the reasons that notions of fairness are deficient.

Even though pursuing notions of fairness does not make everyone worse off, it is still necessarily the case that social welfare is reduced if a notion of fairness is given independent weight. Recall from section II.A just what a reduction in social welfare means. The relevant point is that, however many individuals might benefit from a fairer rule, and however great their benefit might be, the fact that social welfare is lower means that a judgment has been made that the losses borne by those who are worse off under the rule are of greater social importance with regard to consideration of different individuals' levels of well-being.

We now elaborate on this point. To begin with, we have noted that the only difference between the present case and the reciprocal case is that here a distributive effect will arise. It might appear that such an effect could provide a basis for defending some notion of fairness. But the distribution of wealth (or, more generally, well-being) is *already* an aspect of social welfare

---

89. We note, however, that sometimes deviations from welfare economics will make everyone worse off even in the nonreciprocal context. First, many actual situations are not entirely nonreciprocal. In such cases, those who usually lose from choosing, say, the negligence rule rather than strict liability, may lose much less than they gain on those less frequent occasions when they occupy the opposite role. Second, one can imagine (perhaps due to administrative costs) that the rule dictated by a notion of fairness even in a purely nonreciprocal case would make everyone worse off. Finally, we show in note 114 how adopting a rule that is fairer instead of a rule that maximizes social welfare, when the latter rule is joined with a fee or tax, will also make everyone worse off.

as defined under welfare economics. And, as we explain in subsection II.B.1, we use notions of fairness to refer only to principles of evaluation under which policies are assessed, at least in part, on the basis of factors that are independent of the policies' effects on individuals' well-being. (Furthermore, as we emphasize above,[90] one must distinguish the overall distribution of wealth, a matter that is often evaluated under the rubric of distributive justice but nevertheless is an aspect of welfare economics, from the particular, localized distribution between a particular injurer and victim, sometimes discussed under the rubric of corrective justice or other context-specific notions of fairness.[91])

To illustrate the point that the distribution of wealth is included in social welfare, recall our discussion in subsection (c) of how strict liability and the negligence rule would be assessed under welfare economics. As we suggest, strict liability could be superior to the negligence rule in the sense that social welfare is greater under strict liability precisely because it is distributively superior. That is, the negligence rule might result in lower total costs, but the distributive benefit of strict liability, in terms of the ultimate effect on social welfare, may be greater. (Perhaps the negligence rule has modestly lower legal costs but victims are much poorer than injurers, making strict liability preferable on distributive grounds.[92]) Likewise, if a rule that is pre-

90. See subsection II.A.3.

91. If a notion of fairness has independent significance in the manner described in the text, one can see that the notion of fairness could not be incorporated into a social welfare function of the type discussed in subsection II.A.2. See note 15 in chapter II. The reason is that we are assuming that social welfare depends upon individuals' well-being and on nothing else. Thus, being an injurer or victim per se—that is, without regard to the resulting effect on well-being—is of no significance under this formulation of social welfare. See note 52 in chapter II. Put another way, under welfare economics, one necessarily evaluates two regimes equally if literally everyone's well-being is the same under the two regimes, even though such matters as the identity of individuals as injurers or victims may differ between the two regimes. See note 23 in chapter II. (Those who are victims in one regime, for example, would be no better off in the other regime in which they are not victims, whether because they suffer from some other form of bad luck or simply are bestowed with less income-earning ability or some other positive feature. It may be observed that a contrary view, which is implied by a notion of fairness that gives weight (independently of any effects on their well-being) to whether individuals are injurers or victims or to how such individuals are treated, violates equality in the sense that two individuals who are identically situated in terms of their ultimate well-being—who would be indifferent to trading places—would be weighted differently or treated differently.)

92. The very fact of suffering harm may involve a significant reduction in the victim's relative wealth. In a case with uncertainty, the prospect of such a reduction is precisely what is captured by a welfare economic evaluation when it accounts for victims' risk aversion. See

ferred under a correct welfare economic evaluation is distributively inferior, the meaning is that, under the chosen method of social welfare assessment—which entails value judgments about the relative importance of distribution—the distributive cost of the legal rule is not as important as the benefit of the rule in lowering total costs. (We also observe that some notions of fairness might be viewed as providing proxy tools for identifying opportunities to improve the distribution of wealth, rather than as independent evaluative principles potentially opposed to it. For example, a principle requiring that victims be compensated might have this feature if victims are typically poorer than injurers. Nevertheless, it is apparent that such a notion of fairness would at best be a weak proxy indicator, even for this aspect of social welfare.[93])

Thus, just as in the reciprocal case, promoting notions of fairness rather than relying entirely upon welfare economics necessarily entails an avoidable loss in individuals' well-being (here, taken to include both the average level of well-being and its distribution among individuals). The only difference between the reciprocal case, in which giving weight to a notion of fairness makes everyone worse off, and the nonreciprocal case is that the latter raises an additional question concerning the appropriate degree of equality in the distribution of income or well-being. It remains true that a notion of fairness, because it gives weight to factors unrelated to individuals' well-being, necessarily favors policies that reduce individuals' well-

---

section D. When harm is certain, as in the present case, the victim class that in the absence of harm might have the same wealth as the injurer class will have less wealth after harm occurs (assuming no compensation). This resulting wealth difference, to the extent that it means that social welfare would be enhanced by transferring dollars from injurers to victims, will already be taken into account in a complete welfare economic assessment. As we describe in subsections II.A.2 and II.A.3, the welfare economic notion of social welfare will register the social valuation attributable to different levels of individuals' wealth.

93. First, depending upon the kind of injury, either victims or injurers might be wealthier, so favoring victims may not further equalizing redistribution. (For example, ten-year-old automobiles, typically owned by lower-income drivers, may cause more accidents, in which case victims of harm caused by automobiles will tend to be wealthier than injurers.) Second, there will often be substantial heterogeneity within each group. (Those who are usually pedestrians rather than drivers might include those too poor to own cars and those who live in affluent downtown areas and thus do not use cars.) Third, imposing liability on injurers that are firms will actually affect some combination of dispersed shareholders, workers, and customers, a diverse group who are not nearly as rich, on average, as a large corporation with many assets might seem. (And if the firm makes products disproportionately consumed by lower-income individuals, the incidence of liability would not result in equalizing redistribution.)

being as a whole.[94] Again, the reader should ask: what is the point of this sacrifice?

Fairness advocates sometimes do address the possibility that there is a conflict between notions of fairness and social welfare. Proponents typically assert that their notions of fairness are more important; sometimes, a notion of fairness is even said to trump considerations of welfare.[95] This position, however, is a conclusion, not an argument. Because welfare economics takes into account the level of individuals' well-being and also the distribution of income, a conflicting notion of fairness cannot be sustained unless there is a good reason either for making individuals worse off (as in the reciprocal case) or for making the distribution of income less favorable (keeping in mind that, under welfare economics, the analyst must already make whatever judgment about the matter is thought to be appropriate), or for doing both. As in the reciprocal case, the reason for making such sacrifices is not apparent, either in the literature or from inspection of the context under consideration.[96]

D. Welfare Economics versus Fairness in Paradigmatic Accident Situations: The Case in Which Harm Is Uncertain

We now consider the case in which harm is caused only with a probability, so that individuals' risk aversion and the availability of insurance become important. We deferred consideration of this more realistic case because

---

94. Although our argument was particularly clear in the reciprocal case because giving weight to notions of fairness literally made everyone worse off, the logic in the nonreciprocal case is much the same. Although not all individuals are made worse off, thereby introducing a distributive effect, the welfare economic framework takes this fully into account, so the original argument in essence remains valid. One way to illustrate this point is to show that our argument in the text concerning the nonreciprocal case, wherein the welfare economic assessment incorporates a distributive judgment, can be translated into a simpler setting— one in which a direct comparison is made between regimes in which everyone is better off in the one chosen under welfare economics than in the one chosen when weight is given to a notion of fairness (whenever the two lead to a different choice of legal rules). We sketch such a construction in note 75 in chapter II.

95. See note 11.

96. Some may believe that the intrinsic difference between injurers and victims, including the fact that injurers make voluntary choices, provides some basis for giving weight to notions of fairness in the nonreciprocal context. As we discuss at some length in subsection E.3, however, the apparent pull of these concepts can be explained by understanding the relationship between notions of fairness and social norms and, accordingly, does not warrant treating notions of fairness as independent evaluative principles.

introducing these added considerations complicates the analysis, but as we shall see, our central arguments are largely unaffected. It remains true that (1) giving weight to any notion of fairness in the reciprocal case will make everyone worse off whenever one is led to choose a legal rule that differs from the rule preferred under welfare economics, (2) pursuing notions of fairness in the nonreciprocal case will reduce individuals' well-being, and (3) there appears to be no sound justification for such results.

1. Reciprocal Accidents

(a) Description. We reconsider the situation of reciprocal harm (from subsection C.1), assuming now that harm is uncertain. For concreteness, we will assume that there is a 10 percent risk of harm, which, when it occurs, is $1,000—so that the expected harm, namely, 10% × $1,000, is still $100. We will continue to assume that harm can be prevented at a cost of either $25 or $150. Individuals are risk averse, which means that they prefer suffering a certain harm of $100 to suffering a harm of $1,000 with a 10 percent probability.[97]

Finally, we assume that individuals may—and, because they are risk averse, will—purchase insurance on actuarially fair terms against any risk they bear.[98] Thus, a person who faces the risk of being an accident victim and expects not to be compensated will purchase insurance at a premium cost of 10% × $1,000 = $100. Similarly, a person who faces the risk of being held liable will purchase liability insurance at a premium cost of $100. The case in which insurance is purchased is relevant because of the widespread availability and ownership of insurance. However, at the end of our discussion of this case, in subsection (f), we will examine in some detail the situation in which individuals do not purchase insurance.

(b) Effects of the Legal Rules. Our analysis of this case can be brief because essentially everything that was true in the case with certain harm remains true here. First, it is clear that, because any uncertain cost is converted into a certain

97. See note 9 in chapter II.

98. Moral hazard (the possibility that individuals will engage in riskier behavior when insured) is ignored for present purposes. Moral hazard turns out to be unproblematic in our particular example: victims are assumed to be unable to influence the occurrence of harm, and injurers would purchase insurance only when they are subject to strict liability and do not intend to take precautions in any event. More broadly, moral hazard will not raise any difficulty when insurers are able to observe behavior and condition coverage accordingly. When insurers cannot combat moral hazard because they cannot observe the relevant behavior of insured individuals, individuals may choose to purchase only partial coverage, to preserve some incentive for proper behavior, or no coverage at all.

insurance premium, individuals will behave just as we described above. For example, suppose that liability is strict and the cost of the precaution is $25. If injurers do not take care, they will bear the risk of liability and pay $100 in insurance premiums, so they will prefer to spend $25 to avoid having to pay the $100 premium; thus, the outcome is the same as before (when they instead have to pay $100 in damages for certain if they do not take care). If the cost of the precaution is $150, injurers subject to strict liability will prefer not to take care; because they are risk averse, they will purchase insurance at a premium of $100, which is precisely the amount they pay in damages (for certain) in the prior case. Similar analysis applies to the negligence rule and a rule of no liability. Finally, the reasoning about injurers' purchasing insurance is equally applicable to victims in cases in which they would be exposed to the uncompensated risk of harm.[99] And the insurance premium they pay in such cases, $100, equals the amount of damages they suffer for certain in the prior case.

(c) *Choice of Legal Rules Using Welfare Economics.* Because individuals' behavior and the costs they bear in every instance are the same as in the previous (reciprocal) case in which harm is certain, the welfare economic evaluation of the legal rules is also the same. Individuals will all be equally affected by any legal rule—each will bear costs equal to per capita social costs—and thus they will all be best off under the rule that minimizes these costs. Moreover, because the purchase of insurance converts any risky situation into a certain situation for each individual, and one identical to that which we described above, there is no need to take into account risk-bearing costs. For instance, when a rule of no liability is best because the precaution costs $150 and both the negligence rule and strict liability entail legal costs, here as before all individuals will bear lower, certain total costs under a rule of no liability than under the negligence rule or strict liability.

(d) *Choice of Legal Rules Using Notions of Fairness.* With regard to notions of fairness, the evaluation of legal rules is the same as we described above because the conceptions of fairness that we discuss do not make any reference to risk per se. The notion that an injurer should pay for the harm he causes, for instance, does not involve risk. If strict liability was thus favored in the previous case on fairness grounds, it should be here as well.[100]

---

99. Under a negligence rule, when the precaution costs $150, victims will bear the loss and purchase insurance. Likewise, with no liability, victims bear any harm that occurs and thus purchase insurance.

100. If the presence of risk was relevant under a notion of fairness, which rule was fairer might differ. This possibility does not affect our critique, which applies to any method of choosing legal rules that differs from welfare economics.

*(e) Why the Choice of Legal Rules Should Be Based Only on Individuals'
Well-Being.* Because the effects of the legal rules and application of the welfare
economics and fairness-based analyses are the same as in the case in which harm
is certain, our criticisms are the same: whenever notions of fairness conflict with
welfare economics, all individuals are made worse off without accomplishing
anything in the process, and any underlying motivations for notions of fairness
appear to be irrelevant. (Note that, once again, our argument does not depend
on the particular notions of fairness that are involved, or on whether an analyst
employs a pure notion of fairness or a mixed one under which weight also is
given to the effects of legal rules on individuals' well-being.)

We pause to note that our point about notions of fairness seeming to be
moot[101] is even more striking in the present context. As before, all individuals
are unaffected at the end of the day by the relative treatment of injurers and
victims, because each is equally often an injurer and a victim. Here, however,
there is no effect even if one focuses narrowly upon a single case, as many
corrective justice theorists would seem to require. Insurance renders fairness
concerns essentially pointless in each particular accident. Even at the moment
the injurer is punished, he suffers not at all, for in such instances the injurer
is insured, so it is the insurance company that makes the payment. Nor are
victims compensated in any sense by a rule of strict liability, for without such
a rule they would have been compensated anyway, by their insurer. To be
sure, individuals must pay premiums for insurance. But in all cases in which
accidents may happen, everyone will be fully insured, everyone will purchase
exactly one insurance policy under each of the three legal rules, and the premium will be $100. The *only* effect of different legal rules (aside from inducing
individuals to take precautions and imposing administrative costs, both concerns of welfare economics) is to determine whether each individual's insurance policy *bears the label* "liability insurance" or "insurance against injuries
caused by others." Thus, when the precaution is expensive and therefore not
undertaken under any legal rule, either every individual will pay $100 for a
liability insurance policy under strict liability, or every individual will pay $100
for a first-party insurance policy under the negligence rule or a regime of no
liability. It goes without saying that the literature does not offer any reasons
why we should reduce everyone's well-being in the name of fairness when
this is the only identifiable effect of adopting the rule deemed to be more fair.

*(f) The Foregoing Reconsidered When Insurance Is Not Purchased. (i) Vic-
tims Uninsured.* We assume in the foregoing that parties can purchase insurance on actuarially fair terms, but this, of course, may not be the case. We now

101. See subsection C.1(f).

suppose instead that there is a loading (administrative) charge that raises the insurance premium from $100 to $110.[102] (To simplify the exposition, we continue to assume that injurers are able to purchase insurance for $100; the possibility of uninsured injurers is considered below, in subsection (ii).) Note that victims might still buy insurance in this case; if they are sufficiently risk averse—say, they would prefer to pay $120 for sure rather than face a 10 percent risk of losing $1,000—they will purchase insurance priced at $110. Thus, when they choose not to purchase insurance, as we now suppose, it follows that the reduction in their expected well-being from exposure to the risk is less than the price of insurance ($110). For concreteness, assume that this valuation is $105.[103]

The analysis of the effects of the legal rules and the welfare economic evaluation of them will be largely the same as before. The only difference is that uncompensated harm—which would occur under a rule of no liability or under the negligence rule when the precaution cost is $150—will be valued in the economic calculus at $105 rather than $100, because the victim is uninsured and his risk-adjusted valuation ($105) exceeds the expected value of harm ($100), as just explained.[104] Thus, strict liability may become more attractive: social welfare is at the same level as before under strict liability but social welfare is lower by $5 under the negligence rule, when the precaution cost is $150, and under a rule of no liability.

Strict liability might also become more attractive under some conceptions of fairness. In particular, a notion of fairness reflecting concern about compensation of victims would now be meaningful because some individuals actually suffer uncompensated harm. This outcome suggests that such a

---

102. There may be other reasons that individuals would find insurance too expensive, notably due to problems of moral hazard and adverse selection. In these cases, the economic analysis would be modified somewhat but the central point would still be true: welfare economics, through its attention to individuals' well-being, fully captures individuals' aversion to risk, and, therefore, making a notion of fairness decisive can only make everyone worse off.

103. The figure $105 is referred to as the individual's certainty equivalent of being exposed to the risk. If the individual were risk neutral, this certainty equivalent would be the expected value of the loss, $100. The more risk averse the individual, the greater the certainty equivalent—that is, the more he would be willing to pay for insurance to avoid the risk. The argument to follow does not depend upon the magnitude of the certainty equivalent, although we do assume that it is lower than the insurance premium, to present the case in which individuals are uninsured. For further discussion of risk aversion, insurance, and expected utility, see note 9 in chapter II.

104. Observe that, if individuals were sufficiently risk averse to have a valuation (certainty equivalent) of, say, $175, then a precaution that cost $150 would be efficient, unlike in the previous cases (although if insurance were available at a cost of $110, it would be more efficient for individuals to purchase insurance and forgo the precaution).

fairness concept may serve as a proxy indicator of the welfare economic objective of reducing risk-bearing costs. We now demonstrate, however, that the connection is imperfect, which implies once again that pursuing notions of fairness may make everyone worse off.

Suppose, for example, that the precaution cost is $150, so that it is less costly to allow accidents to occur, and that strict liability involves legal costs of $20 (whereas, for simplicity, there are no legal costs under the negligence rule or under a rule of no liability).[105] The notions of fairness under which victims should be compensated favor strict liability, which results in a total social cost, borne by each individual, of $120: $20 in legal costs plus $100 of actual harm (which is valued at $100 rather than $105 because it is paid for by injurers, who we are assuming are insured and incur no loading charge). But all individuals would be better off under either of the other rules, for then the total cost borne by each individual is only $105, the cost individuals associate with being subject to the probabilistic harm when they have no insurance.[106]

Consider, moreover, how counterproductive the fairness-based preference for strict liability is in the present context. Individuals all prefer suffering the probabilistic harm to purchasing insurance, because the cost of insurance, $110, exceeds the risk-adjusted cost of being exposed to the harm, $105. Adopting strict liability in this context essentially amounts to providing these uninsured individuals with insurance that costs $120. (The cost is paid by injurers, but in the reciprocal case they are all the same people.) Therefore, for society to adopt strict liability on fairness grounds is to force each individual to purchase insurance that costs $120 when insurance is already available at a cost of $110 and, even at that bargain price, is a bad deal for everyone.

We further note that the only circumstance in which strict liability would leave individuals better off rather than worse off in the present setting is if the administrative cost disadvantage of strict liability were less than $5, in which case the total cost under strict liability would be less than $105—that

105. We note that the assumption that compensation through the legal system is more expensive than first-party insurance is plausible and borne out by the evidence; indeed, compensation through the tort system may cost on the order of one dollar for every dollar received by victims, whereas the cost per dollar of compensation from insurance companies is far less, often in the range of ten to twenty cents. See section F.

106. We continue to speak of all individuals being worse off because this is true according to an ex ante evaluation. When harm is probabilistic and individuals are uninsured, there will be ex post differences and, on account of luck, some may be better off. But such individuals, given the chance to choose one regime or the other ex ante, would have preferred the regime that maximizes their expected level of well-being (their expected utility). See also subsection VIII.C.1, discussing in general why the ex ante perspective is appropriate.

is, less than the cost when individuals are exposed to the probabilistic harm. But in precisely this case the welfare economic evaluation would favor strict liability, and for this very reason. Thus, we have demonstrated once again that whenever a notion of fairness is decisive—when it leads to choosing a legal rule different from the one chosen under welfare economics—pursuing it necessarily makes everyone worse off.[107]

Observe that, on reflection, the preceding criticism is to have been expected. In the perfectly reciprocal case—with or without risk, or any other complications that one might imagine—the situation of each individual is identical at the outset; hence, individuals' rankings of rules in terms of how the rules affect their well-being will be the same. Moreover, these unanimous rankings will by definition replicate the welfare economic ranking. Therefore, if fairness-based analysis is to differ from that under welfare economics, it must favor rules that are to the detriment of everyone.

(ii) Injurers Uninsured. We now briefly consider the case in which injurers rather than victims are uninsured because loading charges on liability insurance policies exceed the value to injurers of avoiding exposure to the risk.[108] The analysis of this case is largely symmetric with that of the case in which victims are uninsured,[109] and thus the preceding arguments are fully applicable. We note that here the concern for risk tends to oppose strict liability (rather than favor it, as in subsection (i)), for this rule exposes risk-averse injurers to risk. A notion of fairness demanding that there be "no liability without fault" would be consistent with a concern for injurers' risk-bearing costs, although,

---

107. We emphasize that this problem may be important in practice. Many commentators favor tort liability in order to compensate victims, yet the tort system is a far more expensive means of providing compensation than is insurance. See section F. This point is particularly apropos of products liability in settings in which victims are customers, because the customers pay the implicit insurance premium through higher product prices. Of course, arguments for (or against) products liability on account of incentives stand on a different footing.

108. We could also consider the case in which both injurers and victims are uninsured, but this would add little further illumination.

109. The primary difference is that, in the present case, injurers bear risk when they do not undertake precautions and are subject to liability, so they will find precautions more attractive (and, for the same reason, precautions will be more efficient). For example, if the value that injurers place on avoiding exposure to the risk is $175, they would be willing to spend $150 to avoid the chance of causing the harm. (This assumes, of course, that insurance costs more than $150, for otherwise they would rather purchase the insurance.) Using analysis similar to that in the text, it is straightforward to show that in this case it remains true that the ranking of the rules based on total risk-adjusted costs precisely matches individuals' unanimous preferences.

as in the prior case, everyone will be made worse off whenever the notion determines the choice of the legal rule.[110] Observe, however, that this notion of fairness does not address risks borne by uninsured victims; likewise, the principle of compensating victims, which serves as a proxy principle for reducing risk-bearing costs when victims are the ones who are uninsured, does not address risks borne by uninsured injurers, as in the present context. Thus, when one considers a range of cases, each of these two notions of fairness turns out to be an imperfect means of taking into account concerns about risk-bearing.

Finally, we point out that the notion that injurers should be punished is not moot in the present setting because injurers are assumed not to be insured, and unlike in the case of certain harm, it is not the case that every injurer who is punished will be compensated when in the role of victim. Rather than being moot, the demand for punishment has a somewhat perverse quality. Injurers who cause harm are, except for bad luck, identical to members of the larger group of potential injurers who do not cause harm and thus would not be punished, and both groups of injurers are the same people as the class of prospective victims. Thus, the "punishment" is applied neither to particular types of individuals nor to individuals who choose to act differently. It is purely a random penalty, suffered by 10 percent of the population.[111] (And, as we explain above, whenever the pursuit of a notion

110. Because the analysis is almost identical, we do not repeat the argument or offer another numerical example.

111. Some philosophers, notably Nagel and Williams, raise the possibility that there may be some virtue in this apparent vice. See Nagel (1979) and Williams (1981). Essentially, they posit that such luck could in a sense be "moral luck," and this designation (somehow) might be interpreted as making it desirable (rather than pernicious) that serious legal consequences follow from fortuitous events beyond individuals' control. Such a conclusion has been strongly criticized within the domain of arguments about fairness. See, for example, L. Alexander (1987a) and Schroeder (1995). See also Calabresi (1970, 301–04), advancing similar criticisms a decade before Nagel's and Williams's writing; McCarthy (1996), arguing that individuals should be accountable for the extent to which they impose risk on others, independently of whether harm is caused; and Schroeder (1990) (same). Some commentators have also questioned whether such a moral claim implies a duty of compensation:

> For all we can tell, there is nothing to be found in the claim that such a sense of responsibility exists that cannot be fully met internally by feelings of deep regret and externally by apologies or efforts to make amends that still fall dramatically short of full repair. . . . The precise nature of the appropriate response to such reactive attitudes seems more heavily influenced by social custom and convention than by moral imperative. (Schroeder 1995, 357–58)

We believe that the appeal of the moral luck position can readily be understood by reference to the distinction, described in section II.D and elaborated in the tort context in

of fairness leads, contrary to the prescription of welfare economics, to choosing a regime that imposes this punishment, all individuals, including noninjurers and victims, are prospectively made worse off.)

---

section III.E, between social norms designed to guide everyday life and evaluative principles that properly should guide legal policy. Those who attempt to justify the seemingly arbitrary punishment of individuals whose bad luck results in harm often appeal to our feelings of remorse when we cause harm, even when we were not at all at fault, as in an example offered in Williams (1981, 28). Similarly, Nagel refers explicitly to guilt, indignation, pride, and other aspects of the mechanism of social norms. See Nagel (1979, 37). See also ibid. (33), referring to the way that common moral attitudes "reappear involuntarily." Such feelings, of course, are to be expected from individuals who are well socialized to avoid improper behavior that risks harm to others. In addition, we may feel outrage at those who cause great harm, even when their behavior may have been only slightly negligent. All such feelings may well reflect the development of social norms designed to impose social sanctions on those who behave improperly. In this regard, one should bear in mind that it may often be difficult for onlookers to know how bad an injurer's behavior that caused significant harm actually was; furthermore, bad behavior that, fortuitously, causes little or no harm will often go unnoticed. We also suspect that most individuals may overlook the fact that the injurer's behavior was only slightly negligent, and, if they were to focus on this, their sense that severe punishment is necessary would weaken. Relatedly, our intuitions and instincts about wrongdoing and redress originally emerged during periods of history in which intentional harmful acts were relatively more common than accidents. Nagel and Williams do not address such straightforward explanations for the common instincts and intuitions upon which they rest their argument, though these explanations have a prominent lineage. See Smith ([1790] 1976, 92–108). Perhaps in commenting on the existence of moral luck, they only mean to suggest that such feelings are typical in ordinary citizens. Such an observation would not carry the implication that proper normative principles—whether used to assess policy or to examine common morality critically—would give independent weight to moral luck. See also subsection II.B.2(c), suggesting that the ex post perspective of many notions of fairness is incomplete and potentially misleading, and that it may reflect cognitive biases involving the tendency to focus excessively on outcomes and to make improper use of hindsight, and subsection E.3, explaining the pull exerted by the concepts of injurer and victim, as well as whether one is seen as choosing to cause harm, in terms of social norms about wrongful behavior that harms others.

We note that adoption of the moral luck view in the tort context would have a number of stark implications. Liability insurance, even in cases of slight negligence, would be considered an immoral institution because it erases the distinction in treatment of the lucky and the unlucky. Furthermore, once one accepts acts entirely beyond one's control as a basis for bearing significant losses, it would seem that negligence should not be a prerequisite for punishing injurers severely. (Nagel repeatedly suggests that negligence is a necessary condition; however, whether there is any blame depends on fortuitously causing harm and the extent of blame depends entirely on how much harm one fortuitously causes, so it is not clear why the existence "of even a minor degree of negligence" is important. See Nagel (1979, 28–29, 31).) Or, taking a different tack, one could argue that compensation to victims is never appropriate in accident cases because their suffering a loss is similarly due to moral luck arising from their own behavior that exposes themselves to risks.

2. Nonreciprocal Accidents

For completeness, let us review the nonreciprocal case in which harm is uncertain. We continue to assume that a harm of $1,000 will occur 10 percent of the time if the precaution is not taken but, unlike in the immediately preceding case, let us assume that injurers and victims are distinct groups. We can be brief in our discussion of this case because it is simply a combination of the preceding two cases, one involving certain harm in the nonreciprocal case (subsection C.2) and the other involving uncertain harm in the reciprocal case (subsection D.1).

Suppose first that insurance is sold on actuarially fair terms, so that injurers purchase full coverage against any liability they might bear, and victims purchase full coverage against any losses they might suffer. Under these conditions, the behavior of the parties and the welfare economic evaluation of the legal rules are identical to those in the nonreciprocal case with certain harm because the risk of losing $1,000 will be transformed into a certain loss of $100 (through payment of an insurance premium) either for the injurer, if liable, or the victim, as the case may be. Likewise, the evaluation of the rules on fairness grounds will be essentially the same as in the nonreciprocal case in which risk is absent.[112] Therefore, our criticisms of notions of fairness in that case will remain applicable.

If insurance is not sold at an actuarially fair price, then parties will not in general be fully insured. The welfare economic evaluation of the legal rules will now incorporate both the risk that is borne by parties if precautions are not taken and the income distributional consequences of the rules. For example, suppose that victims are poorer than injurers and are very risk

---

112. Arguably, the existence of insurance attenuates the relevance of notions of fairness because injurers do not pay (their liability insurers do) and victims do not bear their losses (their first-party insurers do). Nevertheless, the choice of legal rules will affect the insurance premiums that each group pays: victims pay $100 in insurance premiums under the negligence rule, when the precaution costs $150, and under a regime of no liability; injurers pay $100 in insurance premiums under strict liability, when the precaution costs $150. In the reciprocal case, this effect of the choice of legal rules seemed immaterial because injurers and victims were the same people; here, they are not. Thus, if a notion of fairness treated the payment of $100 in the event of certain harm as equivalent to the payment of $100 in liability insurance in anticipation of the possibility of causing harm, and similarly treated suffering a certain loss of $100 as equivalent to having to purchase insurance for $100 to cover probabilistic losses, the fairness analysis would be the same as in the case of certainty. For our purposes, it is immaterial whether notions of fairness favor the same legal rule in the case with certain harm as in the case with uncertain harm but full insurance, because the criticism we present in subsection C.2 applies to any notion of fairness, whenever it favors a legal rule different from that chosen under welfare economics.

averse. Then strict liability will produce benefits beyond inducing the precaution to be taken; it will also protect victims against risk and help to prevent the income distribution from undesirably favoring the wealthier injurers. The evaluation of legal rules on fairness grounds will not be altered in any clear way in this case.[113] When the fairness-based analysis disagrees with the welfare economic evaluation, the foundation is no clearer than before. The welfare economic analysis already takes into account all that would seem to be socially relevant—including here both risk-bearing costs and effects on the distribution of income, in addition to incentive effects and administrative costs. Accordingly, pursuing notions of fairness once again entails a needless sacrifice of individuals' well-being.[114]

113. Compare note 112, discussing the case in which insurance is purchased.

114. Furthermore, we observe that, when individuals are not insured, notions of fairness such as those concerned with the punishment of injurers or the compensation of victims may favor legal rules that make everyone worse off, in a manner analogous to that explored in the reciprocal case. (For additional reasons that fair rules may make everyone worse off even in the nonreciprocal case, see note 89.) Suppose that injurers (say, polluters or blasters) and victims are risk neutral and thus do not purchase insurance. (If individuals were risk averse, the argument would still hold; certainty equivalents would be substituted for expected values, as we explain in subsection 1(f)(i). We assume risk neutrality here only for convenience.) Assume, moreover, that a notion of fairness requires adopting a rule of strict liability but that this rule is more expensive than the negligence rule because of legal costs: under strict liability, injurers' *expected* payments are $110 ($100 of expected harm and $10 of expected legal costs); under the negligence rule, injurers bear legal costs of only $5, and victims bear an expected harm of $100. (Implicit in the foregoing is that the precaution cost is high, so harm occurs. Otherwise, harm would never occur, and it may then be moot which of the two rules is chosen. Note that if victims bore some of the legal costs, one could simply reduce the amount of the fee described below by that amount, and the remainder of the argument would be unaffected.)

Now, compare strict liability to a negligence regime supplemented by a $103 fee on potential injurers (say, a fee for a permit to conduct operations), the proceeds of which are used to lower each resident's (each potential victim's) taxes by a uniform amount. In this case, individuals would all be better off under the negligence rule: injurers' expected payments are $108 ($103 as a fee and expected legal costs of $5) rather than $110, and victims receive $103 rather than an expected amount of $100. (And, recall, everyone is assumed to be risk neutral, so expected values are sufficient to evaluate each rule.) This regime—the less expensive negligence rule combined with the fee—makes everyone better off. This regime, however, violates any notion of fairness that requires punishment of injurers or compensation of victims in the event of an actual injury, because actual injuries involve harm of $1,000, whereas the fees and tax rebates of the injurers and victims are only slightly more than $100.

We could have made this argument in subsection C.2(e), involving the nonreciprocal case but perfect certainty. In that instance, however, the ex ante fee and tax rebate would equal the subsequent harm (which is certain to occur). Thus, one who believes in a notion of fairness that appears to favor strict liability may take the view that the negligence rule

E. The Appeal of Notions of Fairness and Its Implications

Our analysis in sections C and D suggests that notions of fairness should not be given any weight as independent evaluative principles to be used in assessing tort policy. Nevertheless, notions of fairness undoubtedly have appeal to legal analysts and philosophers, as well as to society more generally. Why does it feel right to us that injurers be punished, at least when they are at fault, and that victims be compensated? In terms of corrective justice, why is it that we feel that those who act wrongfully have a duty to rectify the situation by paying victims for their losses? In this section, we attempt to reconcile our thesis with the widespread attraction of notions of fairness by examining the relationship between these notions and internalized social norms that guide individuals in their everyday lives. In subsection 1, we examine the correspondence between notions of fairness in the tort context and particular social norms along with the functions served by those social norms. In subsection 2, we discuss the implications of this analysis for how legal rules should be assessed. Then, in subsections 3 and 4, we comment on further aspects of notions of fairness in the tort context that we believe help to explain why the notions seem appealing even though they should not serve as independent evaluative principles.

1. Social Norms and Notions of Fairness

As we discuss in subsection II.D.1, social norms are principles that individuals draw upon to guide their behavior in a range of situations in everyday life. Such norms simplify decisionmaking and, importantly, tend to curb opportunistic behavior toward others. Individuals are induced to follow social norms not only because the norms make life easier but also because individuals feel guilty and are subject to disapprobation when they violate social norms, whereas they feel virtuous and receive positive reinforcement when they behave in accordance with the norms. We now consider those social norms that seem most pertinent to settings involving injurers and

---

supplemented by the fee is a fair substitute because the prior financial transfers are equal in amount to the transfers that otherwise would be required on account of an actual injury. With regard to the present case involving risk and no insurance, one also could accept the more efficient rule combined with the fee as fair on the grounds that ex ante well-being, and not the actual punishment of injurers or compensation of victims, is the true focus of the proper notion of fairness. We do not, however, understand most fairness advocates to hold such a view—one that is so similar to the welfare economic approach that we describe and defend here.

their victims and how such norms relate to the notions of fairness that we have analyzed throughout this chapter.[115] Here, we focus on informal interactions that occur largely outside the legal system (sometimes because the stakes are too small, sometimes because the legal system has little effect), or those that took place in human prehistory.

When one individual harms another, there does seem to be a social norm calling for rectification, an apology when the injury is slight or intangible (say, a bump or an insult) and compensation (or various substitutes such as repair) when the injury is more significant or tangible.[116] Thus, if a person playing ball ends up breaking a neighbor's window, he is expected to pay for the damage.[117]

Such social norms obviously serve useful functions. A norm that one must in some manner rectify injuries caused to others will tend to deter harmful acts. Negative attitudes toward injurers who do not compensate their victims serve to punish those who do not comply and to reinforce feelings of guilt that further help to deter wrongful conduct in the first place.[118] Another important benefit of social norms requiring that injurers compensate victims is that, when compensation occurs, victims will be less inclined to seek vengeance, which itself is socially costly and may escalate.[119]

---

115. Also relevant is our discussion in section VI.D of social norms concerning retribution and corresponding notions of fairness in the context of criminal punishment.

116. As Smith observes:

> The person himself, who by an accident . . . has involuntarily hurt another, seems to have some sense of his own ill desert, with regard to him. He naturally runs up to the sufferer to express his concern for what has happened, and to make every acknowledgment in his power. If he has any sensibility, he necessarily desires to compensate the damage, and to do every thing he can to appease that animal resentment, which he is sensible will be apt to arise in the breast of the sufferer. To make no apology, to offer no atonement, is regarded as the highest brutality. (Smith [1790] 1976, 104)

See, for example, Baron and Ritov (1993, 17): "When one person (or group) harms another, people often think that the injurer should compensate the victim."

117. Our argument here is that such a social norm exists, and, as discussed in the text to follow, serves valuable functions. We do not suggest that this norm is always followed in practice.

118. Relatedly, social norms requiring redress for injury reinforce more general norms about concern for others, which themselves tend to produce better patterns of behavior. See, for example, Smith ([1790] 1976, 106–07).

119. See, for example, Baron and Ritov (1993, 18), attributing the view that injurers should compensate their victims to an intuitive desire for retribution against injurers and a sense that compensation is required when injuries are caused by human acts. Richard Posner

In addition to being part of a system that deters wrongful acts and discourages physical retaliation, a requirement of compensation may be valuable because it may encourage victims to seek redress. Victims might otherwise find direct retaliation too costly in some instances, such as when they are weaker than their injurers. A norm that encourages victims to seek redress is valuable in a case like this because deterrence is undermined when victims fail to respond. We further note that victims are often in the best position to know when and how much they have been injured as well as the identity of injurers. Finally, if injurers refuse to provide compensation, victims will be inclined to publicize this refusal,[120] and the prospect of such publicity will induce injurers to pay.

It is also true that, especially before the relatively modern development and widespread availability of private and public insurance, informal systems for compensation of losses were socially valuable. For example, members of a community may have helped an individual rebuild a home lost in a fire. The existence of some altruism toward others probably suggests that there would be sympathy toward the victim of an injury caused by another.[121] In the present setting, however, for the sorts of reasons already mentioned, one might expect the source of compensation to be the injurer rather than the community at large.

Social norms concerning the appropriate behavior of injurers toward victims not only are reinforced through a range of social institutions and interactions involving adults but also are inculcated in children by their parents, teachers, and other authority figures. The motivation for this practice probably involves both a desire to maintain order in the present—in the home, at school—and an attempt to prepare children for their future.[122] Of

---

describes how, in primitive societies, remedies for wrongs tended to change from retaliation to compensation when wealth became sufficient for adequate compensation to be feasible. See R. Posner (1980c, 43). A broader discussion of the relationship between retribution and compensation appears in the synthesis of anthropological and other work in Daly and Wilson (1988, chapter 10). See also Parisi (2001, 107–20).

Trivers indicates a possible evolutionary basis for feelings of guilt and what he terms "reparative altruism," the idea that those who do act wrongfully will be motivated to compensate for their misdeeds and behave better in the future so as not to upset valuable reciprocal relationships. See Trivers (1971, 50).

120. Victims will have this incentive both because, when there is a social norm of compensation, they will feel wronged if they are not compensated, and because publicity may induce injurers to make payments in order to limit the damage to their reputations.

121. Or, even in the absence of altruism, norms of reciprocity may emerge within smaller groups whose members interact repeatedly.

122. See, for example, Baron (1994a, 7).

course children, especially young children, are not usually expected to pay monetary compensation; instead, they are told to apologize, participate in repair, or make partial payment (such as by losing an allowance or forgoing a future opportunity their parents would have paid for), or they may simply be punished. The idea that potential injurers have a duty to avoid harm and to take responsibility when they nevertheless cause damage, and the related idea that victims should be objects of concern, are clearly among the important lessons instilled in children. Moreover, when instruction is successful, these social norms become deeply ingrained; they cannot completely perform their role if they will be cast aside for momentary gain or abandoned in situations where social sanctions will not be severe.

Finally, we observe that social norms about injurers' responsibilities to their victims often involve a fault principle.[123] Of course, deterrence can only occur when injurers have some control over the behavior that causes harm; moreover, society does not wish to deter behavior that is desirable overall.[124] When one considers the process by which parents (and others) inculcate social norms in their children, the attraction of the fault principle becomes even more clear. Because the sanctions for misbehavior often are costly to impose (such as when a child must be punished on account of the harm caused being too great for an apology to suffice), and because those imposing the punishment care about the well-being of the child, parents and others will wish to limit sanctions to cases in which they are truly necessary. In addition, the tutelary function of sanctions is enhanced when there is a clear contrast between the treatment of acceptable and unacceptable behavior.[125]

---

123. See note 135 in chapter VI. One might imagine that, earlier in human history, most serious injuries caused by other individuals were intentional, in which case fault would have been automatic. With increasing population density and the advance of technology, accidents have become relatively more important in modern times, making the fault distinction more significant.

124. With regard to the latter, it is familiar that a rule of strict liability with damages equal to harm will not deter behavior that produces a benefit to the actor that exceeds the harm caused by the act. But with social norms, there is no guarantee that sanctions (guilt, social disapproval, and resulting loss of reputation) will be limited to the magnitude of the harm. Moreover, sanctions for violations of social norms are socially costly (they tend to reduce the well-being of the injurer directly, without a corresponding benefit to the victim, in contrast to when monetary compensation is paid); hence, economizing on the use of sanctions is valuable (compare our discussion regarding punishment of children in the text to follow).

125. One could punish children using a rule of strict liability and leave it to them to figure out what constitutes appropriate behavior. This rationale makes sense in some tort settings in which courts have difficulty observing behavior and when injurers are in a better position to determine what is optimal. When disciplining young children, however, it seems

Nevertheless, it may not always make sense to insist upon fault, in part because fault sometimes cannot readily be determined (either by the parent or, among adults, by victims) and in part because conventional understandings of fault do not encompass the full range of ways that injurers may influence the extent to which they harm others.[126]

In summary, we are suggesting that social norms have developed to address interactions among individuals in which one person may injure another. These norms often require injurers to compensate their victims, and the existence of such social norms has beneficial effects on individuals' well-being. Moreover, and importantly, the social norms concerning the duties injurers owe to victims correspond reasonably well with the notions of fairness—calling for punishment of injurers, compensation of victims, or achievement of corrective justice—that are most influential in assessing legal rules in the tort context.

2. Implications for the Role of Notions of Fairness in Legal Policy Analysis

The preceding discussion suggests that, as socialized individuals in a world where powerful social norms govern the relationship between injurers and victims, we are inclined to have strong positive feelings about corresponding notions of fairness.[127] This tendency provides an explanation for the appeal

---

clear that parents will want to state explicitly what constitutes right and wrong behavior and to reinforce the distinction by punishing violations and excusing harm that results from good behavior, due to bad luck. See, for example, Baron (1993, 158).

126. Notably, injurers decide whether—and the extent to which—they will engage in activities in the first place, and many activities may cause harm even when conducted properly. See Shavell (1980b).

127. Another possibility, different from that explored in subsection 1, is that the intuition behind notions of fairness really derives from feelings about the general distribution of income (an aspect of the welfare economic conception of social welfare, see subsection II.A.3), rather than the particular situation of injurers and victims. Indeed, even corrective justice theorists who have labored at length to distinguish their notions from concerns for distributive justice are often accused (by each other) of slipping into distributive appeals. See, for example, Fletcher (1993, 1668), referring, in a review of Coleman (1992b), to the central problem of modern tort law as "one of distributive rather than corrective justice," and Perry (1992a), criticizing Coleman's earlier corrective justice theory as actually involving distributive justice. See also R. Posner (1981a, 196), describing Epstein's theory as one of distributive, not corrective, justice. (Rakowski's theory of corrective justice differs from others' constructs in that his theory is explicitly parasitic on his view of distributive justice. See Rakowski (1991, chapter 10).) We do not focus on this interpretation because most notions of fairness in the tort context as well as the tort law itself seem concerned with whether injurers should compensate their victims, independent of the relative wealth of the parties.

of the notions of fairness that we have been examining. When the legal context is naturally associated with the setting of our ordinary life, as it often will be, we can expect to have instincts and intuitions about what seems fair due to our internalized social norms. It is therefore not surprising that such principles have the prominence that they do in the minds of legal analysts when they come to examine tort law.[128]

Nevertheless, this source of attraction does not provide any basis for viewing these notions of fairness as independent evaluative principles to be used in assessing legal rules.[129] If, as we suggest, the underlying purpose of social norms in their setting involves the advancement of individuals' well-being (such as by deterring wrongful conduct and quelling the urge of victims to retaliate), it would be illogical and even ironic to give weight to such norms in the evaluation of legal policy when doing so can only come at the expense of individuals' well-being.[130]

To elaborate, it is useful to compare the context in which social norms have developed, informal interactions in everyday life, with the context in which legal rules are used, the formal legal system. On one hand, there surely is overlap in the problems addressed in the two contexts and in the methods of controlling behavior. In both contexts, for example, some sort of sanction is employed to deter harmful conduct.[131] Hence, as we have discussed previously, one would expect notions of fairness—which we now understand to be related to social norms—to serve as proxy principles for the identification of legal rules that promote individuals' well-being.[132] (We also note that this

---

128. To reinforce the idea that notions of fairness are related to familiar social norms, we note that proponents of notions of fairness sometimes explain such notions by reference to community norms and conventions. See, for example, Coleman (1992b, 355–60).

129. The reader should recall from our discussion in subsection B.2 that the literature on corrective justice is not necessarily inconsistent with this view: as we noted, much of the literature is merely taxonomic (in that it focuses on defining what constitutes corrective justice, as distinct from distributive justice or other notions), and many claims are positive rather than normative (in that corrective justice is said to provide a better account—that is, description—of existing doctrine or of judges' thought processes).

130. See Baron and Ritov (1993), suggesting that notions of fairness concerned with punishing injurers and compensating victims result from the overgeneralization of what might otherwise be reasonable heuristics.

131. We have focused throughout this chapter on injurers' behavior, but social norms also clearly reflect the possibility that victims bear responsibility. Correspondingly, fully developed notions of fairness tend to be consistent with some sort of defense in tort suits based on victims' contribution to causing harm.

132. That is, notions of fairness tend to have this characteristic because of their nature, regardless of whether these beneficial consequences for individuals' well-being are what motivates analysts to invoke these notions.

proxy characteristic of notions of fairness helps further explain their appeal.[133])

On the other hand, there are differences between the two contexts; hence, notions of fairness will tend to be only rough guides and thus inferior to a direct welfare economic inquiry into how legal rules affect individuals' well-being. The methods of collecting information are different (social norms often rely on individuals, notably victims, who already know what happened, or on informal means of dissemination, whereas the formal legal system must ultimately provide information to an independent factfinder), the costs of implementing decisions may be quite different, and so forth. Thus, rules that are appropriate in one context will sometimes lead us astray in another. For example, a social norm that works best in informal settings may be too costly to implement through the formal legal system. Or a system that is not employed in informal settings because it cannot be enforced through sufficiently strong sanctions may be feasible when backed by the power of the state. More generally, one presumes that the tort system's existence reflects a belief that social norms alone are inadequate in some instances, whereas the different character of the formal legal system means that it can provide a useful supplement to, or substitute for, regulation through social norms.

In addition, social norms tend to evolve slowly, and hence norms that once may have been optimal may no longer be so (say, after the development of formal insurance schemes as a means of compensation). We also note that social norms—because of the manner in which they are initially taught to children and subsequently enforced and reinforced through informal means—

133. Indeed, commentators who advance notions of fairness sometimes support their argument by making observations that suggest a deterrence rationale. See, for example, Fletcher (1972, 569), explaining, in the course of defending the fairness of strict liability in some contexts with an appeal to autonomy, that the tort system thereby taxes socially useful activities without prohibiting them; Owen (1985, 670), arguing that market-based deterrence is acceptable as a matter of justice because those who benefit from a good or a service should have to pay all of the costs—the call for internalization of costs being a standard economic prescription for dealing with behavior that has external effects; and Schwartz (1997, 1819–20), arguing that behavior that fails the Hand cost-benefit test involves the defendant ranking his own welfare as more important than that of others and thus is ethically improper—an argument that involves presenting one of the standard efficient deterrence arguments as a justice claim. Perry notes that some versions of fairness principles, such as that advanced by Baron Bramwell, can be interpreted as cost internalization, although achieving efficiency does not appear to be the concern. See Perry (1992b, 462). See also Calabresi (1970, 299), stating that "fairness has long been used to support approaches allocating accident costs to the activities that 'cause' them or profit from them" (citing Harper and James (1956)).

usually need to be simple and general, even when a more detailed norm would more closely comport with underlying objectives. In designing a formal legal system, by contrast, it may be possible to incorporate greater complexity (using, say, one scheme for medical malpractice and another for automobile accidents) in order to take into account variations across contexts (such as differences in the extent to which precautions are worth undertaking or in how difficult it is to acquire and process the information needed for adjudication).

Therefore, although there will be some tendency for social norms, and corresponding notions of fairness, to favor policies that promote individuals' well-being, one would expect there to be important divergences.[134] Furthermore, such divergences are an important reason that notions of fairness sometimes favor different policies from those chosen under welfare economics, as we explain in sections C and D (and elaborate, with regard to our actual legal system, in section F). Indeed, we saw in the reciprocal setting that giving weight to such notions will make everyone worse off when they favor policies that differ from those chosen under welfare economics, as they sometimes do. The foregoing discussion of the differences between the setting in which social norms are used and the setting of the formal legal system supports our previous argument that, when such conflicts arise, one should choose the policy favored by welfare economics. Analysts may find that notions of fairness suggest paths of inquiry, but a complete welfare economic examination is required to identify all factors that bear on individuals' well-being and to combine all relevant effects into an overall judgment.

Even though notions of fairness should not be viewed as independent evaluative principles, the existence of corresponding social norms of the sort we have described is relevant for the assessment of legal rules using the framework of welfare economics. One reason is that individuals have tastes concerning social norms that may translate into tastes for the legal system to treat injurers and victims in accord with social norms, and thus in a manner consistent with related notions of fairness.[135] That is, just as individu-

---

134. One could attempt to avoid such divergences by adjusting notions of fairness and permitting them to be traded off against other economic factors in an appropriate manner. This approach, however, will avert the fundamental problem that we have identified only to the extent that one's original fairness principles are abandoned and a concern for individuals' well-being is made the exclusive criterion for evaluating legal policy. For example, as we discuss in subsection C.1(e), involving the reciprocal case, as long as a notion of fairness is given any independent weight—that is, independent of the extent to which it advances individuals' well-being in a particular context—pursuing the notion will make everyone worse off any time that one is led to choose a legal rule different from that chosen under welfare economics.

135. This point is in addition to the fact that notions of fairness may serve as proxy principles, as we discuss above in the present subsection.

als will be upset, leading them to express disapproval, when an injurer does not compensate a victim in informal settings, they may be upset if the legal system does not require an injurer to compensate a victim when the injurer's wrong is within the domain of tort law. Moreover, individuals may have a taste for the institution of tort law itself, because it makes injurers pay compensation to victims.

If individuals do have such tastes, they will be relevant under welfare economics just like any other tastes, whether for material goods or aesthetic pleasures, because welfare economics takes into account all components of individuals' well-being.[136] To illustrate, suppose, as in one of our above examples involving the reciprocal case with no uncertainty,[137] that the negligence rule has an advantage over strict liability because legal costs are only $5 under the former but $10 under the latter. Suppose further that individuals feel that strict liability is more fair (perhaps because their notion that injurers should be punished applies whenever someone injures a stranger), and they each place a value of $7 on imposing the rule that they regard as fair.[138] Then strict liability will in fact be the rule that maximizes social welfare, properly measured. (Alternatively, if individuals place a value of only $2 on being governed by the fair rule, the negligence rule will continue to be superior; choosing the fair rule, in this instance, will make everyone worse off.) Whether, and the extent to which, individuals actually do possess such fairness-related tastes for one or another legal rule is an empirical question. This empirical question, it should be noted, is wholly distinct from the question of whether a philosopher might deem some notion of fairness to be a proper principle for the evaluation of legal rules, independent of individuals' well-being (and thus regardless of their actual tastes concerning the notion of fairness).[139]

A second manner in which social norms may be relevant under welfare

---

136. See subsection II.A.1. For a model in which individuals care about whether tort liability is imposed in accordance with their own notions of fairness, see Lando (1997).

137. See subsection C.1(c).

138. The reader may find it odd to impute such a valuation to fairness. But it should be kept in mind that here we are considering fairness as a taste. Thus, saying that individuals place a value of $7 on fairness simply means that if they could choose between being in a regime with the fair rule and being in one with the unfair rule that also gave them an additional $6, they would prefer the former; but if they were materially better off by $8 in the latter regime, their preference would change. See note 32. Moreover, as we discuss in subsection VIII.D.1, using a common denominator (such as monetary equivalents) is implicit in any consistent decisionmaking scheme, regardless of what is being valued.

139. For further discussion of tastes for fairness, including how they might be measured and the factors bearing on their likely importance, see subsection VIII.B.4.

economics concerns the possibility that the norms will be influenced by legal rules. For example, a legal rule that is seen to embody a social norm—a notion of fairness—may reinforce that norm, which would be desirable to the extent that the norm results in better behavior by individuals in everyday life. Likewise, tort rules determining which acts are subject to liability might communicate messages about right and wrong, which in turn would influence behavior independently of the formal legal system.[140] Once again, however, the relevance of social norms, and thus of corresponding notions of fairness, concerns the ultimate effects of legal rules on individuals' well-being, as part of the welfare economic assessment, not some basis independent of such effects that is to be given weight at the expense of individuals' well-being.

3. Remark on the Concepts of Injurer and Victim

The relationship between notions of fairness in the tort context and social norms used in everyday life pertains to the very concepts of injurer and of victim; indeed, referring to the individual suffering harm as a victim may itself suggest that there is some ground for rectification. These terms seem to play a significant role in the views of many, including some who advance the principle of corrective justice, concerning what treatment is fair.[141] We suggest that the attraction most of us feel concerning the appropriate treatment of injurers and victims can best be understood by reference to the role of social norms in promoting individuals' well-being rather than by suppos-

---

140. See, for example, Baron (1993, 157–59), suggesting a possible advantage of the negligence rule over strict liability in that the former sends clearer signals about proper versus improper behavior. But see Sugarman (1985, 611–13), suggesting that accident law does not in fact provide useful signals about proper behavior, and arguing that other mechanisms, ranging from upbringing to the use of criminal and regulatory law, better fill this need.

In analyzing possible effects of tort rules on notions of right and wrong, one cannot view these rules in a vacuum. For example, under a combined reform of the sort discussed in section F, wherein one might abolish tort liability for automobile accidents but simultaneously raise penalties under traffic laws for dangerous driving, the overall message might heighten rather than diminish the perception that certain driving behaviors are wrong. The experience in the United States with drunk driving may bear on this point. Accidents caused by drunk drivers were always subject to tort liability, but it may be that social perceptions of the wrongfulness of drunk driving changed only when traffic laws regarding drunk driving became stricter, both on the books and as enforced. Of course, another possibility is that social norms concerning drunk driving changed first, and this change led to tougher traffic laws and enforcement.

141. See, for example, Coleman (1992b, 382), referring to the need for corrective justice to draw upon "pre-theoretical conceptions of the terms victim, injurer, and causation."

ing that there exists some underlying evaluative principle, independent of welfare, that explains the force of these concepts.

Initially, we observe that there seems to be an inherent difficulty in any attempt to construct a moral foundation for distinguishing injurers from victims (apart from instrumental considerations relating to individuals' well-being). This is because, from the perspective of those advancing various notions of fairness, the characteristics that lead some individuals to find themselves in the role of injurers and others to find themselves in the role of victims in the present setting appear to be morally arbitrary.[142] For example, suppose that harm arises because those who plant trees—the injurers—need to burn fallen leaves each autumn, which causes harm to their neighbors—the victims—who prefer shrubs (which are conifers that retain their leaves). The identities of the injurers and the victims will be reversed, however, if a new leaf removal technology eliminates the need to burn leaves, but a pest arrives on the scene that is attracted by the shrubs yet causes damage only to the nearby trees. Reflecting on this example and many others, we find that the factors that ultimately determine who are injurers and who are victims—technology, accidents of nature, and particular individual tastes—are not the sorts of differences that are plausible grounds on which to construct an independent evaluative principle.[143] (Another way to put the point is that,

142. In advancing this criticism of moral arbitrariness, we refer to the sorts of moral notions that fairness-minded analysts seem to find compelling. However, even those who examine some notions of fairness in depth do not identify the causes of individuals falling into different groups in basic contexts in which harm occurs; nor do they indicate the criteria for assessing whether the reasons that some are injurers and others victims justify their proffered notions of fairness. Compare note 16, discussing the extent to which commentators recognize that substantive principles outside their analysis must be called upon to provide content to their constructs. Hence, we do not know with confidence what criteria are really implicit in fairness advocates' views; nevertheless, we suspect that having outcomes turn entirely on what seem to be morally arbitrary factors would be viewed as objectionable. For a possible exception, see note 111.

From the perspective of welfare economics, the fact that the distinction between injurers and victims is arbitrary in the sense described in the text is irrelevant. What matters, as we discuss in the text to follow, is whether treating these groups differently will make individuals better off, such as by reducing the number of injuries.

143. Tastes may not be seen as entirely arbitrary to the extent that individuals choose their tastes or can change them in light of legal rules. As we discuss in subsections VIII.B.2 and VIII.B.3, there are, in principle, sound arguments for challenging certain preferences or attempting to modify them over time (for example, preferences to cause harm to others for the sheer pleasure of it). We explain, however, that such arguments are themselves aspects of welfare economics because their force depends on the effect of changing preferences on individuals' well-being. Furthermore, we observe that such arguments do not seem applicable

behind a "veil of ignorance," where individuals would not know which role they would occupy, they would not assign weight to such statuses per se, especially when doing so would reduce their well-being.[144])

Even though the categories of injurer and victim seem to have a morally arbitrary character when viewed as a direct source of an evaluative principle, our discussion in subsection 1 suggests that, for social norms to be effective in promoting individuals' well-being, members of society will need to develop a common understanding about which individuals should be made to compensate others for harms—injurers—and which should receive such payments—victims. Relatedly, when, say, a change in technology alters who is generally regarded as an injurer and who as a victim, it typically will be appropriate to make a corresponding adjustment in who will have to pay compensation to whom, even though the change in technology is of no intrinsic significance.[145] Because an important purpose of the social norm is

---

to many tastes that might lead one to be in the position of a potential injurer, particularly since we are emphasizing the contexts of ordinary accidents and nuisances, not intentional torts like murder; thus, even if some tastes are not taken as given, there is hardly a systematic basis for objecting to the sorts of tastes under consideration here (such as tastes for trees versus shrubs).

144. Compare note 16 in chapter II, explaining that the welfare economic notion of social welfare treats all individuals symmetrically, without regard to aspects of identity, which would include status as a potential injurer or victim. This ex ante view corresponds to the welfare economic approach in the reciprocal case. See subsection C.1(e)(iii), suggesting that the Golden Rule and other approaches to testing moral principles are tantamount to requiring that decisions be consistent with the preferred outcome in the reciprocal case. See also subsection VIII.C.1, offering justifications for an ex ante view.

We also note that even if one found any of these features to be ethically significant, notions of fairness could not be applied in the usual manner. For example, suppose that for some reason tree-lovers were to be favored. Then a rule favoring injurers would be required in the first scenario described in the text, but one favoring victims would be required in the second. Once one goes to underlying characteristics, one would have to favor, say, tree-lovers as a group rather than victims as a group. We are unaware of any proposed notion of fairness in tort law that would produce this pattern of results. Also, as we explain in note 114, if one does wish to favor tree-lovers, one can do this in a manner that makes everyone better off by using direct transfers among groups of individuals rather than choosing welfare-reducing tort rules.

145. We also suspect that the importance given to the status of being an injurer or a victim under social norms would depend to some extent on the context, in a manner that corresponds to the functions that social norms serve. For example, if a victim is clearly at fault (say, when someone walks along railroad tracks listening to music with headphones and is struck by a train whose whistle could not be heard), injurers would not ordinarily be blamed.

to deter harmful acts, changes in technology may well change which acts we wish to deter.[146]

Viewing the categories of injurers and victims functionally, we should keep in mind that there are internalized social norms about the proper behavior and treatment of individuals in various circumstances. Hence, once a type of actor is identified as an injurer or as a victim in the relevant sense, we will have feelings about what treatment is appropriate. That is, the pull exerted by thinking about some people as injurers and others as victims seems to be another manifestation of the role of social norms and their correspondence to notions of fairness.

We now examine another perspective on the present subject. Instead of trying to distinguish injurers and victims based on their underlying characteristics, one might attempt to motivate a notion of fairness by drawing on the fact that individuals, whatever may have put them in a particular position, still make choices, which ultimately affect whether they actually become injurers (rather than, say, tree-lovers who have the option of choosing not to have trees if the only way to dispose of the leaves is by burning them). However, if one abstracts from the welfare-enhancing effects of basing rules on individuals' choices, this formulation also raises difficulties. First, focusing on individuals' choices per se does not tell us whose choice should matter. As Coase emphasized, victims make choices as well.[147] Second, no matter whose choices are under consideration, there must be some basis for objecting to some choices but not to others. After all, most choices are not objectionable, and even choices that harm others, such as outdoing a competitor through hard work, are often to be encouraged rather than condemned. Corrective justice theories make injurers "responsible for those losses that result from voluntary action which is, in some sense to be specified, wrongful,"[148] but as we have previously discussed,

146. In subsection 1, we also identified other purposes of social norms concerning compensation, such as alleviating the desire for vengeance and caring for victims. As with deterrence, when technology or some other factor changes in a manner that affects who is viewed as an injurer and who as a victim, it will tend to be the case that who should pay compensation to whom in order to further the purposes that underlie social norms will likewise change.

147. See Coase (1960). See also Perry (1997), arguing that, in light of the fact that both the injurer and the victim inevitably make choices, the libertarian view that one can assign liability based upon which party made a choice that caused harm cannot be maintained, and Perry (1992b, 463–67), noting the problem that in some corrective justice theories it is difficult to decide which party is the active injurer and which the passive victim.

148. Perry (1992b, 475).

corrective justice theories do not themselves furnish a theory of wrong-fulness.[149]

If, however, one again considers the functions served by social norms, it is easy to understand why members of society would have developed intu-itions about responsibility that focus on individuals' choices: different choices have different effects on other individuals' well-being, and it is vol-untary choices that may be influenced through social norms. Just as the labels "injurer" and "victim" will tend to be applied functionally, so too can we understand how society determines whose choices are most relevant (it will tend to be those whom we wish to deter) and which types of choices will be associated with feelings of guilt and social disapprobation rather than feelings of virtue and social approval (the former will tend to be choices that are socially detrimental and the latter choices that promote individuals' well-being).

In sum, we are suggesting that our intuitions about the basic concepts of injurer, victim, and choice, which seem to underlie notions of fairness in the tort context, can be understood as aspects of social norms applicable in situations in which individuals cause harm to others. If this is the case, then, as we discuss in subsection 2, it would not make sense to pursue notions of fairness, whose appeal derives from our intuitions about these concepts, at the expense of individuals' well-being, particularly when the purpose of the corresponding social norms that underlie our intuitions is to advance welfare.

4. Remark on the Ex Post Character of Notions of Fairness

As we discuss in subsection II.B.2(c), many notions of fairness involve the adoption of an ex post perspective, in which analysis focuses on particular outcomes (omitting or demoting in importance other outcomes, which may be more typical) and tends to ignore the effects of legal rules on the behavior that is responsible for whether or how likely various outcomes are to occur. Notions of fairness in the tort context exemplify this perspective. Under such notions, one is led, for example, to ask after the fact whether an injurer should be punished or a victim should be compensated, or, under corrective justice, whether the state that results when an injurer has harmed a victim is of the sort that calls for correction through compensation. As our analysis in section D notes, this perspective tends to be governed by the fortuity of

149. See pages 93–97.

whether, for a given act, an accident has in fact occurred. Moreover, our analysis in both sections C and D indicates that notions of fairness seem insensitive to how tort rules affect parties' initial behavior, which determines the likelihood of accidents.[150] Indeed, much of the difference between prescriptions based on notions of fairness and those derived from welfare economics is accounted for by the fact that, under welfare economics, a broader view is taken, one that reflects factors that tend to be eclipsed by the ex post perspective of notions of fairness.

As suggested in our previous, more general discussion of the subject, we believe that the tendency to adopt an ex post perspective can be explained by familiar cognitive biases. Thus, when an accident occurs, it is the accident itself and the resulting harm to the victim that are most salient, not the hypothetical (though ex ante often much more probable) outcome in which no accident occurs. Likewise, one is not automatically inclined to focus upon the original choices that led one individual to be in the role of potential injurer and the other in the role of potential victim, and how these choices may have been influenced by the anticipation that one or another legal rule would be applied ex post, in the event of an accident. (The foregoing relates both to our analysis comparing notions of fairness and welfare economics in sections C and D and to our discussion of the prominence of the concepts of injurer and victim in subsection 3 of this section.)

That there exist natural human tendencies to take such an ex post perspective when forming impressions of a situation helps to explain why notions of fairness that embody this perspective seem natural and fitting. These defects in and limitations on our intuition, however, do not justify treating intuitively appealing notions of fairness as independent evaluative principles to be used in place of welfare economic analysis, which involves a more explicit and comprehensive assessment of situations in order to determine which legal rules are more likely to advance individuals' well-being.

F. The Extent to Which the Use of Notions of Fairness Has Led Us Astray

It is self-evident that legal commentators, judges, legislators, and others in the legal arena tend to give significant weight to notions of fairness in assessing tort law and making policy. An examination of legal academic literature,

---

150. In section D we also discuss how notions of fairness do not take account of parties' initial decisions concerning whether to purchase insurance.

teaching materials, and judicial decisions shows that they constantly refer to the primary notions of fairness discussed in this chapter—that the tort system should compensate victims and impose liability on wrongdoers.[151] Although they also devote attention to economically relevant, instrumental factors that bear on individuals' well-being,[152] the emphasis that they place on these factors appears to us insufficient and haphazard.[153]

First, consider victims' actual need for compensation from the tort system. It is manifest that to assess this need, one must know whether victims are already going to be compensated by private or social insurance. In fact, a high proportion of the population of the United States possesses insurance coverage: approximately 85 percent of the population has public or private medical insurance; most of the workforce is covered by Social Security or private disability insurance; and about 80 percent of adults with dependents have life insurance.[154] Yet in many tort policy discussions, insurance coverage is ignored or only briefly mentioned. Apparently, the notion of fairness that requires the victim to be compensated via the tort system is so strong that fairness-minded analysts are not led to ask whether victims actually lack a source of compensation.

Second, consider tort-related deterrence of harm. Although we do see some mention of this factor, one is struck by the casual character of discussion about it and by the frequency with which one encounters essentially

151. See subsection B.1.

152. That prevailing attitudes about tort policy reflect mixed views—which combine pure notions of fairness and consideration of individuals' well-being rather than insist that policy be based entirely on notions of fairness—is clear not only from most discourse on the subject, as we discuss in the text to follow, but also from the legal rules actually in place. For example, if one took corrective justice seriously and gave no regard to administrative costs (following, for example, Fletcher, as discussed in note 11), it would be necessary to make the legal system available to remedy countless small-scale infractions in everyday life, which could consume a substantial fraction of social resources.

153. See, for example, Henderson (1991, 1589–97), presenting evidence that, in products liability cases in which policy reasoning was developed and in those in which such reasoning controlled decisions, appeals to the fairness or rightness of an outcome were more prevalent than appeals to efficiency and cost reduction, especially in cases in which the rationales were seen to conflict.

154. See U.S. Census Bureau (1997), presenting data that indicate that 84.4 percent have private or government health insurance coverage, and American Council of Life Insurance (1996, 36), documenting that, in 1992, 84 percent of husband-wife households with children had life insurance on at least one member, and 72 percent of single-headed families had life insurance. See also Priest (1987, 1552 and n.136, 1586–87), indicating that the vast majority of Americans have health, disability, and life insurance, and Sugarman (1985, 645–48), surveying existing coverage for income replacement and medical expenses.

conclusory statements, such as that tort law simply does not deter.[155] Yet one would surmise that there is sufficient likelihood that tort law can substantially deter harm that analysts should seriously consider the possibility. Notably, firms plausibly take actions to reduce harm in order to lower their liability bill; after all, their usual focus is on profits, and we generally believe that they take actions to reduce their production costs, so there is reason to believe they do the same to reduce their liability costs.

Third, although there seems to be more general awareness of the administrative costs of the tort system, treatment of the issue still seems inadequate. Given that such costs are so high, they can hardly be viewed as a secondary consideration; under the tort system, it costs over a dollar in expenses for each dollar that victims receive.[156]

Against this background, one suspects that tort policy decisions are often incorrectly made or are reached without adequate justification. Indeed, this deficiency seems to exist in specific domains of accident law. A particularly important area is automobile accidents, which generate a substantial fraction of all tort litigation.[157] One might reasonably wonder (as many have) whether this litigation is worthwhile—that is, whether a no-fault system would be superior to the present system of tort liability.[158] As mentioned, many indi-

155. Notable exceptions are Schwartz (1994) and Sugarman (1985, 559–91).

156. See, for example, Forcier (1994, 154), stating that litigation expenses account for half of the total expenditure or insurance cost in contested cases and 70 percent for product liability claims, and that the total cost of the liability system is $40 to $80 billion per year; Hensler et al. (1987, 25–29), presenting data indicating that the net compensation to plaintiffs is 52 percent of total litigation expenditures for auto cases, 43 percent for non-auto cases, and 37 percent for asbestos cases, and that litigation costs consumed about half of the $29 to $36 billion spent on tort litigation in 1985; and Insurance Information Institute (2000), referring to 1995 data indicating that the total cost of the civil liability system was $161 billion and breaking down each dollar of tort costs as follows: 24 cents to litigants for actual losses, 22 cents for pain and suffering; of the remaining 54 cents, 16 cents for claimants' lawyers, 14 cents for defense costs, and 24 cents for administrative costs.

157. See, for example, Hensler et al. (1987, 6–9 table 2.1), presenting data indicating that automobile cases in 1985 comprised 55 percent of total case filings in five state courts and 16 percent in federal courts; Smith et al. (1995, 2), presenting data indicating that 60.1 percent of all tort cases in the nation's seventy-five largest counties involved automobile accidents; and Gross and Syverud (1996, 13), presenting evidence showing that about a third of personal injury trials in a California sample were vehicular negligence cases.

158. Such reforms have been considered, and in some instances implemented, in many countries. In the United States, some states have adopted no-fault automobile accident regimes, but tort liability is typically eliminated only for cases in which the degree of injury is below a modest threshold (such as a few thousand dollars of medical expenses) or in which there is no significant or permanent disfigurement. See, for example, Insurance Information

viduals possess insurance coverage, which costs far less to provide than compensation through the tort system. Moreover, if present coverage is inadequate, alternative insurance schemes rather than the use of tort liability would seem to be a far cheaper solution.[159] Furthermore, it is not obvious that the tort system provides a substantial stimulus for safe driving. Most people have strong incentives to drive carefully in the first place—they do not want to be injured in an accident, and their driving behavior is regulated by enforcement of traffic safety laws.[160] In addition, the incentive created by the prospect of tort liability is attenuated by liability insurance coverage.[161] Thus, serious consideration seems warranted as to whether the merits of tort liability in the automobile accident context outweigh the costs.[162] Yet

Institute (1998), discussing existing no-fault automobile insurance laws in thirteen states and Puerto Rico; White and Liao (1999, 1–2, 30), describing mixed no-fault regimes in fifteen states and pure no-fault systems in other countries; and Schwartz (2000, 617–19), describing different no-fault regimes in various states and emphasizing that none are pure no-fault systems. Schwartz argues that a pure no-fault regime, in which liability for automobile accidents is completely eliminated, is the most promising alternative (although he does not endorse such a change, and instead focuses on its most important advantages and problems in comparison to mixed no-fault systems and traditional negligence liability).

159. Also, the tort regime does not cover a wide range of accidents and other harms, such as naturally occurring disease, accidents one causes to oneself, and, in most cases, non-negligently caused accidents. Hence, if there is a general social problem of inadequate insurance, the tort system, even if not excessively expensive, would be only a partial solution.

160. If a change to a no-fault regime resulted in inadequate residual incentives, traffic enforcement might be increased. See, for example, Benson, Rasmussen, and Mast (1999), surveying literature and presenting further evidence on the effect of increased law enforcement on drunk driving. A range of policies aimed at drunk drivers (including such measures as raising taxes to increase the price of alcoholic beverages) has had significant effects in reducing automobile accidents, especially for young drivers who contribute significantly to the problem. See, for example, Sloan, Reilly, and Schenzler (1994). Another way to provide incentives for safe driving under a no-fault system would be to employ forms of experience-rating in determining drivers' insurance premiums.

161. See, for example, Gross and Syverud (1996, 6, 19, 21–22), stating that, in the typical personal injury trial in California, "the defendant has an insurance policy that covers all defense costs and any likely judgment," and that individual defendants in vehicular negligence cases are most likely to have complete insurance and rarely have none. We note, however, that liability insurance does not entirely eliminate financial incentives regarding driving behavior; not only is coverage sometimes incomplete, but premiums may be experience-rated and some potential drivers (particularly high-risk teenagers) may be induced not to drive on account of high insurance costs.

162. This question has received some serious scholarly attention. See, for example, Carroll et al. (1991); Dewees, Duff, and Trebilcock (1996, 54–62), discussing evidence on the effects of no-fault regimes; Keeton and O'Connell (1965); White and Liao (1999); Schwartz (1994, 393–97), surveying evidence, including data on various no-fault systems, and concluding that

consideration of substantial no-fault automobile regimes has been retarded, in part, it seems, because of the appeal of punishing those who negligently cause harm on the road (even though those who are "punished" typically own liability insurance[163]) and because we ignore victims' ability to obtain compensation from their own insurers.[164]

Another example that raises doubts about our tort policy involves situations in which firms cause harms—notably many health-related environmental harms—that are difficult to trace to their sources. Here there is a danger of too little deterrence because firms anticipate that they are likely to escape liability. To address this problem, we might want to relax liability standards and to augment damages when firms are found liable. Yet the possible advantages of an increase in liability and damages in this area do not appear to be fully appreciated for two interrelated reasons. First, there is a reluctance on fairness grounds to impose liability when it cannot be proved that a particular injurer caused harm to a particular victim.[165] Second,

---

tort law probably has a significant effect on automobile accidents; ibid. (434–36), suggesting that the deterrence benefits of liability for automobile accidents may well exceed the administrative costs; and Sugarman (1985, 559–91), giving reasons to be skeptical of the ability of tort law to deter. See also Atiyah (1997), exploring the merits of abolishing tort liability and leaving individuals in the market to make their own insurance arrangements, and Carroll and Kakalik (1993), examining the effects of no-fault schemes on administrative costs and on the relationship between compensation and loss.

163. See note 161, quoting Gross and Syverud.

164. Compare Bell and O'Connell (1997, 204–06), suggesting social resistance to no-fault proposals. As we note in subsection E.2, notions of fairness would be relevant to the extent that individuals have tastes for seeing such notions reflected in legal policy. We might be skeptical, however, about how upset most individuals would be as a result of a major tort reform that reduced their automobile insurance premiums significantly while also decreasing reliance on lawyers and the courts. The present tort system, as noted in the text, does not directly punish most injurers because they have liability insurance. Compare O'Connell and Simon (1972, 26–27), summarizing surveys of auto accident victims compensated by injurers' insurers, which indicate that fewer than 10 percent remain angry at the other driver. It is true that injurers' premiums may rise in the future, but this would happen as well under no-fault regimes with experience-rating. Also, those who behave egregiously would be subject to traffic laws and possible criminal liability, such as for drunk driving.

Another possibility identified in subsection E.2 concerns the manner in which the law may influence important social norms. Thus, there may be a risk that eliminating tort liability for automobile accidents would, independently of any direct reduction in deterrence, send a message that safe driving was less important. If, however, such a reform were accompanied by tougher traffic laws and enforcement, the net effect might be the opposite. See also note 140, discussing the issue with regard to drunk driving laws and the tort system.

165. See, for example, L. Alexander (1987a, 14–15), criticizing corrective justice because it opposes market-share liability, which stance is problematic when causation is difficult to

the orientation of torts commentators does not give proper attention to deterrence. One does see higher punitive damages being imposed on some firms, but this increase does not seem to be targeted at areas in which there is reason to believe that existing liability may be inadequate, and raising damages when liability is already adequate may cause problems of overdeterrence.[166]

We can also query the soundness of what has been in a sense the major policy decision regarding tort law in the last half century: namely, the growth of tort liability, both in the scope of allowable claims and in the level of awards.[167] This expansion of tort liability has come in the face of several elements that suggest it might have been rational to contract the extent of liability. First, victims' actual need for compensation has been reduced because of the spread of insurance coverage. Second, the need for tort liability as a deterrent has been diminished by the increasing use of regulatory controls by the state. Third, the administrative costs of the tort system are large and greatly exceed those of the insurance system. This is not to say that the general expansion of tort liability definitely has been ill-advised—perhaps tort liability was employed much too sparingly earlier—but it is to say that questions about the expansion of tort liability are of obvious importance and demand further investigation.

At the same time, we can inquire about the wisdom of recent tendencies toward retrenchment in tort liability, including placing limits on punitive damage awards, imposing penalties for supposedly frivolous suits, and shifting legal fees to losing plaintiffs.[168] Such steps to curb litigation seem to be more a generalized reaction against the expansion of liability than a well-considered policy based on an assessment of the need for compensation, the extent of deterrence, and the magnitude of the administrative costs of tort liability in particular contexts.

Mistakes in policy judgments in the area of tort liability seem inevitable if the discourse and analysis are, as they have been, so influenced by notions

---

trace; Strudler (1992), arguing that remedial schemes in mass tort cases are inconsistent with extant interpretations of corrective justice but offering an alternative interpretation; and note 116 in chapter V. But see Kraus (1997).

166. See, for example, Polinsky and Shavell (1998, 899–900, 955).

167. See, for example, Priest (1985, 505–27) and Weinstein and Hershenov (1991, 272–75).

168. See, for example, Priest (1987, 1587–88), describing state tort reform legislation, Weinstein and Hershenov (1991, 322–23), describing efforts to reform tort law and legal procedure, and "Common Sense" Legislation (1996, 1768), describing state tort reform legislation.

of fairness that they fail to incorporate in a systematic and careful manner instrumental factors of central importance to everyone's well-being. Relatedly, we suspect that the influence of notions of fairness also helps to explain why legal academics devote so little effort to empirical work. If analysts believe that tort policy should be guided by notions of fairness that are independent of the effects of legal rules on individuals' well-being, empirical work on the effects of the tort system is just not very relevant. If, however, it were more widely accepted that policy should be assessed under welfare economics, wherein everything depends on how legal rules affect individuals' well-being, the need for empirical work would be more apparent and the relevant research program would be more clearly specified.

CHAPTER IV

────────□────────

Contracts

In this chapter, we focus on basic questions concerning the enforcement of contracts. We begin in section A by describing the application of welfare economics to contract enforcement and continue in section B by discussing relevant notions of fairness. In section C, we examine a paradigmatic contract enforcement problem and consider how contract enforcement rules would be evaluated under welfare economics and according to notions of fairness. Then we explain why welfare economics should be employed. In section D, we consider possible distributive effects of contract enforcement rules and issues of advantage-taking; we also comment on whether fairness-based analysis has led to mistakes in legal policy.

A. Welfare Economics and the Enforcement of Contracts

From the perspective of welfare economics, the purpose of contracts is to promote the well-being of the contracting parties; accordingly, contract law generally should facilitate this purpose.[1] As in other areas of the law, it is true in contracts that legal rules will affect parties' well-being by influencing their incentives. In this regard, there first needs to be an incentive for parties to enter into contracts when doing so would be mutually beneficial.[2] Second,

---

1. There are, of course, exceptions—notably, when a contract would negatively affect third parties (such as a contract to commit a crime).

2. Contract law may affect whether parties enter into prospectively advantageous relationships both by affecting the costs of contracting (such as by providing useful default rules that

it is often important for parties to make investments during the contractual relationship that enhance its value appropriately. Third, and our focus in this chapter, parties need to be induced to perform their contracts when performance would be beneficial, but should not be encouraged to perform when doing so would reduce their well-being.[3]

Contract law may also influence parties' well-being in other ways. The cost of administering different contract rules may affect which rule is best for the parties. Contract rules may affect the allocation of risk, which will be important when parties are risk averse; for simplicity, however, we will assume that parties are risk neutral. Additionally, the division of gain between the parties from contracting may be relevant on distributive grounds, but, in most of the examples we study, contract law will not have any distributive effect because changes in the contract price will offset any tendency of a contract rule to favor one or another party. (In subsection D.1, we do briefly examine a case in which contract rules may have a distributive effect in order to examine how considerations pertaining to the distribution of income might affect our analysis.)

B. Notions of Fairness and the Enforcement of Contracts

We now consider notions of fairness that bear on the legal enforcement of promises, that is, on the choice of contract remedies.[4] We will focus on two sets of views that have received the most attention in modern contracts scholarship, one based on the sanctity of promises and the other premised on the idea that a contract breach is analogous to a tort.[5]

---

reduce the costs of drafting) and by affecting the course of such relationships (which affects their value to the parties).

We also note that parties should have an incentive not to enter into arrangements that would reduce their well-being. Because consent is required, this problem will not usually occur; however, difficulties may arise when the prospect for advantage-taking exists and the party who would suffer is under duress or otherwise lacks the ability to make good decisions. See, for example, subsection D.2.

3. Other incentives could be mentioned as well, such as the incentive to mitigate damages when there is nonperformance.

4. Notions of fairness are thought to be important in addressing other contract doctrines as well. See, for example, Eisenberg (1982). We note, however, that unified views of fairness are not usually offered, and explicit underlying rationales for fairness arguments are not generally presented.

5. One of our motivations for focusing on these views of contract scholars and philosophers is that conventional syntheses of contract law say little about the purpose of contract

1. Promise-Keeping

The first notion of fairness draws on a body of philosophical literature that deems it wrong for a promisor to break his promise. This literature includes work by Kant,[6] Ross,[7] and others.[8] They emphasize the broadly held intuition

---

remedies. See, for example, Corbin (1964, §992), referring to the objective of putting an injured party in as good a position as would have resulted from performance, but not addressing why this should be the purpose of contract remedies; Jaeger (1968, vol. 11, §1338; 3rd ed. of *Williston on Contracts*), insisting that the purpose of damages is to compensate plaintiffs by putting them in as good a position as if their contracts had been performed, but not stating why this is the case; and *Restatement of the Law Second: Contracts* (1981, §344), listing various abstract "interests," which parallel those interests discussed by Fuller and Perdue (1936), see note 32, but not explaining why protecting these interests is desirable. Corbin does, however, suggest that awarding compensatory damages serves to keep the peace and also to deter future harm arising from breaches of contract, thereby encouraging business transactions, both purposes obviously related to individuals' well-being. See Corbin (1964, §1002). See also *Restatement of the Law Second: Contracts* (1981, chapter 16, Introductory Note), suggesting that the contract rule requiring promisees to be compensated for loss, but no more, is in general accord with the economic view of contract breach, but suggesting shortcomings of the economic view, including inattention to "moral obligation."

6. Most famous is Kant's discussion, in the course of elaborating his categorical imperative, of a person who would knowingly make a false promise, such as seeking to borrow money with no intention of repayment. See Kant ([1785] 1997, 15, 32, 38). Kant argues (among other things) that freely allowing false promises could not be admitted as a universal rule, for then no one would believe promises anymore (which he finds problematic because he sees this as a contradictory state of affairs). See ibid. (32). He does not, however, explicitly consider the possibility of allowing promises to be broken only in a narrowly specified set of circumstances, or allowing them to be broken only if the promisor pays damages. It seems unlikely that generalizing such practices or rules would undermine the institution of promising. If appropriately chosen, they would constitute a mutually beneficial social institution. See note 119.

It should also be noted that Kant's discussion, like that of many philosophers, concerns promises rather than formal contracts. Kant does address formal contracts in other work, but not in sufficient detail to determine what contract rules he would favor with regard to most issues and, in particular, whether he would apply an absolute prohibition on breaking promises in the setting of formal contracts. See Kant ([1796–1797] 1887, 100–07, 143–46, 241–43). In any case, consistent with his general emphasis on free will and autonomy, Kant clearly endorses what is now generally referred to as a "will theory" of contract: "The act of the united Wills of two Persons, by which what belonged to one passes to the other, constitutes CONTRACT." Ibid. (101).

7. See Ross (1930, chapter 2), and note 17, quoting Ross.

8. See, for example, Searle (1964). Many philosophers have focused their analysis on the question of how making promises can create obligations; a common answer refers to social conventions about the meaning and implications of the act of promising. See, for example, Melden (1956). Scanlon's position is similar to that of the promise-keeping theorists, although

that promises should be kept, even when breaking them would advance the greater good, often suggesting that this intuition stands as a strong counter-example to the claims of act utilitarians.[9] We do not, however, focus primarily on these scholars because they do not directly address contract law, or, more particularly, the law of remedies with which we are concerned here.[10]

---

there are important qualifications. See Scanlon (1990). Scanlon emphasizes that the moral obligation to keep promises depends not on the existence of a social institution of promise-keeping, but merely on parties creating clear expectations in each other's minds. He suggests, therefore, that one does not need to refer to such an institution to interpret promises, yet he acknowledges that social conventions about meanings (which would include the generally accepted meaning of "I promise") would determine how parties' statements should be interpreted, which is a sufficient foundation for our discussion that follows. See also McNeilly (1972), suggesting, similarly, that what matters is parties' ability to create expectations by showing that they have a motivation to keep their promises, while denying that moral obligation is the only means of doing so.

We also note that much philosophical writing on promises is devoted to issues of definition. See, for example, Árdal (1968), Locke (1972), and MacCormick (1972). Of course, to the extent that promises are understood to involve moral obligations, arguments about what counts as a promise are, at least implicitly, concerned with what should be deemed morally obligatory.

9. See, for example, Atiyah (1981, 30): "[O]ne of the most frequently adduced examples [in arguments against utilitarianism] is the case of promising. To many philosophers, it is manifest that justice requires promises to be kept even where the result is, on balance, to do less good than could be done by breaking the promise."; and Rawls (1955, 17), explaining that, under promise-keeping theories, it is not a general defense to breaking a promise that the promisor truly believes his action to be best on the whole, although there may be a defense when the consequences of keeping a promise would be very severe.

Many have criticized the standard promise-keeping objections to utilitarianism. See, for example, Atiyah (1981, chapter 3); Hare (1964), criticizing Searle's view; Harrod (1936, 147–56), suggesting that prima facie obligations, such as promise-keeping, are consistent with a utilitarian system; Narveson (1971), criticizing arguments, particularly those of Grice, Hodgson, and Searle, that question whether utilitarianism can account for the practice of promising; Rawls (1955, 13–18), responding to the standard objection by distinguishing between justifying a practice, a task for which utilitarian arguments are more compelling, and justifying particular acts falling under the practice, which must be done by reference to the practice itself; Sartorius (1969), criticizing the standard view, of which Ross is a proponent; and Singer (1972), criticizing Hodgson's argument that act utilitarians may not take into account the effect of their acts on the institution of promise-keeping. See also Sidgwick (1907, 303–11), suggesting that the common moral understanding of promising is much less absolute than is sometimes suggested and that it does not contain within itself the criteria for defining its range of applicability.

10. See, for example, Ross (1930, 17–18, 34–39). Nevertheless, our discussion of the promise-keeping theory of contracts—especially in the case of incomplete contracts, in subsection C.2(e)(i), and with regard to its relationship with social norms about promises, in subsection C.2(g)—will bear on philosophers' views about promises.   *(continued)*

The philosophical literature on promises has, however, provided a foundation for modern contract scholars.[11] Notably, Fried views contract as a type of promise. Because breaching a contract involves breaking a promise and because it is wrong to break promises, he argues that it is wrong to breach contracts.[12] This position derives its normative force from the belief that individuals' ability to bind themselves by making promises is an essential aspect of their autonomy.[13] Relying less on promises per se and more on the underlying idea of autonomy, Barnett argues that contracts are the means by which individuals are able to transfer their property rights. From this perspective, contract enforcement is necessary to enable individuals to exercise an important aspect of their sovereignty over that which is rightfully theirs.[14]

We do note that Scanlon differs from many other philosophers who have addressed promising in two respects. First, he discusses the question of remedies and tends to favor requiring performance rather than simply allowing a promisor to break a promise and pay compensation (although he does not take an absolute stand in that he does not believe that the obligation holds without regard to the cost of fulfilling it). See Scanlon (1990, 204–06, 214). Second, one can infer that his analysis is primarily directed toward the obligations of promisors in informal settings rather than what may be the appropriate requirements of contract law, although it is not clear that he would thus limit its application. See ibid. (205), stating that his argument against compensation "is particularly important in the domain of informal personal morality, where (in contrast to the legal domain) there is no presumptively impartial third party with authority to make judgments of equivalence." We also note that Kant's writing that explicitly (though briefly) addresses contract law distinguishes between the requirements of individual morality and the appropriate judgment of a court. See Kant ([1796–1797] 1887, 146). See also MacCormick (1972, 73–78), noting differences between promises and contracts subject to the law of voluntary obligations.

11. See, for example, Barnett (1992a, 1023): "[M]ainstream contract theory is dominated by the conception of 'contract as promise'. . . ."

12. See Fried (1981, chapters 1–2).

13. A different rationale is that promises must be kept, for otherwise the individual breaking a promise, which is a type of prior statement by the individual, will have lied. See, for example, Sidgwick (1907, 303–04), noting that some have viewed the duty of keeping promises as closely related to the duty of veracity and identifying some similarities, but concluding that "the analogy is obviously superficial and imperfect"; Craswell (1989, 501–03), criticizing the truth-telling theory; and Fried (1981, 9) (same). Some inspiration for this view may derive from the fact that Kant's well-known discussion of promising focuses on the case of a false promise—one the promisor has no intention of keeping—rather than a promise intended to be kept when made but subsequently broken. See Kant ([1785] 1997, 15, 32, 38).

14. See, for example, Barnett (1986a; 1989, 628), and Craswell (1989, 497, and n.21), describing Barnett's view and noting its roots in the work of such earlier political and legal theorists as Hobbes and Blackstone. Although Barnett emphasizes the centrality of individuals' consent to be legally bound rather than promises per se (because many promisors intend to keep their promises but do not intend to invoke state enforcement), see, for example, Barnett (1992a, 1024, 1027–33), we do not find it necessary to distinguish among varying strands of

Based on their rationales for the promise-keeping notion, one might imagine that the theory's proponents would have a preference for a remedy of specific performance—requiring the contract to be performed—for such a remedy amounts to a requirement that the promisor keep his word.[15] (Or, if specific performance were infeasible once a promisor had breached, promise-keeping theories would seem to favor supercompensatory (punitive) damages; after all, the greater the sanction, the less likely promisors would be to breach in the first place.) The use of expectation damages[16] appears to be inconsistent with the standard account of the promise-keeping notion because it allows the promisor to breach. Indeed, it is well understood that subjecting promisors merely to expectation damages invites breach whenever the balance of the parties' interests makes breach favorable—a result that does not respect the sanctity of promises, particularly if contracts are supposed to be performed even when their breach would increase the balance of the good.[17] Nevertheless, for reasons that are difficult to identify,

---

this general approach and, due to the long tradition of philosophical writing, we will refer to this broad set of views as promise-keeping theories. For further comments on Barnett's particular views, see notes 18, 23, 24, 96, and 131.

A related view is presented by Friedmann, who argues (in criticizing Fuller and Perdue's tripartite characterization of the possible purposes of contract remedies) that contract damages should protect what he calls the performance interest. Performance is a right of the promisee, so breach is seen as analogous to conversion, private eminent domain, or, more generally, unlawful appropriation of others' property—the ordinary remedy for which would include, in addition to suits for damages, private injunctions as well as state-imposed criminal penalties. Relatedly, he argues that the notion of efficient breach fails to appreciate the right of performance. See Friedmann (1989, 1995).

We also note that the "will theory" of contracts, more popular a century ago, is closely related to the promise-keeping and consent theories. See, for example, Kronman (1981, 404–406), reviewing Fried (1981), and note 6, discussing Kant's view on promises and his advancement of a will theory of contracts. Compare Barnett (1986a), characterizing Fried's view as a will theory but claiming to distinguish his own consent theory on the ground that whether an individual truly consented may be determined objectively, which is advantageous, but whether an individual's will was to enter into a contract can only be determined subjectively.

15. In suggesting that promise-keeping theories seem to favor specific performance, we acknowledge that proponents in some instances would excuse performance altogether (sometimes on the ground that the initial promise is deemed invalid), such as in cases involving improper influence or mistake. See, for example, Fried (1981, 57–63, 93–99) and Barnett (1986a, 309–10, 318–19).

16. Under expectation damages, an individual who breaches a contract is not required to perform, but rather is obligated to pay damages, and the amount of damages is, in principle, set equal to the value of the promisee's expected return had the contract been performed.

17. Not only does the promise-keeping theory call for keeping promises even when the balance of good favors breach, but it also calls for promises to be kept even when breach

some legal scholars who favor the promise-keeping theory endorse expectation damages as a remedy.[18] Our analysis in section C, however, focuses on

---

would increase the good to the *promisee* (an even better result for the promisee than under expectation damages, which would merely make him whole). Consider the following example from Ross (a promise-keeping theorist who nonetheless does not view the theory as absolute):

> If I have promised to confer on *A* a particular benefit containing 1,000 units of good, is it self-evident that if by doing some different act I could produce 1,001 units of good for *A* himself (the other consequences of the two acts being supposed equal in value), it would be right for me to do so? Again, I think not. Apart from my general *prima facie* duty to do *A* what good I can, I have another *prima facie* duty to do him the particular service I have promised to do him, and this is not to be set aside in consequence of a disparity of good of the order of 1,001 to 1,000, though a much greater disparity might justify me in so doing. (Ross 1930, 35)

See also ibid. (36): "Our certainty that it is *prima facie* right [to keep a promise] depends not on its consequences but on its being the fulfilment of a promise."

18. Fried concludes a section entitled "The Moral Obligation of Promise" by stating that "the contract *must* be kept because a promise must be kept." Fried (1981, 17) (emphasis added). But he then begins the next section, on remedies, as follows:

> If I make a promise to you, I should do as I promise; and if I fail to keep my promise, it is fair that I should be made to hand over the equivalent of the promised performance. In contract doctrine this proposition appears as the expectation measure of damages for breach. (Ibid.)

In his brief discussion, he does not even mention specific performance as an alternative to expectation damages. Yet a few pages earlier, Fried had stressed that breaking a promise, even when doing so maximizes utility, is wrong from the perspective of his theory. See ibid., 15. However, it is well understood that expectation damages encourage breach in precisely this situation, whereas specific performance or punitive damages would tend to deter—and, in the case of specific performance, undo—precisely these sorts of breaches. See Contract as Promise (review) (1983, 905–06), noting that "Fried casually endorses the expectations measure of contract damages" even though under his view "breaking an inefficient contract is morally wrong." See also Craswell (1989, 523), stating that "in the case of expectation damages, [Fried] advances no justification at all."

Friedmann seems similarly inconsistent. Despite his explicit criticism of Fuller and Perdue (who recognize the expectation interest but not the stronger performance interest) and of the notion of efficient breach (which is usually associated with the remedy of expectation damages), see note 14, Friedmann states without offering any further explanation that present law, by awarding money damages that seek to place the injured party in the position where he would have been if the contract had been performed—which is to say, expectation damages—protects what he refers to as the performance interest as much as a damages remedy can. See Friedmann (1995, 649). As noted previously, if one adopts Friedmann's view that breach is a serious wrong in itself because the promisee's interest is akin to property that the promisor may not take without consent (even if the promisor is willing to pay), one would think that punitive damages would be required if specific performance were unavailable, as is often the

the more natural interpretation of the promise-keeping view, although we address the other version as well in the margin.[19]

Finally, we suggest that the promise-keeping theory of contract, when

---

case under existing contract law. Friedmann does, however, argue that the performance interest is receiving greater recognition through the increasing availability of specific performance, and he seems to approve of this trend. See ibid. (648–49).

Perhaps one might believe that specific performance is not really required by the promise-keeping notion because, for example, a buyer would be perfectly happy with expectation damages: After all, under expectation damages, the buyer is made as well off as if the contract had been performed because the damages award equals the value to the buyer of what the seller was obligated to deliver. Because, ex post, the buyer would be indifferent between expectation damages and specific performance, and, as our analysis in subsection C.2 will demonstrate, the seller would prefer expectation damages, such damages might be deemed appropriate. This argument, however, is one of welfare economics: It amounts to choosing the legal rule that best promotes individuals' well-being. That is, in assessing whether breach is an evil, as the promise-keeping theory insists, the argument looks only to the consequences of breach, not the fact of breach; moreover, the only consequence it considers is the well-being of the parties. Clearly, such an argument gives no weight whatsoever to whether a promise has been broken. As noted in the text, the use of expectation damages invites breach whenever the balance of the good favors it, and the defining feature of the promise-keeping theory is that it will not do for promises to be broken merely because the consequences of breaking them are beneficial. (One could construct a theory of fairness that was instead concerned with the well-being of the victim of breach, the promisee; indeed, the second theory that we consider in the text, which views breach as akin to a tort, is of this type.)

A possible motivation underlying Fried's preference for expectation damages may arise from his desire to offer a theory that explains existing doctrine. See note 39. Given that expectation damages are the standard remedy, that specific performance is applied relatively infrequently, and that penalties (even when privately agreed to in advance by the parties) are prohibited, a successful descriptive theory will have a strong pull toward expectation damages. See Farnsworth (1999, §12.1), stating that compelling performance is not a goal of existing contract doctrine.

Not all legal theorists who advance notions of fairness similar to Fried's favor expectation damages. Barnett, for example, favors specific performance; his reason for doing so is based on the empirical conjecture (about which we raise questions, see notes 21 and 23) that such a requirement is what most unsophisticated parties believe to be the normal implication of entering into a legally binding agreement. See Barnett (1986b, 180, 183; 1992b, 890). See also Barnett (1986b, 182), suggesting that another factor favoring specific performance is the argument that innocent victims of breach should not bear the risk of adjudicative error. (Barnett would not, however, allow specific performance of personal services contracts because he believes personal services themselves to be inalienable. See, for example, Barnett (1986b, 197). We are unaware of any discussion that addresses whether his theory permits or requires supercompensatory damages in order to discourage breach of such obligations.) Compare note 10, discusssing Scanlon, who favors, in the course of a philosophical discussion of promise-keeping, a requirement of performance over compensation, although giving as one reason a point more relevant to informal settings than to the formal legal system.

19. See notes 68, 71, 74, 88, and 90.

examined more closely, does not necessarily have the aforementioned—or, indeed, any—implications for the rules of contract law because, in an important sense, the theory is incomplete. In particular, most promise-keeping theorists presume that, when making a promise, the promisor invokes a specific social institution or convention—a set of background understandings that determine the meaning of a promise.[20] But what is this social institution that constitutes the conventional understanding of what a promise means? Promise-keeping theorists essentially stipulate that the social institution is one under which a promise entails a firm commitment to perform, but they do not explain why this should be the case.[21]

The failure of promise-keeping theorists to treat the meaning of the social institution of the promise as an open question for analysis has serious implications for the study of the law of contract remedies. This is because the legal rules themselves are part of the social institution of promising, and when legal enforcement is important, they are a central part.[22] Suppose, for example, that the legal rule is "perform, or pay expectation damages." Then one who invokes contract law by entering into a formal contract has promised to perform or to pay such damages. If, instead, the legal rule is "perform, or the state will make you perform," then the party entering into a contract has promised per-

20. See, for example, Raz (1977, 214 and n.4), noting that the view that "promises can exist only if there is a social practice to that effect" is "endorsed by almost all the writers on promising," but nevertheless arguing that it is possible to have promises without such a social practice.

21. They appear to assume that it is an empirical fact that people understand promises to create an unconditional obligation to perform, but, regardless of whether this is true, it does not provide a basis for determining what the convention of promising ought to be. We also note that promise-keeping theorists' empirical assumption is not directly supported. Whatever may be true about their assumption in the informal setting in which legal enforcement is unimportant, see subsection C.2(g), in the context of contract law the suggestion that contracts should be understood as entailing a firm commitment to perform seems inconsistent with current practice, which employs a general remedy of expectation damages rather than specific performance. Barnett suggests that contracting parties do in fact commonly believe that there will be specific performance. See note 18. However, he offers no evidence for this view, nor does he reconcile it with the fact that an award of expectation damages has been the prevailing remedy for centuries. In addition, he does not address the fact that specific performance is often unavailable. For example, we imagine that most overbooked airline passengers with valid tickets would not expect the state to support their efforts to board an airplane when the airline breaches; quite the opposite (the airline calling the police to restrain the promisee) would undoubtedly occur. See also note 23, further discussing Barnett's view.

22. As others have noted, it would involve circular reasoning to use existing practice as a basis for justifying the institution's rules when that practice depends on those very rules. See, for example, Craswell (1989, 505–08) and Fuller and Perdue (1936, 59–60). See also MacCormick (1972, 77), stating that the existence of rules on contract is logically prior to the concept of an enforceable contract.

formance, come what may.[23] Thus, any legal rule can be fully consistent with the social institution of promising with regard to legally enforceable contracts.

It follows that the obligation to fulfill contractual obligations, upon which promise-keeping theory insists, does not tell us anything about what those obligations should be. Therefore, a fairness-minded analyst who wishes to determine which legal rule is socially best must invoke some other substantive moral theory, which promise-keeping theorists have not identified.[24]

---

23. The former interpretation (perform or pay) is usually associated with Holmes's view of the law in general and of contract remedies in particular. See Holmes (1881, 301): "The only universal consequence of a legally binding promise is, that the law makes the promisor pay damages if the promised event does not come to pass."; and Holmes (1897, 462): "The duty to keep a contract at common law means a prediction that you must pay damages if you do not keep it,—and nothing else." Some commentators have criticized Holmes for not giving enough attention to the law's occasional use of specific performance, which fits the latter interpretation in the text. See, for example, Atiyah (1986, 59–60), noting Holmes's failure to account adequately for instances when specific performance is compelled and for various other contract doctrines that presuppose a duty to perform.

Barnett believes that the matter can be resolved empirically by inquiring into what rule individuals ordinarily suppose would be applied to their situation. See Barnett (1992b, 874–97). (He believes that such an investigation will favor specific performance, see note 18, for reasons that we question, see note 21.) Yet, in advancing his argument about specific performance, he does not really address the point that what individuals ordinarily believe to be the applicable legal rule will be influenced—often decisively—by the prevailing legal regime. Implicitly, he supposes that most individuals hold beliefs that are in fact inconsistent with prevailing law and that they believe as well that the law will ordinarily defer to this misinformed consensus. These assumptions do not seem very likely to be true even for relatively unsophisticated parties. Moreover, in criticizing reliance theories of contract for being circular, he seems to acknowledge that a contrary view is more plausible: "[W]hat most persons will do depends on their perception of what the legal rule is concerning the extent of [contractual] liability, and therefore such a prediction [of what a promisor would have reasonably expected a promisee to do] cannot itself determine the legal rule." Barnett (1986a, 316). For further discussion of Barnett's view on parties' understandings, see note 96. See also note 18, noting Barnett's qualification that personal service contracts should not be subject to the remedy of specific performance due to the inherent inalienability of personal services.

For further discussion of this problem with promise-keeping theories in general, see subsection C.2(e)(i).

24. To illustrate the problem discussed in the text, consider Fried's argument:

> I am bound to do what I promised you I would do—or I am bound to put you in as good a position as if I had done so. . . . *Since by hypothesis I chose to assume the obligation in its stronger form* (that is, to render the performance promised), the reliance rule indeed precludes me from incurring the very obligation I chose to undertake at the time of promising. (Fried 1981, 19, emphasis added)

It seems that one could just as easily hypothesize the existence of only a lesser obligation (to perform or pay reliance damages) or an even stronger obligation (to perform, or else). More-

This lacuna in the promise-keeping notion of fairness not only makes it impossible to draw clear conclusions about the implications of the theory but also suggests that the underlying normative justification for adhering to the theory cannot readily be determined. In any event, when we consider the promise-keeping theory in section C, we will assume that it does carry the implication that promises must be kept, that is, that contracts must be performed.

---

over, if the legal rule were in fact reliance damages, then an individual, in making the simple promise, would have incurred the weaker legal obligation. See Craswell (1989, 489), arguing that "analyses such as Fried's have little or no relevance" to many parts of contract law; ibid. (490): "[T]he fidelity principle is consistent with any set of background rules because those rules merely fill out the details of what it is a person has to remain faithful to. . . ."; ibid. (511–28), criticizing Fried's and Barnett's theories as failing to provide any basis for giving content to contract law; and Farber (1982, 564): "Fried's premise is that promises are binding because they invoke an institution of trust. From this one can infer only that the promisor must be faithful to this institution; one cannot infer the institution's rules." As Farber explains:

> Whichever meaning the promise is given by a particular society, the promise principle imposes a corresponding moral duty. Thus, the promise principle is perfectly consistent with any of these interpretations of the promise, and consequently gives no ground for preferring any of them. The promise principle says only that persons who voluntarily invoke their society's rules about promises are morally bound by those rules, whatever they may be. (Farber 1982, 565)

See also Charny (1991, 1818), motivating an exploration of the normative basis for using hypothetical bargains in contract interpretation in part by reference to the indeterminacy of normative theories of contract.

As we argue in subsection C.2(e)(i), it is plausible—given that concerns for autonomy typically motivate those who view contracts as promises—to appeal to individuals' well-being in order to make the promise-keeping theory complete. However, in that case, the notion of fairness reduces entirely to well-being (that is, honoring contracts becomes the command to subject oneself, when entering into contracts, to the set of legal rules that maximizes well-being). Barnett, who is among those motivated by a concern for autonomy, believes that contract law should be concerned with consent as an end in itself. See, for example, Barnett (1986a, 1992b). (His independent theory is one based on "entitlements," and he makes it clear that some other source must define parties' entitlements and provide a justification for them. See also Barnett (1986b), discussing the relationship between rights that individuals may transfer and contract remedies.) Thus, Barnett repeatedly argues for modes of interpretation that will minimize the frequency of instances in which the law does not reflect an actual mutual agreement of the parties, seemingly without any regard for whether the result advances or runs against any or all parties' interests. See, for example, Barnett (1992b, 829), summarizing his position on interpretation, and ibid. (882, 888). We consider this problem further in note 96, where we discuss the failure of contract theorists, including Barnett, to address cases in which their theory conflicts with individuals' well-being and to provide reasons for promoting their notions of fairness at the expense of well-being in such instances.

2. The View That Breach Is Akin to a Tort

We now examine a second notion of fairness, under which the harm caused by a breach of contract to a promisee who has relied on a promise is analogized to the harm caused by a tort to a victim who suffers from an injurer's wrongful act.[25] Fuller and Perdue's famous two-part article provides fuel for this view, which has been advanced in more recent work by Atiyah and others.[26]

Proponents of this view tend to see contract remedies in compensatory terms.[27] However, the concept of compensation is ambiguous in the case of contracts: expectation damages make the victim of a breach whole by reference to a benchmark of performance, whereas reliance damages make the victim whole by reference to the position he would have occupied if no promise had been made.[28] Commentators who believe that contract breach

---

25. Some contracts scholars are also concerned with the benefit promisors may gain at promisees' expense. See, for example, Fuller and Perdue (1936, 53–56). The problems (discussed in the text to follow) with identifying which acts of reliance should be deemed to give rise to liability and what sort of liability is appropriate are similar to the problems with identifying which benefits to promisors give rise to what requirement of restitution.

26. Fuller and Perdue (1936, 1937) and Atiyah (1979, 1981, 1986). See also Gilmore (1974). This view actually has earlier roots; writing before Fuller and Perdue, Cohen described the injurious-reliance theory as the favorite theory of the day. M. Cohen (1933, 578).

A somewhat related view is offered by Raz. He begins by criticizing those who simply see contract law as "based on liability in tort for the prevention of harm[, because it is still necessary for the law to] choose which harms to protect against and which not." Raz (1982, 938). (This criticism is similar to a point we make in the text to follow.) He then distinguishes his own view because he sees contract law as protecting against a distinct set of harms: "harms to the practice of undertaking voluntary obligations and harms resulting from its abuse." Ibid. (Yet it seems to us circular to say that the purpose of contract law is to protect the institution of the making of obligations, that is, of contract.)

27. This outlook is not inevitable, for, as we discuss in chapter III, tort law—to which the analogy is being made—need not be seen in compensatory terms. One might just as well have been led to focus on the punishment of promisors who renege and thereby injure promisees, or on theories that emphasize the relationship between promisees' injuries and promisors' wrongful acts, but such perspectives seem less prominent in the minds of this group of theorists. Nevertheless, one can find in the relevant literature analogues to most of what is raised in the tort context. See, for example, Fuller and Perdue (1936, 56), drawing upon Aristotle's notion of corrective justice. In any event, our argument in section C does not depend on how one chooses to characterize notions of fairness. We do observe that the existence of a close mapping between many notions of fairness in contracts and torts suggests that the criticisms that we raise in our discussion of torts will be applicable here as well (as indeed they are).

28. Compare Corbin (1964, §996), referring to expectation damages as money damages and to reliance damages as restitution. However, as we discuss in note 61, these two measures will be the same in an important set of instances because an aspect of reliance may involve forgoing other contract opportunities.

should be viewed as akin to a tort, however, favor reliance damages,[29] at least in principle.[30]

We also note that the view under consideration suffers from incompleteness because one must first determine the conditions under which various types of reliance by promisees are appropriate in order to know whether compensation should be required and to what extent.[31] That is, one needs

---

29. See, for example, Fuller and Perdue (1936, 52–53). The reason for this choice is not usually made explicit. Reliance damages make reference to the no-contract benchmark, but proponents do not explain why they invoke that benchmark, rather than the performance benchmark. We suspect that the rationale has to do with the lack of an affirmative duty on the part of the promisor to have entered into the contract; the promisor is merely required not to leave the promisee-victim worse off than the promisor found him. Yet it is not uncommon for individuals to take on new or higher duties of care by entering into relationships with others. Thus, even if individuals are deemed to have no affirmative duty to perfect strangers, further argument would be required for applying the same standard to those who have chosen to enter into contractual relationships with each other. For individuals who have embarked on such a voluntary undertaking, it is appropriate to ask what regime they would like to subject themselves to, a question we explore in section C.

Arguably, Friedmann is a commentator who views contract breach as akin to a tort but does not favor reliance damages. We do not classify him in this manner, however, because he presents analogies to intentional torts. Therefore, for present purposes his views seem more like those of promise-keeping theorists, who believe that it is wrong for individuals to break their contracts. See note 14, discussing Friedmann's view.

30. Expectation damages may be favored in practice when reliance damages are hard to measure and expectation damages provide a good proxy measure. Some theorists suggest that expectation and reliance damages will often be nearly the same. See, for example, Fuller and Perdue (1936, 73–75).

31. The very fact that we refer to reliance by promisees rather than by strangers suggests that this entire tort-like approach is parasitic on the promise-keeping approach. See, for example, Fried (1981, 10–11); Fried (1980, 1862–64), arguing, in the course of reviewing Atiyah (1979), that the principle that promises must be kept supplies the ground of commitment that justifies reliance; Barnett (1986a, 275, 315–16); and Craswell (1989, 498–501). Compare Yorio and Thel (1991), arguing that the actual basis for courts' application of promissory estoppel is not in fact Fuller and Perdue's concern about harm to promisees who have relied, but rather involves a decision about enforcing the promises that have been made. However, we have already seen that the promise-keeping approach is itself incomplete.

Another way to put the problem is reminiscent of Coase's discussion of causation. See Coase (1960). To cause harm to the promisee from breach, there are two jointly necessary conditions: the promisee's reliance and the promisor's breach. Thus, one needs some independent basis for determining when promisees should be entitled to rely. See, for example, Atiyah (1981, 64–66). It is often suggested that reliance has to be reasonable, but that term itself begs the question. Moreover, even clearly reasonable reliance is not a sufficient condition for contractual liability. For example, most understandings of "reasonableness" would imply that one may reasonably rely on a weather forecast in deciding to go on a picnic, but it hardly follows that one can sue the forecaster if it unexpectedly rains. One might imagine that other

some independent normative theory, some substantive principle, from which one can determine what contract rules should be chosen. The pertinent literature does not, however, supply such a theory.[32] As is the case with the promise-keeping notion of fairness, this gap makes it difficult to deter-

---

aspects of the definition or the existence of a promise would allow one to avoid these problems, but we find such attempts unsuccessful. For example, MacCormick insists that promises involve not merely reliance but also that "the speaker *intended* the other to rely upon him, or, we may add with equal force, *knew* or *thought it likely* that he would so rely." MacCormick (1972, 66). Of course, weather forecasters surely think it likely that many people will rely on their forecasts; there would be little point in offering forecasts if such reliance was not anticipated.

32. We note that this problem of incompleteness is essentially the same as the one we identified with theories of corrective justice in the torts context. See subsection III.B.2. Hence, the fact that these contract theorists make an analogy to tort does not supply a ready answer. See also Craswell (2000, 128), arguing that "the torts analogy is incomplete without some further account of why its baseline is the appropriate one."

One possible approach, of course, would be to choose legal rules so as to advance individuals' well-being; then, one would compensate those who rely on promises when and to the extent that doing so is welfare maximizing. (And one might not require reliance at all.) One reviewer has suggested that Atiyah's normative view tends to favor such an approach. See, for example, Raz (1982, 918).

In the case of Fuller and Perdue, the reasoning is more obscure. For the most part, they tend to refer to the "purpose" of remedies as protecting the "reliance interest"—Fuller and Perdue (1936, 53–57)—without indicating why it would be desirable to do so. See, for example, Rakoff (1991, 215): "To state that reliance measure damages are awarded to protect the reliance interest self-evidently does not explain a rule in light of its purposes. . . ." As Rakoff observes:

> A further difficulty, at least in epistemological terms, is the "lightness" with which Fuller introduces and defends his normative propositions. . . . The famous, oft-reprinted passages in which he asserts a normative hierarchy, with the restitution interest presenting the strongest claim to judicial relief, and the expectation interest the weakest, cover only about a page of text. In that page, Fuller makes both hypothetical assumptions of value ("If, following Aristotle, we regard the purpose of justice . . ."), and bald assertions ("the promisee who has actually relied . . . certainly presents a more pressing case. . . ."). And then it is over, and the hierarchy is taken as established. (Rakoff 1991, 213)

See also ibid. (214): "Indeed, Fuller never considers the possibility that there might be social policies of the sort he discusses that would support the expectation measure on its own. . . ." In discussing Fuller's position as expressed in Fuller (1941), Atiyah suggests that Fuller "comes very close to saying that all contractual obligations are ultimately referable to prior substantive grounds of duty, and that the contract itself is merely a formal acknowledgment or admission of that fact." Atiyah (1986, 85). Yet this would seem to make all the more clear that such a theory of contract is substantively empty, drawing upon some other source for its content. See also note 26, discussing Raz's theory.

mine the theory's implications and to identify the underlying basis for advancing this notion of fairness.

3. Further Comments on the Literature

Before undertaking our comparison of welfare economics and notions of fairness, we offer three additional remarks about the literature on fairness. First, notions of fairness that bear on the enforcement of contracts appear to have implications that raise questions about the internal coherence of the theories. The reason is that these theories take contracts, and whether contracts have been breached, as given and look solely at whether the resulting remedy seems fair. Accordingly, they do not take into account how the use of a notion of fairness will affect the number of breaches of contract. Yet, as we now explain, it would seem that the breach of a contract is a morally significant event under both types of theories that we consider.[33]

Suppose, for example, that remedies deemed to be fair under the promise-keeping view would make most otherwise sensible promises no longer attractive. It would seem that promise-keeping theorists should be disturbed by such a result because the institution of promise-keeping would have been substantially undermined.[34] Yet such theories do not appear to take such effects into account. And if they did, they would need to specify how the erosion of the usefulness of promises should be traded off against the failure to provide perfectly fair remedies for breach. Making such a determination would necessarily engage the promise-keeping theorists in the sort of instrumental calculus that they reject.

Notions of fairness under which breach is viewed as akin to a tort face a related difficulty.[35] Suppose that, as a consequence of employing the fair remedy, breach is frequent, whereas under some other, unfair remedy, breach is rare. (This situation might arise if the fair remedy provides little deterrence to breach.) Proponents of this notion of fairness view breach as a wrong, yet in the contemplated situation, many wrongs are committed

33. Compare subsection III.B.2, making similar observations about the relevance of consequences of legal rules to notions of fairness in the tort context, and subsection VI.B.2, regarding notions of fair punishment.

34. We say this because promise-keeping theorists motivate their theory by reference to the importance of the institution of promise-keeping. One could, of course, deem promises to be wholly unimportant yet also deem breaches of promises to be important, but the rationale for such a theory seems difficult to imagine.

35. The argument here parallels the one we offer with regard to theories of corrective justice in the torts context. See subsection III.B.2.

under the fair regime and few under the unfair one.[36] Current theories do not address this problem. Were they to take it into account, they too would need to specify how to make tradeoffs between the character of ex ante behavior and the fairness of ex post remedies for breach—an inquiry that seems foreign to the basic nature of these theories.

The foregoing discussion of how these notions of fairness lead one to ignore ex ante concerns about behavior does not imply that it would be impossible to construct much more elaborate, qualitatively different theories of fairness. It does, however, indicate that the existing theories have not been examined in a manner that allows one to appreciate their implications. Moreover, we note that the modifications required to complete the two theories would make them each much closer to the approach of welfare economics.

We now offer a second observation about the relevant literature. Many contributors see themselves as engaged in making positive (descriptive) claims about what notion of fairness is most consistent with the common law of contracts, not necessarily about what notion of fairness is normatively attractive. This descriptive focus is most apparent in the work of Fuller and Perdue; the point of much of their argument is that then-existing contract doctrine protected the reliance (rather than expectation) interest to a greater extent than had been appreciated.[37] This focus is also evident in Atiyah's book, *The Rise and Fall of Freedom of Contract,* which traces the history of

36. That is, we understand fairness theorists to view wrongful acts negatively, which stands in contrast to the outlook under which a state of affairs characterized by widespread wrongdoing is taken to be perfectly fair, as long as all wrongdoers are made to pay the correct amount for their wrongful acts.

37. Their interest in positive analysis is especially apparent in the second of their two articles, which focuses entirely on describing how existing law reflects their view. See Fuller and Perdue (1937). Indeed, they conclude the presentation of their positive claim about contract doctrine by stating: "This makes it necessary to consider whether a wider recognition of the reliance interest would be desirable." Ibid. (418). This pronouncement indicates that they do not see their preceding discussion as constituting a normative argument, but rather as raising a normative question—albeit one on which they clearly have a view, favoring recognition of reliance as a distinct promissory interest. See ibid. (420). See also Rakoff (1991, 230–31), suggesting that the reason Fuller and Perdue take the position that expectation damages should be a ceiling on compensation for the reliance interest, in spite of their belief that the reliance principle is normatively superior, is their desire to support rules that fit well with existing court decisions; and ibid. (245), claiming that the project of the Fuller and Perdue articles was to show that the pattern of legal doctrine was, after all, consistent with the reliance theory previously examined by Cohen.

English contract doctrine.[38] There are strong descriptive aspects in much of the other writing in this area as well.[39] To the extent that the fairness theories are only descriptive, they are irrelevant to our inquiry because our claim is purely normative, involving how legal rules should be evaluated.

However, this literature—including the work of Fuller and Perdue as well as that of Atiyah—is not entirely positive; it also advances normative claims.[40] And surely it is the case that these bodies of literature are generally understood by legal academics as offering accounts of how contract rules

38. Atiyah (1979). See ibid. (6): "In suggesting that these ideas are, at least intuitively or implicitly, gaining much ground today, and in advocating open recognition of these facts, it does not follow that I approve or disapprove of them."; and ibid. (779), referring, as he concludes, to various policy questions and stating that the task of addressing them "is one to which I hope to return."

39. See, for example, Fried (1981, 1), presenting as a central claim that "[t]he promise principle . . . is the moral basis of contract law" (emphasis added); ibid. (6), stating his intent to show that the promise conception "generates the structure and accounts for the complexities of contract doctrine"; Gilmore (1974, 4), posing the central question of his book as: "Whatever happened to the doctrine of consideration?"; ibid. (87), beginning his conclusion by stating: "Speaking descriptively, we might say that what is happening is that 'contract' is being reabsorbed into the mainstream of 'tort.'"; ibid. (101): "This has been a study in what might be called the process of doctrinal disintegration."; and Barnett (1986a, 270–71, 318–19), arguing that his consent theory best explains contract law's objective approach to interpretation and doctrines involving excuses. In addition, much of Barnett's discussion of contract theory is taxonomic, relying on how contract law is distinct from tort law. (For example, he notes that contract law is concerned with voluntary transfer whereas tort law regulates involuntary transfer.) See ibid.

40. For example, in addition to his historical account of contract doctrine, Atiyah has written on the normative theory of contract law. See Atiyah (1981, 1986). See also Raz (1982, 919), criticizing Atiyah's Promises, Morals, and Law for not being clear on whether the aim of the book is positive or normative. Fuller and Perdue, despite their explicit disclaimer at the conclusion of their two-part series that they have not advanced a normative position (see the quotation in note 37), seem, in much of their first part, to offer a normative defense of basing contract law on protection of the reliance interest. See also Fuller and Perdue (1937, 420), stating a normative view at the end of their article that presents positive analysis. (For further discussion of their normative argument, see note 32.) Fried often speaks in normative terms. See, for example, Fried (1981, 6), stating that solutions implied by the promise principle are in accord with "decency and common sense as well"; and ibid. (7), deriving the promise principle from the liberal ideal and discussing what "morality requires." Furthermore, Fried's book is generally critical of the doctrine of consideration, indicating that his account is not entirely a descriptive one. The article in which Barnett presents his theory of contracts purports to be normative, in spite of the strong positive claims for his own theory and his criticism of other theories for failing to be consistent with existing doctrine. See Barnett (1986a, 270 and n.4).

should be chosen.[41] Accordingly, it is important to compare welfare economics and fairness-based analysis as methods of evaluating contract law.

Finally, we have described notions of fairness concerning contract enforcement without regard to considerations of welfare, but it should be emphasized that most analysts who believe that legal rules should be fair would
also give weight to the effects of legal rules on individuals' well-being. Such
mixed views are evident when a promise-keeping theorist would allow a
promise to be broken if the consequences of keeping it would be extremely
undesirable,[42] or when one who views contract breach as akin to a tort would
permit the use of a less preferred remedy (say, expectation damages instead
of reliance damages) in cases in which the cost of determining the ideal
remedy would be excessive.[43] The criticism that we offer in the following
section is applicable to these mixed views, but only to the extent that they
lead one to favor rules that differ from those that would be chosen under
welfare economics.

C. Welfare Economics versus Fairness and the Enforcement
of Contracts

Let us consider a simple situation in which a seller and a buyer contemplate
entering into an agreement about the production and delivery of, say, a
custom-made cabinet.[44] We suppose that there is uncertainty about the cost
of manufacture of the cabinet; it may not be known how long it will take
to construct or what the price of wood will be. For concreteness, we assume
that the value of the cabinet to the buyer is $200 and that there are only
two possible levels of production cost that the seller may incur: a typical
level of $100, the probability of which is 90 percent; and an unusual, high
level of $500, the likelihood of which is 10 percent. We also assume for
definiteness that when the parties make a contractual agreement, they will

41. See, for example, Farber (1982, 561), describing Fried's *Contract As Promise* as arguing
that contracts should be enforced for moral reasons, and Katz (1988, 541), describing Fuller
and Perdue's article as making both descriptive and normative claims, the latter being that
"the reliance interest, rather than the expectation interest, was the appropriate object of judicial
protection."

42. See, for example, note 17, quoting Ross.

43. See note 30.

44. We consider an item that is custom made, because with a standardized product (say,
a toaster) there could be an instantaneous exchange of money for the product, and the issues
we address in our illustration would be unlikely to arise.

bargain to a price that splits equally their expected gains from contracting (though our general conclusions would hold as well under any division of the gains).[45] Finally, to keep matters simple, we ignore various complications, such as the possibility that parties are risk averse, that they may be able to renegotiate after breach, and that remedies will influence actions taken by the buyer in reliance on the contract.[46] We also set aside problems that may arise when one party is not fully informed (but we discuss this issue in subsection D.2).

This example serves to represent any situation in which a contract for production of any sort is contemplated and uncertainty exists in the environment.[47] Using this example, we consider first "complete" contracts—those containing specific, separate provisions for all possible contingencies—and then "incomplete" contracts.[48] Examining both types of contracts will furnish

45. See note 55.

46. In chapter III, on torts, we extend our discussion to consider the case in which individuals are risk averse, both when insurance is and is not available. See section III.D. Were we similarly to extend our analysis in the present context of contract remedies, we would reach analogous conclusions (namely, that when insurance is available and operates perfectly, the analysis is equivalent to that in the risk-neutral case; when it is not, a welfare economic analysis would take into account risk-bearing costs, which could favor different legal rules, but the comparison of welfare economics and notions of fairness would be similar). On the analysis of risk aversion and contract breach, see, for example, Polinsky (1983) and Shavell (1980a, 487–88; 1984, 127–28, 146–47). Renegotiation raises different issues. If renegotiation always occurs and is costless, then any remedy will lead to the same welfare-maximizing result, as well as the same distributive impact on parties, in a model with no reliance. Otherwise, in addition to the effects we identify, we would have to consider how different remedies influence bargaining, which in more complex settings (such as when parties make reliance expenditures) would in turn influence behavior. See, for example, Aghion, Dewatripont, and Rey (1994), Edlin and Reichelstein (1996), O. Hart (1987), O. Hart and Moore (1988), Rogerson (1984), and Shavell (1984, 141–45). With regard to reliance in the absence of renegotiation, remedies that lead to optimal breach decisions tend to induce excessive reliance. See, for example, Shavell (1980a, 477–83, 485–87).

In each case, welfare economics allows one to relax a simplifying assumption, determine the consequent effects on behavior, and assess individuals' well-being. See page 197, noting that, when our assumptions are relaxed, different remedies may well become desirable under welfare economics. In contrast, the aforementioned complications ordinarily are not considered in expositions of notions of fairness, and we are unsure about how various fairness-based analyses should be altered if these additional factors are to be taken into account.

47. Even though uncertainty is not emphasized in the philosophical or legal literature on notions of fairness, it plays a central role in our analysis both because it is important in actual contract problems and because it is essential to consider if one is to understand the relationship between welfare economics and notions of fairness.

48. Our analytical discussion parallels the more general analysis in Shavell (1980a, 1984).

insight into the differences between analysis guided by welfare economics
and that based on notions of fairness.

1. Complete Contracts

(a) Description. By a complete contract, we mean, as just stated, a contract in
which the parties specify separately what their duties are in every contingency
that could arise.[49] At a conceptual level, the notion of a complete contract is
comprehensive; in principle, a complete contract provides for literally every
contingency imaginable. Of course, as a practical matter, contracts do not make
specific provisions for all potentially relevant contingencies, which is why we
examine the case of incomplete contracts at length in subsection 2. Nevertheless,
the complete contract is a valuable conceptual construct, both in economic
analysis (where the concept was developed) and, as we will see, in examining
normative approaches to the formulation of contract law.

In our example, we have intentionally kept matters simple by examining
a case involving only two contingencies: normal production cost and high
production cost. A complete contract in this instance is one that states
whether the seller must produce the cabinet if he learns that the production
cost will be $100 and whether he must produce it if he learns that the cost
will be $500.[50] We will consider two possible complete contracts: one calling

49. To clarify, our notion of a complete contract is one that the parties would make
when there are no constraints in specifying separate provisions for each and every contingency.
Note that a contract might be "complete" in the sense that it has no literal gaps, but it may
still reflect the inability of the parties to write separate provisions for contingencies that matter
to them. For example, a contract might require a single action, such as the delivery of a good,
in all contingencies and thus not have any gaps; yet because it would be too costly to draft
the necessary exceptions or to determine their applicability in court, this requirement of a
single action may cover some contingencies in which the action is undesirable. We emphasize
that, when we use the term "complete contract," we mean that it is feasible and costless to
make different provisions for different contingencies whenever doing so might be desirable.
Likewise, in subsection 2 we use the term "incomplete contract" to refer to cases in which
such specification is not possible.

50. We assume that the seller learns the production cost *before* he actually begins the
production process. Sometimes, this assumption is apposite; for example, the seller will learn
what the price of wood is before he buys it. However, it could be that the seller will begin
his project before learning all relevant costs: He might purchase wood knowing its cost but
still be uncertain about the cost of varnish until after he begins. It would be straightforward
to consider more complicated situations in which the seller first sinks some resources into
performance before learning how various uncertainties are resolved, but this exercise would
not add to our understanding of the fundamental difference between notions of fairness and
welfare economics in the contractual context.

for production only when the cost is $100 and one calling for production both when the cost is $100 and when it is $500.[51] In subsection (b), we assume that whatever contract the parties make will definitely be enforced and that there are no legal costs involved in enforcement. We introduce the standard legal remedies for contract breach and consider enforcement costs in subsection (c).

(b) Examination of Different Contracts. Let us begin with the contract calling for performance only when the production cost is $100. The buyer's expected value of performance will be 90% × $200 = $180.[52] (In the remaining 10 percent of the cases, in which the production cost is $500, there is no performance.) Thus, the buyer would be willing to pay up to $180 to enter into such a contract. Similarly, the seller's expected cost of performance will be 90% × $100 = $90, so he would be willing to enter into such a contract as long as the price is at least $90. What will the contract price be? Given our assumption that the parties split the gains from contracting, the price will be $135 because this amount is midway between the seller's cost of $90 and the buyer's valuation of $180. This price allocates $45 of the gain from contracting to each party; the buyer's gain net of the price paid will be $180 − $135, and the seller's gain net of his expected costs will be $135 − $90. (For simplicity, we assume throughout that the price is paid at the outset, when the parties make their contract, and is not refunded, except implicitly, in the context of some of our later discussions, as part of a damages award.[53])

Now consider the other contract, which requires performance in both contingencies. In this contract, the buyer obtains a certain benefit of $200, the value of performance. The seller's expected costs are (90% × $100) + (10% × $500) = $140. In this case, a price of $170 splits the surplus from contracting; each party will expect to gain $30 from such a contract.

Observe that both parties expect to be better off under the first contract, which calls for performance only when the production cost is $100. Each gains $45 under that contract, rather than $30 under the contract calling

---

51. It will be easy for the reader to verify that the two parties would never choose a contract calling for production only when the production cost is $500, and that all of our conclusions would hold were we to consider this type of contract. Finally, a contract calling for no production under any contingency is equivalent to not contracting at all, so we do not separately consider it (because, in our examples, the contracts that we consider are better for both parties than not contracting).

52. Because we have assumed the parties to be risk neutral, it is sufficient to focus on expected values; we often will omit the qualifier "expected" hereafter.

53. None of our conclusions depend on this assumption. See note 60.

for performance all of the time. Hence, the contract under which the seller performs only when the production cost is $100 is the contract that they will make.[54]

The underlying reason for the conclusion that the parties will not want a contract calling for performance when the production cost is $500 is that the seller's cost of $500 exceeds the buyer's gain of $200 in that situation. Thus, both parties will be made better off if any term calling for performance in this contingency is changed to one excusing performance: the seller is willing to reduce the price by up to $50 to be rid of the requirement to perform (because 10 percent of the time he thereby saves $500), and the buyer will allow the term to be changed if the price is reduced by at least $20 (because 10 percent of the time he forgoes a benefit of $200). In our example, the price is reduced by $35 (from $170 to $135), which simply splits the difference between the seller's savings of $50 and the buyer's loss of $20.

More generally, it can be shown that both parties will prefer a contract calling for the seller to perform whenever the production cost is less than the value of performance to the buyer, and excusing the seller from performance whenever the production cost exceeds the value of performance. Any other type of contract would be rejected by both parties because they would both be worse off than under the contract that we have identified. (It is of particular relevance to our later discussion that even the buyer is better off under this contract than under one in which the seller also performs when production costs are high; this is because the buyer would have to pay more than performance is worth to him to induce the seller to commit to undertake such performance.) The argument demonstrating that this general statement

54. As should be clear from the text, in the present setting in which we ask what contract the parties would like to enter—and, later, how they would like it to be enforced—the relevant perspective is an ex ante one, in which the effect of different contracts and contract law rules is assessed at the time the parties contemplate entering into a contract. It is always possible when there is uncertainty that one or the other party would prefer a different rule ex post, finding a different outcome to his advantage. For example, if the cost of performance rises above the contract price but stays below the value of performance to the promisee, the promisor would wish that he had not entered into the contract; given that he has, he would prefer to breach and only have to return any payments made by the promisee, rather than being subject to specific performance or being required to pay expectation damages (or, for that matter, performing the contract). But this ex post preference does not bear on the contract or legal regime that the parties should choose. For further discussion of why the ex ante perspective is appropriate, see subsection VIII.C.1. See also note 86 in chapter VIII, indicating that taking an ex ante perspective is not actually necessary to our argument.

is true is essentially the one given in the example just discussed.[55] We call the complete contract that both parties would want to make the mutually ideal complete contract.

(c) *Effects of the Legal Rules.* Here, we consider standard contract remedies.[56] While in subsection (b) we took performance for granted, now we focus on how the choice of contract remedies affects performance of the parties' mutually ideal complete contract—a contract specifying production if and only if the cost is $100[57] Also, we allow for the possibility that there may be legal costs incurred when enforcing these rules and that the level of legal costs under each rule may differ; however, for convenience, most of our analysis focuses on the case in which there are no legal costs of enforcement.

---

55. For the general proof, see Shavell (1980a). The argument about when performance is value maximizing in the case of a complete contract is true no matter how many production cost possibilities there are, even though in our example there are only two, and it continues to be true when parties are risk averse. With regard to risk-averse parties, see Shavell (1984, 127).

The reason that the parties will never want a contract in which the seller must perform when production cost exceeds the buyer's value is illustrated in our example. We did not illustrate the reason why the parties will never want a contract in which the seller does not perform when the production cost is less than the buyer's valuation. In such a case, the buyer would be willing to pay sufficiently more to the seller to induce him to agree to produce in the contingency in question.

We have assumed for convenience that the division of gain from contracting is always 50%–50%. But any other division, say 90%–10%, would lead to the same conclusion with regard to the optimal contract terms. The reason is that, as long as each party will receive some given fraction of the surplus from the contract, each party will prefer those contract terms that maximize the surplus created by the contract.

56. In a sense, legal remedies for breach are not separate from the subject of our preceding subsection, in which we determined what would be the parties' mutually ideal complete contract. The reason is that, whatever legal rule is best for the parties, one can think of this legal rule as being specified as part of the mutually ideal complete contract. After all, the definition of a complete contract is one that fully provides for every contingency, and nonperformance is one of the possible contingencies. We find it convenient, however, to abstract from this point in much of our discussion, although we occasionally return to it.

57. In this subsection, we do not examine the complete contract calling for performance in every instance because that contract is not the one that the parties prefer and because discussion of it would not be very illuminating. The only point of interest with regard to such a contract is that damages remedies, notably expectation damages, would not always induce performance because the promisor would rather breach and pay damages of $200 than perform when the production cost is $500. As we discuss in subsection 2 on incomplete contracts, the expectation damages remedy essentially converts the contract requiring performance in every contingency into one that does not require performance when costs are high.

First, consider specific performance, which requires a breaching party to perform the contract. By stipulation, this remedy enforces the parties' complete contract, so the parties would be satisfied with this remedy. Observe, moreover, that specific enforcement of the mutually ideal complete contract does not expose the seller to the risk of having to perform when doing so is expensive, for the very terms of this contract already state that the seller does not have to perform when the production cost is $500.[58] Note also that, although one might be tempted to view the promisee—the buyer—as suffering injury from disappointed expectations in the case in which the production cost is high, such a view would be misleading: under the mutually ideal complete contract (which, recall, is the one preferred by the buyer as well), it is understood from the outset that the seller will not perform when costs are high.

Under expectation damages, a breaching party is required to pay damages equal to the reduction in the other party's valuation caused by the breach. Expectation damages also lead the promisor to honor the mutually ideal complete contract. In the present example, breach would harm the buyer by $200,[59] which would be the amount of expectation damages.[60] And

58. Relatedly, there is no concern about the possibility of a punitive sanction being imposed upon the seller because, in this case, there never would be a breach. The only effect of sanctions is to provide deterrence. Such a depiction may strike the reader as implausible, but this is because our contrary intuitions arise from the incompleteness of real contracts, the topic of subsection 2.

59. To simplify the discussion, we assume that there is no way that the buyer can mitigate damages; alternatively, the value of $200 can be understood to be the net value of performance, after taking into account the possibility of mitigation.

60. We note that damages are $200 because we have assumed that the contract price is paid by the buyer at the outset (and is not refundable, except implicitly in some instances as part of damages payments). As a result, if the buyer receives performance, he receives something worth $200 and pays nothing at that point; hence, if there is a breach, he must receive $200 in damages to be made whole.

If we had assumed that the contract price were paid at the time of performance, expectation damages would be different. For instance, if the contract price under this assumption were $150 (which it would be if the price were due at the time of performance and payable only in the event of performance), then the buyer would receive a net benefit from performance of $200 − $150 = $50, so damages for breach would be $50. In that case, the seller would reason as follows: If he performs, he incurs a cost of C (which in our example could be $100 or $500, although under the ideal contract, it would be $100 whenever performance is required) and receives $150, so his profit is $150 − C; if the seller breaches, he pays $50, which is to say, his profit is −$50; thus, the seller will perform when $150 − C exceeds −$50, or when C is less than $200. His behavior is therefore the same as it is if the price is paid at the outset and expectation damages are, accordingly, $200.

when damages are $200, the seller would not breach; he would prefer to perform at a cost of $100 rather than pay damages of $200. This characteristic of expectation damages—that it leads to performance exactly when called for in the mutually ideal complete contract—is general. As we observe above, the parties' mutually ideal complete contract entails production when and only when the production cost is less than the buyer's valuation; under expectation damages, which equal the buyer's valuation, the seller will choose to perform any such obligation because the cost of performance will be less than expectation damages.

Under reliance damages, there might not be a sufficient incentive to induce performance of the mutually ideal complete contract. By definition, reliance damages are set to restore the promisee's economic position to the level it would have been but for his having entered into the contract. In our example, the buyer does not take any actions in reliance on the contract.[61] However, because we have assumed that the buyer paid the contract price at the outset, reliance damages would require the seller who breaches to return that initial payment to the buyer. Here, that price would be $135. Because this amount exceeds the seller's production cost of $100, he would prefer to perform the contract, just as under expectation damages. But reliance damages do not always operate in this manner. For instance, if the high production cost had been $180 rather than $500, the mutually ideal complete contract—which the parties definitely want enforced—would call for performance when the production cost is $180, because this cost is less than the value to the buyer of $200. In this instance, the use of reliance damages

---

61. More generally, reliance may involve two types of activity: forgoing other contracting opportunities at the initial stage and making investments after the contract is formed, in order best to take advantage of the opportunity created by the contract. We note that reliance of the former type is quite common; indeed, if there are other sellers who would have offered equally good deals but who would not have breached, the buyer's reliance damages—understood in the manner just described—would equal expectation damages. See, for example, Fuller and Perdue (1936, 60). We choose to focus on the more interesting case in which reliance damages are different from expectation damages. Our assumption corresponds to a case in which the seller is uniquely able to meet the buyer's needs.

With regard to the latter type of reliance (investments made subsequent to entering into a contract induced by the making of the contract)—the type most typically envisioned in discussions of reliance damages—our assumption that no subsequent investments are made is a simplification that has no effect on our analysis. Suppose, for example, that the buyer's subsequent reliance expenditures are $10 rather than $0. Then, reliance damages would be $10, plus return of the initial payment; this level of damages would still be insufficient to induce performance in some cases, including the numerical example that we discuss in the text to follow.

would not be sufficient to enforce the parties' mutually ideal complete contract.[62]

Now consider the legal costs of administering different contract remedies, which we assume to be borne by the parties and thus to influence their
well-being. It should be clear that, if the legal costs differed sufficiently
among the legal rules, any of the rules might be in the parties' interests. For
example, both expectation damages and specific performance serve to enforce the ideal contract; whichever is cheaper to use would be to the parties'
advantage.[63] However, if the legal costs of using reliance damages were sig-

---

62. See Shavell (1980a, 479–80, 486–87). This result with respect to reliance damages
would surely follow in our example if the seller's payment in the event of breach equaled the
previously specified contract price of $135, which is less than the production cost of $180.
But in the present context, the seller will have to return the contract price (by paying reliance
damages) when production costs are high. (In the prior case, the complete contract specifies
that there is no obligation to perform in the high-cost scenario; hence, there would be no
breach on account of nonperformance, and no payment of damages.) Nevertheless, at the
price that splits the surplus, which we now show to be $150, the seller would breach when
the production cost is $180.

To demonstrate that the price will be $150 under reliance damages, observe that if the
seller keeps the payment of the contract price (P) and incurs costs of $100 in 90% of the
cases and returns the payment of the contract price in the other 10% of the cases, his expected
benefit will be 90% $\times$ (P − $100). The buyer's expected benefit will be 90% $\times$ ($200 − P).
Thus, the surplus will be 90% $\times$ ($200 − $100), or $90, each party's share will be $45, and
the price that yields this surplus is $150. (For instance, the buyer's expected benefit will be
90% $\times$ ($200 − $150), which is $45.)

In addition, let us confirm the claim that reliance damages cannot sustain the mutually
ideal contract. To do so, consider the possibility that there would be performance when the
production cost is $180. If there would be performance, the seller's production costs would
increase by an expected amount of $18 (10% $\times$ $180), so that total expected production costs
would be $90 + $18, or $108. The buyer's value would be $200 because there would always
be performance, so the surplus would be $92. The contract price that splits the surplus of
$92 would be $154, which would give $46 of the surplus to each party. But if the price were
$154, reliance damages would not be sufficient to induce performance when the production
cost was $180. (In contrast, under expectation damages, which are $200, production would
be induced in this case. Thus, under expectation damages, the price would be $154 and each
party's surplus would be $46, $1 higher than under reliance damages.)

63. For example, in some instances—such as the transfer of land—specific performance
may be easy to effect. However, in others—like labor contracts requiring intense supervision—
implementing the remedy may be costly. Similarly, expectation damages sometimes will be
inexpensive to measure—when there is a reference market price, such as when the buyer will
cover. And in other instances, measurement of expectation damages will be expensive—when
the good is unique and lost profits are difficult to ascertain.

For simplicity, we assume that all legal costs are borne by the parties. The allocation of
costs between the parties is not important because an unequal allocation would be counterbal-
anced by a price adjustment.

nificantly lower[64] and this remedy performed nearly as well, reliance damages would be best for the parties.[65]

(d) Choice of Legal Rules Using Welfare Economics. As shown in subsection (b), both parties are best off under the mutually ideal complete contract if performance will occur as specified by the contract. Thus, any legal rule that ensures performance of this contract will be best for the parties and, accordingly, would be selected under a welfare economic approach (in the absence of administrative costs). As we explain in subsection (c), both specific performance and expectation damages achieve this result. Reliance damages may induce performance in some instances, but they will not do so in general.

But when legal costs are significant, any of the contract remedies might be the best rule for both parties. In particular, reliance damages might be best.

We observe that, in the present context, both the buyer and the seller are identically affected by the choice of legal rule.[66] Through adjustment of the contract price, the two parties share the gains and losses attributable to contract remedies. Thus, whatever legal rule and whatever factual assumptions are considered, the buyer's and the seller's rankings of the rules will be the same. And these rankings, we emphasize, will be the same as the ranking under welfare economics.[67]

(e) Choice of Legal Rules Using Notions of Fairness. The choice of legal rules using notions of fairness will depend on the type of fairness notion under consideration. Promise-keeping notions naturally favor specific performance.[68] Notions of fairness that seek to compensate the victim of breach for his injury,

---

64. Measuring reliance damages may entail low costs (such as in our example, which includes no acts of reliance and therefore requires only returning the purchase price) or high costs (when the buyer undertakes many activities and it is difficult to determine which were done in reliance on the contract).

65. It may seem inconsistent with our definition of the mutually ideal complete contract that reliance damages could be best for the parties even if such damages do not fully enforce that contract. But, as we explain in note 56, in principle the complete contract would encompass the choice of remedy, an important feature when remedies are themselves costly or otherwise problematic.

66. In this respect, our analysis parallels that in the reciprocal context with torts. See subsections III.C.1 and III.D.1.

67. In the simple setting under discussion, this result is general in nature and, in particular, does not depend on our assumption that parties split the surplus equally. See note 55.

68. However, as we note in subsection B.1, some legal scholars who endorse the promise-keeping view favor expectation damages instead.

which proponents of this view take to be the cost of reliance on the contract, are understood to favor reliance damages.

(*f*) *Why the Choice of Legal Rules Should Be Based Only on Individuals' Well-Being.* Our main point is that there is an important objection to fairness-based evaluation, namely, that following its prescriptions rather than those of welfare economics can only make everyone prospectively worse off. As we observe in subsection (d), both parties will have the same ranking of the legal rules (any ranking is possible), and welfare economics requires choosing the legal rule under which each party to the contract is best off. But, as we state in subsection (e), notions of fairness are understood to favor particular remedies; for example, the approach that seeks to provide compensation to promisees who have relied on a contract favors reliance damages, even when specific performance or expectation damages would be best for the parties. Whenever a notion of fairness calls for a different outcome from that under welfare economics, both parties prospectively will be made worse off. Therefore, to the extent that a notion of fairness does not produce the same results as welfare economics, it is objectionable.[69]

We will now explore the extent to which each of the two notions of fairness is likely to conflict with welfare economics in the context of complete contracts and what, if anything, might be gained by pursuing notions of fairness at the expense of individuals' well-being.

(*i*) *In Relation to Promise-Keeping.* When contracts are complete, the prescriptions of promise-keeping notions of fairness tend to align with those of welfare economics.[70] As we explain in subsection (c), the parties always would want obligations to perform under the mutually ideal complete contract to be enforced. This can be paraphrased by saying that they would like to be committed to keeping their promises. And that, in turn, is what the promise-keeping

---

69. See note 54, discussing the ex ante perspective employed in our argument. This objection is, of course, the same one that we raised to notions of fairness in the reciprocal case with torts. See subsections III.C.1 and III.D.1. As before, the socially optimal rule will not depend upon distributive concerns because there is no distributive effect.

70. We remind the reader, however, that the promise that the parties would make, in the form of the mutually ideal complete contract, is not an unconditional obligation for the seller to construct the cabinet but instead is a conditional promise to do so when and only when the production cost is lower than the value of performance to the buyer. This distinction is important in subsection 2, which addresses the more realistic, practically important case of incomplete contracts, in which the promise-keeping approach conflicts with welfare economics.

notion requires. The naturally favored remedy, specific performance, accomplishes this directly.[71]

In these circumstances, adhering to the promise-keeping notion of fairness will necessarily maximize individuals' well-being, so there will be no conflict between welfare economics and that notion of fairness. This alignment in the context of complete contracts is not a mere accident. After all, many who view the keeping of promises as central to contract law are motivated by concerns for individual autonomy; similarly, allowing individuals freely to arrange their affairs in their own interests necessarily results in the maximization of their well-being in the present context. Because only mutually advantageous, welfare-promoting promises will be made, and the fostering of autonomy implies enforcement of all promises, preservation of autonomy serves as a proxy principle for identifying rules that promote individuals' well-being in the case of complete contracts.[72]

The agreement between the promise-keeping notion of fairness and welfare economics, however, is only partial. As we note in subsection (c), when the legal costs of implementing specific performance are sufficiently high, expectation damages or reliance damages might better serve the parties'. interests.[73] In that case, pursuing this notion of fairness—which amounts to insisting on specific performance[74]—would conflict with the prescriptions of welfare economics and, accordingly, would make everyone worse off.

Moreover, it is hard to understand what social value would be served by such a result. Indeed, requiring the use of a remedy that hurts both parties—by substituting an inferior enforcement mechanism for the one that they would have preferred—does not even seem consistent with the principle of autonomy, on which the promise-keeping notion is often premised.[75]

---

71. We also explain that expectation damages, favored by some legal scholars who advance the promise-keeping view, induce the promisor to perform the parties' mutually ideal complete contract.

72. Atiyah makes a similar point from a different perspective. He argues that writers who have found the common law of contracts to be efficient may have really been observing a system that was meant to advance autonomy. See Atiyah (1986, 152–53).

73. See also page 197, indicating that, when various of our assumptions are relaxed, different remedies may be mutually beneficial.

74. Under the view that promise-keeping implies expectation damages, there would be a conflict whenever reliance damages or specific performance was the superior remedy.

75. Arguably, however, the two approaches can still be reconciled. As we state in note 56, the parties' ideal contract can be regarded as encompassing a specification of the remedy for breach (as well as stating the conditions under which performance is required). Moreover, the remedy they would specify will be the one that maximizes their well-being. Thus, if a notion of fairness indeed requires enforcing the parties' complete contract, including the provision on enforcement—*even when that provision conflicts with the remedy that the theory is believed to*

(ii) In Relation to the View That Breach Is Akin to a Tort. Other notions of fairness and contract enforcement, notably those requiring that buyers be compensated through the award of reliance damages, may well lead to outcomes under which both parties are worse off. Put simply, the reason is that reliance damages are not always sufficient to enforce the parties' mutually ideal complete contract.[76] (In a modified version of our example, performance is not induced when it costs $180, which exceeds the contract price but is still lower than the value of performance to the buyer, thereby making performance beneficial.)

Again, it is difficult to understand what is accomplished by pursuing the notions of fairness under consideration. The main concern behind reliance-based theories seems to be the protection of innocent promisees—here, the buyer. Yet the buyer is worse off when the favored reliance damages rule is chosen in the present context, because it results in too little performance by promisors.

A second concern underlying the preference for reliance damages over expectation damages might be to avoid punishing promisors. According to this argument, only the reliance interest is worthy of protection; hence, imposing a greater sanction would punish more than is appropriate in a contractual setting involving an ordinary breach. But, as we have already explained, sellers too are worse off if damages are below expectation damages: ex ante, sellers cannot enter into as favorable a set of agreements with buyers because buyers will anticipate the prospect of excessive breach.

---

require—pursuing that notion of fairness will not conflict with the prescription of welfare economics; instead, the fairness approach will dissolve completely into the welfare economic approach. (We will elaborate this point in subsection 2, on incomplete contracts.) Unfortunately, proponents of promise-based fairness theories do not recognize that their own analysis favors rules that may oppose both parties' interests; nor do they employ a mode of analysis that in principle would allow one to determine the best rule from the perspective of the parties' mutually ideal complete contract. These observations are consistent with our suggestion that the pursuit of notions of fairness by legal academics—here, a notion of fairness that may not even be in fundamental conflict with welfare economics—tends to lead analysts astray by focusing attention on the particular characteristics of situations that are deemed to be of intrinsic importance rather than on the basic ways that legal rules will affect individuals' well-being.

76. It is also possible that the legal costs of determining reliance damages would be so large as to make parties worse off than under some other remedy. In addition, Fuller and Perdue, and some others known to favor protecting only the reliance interest, have suggested that expectation damages will sometimes equal or approximate reliance damages. See, for example, Fuller and Perdue (1936, 73–75). But they do not address how problematic reliance damages would have to be (and thus, as we show here, how much worse off both parties would have to be) before they would be willing to deviate from what they believe to be the fairer rule.

Thus, whether the analyst wishes to be fair to promisees, to promisors, or to both, it is hard to see how the use of reliance damages as a matter of principle leads to fair treatment.[77] Concerns for individuals' well-being—that of both promisors and promisees—may well be at the root of scholars' support for the reliance conception of fairness, but our analysis suggests that pursuing such concerns directly will in fact be more successful.[78]

(iii) Summary. The prescriptions of notions of fairness may conflict with those of welfare economics, and whenever they do, pursuing notions of fairness will make everyone worse off. It should be apparent that this objection does not depend on the particular notions of fairness we have considered. The reason is that, in the present setting, welfare economics always favors whatever rule makes both contracting parties better off than does any alternative; hence, whatever the notion of fairness is, it will make everyone worse off any time it conflicts with the prescriptions of welfare economics. Moreover, this point applies equally to mixed views that accord weight both to notions of fairness and to the effects of legal rules on individuals' well-being: as long as some weight is given to a notion of fairness, one will sometimes be led to choose legal rules

77. Use of reliance damages rather than expectation damages does accomplish the purpose of being more lenient to those promisors who breach. But, as we have already discussed, all promisors are worse off ex ante, which is the proper perspective in this context. See note 54. See also note 85 and subsection VIII.C.1. Yet one may be concerned about mitigating the extent of the loss for promisors who are unlucky ex post. That is, using a lower measure of damages is disadvantageous to promisors as a group, but it is beneficial ex post to the occasional promisor who suffers bad luck. As we discuss in the torts chapter of this book, such a concern would make sense only if parties were risk averse, but a welfare economic analysis fully incorporates this factor. See section III.D. See also note 46, incorporating risk aversion in the contract setting, and subsection VIII.C.1, discussing ex post bad luck generally.

78. There is another argument that could be offered in favor of reliance damages, one opposite to that which seems implicit in the discussions by proponents of this view of fairness. Reliance damages might be seen as furthering the purpose of punishing promisors who induce reliance and then breach, for insisting upon the use of the value-reducing remedy of reliance damages does punish promisors, as we have noted. However, not only does this approach punish promisees as well, but it also yields results that seem perverse from this alternative perspective: Ex post, those promisors who do in fact breach pay *less* than under expectation damages. The punishment is applied ex ante, through a less favorable contract price that reflects the prospect of value-reducing breach; this punishment is incurred by all the promisors who do not breach (as well as by promisees). Finally, it is unclear why one would wish to punish promisors who breach in this setting, for here the reason for breach is merely the bad luck of being faced with atypically high production costs. Compare subsection III.D.1(f)(ii) and note 111 in chapter III, discussing in the tort context the moral arbitrariness of punishing individuals merely for bad luck.

that reduce everyone's well-being.[79] Finally, as we emphasize above,[80] logically consistent adherence to a notion of fairness thus entails the idea that it may be socially desirable for all individuals, here both of the contracting parties, to be made worse off—a conclusion that we find troubling.

As in the reciprocal context involving torts, we are unable to identify reasons for pursuing notions of fairness at the expense of everyone involved, including any supposed beneficiaries of the notions. We explored this point briefly above, with regard to each of the two notions of fairness that we examined. We will consider more directly the literature concerning these notions of fairness and contract enforcement in subsection 2(e), when we discuss incomplete contracts. Similarly, we will defer until subsection 2(g) our discussion of why notions of fairness concerning contract enforcement seem appealing in spite of their defects and of how notions of fairness may have some relevance under welfare economics, although not as independent evaluative principles.

2. Incomplete Contracts

(a) Description. We continue with our example: a contract to produce a custom-made cabinet, with a value to the buyer of $200 and a cost to the seller of either $100 (with a probability of 90 percent) or $500 (with a probability of 10 percent). Here we take into account that parties in fact omit mention of many contingencies in their contracts—their contracts are far from complete. They may either leave gaps in their contracts or group together contingencies that ideally would be distinguished.[81] Reasons for such incompleteness include the cost in time and effort of enumerating and bargaining over contingencies and the problems courts would face in verifying whether a claimed contingency actually occurred.[82] To understand such incomplete contracts more readily, we

---

79. For a numerical example of this point in the tort context, see note 50 in chapter III.

80. See subsections II.C.1 and III.C.1(e)(iii).

81. See note 49.

82. See, for example, Shavell (1980a, 468–69). If the courts cannot verify the occurrence of a contingency—such as the contingency that the production cost is $500 (suppose the reason for this is that an idiosyncratic difficulty arises in the making of the cabinet that would be hard for the court to appreciate)—then a contract excusing performance under that contingency would be unworkable. (Sometimes the seller would benefit from claiming that the high cost contingency occurred so that he could avoid his obligations under the contract, even when breach would not be mutually beneficial.) Relatedly, the parties may omit contingencies that could be verified by an adjudicator, but only at a high cost.

Parties' willingness to enter into incomplete contracts will depend upon how the law deals with such situations. To the extent that the law provides remedies that reflect the costs

consider a contract that does not specify any contingencies.[83] In our example, therefore, we discuss the incomplete contract that simply reads "Seller will build and deliver a cabinet to Buyer" for an agreed-upon price that the buyer pays in advance.

We again examine the effects of three legal rules—specific performance, expectation damages, and reliance damages—allowing in some instances for the possibility of different legal costs under the three rules. In the present context, specific performance would require the seller to perform under both the $100 cost contingency and the $500 contingency because the contract plainly says that the seller will build and deliver a cabinet. The two damages rules permit the seller not to perform the contract, but if he breaches he must pay damages to the buyer—$200 (the buyer's value of performance) under expectation damages and return of the contract price under reliance damages (because, for simplicity, we continue to assume that the buyer has taken no action in reliance on the contract other than to pay the purchase price at the outset).

(b) Effects of the Legal Rules. Under specific performance, the situation is as we described it in subsection 1(b) for the case in which the seller would always have to perform: the value of the contract to the buyer is $200, the seller's expected costs are $140, the contract price will be $170, and each party will obtain $30 in surplus.

Under the expectation measure of damages, the seller will breach when the production cost is $500: paying $200 in damages for breach is better for him than spending $500 on performance. The seller will, however, perform when his cost is $100: spending $100 on performance is preferable to paying $200 in damages. Consequently, the gross value of the contract to the buyer is $200: he either receives performance worth $200 or damages of $200. The expected cost to the seller is $(90\% \times \$100) + (10\% \times \$200) = \$110$. Therefore, the contract price will be $155, and each party will obtain a surplus of

---

and difficulties of entering into complete contracts (such as expectation damages, which are superior to specific performance in certain types of situations that we discuss below), incomplete contracts will be more desirable. If, instead, contract remedies substantially reduce the overall value of exchange, parties may refrain from contracting, or they may incur additional costs in attempting to make their contracts more complete (as well as suffer losses in value that result from the less desirable remedy, which is the harm that we will emphasize in the text).

83. Examination of this case will yield the insight needed to evaluate contracts that address some but not all contingencies. In any event, our example has only two contingencies, so it exhausts the possibilities to consider the cases in which they are and are not distinguished.

$45.[84] As a result, both parties are better off under expectation damages, each obtaining $15 more in surplus ($45 − $30) than under specific performance. (Thus, had they chosen to specify the remedy in their contract, they would have selected expectation damages over specific performance.)

Reliance damages will sometimes reduce individuals' well-being. In particular, under reliance damages, there might be breaches that reduce overall value and thus make the parties worse off. In subsection 1(c), for example, we consider the case in which the high production cost (which arises 10 percent of the time) is $180 rather than $500. In this case, the seller will breach under reliance damages as long as the contract price is less than $180—which it will be—with the result that both parties expect to fare worse under reliance damages than under expectation damages.[85] (In our original example, in which the high production cost is $500, however, reliance damages lead to the same result as expectation damages.)

Finally, if we allow for the possibility of different legal costs under the three rules, it should be clear, just as in subsection 1(c), that any of the rules might be best for the parties. For example, if reliance damages were much cheaper to measure and there were few if any instances in which they would result in value-reducing breach, reliance damages would be superior to ex-

---

84. The price under expectation damages is $155, whereas the price under the complete contingent contract, which specifies performance under the same contingencies, was only $135. See subsection 1(b). The reason for the difference in price is that, in the prior case, performance is excused when the production cost is high; here, the seller must pay damages of $200. Because this contingency occurs 10 percent of the time, the expected cost to the seller of the damages payment is $20, so the price he receives will be $20 higher—again producing the result that each party enjoys a surplus of $45.

85. As we show in note 62, the price in this modified example will be $150, and each party's surplus under reliance damages will be $45. Under expectation damages, each party's surplus in this example will be $46.

Although the seller is better off, ex post, under reliance damages when the cost of performance turns out to be high, an ex ante perspective (indicating that the seller is prospectively worse off under reliance damages) is clearly appropriate in the present context. See note 54, and subsection VIII.C.1, which addresses the general merit of the ex ante perspective. An important reason that the ex ante view is compelling is that this is indeed the perspective the parties would adopt if they were asked to choose the legal rule before entering their contract. See, for example, Craswell (1992, 811 n.7, 813–15). (As another illustration of the difference between the ex ante and ex post perspectives, suppose that the only two possible remedies were specific performance and expectation damages and that the latter involved slightly higher legal costs, borne by both parties. Then, ex post, the buyer would slightly prefer specific performance. Nonetheless, he would prefer—if the contract were to specify a remedy—that expectation damages be employed, because he would share, through negotiation over the contract price, in the net gains from avoiding excessively costly performance.)

pectation damages; that is, both parties would be better off under reliance damages.[86]

(c) Choice of Legal Rules Using Welfare Economics. In the examples we have described, the remedy of expectation damages is best for both parties (in the absence of legal costs) and thus is the preferred rule under welfare economics. In our first, main example, reliance damages are as good and specific performance is inferior; in our modified example, in which the high production cost is only $180, specific performance is as good and reliance damages are inferior.

More generally, allowing for legal costs, any of these rules might be best for the parties. For instance, in our original illustration, reliance damages would be best if legal costs were lower than under expectation damages.

It is also true that, whichever remedy is best, that remedy will be best for both parties because the contract price will adjust so as to split the surplus between them.[87] Just as in the case of the complete contract, both parties are identically affected by the choice of the legal rule. Once again, regardless of the legal rules under consideration and the particular facts assumed to exist, there will be a unanimous ranking of the rules, and this ranking will necessarily be the same as that under welfare economics.

(d) Choice of Legal Rules Using Notions of Fairness. As in subsection 1, promise-keeping notions naturally favor specific performance,[88] and notions that view contract breach as akin to a tort are generally understood to favor reliance damages.

(e) Why the Choice of Legal Rules Should Be Based Only on Individuals' Well-Being. As in the case of complete contracts, our main point is that fairness-based evaluation can only make everyone worse off. This result necessarily arises because, as we explain in subsection (c), welfare economics always leads to the choice of the rule under which both contracting parties are best off (and, depending on the facts, this could be any of the rules). In contrast, as we note

---

86. Using the figures in note 85, pertaining to our example in which the high production cost is $180, expectation damages yield gains of $2 ($1 for each party) over the surplus generated under reliance damages. Accordingly, if the expected value of legal costs under expectation damages is greater than under reliance damages by an amount exceeding $2, each party's surplus will be greater under reliance damages.

87. As we have explained, the argument in the text holds regardless of the share of the surplus that each party receives. See note 55.

88. Alternatively, in the view of some contract law scholars, expectation damages would be favored.

in subsection (d), notions of fairness lead one to favor particular rules without regard to their effects on individuals' well-being. Thus, the two approaches may well conflict. For example, promise-keeping notions tend to favor specific performance even though in the most basic case this rule makes both parties worse off.

Whenever the prescriptions of notions of fairness are followed and they differ from those of welfare economics, each individual's well-being will be reduced. This conclusion necessarily holds true for any notion of fairness as well as for mixed views that are concerned both with satisfying notions of fairness and promoting individuals' well-being, as long as any weight is given to a notion of fairness.[89] Thus, as in the case of complete contracts, if one is logically consistent and endorses a notion of fairness, one must accept that it may be socially desirable to favor a legal rule that makes everyone worse off.

We now elaborate on the conflict between notions of fairness and welfare economics with respect to each of the two types of fairness notions, and we consider whether there is any justification for the reduction in well-being that results from pursuing these notions.

(i) In Relation to Promise-Keeping. Promise-keeping notions look to the character of acts—was a contract made? was it breached?—rather than to the consequences of acts. Such notions do not direct attention to the effects of legal rules on promisors and promisees—their effects on behavior (when will contracts be breached?) and, ultimately, on the parties' well-being. Accordingly, one would expect that following promise-keeping notions will produce undesirable results, and indeed this is the case.

In our example, the expectation measure of damages leads to a greater level of well-being than does specific performance. As we discuss in subsection B.1, consistent with the notion that individuals should keep their promises, one would employ a remedy under which plaintiffs actually carry out their contracts, namely, specific performance.[90] If the promise-keeping no-

---

89. See note 50 in chapter III, presenting an example in the tort context showing that everyone might be made worse off as long as any positive weight is given to a notion of fairness.

90. Similarly, we suggest that, if there is breach and the promisor simply refuses to perform (or has taken actions making performance impossible), promise-keeping would seem to call for punitive damages rather than merely compensatory damages. (Most who believe that promises should be kept do allow for some excuses, such as impossibility. But if the impossibility is of the promisor's own making, excusing the promisor would be inconsistent with the promise-keeping notion.) Imposing punitive damages, like requiring specific performance, would make parties worse off because it would induce performance in some instances

tion of fairness is implemented in this manner, all individuals will be made worse off. Moreover, as we discuss in subsection 1(e), it is difficult to understand the sense in which society can be said to gain by adhering to this notion. The promise-keeping view seems particularly problematic given that it is often motivated by a concern for the autonomy of the very individuals who are subjected to a legal rule under which, when they pursue their plans as best they can, they are made worse off than under the different rule that welfare economics favors.

We now explore two ways to view the application of the promise-keeping notion to the case of incomplete contracts that are different from those in the literature. We suggest that, upon reflection, these alternative perspectives make more sense than the one we have just considered and also resolve the basic conflict between promise-keeping notions of fairness and welfare economics in the present setting.

First, we find it illuminating to contrast the incomplete contract that the parties write to the corresponding mutually ideal complete contract that we examine in subsection 1. The incomplete contract in the present context is an unconditional contract that ostensibly requires performance under any contingency. Yet this is not the promise that the parties really would wish to have made. (Recall that parties write incomplete contracts, which only imperfectly reflect the agreements they truly wish to make, because of various complications that often exist when parties transact—such as the cost of analyzing and providing for every possible contingency, many of which are unlikely ever to arise.) The complete contract that the parties would like to have made calls for performance only when production costs are low; performance is excused when costs are high. Accordingly, when one examines the breach that occurs under expectation damages—in the situation in which costs are high—one can see that it is only a nominal breach in the sense that it does not represent a breach of the mutually ideal complete contract that the parties would really like to have made.

A second way to reconcile the promise-keeping notion with welfare eco-

---

in which performance would reduce value. As we have explained, an excessive incentive to perform may arise whenever damages exceed expectation damages.

    As we note in subsection B.1, some contract law scholars—notably Fried—believe that expectation damages are most consistent with a promise-keeping notion of fairness. We have explained the problems with this view. See note 18. If, however, one were to accept this interpretation, its only effect would be to change the set of circumstances in which the notion of fairness reduces everyone's well being (see our discussion at the end of this subsection). When the notion of fairness does conflict with the well-being of the contracting parties, our criticism of promise-keeping presented in the text remains applicable.

nomics is to interpret contracts as implicitly building in remedies that the parties would have adopted. Thus, one may interpret the contract that reads "Seller will build and deliver a cabinet to Buyer" to mean "Seller will build and deliver a cabinet to Buyer, or else pay expectation damages, at Seller's option."[91] If the parties had been given the choice between the former, more literal interpretation—which would require specific performance—and the latter, both parties would have chosen the latter. (The reader may recognize this argument as involving "hypothetical contract" reasoning, which has been increasingly used by contract analysts.[92]) Another way to express the point is that promises are not, after all, meant by those who make them to be kept in all circumstances; promises are meant to be broken whenever promisors find it in their interest to do so, as long as they pay a "correct" amount of damages.[93] Indeed, under this interpretation, a promisor has not actually broken his promise, because paying damages qualifies as performance. Therefore, if one is concerned about the principle of autonomy that animates many promise-keeping fairness notions, one arguably should reject specific performance in favor of whatever remedy the parties would have preferred—that is, the remedy under which they are better off. And this remedy, in turn, is the one that would be chosen under welfare economics.

This point—and, more generally, the idea that we develop throughout this section that, if given the choice, both parties would favor the legal rule that maximizes their well-being—raises a problem for all fairness-based normative theories of contract: If the parties *do* specify the legal rule favored by welfare economics in their contract, is this rule to be enforced? On one hand, failure to enforce such a provision, in addition to making both parties

---

91. Compare note 23, noting Holmes's view, which in a sense interprets all contracts in such a manner.

92. See, for example, Charny (1991), addressing the normative basis for use of hypothetical bargains in contract interpretation; ibid. (1815–16), referring to hypothetical bargains as the standard method of contract interpretation; and Craswell (1992, 813–15). Charny discusses at length the relationship between autonomy-based normative theories of contract law and the use of reasoning that makes reference to hypothetical contracts. See Charny (1991, 1825–35).

93. As we discuss in subsection B.1, proponents of the promise-keeping view essentially stipulate that the more literal interpretation is the only one consistent with the institution of promising, whereas in fact both interpretations are consistent with it and, moreover, theorists' invocation of the institution of promise-keeping gives no basis for embracing one version of the institution rather than another. This helps to explain why the existing literature does not offer any affirmative justification for its approach, much less one that will withstand scrutiny when it is revealed that the approach in the literature is one under which all parties are made worse off.

worse off, would conflict with many of the motivations for these theories—such as advancing parties' autonomy or protecting promisees' legitimate reliance interests. On the other hand, to enforce the provision would suggest that contract law's remedies (and, in fact, all matters of interpretation and determination of default rules) should be based entirely upon welfare economics whenever parties make the effort to say that they want their interests to be advanced to the maximum extent possible. (Parties might include a boilerplate clause in all of their contracts to that effect.) But, when the parties fail to make such a provision, whether because of error or simply to save time, then some conflicting theory, contrary to the parties' interests, should govern their contracts. We find it hard to understand how this latter outcome furthers parties' autonomy or other values that one might suppose underlie contract law.[94]

The two foregoing perspectives on promise-keeping notions of fairness—reference to the mutually ideal complete contract as a benchmark for determination of what the parties really want and interpretation of the contract such that paying damages constitutes performance—have much in common. They both make clear that there is more than one way to construe the parties' promise, and they both suggest that the most sensible solution resolves the ambiguity latent in the parties' incomplete contract by favoring the construction under which both parties are better off. This approach always comports with the recommendations of welfare economics. If this understanding of promise-keeping is compelling, one should view promise-keeping theories as collapsing into—not conflicting with—welfare economics.[95] If, however, one does not so interpret or modify the conventional

---

94. The welfare economic approach is not subject to this criticism because, in the present context, parties will find it in their mutual interest to adopt such an approach to govern their contract and will reject any approach that produces a different outcome. (In contrast, in subsection D.2, we consider situations in which contracts may contain terms that reduce individuals' well-being; in such instances there may accordingly be a good reason under welfare economics to reject the terms.)

95. Such a result is not entirely surprising because, as we emphasize in subsection B.1, the promise-keeping view is fundamentally incomplete, giving rise to a need to draw upon some other substantive theory to reach normative judgments about legal rules. Compare Kronman (1981, 416), noting Fried's argument that self-interest and utility are not the moral basis of the promise-keeping notion but arguing that they play an important role in constructing the hypothetical agreements that one must consult to determine what rational parties would have wanted, the content of which cannot be extracted from the promise-keeping principle alone.

Another way to express our argument is to state that promise-keeping is not valued per se; rather, at most it has instrumental value. In our example, buyers prefer a regime in which

understanding of promise-keeping notions, incomplete contracts will be enforced in a manner that may well thwart both parties' interests. In that case, promise-keeping theorists would need to present a normatively compelling justification for their views—one that would be difficult to ground in autonomy or related ideas that they have advanced.

When we examine the literature on promise-keeping notions, we do not find any sound reason to adhere to these notions at the expense of individuals' well-being. Legal scholarship on contracts does not directly confront the fundamental conflict between the keeping of promises associated with incomplete contracts and the promotion of individuals' well-being, much less explicitly defend pursuit of this notion of fairness at the expense of individuals' well-being or explain how doing so could possibly enhance parties' autonomy despite making them worse off.[96] Nor does the legal literature on

---

promises are kept only when it is mutually beneficial to do so; they are worse off in a regime where promises are kept more often than this. It may be said that proponents of promise-keeping themselves cannot but understand promise-keeping in instrumental terms, given that their motivation derives from a concern for individuals' autonomy. See also note 131, noting fairness theorists' references to the welfare-enhancing function of promises. To apply such a view, however, one must provide additional content. Two competing contract remedies each make available to individuals—potential promisors and promisees—a *different* set of options. (That is, the contracts that will be viable, the prices paid, and the resulting performance will depend upon the legal regime.) Accordingly, one must decide which set of options is best. The welfare economic approach favors the set that is most advantageous to the individuals concerned, and in the present setting all would agree on which set that is: the one given by the legal rule that maximizes total value to the parties. If the same criterion is used to identify which regime best promotes autonomy, then the promise-keeping notion and the notion of autonomy underlying it would not differ from the evaluative approach of welfare economics; the latter would simply be a more precise, operational way of stating the criterion. Compare Charny (1991, 1830–35).

96. As far as we can tell, none of the simple, direct conflicts that we examine are considered in any of the literature, even though some theorists understand that they are advancing theories that differ, in principle, from (and thus are in potential conflict with) one concerned exclusively with welfare. For example, Barnett contrasts his theory, which emphasizes objective manifestations of the parties' consent, with, among others, an efficiency-based theory, see Barnett (1986a), and in one of his articles he responds at length to criticisms from Craswell, who favors an economically oriented outlook, see Barnett (1992b, 874–97). Yet Barnett does not present basic cases in which the two approaches conflict and then suggest reasons for preferring his theory.

Now, because Barnett's theory is based on the parties' mutual understanding, and because welfare depends on what is mutually beneficial to the parties, these two approaches will tend to overlap significantly. The simplest case of conflict between the theories is one in which the common understanding of the parties is that they are subject to a mutually bad rule, yet they fail to include an alternative term in their contract due to the costs of providing for an unlikely contingency. In this case, it seems that Barnett's theory demands—out of concern for the

fairness in contracts suggest that, upon reflection, the promise-keeping notion is one that dissolves (entirely) into a concern for maximizing individuals' well-being, in the manner suggested by our preceding discussion.[97]

---

parties' autonomy—that they be subject to the bad rule, for to apply a mutually preferred rule, thereby making them both better off, is not something to which they ever consented. We see no basis for this normative stance. Moreover, Barnett emphasizes that his theory has its greatest force when the parties are unsophisticated and have given very little thought, or none whatsoever, to the contracting problem in question. Consequently it seems all the more strange that he would insist on enforcing the courts' best guess as to what they thought was the rule, rather than the rule that would actually make them better off. (Indeed, at one point he explicitly contrasts his theory and the efficiency theory by explaining that the latter seeks to discern the term that most parties would have attempted to provide had they thought about it, but he does not pause to explain why this should be seen as a vice rather than as a virtue. Barnett (1992b, 893).) To take another case, when two unsophisticated parties turn out to hold reasonable but inconsistent views, Barnett favors rescission because the requisite consent is lacking. See ibid. (896). However, he does not comment on the fact that it is entirely possible that under one or both of the parties' inconsistent views, parties may be (prospectively) better off than under rescission. In choosing legal rules, Barnett seems solely concerned with his notion of consent, and thus he pays no attention to whether the parties whom he apparently believes he is protecting are benefitted or harmed by the approach he advocates.

In addition, Barnett's view seems vulnerable to the sort of interpretive argument made in the text: That is, one could ask whether the parties consented to the bad rule, period, or whether they consented to an agreement believing generally that a bad rule likely would govern them but consenting implicitly to a good rule should the legal system exceed their expectations. Of course, such difficulties with a consent theory are avoided if the role of consent, however important, is understood as instrumental to enhancing parties' well-being rather than as an end in itself, to be pursued regardless of their well-being. It appears, however, that Barnett adopts an intrinsic rather than an instrumental view of the principles he advances. This interpretation is suggested by his failure to identify explicitly the goals to be achieved by his approach and also by his insistence that personal services contracts can never be subject to specific performance, apparently without regard to whether parties would benefit from that. See Barnett (1986b). In the end, Barnett gives no reason that a party should consent to application of his consent-based approach, and our analysis suggests that no one would wish to do so. For further discussion of consent and the ex ante view that we employ here, see subsection VIII.C.1.

97. More generally, this literature is not sufficiently explicit about the rationale for a promise-keeping notion of fairness to enable one readily to infer the understood relationship between the proffered views and the welfare economic approach. The value of individual autonomy is cited most often, yet this concept can be understood in a number of ways, including one in which it is nearly congruent with maximizing individuals' well-being, as suggested by the preceding discussion. See, for example, Craswell (1989, 524 n.86), discussing how welfare seems to underlie Barnett's autonomy-based view. Part of the explanation for the failure of the legal literature on promise-keeping to explain differences between it and the welfare economic approach is that the literature is substantially directed to internal debates among contracts scholars over particular notions of fairness. See, for example, Fried (1981, chapter 1), and Contract As Promise (review) (1983, 904).

In contrast, some of the general philosophical literature on promising does, as we note in subsection B.1, indicate that notions of fairness conflict with overall welfare. But this literature largely assumes that its promise-keeping view is correct, and it does not consider the type of problems that we have raised. Moreover, this literature often supports its view by reference to the obvious fact that the institution of promise-keeping advances individuals' well-being, but the virtues of an institution that respects promises are implicitly compared to the vices of a regime in which no promises are possible. That contrast, however, provides no basis for insisting on a version of the institution that reduces individuals' well-being relative to the level achievable under an intermediate version in which most promises would be kept, such as welfare economics would favor.[98]

These shortcomings in the philosophical and legal literature are not surprising in light of our observation in subsection B.1 that the promise-keeping theories expounded by philosophers and legal academics are incomplete. As we have explained, these theories require upholding promises that invoke society's institution of promising, but they do not tell us what the contours of that institution—which in the case of contracts are determined by the legal rules in question—should be. (We also have suggested that the theories have serious problems of internal coherence, which could only be addressed by fundamental alterations.) To the extent that theorists arrive at a determinate answer without addressing its normative basis, there is no justification for adherence to their position once its defects are made apparent. Thus,

---

98. To elaborate, some of the literature argues essentially that failing to keep promises—even when the balance of interests favors breaking them—will ultimately undermine the institution of promising, which in turn is understood to advance individuals' well-being. See sources cited in note 131. (If the institution of promise-keeping did not affect anyone's well-being or actually made members of society worse off, it would be hard to understand why acts that undermined the institution would be subject to moral opprobrium rather than indifference or praise.) This argument does not hold in the legal context because it relies on an implicit assumption that there are only two possible ultimate outcomes: keeping (virtually) all promises, regardless of the consequences, or doing without the institution of promising. The philosophical literature does not usually consider intermediate solutions such as those employed by the legal system in enforcing contracts, namely, damage remedies like expectation damages. Compare note 6, noting that, as an alternative to keeping all promises, Kant considers only the possibility that false promises may freely be made. In the present context, we have already demonstrated that this intermediate alternative makes everyone better off than does rigid adherence to the literal terms of parties' incomplete contracts. (We also note that the philosophical literature seems more influenced by, and in some instances more concerned with, fairness principles as internalized social norms than as evaluative principles for policymaking, as we discuss in subsection (g). See also note 6, comparing Kant's discussions of promising and of formal contracts, and note 134, suggesting that, even in the realm of social norms, the view of many philosophers that promises must be rigidly followed is mistaken.)

we do not consider the existing literature to provide grounds for an analyst to deviate from the objective of advancing individuals' well-being.

Remark on the role of expectation damages in our argument. Before concluding our discussion of promise-keeping notions of fairness in the context of incomplete contracts, we wish to observe that, although our critique has focused on an example in which welfare economics favors expectation damages, this preference is not essential to our argument. As we have noted, when one takes into account legal costs, it might well be that some other rule, such as reliance damages, would make both parties better off than do expectation damages. Other factors, such as parties' reliance expenditures or risk aversion, also might make rules other than expectation damages in the interest of both parties.[99] In such cases, just as in our original case, pursuing notions of fairness, which are understood to favor a particular remedy (whatever that remedy may be), will make all parties worse off, unless, by coincidence, the remedy favored by a notion of fairness happens to be the best remedy for the parties.[100] All of our preceding analysis—which indicates that one should make reference to the mutually ideal complete contract rather than to the literal terms of the parties' incomplete contract, that one should interpret incomplete contracts to promote individuals' well-being rather than to reduce it, and that there is no good reason (including the advancement of autonomy) to make everyone worse off by slavish adherence to an abstract principle—continues to apply with equal force.

(ii) In Relation to the View That Breach Is Akin to a Tort. Notions of fairness that are based on the view that contract breach is similar to a tort focus on the harm to the victim, the promisee, who is said to be entitled to compensation for wrongful acts of the injurer, the promisor.[101] This approach, like that dictated by promise-keeping notions, is concerned with the character

---

99. See, for example, Craswell (2000, 110), Macneil (1982), and the sources cited in note 46.

100. As we have already noted, if autonomy is understood as requiring the choice of remedy that maximizes individuals' well-being—the remedy that the parties would have chosen to govern themselves—then a notion of fairness interpreted always to favor autonomy would fully coincide with the welfare economic approach in the present setting. To differentiate the two approaches would require varying the context in such a manner as to generate true conflicts—such as by introducing heterogeneity or externalities, both of which present the need to trade off the well-being of different parties. See subsection D.1, discussing a case involving heterogeneity. See also subsections III.C.2 and III.D.2, discussing these issues in the context of nonreciprocal torts.

101. As we discuss in note 27, these fairness theories of contract are analogous to fairness theories of tort law. Consequently, there are parallels between the criticism advanced here and that offered in chapter III.

of acts. To the extent that consequences are addressed, there is still little attention paid to behavior (how the legal rule will affect whether breach occurs or whether contracts will be advantageous to enter) or to the ultimate effect on each party's well-being (which will depend not only on behavior but also on the different contract prices that will prevail under different regimes). As a result, one again would expect the pursuit of notions of fairness to reduce individuals' well-being. We will now examine the extent to which this is the case and whether any resulting reduction in individuals' well-being can be justified.

Recall that many who view contract breach as akin to a tort believe that the cost incurred in reliance on the contract is the proper measure of injury. As we have noted, reliance damages are not always sufficient to induce performance when that is desirable (this occurs when the effects of reliance damages differ from those of expectation damages[102]), and, in such cases, both buyers and sellers will be made worse off.[103]

The insufficiency of reliance damages may not seem problematic to theorists who view contract breach as akin to a tort, because they may believe that only a certain minimum level of protection is morally required. Nevertheless, as we discuss in subsection 1(f)(ii), it is difficult to discern an affirmative argument against raising damages further—even from the perspective of such fairness theorists—when stricter enforcement would benefit both the promisee, whom they wish to protect, and the promisor, whom they may wish to avoid punishing excessively. These theorists do not directly confront this fundamental problem because they do not analyze basic cases in which following their preferred conceptions of fairness conflicts with the prescriptions of welfare economics.

On reflection, it should not be surprising that there seems to be no good reason to pursue these notions of fairness at the expense of individuals' well-

---

102. Recall that in our main example, with production costs of $100 and $500, reliance damages and expectation damages have the same effect, but in our modified example, in which the high production cost is only $180, expectation damages lead (appropriately) to performance in the high-cost case whereas reliance damages lead (undesirably) to breach. See also note 61, explaining that reliance damages may equal expectation damages when reliance involves forgoing other contracting opportunities.

103. As we note in subsection B.2, however, it is possible to adopt the view of fairness under which contract breach is akin to a tort while believing that expectation damages, not reliance damages, are the appropriate remedy. Under this approach, there would be no conflict in our example between notions of fairness and welfare economics. Nevertheless, pursuing notions of fairness would make both parties worse off in other instances—namely, when specific performance or reliance damages are superior to expectation damages because of administrative costs or other complications—without serving any identifiable purpose.

being. As we discuss in subsection B.2, notions of fairness that call for compensation to protect promisees who have been wronged by promisors' breaches are incomplete: it is necessary to go further and specify some substantive theory that explains which refusals to perform should be deemed wrongful and that provides an explicit justification for choosing a particular remedy.[104] In the absence of an underlying normative foundation for this view of fairness, it is hard to understand why one should seek to adopt certain rules when doing so makes everyone worse off.

As in the case of promise-keeping theories, thinking about the mutually ideal complete contract that the parties would have wished to enter helps illuminate our understanding of the incomplete contract that they did adopt.[105] Analysis of the complete contract both provides a substantive basis for addressing the gaps in the tort-fairness theory and clarifies the true purposes of contract remedies. First, an answer can be given to the question of when failure to perform wrongfully harms the promisee: nonperformance is improper when, and only when, the complete contract—which reflects the true wishes of the parties and which would make them both better off—calls for performance.

Second, the purpose of contract remedies is to implement, as best one can, the mutually ideal complete contract, because it is the underlying agreement that the parties truly want to enforce. One implication is that the primary purpose of remedies is not to compensate for wrongful breach but to prevent it from happening in the first place.[106] (Recall that in our example

104. Most attention in the literature is devoted to borderline cases (such as when there is no explicit promise). The more basic question of the extent to which reliance is appropriate in the case of a simple, explicit promise in a world of some uncertainty—the most conventional sort of case, which we address here—usually receives scant attention. Statements such as Fuller and Perdue's, to the effect that reliance damages serve the purpose of protecting the reliance interest, provide no answer. See note 32.

105. The failure to appreciate this approach is apparent in standard accounts of contract theory. For example, Fuller and Perdue dismiss the relevance of the "will theory" of contract law primarily because they believe that it only provides a basis for ascertaining the substantive content of a contract and does not allow one to determine the remedy for its breach. See Fuller and Perdue (1936, 58). But this reasoning makes little sense; it suggests that parties have strong views on what they hope to accomplish in a contract but are indifferent to the remedy, despite the fact that it affects whether the contract is performed and determines the consequences that they must live with in the event of breach.

106. Compare Farnsworth (1999, §12.1), indicating that contract damages doctrine has the opposite purpose. We do not mean to suggest that there never could be a compensatory function. Because breach sometimes will occur (in our example and with expectation damages, only when breach is desirable), and because promisees may be risk averse and uninsured, awarding damages may enhance well-being. At the same time, however, requiring payment

undesirable breach is always deterred with expectation damages, whereas such breach might occur under reliance damages.) We also observe that, when promisors are required to pay damages, the payment is not to punish wrongful conduct, as is typically imagined in the literature. Rather, when damages are paid, it turns out that no wrong has in fact occurred—again, by reference to the complete contract by which the parties would like to be governed. After all, wrongful breaches are deterred, so nonperformance arises precisely when nonperformance is desirable.[107] The fact that the direct effect of damages may be to punish promisors who have behaved properly (a point that does not seem to be widely appreciated) may seem ironic from the point of view of fairness-minded scholars. Nevertheless, this is a price that both parties are willing to pay—rather than be in a situation in which no remedy (or a lesser remedy) is provided—precisely because they wish to deter value-reducing breach.[108]

In sum, we suggest that fairness theories do not really address what is actually at issue: they fail to take proper account of the value of deterring undesirable breach and they fail to reflect that the actual imposition of damages may not be for engaging in wrongful behavior, but instead is likely to be a necessary feature of a system designed to deter such behavior. Nor does it appear that any social purpose would be served by allowing undesirable breach to occur or by attempting to reduce the damages that must be paid

---

of damages may reduce well-being if the breaching party is more risk averse than the victim. Allowing for these possibilities may, as in our discussions of risk aversion in the tort context in section III.D, affect which rule best promotes individuals' well-being, but the welfare economic framework fully accounts for risk aversion, and, accordingly, our analysis of notions of fairness would not be fundamentally altered. See note 46.

107. Even under reliance damages, many breaches that do occur will not in fact be wrongful by reference to the mutually ideal complete contract (and, in our original example, none of them will).

108. Compare our discussion of the analogous situation in the tort context in subsection III.C.1. The assumption here is that courts are unable to determine when breach would have been appropriate. To determine when a breach maximizes value, a court must be able to observe the seller's cost of performance, in addition to the harm to the buyer (which is all that must be observed in order to apply expectation damages). If the court is able to do this, then it can excuse beneficial breaches, which is what the first complete contract that we considered provides. In our example, the parties would be indifferent between this outcome and the outcome under expectation damages. The choice would depend on legal costs, namely, whether it was cheaper to determine whether breach was justified or to assess damages. (This comparison between allowing excuses for breach and simply requiring the payment of expectation damages is analogous to the comparison between the negligence rule and strict liability in the tort context.)

by a class of parties who would actually be better off under the remedies favored by welfare economics.[109]

(f) The Apparent Mootness and Arbitrariness of Concerns for Fairness. In the contract problems that we have been examining, any notion of fairness that reflects concerns for rewarding, punishing, or protecting a party to a contract will in an important sense be moot. The reason is that different contract remedies will result in different contract prices.[110]

Consider choosing a remedy that is more favorable to the promisee, the buyer in our example—whether the choice is motivated by a desire to protect the promisee, as under reliance-based theories, or by a concern about the misbehavior of the promisor, as under promise-based theories.[111] One effect of such a choice will be a higher contract price, which will be to the buyer's detriment. As our previous discussion suggests, the only way that the buyer ultimately will benefit from a rule that nominally is more favorable to him is if the rule is mutually beneficial. Thus, if one is concerned with helping the buyer, one should attend only to maximizing individuals' well-being.[112] To illustrate, suppose in our example that damages are set at $600 rather than $200.[113] This will induce the seller to perform when the cost of performance is

109. Recall that, although the seller pays more under expectation damages when production costs are high, he is more than fully compensated for this contingency ex ante through a higher contract price.

110. See, for example, Craswell (1992, 833–35). Our point about mootness in this subsection is independent of the arguments in subsection (e), which suggest, for example, that if incomplete contracts are interpreted appropriately, concerns about keeping promises or wrongful breach evaporate (because nonperformance will then arise only when the contract is understood not to require performance).

111. Admittedly, proponents of these theories may be concerned about both parties, but this possibility merely reinforces the point in the text.

112. More familiar concerns for compensating victims similarly go awry in the present setting, because potential victims of breach are, as a class, made worse off by the rule that might seem to protect them. Of course, if promisees are risk averse, compensation will serve a function. But this function is explicitly a component of individuals' well-being, as we emphasize in section III.D on torts and apply to contracts in notes 46 and 106. We also observe, as we do in subsection III.C.1(f), that concerns about compensation may often be moot because of insurance and because victims may be firms, in which case the ultimate impact of injury is often diffuse and risk may not be an important concern.

113. If damages were higher than expectation damages of $200 but less than $500, there would be no effect on the buyer's well-being in our simple example: The buyer would get more in the event of breach—which would happen in the same circumstances as under expectation damages—and the contract price would be higher by an amount that just equaled the increase

$500, just as under specific performance. As we explain above, in that event the contract price settles at $170 rather than $155, as it is under expectation damages, and the buyer is worse off by $15.

The same analysis implies that any rule designed to punish the promisor for his breach will make him worse off only if the rule reduces value, and such a rule will make the promisee worse off as well. One can favor such an outcome if one wishes to inflict punishment for its own sake, but this is an arbitrary—indeed, perverse—justification. First, all concerned will be made worse off. Second, the attempt to punish particular behavior ex post will be reflected in the price negotiated ex ante, so that the class that is to be subject to the prospect of punishment is compensated for this possibility at the time of contracting. Also, the punishment will not be applied (ex post) to sellers who are in any real sense evil; rather, those punished are simply those who had the misfortune to suffer atypically high production costs.[114] The welfare economic approach does, in a way, punish this group of sellers: in our example with incomplete contracts, the unlucky sellers pay $200 in expectation damages, whereas the rest of the sellers perform at a cost of $100. This punishment, however, is assessed for a purpose: to induce sellers to breach when and only when breach is desirable (that is, only in cases in which the parties' mutually ideal complete contract would call for nonperformance).[115] And prospective sellers will wish to subject themselves to such punishment because they thereby maximize the expected surplus produced by their contracts and thus maximize their own benefit.

Notions of fairness that would penalize or compensate for reasons unrelated to the promotion of individuals' well-being will fail in their purpose (because of contract price adjustments) or prove perverse (because the combination of the behavioral effects and contract price adjustments will detrimentally affect promisors and promisees). Thus, even from the perspective of many fairness proponents, notions of fairness seem to be defective.[116]

---

in expected damage payments. More generally, when there is a range of possible costs of performance, damages higher than expectation damages will affect behavior by discouraging value-maximizing breach and thereby make the buyer, in addition to the seller, worse off (by causing an increase in the contract price).

114. See subsection (e)(ii). Compare subsection III.D.1(f)(ii) and note 111 in chapter III, discussing the nature of punishment in the accident context when those who actually cause injury differ from others only in their luck.

115. Such punishment, rather than excusing performance, tends to enhance value for the parties because determining when sellers' behavior is proper rather than opportunistic may be costly and subject to error, if it is possible at all. See note 108.

116. Compare note 142 in chapter III, explaining that we are concerned only with the extent to which a notion of fairness promotes well-being and that we note problems of moral

The shortcomings examined in this subsection and in the preceding ones appear to arise on account of a phenomenon we initially identify in subsection II.B.2(c), namely, that notions of fairness often are associated with an ex post perspective. In the present context, the promise-keeping theory asks what should be done in light of the fact that a promise has been broken. The view of breach as akin to a tort asks what compensation is due to a victim of a given breach. Neither theory focuses on how the rule one adopts will affect ex ante behavior, such as whether parties will find it worthwhile to enter into contracts, what price will be agreed upon, or what the parties' incentives will be to breach in the first place. Inattention to such effects— which, by contrast, play an important role under welfare economics—helps explain the differences between the prescriptions of fairness-based analysis and those of welfare economics, and underlies much of the reasoning in favor of the latter. In our earlier discussion of the ex post character of many notions of fairness, we also suggest that this feature helps explain the notions' appeal, for when assessing a situation, we are all naturally inclined to focus on what in fact has happened, even when upon more careful analysis we would discover that such a focus omits important factors. We now consider another aspect of what we believe to underlie the attraction held by notions of fairness in contract law.

(g) The Appeal of Notions of Fairness and Its Implications. The defects that we have identified in normative theories of contract that rely on notions of fairness rather than welfare economics raise the question of why notions of fairness have the appeal that they do. In addition to the point made in the preceding subsection concerning the ex post perspective taken under notions of fairness, we believe that a potentially significant part of the answer lies in the fact that notions of fairness concerning contracts correspond to internalized social norms.

The view that contract breach is akin to a tort immediately suggests that our analysis of social norms in the tort context, in section III.E, should apply here as well, and we believe this to be the case. As our prior discussion indicates, instilled or inborn social norms concerned with punishing wrongdoers or compensating innocent victims help explain why it seems fair to insist that legal rules be designed to serve these purposes. Nevertheless, there are important differences between individuals' decisions in everyday life, the domain of internalized social norms, and decisions about legal policy. As a

---

arbitrariness because they seem independently relevant from the perspective of fairness theorists.

result, basing policy on the apparent implications of internalized social norms will sometimes lead us astray and thus is not the proper method for choosing legal rules when the social norms seem to favor policies different from those chosen under welfare economics. In the present context, the wrongful act involves breaking a promise or breaching a contract and the victim is a promisee, but the analysis is much the same.

The promise-keeping view of contract requires more extensive discussion because it involves a social norm qualitatively different from the one that we considered previously. In particular, the promise-keeping notion of fairness corresponds to the social norm that governs promises made in everyday life. Indeed, the internalized social norm regarding promises in informal settings—that is, in the absence of enforceable contractual rights—lies behind many of the arguments of both philosophers and legal scholars who promote this view of contracts. The connection between their analysis of promise-keeping and the social norm is often quite explicit, and in other instances seems to lie just below the surface.[117]

The social norm that promises must be kept is widely instilled in members of society and serves a valuable function in channeling behavior in everyday life.[118] Many commitments are made in settings in which formal contract enforcement is essentially unavailable. This absence of formal enforcement creates the problem that individuals might feel free to break their commitments opportunistically—that is, whenever they find it in their interest to do so, without regard to whether a change in course is beneficial overall.[119] This problem, in turn, would make individuals reluctant to rely on

117. See, for example, Melden (1956). Most philosophers are directly concerned with the social norm and do not even address the question of formulating legal rules for contract law. See page 158 and note 10. Therefore, many of the arguments in this section are not necessarily critiques of the philosophers' views, because it is possible that they would recognize that their views about promise-keeping have limited relevance to contract law. In the case of legal scholars, we note that Fried, the principal advocate of the promise-keeping view, centers his analysis on the connection between the social norm and the notion of fairness that he believes should guide legal policy. See Fried (1981, chapters 1–2).

118. A number of points we make about promise-keeping as a social norm are developed in Hume ([1739] 1992, §III.II.V).

119. Our emphasis on the problem of individuals opportunistically breaking their promises differs from the focus in much of the philosophical literature on promise-keeping, which is on individuals who would break their promises to promote overall well-being (and not just to advance their own interests, possibly at greater cost to promisees). See, for example, note 17, quoting Ross. We believe, on one hand, that a substantial inability to deter opportunistic behavior would seriously undermine the value of promises (and contracts) because individuals, after undertaking obligations, will often find that better opportunities come along or that performing as promised will be more expensive or less rewarding than anticipated. Moreover,

promises in the first place. The net result would be a sacrifice of the substantial gains that are available through cooperative interaction.

To realize the benefits of exchange, there must be real impediments to the breaking of promises. Some deterrent is produced by the fear of losing future opportunities with individuals who come to believe that one is an unreliable partner. An important supplement[120] is provided by the promise-keeping social norm: to the extent that individuals will feel virtuous if they keep their promises but will feel guilty and subject themselves to social sanc-

---

once the other party has relied on the promise—by forgoing alternative contracting opportunities or making investments that are valuable only if the contract is performed—it is often possible to take advantage of his position. If promisors freely ignored their obligations whenever they found it in their self-interest to do so, and thus with no regard for the harm imposed on promisees, promisees' ability to rely on promisors' undertakings would be greatly undermined.

On the other hand, it is hardly obvious that the institution of promise-keeping (or contract) would be seriously undermined if promisors were relieved of their obligations only in those cases in which the overall social good would in fact be promoted. For example, lunch dates broken because a person needs medical treatment—or even because of less pressing reasons (such as when an out-of-town relative unexpectedly drops by)—would occur far less frequently than lunch dates broken whenever it is in the promisor's self-interest to do so, without regard to the loss suffered by the promisee. Moreover, there would be mutual social advantage from an institution allowing exceptions in such atypical situations, whereas there would be no such mutual gain from permitting purely opportunistic breach.

We should emphasize, however, that a proper welfare economic analysis of the role of such exceptions would take into account the effect on parties' expectations of permitting them. Furthermore, as a practical matter, it may be impossible to allow exceptions freely whenever it would in principle be socially desirable to do so, particularly in informal settings where social norms help to enforce obligations. As we discuss in note 123, it may be difficult for others to know when a valid exception exists, and promisors may often convince themselves that they qualify for a valid exception when in fact they are responding to self-interest. To be effective in discouraging opportunistic behavior, social norms need to be simple and strong, in the sense that they are resistant to promisors making case-by-case exceptions. Hence, it should be no surprise that well-socialized individuals would feel some compunction about breaking all promises, even those whose breach would be socially desirable. Accordingly, our moral instincts and intuitions may well not be fully aligned with the apparent prescriptions of welfare economics in particular cases, but this in no way would indicate that our proper concern should be with promise-keeping in and of itself, rather than with individuals' well-being, which the institution of promise-keeping tends to promote. For further discussion of these and related issues and of how they are often overlooked by promise-keeping theorists, see the sources cited in note 9 and also Hare (1988, 242–44).

120. A supplement is important because parties often will wish to enter agreements with individuals whom they do not yet know through prior interactions, and because parties will sometimes find themselves in endgame situations in which a party's gains from opportunism exceed the losses from being unable to deal with a particular partner in the future.

tions if they break their promises, they will be more reliable partners.[121] In order for the norm to operate in this manner, it is important that society instill in individuals the idea that keeping promises is a virtue and breaking promises is an evil in and of itself.[122] If the norm merely reminded individuals to keep others' well-being in mind, there would be a tendency for self-interest to color the outcome of their internal analysis of whether to break a promise. (We note, however, that the social norm that prohibits the breaking of promises is hardly so absolute as to admit of no exceptions—consider a person who misses a lunch date due to a sudden illness—but it nevertheless does carry independent weight in many settings.[123])

121. See Romer (1996, 206–09), linking the usefulness of a taste for punishing others to whether they have made a promise. Compare McNeilly (1972, 75–79), emphasizing that there are many sources of the motivation to keep promises other than the notion that one is morally obligated to do so but, because this notion of moral obligation is not defined, failing to make clear how his view differs from the sorts of phenomena described in the text.

122. As one commentator explains:

> [T]he practice of promise-keeping is made an important part of moral education. It is attempted to inculcate this as a habit in the young. They are made to promise various things they don't want to do, and are made to feel that it is completely irrelevant to the binding force of the promise that they don't want to perform it. Since part of the point of promising is to encourage trust in the promisee that what is promised will be performed, absolute dependability, even when you are not being watched, is to be counted a virtue. (Árdal 1968, 236–37)

123. See Sidgwick (1907, 304–11, 353–54), emphasizing this theme. See also Árdal (1968, 237): "But a man who feels he must keep all promises, however trivial they may be, is either a fanatic or morally immature."; and note 134, explaining why an absolutist social norm on promise-keeping would be detrimental. In our consideration of contract doctrine, we have chosen for the sake of simplicity not to examine the corresponding issue of the excuses recognized in formal contract law. (In addition, we may suppose that courts often are unable to determine when a valid excuse exists.) Our analysis could, however, be extended to examine such doctrines. See note 108.

Relatedly, one may ask why the promise-keeping social norm does not generally excuse socially beneficial breaches (that is, when the mutually ideal complete statement of the promise would provide for nonperformance). The answer is two-fold. First, it will often be difficult for the promisee or for third parties (who also are involved in the imposition of social sanctions) to observe whether such an excuse really exists. For example, when someone who misses an appointment says there was an "office emergency," it is often difficult to know whether this is really the case. Second, if such a general excuse was widely extended, promisors might too readily imagine that a good excuse exists when breaking their promises would advance their self-interest. (It seems to us that many philosophers who have advanced strong promise-keeping notions, sometimes to critique a certain species of act utilitarianism, are implicitly motivated by this sort of concern. See note 119.) Contrast the case of formal contract law and expectation damages; a promisor contemplating breach, even when breach is cost-justified, will

Given that social norms about promise-keeping are an important means of enhancing individuals' well-being, it is unsurprising that such norms have emerged. And in many settings—either when stakes are low or when there exists a tight local network in which reputation is important and information about others is abundant and reasonably accurate—such social norms may suffice to ensure that promises usually are kept. But informal norms often will not be enough, and the formal legal system will be needed to induce individuals to honor their obligations.

Unfortunately, the norms that govern everyday life may be inadequate as rules of formal contract law, for reasons that we have explored previously.[124] First, such norms have developed in informal settings in which the subjects of contractual arrangements and the manner of enforcement differ from those in contexts in which formal legal enforcement is typically employed.[125] In particular, the primary means of enforcement in the informal setting involves guilt and shame, so it is necessary for people to feel that it is intrinsically wrong to break a promise. In contrast, the most important remedy in the legal context involves the state using its power to coerce the promisor to pay damages to the promisee.[126] Second, social norms about promise-keeping tend to be simpler than the rules of a fully articulated regime that is best suited to the regulation of large-scale activities.[127] Hence, we should not be surprised if our intuitions about social sanctions for breaching promises, formed in the context of social norms, are sometimes inapposite or misleading when applied to the formal legal enforcement of contracts.

---

be required to pay for the loss to the promisee and therefore will not be so tempted to underweigh the promisee's interests.

124. See subsections II.D.2 and III.E.2.

125. Even regarding contracts that are often legally enforced, parties may choose to use only nonlegal sanctions because of important differences in the manner in which formal and informal enforcement regimes operate. See Charny (1990).

126. Compare note 10, quoting Scanlon (1990), who suggests that compensation is particularly inappropriate in the domain of informal personal morality because there is no neutral party available to determine the appropriate amount to pay.

127. We acknowledge that not all social norms will be simple. For example, elaborate and subtle norms of etiquette may have developed concerning when one may cancel a lunch date. Nevertheless, such norms are unlikely to be helpful in addressing complexities that arise in, say, construction contracts or intricate financial arrangements, realms where analogous everyday norms are unlikely to be very elaborate. A contrasting case may arise when a group of sophisticated parties have regular interactions. Nevertheless, such parties do not usually rely solely on evolved customs, which even in such circumstances may not be so well defined. Often, they also decide explicitly on the rules under which they wish to be governed, and these rules may differ from their customs. For recent studies of the practices of particular industries, see, for example, Bernstein (1992; 1996, 1771–87; 1999, 717–40).

For these reasons, popular conceptions of fairness will tend to diverge from the prescriptions of welfare economics and, when they do, the reasons for the divergence imply that welfare economics should be used by analysts who investigate how to improve the legal system. Notions of fairness with regard to contract enforcement are best understood as the by-products of instilled social norms and, as such, have no special status as independent evaluative principles, to be pursued at the expense of everyone's well-being.[128]

128. This conclusion raises the question that we discuss more generally in note 121 in chapter II, concerning whether philosophers' discussions of morality, often aimed at individual morality (which corresponds to social norms in our present discussion), are intended to be applicable in the qualitatively different domain of policy assessment. This distinction between contexts also is not usually addressed directly by legal commentators, and, when they do consider the issue, we find it difficult to interpret their positions. For example, Fried refers to individuals' inhibitions against opportunistic promise-breaking as involving a "moral obligation" (Fried 1981, 15), and he states that he is concerned with "individual obligation, that is, moral obligation" and not a "legislative perspective," ibid. (16). Thus, it would seem quite clear that his focus is on individual morality and not legal policy. Yet the subject of his entire book is contract law; that is, it is concerned with legal policy and not with personal morality. And Fried presents the chapter in which the quoted discussion appears as a foundation for his discussion in the rest of the book. He does not consider that the two contexts differ in important ways and that, consequently, the best social norms in the context of personal morality may well not be the proper evaluative principles in the context of designing a formal legal system.

Atiyah, in an essay on "Promising and Utilitarianism," distinguishes social norms (which he refers to as "morals") about promising from their underlying justifications in a manner that parallels our discussion. See Atiyah (1981, chapter 3). He states:

> The notion that promises are "binding" is an artificial contrivance created and kept alive by those who mould society's moral system. It is inculcated and propagated by education and example, and, to some degree, by the legal sanctions which themselves lie behind the moral ones.
>
> . . . .
>
> [M]oral training is often designed to inculcate habits of behaviour which are un-questioning. Indeed, moral training is often so powerful that it overshoots the mark. . . . Indeed, one may still *feel* one should keep a promise even where there is no real utilitarian case for it at all. . . . But feelings of this kind may be no more than residual nagging doubts arising from irrational sentimentalism or a confused intellect. (Ibid., 31–32, 52)

Drawing an analogy to the obligation to tell the truth, Atiyah notes that many people's reluctance to tell even "white lies" "does not prove that it is wrong to tell such a lie; it may merely demonstrate how hard it is to act in unaccustomed ways." Ibid. He does not, however, use this analysis in the way that we do. (His primary purpose is to refute the criticism of utilitarianism by moral philosophers who argue that, because we all know that breaking any promise

This conclusion is reinforced by the very reason for the existence of internalized promise-keeping norms—to promote the well-being of individuals who seek to benefit from cooperative relationships—a purpose that many fairness advocates seem to recognize.[129] Hence, it is illogical to cite the existence of such norms as a basis for adopting rules that reduce contracting parties' well-being.[130]

We now consider three additional implications of the relationship between notions of fairness and social norms. First, notions of fairness may serve as a proxy device for identifying rules that promote individuals' well-being in a range of familiar settings. Promise-keeping, as we have noted, does improve individuals' well-being in an important sense; if there were no social norm requiring that promises be kept, it is conceivable (in settings without legal enforcement) that they would generally be ignored. Likewise, if formal contractual commitment meant nothing, contracts would serve

---

is morally wrong and because utilitarianism allows for exceptions, utilitarianism must be incorrect.)

In addition to distinguishing social norms from their underlying justifications, Atiyah discusses the closely related distinction between what he calls the internal and external views of the purposes of morality—the former referring to the question of what is the right thing for an individual to do and the latter to the question of why moral rules should exist and be respected. See ibid., chapter 5. As we discuss in note 121 in chapter II, this distinction is analogous to our distinction between how an individual should decide what is the right thing to do and how legal policy should be assessed (the latter differing from the question of which moral rules should govern informal interactions among individuals).

Hart does briefly distinguish legal obligation, characterized by enforcement through the infliction of harm or use of force, from the moral obligation to keep promises, enforced by exposing individuals to reactions from a social group. See Hart (1958a, 102–03).

129. See sources cited in note 131.

130. Compare Hume ([1739] 1992, §III.II.V), arguing that moral sentiments that favor keeping promises should be understood as instrumental rather than as independent principles of an underlying morality. Adam Smith distinguished between rules of contract enforced by the formal legal system and norms of everyday morality, stressing that what is obligatory in the latter context may properly be unenforceable in the former. See Smith ([1790] 1976, 330–33). Moreover, he criticized his contemporaries in the field of law for confounding the two settings:

> But though this difference [between casuistry—referring to the analysis of rules of everyday morality—and jurisprudence] be real and essential, though those two sciences propose quite different ends, the sameness of the subject has made such a similarity between them, that the greater part of authors whose professed design was to treat of jurisprudence, have determined the different questions they examine, sometimes according to the principles of that science, and sometimes according to those of casuistry, without distinguishing, and, perhaps, without being themselves aware when they did the one, and when the other. (Ibid., 333)

little purpose. Thus, in settings in which contract law is important, having the law follow social norms about keeping promises—when compared to the alternative of having the law give little or no weight to contractual commitments—would tend to promote individuals' well-being. Indeed, fairness theorists often refer to the welfare-enhancing function of the institution of contract when motivating their purportedly non-welfarist positions.[131]

It should be clear from our prior discussion, however, that internalized social norms about promise-keeping provide only a crude basis for formulating contract law. The promise-keeping norm correctly tells us that enforcement of contracts is superior to nonenforcement, but it has little to offer beyond that; indeed, as applied by some promise-keeping theorists, the norm

131. See, for example, Atiyah (1981, 135–36), explaining that individuals gain from the institution of promise-keeping; Fried (1981, 8), discussing how the pursuit of others' trust, for its own sake, is a powerful tool for cooperative action that benefits individuals; ibid. (13), identifying the benefits of the promising convention, which is supported by the promise principle, as the ability to facilitate the projects of others and, more centrally, the ability to "facilitate each other's projects, where the gain is reciprocal"; and Fuller and Perdue (1936, 62–65). See also Rawls (1971, 348): "[G]iven the principle of fairness, we see why there should exist the practice of promising as a way of freely establishing an obligation when this is to the mutual advantage of both parties. Such an arrangement is obviously in the common interest. I shall suppose that these considerations are sufficient to argue for the principle of fairness."; Rawls (1955, 16), identifying, in the course of a discussion of philosophical literature on promise-keeping, the obvious utilitarian advantages of a practice that does not allow promisors the defense of a general appeal to utilitarian considerations; and Raz (1972, 101): "[P]romises are binding because it is desirable to make it possible for people to bind themselves and give rights to others if they so wish. It is desirable, in other words, to have a method of giving grounds for reasonable reliance in a special way. . . ." Nevertheless, it seems clear that most fairness theorists do not in fact adopt a view that they see as reducing entirely to welfare. See, for example, Fried (1981, 15), contrasting his theory with the utilitarian view, and Farber (1982, 561), claiming that Fried "argues that contracts should be enforced, not because enforcement facilitates socially useful conduct, but because individuals are morally obligated to keep their agreements."

Barnett is a mixed case: He seems to view efficiency or increasing the contracting parties' welfare as the reason for contracting, but he rejects such motivations as reasons for imposing obligations in the absence of consent (although this may be a mere semantic point, to the extent that he would allow other branches of law—permitting driving though it may infringe others' rights, allowing compulsory taxation to pay for public goods—to impose such obligations without the need for consent). See, for example, Barnett (1986a, 320; 1992b, 876). See also Craswell (1989, 524 n.86), characterizing Barnett's reason for giving individuals authority over transferring their property rights as libertarian, but adding that "[i]f one asks why freedom of action is itself a desirable thing, his answer sounds closer to economic or utilitarian notions of preference-satisfaction." Barnett also determines which rights can be transferred and how this may be done by invoking moral rights, without taking account of effects on individuals' well-being. See Barnett (1986b).

is affirmatively misleading. As we explain in subsection (e)(i), the promise-keeping notion of fairness does not, upon reflection, help us to choose among contract remedies. Moreover, the previously described difference between the contexts of everyday life and legal policy assessment make any prescriptions one may derive from the norm of doubtful value. Thus, when designing a formal system of contract enforcement, it is better to undertake the type of analysis that is expressly designed to assess the effects of legal rules on individuals' well-being rather than to debate which is the correct fairness-based theory of contract and what that theory really implies. Our instincts about what is fair may well suggest some valuable lines of analysis, but an understanding of the origins of such instincts should warn us against treating social norms about promise-keeping as though they were independent evaluative principles.

Second, in light of these social norms about keeping promises, it is possible that members of society have a taste for legal rules that reflect these norms: they might feel better off when the legal system implements some particular remedy if they generally understood that remedy to respect social norms. As we note in other contexts, however, the importance of this consideration depends upon empirical evidence about the prevalence of such a taste, not upon philosophical theorizing about contracts. We also observe that, for reasons we offer in connection with the following topic, individuals do not seem very likely to have a strong taste for remedies that differ from those that best promote parties' well-being.

The present inquiry suggests a third respect in which social norms about promise-keeping may be relevant under welfare economics: using one or another contract remedy may tend, over time, to reinforce or erode these social norms, which are, as noted, valuable in certain settings.[132] For example, using a remedy of specific performance rather than expectation damages may reduce the well-being of parties to contracts, but over time it may reinforce individuals' sense that keeping promises is important, thereby leading to improved behavior in everyday life, where legal remedies are not used. In such a case, a complete welfare economic evaluation would favor the stronger remedy if the benefits with regard to reinforcing useful social norms were sufficiently great.

The relevant empirical psychological and sociological inquiries into this issue have not been made, but we are doubtful that the results of such investigations would lead to a significantly different approach to contract enforce-

---

132. This illustrates the general possibility, which we explore briefly in subsection VIII.B.2, that the law may have an educative function, such that particular legal rules may support or undermine certain social norms.

ment. As we have noted, the normal alternative to performing contracts (keeping promises) in the formal legal setting is being held legally liable and being forced to pay full damages to the promisee, not avoiding one's obligation entirely. It is hardly obvious that individuals' awareness that the legal system generally uses expectation damages rather than specific performance has diminished their sense of the importance of keeping promises.[133] We also note that too strong a belief in the necessity of keeping promises—which might be conveyed by observing a legal system that insists on performance even when it would obviously be wasteful—probably would not produce ideal social norms.[134] Another relevant factor is that many legal rules regard-

133. In contrast, if the legal system were to permit a broad array of excuses, relieving promisors of any obligation to perform or to pay damages in most instances when breach appeared to be desirable overall, it would seem more plausible that the symbolic message would interfere with the social norm supporting promise-keeping.

134. We have already noted that prevailing social norms about promise-keeping often permit excuses where it is reasonably clear that performance would reduce individuals' well-being. See page 206 and note 123. It seems likely that successful inculcation of an absolutist view about the sanctity of promises would be detrimental rather than desirable. We would be worse off, not better off, if people took their own promises so seriously that they attempted to keep them even when performance was rendered very costly by a change in circumstances. Moreover, if too rigid a promise-keeping norm prevailed, people either would be excessively reluctant to make promises or would be induced to spend (waste) extra effort, whenever making simple promises, to offer a lengthy series of caveats. These caveats, as we have explained, are implied by welfare economic analysis. Moreover, we believe that they are already understood as part of many informal "promises" that people make. For example, a promise to meet for lunch would be understood by almost anyone to excuse nonperformance in the event of serious illness, or even for less extreme reasons.

This rather straightforward description of promise-keeping differs from the more rigid depiction of the notion by most promise-keeping theorists. Our impression is that they have observed the practice of promise-keeping—which does have some rigidity in the sense that it does not permit an open-ended excuse whenever the balance of good favors breaking a promise—and distilled from it a more pure, extreme version of the practice that they put forward as their favored moral principle. Because this difference between actual promise-keeping behavior and the theorists' ideal type is not recognized, however, the theorists do not attempt to defend the proposition that society would be better off under their idealized notion than under the prevailing one. Some writers do seem to express the concern that, once slippage from an extreme position is allowed, the game is over. Yet most would allow some slippage. Moreover, greater flexibility has in fact characterized the actual institution of promise-keeping, yet the practice has persisted for ages without obvious signs of an inevitable tendency to self-destruct. See also Gibbard (1982b, 72): "But if *in fact* . . . keeping promises in that class generally led to unhappy results, the moral aura that attached to keeping promises of that sort would fade, and the class would come to be regarded as an exception to the rule enjoining promise-keeping."

ing contracts are not very visible to most citizens; consider, for example, the rules regulating electronic funds transfers between financial institutions or those governing responsibilities between traders on an organized exchange. Finally, we are unsure of the extent to which the spillover process occurs in the first place, for it is possible that most individuals compartmentalize their thinking, taking the view that different rules are applicable in their informal interactions (say, with family and friends) than in their legally enforceable contractual relationships (with a bank or an airline).[135]

D. Additional Considerations

1. Distribution of Income

We have not emphasized the distributive effects of legal rules concerning contract enforcement[136] because there are none in the situations that we have examined. As we explain in subsection C.2(f), adjustment of the contract price to reflect the impact of legal rules always leads to a result in which both parties have the same interests (either both gain or both lose). This common feature of contractual settings tends to render moot many fairness considerations and also to make irrelevant any concerns about the distribution of income.

If one modifies our examples, however, it is possible that certain legal rules will help some individuals at the expense of others. For instance, suppose that, for one set of buyer-seller pairs, expectation damages are easy to determine from readily observable market prices, whereas reliance damages would provide too little incentive for performance in some situations. For a second set of buyer-seller pairs—who are contracting, say, about advertising campaigns for new products—expectation damages would be very difficult to calculate, but reliance damages are both more readily computed and sufficient to provide reasonably good incentives for suppliers of advertising services. Buyers and sellers in the first group would prefer expectation damages, whereas buyers and sellers in the second group would favor reliance damages. If courts cannot readily distinguish between the two sets of cases, a single rule will have to govern both types of situations. Whichever rule is

135. For further discussion of some of the issues addressed in this paragraph, see section VII.C and subsections VIII.A.3 and VIII.B.2–4.

136. Distributive effects have been emphasized in some prior writing. See, for example, Kennedy (1982) and Kronman (1980a).

chosen will benefit one group of buyers and sellers at the expense of the other.[137]

Our analysis of this type of case is essentially the same as our analysis of the nonreciprocal case in our discussion of tort law.[138] First, we would assess the relative magnitude of the costs and benefits to all parties under each rule in order to determine which group of buyers and sellers would benefit more from its preferred rule.[139] Second, if the choice of legal rules has a systematic effect on the distribution of income, this factor could also affect which rule is better under the framework of welfare economics.[140]

Now, aside from the possible effects on the general distribution of income just noted, we do not see any normatively relevant respect in which the present case differs from those that we examine in section C, in which individuals have unanimous rankings of the legal rules and those rankings are followed by welfare economics. In particular, the posited change in the situation does not present any apparent reason to favor a legal rule that reduces overall well-being on account of the fact that some particular individuals gain and others lose. In the present example, under whatever rule turns out to be best for society as a whole, the identity of gainers and losers will depend on the fortuity of whether an individual buyer or seller happens

137. As Craswell emphasizes, those who benefit under one legal rule, say, expectation damages, will not generally be buyers as a whole or sellers as a whole, but rather (as in our example in the text) one group of buyer-seller pairs, who gain at the expense of another group of buyer-seller pairs. See Craswell (1991, 372–84; 1992, 815–16, 835).

The disfavored group might contract around the rule that is undesirable for it. For example, if expectation damages apply in both cases, the second group may specify reliance damages in its contracts. Assuming, however, that this entails some cost (see our discussion of incomplete contracts at the outset of subsection C.2), the second group will still be somewhat worse off than if the general rule is reliance damages (and, perhaps, the first group contracted around that rule).

138. See subsection III.C.2.

139. The main factors affecting which rule maximizes total value for all parties combined (which is only part of the analysis when there are distributive effects) are the magnitude of the cost or benefit of one rule versus the other for each pair of contracting parties and the number of each type of party. To account for the possibility of contracting around undesirable rules, see note 137, the cost of so doing would be relevant as well.

140. In light of the preceding analysis, such an effect would not necessarily arise, for price adjustments tend to cause costs and benefits to be shared among contracting parties. (It would be possible, however, for one type of contracting pair—say, buyers and sellers contracting about advertising campaigns—to be richer or poorer than other groups of buyers and sellers.) Even when there are distributive effects, rules of contract law should take them into account only if the tax system is somehow unavailable for redistribution or is inferior to the use of legal rules. See subsection II.A.3.

to be one who stands to benefit from a contractual relationship in which the legal costs of administering a particular remedy are high or low. This essentially arbitrary characteristic seems unrelated to any plausible normative ground for favoring some individuals at the expense of others. And, in particular, it seems unrelated to either of the two notions of fairness regarding contract law that we have examined.[141] Thus, when we take distributive effects into account, our conclusion that normative analysis of legal rules should be guided exclusively by welfare economics remains unchanged.

2. Advantage-Taking

We have also assumed in this chapter that both parties to a contract are fully aware of all of its provisions and appreciate their implications. In these situations, it is not possible for one party to take advantage of the other by inserting one-sided terms into the contract. Whenever such terms are value-reducing, both parties are made worse off, as a consequence of an adjustment in the contract price. We now address briefly how our analysis applies to situations in which one of the parties is not fully informed.

For concreteness, suppose that one party, say, the buyer, will not read or understand all of the terms in a contract. This situation may arise, for example, when the seller presents a detailed form contract in connection with the sale of an inexpensive good or service. (Consider a car rental agreement or the warranty accompanying a hair dryer.) In a setting of this type, it generally would be irrational for the buyer to take the time to apprehend the contract's minutiae. Recognizing that fact, sellers may well include pro-seller provisions even though these terms reduce the overall value of the contract.[142]

---

141. See especially our discussion of income distribution and, more generally, of asymmetric situations in the tort context in subsections III.C.2(e) and III.E.3. We observe that the present example, in which some individuals gain at the expense of others regardless of which rule is selected, raises a problem for certain notions of autonomy that may underlie promise-keeping theories. The reason is that some theorists who invoke autonomy find it impermissible to use legal rules to help some when others who have done no wrong must be hurt in the process. Yet, in the present setting, this is precisely what will happen regardless of which of the two legal rules is chosen. We see no way to avoid doing what such theories forbid, short of choosing a regime that equally thwarts everyone's interests, if that were possible.

142. There may be a "race to the bottom." Sellers who offer biased but value-reducing provisions have lower costs and thus can charge lower prices, attracting customers from sellers who offer terms more valuable to buyers. Sellers of the latter type are unable to distinguish themselves (that is our assumption), so they are unable to keep customers from switching to lower-priced competitors.

Note that the analysis of contract terms is applicable to matters concerning the quality of contractual performance. For example, a value-reducing pro-seller term can be understood

In such situations, the question arises whether the law should uphold the contract as written or should in effect substitute more reasonable contract terms for those that the seller has drafted. Notions of fairness may be invoked in favor of the latter approach, which would prevent one party from taking advantage of another, something that seems quintessentially unfair—although the particular notions of fairness applicable here may well differ from those discussed with regard to contract remedies, and the pertinent notions are not generally stated in very precise terms.[143]

---

to cover the case in which a seller's product is of lower quality than the buyer perceives at the time of contracting, and the contract contains a disclaimer of liability regarding product quality.

143. See, for example, Eisenberg (1982), criticizing the bargain principle because it yields unfair results in settings involving exploitation. Some commentators view distributive concerns as central in such contexts, see Kronman (1980a), on which see note 144.

One could attempt to apply in the present setting the notions of fairness that we discuss in the context of remedies. For example, under one interpretation, the promise-keeping notion of fairness would hold uninformed parties to their literal contracts, for this is, after all, what they promised. Arguably, this interpretation is implied by the autonomy-based rationale that theorists often advance in support of the promise-keeping notion of fairness: When presented with a written contract, individuals are free to read it, and they may choose simply to ignore it; hence, if they sign it, they have promised to be bound by it. Another view is that uninformed parties' promises should be reinterpreted in light of the contracts they truly (or plausibly) intended, a concept that might be made more precise by reference to the mutually ideal complete contract. Under this interpretation, however, following the notion of fairness would be tantamount to adopting the welfare economic approach. Compare subsection C.2(e)(i), using the same approach to suggest that a contract stating that a party shall perform may be interpreted, under the promise-keeping view, to contain an option to pay damages or an implicit exception for when performance would be excessively costly. This interpretation could be reconciled with an autonomy-based rationale if autonomy is not understood in terms of actual willful choices but rather with regard to maximizing individuals' ability to realize their objectives. But this understanding would make preserving autonomy nearly synonymous with promoting individuals' well-being.

Unless one interprets the promise-keeping notion of fairness (or others) in a manner that gives it no significance independent of welfare economics, however, it seems that different notions of fairness need to be (and are) advanced in different settings, even within contract law. Thus, promise-keeping may be invoked with regard to issues of breach, and some advantage-taking notion of fairness may be applied to assess the validity of contract terms. When there are multiple and potentially conflicting notions of fairness—as is true even if one looks only to notions of fairness explicitly applicable to promises or contracts, or even just to remedies for breach—the fairness-based method of analysis is not complete until one provides some theory that determines the domain of each notion of fairness and reconciles any conflicts among them. For example, if a contract term concerns breach, does one apply the notion of fairness governing breach or that governing the validity of contract terms? (Furthermore, it could be argued that the method used to select which notion is most pertinent is implicitly based on a concern for which outcome advances individuals' well-being. Sidgwick advances this view with respect to a broad range of principles. See Sidgwick (1907).)

Welfare economic analysis may favor a similar result—replacing one-sided contract terms with more reasonable ones—for, under the stated conditions, enforcing the original terms may reduce parties' well-being.[144] That unsophisticated buyers may become subject to value-reducing arrangements is obvious. Welfare would also tend to decrease even for buyers who were sophisticated enough to know when sellers would probably attempt to take advantage of them (although not sufficiently informed to know how this may come about in a given transaction). A generalized awareness of the prospect of advantage-taking may lead buyers to avoid certain transactions (thereby reducing their well-being as they forgo otherwise valuable opportunities), to expend additional resources on investigation (a costly process that directly reduces well-being), or simply to lump it (in which case they will enter into contracts that are not value maximizing).[145] Less sophisticated parties will fare no better; unaware of the first two options, they are simply left with the third. If reasonably accurate legal intervention were possible at low cost,[146] then parties would generally be better off under the rule favored by notions of fairness.[147]

---

144. See, for example, Katz (1990a, 282–93; 1990b). See also *Restatement of the Law Second: Contracts* (1981, §211(3) and comment f), stating the conditions under which terms of form contracts will not be enforced.

In this subsection, we will not focus on whether the reduction in parties' well-being makes every person worse off or merely reduces overall welfare. As we note in the preceding subsection, if a legal rule has a distributive effect—for example, if sellers gain at the expense of buyers and sellers are, say, poorer than buyers (a sort of Robin Hood effect)—then the additional factor of distribution would have to be considered under a welfare economic analysis, unless, as may be the case, distributive effects are best achieved or offset through adjustments to the tax and transfer system.

145. Indeed, if literally anything a seller included in fine print were enforceable provided that the buyer signed on the dotted line, contracting would become a perilous activity. If buyers continued not to read, there would be no limit to what sellers might include as hidden terms. For example, they might require the buyer to surrender all of his assets in thirty days. Anticipating this possibility, buyers may be forced either not to enter into contracts at all or to read all contracts with painstaking scrutiny. The latter option would be very expensive, in relative terms, for the myriad small transactions that parties might wish to enter, and it would undoubtedly redirect much activity in ways that would prove costly. Perhaps a more likely outcome is that reasonably sophisticated parties would usually be willing to sign only extremely short contracts that left virtually everything open, to be supplied through default rules or in adjudication.

146. It is often imagined that courts would, in essence, rewrite contracts as necessary, on a case-by-case basis. An alternative would be for some legal body, perhaps a regulatory agency, to write standard form contracts, the use of which would be mandatory in certain settings. (Some compulsory disclosure rules perform a similar function.)

147. The analysis in the text is oversimplified in a number of respects, some of which we consider later in this subsection. The analysis also is incomplete and potentially mislead-

The preceding discussion suggests that, in the present context, there may be little difference between welfare economic analysis and that based on notions of fairness.[148] However, the alignment probably will be incomplete. One problem with notions of fairness concerns their definition and range of application. Just what should qualify as the "advantage-taking" that would constitute the basis for rejecting the contract terms nominally agreed to by the parties? Our consideration of advantage-taking in this subsection has focused on the problems that may arise when one party is imperfectly informed. The reason, as we note at the outset, is that when both parties fully understand all the effects of their contracts (including the legal rules that will be applied in interpreting them), both parties tend to gain from contract terms and legal rules that increase the size of the contractual pie; hence, the presence of imperfect information indicates when legal intervention may be beneficial. Fairness-minded commentators concerned about various sorts of advantage-taking, however, do not always identify the relevant conditions and often focus on rather different factors, such as the presence of monopoly power (or so-called unequal bargaining power)[149] or the use of "contracts of adhesion" (that is, take-it-or-leave-it offers that prevent offerees from individually negotiating the terms of the contracts).[150] As we discuss in the margin, however, neither of these factors is a necessary or sufficient condi-

---

ing because it may appear that, in the present setting, sellers necessarily gain from the ability to take advantage of uninformed buyers. This, however, need not be the case. First, to the extent that buyers are generally aware that the terms of many contracts are likely to be stacked against them, they may be unwilling to pay as much for goods and services as they otherwise would. Second, regardless of buyers' reactions, competition among sellers will lead them to charge lower prices because pro-seller provisions presumably lower sellers' costs (which makes attracting customers away from their competitors more profitable than would otherwise be the case). Thus, in equilibrium, sellers may not make excess profits, whether because buyers are inclined to pay less for what they anticipate to be inferior deals or because competition erodes profits. Even if sellers do not profit at buyers' expense, buyers may nevertheless be worse off because they face inferior contractual opportunities, as we describe in the text.

148. Indeed, it seems plausible that the concerns for fairness under discussion are motivated, at least in part, by a concern for individuals' well-being. To that extent, it is not surprising that notions of fairness should serve as a proxy device for identifying legal rules that advance individuals' well-being with regard to advantage-taking, just as we observe with regard to other notions of fairness applicable to contract remedies and other sorts of legal rules. As the text to follow emphasizes, however, these fairness principles are likely to be imperfect proxy tools, as are other fairness principles in different contexts.

149. See, for example, Kessler (1943).

150. See Kessler (1943) and Rakoff (1983).

tion for problematic contractual terms to arise.[151] As a consequence, notions of fairness that use these considerations to determine the existence of advantage-taking are likely to lead us astray by favoring legal rules that make both parties worse off—for no apparent reason.

Indeed, even the factor of imperfect information is not by itself a sufficient indicator of when contract terms should be modified. First, bad contract terms may not arise. Even when some buyers are uninformed, if enough

---

151. First, consider monopoly power. Its presence is not a necessary condition for welfare to decrease, because, as we explain in the text and in notes 142 and 147, when one party is imperfectly informed, individuals' well-being may decline even when there is competition. Nor is monopoly power a sufficient condition, because, if consumers are aware of quality levels, a monopolist will generally have strong incentives to offer appropriately high quality, whether with respect to goods and services or contract terms.

To see that this is true in simple cases, suppose that a monopolist offered a contract of too low quality, which is to say that higher quality would be worth more to each buyer than it costs the monopolist to provide. Under these circumstances, if the monopolist were to raise the level of quality, it could raise its price by more than its incremental cost and still sell the same amount to buyers. This possibility means that the monopolist's profits are not maximized when quality is too low. There are a range of qualifications to this point, see, for example, Spence (1975, 417–22), but they may lead monopolists to choose quality that is either too high or too low. These qualifications are therefore not inconsistent with the basic argument that the presence of monopoly power is not a sufficient condition for quality to be too low; in addition, the qualifications appear to be unrelated to any notions of fairness of which we are aware.

As a final note, we observe that the existence of monopoly power may justify some types of government policy, such as antitrust laws or price regulation; our point here is that the existence of such power is not a reliable indicator of when it makes sense to rewrite parties' contractual terms.

With regard to contracts of adhesion, we first observe that, when parties subject to such contracts, say, buyers, are fully informed, sellers have an incentive to offer value-maximizing terms. For example, consider the related case (see note 142) of observable product characteristics. If sellers of hair dryers offer one color or style of hair dryer, they will sell more hair dryers or be able to charge higher prices by selling the color or style that buyers most prefer; sellers who make ugly or clumsy hair dryers—characteristics that we are assuming buyers can observe—will not fare as well. (Likewise, if buyers are sufficiently diverse in their contractual preferences and if the cost of offering more choices is sufficiently low, sellers have an incentive to provide more individualized treatment, for sellers who offer such variety can profitably lure customers away from their competitors who do not.) Second, when buyers are unable to understand contract terms or other product characteristics or, alternatively, would not rationally take the time to ascertain them, the opportunity to negotiate over details would not improve their situation because sellers would take advantage of them in any negotiations. That is, as we discuss in the text, the existence of imperfect information is sufficient to raise questions about the desirability of contract terms and other aspects of contractual arrangements.

others are informed, sellers may be induced to offer value-maximizing terms.[152] In addition, companies' concern for their reputations may lead them to offer good contract terms; similarly, fear of adverse publicity may lead them to forgo the enforcement of onerous terms when such enforcement would be inappropriate. Second, it may be costly to determine when and how contract terms should be modified, and such calculations are susceptible to mistake. Under a welfare economic analysis, modification of contract terms would only be endorsed when the expected gain from doing so was sufficient to justify the costs.[153] Rigorous application of notions of fairness, by contrast, may favor intervention even when it would make parties worse off.

Notions of fairness pose another problem: even if it were possible to identify the conditions conducive to undesirable advantage-taking, it remains to be determined *which* contract terms require modification and *how* they should be revised. Notions of fairness concerned with advantage-taking do not offer a clear method of finding answers to these questions.[154] By con-

152. See, for example, Schwartz and Wilde (1979).

153. Moreover, in performing the relevant analysis, a welfare economic approach would take into account how legal rules would affect parties' incentives to write better contracts in the first instance and parties' incentives to read contracts before accepting them.

154. See, for example, Slawson (1971), presenting part of the economic explanation of why form contracts may be problematic but offering as the only guidance to courts, in determining what terms to enforce, the suggestion that the terms be fair, democratic, and in the public interest. Indeed, as we discuss above, leading writers on the subject who do not explicitly adopt a welfare economic approach, which focuses on how rules affect parties' well-being, tend to emphasize the wrong factors in diagnosing the situation. (It is possible that the factors they emphasize are relevant under some notion of fairness even though they provide misleading results with regard to assessing parties' well-being.)

To illustrate the problems that may arise, consider the doctrine that ambiguities in insurance policies are to be construed against the drafter. See, for example, Russ and Segalla (1997, vol. 2, §22:14): "The words, 'the contract is to be construed against the insurer' comprise the most familiar expression in the reports of insurance cases." This doctrine seems rooted, at least in part, in notions of fairness. See ibid. (§22:18), noting that the common view that the rule of construction is based on the insurer having been the drafter sometimes "is simply stated in terms of fairness, namely, that since the language of the policy is that of the insurer it is both reasonable and just that its own words should be construed most strongly against it," and citing cases from most U.S. jurisdictions. But this notion of fairness does not adequately deal with the problem at hand. First, because it is often irrational for the insured to read most of the contract, the notion that ambiguity somehow inhibits communication of the content of the bargain is misconceived. Indeed, the doctrine itself may well suppress communication, for any attempt by an insurance company to communicate the gist of an agreement, in simple language that one might actually read and understand, may expose the company to liability for risks against which it does not make sense to insure. Second, it obviously

trast, welfare economics does offer a framework for addressing the questions. Just as in the case of contract remedies, one would refer to the parties' mutually ideal complete contract as a source for terms that would make the parties better off. Thus, in another important respect, notions of fairness in this context seem to diverge from welfare economics, to parties' detriment.[155]

3. The Extent to Which the Use of Notions of Fairness Has Led Us Astray

As we discuss in section B, the leading notions of fairness seem to call for specific performance or reliance damages. If contract law did in fact consistently embody one of these notions of fairness—which it clearly does not, as expectation damages (a remedy neither fairness theory implies) is the standard remedy[156]—we believe that we would indeed have been led astray.[157]

---

will not generally be optimal to construe contracts in this manner. Many reasons dictate that certain risks and contingencies not be covered by insurance contracts. (Some of these relate to the insured's incentives or pricing problems concerning risks about which the insured knows more than the insurance company.) The familiar notion that the pro-insured rule of construction makes sense because the purpose of insurance is to provide the fullest possible protection, see ibid. (§22:19), is therefore incomplete in a critical sense. Third, if rigorously enforced, the doctrine would induce insurance companies to spend substantial resources writing detailed language to cover remote contingencies although it makes no sense to do so. Finally, the problem described in the text—that terms will tend to be skewed when contracts are not read by most signatories—is not substantially addressed in any event, because the doctrine does not apply to language that undesirably restricts coverage as long as such language is clear. (A conjecture as to the explanation for this rule is that courts are unsure how to construe ambiguous clauses. This uncertainty, however, may in turn be attributable to analysis that draws upon notions of fairness—which may provide little guidance in all but the most obvious cases—rather than one that uses a welfare economic approach.)

155. The problems identified in this section could be avoided only if one endorsed a notion of fairness that took all welfare-relevant factors into account and gave them proper weight, but then one's notion of fairness would call for analysis equivalent to that under welfare economics.

156. See, for example, Farber and Matheson (1985), surveying promissory estoppel cases and finding that enforcement does not strongly depend on the detriment to the promisee and that reliance-based damages are exceptional, which makes these cases much more like the larger category of cases involving bargained-for exchange; Friedmann (1995), arguing that Fuller and Perdue's writing has been very influential in the legal academy but has not substantially influenced the law; and Yorio and Thel (1991, 130–51), showing that, even in promissory estoppel cases under section 90 of the *Restatement (Second) of Contracts*, expectation damages are the ordinary remedy and damages are computed according to the reliance formulation only in anomalous cases.

157. That contract doctrine appears less influenced by notions of fairness than are other legal doctrines calls for some explanation. One conjecture is that many judges (through prior

This is most apparent under the promise-keeping notion, which in principle favors specific performance. Requiring contracts to be performed, even when performance would be highly undesirable, would result in needless social waste.[158] Likewise, a standard rule of reliance damages would appear to induce breach more often than necessary.[159]

Although notions of fairness may not have led us seriously astray—because basic rules of damages do not seem to reflect such principles[160]—we suspect that the law would be improved by greater attention to the consequences of contract rules for individuals' well-being. First, even if the basic rule of expectation damages is generally desirable, various subsidiary doctrines may not be advantageous.[161] Second, as we note at various points

---

experience representing clients) and others charged with formulating contract rules have sufficient exposure to commercial dealings governed by the formal legal system that they are less vulnerable to the influence of internalized social norms corresponding to notions of fairness and more likely to adopt an explicitly instrumental outlook. Another explanation is that social norms about promise-keeping are not as rigid as the notions of fairness advanced by philosophers and some legal commentators, and that the norms' actual contours are fairly close to those that welfare economics would prescribe.

158. The actual extent of such waste would be limited, for example, by the parties' ability to renegotiate their obligations (for example, a party under a duty to perform may pay the promisee to waive the obligation), but renegotiation will not always be possible or successful.

159. This problem is likely to be mitigated, but not eliminated, by the possibility of renegotiation. See note 158. The extent to which this problem would arise is also limited by the fact that reliance damages, properly understood, would be equivalent to expectation damages in many instances. See note 61. We also note that another aspect of the reliance-based fairness notion—that any reasonable reliance should provide a basis for contractual liability—may well (if it were to become generally reflected in the law) lead us badly astray. See note 31, suggesting that such a notion would create a vast range of liability.

160. In other areas of contract doctrine, such as those pertaining to information disclosure and the interpretation of form contracts, we believe that there is somewhat more attention to notions of fairness and a corresponding neglect of the actual consequences of legal rules. See, for example, note 154. The extent to which bad rules result depends on how well the notions of fairness relevant in those contexts serve as a proxy device for identifying welfare-relevant concerns.

161. For example, courts are hostile to liquidated damages clauses deemed to be penalties (because they provide for damages in excess of actual harm), although parties may have good reasons—to their mutual benefit—to adopt such clauses. By contrast, certain doctrines, such as the requirement to mitigate damages, seem to reflect a welfare economic perspective rather than one based on notions of fairness. (Why, if not out of concern for welfare, must a promisee, who justly relied upon a promisor bound to keep his promise, have to undertake efforts that, in the end, benefit the promisor by reducing the damages he must pay to the promisee?) We do not here take a position on the extent to which contract law (or any other field of law) is more consistent (in its content or stated motivation) with one or another justificatory theory; we merely suggest that there seems to be evidence of the influence both of various notions of fairness and of a concern for individuals' well-being.

above, the rule of expectation damages is best only in certain circumstances: administrative costs, risk aversion, problems of excessive reliance by prom- isees, and other factors could well render different remedies superior.[162] It is not at all clear that existing doctrine (as reflected in both the common law and in relevant provisions of the Uniform Commercial Code) is sufficiently sensitive to context-specific factors that may favor other rules.[163]

162. See page 197.

163. On one hand, standard doctrine is relatively insensitive to some factors relevant to contracting parties' well-being. On the other hand, case-by-case litigation over damage rules is costly, and when remedies reduce value substantially, parties will be inclined to contract in advance for different remedies or to renegotiate when problems arise. Accordingly, we do not suggest that existing doctrine is necessarily mistaken or, if so, that it has serious negative consequences. Nevertheless, it does not appear to reflect careful analysis of the relevant consid- erations.

We also note that a significant portion of contract disputes arise outside the formal legal system and are governed instead by trade association regulation, arbitration systems (selected through contractual provisions), and even informal networks. Perhaps sophisticated parties' consistent bypassing of the legal system evidences serious problems in contract law. It seems likely, however, that an important (and perhaps the primary) explanation for opting out of the formal legal system lies in perceived procedural deficiencies—notably, procedures that result in excessive litigation costs and inaccurate, unpredictable decisions—rather than prob- lems with the substantive law of contract. For investigation of these and related issues, see the sources cited in note 127.

CHAPTER V

Legal Procedure

In this chapter, we consider two important aspects of legal procedure.[1] In section A, we examine the basic question of when individuals should be permitted to bring suit. In section B, we address the accuracy of legal procedure once a suit is brought. The issue of accuracy bears on a whole range of procedures—rules governing preliminary disposition, discovery, the conduct of trial, and appeal—that affect the ability of the legal system to produce correct outcomes at a reasonable cost. In each of these two sections, we explain how the approach of welfare economics applies, describe the pertinent notions of fairness, and then assess in paradigmatic settings whether the evaluation of legal procedures should be based on welfare economics or notions of fairness. We also discuss why notions of fairness seem appealing in spite of the problems that we identify.

Both of these sections focus on how different legal procedures affect legal costs and help to determine how underlying substantive legal rules ultimately affect behavior (for example, the ease of bringing suit will affect the extent to which a legal rule deters harmful conduct).[2] In section C, we consider other ways that procedural devices may influence individuals' well-being, such as by limiting abuse of power or by enhancing the legitimacy of the legal system.

Before commencing our investigation, we think it useful to highlight

---

1. We generally discuss civil procedure, although some of our analysis and the literature that we cite relates to the criminal context. As in our treatment of other areas of law, our goal is to examine certain basic questions, not to cover all important topics in the field.

2. We also briefly discuss the compensation of victims and the distribution of income.

the relationship between legal procedure and the substantive law that provides the underlying basis for lawsuits. Under welfare economics, this connection is central, for legal procedure is primarily viewed as providing the means by which substantive legal rules are ultimately enforced. For example, the effect of tort law on the deterrence of accidents will depend on which victims actually sue and the expected outcomes of the resulting litigation.

In contrast, the literature on the fairness of legal procedures does not usually emphasize the link between procedure and substance. Nevertheless, we believe that this interdependence should also be viewed as central from the perspective of those concerned with notions of fairness.[3] For example, it seems that the existence and importance of a right to sue ought, in principle, to depend upon the underlying basis for the legal rule that provides the grounds for a lawsuit. Thus, if the substantive interest were trivial, failing to make available an elaborate system for adjudication might not be deemed unfair—or at least not as unfair as when the substantive interest is great. The inherently instrumental character of procedure suggests that largely nonconsequentialist notions of fairness in procedure are inappropriate to employ. At a minimum, it seems clear that independent notions of fairness regarding legal procedure cannot be viewed in a vacuum when determining how the legal system should operate.

To the extent that the normative evaluation of legal procedure depends on an evaluation of the substantive legal rules that the legal system is designed to implement, our analysis in prior chapters suggests that notions of fairness should be given no weight in the evaluation of legal procedure. For example, our analysis of torts in chapter III is applicable to any legal rule, including any procedural rule, and to any notion of fairness, including one pertinent to legal procedure in torts cases. Hence, if our argument there was convincing, we will have already established that notions of fairness regarding procedure are not acceptable evaluative principles, at least in tort cases.[4] Nevertheless, because somewhat different notions of fairness are often advanced with regard to procedure, and because the welfare economic analysis of legal procedure may be less familiar to many readers, we take up the subject independently.

3. See, for example, L. Alexander (1998), arguing, from a rights perspective, that procedural rights are components of substantive rights and have no independent status.

4. Similarly, our analysis of contracts in chapter IV shows that, when parties are informed about the effects of legal rules and therefore take them into account when bargaining over the contract price, both parties would always be better off with welfare-maximizing provisions, which would include all provisions pertaining to the resolution of any disputes that may arise.

A. Ability to Bring Suit

1. *Welfare Economics and the Ability to Bring Suit*

In many areas of law, including those we examine in this chapter, a primary reason to permit individuals to sue is that the prospect of suit provides an incentive for desirable behavior in the first instance.[5] Thus, an assessment of rules governing when parties may sue depends on how the provision of such an incentive affects parties' well-being. The central concerns are the costs to potential parties of their actions (the cost of precautions, of performing contracts, and so forth) and the effects of their behavior on other individuals (the extent of harm caused, whether promised goods are delivered). In addition, the costs of legal proceedings themselves matter— whether those costs are borne by plaintiffs, defendants, or the state (in which case individuals ultimately bear the burden through taxes).

Permitting suit may have other direct effects on individuals. First, by providing compensation to injured parties, a right of action can serve a valuable insurance function when individuals are risk averse and uninsured. (However, the prospect of having to make payments may impose risk on potential defendants.) Second, in some settings, lawsuits may affect the distribution of income, which would be important if other means (notably, tax and transfer programs) were unavailable or inferior. For the most part, we set aside these two effects by assuming that individuals are risk neutral and by considering reciprocal settings (in which income distribution is never affected); extending our analysis to consider these factors would lead us largely to repeat our corresponding discussions of tort law from chapter III. (Moreover, there are additional effects of suit, which we consider in section C.)

---

5. In some settings, such as suits for injunctions or licensing proceedings, the goal is to control future behavior. Although the particular analysis may differ, the general principles of welfare economics remain largely the same. See, for example, Kaplow (1994b, 369–381).

Another general function of permitting aggrieved individuals to sue is that it substitutes for self-help, which may be costly or violent. See, for example, Fuller (1978, 357, 372), subsection III.E.1, and subsections V.A.6 and VI.D.1. Compare Carrington and Babcock (1983, 1): "Essential to any civilization is control of conflicts among its members." For the most part, we suppose that individuals will accept the results that the legal system provides, including the possibility that no legal redress may be available. In subsection C.2, however, we consider how legal procedures may affect the perceived legitimacy of the legal system, thereby affecting individuals' well-being.

2. Notions of Fairness and the Ability to Bring Suit[6]

The most relevant conception of fairness is the idea that individuals who have suffered injuries for which the law provides a remedy should be permitted to sue to recover for their losses.[7] That is, it would be unfair to bar a potential plaintiff with a valid claim from bringing a lawsuit. Moreover, the

6. A difficulty we face here (and in subsection B.2, on notions of fairness and accuracy in adjudication) is that there is no body of literature by legal scholars or philosophers on the subject—unlike with torts, where there is a literature on corrective justice; with contracts, where there is a literature on promise-keeping and also on reliance by promisees; and with crime and law enforcement, where there is a literature on retributive justice. This gap in the literature exists despite what one would think to be the centrality of procedural justice to the fairness of any legal system. However, some writing exists on particular procedural subjects, such as the appropriateness of encouraging settlement, see, for example, Fiss (1984); the fairness of group versus individual justice (usually with reference to class actions), see, for example, the sources cited in note 7; and the need for particular procedural protections in determinations that involve government welfare benefits (the literature spawned by the Supreme Court's decisions in Goldberg v. Kelly, 397 U.S. 254 (1970), and Mathews v. Eldridge, 424 U.S. 319 (1976)), see, for example, Mashaw (1976). Selections from these literatures and other writings—as well as impressions of common understandings that we have absorbed during our years in the legal academy—provide the background for our discussion of notions of fairness with regard to legal procedure. (We note, however, that many of the arguments in the scholarship on procedure are rooted in concerns for individuals' well-being. Consider, for example, many of the concerns raised by Fiss (1984), and see also the discussion of literature in the notes to subsection C.2.) Many of the internal problems that we have found in the literatures on notions of fairness and other legal subjects are even more pronounced here because few writers on procedure have attempted to elaborate any detailed theory of fairness, and because most who draw on notions of fairness make their points briefly or leave their ideas about fairness implicit.

7. See, for example, R. Dworkin (1985, 73), and Michelman (1973, 1177): "However articulated, defended, or accounted for, the sense of legal rights as claims whose realization has intrinsic value can fairly be called rampant in our culture and traditions." The statement in the text assumes that claims are valid; we consider claims of uncertain validity at the end of this subsection.

The right to bring suit can arise in other settings, such as that addressed by the Supreme Court in Martin v. Wilks, 490 U.S. 755 (1989), in which individuals not party to the original proceeding challenged the remedy as a violation of their constitutional rights. Ibid. (762), referring to the tradition that everyone is entitled to his own day in court and citing Wright, Miller, and Cooper (1981, vol. 18, §4449). See Ortiz v. Fibreboard Corp., 527 U.S. 815, 846 (1999), invoking the same principle in the context of class certification; Bone (1992); and Fiss (1993). See also Cottreau (1998, 510–21), advocating broader opt-out rights on grounds that each individual should be able to have his own day in court; Transgrud (1989), offering fairness arguments, among others, in favor of allowing each victim to pursue claims individually in the mass tort setting; and Woolley (1997), arguing that each class member should have an individual right to be heard and to participate in litigation affecting his rights.

notion that there is a right to sue, as this fairness notion is often expressed, may be deemed applicable to cases in which the complaining party has a valid claim but may be discouraged from pursuing it because of the costs of suit.[8]

Most analysts, however, recognize a need to trade off the right to bring suit and legal costs.[9] One may justify limiting the right to recovery on the ground that lawsuits themselves impose costs on others—the defendant and the state (and thus other citizens)—which can be seen as involving a sort of unfairness. Whatever the precise limit, one imagines that fairness advocates who favor anything short of an unfettered ability to bring any valid claim would base their limit in some manner on the size of legal costs relative to the magnitude of the grievance, perhaps confining suit to cases in which plaintiffs can afford their own legal costs. For convenience, we will hereafter refer to notions of fairness that would, in some manner, condition the right to sue on the magnitude of legal costs as "moderate" and notions that favor an unconditional right to sue, supported by subsidies when necessary, as "strong."

8. As some commentators have stated:

> The American citizen's access to the courts is one of the pillars of a government of laws. "Access to the courts" must mean more than some abstract or theoretical right to use the courts. It means they must be accessible in the practical sense of being financially affordable as well as physically approachable. People are entitled to pursue their claims or interpose their defenses for financial outlays that are not terrifyingly high or disproportionate to the stakes. (Rosenberg, Smit, and Dreyfuss 1990, 46)

See, for example, Brickman (1973); Leubsdorf (1984, 631–37), arguing that the Constitution supports subsidization of parties who cannot afford civil litigation; and Michelman (1974, 530): "'[L]iberty' encompasses the interest in pressing litigation as far as the provable facts and prevailing law will carry you, and . . . the state deprives you of that part of liberty without due process when it exacts a price for enjoyment which you are unable to pay." Indeed, given the importance that many attach to the right to sue, it would seem surprising if the right were effectively available only to those who expected to profit more by investing in a lawsuit than in other ventures.

9. See, for example, Hazard and Taruffo (1993, 215): "The fundamental problem for American civil justice is to accommodate these ideals—equality, access, autonomy, and openness in civil justice—to the reality that their fulfillment entails economic, political, and moral costs."; Burbank and Silberman (1997), examining two goals of reform—reducing expense and delay and ensuring access to justice—and noting how the former can assist with the latter; and Resnik (1984, 844–59). Compare Trangsrud (1985, 779–80), suggesting an "inescapable tension between the interest of individual litigants in preserving individual control of claims and procedural fairness, on the one hand, and the interest of the judicial system in the efficient joinder of related claims, on the other."

Before evaluating these notions of fairness, we note that they are incomplete in important respects.[10] First, the suggestion that individuals should be permitted to sue whenever the law provides a remedy begs the question: If no suit were permitted, or if the right to bring suit were somehow circumscribed, then it would no longer be true that the law unconditionally provides a remedy; hence, the posited right to sue would be inapplicable.[11] (For example, if playing loud music outdoors during daytime hours is not legally deemed to be a nuisance, a complaining party whose suit was dismissed could not object that his right to sue was thereby violated.) Thus, the view that a notion of fairness requires permitting individuals to sue in order to seek legal redress presupposes some independent reason for there to be a substantive provision making legal redress available in the first place.[12] This

10. We believe that the problems that we describe in the text to follow largely derive from the previously noted point that any coherent view of the value of legal procedures must relate intimately to the purpose for the underlying substantive legal provision, whereas fairness-based analysis of procedure does not usually refer to the purposes of the substantive law.

11. This form of argument is analogous to the familiar difficulty of establishing procedural due process rights under the Constitution in cases in which there is no constitutional basis for the underlying substantive right. See, for example, L. Alexander (1987b, 325–26, 341–43; 1998, 26–31) and Grey (1977, 187–97). Most such disputes, however, concern when due process rights trigger once a substantive right is provided (such as when a legislature enacts a welfare program); when no substantive right exists, it is generally accepted that there is no procedural right to the substantive right's creation.

12. Dworkin's argument recognizes this problem. See R. Dworkin (1985, 73–77). His answer seems to be based entirely on the distinction between statutes, which create "rights"— a realm in which welfare maximization is appropriate—and adjudication, which vindicates them—a realm in which one must adhere to principle. This approach, however, is unsatisfactory. First, most procedures affecting—and potentially limiting—the right to sue (as well as those affecting accuracy, as we discuss in section B) are determined in advance, through legislation or equivalents. (This includes, for example, the rules of civil procedure, the rules of evidence, laws governing fee-shifting, rules determining what costs parties must bear, and whether suit is subsidized.) Since Dworkin concedes that initial rights may be set to promote welfare, the only import of his view is that, once the rules are in place, judges must follow them. (This position too follows readily from a welfare economic approach: If the rules are set to maximize welfare, then it is welfare maximizing for them to be followed; moreover, even if occasional deviations might further increase welfare, one presumes that the decision that a rule that permits no exceptions is welfare maximizing encompasses the judgment that more harm than good would result from permitting agents implementing the rule to deviate at their discretion. See also subsection C.2, discussing how controlling possible abuse of power by government actors, such as judges, can advance welfare in the context of adjudication.) We further note that even Dworkin's more limited claim about judges fails if the original rules, which create the rights, themselves contain provisions that delegate authority to judges (including the possibility that judges may be given discretion to dismiss suits when this would promote the general welfare), for then it would simply be the case that no "rights" in Dworkin's

observation suggests that any theory of fair procedure derives from other principles regarding the underlying substantive law.[13] (We observe further that most fairness-based analysis of substantive law tends to ignore both the costs of lawsuits[14] and whether, under the substantive rules deemed to be fair, aggrieved parties would have an incentive to bring suit. As a result, even if one understood the grounding in notions of fairness for given rules of substantive law,[15] it would still be unclear whether one could infer a particular position with regard to the right to bring suit.)

In addition, fairness proponents have not explained how they believe the right to bring suit should be limited. On one hand, it seems that many who believe in a right to sue also favor substantial limits on that right because of the already noted concern about imposing costs on defendants and the state. In any legal system, countless suits over minor matters either are not permitted or are permitted in principle but rarely brought in practice due to the unrecoverable costs that the plaintiff would have to bear. If a notion of fairness required suits in all such instances, operating the legal system could bankrupt society.[16] On the other hand, fairness proponents usually do not address how limits on suits should be determined, even in the clearest cases in which the potential plaintiff's claim is fully meritorious. Thus, our suggestions above that many fairness proponents would limit suits as a func-

---

sense would have been created in the first place. See also notes 63 and 65, further discussing Dworkin's views, and note 47 in chapter VI, discussing similar problems with mixed views regarding the setting of punishment by legislatures and the application of punishment by courts.

13. The same logic suggests that this link between procedure and substance will exist under welfare economics as well, and our analysis indeed bears out the existence of such a connection.

14. See, for example, subsections III.C.1(e)(i) and III.D.1(f)(i), presenting examples in the torts context.

15. One can imagine that substantive rules could be based on welfare economics whereas procedures would be based (at least in part) on independent notions of fairness, but such a position would be internally inconsistent. If, for example, a welfare economic analysis showed lawsuits to be undesirable in some set of circumstances, the substantive law would optimally provide that there is no violation in those cases; hence, prohibiting suit would not violate any notion of fairness that required permitting individuals to bring suit whenever they had a legitimate legal grievance. See also note 12, discussing Dworkin.

16. Much of the literature on fair procedures seems on its face to indicate that the authors implicitly favor such an extreme result. We assume, however, that if confronted with this point, they would retreat to a moderate position. The problem that we identify in the text is that we cannot infer what such an intermediate position really is. We also note that the concession to costs that fairness advocates would make means that they implicitly give substantial weight to welfare, in spite of their frequent claims to the contrary.

tion of the costs and the stakes, or that they may favor allowing suits only when plaintiffs find them profitable, are speculative.[17] We do not know what limits would actually be favored if this basic tradeoff were directly confronted or what supplementary normative principles would be invoked to justify those limits.

Another subject that raises serious problems for fairness theories in the present context is uncertainty regarding the validity of legal claims. To simplify our exposition and to consider the best case from the perspective of fairness theorists, we examine legal claims that are clearly valid.[18] A complete theory, however, would have to indicate when it was fair for suits with a given probability of validity (perhaps perceived differently by the plaintiff, the defendant, and, ultimately, the court) to proceed, and with what attendant costs. Whether the plaintiff will find it profitable to proceed, which can happen in some contexts even with wholly meritless suits, can hardly be a dispositive test. Moreover, there is always the prospect of encouraging suits (through free legal services, subsidies to the filing of suits, cost-shifting, and damage multipliers) or discouraging them (through opposite policies), so a profitability test cannot answer basic questions of procedural design. By and large, commentators do not even attempt to resolve this endemic problem when they invoke notions of fairness to assess legal procedures.[19]

3.   Description of a Basic Case

We will build upon the simplest case that we presented in subsection III.C.1 of our torts discussion, which involves reciprocal accidents that impose cer-

---

17. In addition, it is rather difficult to interpret what such cost or profitability limitations might mean because legal rules themselves determine whether the plaintiff can afford his legal costs—for example, by deciding what (if anything) to charge to bring a case or whether the plaintiff is responsible for the defendants' costs. Likewise, various aspects of procedural design not directed at the plaintiff's choices will nevertheless affect the plaintiff's costs.

18. Relatedly, in section B we consider the presentation of evidence that is valid and that the factfinder will properly assess.

19. In contrast, under welfare economics, the principles applicable to invalid claims are clear, even if the analysis is more complicated. Invalid claims tend both to waste the resources involved in suit and to undermine the purposes of the substantive provisions—for example, if even those who behave properly are sued sometimes, the incentive to behave properly is diluted. One would assess the costs of procedures to weed out invalid claims and compare them with the resulting benefits. In addition, one would compare alternatives, which include adjusting substantive rules in an attempt to restore the deterrence lost on account of allowing some invalid claims or screening out some valid ones.

tain harm.[20] To remind the reader, in the reciprocal case that we considered, each individual is once in the role of potential injurer and once in that of potential victim. As before, concreteness is helpful: Suppose that the harm is $100 and that the costs of precaution (which would prevent the harm entirely) are $25 in one situation and $150 in another. In addition, we assume that there are costs of bringing suit: We consider cases in which the plaintiff's costs are $10 or $110; the defendant's costs will always be $10.[21]

In a regime of strict liability, we examine three procedural rules regarding the right to bring suit. First, we examine the standard regime in the United States: Plaintiffs make their own decisions whether to bring suit, and parties bear their own legal costs. Second, in those instances in which a plaintiff would choose not to sue, we consider the possibility of a subsidy to plaintiffs sufficient to induce them to sue.[22] Third, when a plaintiff would otherwise sue, we consider the possibility of prohibiting suits (or taxing suits sufficiently to discourage them).

4. Effects of the Legal Rules[23]

The different procedural rules will affect when potential plaintiffs will choose to sue and whether potential injurers will take care. The analysis of each

---

20. It should be clear that our analysis applies more generally than to this simple tort setting. Thus, one could apply our analysis in section III.D, which shows that our results hold in cases involving risk, both when parties are insured and when they are not. Likewise, one could draw upon our analysis in subsections III.C.2 and III.D.2 to extend our present analysis to the case of nonreciprocal accidents. See also subsection III.C.1(e)(iii), indicating the importance of conclusions in the reciprocal case for nonreciprocal cases. Moreover, our example translates to wholly different contexts, such as a suit for contract breach: The harm would correspond to the value lost by the victim of breach, and the cost of precaution would correspond to the breaching party's cost of undertaking performance rather than breaching the contract. See subsection 7, on the generality of our results.

21. For simplicity, we assume that the state incurs no costs. In the perfectly reciprocal situation that we examine, this assumption has no effect: Individuals would also be symmetrically situated as taxpayers and hence would ultimately bear equal shares of any costs initially incurred by the state; accordingly, one can view the state's costs as included (half each) in the costs incurred by each of the two parties.

22. We could instead consider fee-shifting, a more commonly employed device. The analysis would be largely the same. The only difference would be that, in a fee-shifting regime, potential injurers' net liability would be greater, which would further increase their incentive to take care. In some instances, this change would modify our particular characterizations of the effects of encouraging suit, but essentially the same general results could be obtained.

23. The analyses in this subsection and in subsection 5(a) illustrate results originally presented in Shavell (1982b, 1997, 1999).

rule is straightforward in our example. Under the standard rule by which plaintiffs must pay their own way, they will sue if and only if the harm (and thus the prospective damages recovery) exceeds their litigation costs. Here, they sue when their litigation costs are $10 but not when they are $110 (because the harm, and thus the prospective damages award, is $100). In the latter case, however, plaintiffs will be induced to sue if there is a sufficient subsidy (exceeding $10). In the former case, they would not sue if there were a prohibition (or a sufficiently high tax, exceeding $90).

Injurers will take care when, if they did not, they would be sued for causing harm and their cost of care is only $25; in this instance, their cost of care is less than the $100 in damages they would otherwise have to pay (plus the $10 in legal costs that they would incur). If the cost of care is $150, however, they will not take care, preferring to pay $110 ($100 in damages and $10 in legal costs). Also, if injurers will not be sued, they will have no incentive to take care and thus will not do so, regardless of whether care costs only $25 or it costs $150.

Litigation costs will be incurred when, and only when, injurers do not take care, thus causing harm, and victims sue.

Finally, because the setting is reciprocal, the well-being of individuals is determined by the total costs incurred (per instance) under each regime for each possible case, as each individual will be once in the position of injurer and once in that of victim.

In light of the foregoing, we can readily analyze each of the four possible cases.

Case 1: Cost of care is low ($25) and plaintiff's cost of suit is low ($10). The standard rule (under which plaintiffs bear their own litigation costs) or any subsidy leads to the result that total costs (per instance) will be $25. Because the plaintiff will sue if injured, the defendant will take care, spending $25, and no legal costs will be incurred (because there is never any harm, there will be no suits). If suit is prohibited, the defendant will not take care, harm of $100 will occur, and there will be no legal costs incurred.

Case 2: Cost of care is low ($25) and plaintiff's cost of suit is high ($110). Under the standard rule, victims will not sue; hence, injurers will not take care, so total costs will be $100, the amount of harm imposed. If suit is prohibited, the result is the same. If, however, suit is subsidized, potential injurers will take care, and there will be no harm and thus no suits, so total costs will be only $25.

Case 3: Cost of care is high ($150) and plaintiff's cost of suit is low ($10). Under the standard rule, plaintiffs will sue. Nevertheless, injurers will not be induced to take care, so harm will arise. Accordingly, total costs will be $120 (harm of $100 plus litigation costs of $10 for each party). If suit is subsidized, the result is the same. However, if suit is prohibited, total costs will be only $100 (because the parties avoid incurring the litigation costs of $20 in total).

Case 4: Cost of care is high ($150) and plaintiff's cost of suit is high ($110). Under the standard rule, plaintiffs will not sue, care will not be taken, harm will occur, and the total cost will be $100. The result is the same if suit is prohibited. If suit is subsidized, victims will sue, so the cost of suit ($110 for plaintiffs and $10 for defendants) will be incurred, but injurers still will not take care, so total costs will now be $220 ($120 in legal costs plus harm of $100).

The following table summarizes these results. (For each case, the rules with the lowest total cost—and thus the highest level of well-being—are underlined.)

Injurer's Cost of Care	Plaintiff's Cost of Suit	Total Costs: Standard Rule	Total Costs: Subsidy	Total Costs: Prohibition
$25	$10	$25	$25	$100
$25	$110	$100	$25	$100
$150	$10	$120	$120	$100
$150	$110	$100	$220	$100

5. Normative Assessment

(a) Choice of Legal Rules Using Welfare Economics. As in the reciprocal case in the torts section, everyone will rank the legal rules identically, this ranking will favor the rules with the lowest total costs, and this is the ranking that will determine the choice of legal rules under welfare economics. (To remind the reader, the reason is that, because each individual occupies each of the two roles once, each person's total costs will equal the total costs per case, as reported in the above table. Therefore, every individual has the same interest in minimizing costs. And, finally, welfare economics favors the rule or rules that maximize individuals' well-being.) The choices underlined in the table would therefore be selected.

Observe that the standard rule under which each side bears its own legal costs makes everyone better off in two of the four cases: when the plaintiff's cost of suit is low and the cost of care is low (the latter of which makes suit desirable) and when the plaintiff's cost of suit is high and the cost of care is high (the latter making suit undesirable).[24] However, when the cost of care

---

24. In each case, one of the other rules performs equally well.

is low but the cost of suit is high, suit is desirable, but it will not occur unless there is a subsidy. And, when the cost of care is high but the cost of suit is low, suit is undesirable but will occur unless suit is prohibited (or sufficiently taxed). Accordingly, any of the rules may be best under welfare economics, depending on the cost of suit and whether the prospect of suit will induce cost-effective precautions to be undertaken. Under welfare economics, these factors are considered together in a manner that leads to the selection of the rule that produces the highest possible well-being for all individuals.

(b) Choice of Legal Rules Using Notions of Fairness. Under a simple, strong notion of fairness—holding that there is a right to bring any valid suit, and that the state should subsidize suit if necessary to accomplish this—the optimal rule is either the standard rule or, when this is not sufficient to induce suit, subsidy. Under the weaker notion of fairness—stipulating that plaintiffs have the right to sue whenever they find it in their interest to do so (bearing their own legal costs)—the standard rule is always best, by definition.[25]

(c) Why the Choice of Legal Rules Should Be Based Only on Individuals' Well-Being. As in some prior sections of this book, we find that fairness-based evaluation of legal rules is troubling because the pursuit of notions of fairness makes everyone worse off whenever it favors a rule different from that chosen under welfare economics. This result can be seen by examining the four cases in our example.

In the first case, when the costs of care and of suit are both low, welfare economics and fairness-based analysis are in accord: Suit makes everyone better off (because the prospect of suit deters harm at low cost and litigation costs are never incurred) and hence is favored under welfare economics, and it is favored by the identified notions of fairness as well.

In the second case, when the cost of care is low but the cost of suit is high, a subsidy makes everyone better off: The high cost of suit is not actually incurred due to the deterrent effect, and the harm of $100 is prevented at a cost of only $25.[26] It is worth pausing to emphasize a feature of this result:

25. Under further variants, it might be deemed fair, for example, to allow suit only when the plaintiff's recovery would exceed total litigation costs, not just the plaintiff's. In our example, this change would have no effect because, when the plaintiff's costs are low relative to the stakes, so are total costs; therefore, our example suffices to show the deficiency of such variants as well. (Some other moderate versions of fairness may require a modified example to demonstrate their shortcomings.)

26. The results would be qualitatively similar, although less stark, had we assumed that care reduced the probability of harm rather than eliminated harm entirely (or that care abso-

Welfare economics may favor subsidizing suits in which the stakes are lower than the plaintiff's litigation costs.[27] In contrast, notions of fairness may or may not favor this desirable result. A strong belief in the right to sue—maintained even when the plaintiff's litigation costs exceed the stakes—would lead to a similar conclusion.[28] In contrast, a more moderate view of the right to sue, which recognizes the right only when the party is willing to incur the cost of pursuing a remedy, would not favor a rule subsidizing suit. Thus, pursuing the moderate notion of fairness would make everyone worse off in this case.

In the third case, when the cost of care is high but the cost of suit is low, prohibition of suit makes individuals better off than does the standard rule, because allowing plaintiffs to sue, which they will do, does nothing to reduce harm but involves a wasteful expenditure on litigation of $20 ($10 by each party). That is, it is in everyone's interest to deprive individuals of the right to bring a suit, even though the suits would be entirely meritorious and even though the total litigation costs are only a modest fraction of the stakes (here, 20 percent). Indeed, even if the defendant bore no litigation costs—so that the only legal costs were incurred by the plaintiff, who under the standard rule chooses to sue—it would be in everyone's interest to prohibit suit.[29] (The reason is that suits are a waste of resources; an individual would happily give up the opportunity to bring such a suit if others would similarly forbear if the individual harmed them.) In contrast, such a result would be viewed as unfair under both the strong and the moderate notions of fairness. From the perspective of the right to sue, this is a clear case for

lutely prevented the possibility of harm but some individuals did not take care due to mistake or because they had atypically high costs of precaution). Then, for example, when litigation costs were high and suit was subsidized, the high litigation costs would sometimes be incurred, but encouraging suit would still be desirable if the benefit from improved behavior were sufficiently great.

27. This result clearly belies any notion that a proper economic approach is narrow-mindedly concerned with reducing costly litigation. It also suggests that it is inappropriate to regard suits with a negative expected recovery to plaintiffs as necessarily "frivolous."

28. The fact that subsidizing suit does not actually result in anyone suing may seem odd from a fairness perspective, if the whole point was for victims with valid claims to recover. In the present situation, the deterrent effect eliminates harm, so there are no victims left to exercise their right to sue. As we discuss toward the end of this subsection, the ex post perspective that typifies fairness-based analysis in this context can thus be quite misleading.

29. It seems to be a common view that the central (or only) problem leading to potential divergences between plaintiffs' and society's interest in bringing suit arises from the fact that plaintiffs impose costs on others. As our discussion should make clear, however, this explanation is only part of the story. See Shavell (1982b, 1997). See also Kaplow (1986).

permitting suit.[30] Hence, in this case, pursuing either of the notions of fairness requires that one embrace an outcome under which everyone is worse off.

Finally, in the fourth case, when costs of care and of suit are both high, suit is again wasteful. This time, suit would not be brought under the standard rule, so the moderate notion of fairness and welfare economics are in accord. In contrast, the strong notion of fairness, which would encourage all meritorious suits, would endorse a subsidy, under which everyone is worse off.

In summary, in each case, welfare economics favors an outcome under which everyone benefits. In contrast, both the strong and moderate notions of fairness favor outcomes that in half of the cases (cases three and four for the strong notion, two and three for the moderate notion) make everyone worse off.

What, if anything, is accomplished by pursuing these notions of fairness? The purpose, one presumes, is to enable individuals to vindicate their rights by pursuing valid claims. Yet why should individuals be subject to a regime that achieves this goal when doing so harms the very people to whom one purports to be fair? In two of our cases (when the cost of care is high), suits are an outright waste, and, consequently, individuals would benefit by forgoing the opportunity to bring such suits if others similarly were to refrain. Adopting the rules favored by welfare economics accomplishes precisely this result.

Our analysis further reveals that perverse results cannot be avoided under notions of fairness, regardless of how one might attempt to refine them by taking into account the cost of suit and the plaintiff's willingness to pay it. On one hand, suit may make everyone better off even when the cost of litigation exceeds the stakes (our second case), so any general principle that would encourage suits must be very generous with regard to the permissible level of litigation costs (to the extent of subsidizing very expensive cases). On the other hand, suit may make everyone worse off even when the costs are only a small fraction of the stakes (our third case), so even a stringent general principle limiting suits would be insufficiently strict in some cases.

The problem is that looking solely to whether a legal claim is valid, or factoring in as well the cost of suit, fails to capture all that is relevant to individuals' well-being. As a result, any general principle that determines whether suit should occur as a function of the merits of the suit and litigation

---

30. Namely, the suit is certainly meritorious, and both the plaintiff's costs and total litigation costs are a small fraction of the stakes. Relatedly, the plaintiff would sue even if he bore all the legal costs, so that none would be imposed on the defendant or on the state.

costs (in total, or for a given party) will be inferior to welfare economics in important instances. Only the welfare economic approach considers all the pertinent factors—including, importantly, the effect of suit in channeling behavior—and combines them in a manner that ensures that the preferred legal rule is the one that best enhances individuals' well-being.[31]

We emphasize that our conclusion holds as long as notions of fairness are given any independent weight. The preceding discussion indicates that, whenever a notion of fairness is decisive and thereby leads to a result different from that favored under welfare economics, everyone will be worse off. Moreover, it can readily be demonstrated that, if a notion of fairness has any weight, one can construct scenarios in which the notion of fairness will in fact be decisive, thus making everyone worse off.[32] Therefore, to avoid the prospect of selecting legal rules that hurt everyone, it is necessary to give no weight to any notion of fairness.

When we examine the literature that invokes notions of fairness, we find no basis for questioning this critique. By and large, although commentators recognize that there is some inevitable tension between approaches based on notions of fairness and welfare economics, they do not address the direct conflict that we identify, under which a notion of fairness can only make everyone worse off. It would appear that, in considering individuals' procedural right to sue when they have valid claims, commentators have lost sight of the substantive purposes of the laws that create the underlying legal right. If, in some instances, suit fails to serve these purposes and simply wastes everyone's time and money, it should not be allowed. Alternatively, if plaintiffs would not find it in their interest to sue when suit would advance these purposes, suit should be subsidized.

31. To clarify our meaning with regard to the practicalities of designing legal rules, we suppose that case-by-case determinations of whether to allow suit may involve high costs and be prone to mistake. Therefore, decisions about whether to permit suit should probably be made categorically, perhaps depending on the type of legal claim, the nature of the injury, and the magnitude of the stakes. Such a policy will, of course, result in errors in particular cases, but it may be the best course practically available. In contrast, under notions of fairness, it is likely that the chosen policy for entire classes of cases would be erroneous, because the rules would not be selected in light of all the relevant factors, each given the appropriate weight.

32. To illustrate this idea, which we develop more fully in our torts discussion, see note 50 in chapter III, suppose that a notion of fairness has a weight equivalent to only $1; then, there still will exist figures for costs of care, costs of lawsuits, and levels of harm such that, under the more fair rule, each party is made worse off by, say, $0.25. (Of course, if the weight given to a notion of fairness is trivial, taking the notion of fairness into account will cause little harm.)

It is no answer to offer such assertions as "for every legal right there must be a remedy,"[33] for if it were decided that suit should be prohibited in certain instances, then there would no longer be any legal right. As we discuss in subsection 2, reasoning from preexisting rights to remedies is circular when one considers legal rules that can be understood to define the legal rights themselves.[34] One could attempt to avoid this sort of problem by deeming every wrong (however trivial) a legal wrong giving rise to a right to sue. But, as we note in subsection 2, implementing such a strong notion of fairness would bankrupt society. We suspect that the foregoing points have not been sufficiently salient to many fairness-minded analysts because their thinking on procedural questions displays an ex post perspective, under which rights are taken as given and behavior is in the past, making it appear that the only question is how to satisfy claims that have previously been deemed to be worth bringing. Such a view, it should now be clear, can easily lead the analyst astray.[35]

In this subsection, we have explained that, under a more moderate notion of fairness, like one that limits suits to instances in which plaintiffs find it profitable to sue or those in which the stakes exceed total legal costs, we cannot avoid the possibility of making everyone worse off. Furthermore, in some settings this more commonly held notion of procedural fairness seems counterproductive with respect to its apparent underlying motivations. This problem can be seen in our second case, in which the cost of care is low ($25) and the plaintiff's cost of suit is high ($110) relative to the stakes ($100). There, under the moderate notion of fairness, suit is disfavored because litigation costs are excessive relative to the stakes. And yet, when one follows the prescription of welfare economics, which would involve subsidization of suits in this instance, all harm is deterred. As a consequence, no suits would ever need to be brought. Thus, under the moderate notion of fairness, which one presumes is concerned as an initial matter with providing legal redress, the analyst is led to favor a rule under which harm is widespread

33. This view is commonly traced to Marbury v. Madison, 5 U.S. (1 Cranch) 137, 162–63 (1803).

34. Thus, using our example in subsection 2, if annoyed individuals do have a legal right to sue those who play loud music during daytime hours, one can confidently say that prohibiting suit (because the cost of such suits vastly exceeds any benefits from regulating behavior) violates their right to sue. But this conclusion obviously is based on circular reasoning. If such suits are undesirable, the government can change the law such that the behavior is no longer a violation, and, accordingly, one can say that there no longer exists a legal right to sue. That is, when the law no longer deems such behavior to be a nuisance, disappointed victims cannot properly object that courts violate their rights when disallowing their lawsuits.

35. See subsection II.B.2(c).

and redress is never in fact provided. In contrast, when this notion of fairness is cast aside in favor of welfare economics, the result is a world in which there are no unredressed injuries.[36] Moreover, no litigation costs are in fact incurred under the unfair rule that is favored by welfare economics, even though the reason for subscribing to a moderate notion of fairness rather than a strong one is, one supposes, to avoid excessive litigation costs.[37] These results further illustrate how notions of procedural fairness that tend to focus on the redress of wrongs that have already occurred—thus failing to attend to the consequences of rules in the manner prescribed by welfare economics—may well favor counterproductive legal rules.

6. The Appeal of Notions of Fairness and Its Implications

As we have just noted, one explanation for the appeal of notions of fairness concerning procedure is that commentators mistakenly adopt an ex post perspective. When adopting such an outlook, the analyst implicitly takes as given what wrongs have occurred and which claims parties should be permitted to pursue. Such assumptions, we suggested, are problematic given that an important function of making remedies available is to curb wrongful behavior and that the question of what claims to permit is at the core of what is to be decided. From an ex post perspective, however, these shortcomings are obscured, and consequently one may be attracted to legal rules that seem fair under the circumstances.[38]

---

36. Had we considered more realistic and complex situations in which the rule that maximizes individuals' well-being did not deter all harm, the same perverse results could readily have arisen. If, for example, some potential injurers had high costs of precaution, the rule that subsidizes suits would prevent most injury but result in a small number of lawsuits (which would be unfair under the moderate notion of fairness). In this case, the moderate notion of fairness implicitly favors a world with widespread unredressed wrongful imposition of harm over the one in which most harm never occurs, but what harm does occasionally occur is redressed even though the accepted notion of fairness does not recognize a right to sue because of the costs of suit.

37. As the preceding note indicates, more realistically there would be some suits in a regime that subsidized suit, because deterrence would be incomplete. Nevertheless, the impression one obtains with respect to legal costs under different regimes is misleading when one fails to take deterrence into account. (We also note the possibility that legal costs could be *lower* under the regime that subsidizes suits. For example, with no subsidy, some plaintiffs may have sufficiently low costs that they will be induced to sue, but the frequency of such lawsuits may be too low to produce much deterrence. In contrast, with a subsidy and the resulting increase in deterrence, there could be fewer total suits, even though a higher proportion of those ultimately injured would sue.)

38. See subsection II.B.2(c).

A further—and we believe important—explanation for the appeal of notions of fairness is that they may well originate in internalized social norms that regulate informal interactions in everyday life. Although such norms are functional in the setting in which they emerged, they may be ill-suited to the different context of costly formal legal proceedings.

Consider the internalized social norms that govern the availability of remedies for wrongful acts (such as causing injuries or breaking promises) in daily life. When one individual harms another—a family member, a neighbor, a business associate, or even a stranger—certain redress may be deemed appropriate, whether in the form of an apology or of some type of compensation or correction. Individuals are induced to remedy their wrongs by feelings of guilt and concern for others' disapprobation as well as by the possibility of other social sanctions, such as the loss of future opportunities for interaction.

The existence of internalized social norms of this type serves a number of functions. First, such norms tend to discourage wrongdoing because forbearance allows one to avoid the costs of rectifying the situation. (Even an apology may bring embarrassment.) In addition, such norms for redress tend to reinforce behavioral norms; the processes of apology and remediation remind everyone of the importance of correct behavior toward others. We would expect this function to be especially important in teaching children— to allow wrongful behavior to go unremedied would send the wrong message. Furthermore, assuring that there is an appropriate response by the injurer tends to preserve valuable relationships with victims and to make victims (including those not in preexisting relationships with their injurers) less inclined to retaliate in undesirable ways.[39] This factor also seems important for instructing children, who may have complaints about the behavior of siblings or classmates. Children who misbehave are supposed to take responsibility for their acts. If they do not, victims are encouraged to take the matter to authority figures for resolution rather than to respond with physical aggression.

In such informal settings, the analogue to legal procedure may take a simple form. If the offender is aware of his improper behavior, he just takes the corrective action. If he is unaware or if a proper response is not forthcoming, a victim (or an onlooker) may demand an apology or otherwise express disapproval and the need for redress. The costs of such "procedures" will often be trivial, in which case there is no need to develop elaborate rules prescribing when they are worth undertaking. The basic principle that

---

39. Compare our discussions of the functions served by social norms involving corrective justice in subsection III.E.1 and retribution in subsection VI.D.1.

wrongs merit redress usually suffices.[40] Moreover, for children, informal adjudication by parents and teachers costs little and is inherently valuable as part of the process of inculcating social norms that help to maintain order in the present and to prepare children for their adult lives as members of society.

Internalized social norms thus seem to provide victims with remedies of sorts for the wrongful behavior of others. Injurers who do not respond accordingly should (and one hopes often do) feel guilty, and onlookers are inclined to disapprove of those who violate society's norms.

Hence, it should not be surprising that, upon turning to the analysis of legal procedure, we are inclined to apply similar instincts and intuitions—which correspond to prevailing notions of fairness—about what victims are entitled to expect and how society should respond to injurers who do not voluntarily make amends. As we explain in subsection II.D.2 (and explore in other legal contexts), however, it does not follow from the existence of such social norms that corresponding notions of fairness should be treated as independent evaluative principles when designing legal institutions. Such treatment seems particularly misguided to the extent that the social norms exist in order to promote individuals' well-being, whereas giving weight to notions of fairness in the evaluation of legal procedure can only come at the expense of their well-being.

Our conclusion is reinforced by the fact that there are important differences between the context of everyday life—the realm of social norms—and that of formal adjudication, where notions of fairness are often employed. There are, of course, some similarities between the two settings, in that both social norms and the formal legal system are designed to discourage wrongdoing and, by providing victims a remedy, to dissuade them from seeking vengeance. This parallel suggests that, to an extent, notions of fairness that correspond to social norms will serve as proxy devices for identifying welfare-promoting policies. Indeed, the entire system of legal procedure that provides remedies for a variety of undesirable acts is socially valuable—particularly in a modern society where many interactions involve

40. In fact, even these informal norms involve some complexity. For example, an elaborate apology would be considered unnecessary, even inappropriate, for a trivial violation; likewise, individuals who are tremendously aggrieved by insignificant acts and who insist on redress are viewed as behaving somewhat outside the bounds of proper social interaction. Note, however, that acts that are small in the context of formal legal proceedings may be substantial relative to those that ordinarily trigger appropriate demands in informal settings. (Missing a lunch date warrants an apology, whereas a lawsuit would hardly be an appropriate means of redress.)

individuals not in tight-knit communities or otherwise in long-term relationships, which tends to make social norms less effective. (We also note that this tendency for notions of fairness in many settings to favor welfare-promoting policies may contribute to the notions' appeal.)

Nevertheless, it is hardly the case that the proxy function of notions of fairness is perfect, or even nearly so. Most importantly, the low cost of determining appropriate remedies in many informal settings is not matched in the formal legal system, in which procedural costs can readily be of a similar order of magnitude to the stakes in cases that are litigated, and costs undoubtedly exceed the stakes in many cases that potential plaintiffs choose not to bring.[41] Moreover, even when legal costs are a low fraction of the harm, they may well be significant in absolute terms.[42] Thus, although the principle that there should be a remedy for every violation makes a good deal of sense when procedures are nearly costless, such a notion of fairness can readily lead us to favor undesirable policies when procedures are costly. Additionally, we have previously explained that, once costs are factored in, there is no simple relationship between the cost of a lawsuit and its desirability, because the benefits of lawsuits vary tremendously and in ways that are not reflected in litigation costs alone. Hence, even moderate notions of fairness that take costs into account will not be reliable indicators of when legal rules governing procedure make sense.[43]

The relationship between internalized social norms about the redress of wrongs and notions of fairness regarding the right to sue suggests two further respects in which notions of fairness may be relevant under welfare economics: Individuals may have a taste for a legal system that allows suit whenever there is a valid claim, and making legal remedies available may reinforce substantive social norms regarding proper behavior.[44] We consider these and related possibilities in section C.

41. See, for example, R. Posner and Rasmusen (1999, 380), suggesting that enforcement using social norms is superior to that using the law when individual violations are small or costs of proof are too great to justify the use of formal legal procedures.

42. In our initial example, costs in some cases are only 20 percent of the harm, but when the cost of precautions is high and thus there is no benefit from suit, they constitute a pure—and potentially significant—waste of social resources.

43. In this respect, we note that social norms often tend to be simple for a number of reasons: They must be taught to children, individuals tend to apply them almost automatically, and third parties' reactions are more predictable if determining the applicability of a social norm is not very complex. By contrast, the rules that determine when and what type of legal remedies are available for various wrongs can be fine-tuned a good deal, and the stakes are often sufficient to make more refined rules worthwhile.

44. This potential benefit is not entirely straightforward. On one hand, if social norms about behavior are important because the legal system is too expensive a means of inducing

7. Remarks on the Generality of Our Results

We have focused on a perfectly reciprocal case involving certain harm. These results can readily be extended—pursuant to our arguments in chapter III on torts—to nonreciprocal cases (in which some individuals are more likely to be plaintiffs, and others defendants) and to cases in which the prospect of harm is uncertain and individuals are risk averse (both when insurance is purchased and when it is not).

For the nonreciprocal case, the analysis under welfare economics may differ because of the possibility of distributive effects. For example, potential plaintiffs may be poorer than potential defendants. As we explain in subsection III.C.2, in such instances distributive effects can influence the determination of which legal rule is best.[45] But once distributive effects have been taken into account, the situation becomes much like that in the reciprocal case. In particular, giving weight to notions of fairness will continue to make individuals worse off overall, and there is no apparent reason to do so.

Introducing considerations of risk, as we do in section III.D, has even less effect on our analysis. Uninsured, risk-averse individuals do value the protection against risk that may be provided when they can be compensated through bringing lawsuits. But such gains can be combined with the behavioral benefits of allowing suit, thereby producing an overall measure of the extent to which permitting suit may increase individuals' well-being.[46] Once risk-bearing costs are included, the welfare economic analysis of legal rules proceeds in essentially the same way, and the conclusion that giving weight to notions of fairness can only make individuals worse off continues to be true. Moreover, we are unable to identify any respect in which the fact that harm is uncertain provides a good basis for giving weight to notions of fairness that are unsound in cases in which risk is not involved.

There is another dimension in which our analysis is more general than may initially appear to be the case. Although our example involved a setting

---

good behavior, it is self-defeating to channel all disputes through the legal system (because then the informal norm may be unnecessary and the excessive costs will be incurred in any event). On the other hand, creating a formal right to sue, which will only occasionally be exercised (when the stakes are unusually high, so as to motivate the victim to sue) and thus will not generate substantial costs, may reinforce a social norm enough to justify what would otherwise be a socially excessive expenditure on litigation.

45. As we note in subsection II.A.3, this will tend to be true only when superior means of adjusting the distribution of income—notably taxes and transfer programs—are unavailable for some reason.

46. We also note that legal rules that may reduce victims' risk-bearing costs, by requiring injurers to compensate them, may raise injurers' risk-bearing costs if they, too, are risk averse and uninsured.

that is most readily interpreted as embodying the kind of problem governed by tort law, our argument does not depend on this interpretation. For example, the harm could be interpreted as the loss of value when a contract is breached and the cost of the precaution as the cost of performing a contract.[47] More broadly, the main points raised here involve two types of situations. On one hand, when behavior would respond little to the incentives provided by the prospect of suit, suits will tend to be wasteful, even when the litigation costs are well below the amount of any loss incurred; hence, notions of fairness involving a right to bring suit will sometimes favor regimes under which individuals are worse off. On the other hand, even when the costs of suit are high relative to the stakes, encouraging suits may have a substantial benefit in terms of improving defendants' prior behavior (and in such a manner that would reduce the number of harmful acts, making actual subsequent suits less necessary). In these instances, moderate notions of fairness, which tolerate suit only when costs are not too high relative to the stakes, will fail to favor regimes that subsidize suit. This logic is valid regardless of the nature of the injury and the governing body of substantive law.

8. The Extent to Which the Use of Notions of Fairness Has Led Us Astray

Numerous proposed and enacted legal reforms over the past few decades have related to the right to bring suit. Initially, many reforms that were designed to promote fairness tended to increase access to the courts. In addition to creating new legal rights, reforms have included expansion of class actions,[48] numerous pro-plaintiff fee-shifting statutes,[49] and subsidization of legal assistance to the poor.[50] These reforms, in turn, were forerunners of the wave of mass tort litigation that we have recently experienced—involving asbestos, cigarettes, certain pharmaceuticals, and other products—which in turn is responsible for substantial legal costs and may have significant effects on the operation of many businesses.[51] From a welfare economic point of

47. See note 20.

48. Federal Rules of Civil Procedure (2001, rule 23) (major amendment in 1966); see Yeazell (1987, 238–45, 261–66).

49. See, for example, Derfner and Wolf (1999), listing federal fee-shifting statutes; Vargo (1993, 1588–90); and State Attorney Fee Shifting Statutes (1984, 330), identifying state fee-shifting statutes.

50. See, for example, Quigley (1998). Subsidization may not traditionally be classified as a procedural reform, but, like fee-shifting, it directly affects the willingness of potential parties to sue and so, like standing rules, can be seen as a central part of the legal system's apparatus that governs whether "rights" to sue are realized.

51. See, for example, Garber (1993) and Hensler (2000).

view, concerned with promoting individuals' well-being, some of these reforms appear to make sense.[52] But because fairness-based analysis seemed
to motivate the reforms, some are probably ill-advised. In particular, the
arguments for reforms usually take as a given that the underlying substantive
legal rules are desirable, implicitly assessed without regard to the legal costs
involved in their implementation. However, our analysis suggests that even
if the rules might, in a vacuum, be desirable and even if all claims brought
would be valid, it does not follow that expansion of the right to bring suit
will increase individuals' well-being. In fact, such expansion may have the
opposite effect.[53]

More recently, there has been a growing sense of a "litigation explosion"
and hence of a need to reduce access to the legal system.[54] As we note in
subsection 2, it seems that most analysts hold moderate views about the
right to bring suit, giving weight to legal costs because they are intrinsically
important or because imposing costs on other parties to lawsuits or on the
state is itself understood to be potentially unfair. Although the increased
attention to the cost of litigation is appropriate, our analysis explains that
moderate notions of fairness, which make some sort of tradeoff between
rights to sue and legal costs, do not adequately guide legal policymaking.
The reason, as we emphasize in subsection 5(c), is that there is no simple
level of cost or relationship between cost and stakes that indicates which
lawsuits are socially desirable. For example, if the behavioral effects are large,
lawsuits can be desirable even when the plaintiff's costs exceed the stakes.
Thus, we can have little confidence that various reforms will reduce access

52. For example, class actions are valuable when they allow claims that would otherwise
be brought individually to proceed jointly at lower cost due to the realization of economies
of scale. In addition, our analysis emphasizes that, when legal costs exceed the stakes, there
may be no suits and thus no deterrence; aggregating claims also solves this problem (although
it is still possible that the aggregated claim may not be socially desirable if the benefit from
improved behavior is sufficiently small).

53. Another problem, of course, would arise if the substantive rules themselves did not
make sense, even in a vacuum that ignored litigation costs. In that case, however, one would
more likely take issue with the substantive law than with the procedural reforms. Yet another
difficulty concerns claims of questionable validity.

54. See, for example, Burbank and Silberman (1997, 683–99), documenting the ebb and
flow of access reforms; Tobias (1995), discussing the Common Sense Legal Reforms Act, part
of the Republican Party's 1994 Contract with America; and Weinstein and Hershenov (1991,
323). In the 1990s, Congress considered a number of proposals to limit litigation, and some
passed one or both Houses, the latter group producing some presidential vetoes but also
enactment of the 1995 Private Securities Litigation Reform Act and the Securities Litigation
Uniform Standards Act of 1998. For surveys of recent reform efforts, see, for example, Tobias
(1994, 1998).

only in those areas where it makes sense.[55] Determining which reforms are most likely to increase individuals' well-being requires a welfare economic analysis of legal procedure.

Even in familiar areas of legal dispute, such as auto accident claims, it is not clear whether litigation is socially desirable given its cost, as we explain in section III.F.[56] We also note there that most discussions of reforms do not seem to reflect a proper appreciation of the relevant factors and mode of analysis.

In all, our legal system is very expensive, and the range of behavior it attempts to control is extremely important, so decisions about the scope of the right to bring suit are of great social consequence. Unfortunately, most analysis in the legal academy and outside it seems guided by loose notions of fairness, notions that we have reason to believe will often lead us to the wrong policy decisions.

B. Accuracy in Adjudication

Once the legal system permits a plaintiff to bring suit, as we discuss in section A, there remains a wide array of problems concerning the design of the system that will govern subsequent litigation. A central question underlying these legal procedures is how to make tradeoffs between the accuracy and the cost of adjudication.[57] On reflection, this consideration is fundamental

55. There has been much attention devoted to the need to reduce "frivolous" litigation. Although everyone can agree that wholly meritless cases should be weeded out, if possible, we are unaware of any coherent attempt to define what in principle counts as a frivolous case within the large class of claims that are not entirely without merit. As we note in subsection 2, commonly invoked notions of fairness neglect this question. In contrast, a proper application of welfare economics would allow one both to determine which claims should not be brought and to evaluate procedures that are designed to discourage some claims.

56. Observe that many reforms, such as substituting no-fault auto insurance for traditional negligence liability, can easily be viewed either as reforms of substantive law ("tort reform") or as procedural reforms (scaling back the right to sue—with auto no-fault, usually by keeping low-stakes cases out of court). The ease of dual characterization is hardly surprising in light of our emphasis in the introduction to this chapter on the close interdependence between legal procedure and substantive law.

57. We do not mean to suggest that effects on accuracy are the only relevant features of procedures besides cost. Indeed, we consider some other effects in section C. Nor is it the case that the literature on procedure usually phrases the problem as one involving accuracy and cost. More common are vague statements of the purpose of procedures, such as references to the quality of the "administration of justice," or no statement of purpose at all. See, for example, Amendments to the Federal Rules of Civil Procedure (1993, 132) (advisory commit-

to the assessment of the criteria for deciding motions for disposition prior to a final verdict (motions to dismiss, for summary judgment, for a directed verdict), the extent of and limits on discovery, pretrial orders (which may limit trial days or the use of expert witnesses), many rules of evidence (which may limit hearsay, thereby requiring additional witnesses to be called, or may permit introduction of business records, thereby eliminating the need for other witnesses to testify directly), and appeals (rules on when appeals are permitted and on the standard of review).[58] We now consider the difference between evaluations of the accuracy of legal procedures under welfare economics and under notions of fairness.

1. Welfare Economics and Accuracy in Adjudication

The relevant considerations here are similar to those bearing upon the ability to bring suit. Legal procedures that produce more accurate outcomes typically will lead to more desirable behavior. Consider the extreme example of a purely random procedural system. It would do nothing to channel behavior in accord with substantive legal rules: A person would be just as likely to have to pay damages if he obeyed a legal rule as if he did not. Generally speaking, the more accurate the legal system, the greater will be the extent to which individuals will conform their behavior to legal rules. The primary disadvantage of more accurate legal procedures, of course, is that they usually increase the costs of the legal system, which reduces the well-being of the parties (or of citizens generally, to the extent that financing court costs requires higher taxes).

Other factors are also relevant under welfare economics. As we explore more fully in subsection 4, greater accuracy will lead to more finely-tuned

---

tee notes): "The purpose of this revision . . . is to recognize the affirmative duty of the court to exercise . . . authority . . . to ensure that civil litigation is resolved not only fairly, but also without undue cost or delay." Nevertheless, we believe that the accuracy-cost tradeoff is indeed central to many procedural choices, whether or not this feature is well recognized.

Another aspect of legal procedure, concerning the burden of proof, is often bound up with discussions involving the accuracy of procedural provisions, even though accuracy and the burden of proof are conceptually distinct. For example, provision of subsidized counsel to criminal defendants may both affect accuracy and shift the implicit burden of proof. We will not address the subject of proof burdens here. For an analysis of the relationship between these topics, references to some of the economic literature on the subject, and a suggestion that some arguments for fair procedures are better understood by disentangling effects on accuracy and on the burden of proof, see Kaplow (1994b, 356–62, 375–78).

58. Likewise, issues concerning the use and design of alternative dispute resolution mechanisms often involve the tradeoff between accuracy and cost.

compensation of plaintiffs, which will be important for their well-being when they are risk averse and uninsured—although greater accuracy may also impose more risk on defendants. Also, in section C, we consider the possibilities that individuals may have a taste for particular procedures and that procedures may have broader instrumental benefits, such as controlling the abuse of power.[59]

2. Notions of Fairness and Accuracy in Adjudication

The notions of fairness pertinent to accuracy in adjudication are analogous to those we consider in section A concerning the ability to bring suit. First, theories of fair procedure may hold that individuals have a right to invoke all manner of procedures or are entitled to procedural rules under which they may advance their cause. If they have potentially valid arguments, they have a right to be heard. If they have probative evidence, they should be permitted to present it. If a party's opponent has relevant evidence, the party should be allowed to discover it. If cross-examination might reveal the failings of the opponent's witness, such questioning should be authorized. Procedural rules that deprive a party of the opportunity to offer valid arguments and evidence are unfair.[60] (We observe that notions of fairness that favor making such procedures available to parties are often rationalized by reference to the parties themselves rather than to a systemic interest in providing

---

59. In addition, concerns about the distribution of income could arise. See, for example, note 108. It will become apparent below that there are no distributive effects in many of the cases that we consider here. In some instances, even when one considers a nonreciprocal setting, one rule may be best for both potential plaintiffs and potential defendants or at least may benefit one group at no cost to the other. See subsections 4(a) and 4(b) and note 82. Moreover, as we discuss in subsection A.7 and elsewhere in this book, taking distributive effects into account would not directly affect most of our analysis.

60. As one commentator has described the standard view:

> Fairness is the fundamental concept that guides our thinking about substantive and procedural law. . . . We strive to provide each side with a fair opportunity to achieve that outcome, by which we mean the chance to initiate and pursue any plausible claim or defense, the availability of elaborate means for producing and testing evidence, and the assurance of appellate review to enforce the rules of the present system. All of this we do in the name of fairness. (Newman 1985, 1646)

See, for example, Bone (1992, 232): "[M]any procedure scholars today assert, or, more frequently, assume, that the day in court ideal guarantees individuals a strong prima facie right to freedom of strategic choice in all cases."; Fiss (1993, 967): "At the heart of *Martin v. Wilks* is what I call 'the right of participation': the notion that every person is entitled to a day in court and that no one can have his or her rights determined by a court without having participated in the proceeding."; and note 64, quoting Fuller.

accurate results, although the notions are frequently motivated by examples or arguments that suggest a concern for an increase in accuracy.[61])

It is generally accepted, however, that there must be some limit to what parties may do during dispute resolution, particularly because their arguments and evidence may be invalid[62] and because legal proceedings impose costs on a party's opponent and on the state, which administers the legal system.[63] One may refer to some such concerns as involving fairness to the adversary. Accordingly, provisions for summary disposition of meritless

61. See, for example, the illustrations cited in note 149.

62. We focus on the case in which the evidence a party wishes to offer is both valid and will be properly understood by the factfinder. As we note at the end of this subsection, however, fairness theories are seriously incomplete (whereas welfare economics is not) when applied to the realistic setting in which not all demonstrations will be valid.

63. See, for example, Federal Rules of Civil Procedure (2001, rule 1), stating, in a rule entitled "Scope and Purpose of Rules," that the rules "shall be construed and administered to secure the just, speedy, and inexpensive determination of every action"; Federal Rules of Evidence (2001, rule 102), stating, in a rule entitled "Purpose and Construction," that the "rules shall be construed to secure fairness in administration, elimination of unjustifiable expense and delay, and promotion of growth and development of the law of evidence to the end that the truth may be ascertained and proceedings justly determined"; Mathews v. Eldridge, 424 U.S. 319, 348 (1976): "At some point the benefit of an additional safeguard to the individual affected by the administrative action and to society in terms of increased assurance that the action is just, may be outweighed by the cost."; Babcock and Massaro (1997, 2), observing that decisional process is a scarce resource and stating: "If the cost to the individual is too high, the 'right' is a deception and the game is unfair and ungratifying. But if the cost to the public is exorbitant, the right is contrary to the general interest."; ibid., arguing that "we cannot be too fastidious about costly adversary procedures [and] we cannot be excessively demanding about the absolute accuracy and consistent application of substantive principles"; Wright and Miller (1987, 4:124), finding it noteworthy that "Rule 1 places the objectives of 'speedy' and 'inexpensive' on a plane of equality with 'just'"; L. Alexander (1998, 23–26), stating that procedural rights protect against risks, but also involve costs that must be taken into account; Brunet (1991, 274): "All litigation . . . involves a balancing of process values between fairness and efficiency."; Coleman and Silver (1986, 104–05, 108), acknowledging that settlements have the virtue of reducing costs but suggesting that the price of trial may be worthwhile to enhance justice; and Grey (1977, 184), stating that procedural fairness favors correct resolution of disputes, but only "at a cost commensurate with what is at stake in the dispute."

Dworkin's essay on legal procedure is an instructive example. He devotes the essay almost entirely to the proposition that the right to greater accuracy must be traded off against cost, see R. Dworkin (1985), in spite of the fact that he is most known for the view that matters of principle (which he acknowledges would seem to place absolute weight on avoiding incorrect outcomes) should trump considerations of policy (such as concerns for costs) in adjudication. See Raz (1986, 1103), stating, in the course of reviewing the book in which Dworkin's procedure essay appears, that the essay "seems to undermine Dworkin's apparent view that in adjudication, rights should take precedence over issues of public policy, such as administrative expedience."

cases may protect a party from having to respond to intrusive discovery requests, and rules of finality may shield a victorious party from repetitive appeals or relitigation.

The concern that parties should be permitted to engage in activities that will promote their causes and the desire to avoid the imposition of unreasonable costs on adversaries and the state are generally set off against one another in some fashion. Summary disposition is available, but only in certain circumstances; discovery is permitted, but subject to limits; appeals are allowed, but limited in number. This attempt at accommodation can be viewed as a balancing of competing notions of fairness or conflicting rights, or as a contest between notions of fairness or rights on one hand and costs on the other. Either way, some framework is necessary for making the choice.

In this respect, theories of fair procedure are incomplete. Notions of fairness or rights are often presented as if they were absolutes, which cannot comprehend consideration of legal costs.[64] However, as already noted, we suspect that few fairness proponents actually hold absolutist views. Therefore, implicit in most notions of fairness must be some manner of resolving the tension between accuracy and legal costs and thereby yielding concrete results, but this mechanism is generally unspecified.[65] As a result, it is difficult

64. For example, Fuller (1978, 364) states that "[w]hatever destroys the meaning of [individuals'] participation destroys the integrity of adjudication itself"; see ibid. (382). Compare note 63, discussing Dworkin's views.

65. Dworkin states (consistently with our own research) that he is "not aware of any systematic discussion of [questions involving the tradeoff between accuracy and cost] in political philosophy." R. Dworkin (1985, 73). Then he presents an approach to the problem that we mention in note 63. He begins by positing a notion of "moral cost" or "moral harm," which he deems to be necessary to give any weight to fairness, as distinct from considerations of welfare. See R. Dworkin (1985, 81), stating that, because "we want to be able to say" a particular view, "we need a notion of a moral cost"; and ibid. (87), referring to our recognition of "moral harm." Then, he invokes "[o]ur common moral experience" to suggest that moral harm is not given absolute weight. Ibid. How much weight should it be given? Dworkin's only answer is to suggest that the matter be left to democratic institutions to decide. See ibid. He presents no argument as to how a responsible voter or legislator (including himself) might go about answering this question. Indeed, aside from raw appeal to our intuitions and his statement that we need the notion of moral cost to reach his desired normative conclusion, he gives no defense of his concept of moral cost. Ultimately, Dworkin argues that procedural rights involve primarily an injunction that the weight given to "moral harm" be consistent across cases and areas of law, see ibid. (96), which leaves entirely open the question of proper weight (indeed, a weight of zero in all instances would be consistent). Moreover, as our analysis shows, procedures that enhance accuracy to a given extent may be desirable in some settings but may make everyone worse off in others, so Dworkin's insistence on consistency of applica-

to determine what regime notions of fairness would actually support (just as in section A, where we consider a moderate rather than absolute principle favoring the ability to bring suit). Nevertheless, we show that any formulation—that is, any that does not essentially convert notions of fairness into welfare economics—will sometimes favor undesirable outcomes, under which both parties are made worse off, for no good reason.

Theories of fair procedures are also incomplete in two additional respects that we identify in subsection A.2, in connection with the right to bring suit. First, it seems that any theory of fair procedures should depend on the underlying justifications for the legal rules that provide the basis for a lawsuit. Thus, to the extent a procedure furthers the purpose of the legal rule, it would tend to be favored, and if it does not, it would tend to be disfavored.[66] This connection is largely left unaddressed in the legal literature. The apparent need for a theory of fair legal procedure to depend on the underlying purposes of substantive law raises the question of whether there can be a coherent normative basis for notions of fairness regarding legal procedures. This dependency also makes it difficult to know which procedures in what contexts would actually be favored by notions of fairness, properly understood.[67]

Second, when parties might proffer invalid or misleading information or arguments—which occurs under virtually any procedure—theories of procedural fairness require further specification because one supposes that the right to present valid evidence does not extend to attempts to mislead

---

tion—regardless of the consequences—will itself prove to be detrimental. (Another difficulty with Dworkin's argument about accuracy with regard to legal procedures is that it suffers from the same type of logical problems as does his argument about the right to bring suit. See note 12.)

66. In this spirit, Fiss argues that "fairness is a pragmatic ideal. [We must] acknowledge that the fairness of procedures in part turns on the social ends that they serve." Fiss (1993, 979), arguing that individuals should not be given procedural rights that interfere with rather than promote enforcement of civil rights laws. See also Arenella (1983, 197), stating that criminal procedure must promote the goals of substantive criminal law, so analysis of procedure is "inextricably interwoven" with substantive goals.

67. Relatedly, just as we observe in subsection A.2 that there is an inherent circularity in arguments about the right to bring suit to redress violations of substantive law (because denial of a right to sue can be recharacterized as a change in the substantive law such that a violation is no longer deemed to exist), it is possible to define substantive rules to include or preclude the right to particular procedures. Thus, attempts to posit procedural rights that are independent of the justification for the substantive claim at issue are problematic even at the level of definition. See also note 11, discussing the relationship of the foregoing point to arguments about the scope of the constitutional guarantee of procedural due process.

the tribunal.[68] For example, if a procedure results in parties behaving sometimes in a manner that correctly informs a tribunal and other times in a manner that misinforms it, is permitting parties to use the procedure fair or unfair? How, if at all, does this answer depend on the frequency of each result, the likely effect on the outcome of cases, and the cost of the procedure, among other factors? Those who favor fair procedures generally do not address such basic questions, so it is difficult even in principle to know what procedures to regard as fair.[69] Moreover, the inability to infer how notions of fairness should be applied to typical problems involving the choice of legal rules is symptomatic of the failure of fairness proponents to identify the rationales underlying notions of fairness.

3. Basic Case: Accuracy in Assessing Damages and the Benefit of Inducing Behavior in Accordance with Legal Rules[70]

To begin our discussion of procedural fairness and accuracy, we consider the problem of accuracy in assessing damages. We start with this case because it is reasonably straightforward to analyze and is of great practical importance (a large proportion of expenditures in tort cases, for example, involves disputes over the extent of damages). We supplement this discussion in subsection 5 by commenting on the problem of accurately determining liability. Also, in subsection 4, we consider variations of the basic case in this subsection, including one in which plaintiffs are risk averse and uninsured, so that more accurate damages provide a valuable compensatory function in addition to inducing better behavior by potential injurers.

(a) Description. We again consider a perfectly reciprocal situation in which each (risk-neutral) individual is once a potential injurer and once a potential victim.[71] The injurer will cause harm unless he takes care. In one set of

---

68. Compare our discussion in subsection A.2 of the incompleteness of notions of fairness regarding the right to bring claims of uncertain validity.

69. As we discuss in note 19, welfare economics does, in principle, offer a way to analyze situations involving claims of uncertain validity; analogous reasoning applies to presenting information or arguments of uncertain validity.

70. For prior formal analysis of accuracy in determining damages, see Kaplow and Shavell (1996), and for further, less formal discussion, including remarks on notions of fairness, see Kaplow (1994b, 311–45, 383–86).

71. Although our discussion's use of the language of injurer and victim calls to mind the tort context, the analysis applies more broadly. For example, the injurer may be one who breaches a contract, the harm the loss in value to the promisee, and the cost of precaution the incremental cost of performance. See note 20.

cases, taking care is assumed to cost $80 and, in another, $120. Harm to the victim will be either $50, $100, or $150, with equal probability.[72] The injurer is assumed to know what the actual level of harm will be before he decides whether to take care.[73]

Let us examine two legal regimes. In the inaccurate (and therefore inexpensive) regime, in which litigation costs will be assumed for simplicity to be $0,[74] the tribunal simply awards damages of $100 in all cases in which the injurer has harmed the victim. In the accurate regime, the parties are given the opportunity to demonstrate the true extent of damages. In one set of cases, they can do this at a cost of $15 (borne, for simplicity, entirely by the party undertaking the demonstration),[75] and, in another, at a cost of $45.

To motivate this set of assumptions, we observe that it often will be relatively cheap for a tribunal to determine the approximate level of harm. For example, the tribunal might simply observe that the plaintiff has a broken leg, and from experience (or making reference to a damages table based on others' experiences) the tribunal may know the average level of harm in that type of case. The actual harm, however, may be higher or lower than average due to the particular characteristics of the victim's situation (such as preexisting health problems or the extent to which the impairment is relevant to the plaintiff's occupation), and it will typically be costly to collect and introduce evidence that would establish this. More permissive procedures (allowing broader discovery, additional expert witnesses, and the like) would make a demonstration of actual harm possible. To simplify the exposition, in our example we abstract from these details and present an all-or-

---

72. That is, each individual, when in the role of potential victim, may suffer one of these three levels of harm, although, of course, each actual victim will suffer only one level of harm. Because we are, for simplicity, assuming that individuals are risk neutral, only victims' expected harm will matter. See also subsection VIII.C.1, discussing the appropriateness of adopting an ex ante perspective.

73. We consider in subsection 4 the case in which the injurer does not know in advance the actual level of harm.

74. Our analysis in the text depends on the difference between litigation costs in the inaccurate and accurate regimes. Thus, for example, if we assume that litigation costs are $10 in the inaccurate regime and add $10 to the litigation cost figures in the accurate regime (that is, if litigation costs of $10 are incurred regardless of whether a party demonstrates actual harm, in addition to the demonstration costs), the results for our illustration concerning the comparison of the two regimes will be the same.

75. If, for example, each party bears half the costs, our results will be the same in our example. (If, however, we consider an example in which costs are sufficiently high—above $50—it would matter whether the party seeking to make the demonstration bears all of the costs, because the party will proceed only if his expected benefit in improving the outcome exceeds his own litigation expenditure.)

nothing situation in which actual harm either is fully demonstrated or is not proved at all.[76]

(b) Effects of the Legal Rules. We initially consider the case in which the cost of taking care is high ($120). First, let us examine the inaccurate regime. The injurer who does not take care will cause harm of $50, $100, or $150, but in any event he will be required to pay damages of $100. (He will pay this amount even if harm is only $50, or if it is really $150, because the tribunal will not allow actual harm to be demonstrated.) This cost ($100) is less than the cost of taking care ($120), so he will not take care. Total expected costs are thus $100 in this inaccurate regime.

Second, in the accurate regime in which demonstrating actual harm costs $15, the plaintiff will demonstrate harm whenever it is $150 (he recovers an additional $50, at a legal cost of $15), and the defendant will demonstrate harm whenever it is $50 (he pays $50 less in damages, at a legal cost of $15). As a consequence of the former prospect, an injurer will take care in those instances (and only in those instances[77]) in which he knows that harm would be $150 (recall that we here assume that the injurer knows ahead of time the level of harm he will cause if he does not take care). There is a benefit from improving behavior of $30 (the harm avoided, $150, minus the cost of avoiding it, $120); moreover, the demonstration cost is not incurred because harm does not actually arise in this case. Hence, one-third of the time, there is a net savings of $30, yielding an expected benefit of $10 relative to the situation under the inaccurate regime. On the other hand, when harm would be only $50, the defendant will spend $15; this result occurs one-third of the time, for an expected cost of $5 relative to the situation under the inaccurate regime. In sum, total expected costs are only $95 under this accurate regime ($100 under the inaccurate regime, minus the $10 in expected savings from improved behavior when harm would be $150, plus the $5 in expected demonstration costs when harm is $50).[78]

Third, in the accurate regime in which demonstrating actual harm costs $45, the plaintiff again will demonstrate harm whenever it is $150 (damages

76. The qualitative results would not change if we were to admit intermediate levels of demonstration at intermediate costs.

77. When harm is $100, the injurer would rather pay damages of $100 than avoid harm at a cost of $120. When harm is $50, the injurer's total expected costs if he does not take care are $50 in damages plus $15 in legal costs, totaling $65, which is also less than the cost of care of $120.

78. Alternatively, one can simply compute the expected total costs: $(1/3 \times (\$50 + \$15)) + (1/3 \times \$100) + (1/3 \times \$120) = \$95$, compared to $100 under the inaccurate regime.

are $50 higher, at a legal cost of $45), and the defendant again will demonstrate harm whenever it is $50 (damages are $50 lower, at a legal cost of $45). Behavior will, accordingly, be the same as in the preceding case, and thus all the results are also the same except that higher demonstration costs of $45 (rather than $15) are incurred one-third of the time. Therefore, expected legal costs are $15 (rather than $5), and total costs under the accurate regime are $105 (rather than $95).[79]

Our initial description also included the case in which the cost of care is low ($80). This case differs mainly because, under the inaccurate regime, the cost of care is less than the expected damage payments, so injurers will take care (whereas they do not take care under this regime when the cost is high). Nevertheless, it turns out that the analysis of the effects of accuracy is much the same, so we examine this case only in the margin.[80]

(c) Choice of Legal Rules Using Welfare Economics. When the cost of accuracy is low ($15), achieving accuracy reduces expected total costs, making all individuals (prospectively) better off. When the cost of accuracy is high ($45),

---

79. Alternatively, one can simply compute the expected total costs: $(1/3 \times (\$50 + \$45))$ + $(1/3 \times \$100)$ + $(1/3 \times \$120)$ = $105, compared to $100 under the inaccurate regime.

80. The case in which the cost of care is low ($80) is entirely symmetric to the case in which the cost of care is high ($120), except in one respect. A sketch follows:

(1) Under the inaccurate regime, expected damage payments are $100, so the injurer always (rather than never) takes care.

(2) Under the accurate regime in which the cost of proving damages is $15, the injurer will take care except when harm would be only $50, because taking care costs $80 and not taking care costs $50 in damages plus $15 in demonstration costs. In the other cases, the injurer will take care because he otherwise would pay $100 or $150 (the victim demonstrates harm when it is $150).

(3) But when the cost of proving damages is $45, the injurer will not choose to prove that damages are only $50 rather than $100 (even though, ex post, this saves $50 at a cost of $45) because he would do better simply by taking care in this case (at a cost of $80 rather than an expected cost of $95, the sum of $50 in damages and $45 in legal costs). In sum, the accurate regime will have the same effect as the inaccurate regime in this final instance because the injurer will always take care, there will never be harm, and thus no legal costs will ever be incurred. However, the scenario would change if the cost of $45 to demonstrate harm were borne equally by the two parties. In this case, the injurer would not take care when harm was $50, harm would be demonstrated, and the net result would be a benefit of $30 (the net benefit of not taking care in this instance) obtained at an ex post legal cost of $45. This outcome is symmetric to the result in the text, for the case in which the cost of care is $120. (Alternatively, had we considered a case in which care reduced the probability of harm rather than made harm impossible, the accurate regime with high costs of demonstrating harm could have been undesirable even when all the costs were borne by the party demonstrating harm.)

achieving accuracy raises expected total costs, making all individuals (prospectively) worse off. Simply stated, the benefit of accuracy in this example is that it may improve behavior, the value of which is $30 in those instances in which the benefit arises.[81] Equally often, however, additional legal costs are borne in the accurate regime in situations in which there is no benefit in terms of improved behavior. Thus, if the legal costs are low ($15)—lower than the benefit from improving behavior ($30)—accuracy is desirable; if legal costs are high ($45), accuracy is undesirable.

In this perfectly reciprocal setting, everyone shares equally in the net benefits or net costs of greater accuracy.[82] Welfare economics provides an explicit method for assessing whether the benefits of accuracy are worth the costs: It favors whichever rule—procedural accuracy when its costs are low, and no accuracy when its costs are high—is best for the individuals affected by the rule.

(d) Choice of Legal Rules Using Notions of Fairness. Notions of fairness would ordinarily be understood as favoring accuracy in the present context. This conclusion holds both under strong notions that favor accuracy whenever achievable and under more moderate notions that favor accuracy when the costs of obtaining it are less than the stakes, that is, when a party would use a legal procedure (here, the opportunity to present valid evidence) even if that party bore the entire cost of the procedure.[83] (Recall that, in our example, even

81. As we discuss in note 80, when the cost of care is low ($80), this benefit would arise in our example under the accurate regime only when legal costs are low. It would, however, also arise when legal costs are high if, unlike in our example, these costs were shared equally by the parties rather than being borne entirely by one party.

82. We observe that in this example potential victims do equally well under each regime. (In the inaccurate regime, expected harm is $100 and damages are $100; in the accurate regime, whether costs are low or high, potential victims are harmed only when harm is $50 or $100, and they recover an amount equal to actual harm in both instances.) Accordingly, all of the gains in this particular example go to potential injurers. Hence, even if we had considered a wholly nonreciprocal case in this example (in which some individuals occupied only the role of potential injurers and others only that of potential victims, rather than each person occupying each role once), the rule that minimizes costs would indeed have made one class of parties (potential injurers) better off without making anyone worse off.

83. In subsection 2 we indicate that there may be a notion of fairness that competes with the right to invoke procedures that may enhance accuracy, namely, a right of the opposing party not to be imposed upon excessively. For simplicity, we include this notion among what we call "moderate" views on fairness, which take into account legal costs in some manner. In our present example, all the legal costs of the more accurate procedure are borne by the party invoking it, so a concern for imposing costs on the opponent would be moot; accordingly, under a range of formulations for a moderate notion of fairness, the favored rule in our example would be the same.

when costs are high ($45), they are still less than the stakes, a change of $50 in the damage award; moreover, we do assume that the entire cost of accuracy is borne by the party seeking to gain from it.)

(e) Why the Choice of Legal Rules Should Be Based Only on Individuals' Well-Being. Our discussion here will be brief because the analysis is similar to that offered in section A, regarding the bringing of suit. First, it is apparent that choosing the fairest rule will once again make all individuals worse off whenever the fair rule is not the same as the rule that would be chosen under welfare economics. When the cost of demonstrating actual harm is high ($45), the accurate regime is fairer, but it makes everyone (prospectively) worse off.[84]

We also note that there is no straightforward way to avoid the problem that pursuing even a moderate notion of fairness, under which the desirability of accuracy depends on the magnitude of legal costs, will make everyone worse off. In our example, one might set the cost cutoff (indicating the cost below which more accurate procedures would be deemed fair) at $30 rather than, for example, at the level of the stakes, $50. Because the behavioral benefit was $30, this cutoff would ensure that only desirable procedures are deemed fair. But if the cost of care were $110 rather than $120, this $30 cutoff would be too stringent (because the behavioral benefit of accuracy would then be $40), and if the cost of care were $130 rather than $120, this $30 cutoff would be too lax (because the behavioral benefit of accuracy would then be only $20). More generally, the only way we can give weight to a fairness principle and still avoid the possibility of making all individuals worse off is to require the principle to satisfy the following conditions: The principle must depend not only on the costs of accuracy but also on its behavioral benefits (considering both the costs of precautions and the benefits of avoiding harm). Furthermore, the manner in which the principle depends on these factors must attend precisely to how individuals' well-being is affected. But these conditions, of course, are met when, and only when, the evaluative principle is formulated to implement a welfare economic assessment.[85]

84. As elsewhere, we adopt an ex ante perspective, asking what rule individuals would find beneficial before they know whether, by chance, they will gain or lose in a particular instance. As we discuss in subsection VIII.C.1, there are a number of reasons that this perspective is compelling in the present context. (We also note that, because we are assuming that individuals are risk neutral, it is straightforward to determine which rule individuals would find advantageous ex ante.) See also note 86 in chapter VIII, indicating that illustrations such as the present one could be modified in a manner that would allow us to make our argument even without relying on an ex ante perspective.

85. As we discuss in note 31, as a practical matter the analysis may be most relevant to the selection of rules for types of procedures and classes of cases rather than to the choice of

Second, we wish to emphasize that we have demonstrated this point in a case in which the legal procedure in question is clearly and unambiguously fair. We have confined ourselves to an instance involving an entirely valid demonstration that would be properly evaluated by the factfinder. (In more realistic situations, what is otherwise deemed a fair procedure would sometimes, perhaps often, produce less desirable results.) Moreover, we have considered a case in which all of the costs are borne by the party seeking to benefit from invoking the fair procedure. (More typically, parties who take advantage of various procedures also impose costs on their opponent and on the court.) Thus, pursuing notions of fairness at the expense of individuals' well-being can be troubling even under the most favorable conditions.

Third, we are unable to identify any good reason for insisting on what are deemed to be fair procedures, at the expense of all individuals' well-being. Although some analysts may find a more accurate legal system more aesthetically pleasing, the insistence on procedures that improve accuracy when the result is to hurt everyone, including the purported beneficiaries of fair procedures, requires a more substantial justification.

When we examine the legal literature that favors one or another procedure on grounds of fairness, it often appears that the motivation is indeed to improve accuracy. However, the social benefits of greater accuracy are largely taken for granted; they are usually unspecified, and, accordingly, no basis is given for assessing their importance.[86] (Quantification would be unnecessary only if one were to insist on greater accuracy regardless of the cost, but this is an untenable position that nobody seems to endorse.[87]) Moreover, commentators do not seem to appreciate that the benefits of accuracy that do exist, such as improved behavior, depend on contingent factors, notably, the extent to which behavior is responsive to the prospect of having to pay damages.

Relatedly, as in the case of bringing suit, we believe that it is common for commentators to adopt an ex post perspective, which views legal proce-

---

particular procedures on a case-by-case basis; accordingly, our claim about the superiority of welfare economics over any notion of fairness applies to the selection of such rules.

86. For example, in his famous essay "The Forms and Limits of Adjudication," Fuller advances strong views about the core purposes of adjudication and suggests which aspects of procedure are central, see note 64, but he does not even purport to explain the normative basis for his views. Indeed, many of his arguments seem to be little more than assertions about what *defines* adjudication. See Bone (1992, 202–03 n.25): "Fuller failed to give a reason why individual participation should be treated as constitutive of adjudication," or at least failed to provide one that would now be viewed as persuasive.

87. See subsection 2.

dures and their accuracy at the time when litigation occurs.[88] Analysts concerned with notions of fairness seem to understand that the purpose of legal procedures is to produce correct outcomes. In so doing, however, analysts seem to forget the purposes of providing legal redress in the first place— the main one, upon which we focus here, is to channel behavior appropriately (we discuss others below). This oversight helps explain why analysts neglect the subtle relationship between particular procedures employed after the fact and the decisions that individuals make against a backdrop of possible litigation.

Indeed, because of their ex post character, which implicitly takes as given that litigation has reached the stage at which the procedure in question may be employed, notions of fair procedure can easily be counterproductive even with regard to their apparent underlying motivation. To illustrate, suppose that in a given setting a notion of fairness favors more accurate procedures at trial because, once parties reach that stage, additional procedures would permit a better assessment of damages. But suppose it also turns out that the increase in expected litigation costs, once such procedures are regularly available, renders suit unprofitable for many plaintiffs.[89] Then, for most potential plaintiff-defendant pairs, the ultimate outcome will be no award at all. This result, however, is often much less accurate than the recovery that would have been provided under the seemingly less accurate regime with more limited procedures.[90] Moreover, the prospect of a recovery—however imprecise—may have deterred much injury in the first place, in which case inaccurate damages would have been awarded infrequently, whereas when few are induced to sue, harm may be more frequent (and, in many instances, wholly uncompensated). Thus, as a matter of both procedural fairness and concern for the principles underlying the substantive law in question (whether based on notions of fairness or not), pursuing notions of fairness may have perverse effects, reflecting again the problematic nature of evalua-

88. Judge Newman similarly ascribes the general misunderstanding of the social value of legal procedures to the weight given to notions of fairness that embody an ex post perspective. See Newman (1985).

89. This scenario is not far-fetched. Individuals with claims of a few thousand dollars often cannot practically pursue legal remedies due to the high cost of legal proceedings. One assumes that this problem provides the rationale for small claims courts and helps explain the increasing use of other forms of alternative dispute resolution that do not employ many standard procedures.

90. This potential perversity has previously been noted, see, for example, Menkel-Meadow (1995, 2688), although we are unaware of any attempt to articulate a coherent theory of fair procedure that is responsive to such problems.

tive principles that embody an ex post perspective and, accordingly, are insufficiently attentive to consequences.

(f) The Appeal of Notions of Fairness and Its Implications. As with the ability to bring suit, we believe that the appeal of notions of fairness exists in part because analysts improperly take an ex post perspective[91] and, as we now explore, in part because these notions of fairness derive from internalized social norms, here, about adjudication.[92] In informal settings in everyday life, parties naturally wish to resolve their disputes accurately. They do not wish to impose costly punishments, such as cutting off future relationships, unless real misbehavior has occurred, and they do not want actual wrongdoers to avoid punishment, for that would undermine the channeling effect of substantive social norms. It also seems that informal dispute resolution does not ordinarily involve the costly interaction that is common under the formal legal system. Often a controversy is confined to the injurer and the victim, who already know the relevant facts. If one party is not adequately informed—perhaps a victim is upset about an injurer's seemingly inappropriate behavior and contemplates severing future relations—then the other can provide information quickly. Denying the other party the opportunity to provide information would often be counterproductive; for example, one might terminate valuable relationships on account of a misunderstanding.[93]

The earliest and perhaps strongest lessons about adjudication arise from disagreements between children or between parents and children that parents resolve. Here, the primary cost of permitting additional procedures (for example, allowing a child to give further factual details or to offer excuses) is the additional time involved in hearing out the parties and providing more complete explanations for the final outcome. This cost is likely to be low. Furthermore, the additional effort required to provide more elaborate adjudication is likely to be viewed on balance as a beneficial educational investment in one's children.

---

91. In subsection II.B.2(c) we discuss this common feature of notions of fairness and address why they tend to be appealing in spite of their deficiencies.

92. See, for example, Grey (1977, 182): "[I]t seems clear that the basic core of what lawyers call 'procedural due process' is formed around the popular conceptions of procedural fairness manifested in the common judgments of conventional morality."

93. In some instances, easy and reliable exchange of information is not possible, and some misunderstandings are inevitable. Nevertheless, in most informal settings, it is not common for the parties to engage in elaborate collection and exchange of information or to undertake costly efforts to inform independent third parties, as formal adjudication requires. More elaborate information exchanges may be more common in business dealings, often as a substitute for formal adjudication, which may be in the background.

From such experiences, we all may have internalized the notion that fair procedures are those that are reasonably exhaustive. It does not follow, however, that notions of fairness based on these norms of social interaction should be adopted as independent principles for use in designing the formal legal system.[94] This conclusion is especially compelling because the purpose of these social norms is functional, to improve individuals' well-being, whereas giving independent weight to notions of fairness can only have the opposite effect.

Our conjecture about this important source of social norms regarding fair procedure also suggests that such norms may serve as a proxy device for promoting welfare. The main appeal of providing additional procedures to enhance accuracy is, we believe, the simple belief that greater accuracy tends to be desirable. And, of course, greater accuracy often is beneficial, both in everyday interactions and in the formal legal system (for the reasons that we have already given and for others that we explore below). Hence, insistence on procedural fairness, which usually entails improving accuracy, will tend to serve as a proxy instrument for identifying policies that enhance individuals' well-being.

As we have explained, however, the benefits of accuracy are indirect (they are only properly appreciated from an ex ante perspective) and they must be weighed against the costs of more accurate procedures, which are often substantial in the formal legal system, in contrast to the informal resolution of disagreements in everyday life. In addition, the tutelary function served by greater investment in dispute resolution seems a good deal less important with regard to the formal legal system than in the education of children.[95] Thus, pursuing notions of fairness in the design of legal proce-

94. See Kearns (1977, 230), stating that "applying moral precepts to anything as complicated as a legal system is almost never a simple matter," suggesting that "our moral rules and principles apply, in the first instance, not to normative systems, but to persons[, and between] the law, one kind of normative system, and persons, there obviously are substantial differences," and warning that "it might well be that . . . applying our usual moral commitments directly to normative systems actually tends to imperil the moral ends we hope to achieve." A contrary view is sometimes taken for granted. See, for example, Grey (1977, 183), asserting, without any discussion, that "where the law of due process departs from the broad outlines of [lay notions of] the morality of procedural fairness, producing results strongly contrary to widely shared intuitive judgments, it seems right to presume that it has gone astray."

95. Formal adjudication may sometimes serve an educational purpose. We suspect that the importance of this function, relative to the litigation costs involved, is likely to be of some significance, say, in traffic court or in a dispute as to what is proper conduct by police officers, but it has little applicability to the expenditure of tens of thousands of dollars by parties

dures, though appealing, is not a good substitute for explicit welfare economic analysis.

The fact that internalized social norms may favor extensive dispute resolution procedures also implies that individuals may have a taste for fair procedures; that is, they may feel better off living under a regime that provides what they understand to be fair procedures.[96] We consider this possibility further in subsection C.1.

4. Variations: Accuracy in Determining Damages

In this subsection and the next, we consider a number of variations on the example examined in the preceding subsection. Our purpose is to elaborate on the ways in which fairer (and more accurate) procedures may be detrimental on balance, in some instances even when there are benefits to accuracy that were not present in the previous example. We confine ourselves to a brief sketch and do not repeat our analysis of why pursuing a notion of fairness when it makes individuals worse off is undesirable despite the apparent attractiveness of fair procedures.

(a) Case in Which Injurers Do Not Know in Advance How Much Harm Victims Will Suffer. Let us make one modification of the previous example by assuming that the injurer does *not* know in advance how much harm the victim will suffer. This assumption is often realistic; for example, a driver may be unable to predict how badly a pedestrian whom he may strike will be injured or the resulting extent of damages, which would depend on the victim's occupation, among other things. We now demonstrate that, in this setting, legal proce-

---

contesting the magnitude of damages in a routine auto accident case or in many other settings. Compare subsection C.2.

Another reason that greater accuracy may have value in many informal settings but seldom in those involving formal adjudication concerns parties' interest in learning about each other when they expect to interact in the future. Thus, in disagreements among friends, relatives, and business associates, it is important to know whether one's counterpart is the type of person who behaves properly—by avoiding injury when possible, by responding decently when injury nevertheless occurs, and by not reacting excessively or without justification to alleged wrongdoing by others. Formal adjudication, in contrast, more often involves interactions between strangers or disputes that arise at the termination of relationships.

96. Such benefits—which arise from a per se taste for fair procedures—must be distinguished from direct effects on individuals' well-being that are already included in a welfare economic analysis, such as the benefit of freedom from potential harassment provided under a legal regime that is good at sifting out frivolous claims.

dures that enhance accuracy at some cost are always detrimental.[97] Indeed, each of the parties, viewed in isolation, will be worse off in expected terms under the accurate regime, no matter how low the cost of accuracy. That is, even in a perfectly nonreciprocal case—in which some individuals will only be injurers and others only victims—everyone would (prospectively) be worse off under a more accurate regime. In this instance, the conflict between notions of fairness and individuals' well-being is stark.

When injurers do not know victims' level of harm in advance (whether it will be $50, $100, or $150), their decisions must be based entirely on the expected harm, or more precisely, on their expected damage payments and litigation costs. Consider again the case in which the cost of care is $120 and the cost of demonstrating actual harm is $15.[98] Under the inaccurate regime, injurers will pay $100 if there is harm, regardless of its level, so they will not take care and will incur costs of $100. Victims, as before, are made whole on average (and they are risk neutral), so their expected costs are $0.

Consider how the parties' well-being differs under the accurate regime. Suppose that injurers again would not take care (which, as will be apparent momentarily, they will not). When harm is $150, victims will spend $15 to demonstrate the true level of harm (because they would rather recover $150 − $15 than the $100 they otherwise would receive if they did not prove actual damages). When harm is $50, injurers demonstrate this fact, and their total cost is $65 (that is, $50 in damages plus $15 in legal costs). As a result, victims' expected net recovery is $5 lower than under the inaccurate regime: Their expected gross recovery is $100, as before, but one-third of the time they must pay $15 in legal costs, thereby reducing their expected net receipts by $5.[99] Similarly, injurers' expected net payments are $5 higher than under the inaccurate regime: They still make expected payments to victims of $100 but also pay legal costs of $15 one-third of the time.[100] Hence, on an expected

---

97. If the procedure is so costly that neither party would ever choose to take advantage of it, allowing use of the procedure will be irrelevant rather than detrimental. For another instance in which accuracy may be irrelevant, see note 98.

98. When the cost of care is $80, the injurer will always take care under the present assumptions, regardless of whether the accurate or inaccurate regime is employed. Hence, there will never be harm, and the inaccurate and accurate regimes will have identical effects. If we considered care that reduced rather than eliminated the probability of harm, however, this would no longer be true, and it can be demonstrated that the accurate regime would be worse. See Kaplow and Shavell (1996, 193–94, 204–05).

99. Victims' expected recovery is $(1/3 \times \$50) + (1/3 \times \$100) + (1/3 \times (\$150 − \$15))$ = $95, rather than $100, as in the inaccurate regime.

100. Injurers' expected payment is $(1/3 \times (\$50 + \$15)) + (1/3 \times \$100) + (1/3 \times \$150)$ = $105, rather than $100, as in the inaccurate regime.

basis, each party is worse off by $5. (Finally, observe that injurers' expected costs if they do not take care are $105, which indeed are insufficient to induce them to take care, which would cost $120.)

In this case, in which injurers do not know victims' harm in advance, procedures that provide greater accuracy make everyone worse off, even when legal costs are low. (Legal costs were $15 in our example, much less than the effect of demonstrating harm on the outcome, $50; note further that both parties would be worse off even if legal costs were only $1, that is, just 2 percent of the amount by which demonstrating harm affects the outcome.) Nevertheless, notions of fairness are served by greater accuracy. In this setting, it is assumed that only valid demonstrations are made, that the entire cost of making a demonstration is borne by the moving party, and that the costs are only a moderate fraction of the stakes—in combination, a very compelling case for deeming fair those procedures that enhance accuracy by permitting demonstrations of actual harm. Thus, pursuing notions of fairness, even in a setting that is highly favorable to the procedures from the perspective of fairness, is again undesirable for individuals.

We pause to observe that this type of situation—in which injurers do not know the particulars of victims' harm in advance—is probably a very important one. After all, billions of dollars are spent annually contesting details of tort damages (such as the specifics of lost future earnings) that injurers could not possibly have anticipated at the time they decided upon precautions and acted.[101]

(b) Case in Which Victims Are Risk Averse and Injurers Do Not Know in Advance How Much Harm Victims Will Suffer. We now modify the preceding example in order to consider the case in which victims are risk averse. (Because we are examining a reciprocal case, this implies that defendants also are risk

---

101. For further discussion, see Kaplow and Shavell (1996, 201–03).

Our analysis also applies directly to disputes about the use of sampling to determine awards in mass tort cases. See, for example, Bone (1993), Saks and Blanck (1992), and Walker and Monahan (1998). Note that our analysis suggests that the plaintiffs who are left out of the sample—who are included in the class but do not personally receive their "day in court"— are the fortunate ones, contrary to the normal suggestion, because they save costs but on average obtain the same recovery. (Even if costs are reimbursed, time and hassle are unlikely to be.) An important exception involves the problem of adverse selection, that is, when those who suffered an atypically high level of harm will want to litigate—like those opting out of a class action—and others who suffered less harm will not. But ex ante they would all prefer the averaging regime—subject to the analysis of risk aversion in the subsection that follows. See generally Hay (1997) and Hay and Rosenberg (2000).

averse. To keep matters simple, however, we will suppose throughout that individuals have liability insurance so that defendants' risk aversion can be ignored.[102]) In this case, accuracy in compensation—making sure that we do not overcompensate some victims and undercompensate others—has the potential to enhance individuals' well-being. Of course, to the extent that victims have first-party insurance, accuracy will confer no such benefit.[103] Although insurance is important in practice, there is little more to say about this subcase, which is essentially the same as the previous one: Costly legal procedures that enhance accuracy would again be wasteful; adopting them on grounds of fairness would only make everyone worse off.

Accordingly, we focus on the situation in which victims remain uninsured, say, due to the high administrative costs of insurance.[104] Analysis of this situation largely follows the prior example, except that, when care costs $120 so that injurers do cause harm, the accurate regime will now have the benefit of providing more accurate compensation to victims. (In particular, when harm is $50, the inaccurate regime overcompensates victims by $50, and when harm is $150, the inaccurate regime undercompensates them by $50.[105]) One can measure this benefit to victims, as in subsection III.D.1(f),

102. When defendants are risk averse and uninsured, they tend to be better off under the inaccurate rule because accuracy exposes them to greater risk. Under the accurate regime, damages turn out to be $50, $100, or $150; under the inaccurate regime, damages are always $100. Hence, a more complete analysis of risk aversion when parties are uninsured is less favorable to accuracy than the discussion in the text suggests. Indeed, in our example, the defendant's risk under the accurate regime is symmetric to the plaintiff's under the inaccurate regime, so risk-bearing costs under the two regimes would, all else being equal, tend to be similar. Nevertheless, because there are important instances in which defendants are systematically less risk averse than plaintiffs—they may have insurance or be entities owned by individuals whose investments are diversified—and because the case of risk-averse plaintiffs is more prominent in the minds of many commentators regardless of its real-world accuracy, we focus on it in the text.

103. Indeed, if victims have first-party insurance and their legal recoveries are not fully subrogated (that is, not captured by the insurance company), then more accurate compensation would actually increase the risk they bear. In addition, when losses are nonpecuniary, more accurate compensation would also raise risk-bearing costs in the plausible case in which the losses do not affect individuals' marginal utility of income. See, for example, Shavell (1987, chapters 8–10).

104. For further discussion of insurance in this and other cases, see subsection III.D.1(f).

105. In terms of the final position of victims, there is a one-third chance that they will have a net gain of $50 and a one-third chance that they will suffer a net loss of $50. Exposure to such a gamble (though its expected value is zero) reduces the well being of risk-averse individuals. See note 9 in chapter II.

using a risk premium, which is simply the monetary equivalent of the benefit of avoiding risk.[106] We now examine cases in which this risk premium is $20 and in which it is $2.

When the risk premium is $20, the victim's gain under an accurate regime exceeds his expected demonstration cost of $5,[107] and it does so by more than the injurer's additional expected cost of $5. Accordingly, in our reciprocal setting, individuals would be better off under a regime incorporating the procedure that improved accuracy.[108]

In contrast, if the risk premium is only $2, it is not worthwhile for the victim to have the more accurate regime because his expected demonstration cost of $5 exceeds the benefit of protection against risk.[109] (This preference would be heightened if the plaintiff were insured, as we note above.) Moreover, the defendant is also worse off under the accurate regime. Thus, adopting more accurate procedures would be to everyone's detriment even though such procedures better tailor compensation to victims.

We now compare analysis based on notions of fairness, which, as we explain in the preceding subsection, would favor the more accurate regime. In the present case, accuracy is not always a bad prescription, because if uninsured plaintiffs are sufficiently risk averse, the benefit of accurate compensation may justify the cost of more accurate procedures. Thus, a notion of fairness may have appeal not only because it serves as a proxy device

106. The risk premium is equal to the difference between the certainty equivalent of exposure to a risk and the expected monetary value of the risk, which is to say the amount by which exposure to a risky prospect is worse than exposure to a certain outcome with the same expected value. See note 103 in chapter III.

107. Strictly speaking, the demonstration cost is also uncertain. The accurate regime provides incomplete recovery when harm is $150, because the plaintiff must spend $15 to demonstrate the harm. To simplify the exposition, we can interpret the risk premium as taking this detail into account.

108. Had we considered the nonreciprocal case, the victim's expected net gain of $15 would have to be balanced against the injurer's expected loss of $5. This result could favor the inaccurate regime if, say, plaintiffs were much wealthier than defendants and alternative means of redistribution (notably, taxes and transfers) were unavailable. Then we would have another instance in which procedural fairness would come at the expense of overall well-being.

109. Following our analysis in subsection III.D.1(f)(i), it is easy to see that the implicit provision of insurance by improving accuracy may be perverse. Suppose, for example, that the administrative cost of private insurance were $4, but individuals did not purchase the insurance because, as stipulated in the text, their risk-bearing cost was only $2. In this case, providing greater accuracy as a means of improving compensation for risk-averse individuals involves charging those individuals $5 for an implicit insurance policy that they could have purchased for $4, but had found to be undesirable even at that price.

for identifying procedures that make substantive rules guide behavior more effectively, as we imply in subsection 3, but also because the notion of fair compensation is suggestive of a possible increase in the well-being of uninsured victims. But in other important cases—when plaintiffs are not as risk averse or when they are insured (in which case the notion that accurate compensation is fairer appears to be moot[110]), and when the benefit of more accurate compensation is less than the cost of greater accuracy—pursuing notions of fairness will again lead us astray. Adopting the more accurate regime because accurate compensation is fair compensation only makes worse off the individuals to whom one seeks to be fair.

Nor can notions of fairness be redeemed by invoking the competing idea that fairness principles also require limiting the imposition of costs on others. Here, no procedural costs are imposed on the opposing party, so the competing notion of fairness is inapposite. Moreover, if one admits a competing notion of fairness under which total legal costs relative to the stakes are considered, the same problem that we address when we examine the behavioral benefits of accuracy arises: No simple tradeoff, such as may be embodied in a stipulated ratio of permissible costs to stakes, effectively indicates when more accurate procedures are desirable.[111] To avoid results that may be to everyone's disadvantage, it is necessary to undertake a complete welfare economic analysis and not to give weight to possibly conflicting notions of fairness.

5. Variations: Accuracy in Determining Liability

We have focused thus far on cases involving accuracy in the assessment of damages. Of course, contested issues often involve liability: determining who committed an act, whether that act caused the victim's injury, and whether that act violated the relevant legal standard. Although a complete analysis of these cases is beyond the scope of our investigation, we offer a number of observations.[112]

---

110. See subsection III.D.1(e), discussing this point in the tort context. In addition, when defendants also are risk averse and uninsured, greater accuracy would involve an additional cost with respect to imposition of risk. See note 102.

111. See subsection 3(e).

112. We analyze accuracy in determining liability in Kaplow and Shavell (1994a), and the topic is discussed further, with some reference to notions of fairness, in Kaplow (1994b, 345–69, 386–88). We also note that some issues concerning liability can be seen as special cases of accuracy in determining damages. If, say, true damages were either $0 (wrong actor, no causation, and so forth) or $200 (if, in fact, there truly should be legal liability), one can imagine an inaccurate system that does not distinguish between two groups of actors, only

Our central point is that welfare economics accommodates a whole range of possible benefits of accuracy. Greater accuracy tends to enhance deterrence of harmful behavior,[113] to avoid chilling desirable behavior, and to reduce any direct costs of misapplied legal sanctions (such as mistakenly sanctioning the innocent). The welfare economic framework will, as in the previous cases that we have considered, evaluate these effects in terms of their impact on individuals' well-being. Hence, if an accurate regime makes everyone better off, welfare economics will always favor it, but if greater accuracy makes everyone worse off (because the costs of accuracy exceed the benefits), welfare economics will necessarily oppose it.[114] Notions of fairness may serve as proxy devices for ascertaining these effects on individuals' well-being, but giving weight to a notion of fairness when it conflicts with the dictates of welfare economics can only decrease individuals' well-being.

To illustrate this point, consider market-share liability.[115] Suppose that a number of firms undertake identical activities and thereby contribute to risk in direct proportion to their shares in the market. Moreover, assume that each victim is able to determine which firm caused his harm, but that determining causation accurately involves some cost. Assume that this cost is modest and is borne primarily by the victims who must make this demon-

---

one of which is truly responsible for causing harm, and subjects them both to an intermediate level of liability. Indeed, this hypothetical approach corresponds to certain situations involving multiple sources of risk. Suppose, for example, that an actor released toxic substances and that background sources of risk also existed. Awarding damages proportional to contribution to risk would be consistent with the foregoing description of the inaccurate regime. In contrast, an accurate regime would entail spending the resources necessary to determine the true cause of harm—the actor or some background factor—and awarding full damages in the former case and nothing in the latter case.

113. There are two reasons for this conclusion: the familiar one, that if some truly liable parties go free, potential injurers have less incentive to behave properly, and a less familiar one, that if some innocent parties will be held liable, there is less incentive for individuals to avoid causing harm.

114. We have, for simplicity, focused on the reciprocal case, in which the effect (in direction and magnitude) on all individuals is the same. If we were to consider the nonreciprocal case more fully, effects on the distribution of income (if other, better means of income redistribution were unavailable) would also be relevant. Some of our discussion does address the nonreciprocal case, either explicitly, see notes 82 and 108, or implicitly, see subsections 4(a) and 4(b), analyzing examples in which both potential victims and potential injurers are made worse off by the use of fair procedures that enhance accuracy.

115. See Rosenberg (1984) and Shavell (1985b). Compare Walker and Monahan (1999), emphasizing the cost savings obtainable by using sampling methods to determine liability-related issues in cases with large numbers of claims.

stration. In such a case, notions of fairness, as generally understood, dictate that each victim prove causation, for otherwise some defendants might pay for more harm than they actually caused and others might pay for less.[116] In the hypothesized case, however, this expenditure is wasteful. Each plaintiff recovers the same amount regardless of whether harm is traced to the defendant who actually caused it or market-share liability is employed, yet the accurate tracing of harm leaves all plaintiffs worse off because they must bear greater legal costs.[117] Defendants have the same expected payments, and thus the same incentives (assuming that they are risk neutral) under both regimes. Defendants, however, would all be worse off if, as is realistic, they bore greater legal costs in a regime that required tracing of harm (for example, as a consequence of having to respond to plaintiffs' discovery requests).

116. See, for example, Zafft v. Eli Lilly and Co., 676 S.W.2d 241, 246 (Mo. 1984): "[M]arket share liability continues the risk that the actual wrongdoer is not among the named defendants, and exposes those joined to liability greater than their responsibility."; L. Alexander (1987a, 14–15), criticizing corrective justice's emphasis on tracing causation; Fischer (1981, 1629–30, 1638–39), arguing that proof of actual causation is important because liability should be based upon moral blame; Rosenberg (1984, 857–58), describing the law regarding proof in cases involving causal uncertainty and discussing the conventional rationale for it; and Strudler (1992), arguing that remedial schemes in mass tort cases are inconsistent with extant interpretations of corrective justice but offering an alternative interpretation. But see Kraus (1997), disagreeing with Strudler's interpretation of corrective justice. The usual fairness-based arguments that favor market-share liability tend to assume both that fairness principles ordinarily demand proof of causation and that an exception is made, based on a competing fairness principle (such as one favoring compensation of innocent plaintiffs or punishment of negligent defendants, see, for example, Sindell v. Abbott Labs., 607 P.2d 924, 936 (Cal. 1980)), precisely because causation, in the sense of tracing harm to particular defendants, cannot reasonably be established. If so, then in the example in the text in which causation can be established at a moderate cost, even notions of fairness favorable to market-share liability may demand proof of causation, to everyone's detriment.

117. Requiring accuracy could be even worse in practice than suggested by the discussion in the text. Assume, for example, that some of the injuries—say, 10 percent on an expected basis—are caused by background risk factors. Also suppose that plaintiffs are risk averse and not insured. Proportional market-share liability would compensate each victim for 90 percent of the harm. Accurate tracing would give 90 percent of victims full recovery and 10 percent of victims no recovery. On an expected basis, victims are now even worse off, because they face the same expected recovery under an accurate regime (actually, somewhat less, due to added litigation costs), but now they also face a serious risk of no recovery.

Moreover, once risk is taken into account, the fact that defendants may be risk averse, see note 102, can contribute to the undesirability of more accurate procedures. For example, a firm's market share may be 10 percent, but its actual share of the harm might be greater or less than 10 percent; accurately tracing damages would require defendants to bear this risk, an additional cost of accuracy.

Therefore, pursuing notions of fairness in this context helps no one and merely exhausts legal resources, a cost borne by everyone involved.

6. Remarks

(a) The Generality of Our Results. The preceding analysis is applicable to the evaluation of a wide variety of legal procedures and legal issues. Essentially any procedural question that involves a tradeoff between accuracy and cost is encompassed by our discussion. Our framework is also relevant to the evaluation of a variety of legal questions, including identifying the injurer, establishing causation, assessing whether a standard of care has been met, and measuring damages.[118] In addition, although we have considered the tort setting, our analysis carries over to consensual interactions as well. In examining contracts,[119] for example, one would take into account how the anticipated effect of legal procedures in the event of a dispute will be reflected both in behavior under contracts (for example, the decision to breach) and in parties' ex ante contract negotiations.[120]

(b) Parties' Excessive Incentives to Invoke Procedures in Litigation. We also wish to emphasize a point implicit in much of our analysis in this section: procedures that, from an ex ante perspective, would make parties worse off (in an expected sense) often will be favored by one party or the other ex post, once it is learned which of the possible outcomes has been realized.[121] For example,

---

118. Of course, the details of the analysis will vary by context. To illustrate, some random variation in ex post damages assessment, even when anticipated, will have little effect on behavior under a rule of strict liability, whereas anticipated random variation in negligence determinations could have a nontrivial effect on behavior. See, for example, Craswell and Calfee (1986). Nevertheless, the points we emphasize in the text remain applicable.

119. See note 20.

120. With respect to the latter, as we note in chapter IV, contract prices will tend to adjust to reflect any distributive effects of different enforcement regimes; hence, it is all the more likely that adopting a welfare-reducing procedure on grounds of fairness would make *both* parties worse off (even in a fully nonreciprocal case).

121. The general tendency that we identify—that private parties' incentives to spend in litigation are socially excessive—arises in a range of contexts, but it is not universal. To illustrate this qualification, truly innocent criminal defendants may well have a socially insufficient incentive to establish their innocence (because, among other reasons, they do not bear the costs of operating prisons). Whether incentives are excessive or inadequate is explored in Kaplow and Shavell (1996, 195–98, 206–09) and Kaplow (1994b, 338–45, 367–69). See also Hay (1997), emphasizing that parties' ex post preferences diverge from their ex ante assessments, and Hay and Rosenberg (2000), expressing a similar view with regard to whether parties would prefer individualized treatment or averaging.

we identified settings in which both parties would be worse off (on average) if permitted to establish damages more accurately ex post.[122] But when damages actually turn out to be above average ($150 rather than $100 in our example), the plaintiff would want to expend resources ($15 or $45 in the example) to establish this fact. Similarly, when damages are below average ($50 rather than $100), the defendant would wish to demonstrate this fact. Accordingly, at the time of adjudication, we often would expect that one or the other party would wish to invoke some procedure or to be given various opportunities to present its case; our analysis suggests that such preferences often will reflect self-interest, viewed ex post.[123] We believe that the failure to appreciate this difference between the ex post view, under which additional procedures may misleadingly appear attractive, and the ex ante view helps explain, as we have suggested previously, the perceived attractiveness of notions of procedural fairness that in fact provide a poor basis for setting legal policy.

7. The Extent to Which the Use of Notions of Fairness Has Led Us Astray

The preceding analysis clearly suggests that pursuing notions of fairness in the design of legal procedures may lead us to make unsound decisions. Con-

---

122. The reader should recall that we show this result in instances in which the party making the demonstration bears the whole cost of doing so and in which only entirely valid demonstrations are possible. The danger of excessive ex post incentives in adjudication is, one presumes, more serious when these favorable assumptions are relaxed.

123. Additionally, in settings such as those we have posed, such a self-interested view would be advanced even if the party were required to make the same opportunities available to its opponent because, once a concrete case arises, there often will be reason to believe additional procedures would favor a particular party.

This point illuminates debates about which procedures should be available to claimants who contest determinations under government entitlement programs. First, ex post, such claimants may favor procedures that essentially are available only to themselves (because the government case is developed internally, by the staff of the relevant agency). But even if this were not so, there would generally be a socially excessive ex post incentive to contest adverse determinations, and potential claimants would be worse off if greater challenges were allowed and the costs of such challenges were reflected in the generosity of the program. Prior analyses, many of which focus on the Supreme Court's decision in Mathews v. Eldridge, 424 U.S. 319 (1976), generally fail to appreciate these points. For a discussion of the commentary and its shortcomings, as well as an explanation of why the Court's cost-benefit test is not properly formulated, see Kaplow (1994b, 369–78). Compare Kaplow (1994a), modeling the problem in the analogous case of private insurance, where claimants may wish ex post to appeal insurance company determinations that underestimate actual losses but ex ante would prefer an insurance policy that disallowed some such appeals.

sider the case (examined in subsection 4) in which more accurate damage determinations will have no effect on behavior because potential injurers, at the time they act, do not know the precise level of damages that they will cause but rather have only an average sense of the harm that might result from their actions. As we observed, this is probably typical of many accident cases, in which most of the billions of dollars spent litigating the level of damages are devoted to establishing details of particular victims' injuries, the effects of these injuries on future earnings potential, and so forth—matters that injurers could not possibly have anticipated.[124] Although we noted that there may be some benefit in providing more accurate compensation when victims are risk averse and uninsured, it seems unlikely that this benefit is sufficient to justify the high level of litigation costs that are incurred.[125] In any event, the significant possibility that accurate damage assessments may not be worth the cost—and indeed may not be worth much at all in some settings—does not seem to be appreciated. This oversight seems to be shared even by those advocating such reforms as the use of damage tables, partly as a means to increase accuracy by reducing arbitrary variation in jury awards.[126]

Additionally, the set of trends that we identify in subsection A.8—the general increase in access to the courts followed by more recent attempts to restrict access—have analogs with regard to procedural protections as well. For example, the twentieth century saw the creation and expansion of discovery, followed by increasing limitations on it.[127] In the present setting involving accuracy in adjudication, we also find, unfortunately, that notions of fairness seem to influence legal procedure.[128] Accordingly, neither the earlier nor the more recent reforms seem to be guided by careful attention to the relevant effects on individuals' well-being that we have identified in this

---

124. This point may not hold in intentional tort cases in which the victim is known to the injurer, but for most accidents, such as those caused by automobiles, the description in the text seems apt.

125. In note 103, on risk aversion, we also indicated that more accurate compensation tends to impose more risk on defendants who are not fully insured, on plaintiffs who are insured but whose recoveries are not fully subrogated, and possibly on plaintiffs whose losses are nonpecuniary.

126. See, for example, Blumstein, Bovbjerg, and Sloan (1990) and Bovbjerg, Sloan, and Blumstein (1989). See also Rutherford, Knetsch, and Brown (1998), suggesting that damage schedules reflecting citizens' judgments would be more accurate and less costly than case-specific post-incident assessments.

127. See, for example, Amendments to Federal Rules of Civil Procedure (1993, 203–89) (1993 discovery reforms), and Resnik (1986), documenting both phases of the history.

128. See, for example, Newman (1985, 1643): "[T]he way we think about fairness . . . is a root cause of many of the undesirable aspects of our modern process of litigation."; ibid. (1646), arguing that a "more fundamental explanation for the time-consuming and expensive nature of our litigation system [is] the centrality of fairness as our governing standard."

section.[129] Thus, one can have little confidence that sensible reforms have been adopted in appropriate contexts.

C. Additional Reasons Why Legal Procedures May Be Valued

1. Possible Tastes for Procedural Fairness

As in other areas we have examined, it is possible that individuals have tastes regarding legal procedures governing both the availability of legal redress and the manner in which adjudication is conducted. If such tastes exist, they would be valued under welfare economics, that is, they would be weighted according to the extent individuals actually would be willing in principle to expend resources to benefit from procedures rather than, say, more recreational activity.[130] As we have emphasized since our introduction,[131] however, the presence of such tastes must be distinguished from the idea that a notion of fairness is an independent evaluative principle, to be pursued at the expense of individuals' well-being (including the possibility that a component of well-being may be a taste for some notion of fairness being reflected in the legal system).[132] Thus, under welfare economics, the relevant valuations

129. Compare Newman (1980, 1650–51), lamenting the lack of social scientific assessment of legal procedure and suggesting that many expensive aspects of procedure may contribute little to accuracy.

130. This possibility could be included in our analysis in a straightforward manner. For example, when we state that the cost of demonstrating actual harm through more involved procedures is $15, one could take $15 to be the aggregate *net* cost, combining legal fees, the cost of time expended in the process, and any positive or negative utility directly attributable to engaging in the proceedings. (For example, if the direct cost were $20 and individuals derived an experiential benefit of $5, the net cost would be $15.) This net cost figure for each party could then be used in conducting the analysis to determine whether the behavioral benefits of a procedure were sufficient to justify its (net) cost.

131. In particular, see subsection II.A.1.

132. The potential for confusion is clear. For example, Dworkin's argument for an independent concept of moral harm, discussed in note 65, which he insists is distinct from people's preferences, is motivated primarily by reference to such phenomena as feelings of sympathy and our impressions of others' suffering. See R. Dworkin (1985, 80–81). See also ibid. (86), positing the existence of moral harm and arguing that it is the reason that we feel guilty in certain circumstances. Although the logic of the distinction is clear enough, the manner of argument is problematic, for Dworkin repeatedly calls upon our feelings to motivate his concept and then suggests that we accept his concept even after he defines it to be wholly apart from any feelings we may have. But it seems entirely possible that our moral intuitions are explained by the feelings themselves, that is, by our tastes. Moreover, our prior discussion suggests that such tastes may derive from internalized social norms, and, as we have explained, it is a logical error to infer from such intuitions about notions of fairness that there exists some welfare-independent evaluative principle. See subsections A.6 and B.3(f).

depend on what individuals actually favor and to what extent, not on what an analyst engaged in philosophical inquiry might stipulate to be appropriate as a matter of principle. We now explore briefly some factors bearing on the likely empirical importance of a taste for fair procedures.

Initially, we raise a caution about a further distinction. The possibility that individuals have a taste for fair procedures should not be confused with the possibility that we discuss in subsection B.6(b)—that individuals, ex post, tend to value legal rights to redress and particular procedural protections because of their self-interest in securing a favorable outcome rather than because of any social value of the procedures or any intrinsic value that they may have.[133] Hence, in conducting the empirical inquiries necessary to ascertain whether and to what extent individuals have a taste for procedures, one must be careful to isolate the true, independent taste, positive or negative, if any.

Although the empirical evidence is limited,[134] we are somewhat skeptical

133. Compare Resnik, Curtis, and Hensler (1996, 369): "[P]ost hoc explanations by plaintiffs of their reasons for pursuing remedies may be influenced by a desire to downplay certain motives and highlight others perceived to be more socially desirable or noble."

134. The basic problem is that most prior empirical work does not seem to have been designed in a manner that could identify or quantify actual tastes for procedures. One set of studies using experiments with paid student subjects, conducted by Thibaut and Walker and some additional investigators, see, for example, Thibaut and Walker (1975) and Houlden et al. (1978), is discussed in Kaplow (1994b, 392 n.253). The points to be noted include the following: Preference rankings in hypothetical laboratory settings give no evidence about the magnitude of any preference; the questions participants answer are ambiguous in many respects (for example, the procedure on which opinions are being elicited is often unclear, and it is difficult to determine whether the opinions offered indicate the presence of a taste, a belief about what advances self-interest, or a view about what is good policy); the source of any taste is difficult to discern (for example, respondents are described as liking direct participation, yet they actually choose schemes in which lawyers stand between them and the decisionmaker); and there is little attempt to reconcile the interpretations with real-world behavior (such as the frequency of settlement and the use and design of alternative dispute resolution mechanisms). Also, many of these studies mean to address the distinction between adversarial and inquisitorial systems, but the actual differences between those systems do not appear to correspond to what was in fact studied. See, for example, Langbein (1985, 824 and n.4). Other critiques have been advanced as well. See, for example, Gross (1987, 740 n.22), suggesting that it is inappropriate to use untrained students to play the roles of judges and lawyers in litigation because both adversarial and inquisitorial systems are justifiable in large part by the expected performance of professionals, lawyers in the former and judges in the latter; ibid. (747 n.43), suggesting that none of Thibaut and Walker's procedures fairly depicts the inquisitorial system because they postulate no right to legal representation and no role for parties in producing evidence; ibid. (747), arguing that the experiments provide "no useful information" on how real litigants feel about their systems as they actually operate; and Hayden and Anderson (1979), presenting a long series of objections, including some concerning the

of the suggestion that most procedural issues are matters about which most individuals would have strong tastes. Myriad procedural details are unknown

---

correspondence of the experiments to actual inquisitorial and adversarial systems, aspects of experimental design that biased the results, the authors' interpretations of their experiments, and the failure to account for the various costs of the different procedural systems.

Tyler and others have conducted surveys to assess people's attitudes toward procedures. See, for example, Lind and Tyler (1988) and Tyler (1987, 1990, 1997). Similar problems arise involving the proper interpretation of responses. First, views may reflect tastes, self-interest, or opinion about good policy (for example, that individuals think it important for parties to be able to have the decisionmaker consider their views could readily reflect a belief that this opportunity is necessary to produce good outcomes). Second, it is often unclear which aspects of procedure individuals care about, or even whether it is the procedures rather than aspects of the relevant substantive law that influence attitudes (such as when individuals express discontent with lenient treatment of criminals, which one presumes does not reflect a view that there is too little procedural protection but may instead combine distaste for procedural protections and displeasure with excessively lenient sentencing rules). Third, individuals' preferences that procedures be unbiased, consistent, and open to correction in cases of error may reflect a concern for the resulting accuracy that such procedures tend to produce. Finally, there is no attempt to determine the extent to which anyone may value greater procedural fairness per se (for example, by simply asking how much, if anything, individuals would have been willing to pay in litigation costs for greater participation or procedures that in other respects were viewed as fairer). One theme in this work is that it is important to individuals that their "opinions are considered by the decision-making authority," and that this "process control" is distinct from "decision control," the latter taken to capture individuals' concerns about outcomes. Tyler (1987, 52–53). Yet it seems plausible that individuals who strongly prefer that decisionmakers consider their arguments are in fact expressing a concern about outcomes. Relatedly, the terms "process control" and "decision control" are not defined in the surveys. One can imagine, therefore, that individuals surveyed about their experiences when calling the police for assistance (one of the components of the survey that provides the basis for much of this literature) would report a high level of satisfaction if they found that the police listened to their requests and responded promptly and appropriately, even though such callers would not feel that they (rather than the police) had control over the actual response decision. See also ibid. (56): "[P]rocess fairness judgments are almost always found to be linked to some extent to judgments about the fairness of the outcomes a procedure produces."

Other surveys of attitudes about fairness pose related difficulties. For example, in a study of views on arbitration, judicial settlement conferences, trial, and settlement, interviewers simply asked, "how fair did you think [the procedure in question] was?"; no definition or guidance as to the intended meaning or sense of "fairness" was provided. Lind et al. (1990, 991–92). See also Chevigny (1989, 1212) reviewing Lind and Tyler (1988), expressing two concerns about the reliability of responses: that students in experiments may have expressed stronger preferences for fair procedures when the outcomes did not actually matter to them, and that respondents in surveys may have expressed views that they thought it would be best to appear to hold; and ibid. (1218–21), observing that litigants may perceive, correctly, that the power to advance their views will affect outcomes because decisionmakers are ordinarily expected to take views they hear into account, and that this belief is so habitual that it may influence answers even in constructed experiments in which normal effects on outcomes are absent.

except among legal experts. Even those who actually participate in a lawsuit may be unaware of much of what transpires: Most cases settle before many procedures come into operation, information is filtered through lawyers, and alternative regimes are unlikely to be the focus of attention. If one had to speculate from current opinion polls and recent trends in legal reform, one might infer that there is a general public taste for "less" procedure, that is, for limiting the means of legal redress and scaling back costly litigation activities.[135] But any such guess must account for the further difficulty that individuals' views on these issues may reflect not true tastes, but instead opinions about what they suspect would be good policy. (That is, individuals may think that too much is spent on litigation not because they find lawyers or courtroom proceedings particularly unpleasant but rather because their understanding—which may be a misunderstanding—is that many proceedings are wasteful or counterproductive.[136])

Consider now, in greater detail, the tastes of actual participants in lawsuits. Parties bear large costs in their own time and make expenditures on lawyers and on other incidents of litigation (experts, transcripts, filing fees). Also, one suspects that parties are typically anxious about their involvement in litigation, rather than entertained or relieved by the prospect of prolonged legal conflict.[137]

Of course, most cases settle for just these reasons.[138] Also, because they

135. See generally Brookings Institution (1989); Galanter (1994), discussing popular sentiments about lawyers, many of which relate to attitudes about the extent of litigation; ibid. (664–66), presenting survey results showing that the portion of the population believing that there are too many lawyers has risen to 73 percent and that 74 percent believe that the prevalence of litigation is hurting the nation's economy; and Tyler (1997, 872), noting concern about excessive procedural protections for criminal defendants. For example, the Republican Party's inclusion of the Common Sense Legal Reforms Act as part of their 1994 Contract with America, see Tobias (1995), presumably reflected a belief of many politicians that scaling back procedural redress rather than expanding it would be popular with their constituents.

136. See Galanter (1994). For further discussion of the distinction between tastes and opinions about policy and its relevance for policymaking, see section VII.C, on whether government officials should credit popular opinion when assessing legal policy, and subsection VIII.B.4, on tastes for notions of fairness.

137. See, for example, Trubek et al. (1983, 120), stating that the psychological costs to parties of litigation may in part motivate the interest in alternative dispute resolution.

138. It is well known that fewer than ten percent of cases go to trial and reach a verdict. On one hand, this figure overstates the extent of settlement because a portion of the cases not going to trial are not settled but instead are disposed of through other binding determinations, such as dismissals or decisions in alternative dispute resolution. See, for example, Galanter and Cahill (1994, 1339–40) and Resnik (1986, 511–12). On the other hand, a very large portion of all disputes "settle" before the victim files a complaint, whether by voluntary

appear primarily through paid advocates, individuals often are insulated from many aspects of the litigation that does occur. Some positive elements may enter into a litigant's personal calculus, such as the desire for vindication, but this ambition seems unlikely to be strong except in a limited class of cases, such as libel disputes.[139] Observe as well that if procedures had great independent value to parties, beyond promoting their self-interest ex post by securing desirable outcomes, one should expect to hear complaints about the inadequacies of procedures not only from losing parties, but also from victors.[140]

Additional evidence suggesting that litigants do not have a strong independent taste for experiencing more elaborate legal procedures comes from the design of alternative dispute resolution mechanisms, which parties often specify consensually. Here, the consistent pattern is to provide for simpler procedures than are typical of the formal legal system.[141]

---

compensation provided by the injurer or by some other means. See Galanter (1983, 11–18). Thus, the ratio of dispositions by tribunals to underlying disputes, broadly understood, is probably even lower than widely cited settlement rates indicate.

Our point in emphasizing the prevalence of settlements is not to argue that they are desirable in every respect but merely to indicate how this widespread pattern of behavior tends to suggest that litigants place little positive value and, more probably, a negative value on the experience of litigation per se. For a more detailed look at the evidence on why cases settle, see Galanter and Cahill (1994).

139. See, for example, Gross and Syverud (1996, 57–58), presenting a result that, in 735 attorney interviews, only three attorneys, two of whom had been on opposite sides of the same case, mentioned vindication as an explanation for why a case proceeded to trial, but noting that this was a survey of attorneys, not clients, thereby raising a question about the appropriate inference to be drawn; ibid. (58–59), noting that medical malpractice is an exceptional category, in which the evidence of a high trial rate and other factors suggest that doctors seek vindication, plausibly because of their reputational interest; and Mayhew (1975, 413), presenting survey results showing that very few individuals with serious problems had sought legal vindication, except for victims of discrimination.

140. One would expect successful litigants who have a significant positive taste for legal proceedings to attempt to "throw" motions for reconsideration or appeals in order to prolong the experience, or at least to abstain from making motions to dismiss and the like. The lack of even anecdotal evidence of such behavior, however, casts doubt on the idea that many litigants have such tastes.

141. Although the preference for alternative dispute resolution may reflect its lower direct costs and its possibly greater accuracy, it is also suggested that the less formal approach that eschews many of the procedures used in traditional courts contributes to a positive reaction by litigants. See, for example, Lind et al. (1990, 959–60); Steering Committee Report (1989, 817); Trubek et al. (1983, 120); and Tyler (1987, 44–45), suggesting that litigants' concerns for fair dispute resolution often do not entail a need for a formal trial and can be accommodated in informal dispute resolution settings.

None of this evidence, however, is definitive. Settlement and the use of alternative dispute resolution offer cost savings and possibly other benefits. Regarding the latter, settlement may reduce litigants' exposure to risk, and some alternative dispute resolution mechanisms may increase accuracy by substituting more expert decisionmakers for jurors. Consequently, the widespread adoption of such alternatives to formal trials in court merely indicates an upper bound on the extent to which individuals may have positive tastes for legal procedure. Nevertheless, the fact that settlement rates are so high, despite various obstacles, makes it unlikely that most individuals place a substantial positive value on procedures for their own sake.

To test our intuitions about the importance of tastes for fairness, suppose that a reform was enacted for automobile accident cases that eliminated most opportunities to present evidence of victim-specific harm (concerning, for example, preexisting conditions or the effect of an injury on future earnings) and substituted damages tables, compiled by a body of citizens and relevant experts and designed to measure the average harm associated with different types of injuries. One then may ask what decrease in annual automobile insurance premiums ($1?, $10?, $100?) would convince most individuals to favor such a reform, which would entail forfeiting their right to present certain information in court. (One might point out to such individuals other relevant factors, including the likelihood of settlement and the time required for litigation.) We suspect that individuals do not have sufficiently positive tastes for legal procedures of this type that they would forgo such a reform if it promised significant savings. But this is simply our conjecture.[142]

In any event, in assessing legal policy regarding procedures, a relevant question is the extent to which litigants' overall well-being is positively or negatively influenced by the direct effect of the process on the litigants themselves, because this influence will be one benefit or cost, to be considered along with more tangible costs of litigation. This factor is relevant under welfare economics to an assessment of the desirability of procedural alternatives. Furthermore, to the degree that invocations of fairness notions reflect such tastes rather than assert the existence of independent evaluative principles, to be fostered at the expense of individuals' well-being, there is no underlying conflict between notions of fairness and welfare economics.

---

142. The discussion in the text oversimplifies the comparison in many respects. For example, we note in subsection B.4(b) that, to the extent individuals are uninsured, there will potentially be a reduction in risk-bearing costs due to the more accurate compensation. Assessing this factor is not straightforward, however, because it is not obvious whether use of damages tables will make compensation less rather than more accurate. Which result is more likely will depend on the level of detail in the tables and on the extent of randomness in the current system.

2. Other Ways in Which Procedures May Enhance Individuals' Well-Being[143]

Commentators favor various procedural protections for a variety of reasons. Many speak of the dignity of individuals whose cases are to be adjudicated.[144] Other analysts emphasize litigants' right to be heard, to confront accusers or opposing witnesses, or to receive a reasoned explanation for an adverse decision.[145] The literature does not, however, usually state why particular procedures are accordingly thought to be desirable.[146] For instance, commen-

143. Many of the points in this section are developed in Kaplow (1994b, 389–99).

144. See, for example, Allison (1994, 680): "The most commonly identified noninstrumental value of procedure is the elevation of individual dignity."; Arenella (1983, 200–01), addressing criminal procedure; Bone (1992, 279–80): "Most writers trace [process-oriented values in the administrative due process field] back to respect for the dignity of individuals adversely affected by agency action. . . . Many scholars assume that this dignity argument extends unproblematically to civil adjudication as well."; Mashaw (1981); and Resnik (1984, 847).

145. See, for example, Arenella (1983, 201), suggesting that the right to counsel in the criminal context is valued "because it promotes the individual's meaningful participation in the process"; Bone (1992, 287–88): "[T]he intuition that certain cases call for personal participation remains strong, and it is one that many others share in one form or another."; Fuller (1978), emphasizing the centrality of participation, including the presentation of proofs and reasoned arguments in favor of one's position, but not explaining the ultimate reason that participation is important and, accordingly, not distinguishing instrumental benefits related to accuracy from other possible reasons; Resnik (1984, 847–49), discussing the importance of being heard; Summers (1974); and Woolley (1997), suggesting the need to allow class members to participate in litigation and to be heard. Some of the arguments presume unrealistically that the litigants themselves, rather than their lawyers, are in control, a point emphasized in Rosenberg (1987, 582–83; 1989, 701–02).

146. See, for example, Bone (1992, 217): "Indeed, to have offered more guidance would have required the Court to give a normative account of the process-oriented values served by an individual day in court—something the Court has never been willing to provide in the context of civil adjudication." See also ibid. (279): "A number of commentators writing in the constitutional due process field have raised serious doubts about the coherence of any process-oriented participation theory."

Dworkin, himself a defender of non-welfare-based values of procedure, notes a deficiency in arguments suggesting that procedure has benefits apart from accuracy. Thus, in response to Tribe's claim that procedures are intrinsically valuable, Dworkin states: "The intrinsic interpretation points to a different form of moral harm. But what? The language about talking to people rather than dealing with them, and about treating them as people rather than things, is of little help here, as it generally is in political theory." R. Dworkin (1985, 102). He suggests that most arguments about the intrinsic value of procedure really involve concerns about accuracy, and he concludes that "more work needs to be done to establish a relevant head of moral harm distinct from inaccuracy." Ibid. See also ibid. (103), asking "what moral harm, distinct from the risk of substantive injustice [from an incorrect outcome], lies in these [hypothetical] *ex parte* determinations of guilt that offer no role to the individual condemned."

tators usually do not explain what they mean by "dignity" and why it is important, aside from how individuals feel (their tastes?).[147] Similarly, they largely take for granted that one has a right to be heard.[148] In this subsection, we suggest that much of the motivation—and, more importantly, the ultimately sound reasons—for favoring procedures depends on how they promote accuracy or enhance individuals' well-being in other ways.

At the outset, we observe that the examples offered in the literature on fair procedures almost inevitably are ones in which making available the procedure in question serves an obvious instrumental purpose, namely, providing better information to the decisionmaker or otherwise enhancing the availability of remedies (ability to bring suit) or the likely quality (accuracy) of the ultimate outcome.[149] This conjunction immediately suggests that the

147. Indeed, one can readily interpret individuals' dignity in a manner that makes it a component of their well-being. To the extent that dignity is taken to be independent of well-being, however, commentators do not explain why they think dignity is important. According to Mashaw, who has probably written more extensively than anyone else about how dignitary values are implicated by legal procedure: "The values that fit our intuitions are vague at the margins and potentially contradictory at the core." Mashaw (1981, 899).

148. One commentator even argues that the fact that "some process values are so taken for granted in our own society" supports his position. Summers (1974, 33). This reasoning, however, is deficient because the contribution of procedures to good results—or a misapplication of internalized social norms—could readily explain prevalent views without offering any support for the argument that there exist process values independent of instrumental objectives. We also note Summers's inconsistency in grounding process values on the alleged existence of public support even as he criticizes society for failing to act on such values. See ibid. (39, 42).

149. Summers illustrates the virtues of procedural fairness with an example in which the adjudicator gives advantages to one party. Although he recognizes that this approach would bias the results (thereby suggesting an instrumental basis for objecting to such a procedure), he simply asks the reader to imagine that no such effect would occur and then to contemplate whether the procedure would still seem unfair. Summers (1974, 24–25). See also ibid. (46), acknowledging that "most process features capable of implementing process values are at the same time capable of serving as means to certain outcomes." In his discussion of Summers's article as illustrative of other writing that purports to offer independent grounds for procedural rights, Alexander makes similar observations. See L. Alexander (1998, 35), stating that many of Summers's examples of process values involve substantive rights, and ibid. (36): "Other process values that Summers invokes . . . seem to be bound up with increasing the accuracy of adjudicative fact determinations." See also Magat and Schroeder (1984, 317): "Fairness and accuracy are interrelated, because techniques for ensuring fairness—adequate notice and the opportunity to participate meaningfully in proceedings affecting one's interests—will also ensure accuracy. Actually, accuracy may be the primary value."; Redish and Marshall (1986, 482–91), claiming that an independent adjudicator offers both instrumental and noninstrumental benefits but acknowledging that, for the most part, the latter benefits are inherently tied to the former; and Woolley (1997, 597–98), arguing explicitly that the purpose of the right to participate is to promote accuracy.

underlying motivation for arguments that on their face appeal to notions of fairness, justice, or individual rights is in fact the promotion of individuals' well-being.[150] Moreover, some analysts who invoke notions of fairness that are purported to be independent of a desire to promote individuals' well-being support their position by citing benefits of procedures that seem grounded in instrumental concerns for welfare.[151] In sum, it remains unclear the extent to which proponents of notions of fairness actually believe in or have presented arguments in favor of non-welfarist procedural values.

Thus far, we have focused on the instrumental benefits that providing a right to sue or improving the accuracy of adjudication may have with regard to improving parties' ex ante behavior and, more briefly, on how procedures may affect the suitability of compensation to uninsured, risk-averse victims of harm. In addition, in subsection 1, we considered the possibility that individuals may have tastes regarding various procedures. Although we believe that these are usually the primary ways in which legal procedures can promote individuals' well-being, they are not the only ways,

---

150. See, for example, Mashaw (1981, 887): "We all feel that process matters to us irrespective of result. This intuition may, of course, be a delusion."; and Scanlon (1977, 95, 97–100), describing due process as a "moral requirement" but engaging essentially in a welfare economic assessment by stating that the requirements of due process should depend on the likelihood that power will be abused, the seriousness of harm from abuse, the degree to which due process would reduce abuse, and the cost of providing due process. The most direct way to test the proposition that independent process values exist is, contrary to standard practice in the literature, to consider procedures or hypothetical situations in which procedure definitely cannot affect outcomes. Compare Redish and Marshall (1986, 487–88): "This participation only makes sense, though, if the individual harbors some hope of bringing about substantive change in the state agent's action or attitude. . . . The connection that many have drawn between 'control' and 'participation' demonstrates the inseparable connection between participation and result efficacy." We also note that some commentators who use the language of fairness seem rather clearly to be advancing the idea that legal rules should be designed to advance overall well-being. See, for example, Newman (1985, 1649–52), advocating that more attention be paid to "system fairness," which "reflects the aggregate impact of the litigation process upon the lives of all actual and potential litigants." For many commentators, however, the underlying motivation is more difficult to identify. See, for example, Resnik (1984, 842–59), presenting twelve "valued features" of procedure but eschewing attempts to identify whether the value of most of the features is rooted in justice or efficiency, whether they reflect intrinsic or instrumental concerns.

151. See, for example, Allison (1994, 680–82), noting, in the course of discussing values of procedure explicitly described as "noninstrumental," such benefits as "norm communication," which "promotes future modification of behavior so as to conform more closely with society's legitimate expectations," and "institutional legitimacy," the perception of which is important "in order to avoid the social instability and its many associated costs that would likely result otherwise"; and Leubsdorf (1984, 595), describing as nonutilitarian the benefit of "the rule of law as a means of taming government for the benefit of citizens."

and we now consider some others.[152] To the extent that the actual value of
legal procedures inheres in their effects on individuals' well-being, however,
confining normative analysis of procedure exclusively to welfare economics
is appropriate.[153]

It has long been understood that some procedures may be more effective
than others in controlling government officials, and, in particular, in preventing the abuse of power.[154] For example, granting the public access (per-

152. In addition to the benefits mentioned in the text to follow, adjudication may directly
affect future behavior in important classes of cases. See note 5.

153. Even with regard to seemingly loose and wide-ranging notions like abuse of power
and legitimacy that we discuss in the text to follow, explicit welfare economic analysis is
important. One recurring problem in the literature, which does not provide such explicit
analysis, involves overgeneralization. Thus, many commentators who advocate various procedural safeguards rely on arguments or examples raising problems of abuse of power; yet concerns about abuse of power do not obviously necessitate providing for expensive, case-by-
case determinations of harm that entail high levels of participation by the parties rather than
substituting damage tables (perhaps determined by an accountable panel that conducts open
proceedings).

Likewise, Fiss's well-known arguments against settlement invoke institutional benefits of
adjudication that seem to arise only in exceptional cases, see Fiss (1984), even though most
of the push to settle litigation involves the mass of cases in which the elements he emphasizes
seem largely absent. For a description of the more typical case and how it differs from the
extraordinary lawsuits upon which Fiss focuses, see Trubek et al. (1983, 83–84). Fiss disagrees
with this assessment, see Fiss (1984, 1087), but the main argument he offers that might cover
the bulk of routine accident cases is that plaintiffs will be unduly pressured to settle on account
of their limited resources with which to finance litigation and their immediate need for funds.
See ibid. (1076–77). Yet removing the settlement option, which plaintiffs prefer to trial, will
only make them worse off. Fiss suggests that judges can help litigants at trial, citing a single
case involving a constitutional challenge to prison conditions. See ibid. (1077–78 and n.14).
The actual prevalence of judicial assistance remains unclear, particularly in routine cases outside the constitutional context. In any event, the prospect of such assistance would mean that
plaintiffs who settle would correspondingly benefit if indeed it were generally the case that
judges did help plaintiffs at trial. (Because parties bargaining over settlement would anticipate
the judge's behavior, its influence on expected trial outcomes would be reflected in settlement
amounts.) We also note that such plaintiffs usually have contingent-fee lawyers, making Fiss's
point about financing litigation moot. (For differing views on settlement, see, for example,
Menkel-Meadow (1995).)

154. See, for example, Aristotle (1980, book V, chapter 6): "This is why we do not allow
a *man* to rule, but *rational principle,* because a man behaves thus in his own interests and
becomes a tyrant."; Gross (1987, 744–45), stating that perhaps the most common political
argument for the adversary system is distrust of government, that the argument has deep
historical roots, and that it usually focuses on criminal litigation; Resnik (1984, 849–54), citing
control of decisionmakers' exercise of power as an important aspect of procedural values; and
Scanlon (1977, 93–100), noting the "truism that due process is concerned with protection

haps via the press) to trials, using juries, providing counsel to indigent criminal defendants, allowing appeals, and various other techniques have been defended in significant part because of a belief that they inhibit certain forms of corruption and political interference or other misbehavior in the prosecution of criminal cases. We observe that this sort of objective is fully embraced by welfare economics.[155] In a sense, these concerns suggest another respect in which using more costly procedures may improve accuracy.[156] The major difference between these sorts of contributions to accuracy and those we consider above in section B is that analyzing the probability of inaccuracy due to corruption in a less protective system may prove more difficult than identifying routine error,[157] and quantifying the social cost of corruption is

against arbitrary decisions," suggesting that due process is concerned with the improper exercise of power, and referring to due process as "one of the strategies through which one may seek to avoid arbitrary power." The procedural protections in the Bill of Rights are grounded in significant part in concerns about abuse of power. See, for example, Wolff v. McDonnell, 418 U.S. 539, 558 (1974): "The touchstone of due process is protection of the individual against arbitrary action of government."; Dan-Cohen (1984, 650), discussing "the need to shape, control, and constrain the power wielded by [official legal] decisionmakers"; and Raymond (1998), suggesting that post–World War II constitutional procedural doctrine is driven by concerns about totalitarianism that are analogous to the concerns about tyranny that originally led to the constitutional amendments. See also Boadway and Bruce (1984, 177); Hammond (1982b, 90); and Hardin (1986, 47), arguing that rights are important because institutions that leave agents free to judge outcomes based on well-being would be unreliable. Many problems presenting the issue of equal treatment, which we discuss in subsection VIII.C.2, involve concerns about possible abuse of power. In addition, some commentators who advance noninstrumental process values motivate their claims by reference to fears about abuse of power. See, for example, Tribe (1988, §10–7, pp. 666–67, §10–13, p. 718) and Subrin and Dykstra (1974, 456–57, 458–59). More generally, the idea that individual rights should be viewed instrumentally, as promoting well-being, because they are important protections against government abuse, has long been familiar, such as from Mill's *On Liberty*. See Mill (1859, chapter 4).

   Within the economics literature, we believe that the concern about abuse of power underlies Peter Diamond's concern with the "process" by which social decisions are made. See Diamond (1967, 766), expressing this concern in a well-known example crafted to counter one of Harsanyi's arguments for utilitarianism. For discussion of situations like that sketched by Diamond and analyses that offer an interpretation similar to ours, see Baron (1993, 85–86), Mirrlees (1982, 82), Ng (1981a, 244), and Strotz (1958, 194). For additional views, see Broome (1984) and Harsanyi (1975, 326–28).

   155. For further discussion, see subsection VIII.A.2.

   156. See sources cited in note 154. There need not, however, be a direct relationship between enhancing accuracy and controlling the abuse of power. Consider, for example, rules that exclude evidence obtained by improper government searches.

   157. Indeed, a more closed system may itself make assessment more difficult.

hardly a straightforward task.[158] Hence, deciding on the best procedures to combat potential abuse may be a more speculative endeavor. It is, nevertheless, an important one. Moreover, it is a welfare economic one—focused ultimately on determining which set of procedures will, all things considered, best promote the well-being of members of society.[159]

Another, partially related concern about procedures involves the perceived[160] legitimacy of legal institutions.[161] "Legitimacy" may denote different issues. It could simply be another rubric for tastes regarding procedures, which we consider in subsection 1. Or legitimacy may have a further implication regarding the extent to which individuals will voluntarily comply with the law and otherwise assist legal authorities (such as by cooperating in the identification and prosecution of criminals) or will refrain from seeking personal retribution through the use of force.[162] If some procedures generate

158. On the social costs of corruption, see Klitgaard (1988), Rose-Ackerman (1978), Bardhan (1997), and Shleifer and Vishny (1993).

159. Another instrumental benefit of reducing abuse of power, as we consider next, is perceived legitimacy (and its effects on behavior). See, for example, Olmstead v. United States, 277 U.S. 438, 485 (1928) (Brandeis, J., dissenting): "If the government becomes a lawbreaker, it breeds contempt for law; it invites every man to become a law unto himself; it invites anarchy."

160. We emphasize the *perceived* legitimacy of the system because legitimacy, in the present context, is by definition a matter of perception. We also note that, if legitimacy is understood to depend exclusively on the actual quality of the legal system, in terms of best promoting individuals' well-being, then giving weight to legitimacy will be largely redundant under welfare economics—although not entirely so because improvement in the quality of adjudication may thus be all the more important and thereby warrant expending greater resources to achieve it. (Under approaches that largely ignore consequences pertinent to welfare, introducing legitimacy may be a way—albeit indirect—to bring under consideration some of the relevant effects of legal reforms.)

The concept of legitimacy may also be a surrogate for other institutional concerns, such as enhancing accountability, which would often be important because of the need to control government officials, as we discuss above. There we emphasize the benefit of minimizing the abuse of power by those who operate the legal system. Here, by contrast, the benefit is that a legal system that is understood to be more legitimate will induce better behavior by the individuals governed by the system.

161. See, for example, Arenella (1983, 200–08), identifying a legitimation function of criminal procedure; Bone (1992, 233–35), noting the argument of proceduralists that a right to participate in proceedings enhances the appearance of legitimacy; Gross (1987, 746–47), suggesting that a concern for legitimacy provides the basis for an argument favoring adversarial procedures that may be more expensive; and Resnik (1984, 844–59), referring frequently, in her description of twelve valued features of procedure, to ways in which procedure may increase the perceived legitimacy of the legal system.

162. See, for example, Marcus, Redish, and Sherman (2000, 2–3), suggesting that litigants who believe the legal process to be fair will be less inclined to gratify "more destructive motivations like self-help and personal retribution," and Tyler (1990).

positive feelings among citizens that inspire them to engage in more socially constructive behavior, the effects on individuals' well-being would, by definition, be included in a proper welfare economic analysis.[163] It will not be easy to determine these effects. However, it is unlikely that the many procedural details that are essentially unknown to most individuals (as we note in subsection 1) significantly affect the perceived legitimacy of the legal system. But some events, such as the rioting that has followed certain jury verdicts, suggest that certain aspects of legal procedure may influence perceived legitimacy in important ways.[164]

Other possible effects of procedure on individuals' well-being include the possibility that some cases may produce external benefits by serving as precedents, especially when a written opinion is produced on an issue that is likely to recur.[165] In addition, as we have noted in our discussion of social norms,[166] legal proceedings may reinforce underlying norms of proper behavior. For example, deeming a wrong to be a legal wrong, in principle subject to remedy in court, may contribute to the idea that certain acts are inappropriate. Even if few would sue when such acts are committed, and even if those suits would do little to deter such acts, many individuals may choose to abstain because the law leads them to view the acts as wrongful. (By contrast, disallowing suit may be regarded as signifying that the acts may not be wrongful after all, rather than as merely representing a policy judgment that lawsuits are not cost-effective ways to control wrongful behavior.[167]) Although many aspects of legal procedure do not confer such benefits—for example, most legal costs are incurred to find facts in individual cases rather than to set precedents or send messages—these effects may

---

163. One can guess that employing otherwise sensible procedures (say, because they provide reasonably accurate results at modest cost) would tend to enhance legitimacy, in which case procedures that already appear best from a welfare economic perspective may be all the better because they enhance legitimacy. Unfortunately, so convenient a coincidence will not always exist. Most of the public is not aware of many procedures, and, to the extent that it is, it probably does not understand their effects. Moreover, procedures that mask deficiencies in the legal system (perhaps thereby making abuse of power more likely) may enhance legitimacy, at least in the short run. See, for example, Kaplow (1994b, 396 n.265), explaining how the requirement of proof beyond a reasonable doubt in the criminal context may have this character. See also Summers (1974, 39, 42), lamenting that lay ignorance results in a failure to appreciate the value of legal procedures that seem to many to be mere technicalities.

164. See, for example, Porter and Dunn (1984, chapter 2) and Riordan (1994).

165. One of Fiss's main themes in his well-known essay, "Against Settlement," is the need for courts to provide authoritative determinations in matters of concern to society. See Fiss (1984). See also Coleman and Silver (1986, 114–19), discussing precedents as public goods, and W. Landes and R. Posner (1976).

166. See subsections A.6 and B.3(f).

167. See also note 44, offering qualifications.

sometimes prove important. In each of the instances canvassed in this sub-section, the important point is that the analyst should carefully identify the relevant effects on individuals' well-being, lest the analyst be led astray.[168]

We close with a brief example designed to show how procedures that commentators have defended as intrinsically valuable or necessary to pre-serve litigants' dignity can be better understood in the welfare-related terms outlined in this subsection and elsewhere in this chapter of our book. Con-sider the commonly advanced notion that a losing party is entitled to an explanation from the tribunal of the grounds for its defeat.[169]

Observe that such a procedure offers a number of possible instrumental benefits.[170] First, a requirement to state reasons may directly improve accu-racy: Decisionmakers may be more careful if they know that they will have to explain their analysis. Second, making explicit the reasons for the initial decisions may facilitate appeals to correct error. Building on these two points, requiring statements may generally be useful in controlling abuse of power: Corruption would be more difficult to hide, thereby making it less likely to occur and easier to correct, either by changing a particular decision or by identifying the need for reforms designed to reduce corruption or to remove corrupt officials. Third, unsuccessful litigants may lose respect for the legal system if they do not understand the basis of their defeat; offering reasoned explanations may therefore avoid erosion in perceived legitimacy that would reduce future compliance with legal rules and cooperation with legal authorities. Fourth, explanations may guide a litigant's future behavior, both narrowly, in deciding whether to appeal, and more broadly, in deciding how to conduct future affairs that are governed by the very rule explained in the legal opinion. Finally, in some instances, a formal statement of reasons may serve as a valuable precedent, thereby guiding the future behavior of others as well.

---

168. See, for example, note 153, discussing the need for explicit welfare economic analysis.

169. See, for example, Fuller (1978, 387–88), arguing that a statement of reasons ordi-narily increases the fairness and effectiveness of adjudication, offering some of the instrumental arguments noted in the text to follow, but failing to explain what an independent notion of fairness might be or how it would be promoted; and Michelman (1977), arguing that decisionmakers should have an obligation to explain their decisions in certain contexts and suggesting that there are values served that are distinct from protecting claimants' substantive legal rights.

170. We note, too, that there are obviously good reasons for not always providing rea-soned decisions to litigants: explanations take time and involve costs, and we may not wish to require certain decisionmakers (such as jurors) to undertake such a task (which also may not be as meaningful when a large group reaches a common conclusion through possibly disparate reasoning).

Welfare economics readily comprehends each of these points. The key challenges are to assess empirically the importance of these effects and to provide better analytical frameworks for understanding their ultimate impact on individuals' well-being. If, instead, analysts merely invoke vague notions of fairness, there will be no sound basis for determining what procedural safeguards are indeed socially beneficial in any given context. Accordingly, attempts to base procedural reform on notions of fairness may well lead us astray.[171] This argument does not constitute a decisive objection if the notions of fairness are independently valuable. But if they are, analysts must identify the notions more precisely and indicate why the notions should be given weight, especially given that their pursuit comes at the expense of individuals' well-being.[172]

171. See, for example, note 153.

172. See, for example, Fiss (1982, 122), stating that instrumental issues in litigation involving structural reform of institutions are important, "but I believe the question of legitimacy is primary," yet not explaining why he believes legitimacy to be important or how its benefits are other than instrumental.

CHAPTER VI

---□---

Law Enforcement

We begin in section A by reviewing the application of welfare economics to basic issues in law enforcement, focusing, as we will throughout this chapter, on the question of how the state should set sanctions for wrongful acts.[1] In section B, we examine the dominant notion of fairness that is pertinent to setting punishment—retributive justice—and in particular the principle that punishment should fit (be proportional to) the crime. In section C, we consider a basic setting of law enforcement and a number of variations of it (including one in which innocent people might be punished). In each case, we ask what sanction would be appropriate according to welfare economics and according to the notion that the punishment should fit the crime. Then we supply reasons that the welfare economics approach should guide legal policy. In section D, we discuss possible origins of notions of fairness regarding punishment and how these origins bear on the notions' relevance in

---

1. There are a number of respects in which our treatment of law enforcement is not general, but we focus on certain issues and on paradigmatic examples to achieve clarity and to conform our discussion to the relevant literature on fairness in law enforcement. We confine our attention to public enforcement, although many of our points also apply to the context of private enforcement, in which sanctions are monetary and are paid to victims. (In particular, much of what we say concerning deterrence of, and retribution against, potential injurers does not depend on whether a monetary sanction is a fine or a damage award.) We usually speak of enforcement of the criminal law, and thus of wrongs as crimes, although much of the analysis would be applicable to public civil enforcement of regulatory schemes and the like. We limit most of our discussion to the appropriate level of sanction, ignoring the form of sanction (whether, say, fines or imprisonment are best), the level of enforcement effort, and a host of other factors. (We also note that many aspects of enforcement involve issues of legal procedure similar to those we examine in chapter V.)

evaluative analysis. Finally, in section E, we inquire into the extent to which the use of notions of fairness may have led to mistakes in law enforcement policy.

A. Welfare Economics and Law Enforcement

From the perspective of welfare economics, the central purpose of law enforcement is to reduce harmful activity. One way to accomplish this goal is through deterrence: the reduction in the commission of harmful acts through the threat of sanctions.[2] Another is through incapacitation: isolating potential violators from the population, principally through incarceration, so that they cannot commit harmful acts. Incarceration may also influence the level of harmful activity, for better or worse, by changing the character of punished individuals through their reform and education or, alternatively, through their becoming hardened or learning bad habits in prison.[3]

Although the purpose of punishment under welfare economics is to reduce the commission of harmful acts, social welfare also depends on the costs of punishment. One cost factor is the public expense of law enforcement, by which we mean the resources devoted to apprehending violators and to imposing sanctions, such as incarceration. Of course, these costs influence the well-being of individuals because citizens must finance the public sector through tax payments. A second cost factor is the disutility that punished individuals suffer as a result of sanctions.

The social welfare evaluation also includes the satisfaction of any tastes that individuals might have for correct punishment: For example, the gratification they experience when guilty parties are appropriately punished, and the upset they experience when innocent individuals are mistakenly pun-

2. The prospect that criminal conviction will result in stigma may be an aspect of the threat of sanctions that contributes to deterrence beyond the direct cost of the formal sanctions themselves. See, for example, Rasmusen (1996).

Many authors, including Andenaes in his classic article on deterrence, would explicitly include in the preventive effects of punishment not only the deterrence that arises from the fear of sanctions but also the deterrence that results from the "moral" effect of the criminal law. See, for example, Andenaes (1966, 949–51), discussing both effects, although classifying only the former as deterrence, and Andenaes (1983, 591), using the term "general deterrence" to encompass both effects. For expositional purposes, we will discuss separately (later in this section and in subsection D.2) the effect of the law on compliance through its influence on individuals' attitudes and related social norms.

3. In addition to affecting the level of harmful activity, such changes in character also may be directly relevant to the well-being of the affected individuals.

ished. These elements enter into social welfare because they are components of individuals' well-being.[4] (Such satisfaction of individuals' tastes for correct punishment must, as we have emphasized, be carefully distinguished from the notion that punishment according to some principle is inherently good or inherently bad, regardless of individuals' tastes.) In addition, if individuals have a strong taste for punishment in certain settings and the legal system does not provide such punishment, they may seek revenge outside the law in ways that would be socially detrimental.[5] Finally, we note that punishment practices may influence individuals' views about the wrongfulness of acts and the legitimacy of the legal system, which may in turn affect individuals' compliance with the law.[6]

4. Compare Bentham ([1781] 1988, 177), suggesting that, in an exceptional case, society should not punish if a large number of people would be displeased. See also Kahan (1998, 615–22).

5. See, for example, Holmes (1881, 41–42) and subsection D.1.

6. See, for example, Andenaes (1974, chapter 4), discussing but expressing skepticism about the educative influence of the criminal law on compliance; Bentham ([1781] 1988, 184 and n.1), stating that "sometimes . . . the punishment proposed is of such a nature as to be particularly well calculated to answer the purpose of a moral lesson," suggesting that this is so "when, by reason of the ignominy it stamps upon the offence, it is calculated to inspire the public with the sentiments of aversion towards those pernicious habits and dispositions with which the offence appears to be connected; and thereby to inculcate the opposite benefi-cial habits and dispositions" (emphasis omitted); LaFave and Scott (1986, 25), describing the theory that the purpose of criminal punishment is "to educate the public as to the proper distinctions between good conduct and bad—distinctions which, when known, most of society will observe"; Benn (1967, 30), presenting Lord Denning's view that "punishment reinforces the community's respect for its legal and moral standards, which criminal acts would tend to undermine if they were not solemnly denounced," and noting Rashdall's view that criminal law is important in promoting the moral education of the public mind; and Greenawalt (1983, 351): "Serious criminal punishment represents society's strong condemnation of what the offender has done, and performs a significant role in moral education."

Indeed, Robinson and Darley argue that deterrence through moral condemnation is the most important function of punishment and accordingly advocate, on welfarist grounds, that sanctions be set according to community views of just punishment. See Robinson and Darley (1995, 1997). Similarly, Hampton has suggested that punishment can be fully justified by its educative effect, although she does not explicitly ground her approach in welfarism or any other perspective. See, for example, Hampton (1984). For discussions of theory and evidence concerning how punishment is related to social influences on compliance with the law, see Kahan (1997), and Walker and Argyle (1963–1964), presenting survey evidence indicating that knowledge of actual or hypothetical laws does not affect individuals' disapproval of vari-ous acts.

We also note that, when the law influences individuals in the manner just described and in the process changes their tastes, the law thereby exerts a different and direct effect on individuals' well-being. See subsection VIII.B.2.

Although there are many ways in which punishment may influence individuals' well-being, we will focus on deterrence and the direct costs of punishment in our comparison of fairness and welfare economics in section C.[7]

B. Notions of Fairness and Law Enforcement

1. Notions of Fairness

The central notion of fairness that is employed as a justification for punishment is usually referred to as. retributive justice.[8] The retributive theory of justice holds that "the punishment of crime is right in itself, that it is fitting   ·
that the guilty should suffer, and that justice, or the moral order, requires

---

7. In choosing this focus, we are not making any empirical claims about the importance of deterrence. Rather, we seek to achieve greater clarity by reducing the number of phenomena under discussion. Moreover, most retributive theory that seeks to offer an alternative to consequentialist approaches to punishment has been chiefly concerned with criticism of deterrence *as a matter of principle.* Thus, it is natural, in comparing the two types of evaluation, to concentrate on deterrence.

8. See, for example, LaFave and Scott (1986, 26, 29), stating that the theory of retribution was once least accepted by theorists but has recently risen in approval and is now viewed perhaps as the strongest justification for punishment, and discussing the growing rejection of rehabilitation and the rising support for retribution as the leading justification for punishment; and Dolinko (1992, 1623), claiming that retributivism "has enjoyed in recent years so vigorous a revival that it can fairly be regarded today as the leading philosophical justification of the institution of criminal punishment."

Another theory of punishment, which seems to have received a good deal of attention in the 1960s and 1970s, is that "we ought never punish persons who break the law and that we ought instead to do something much more like what we do when we treat someone who has a disease." Wasserstrom (1977, 180). See also Wootton (1963) and Menninger (1968, 253–68; 1973). Two possible rationales for this approach are that it serves retributive justice (the notion being that offenders are not truly responsible for their acts and thus do not deserve punishment) and that it promotes individuals' well-being (because punishment may be thought to cause more harm than good, whereas humane treatment may benefit the criminal and also reduce future crime more effectively). See, for example, Wasserstrom (1977, 181). Because the treatment view is not currently prominent, does not have the same academic lineage as the theories that we consider, and possibly can be reduced to the other views in terms of its underlying rationale, we do not address it here.

Yet another theory concerning law enforcement is that punishment is not justified; instead, it is proper for the criminal to make restitution to the victim. See Barnett (1977). We will not address this theory here, although we observe that it has much in common with the theory of corrective justice examined throughout chapter III, on torts.

the institution of punishment."[9] This notion of fairness was advanced by

9. Benn (1967, 30). See, for example, Fletcher (1978, 416–17): "Retribution simply means that punishment is justified by virtue of its relationship to the offense that has been committed." Holmes states:

> [Retribution] is the notion that there is a mystic bond between wrong and punishment. . . . Hegel, one of the great expounders of [this] view, puts it, in his quasi mathematical form, that, wrong being the negation of right, punishment is the negation of that negation, or retribution. Thus the punishment must be equal, in the sense of proportionate to the crime, because its only function is to destroy it. Others, without this logical apparatus, are content to rely upon a felt necessity that suffering should follow wrong-doing. (Holmes 1881, 42)

Rawls offers the following characterization:

> What we may call the retributive view is that punishment is justified on the grounds that wrongdoing merits punishment. It is morally fitting that a person who does wrong should suffer in proportion to his wrongdoing. That a criminal should be punished follows from his guilt, and the severity of the appropriate punishment depends on the depravity of his act. The state of affairs where a wrongdoer suffers punishment is morally better than the state of affairs where he does not; and it is better irrespective of any of the consequences of punishing him. (Rawls 1955, 4–5)

Although the text and preceding sources refer to the standard retributive view under which wrongdoers should be punished, there is another view (one of a number of mixed views, see sources cited in note 46, on which we will elaborate below) that holds only that punishment of wrongdoers is *permissible*. See generally Brandt (1959, 501–03), describing such a theory and attributing it to Ross (1929)—an attribution that we do not find entirely apt; Hart (1968a, 230–36), suggesting that contemporary retributivists do not adhere to the "fiercest" form of the theory that, following Kant, insists that punishment is obligatory, yet also arguing that an essential aspect of retribution is that the doing of wrong itself calls for punishment; and McCloskey (1967), discussing the permissive view of retributivism at length, suggesting some inconsistency in his own statements on the subject, and ultimately concluding that "there is at least a duty to punish, although not necessarily to the full extent deserved."

Such a theory, of course, must be complemented by another theory that indicates when punishment that is permissible should in fact be meted out; ordinarily, it seems to be understood that some form of consequentialist theory would be employed to do so. The primary import of such a retributive theory would not be to determine what punishment should be, but rather to operate as a constraint on what punishment could be employed when following the other theory. We do not examine this view in detail because most of our analysis of the standard retributive view (including our main critique in section C) is applicable to the permissive view as well (although the difference between this retributive conception of fairness and welfare economics is obviously smaller). See also note 41, addressing a context in which the offered criticism applies only to a retributive theory under which punishment is required, and suggesting the implausibility of the view that retributive theory would merely authorize punishment, and note 68, discussing unfairness with regard to criminals who are

Kant[10] and Hegel[11] and has been developed by numerous twentieth-century

---

not apprehended. We do note that the view that imposing punishment produces a more just state of affairs and that justice should be an important basis for policy does seem inconsistent with the position that justice provides no affirmative basis for imposing punishment. See, for example, Moore (1987, 182): "For a retributivist, the moral culpability of an offender also gives society the *duty* to punish. Retributivism, in other words, is truly a theory of justice such that, if it is true, we have an obligation to set up institutions so that retribution is achieved."

Finally, we note that, for some philosophers, retributivism is not a normative theory of when punishment should be imposed (and to what extent), but rather a view about how, as a linguistic matter, the term "punishment" should be defined. For example, it is sometimes posited that punishment of the innocent is not possible because, if the person is innocent, then what is meted out cannot properly be deemed punishment. See, for example, Quinton (1954). See also Flew (1954, 293), presenting an often-cited definition of punishment that includes the requirement that "it must (at least be supposed to) be for an offense," and Baier (1955), presenting a similar view, but one that allows the imposition of a sanction on one found guilty but not in fact guilty to be called punishment. But see Armstrong (1961, 475–81), criticizing others' treatment of the problem of defining punishment, and McCloskey (1962, 322–23), criticizing definitions of punishment that attempt to incorporate within them whether the punishment is deserved. Because our book concerns normative theory, however, such understandings of retributivism are not pertinent for our purposes. Also, we follow conventional interpretations of the term "punishment" in our discussion so that technical semantic points do not obscure potentially real normative differences between alternative justificatory theories. See Feinberg (1960, 156–57), advocating that legal punishment not be defined in moral terms, which would cloud the discussion of the justification of punishment.

10. See Kant ([1797] 1996, 104–09, 130); and Pincoffs (1966, 4), summarizing Kant's position as holding that criminals should be punished according to their desert, punishment should "equal" the crime, and only criminals may be punished. See also note 17, discussing Kant's rationale.

11. See Hegel ([1821] 1952, 66–73). Hegel notes:

> In discussing this matter the only important things are, first, that crime is to be annulled, not because it is the producing of an evil, but because it is an infringement of the right as right, and secondly, the question of what that positive existence is which crime possesses and which must be annulled; it is this existence which is the real evil to be removed, and the essential point is the question of where it lies. (Ibid., 70)

See Pincoffs (1966, 10, 11), noting Holmes's view that "Hegel professes to establish what is only a mystic (though generally felt) bond between wrong and punishment," and interpreting Hegel as arguing that a failure to punish a crime is an admission that the crime is "valid," and that the only way of showing that instead the crime conflicts with justice is to pay back the deed, to "coerce the coercer"; Anderson (1999, 372–80), interpreting Hegel as arguing that criminal acts entail the claim that the perpetrators had a right to act as they did, so that society must punish them in order to annul this claim; Benn (1967, 30): "For Hegel punish-

scholars.[12] The retributive view of punishment is normally taken to be non-

---

ment is necessary to annul the wrong done by the criminal . . . [because] the criminal has upset the balance of the moral order. . . ."; and Mackie (1982b, 5): "[T]he suggestion made explicitly by Hegel, but perhaps anticipated by Kant, [is] that an appropriate penalty annuls or cancels the crime. . . . But this really is incoherent. The punishment may trample on the criminal, but it does not do away with the crime." See also Ezorsky (1972, xii), noting the view that Hegel sees the purpose of punishment as producing the repentance of sin, and McTaggart (1896), suggesting that punishment can be seen as inducing repentance.

Hegel is often understood as believing that punishment is in some sense the "right" of the criminal because the criminal, in willing the crime, willed that he should suffer punishment similar in degree to his act:

> The injury [the penalty] which falls on the criminal is not merely *implicitly* just— as just, it is *eo ipso* his implicit will, an embodiment of his freedom, his right; on the contrary, it is also a right *established* within the criminal himself, i.e. in his objectively embodied will, in his action. The reason for this is that his action is the action of a rational being and this implies that it is something universal and that by doing it the criminal has laid down a law which he has explicitly recognized in his action and under which in consequence he should be brought as under his right. (Hegel [1821] 1952, 70; bracketed material in original)

See ibid., 71: "[P]unishment is regarded as containing the criminal's right and hence by being punished he is honoured as a rational being."; and Pincoffs (1966, 13): "For a man to complain about the death sentence for murder is as absurd as for a man to complain that when he pushes down one tray of the scales, the other tray goes up; whereas the action, rightly considered, is of pushing down *and* up." This perspective, however, seems to beg the question, for if some other level of punishment—or no punishment—were deemed appropriate, then willing the crime would entail willing such other treatment. This problem, it would seem, could only be avoided by adopting the rule that the state should always do to individuals what they do to others, but such an approach obviously makes no sense. (If an individual wastes all of his resources in a silly attempt to help others, is the state compelled likewise to waste all of its resources?) See also note 17, further discussing the idea that the state should do to the criminal what the criminal has done to others. As suggested in the text to follow, Hegel, like others, seems to rely on metaphors rather than to engage in substantive argument.

12. For discussions and surveys of the views of Kant, Hegel, and other retributivist writers, see Brandt (1959, chapter 19), Pincoffs (1966), Benn (1967), and Greenawalt (1983). Representative writers and statements of the retributive view include Hall (1947); Moberly (1968, chapter 3); Nozick (1981, 363–97); Von Hirsch (1976); Armstrong (1961); Burgh (1982), criticizing Morris's and other retributivists' views but seeming to believe that some sort of retributive theory would justify punishment and the proportionality notion; Doyle (1967), stating that punishment satisfies a just claim that arises from the crime; Gendin (1971), stating that the principle of retributive justice requires that those who commit crimes should be punished unless there is a good reason not to do so, by analogy to the requirement of providing equal treatment unless there is a good reason not to; McCloskey (1967); Moore (1987); Morris (1968, 478–79), stating that the offender should be punished because his offense creates an imbalance between benefits and burdens in society; Mundle (1954); Pius XII (1960, 94): "The

consequentialist; the appropriateness of punishment (and, as we will discuss shortly, its proper level) depends on the character of the act that has been committed, not on the consequences of punishment, including, importantly, effects on individuals' well-being.[13] (Of course, many theorists and most modern analysts who endorse the retributive notion of fairness hold a mixed normative view under which punishment is evaluated according to its consequences as well;[14] as in the rest of this book, our analysis and criticism of

order violated by the criminal act demands the restoration and re-establishment of the equilibrium which has been disturbed. It is the proper task of law and justice to guard and preserve the harmony between duty, on the one hand, and the law, on the other, and to re-establish this harmony if it has been injured."; and Ross (1929).

Mabbott is often cited for his retributive views. See Mabbott (1939, 152): "I propose in this paper to defend a retributive theory of punishment and to reject absolutely all utilitarian considerations from its justification." Yet his theory seems different from standard retributive views in that he endorses a utilitarian basis for criminal law and merely insists that, once the law prescribes a particular punishment, it must be applied (a mixed view that is discussed in note 47). See Flew (1954, 299): "[I]nsofar as Mabbott's view can be called retributive it is not a justification . . . and insofar as any sort of justification is offered it is . . . utilitarian." Others have noted strongly anti-retributivist statements in Mabbott's later writings. See Armstrong (1961, 471–72), quoting Mabbott's remarks that retribution is a polite name for revenge, that the theory is morally indefensible and completely inadequate to determine levels of punishment, and that the theory is discredited.

Additional commonly cited theorists who originally wrote in the nineteenth century are Bosanquet ([1899] 1965, 208–12), discussing retributive theory favorably, but concluding that gradations of punishment should be determined by considerations of prevention and deterrence, and Bradley ([1876] 1927, 26–41), describing, but not endorsing, the view of common people that punishment may be imposed only when deserved.

13. As Kant put it, punishment is not "a means to promote some other good . . . for civil society." Kant ([1797] 1996, 105). Kant emphasized this point by stating that an island society about to disband must still execute the last murderer in prison. Ibid. (106). (Curiously, though, Kant expresses views of punishment that are frankly consequentialist in his other writings. See note 17.) Additional statements of retributivists' anti-consequentialist position are found in Bedau (1977, 53), stating that the focus of retributive theory "is on the offense and nothing else, especially not any social cost/benefit or individual eugenics that can be calculated to result from punishments"; Benn (1967, 30): "Characteristically, the retributivist stresses guilt and desert, looking back to the crime to justify punishment and denying that the consequences of punishment, beneficial or otherwise, have any relevance to justification."; Dolinko (1992, 1626), stating that the permissibility of punishment under retributive theory depends on what criminals deserve regardless of any beneficial consequences; Ezorsky (1972, xi), stating that retributivists hold that the imposition of deserved punishment "is either just or intrinsically valuable, irrespective of any further good consequence"; Fletcher (1978, 415) (same); and Rawls (1955, 4–5) (quoted in note 9).

14. We elaborate and provide references at the end of subsection 2.

notions of fairness—here, of retribution—should be understood to apply only insofar as a notion of fairness is given weight, at the expense of individuals' well-being.)

The rationale for the retributive conception of fairness has proved difficult to identify.[15] It seems that some defenders of the retributive view take it to be self-evidently correct. Most proponents of retributive theory do little more than assert that "justice demands" the punishment of criminals, that criminals "deserve" punishment, that crimes need to be "annulled" through punishment, or that the moral order is "upset" when a wrongful act is committed and must be restored through punishment.[16] Although the basic justification for the use of punishment is not the aspect of retributive theory that is most relevant to our inquiry, we do note that, to us (and to many others),

15. See, for example, Pincoffs (1966, 46): "I have not found an explicit defense of the traditional view" of retributivists that their theory provides a justification for punishment, apart from satisfying the desire for vengeance; Benn (1958, 327): "Consequently, what pass for retributivist justifications of punishment in general, can be shown to be either denials of the need to justify it, or mere reiterations of the principle to be justified, or disguised utilitarianism."; Benn (1967, 31), noting that retributivist justifications might also involve appeals to religious authority; and Mackie (1991, 679): "'Desert' is not such a further explanation [for the retributivist view that wrongs should be punished], but is just the general, as yet unexplained, notion of positive retributivism itself." See also Mackie (1982b), arguing that the principle of retribution cannot be developed in a reasonable system of moral thought.

16. See, for example, Benn (1967, 30), using such terms to describe the basis of the retributive view. See also Bedau (1977, 52): "Probably the most widely held assumption about retribution in punishment is the idea that it makes desert the central feature of just punishment."; Greenawalt (1983, 347): "[A] retributivist claims that punishment is justified because people deserve it. . . ."; Hampton (1984, 236), discussing views of Hegel and Mackie; and note 11, describing Hegel's annulment view.   .

We observe that the notion that punishment is morally appropriate because a state of affairs with "moral balance" is more just than one in which wrongful acts and punishment are imbalanced—a view associated with Kant and other retributivists—appears, on its face, to have an odd implication: If someone were excessively punished (whether truly innocent or guilty but subjected to an unduly severe punishment), the individual's committing a new crime would produce a moral balance that would otherwise be absent. See Ezorsky (1972, xvii). Although we can readily imagine ways to amend retributive theories to avoid this implication, the point suggests that those who for so long have sought to justify retributive punishment in this manner may have been guided more by a seemingly attractive metaphor than by careful scrutiny of their own argument. See also Murphy (1973), arguing that, as long as many individuals become criminals because of economic necessity caused by social inequity, retributive theory cannot justify punishing them in the name of paying a debt owed to society.

the justifications usually offered seem virtually indistinguishable from restatements of the definition of the notion of retribution.[17]

17. "[T]o say 'it is fitting' or 'justice demands' that the guilty should suffer is only to
reaffirm that punishment is right, not to give grounds for thinking so." Benn (1967, 30). See
ibid.: "But in what sense can punishment [in Hegel's theory] be said to restore the balance
or annul the wrong, unless it is taken for granted that criminals deserve to be punished? This
is precisely the point in question."; Hart (1968b, 9), agreeing with Benn "in thinking that
these [formulations] all either avoid the question of justification altogether or are in spite of
their protestations disguised forms of Utilitarianism"; and Dolinko (1991, 538–39): "Notoriously, proponents of retributivism have frequently relied heavily on metaphor and imagery
whose suggestive power exceeds its clarity. [Retributivists have not] transform[ed] such enig-
matic utterances [as nullifying crime, paying a debt to society, giving the wrongdoer what he
has willed] into a rationally defensible theory of punishment . . . and are not likely to do so."
See also note 11, discussing Hegel's views.

Bedau questions whether the concept of desert gives much content to the retributive
justification for punishment:

> On this view, a retributivist holds that a punishment is just if and only if the offender
> deserves it. It seems not to be noticed how essentially trivial this doctrine is; it
> cannot be central or unique to the theory of retributive punishment. Any theory
> of the distribution of benefits and burdens, rewards and punishments, can incorpo-
> rate a notion of desert if it wants to; whatever is said to be properly allocated to
> (or withheld from) a person under the theory can be said to be therewith deserved
> (or not deserved) by that person. (Bedau 1977, 52)

Because so much of the writing on retributive justice is inspired by Kant (even though
his rigoristic approach is not generally followed today), it is worth examining his discussion
with some care. What is most apparent from reading his famous section on punishment is
that he really does not purport to offer any justification for the basic retributive principle.
See Kant ([1797] 1996, 104–09, 130). He appeals repeatedly and explicitly to principles of
retribution but does not explain why they should apply. See Benn (1967, 30), stating that
the most thoroughgoing retributivists, such as Kant, do not "justify punishment but, rather,
. . . deny that it needs any justification." See also Benn (1958, 327): "Assertions of the type,
'it is fitting (or justice requires) that the guilty suffer' only reiterate the principle to be justified. . . ." In addressing Kant's justification for punishment, Pincoffs (drawing, one presumes,
in part on Kant's general writing to interpret the passages on punishment) describes it as
follows: "What we do to him he willed, in willing to adopt his maxim as universalizable. To
justify the punishment to the criminal is to show him that the compulsion we use on him
proceeds according to the same rule by which he acts. This is how he 'draws the punishment
upon himself.'" Pincoffs (1966, 9). This rationale, however, is logically flawed. Most notably,
it does not follow from the fact that the criminal acted wrongly—and, following Kant's view,
thereby willed that his maxim be adopted universally—that the state acts rightly, rather than
committing a further wrong, in imposing punishment. See, for example, Dolinko (1991, 543–
44; 1992, 1628–30), and Hampton (1984, 236): "How is the society that inflicts the second
evil any different from the wrongdoer who has inflicted the first?" Compare Hart (1968a,
234–35), noting that some critics regard such retributivist arguments as involving "a mysteri-

To continue with the description of the retributive conception of fairness, we move to the question that is central to our discussion: If a person has done wrong and deserves punishment, how much punishment should be meted out? The basic answer offered by retributivists is that the magnitude of punishment should fit the crime, which is to say that punishment should

---

ous piece of moral alchemy, in which the combination of the two evils of moral wickedness and suffering are transmuted into good." Nor does the state, when it thus acts, merely proceed by the same rule by which the criminal acted, for the criminal acted in self-interest to harm another who had done (one presumes) no wrong. The principle of retributive punishment has a different motivation and uses an entirely different criterion in choosing the object of harm. Kant's rationale has additional difficulties as well. See, for example, Goldman (1979, 43): "[N]o wrongdoer would construe his action as a consent, tacit or otherwise, to his own punishment."

In assessing Kant's position, we note the remarks of Murphy, who had previously written extensively on Kant and, in particular, on his theory of punishment. On the occasion of revisiting Kant's writings for purposes of a conference, Murphy writes:

> Not only am I no longer confident that the theory is generally correct; I am also not at all sure that I understand (or find understandable) much of what Kant says on crime and punishment. It is no longer clear to me to what extent it is proper to continue thinking of Kant as a paradigm retributivist in the theory of punishment. Indeed, I am not even sure that Kant develops anything that deserves to be called a *theory* of punishment at all. (Murphy 1987, 509)

Some of Murphy's concerns arise from the contrast between the *Rechtslehre* (Kant's writing that most directly addresses punishment, Kant ([1797] 1996, 104–09, 130)) and Kant's other writings that address the purposes of punishment. The theory of punishment "we would predict on the basis of all Kant's writings other than the *Rechtslehre* (precritical, critical, and postcritical) is radically different in both detail and spirit from the one actually present in the *Rechtslehre* as his 'official' theory of punishment." Murphy (1987, 512). Murphy proceeds to present quotations from many of Kant's other writings, including some explicitly stating that the purpose of punishment imposed by the government is to deter! See ibid. (513–16). For example, in Kant's *Lectures on Ethics* ([1775–1780] 1963), he writes that punishments are "either deterrent or else retributive. . . . Those imposed by governments are always deterrent. They are meant to deter the sinner himself or deter others by making an example of him." Murphy (1987, 513). Murphy identifies many passages in Kant's writings that are critical of making retribution the basis for punishment by the state. "To summarize, justified punishment is a deterrence system functioning to maintain a system of ordered liberty of action. To set any more morally ambitious goal for punishment would be to adopt an unacceptable theory of the role of the state and would represent an attempt to play God. . . ." Ibid. (517). See also Byrd (1989), citing similar inconsistencies in Kant's theory of punishment to those noted by Murphy, but arguing that they can be reconciled into a consistent, mixed view of punishment—which we discuss at pages 314–17 and in notes 46 and 47—that has deterrence as its purpose but is restrained in its application by the requirements of retributive justice. Such inconsistency in Kant's writings on moral theory is not confined to his treatment of punishment. See note 55 in chapter II.

be proportional to the gravity of the offense.[18] The clearest and simplest version of the proportionality principle is *lex talionis,* the Biblical maxim of "an eye for an eye." *Lex talionis* entails both the view that punishment should be in kind (a view not often endorsed by modern retributivists) and that the magnitude of the punishment (in whatever form) should in some sense be equal to the wrongfulness of the act.[19] We observe that retributive theory's

18. See, for example, Hegel ([1821] 1952, 71–73); note 9, quoting Holmes's discussion of Hegel's formulation; L. Alexander (1980, 208), observing that "all retributivists agree [that] no punishment [may be] greater than culpability," which he labels "the principle of proportionality"; Benn (1967, 32), stating that the "retributivist insists that the punishment must fit the crime"; Burgh (1982, 197), stating that "it is not enough that we restrict punishment to the deserving, but we must, in addition, restrict the degree of punishment to the degree that it is deserved," that offenders deserve "a degree of punishment that is proportional to the gravity of the offense committed," and that "any punishment in excess of this should be considered as objectionable as imposing an equivalent amount on an innocent person"; Greenawalt (1983, 347–48), describing retributive theory as holding that "the severity of punishment should be proportional to the degree of wrongdoing"; Mundle (1954, 227–28); and Ross (1929, 207–08). Compare Daly and Wilson (1988, 251): "Everyone's notion of 'justice' seems to entail penalty scaled to the gravity of the offense."

19. *Lex talionis* was endorsed by Kant: "[W]hat amount of punishment is it that public justice makes its principle and measure? None other than the principle of equality. . . . Accordingly, whatever undeserved evil you inflict upon another . . . , that you inflict upon yourself. . . . [O]nly the *law of retribution (ius talionis)* . . . can specify definitely the quality and the quantity of punishment. . . ." Kant ([1797] 1996, 105–06). For example, he says that if a person has committed murder, "he must *die."* Ibid. (106).

Bedau suggests that contemporary retributivists do not defend *lex talionis* because sometimes it is literally impossible to respond in kind (for instance, when a kidnapper has no children of his own). Bedau (1977, 63). Also, retribution in kind is often regarded as involving unjust action by the state. Blackstone offers a classic statement of these problems: "[T]here are very many crimes, that will in no shape admit of [*lex talionis*] penalties, without manifest absurdity and wickedness. Theft cannot be punished by theft, defamation by defamation, forgery by forgery, adultery by adultery, and the like." Blackstone (1769, 4:13). See Hegel ([1821] 1952, 72), and Benn (1967, 32): "[T]o try to apply it literally might be monstrously cruel, or, as Kant recognized, it might be absurd." See also Waldron (1992), suggesting ways to interpret or modify the notion of *lex talionis* such that its application is more plausible than has generally been thought; and Wertheimer (1975, 404–05), suggesting that, even though most reject *lex talionis* because it is thought to require unduly harsh punishment, there is wide acceptance of a general notion of proportionality. As indicated in the text, however, we consider the more relaxed notion that the punishment should in some appropriate sense be equivalent to the gravity of the crime (that is, that the proportion between crime and punishment should be one), even if the mode of punishment is not the same as that of the act being punished (such as when a thief is put in jail rather than having an object stolen from him), and also the more general idea that there should be *some* proportion between punishments and the gravity of offenses.

rationale for the degree of punishment, like its rationale for imposing punishment at all, is difficult to identify. It seems that most retributivists believe that the proportionality principle is self-evident or follows directly from the understanding that the purpose of punishment is to restore moral balance in the universe; consequently, the principle is not seen to require explicit justification.[20]

Various subsidiary principles of fair punishment are associated with the general notion of retributive justice, including that a person must have intended to act wrongfully to deserve punishment and that certain conditions might excuse a person from punishment.[21] We will not, however, examine subsidiary principles because, for our purposes, it is sufficient to focus on the basic character of the retributive notion of fairness.

2. Comments on the Literature

Having summarized the retributive view of punishment, we now wish to describe a number of its features that appear to be problematic even from the perspective of the theory's proponents. (Our discussion and central criticism of the retributive conception of fairness in punishment, which concerns its implications for individuals' well-being, is independent of the present discussion and will be taken up in section C.) We begin with a number of remarks about the incompleteness of the retributive theory of punishment.

First, the theory does not include a definition of what constitutes wrongful behavior deserving punishment.[22] Most writers on retributive justice have in mind a core category of acts that they assume to be wrong, such as murder and rape, but they do not independently characterize what behavior deserves punishment. This omission raises immediate difficulties in determining whether certain acts are wrong and deserve punishment. For example, why is breaking a contract or a promise about a dinner engagement not deemed to be a wrong deserving punishment (or is it)? Is sex out of marriage a wrong

20. See, for example, Murphy (1987, 532): "And why should we aim at proportionality so characterized? Kant does not attempt to argue for this view, but seems to think that the claim is self-evident or intuitively obvious. . . ."

21. For discussions of intent, excuse, and other aspects of criminal punishment from the retributive and other perspectives, see Bentham ([1781] 1988, 172–75), Fletcher (1978), Hart (1968c, 13–24, chapters 4–6), Hart (1958b), Holmes (1881, lecture 2), Moore (1993a), Benn (1967, 32–34), Brandt (1969), Ezorsky (1974), Lyons (1969), R. Posner (1985, 1214–30), Shavell (1985a, 1247–59), and Wasserstrom (1967).

22. Compare subsection III.B.2, explaining that the theory of corrective justice invoked in tort law is dependent on some separate substantive theory of wrongful conduct that is neither specified nor defended.

deserving punishment? Is failing to stop a crime from occurring?[23] In the absence of a definition of a wrong that merits punishment, it is not evident how to answer such questions.[24] We also note that this incompleteness makes

23. There are other closely related aspects of the notion of wrongful acts in which retributive theory is either incomplete or potentially misleading. For example, is one who is insane appropriately subject to punishment? It is often suggested that he is not because his acts would not be deemed wrongful (and, under retributive theory, wrongfulness is a necessary condition for punishment). Nevertheless, this same individual may be viewed as properly subject to a form of incapacitation (incarceration in an institution for the insane) that is similar to—and possibly harsher than—the punishment that would be imposed on a sane actor who commits the same act. Such incapacitation, however, would not be called "punishment." See, for example, Wertheimer (1977, 47), arguing that if the sole purpose of incarceration is prevention of future crime rather than deterrence, then dangerous persons should be thought of "as somehow diseased" and "[i]ncarceration would, therefore, no doubt be regarded as a system of social quarantine rather than a system of punishment." To this extent, retributive theory is concerned merely with how incapacitation by the state is labeled, not about the circumstances in which, say, the state may incarcerate individuals to prevent them from causing harm in the future.

24. That the retributive theory does not state a definition of wrongfulness deserving of punishment, and is therefore incomplete, is frequently noted. See, for example, Braithwaite and Pettit (1990, 36), stating that retributive theory does "not offer guidance on what is to be criminalized, on what is to be policed, on what offences are to be investigated, or even on what offences are to be prosecuted"; and Pincoffs (1966, 16): "[T]here is the problem *which* transgressions, intentionally committed, the retributivist is to regard as crimes. Surely not every morally wrong action!" Moreover, appeal to our moral intuitions is not a substitute for a clear definition of a wrong deserving of punishment, as we emphasize in subsection II.D.2 and discuss further in subsection D.2 of this chapter.

To elaborate on this problem with retributive theory, note that the theory holds that individuals should be punished if and only if they commit a wrongful act; hence, once we determine what acts are wrongful, we would know when to punish. Yet most commentators seem implicitly to accept that committing a wrongful act is neither a necessary nor a sufficient condition for punishment. This stance is suggested by their lack of objection to widespread practices that violate the condition of retributive theory. On one hand, many modern crimes (those in the *malum prohibitum* class) involve a range of technical violations that would not be viewed as "wrongs" in the sense intended by retributivists. On the other hand, there are many wrongful acts that everyone agrees should not be crimes (ranging from many civil wrongs, such as breaches of contract, to wrongs in contexts such as intrafamily interactions where punishment by the state would be viewed as intrusive).

> Personal wrongs that members of families and acquaintances do to one another may be of greater magnitude morally than some petty crimes, even though they do not carry publicly imposed penalties. If the purpose of punishment were truly to redress moral guilt, justifying this variance in treatment would be difficult, but few people believe that a liberal society should make the punishment of all serious moral wrongs its business. (Greenawalt 1983, 348–49)

> [T]he government, state, or "society" does not automatically take it upon itself to give people what they deserve in other respects. People, for example, who do good

it even more difficult to ascertain an underlying rationale for the retributive conception of fairness: If we do not know the criteria for deeming acts wrongful or the reasons why the particular criteria were chosen, it is hard to understand why punishment is socially justified if, but only if, acts meet the pertinent criteria.

Second, even if we are able to identify wrongful acts that deserve punishment, the question then arises of how to assess the degree of wrongfulness. Is assaulting somebody worse than stealing a car, and if so, by how much? Also, we do not know the importance of the character of the act itself as opposed to the harm that results from the act: Is it worse to punch one's neighbor in the heat of passion or to carry out a premeditated plan to steal his morning newspaper? Is it worse to succeed in bloodying someone's nose than to shoot to kill but to miss?[25]

---

deeds . . . might be thought to deserve reward, yet the state does not routinely administer such a reward system. For that matter, people who engage in behavior that might be thought to deserve or merit censure or ill-treatment but which does not violate a criminal law are not generally subjected to such sanctions by the state. Why, then, should it be thought so important for the government, the state, or "society" to make sure that people who violate criminal laws receive their "just deserts"? Why single out precisely this one category of persons and insist that the state must give them what they deserve? (Dolinko 1991, 542)

Compare M. Cohen (1940, 988–89), contrasting acts punished by the criminal law with acts regulated by the civil law. Hence, we suspect that most retributivists would not, on reflection, adhere to their basic notion that wrongful behavior and punishment are so directly linked. If they do not, however, the degree to which retributive theories are incomplete is greatly magnified. We note further that this difficulty cannot be circumvented by holding that individuals deserve punishment if and only if they violate the criminal law, because such a stance begs the question of what acts should be covered by the criminal law, that is, what acts should be subject to punishment.

In contrast, the question of which acts to punish is amenable to direct analysis under welfare-oriented theories, as amply illustrated by Bentham's discussion of the subject. See Bentham ([1781] 1988, 309–23). Acts that should be penalized are those that reduce individuals' well-being and that can be controlled most usefully by the threat or imposition of official punishment. We note that core crimes, like murder and rape, have both qualities: Killing and nonconsensual sexual invasions are highly detrimental to overall well-being, and these acts generally cannot be adequately reduced in incidence without the use of strong penalties.

25. In particular, one can ask whether retributive theory implies that there must be no punishment in the latter case, because no harm was done, or severe punishment, because great harm was intended. One can also ask whether, when A kills B through negligence during hunting, whereas C kills D in a premeditated act, A and C deserve equal punishment because they each act wrongly and cause the same harm. See, for example, Van den Haag (1987, 1253–54), reviewing Von Hirsch (1985): "Professor von Hirsch, therefore, remains wisely silent on culpability versus harm." See also Dolinko (1992, 1636–42), noting shortcomings of the litera-

Third, apart from the foregoing difficulties, how do we determine the proper punishment given a view of the magnitude of the wrong? This question may be hard to answer even when *lex talionis* applies, in which case the correct proportion between the wrong and the punishment is said to be one. The reason is that often, if not usually, there is no natural metric for translating the wrong into the punishment. If the wrong is theft or treason, how does this translate into a jail sentence under *lex talionis?* Unless the harm and the punishment are denominated in like units[26]—the harm is

---

ture that has attempted to determine the level of punishment that various crimes deserve, and Sprigge (1965, 290), noting the incompleteness of retributivism with regard to identifying criteria for determining the gravity of offenses.

Expressed more generally, once acts vary with respect to more than a single dimension (and one that itself admits of a natural ordering), a theory holding that more serious acts should be punished more severely requires a common denominator for defining seriousness if the theory is to be meaningful. For example, in order to make battery and theft comparable, one might, as under welfare economics, specify harm to individuals' well-being as the metric. Likewise, when one looks to probability of harm, intention of the actor, and other factors, one also would have to make a conversion in order to be able to say in principle which acts deserve more serious punishments. See Bedau (1977, 64), noting the difficulty in retributive theory of combining culpability and harmfulness, which "seem to be not even as like each other as the proverbial apples and oranges."

We acknowledge that for many acts, there seems to be common agreement on the ordering. But even if there were perfect agreement, analysts still would have to specify the rationale behind their ordering for retributive theory to be complete. Moreover, despite substantial agreement, in fact there remain ambiguities. (For example, McCloskey suggests that "[m]ost of us would agree" on some rankings but that disagreements and doubts would exist with regard to others. McCloskey (1965, 261–62). To address these difficulties, he proposes that we "look to the nature of the offence itself." Ibid. (263). But because that is the final sentence of the article, the reader is given no indication of what about the offense's "nature" should be examined and how it would indicate the degree of wrongfulness.) In addition, the ranking varies over time and across cultures. See, for example, M. Cohen (1940, 993), observing that moral views change over time as conditions change. (In ancient Egypt, for example, the intentional killing of a cat would have been regarded as an act of great sacrilege, but in societies today it would not.) If retributivism does not merely endorse punishment for whatever acts are currently subject to punishment, and to whatever extent is currently authorized (or believed as a matter of public opinion to be appropriate), there must be an independent foundation for retributivist theory. (We also suspect that much of the agreement that exists in a given society about the seriousness of offenses largely reflects the harm they do to individuals; if so, this raises questions about the extent to which the retributive conception of fairness actually constitutes an independent theory of punishment.)

26. Even this condition is insufficient because it is further required that the wrong be measured solely by the amount of harm (and in the same units), which often will not be the case. Notably, actors who cause the same harm may not be deemed equally culpable. In the extreme case of failed attempts, the harm is zero—the same level of harm associated with benign acts—but the degree of wrongfulness is not generally viewed to be zero.

monetary and so is the punishment, or the harm is physical and the punishment is in kind (an eye for an eye)—the interpretation of *lex talionis* is not clear.[27]

With regard to the many retributivists who do not endorse *lex talionis,* our ability to infer the correct magnitude of punishment is made more problematic because we do not even know the proper proportion between wrong and punishment.[28] Retributivist writers do not mention specific proportions, and they provide little basis on which to decide the proper proportion. For example, retributivists furnish no definite way of ascertaining the correct magnitude of punishment for car theft—whether it might be a fine, a suspended sentence, a year in prison, five or ten years in prison, or, for that matter, the death penalty.[29] Nor can the answer be derived from experience or consensus (even if these factors were to count under retributive theory), because the actual proportion between, say, harm and punishment has varied

27. And, of course, in the view of most retributivists, the wrong and the punishment are not denominated in similar units. For example, Hegel states that crimes should be assessed with regard to the nature of the wrongdoer's will. See, for example, Hegel ([1821] 1952, 68–73). But whatever units one may use in attempting to measure this dimension of wrongfulness, they will not translate in any obvious manner into units of tangible punishment.

A possible answer to these difficulties of commensurability is to interpret *lex talionis* not as requiring literally the same penalty as the harm, but as requiring a penalty that creates disutility equivalent to the disutility experienced by the victim. This solution has not been commonly advanced, however. (For an exception, see Goldman (1979, 45).) The reason may be that there would be tension between insisting that the level of punishment be commensurate with the extent of wrongdoing for reasons wholly unrelated to individuals' well-being, and then measuring both the level of punishment and extent of wrongdoing solely by reference to their effects on individuals' well-being.

28. See, for example, Brandt (1959, 499), stating that the typical retributivist view of punishment "agrees with Kant in proposing that the more serious offense should be punished *more* severely, but it does not tell us *how* severely any action should be punished." It may be that most of the retributivists who reject *lex talionis* object only to the requirement that punishment be in kind but not to the requirement that punishment be equal to the crime in some sense. If this is indeed the typical view, it is not made explicit.

29. See, for example, Braithwaite and Pettit (1990, 174–75, 178–79), and Mundle (1954, 223), acknowledging the incompleteness of retributive theory and eschewing any attempt to address it. In saying that retributive theory is incomplete, our objection is not only that retributivists (except those endorsing *lex talionis*) have not stated a particular proportion, but also that they have not identified the principles from which the proper proportion might be derived. For all we know, the correct proportion between the seriousness of the offense (somehow measured) and the severity of punishment (assuming a common metric) should be 100 to 1, 10 to 1, or 2 to 1; in fact, once we no longer insist on equality, we do not even know which should be greater, the magnitude of the offense or that of the punishment. And with regard to proponents of *lex talionis,* they do not explain why the correct ratio is 1 to 1. Although this ratio is obviously attractive as a focal point, a reason must still be provided.

greatly across societies and over time[30] and, even within our society today, the proportion between harm and punishment differs greatly from one offense to another.[31] We also observe that the retributive view of just punishment would be rendered meaningless if the proportion between punishment and the wrongfulness of an act could change freely from one offense to another.[32]

Fourth, let us put the above problems to the side and suppose that we have a definition of wrongfulness and are also able to determine the fair punishment for any wrongful act. A difficulty still arises from the fact that, in reality, errors inevitably will be made in punishment: Punishment will sometimes be too high, including when the innocent are mistakenly punished, and punishment will sometimes be inadequate, including when the guilty are acquitted and thus go without punishment. Given that errors will be made in punishment and that errors can be reduced by the expenditure of social resources to improve the accuracy of the judicial process, the question arises: What level of expenditure is the retributivist willing to make to reduce the rate of error? We presume that he would be willing to spend, say, one penny to ensure that an innocent individual be acquitted rather than executed by mistake. But what is the most he would spend—the entire GDP? To say how much the retributivist is willing to spend to reduce the level of error, he must articulate how much error matters and how valuable social resources are. That is, the retributivist must articulate how the social value of imposing punishment according to the retributive conception of fairness compares to the value of devoting social resources to other uses.[33]

30. For example, theft has been subject to very light punishments (such as suspended sentences), long prison terms, amputation of hands (in Saudi Arabia), and the death penalty.

31. One observes the imposition of fines of $15 for failing to put $0.25 in a parking meter, a proportion of 60 to 1. At the same time, a short prison term might be imposed for vehicular homicide, implying a proportion of much less than 1 to 1. See also note 25, discussing difficulties of attempting to make retributive theory complete by reference to consensus.

32. See, for example, Crocker (1992, 1104), suggesting, in the course of arguing for an approach closer to *lex talionis*, that proportionality is not really invoked in numerical fashion, but instead the proportion varies: "To say that the proportions themselves may vary is to divest the proportionate theory of content as well as of any connection to principles of justice."

33. Dworkin is one of the few writers who explicitly identifies this problem and attempts to address it. See R. Dworkin (1985). In essence, Dworkin simply posits that there is some "moral cost" to be weighed along with welfare (in a manner that seems, as a review by Raz has pointed out, see note 63 in chapter V, to be inconsistent with the rest of Dworkin's work, which advances the view that principles trump considerations of policy). He also distinguishes aspects of bare harm (such as resentment or outrage) from what he describes as an independent factor of justice, a "moral fact" distinct from individuals' emotions, although he relies on common views to establish that the injustice factor even exists. R. Dworkin (1985,

Similarly, we face a difficulty because not all wrongdoers are caught and more social resources could be devoted to apprehending and punishing a greater number of them. Inasmuch as it is more just to impose a positive and appropriate punishment on a wrongdoer than not to impose any punishment, we assume that the retributivist would be willing to spend some social resources to catch more wrongdoers, but, again, we have no idea how much he would be willing to spend.[34] Just as in the case of errors, answering this question requires articulating the social value of punishment according to retributive principles relative to the general value of social resources.

The questions we have considered—how to define wrongfulness deserv-

---

80). For further discussion of Dworkin's analysis of these points, see notes 63, 65, and 132 in chapter V, and for a general treatment of the use of intuition and common morality as a basis for grounding retributive theory, see subsection D.2. See also note 12 in chapter VII, addressing the notion that the right is prior to the good, of which Dworkin's view on principles and policy is an example.

Wertheimer offers another analysis. See Wertheimer (1977). He argues that the problem of determining a morally acceptable probability of mistakes in punishment is best addressed through "utilitarian judgments, as opposed to considerations of justice." Ibid. (45) (abstract of article). Yet, in choosing the level of mistakes, one available level is zero—which, as Wertheimer emphasizes, entails as a practical matter the elimination of punishment, due to the inherent imperfection of judicial procedures. However, it is hard to understand how utilitarian principles could govern this choice, which by definition includes the choice of whether to permit any punishment, while at the same time adhering to a retributive theory of punishment wherein that same decision is made on other grounds. (Of course, one could modify the approach so that retributive concerns receive some weight, as Wertheimer admits at various points might be possible. In this case, the structure of the analysis would be very similar to that under welfare economics, but the weight given to certain factors may differ. See note 36.)

34. As one commentator explains:

How does the retributivist know that we should try to secure retribution at any cost? . . . In the real world of criminal justice, we do not believe that we should sacrifice whatever it takes to secure retribution, and it is not clear that we are morally wrong to believe this. In the real world, no matter how much weight we attach to retributive justice, given a sufficiently large volume of criminal activity and a sufficiently large volume of other claims on social resources, we will have to underfinance the criminal justice system in those respects where its perfect operation is a necessary condition of securing retributive justice. This will guarantee that prosecutorial and judicial choice will often leave some convictably guilty persons untried, some convictable guilty persons underpunished or unpunished, and still other guilty persons unapprehended or unconvicted, and so unpunished. (Bedau 1977, 58)

See also Avio (1993, 263–66), noting the incompleteness of retributive theory regarding the extent of resources that should be devoted to criminal justice, and arguing that to make the view more complete by requiring that all offenders be punished would probably consume all of society's resources.

ing of punishment, how to determine the degree of wrongfulness, how to translate wrongfulness into proper punishment, and how to determine the appropriate amount to spend on judicial accuracy and on catching violators—must be addressed before the retributivist can tell us how to punish and, more generally, how to decide on a law enforcement policy.[35] In the absence of either satisfactory conceptual answers to these questions or even a sense of how such answers might be derived, the retributive conception of fair punishment is seriously incomplete.[36] Furthermore, the substantial incompleteness of retributive theory makes it difficult to identify the norma-

35. In these regards, it is instructive to contrast welfare economics with retributive theory. Under welfare economics, the question of which acts should be subject to punishment is answered by comparing the level of social welfare under the best punishment scheme with that under a regime that does not punish a type of act. The degree of wrongfulness is generally determined by the harm caused by a type of act, and harm is understood in terms of how much victims' (or others') well-being is reduced by an act. Proper punishment is derived by comparing the costs and benefits of different levels of punishment, and likewise with regard to determination of the resources that should be spent on accuracy and on catching violators. For each of these questions, an analyst would ascertain the relevant effects on individuals' well-being, which are identified in section A, and then make an overall appraisal to find the best punishment policy. As we emphasized in subsections II.A.2 and II.A.3, when there are distributive effects involved, this overall appraisal will incorporate a distributive judgment and not merely a summing of costs and benefits. We acknowledge that the relevant data may often be unavailable and that the analysis may be complex, see subsection VIII.D.4(a), but we emphasize that, in principle, the welfare economic framework provides answers to the types of questions that we are suggesting retributive theory generally does not address.

36. Although the literature on retributive justice says very little about most of the questions we have identified, some questions, primarily those relating to aspects of culpability, have received attention, usually when writers have discussed doctrines of intent, excuse, and the like. See sources cited in note 21. Even in such instances, however, the reasoning of writers often appears to be ad hoc, not consistently grounded in a particular notion of retributive justice, and often leaves many issues unresolved (for example, the extent to which various factors should mitigate punishment).

It also seems that, if the retributive conception of fairness were to be made more complete, it would have more of a consequentialist character and thus resemble the kind of theory that retributivists have resisted. For example, it is hard to imagine that any theory could help us to decide how much to spend to catch violators without regard to the number of additional violators that might be caught as a consequence. Likewise, one would suppose that it would make a difference whether the additional violators that would be apprehended had committed serious or relatively trivial wrongs, suggesting that different value weightings would be put on different wrongful acts. The points raised in the text to follow will provide additional reasons that a complete retributive theory would probably have to be a complex consequentialist one, much less different *in structure* from welfare economics than one would have suspected. (It would still be different *in substance*, in that some criteria other than effects on individuals' well-being would determine the value of punishing offenders.)

tive foundation for the theory, a problem that assumes great significance when one attempts to compare the theory's merits to those of welfare economics. These points are closely related, for if a normative basis for retributive theory existed and was made explicit (which, we note in subsection 1, has not been done), one would suppose that it would be easier to determine, at least in principle, what law enforcement policy the theory requires in the standard sorts of situations that we have just examined.[37]

Even ignoring the incompleteness of the retributive notion of fairness, there are important implications of the theory that raise questions about its internal coherence. As we explain in subsection 1, it is intrinsic to the retributive view that proper punishment be determined by examining the character of the particular act that occurred rather than by assessing the consequences of punishment.[38] Therefore, the retributivist does not pay attention to the effects of punishment on the number of wrongful acts committed. Yet a wrongful act is, by definition, something that is wrong on the retributivist's own terms. A world with more wrongful acts would therefore seem to be a less just world, one that the retributivist would not want to exist.[39] But if the retributivist is bothered by the occurrence of wrongful acts, he cannot be indifferent to whether punishment will result in fewer wrongful acts. To illustrate this problem, suppose that if the fair punishment for murder is applied, ten murders will be committed, whereas if a greater and unfair punishment is threatened, none will be. Given that murder is considered by the retributivist to be a wrongful act—that the world in which an act of murder occurs is less just than one in which it does not—it is hard to understand how the retributivist can say that it does not matter in de-

---

37. Compare Dolinko (1997, 527): "That [desert-based and intrinsic-good] claims, each of which carries impressive retributivist credentials, should nonetheless prove incompatible strongly suggests that despite the present-day prominence of the retributive theory, we are still far from a satisfactory account of just what that theory *is*."

38. We remind the reader that, with regard to mixed views of punishment, which would give some weight in setting sanctions to fairness and some weight to consequences, we are only addressing the component that is based on the retributive conception of fairness.

39. Our suggestion that a world with more wrongful acts is less just than a world with fewer wrongful acts is not, of course, required as a matter of pure logic. It is logically possible to say that murder and rape, for example, are "wrong" and should accordingly be punished, yet to be indifferent to whether we live in a world in which these acts occur. Under this view, all that retributivists would mean by "wrong" would be that quality which, when possessed by an act, is deemed to warrant punishment. Such a view seems problematic when one moves beyond internal logical consistency to the matter of moral justification. For if a "wrong" is not an act that is undesirable in any sense, the rationale for insisting on punishment becomes difficult to comprehend even from the deontological perspective.

termining whether the supposedly fair punishment is indeed fair that, as a consequence of insisting on fair punishment, ten murders will occur. We emphasize that this point seems to apply within retributive theory—that is, the occurrence of murder should be relevant from a perspective that views murder as immoral even if that judgment of immorality is not itself based on consequences for individuals' well-being.[40]

Not only does the nonconsequentialist aspect of the retributive conception of fairness imply that the number of wrongful acts committed is irrelevant, but it also means that the number of instances of unfair punishment is irrelevant. In the example just mentioned, when the fair punishment is employed and ten murders occur, some of the murderers may escape punishment (indeed, this possibility of escape may explain why the murderers were not deterred), and let us say that five do so. Thus, for the retributivist to recommend the fair punishment for murder means that he favors a regime under which five people suffer no sanction for their wrong, which itself is unfair under retributive theory.[41] But if the unfairly high sanction is an-

40. See, for example, Nozick (1981, 379): "Punishment does not wipe out the wrong, the past is not changed, but the disconnection with value is repaired (though in a second best way). . . ."; Burgh (1982, 203–04 n.18): "Paying the debt in the form of punishment does not legitimate what has been done—it is still unfair."; and Wertheimer (1977, 61), stating that reducing crime is relevant "[o]n grounds of justice alone" because "if we assume that the victims of crime do not deserve to be the victims of crime, it is unjust that people are victimized by crimes." The view that deterrence should matter from a retributive perspective is suggested by Hart (1968b, 8), who argues that "it would be paradoxical to look upon the law as designed not to discourage murder at all (even conceived as sin rather than harm) but simply to extract the penalty from the murderer."

To test further our conjecture about the retributive conception of fairness, consider a world in which half of the population murders the other half and then itself is executed (assuming, for purposes of the illustration, that this is deemed to be the appropriate punishment for murder). Retribution is perfect in this world; no crime fails to receive the fitting punishment. Is this world, in which everyone is dead, as just as a world in which there is no murder in the first place? If this world is indeed less just, it must be that wrongful acts that are met with full retribution still leave us with a less just state of affairs than if the wrongful acts were never committed. But see Bedau (1977, 69): "It is too rarely noticed that retributivists in principle are fundamentally indifferent between the state of the world in which there is no crime, and the state of the world in which there is a wide variety of horrible crimes each of which is punished fully and exactly as retribution requires."

41. Compare Wertheimer (1977, 61), stating that under retributive theory "it is also unjust to not punish a guilty person" by mistake. This is one of the few places where we make a criticism that depends on retributive theory entailing the view that punishment affirmatively should be meted out to wrongdoers, rather than being equally applicable to the variant of retributive theory under which punishment is merely authorized. See note 9, discussing the literature, and note 68, further discussing unfairness with regard to criminals who are not apprehended. Obviously, if one holds the view that wrongdoing may justify punishment, even

nounced, it will by hypothesis discourage all murders, so that no individuals will in fact experience an unfair sanction (either too high a sanction or getting away scot-free). The more general point is that, because retributivists ignore deterrence and thus changes in the number of wrongful acts that are committed, they by the same token ignore changes in the number of occasions on which wrongdoers unfairly go free. By similar reasoning, the retributivist approach seems to ignore the number of occasions on which wrongdoers are punished to an unfair degree.[42] This point, that retributive notions of fairness are associated with indifference to the number of instances of unfair treatment, is in tension with the demand of retributive justice that fair punishment be imposed on everyone who commits a wrongful act.

The foregoing two arguments suggest that many retributivists might, on reflection, concede that the consequences of punishment—in terms of the number of wrongful acts and the number of instances of unfair punishment—do matter to normative evaluation.[43] Otherwise, their position is inconsistent with their belief that the occurrence of wrongful acts and the imposition of unfair punishment each involve injustice. But if such consequences matter, then deterrence would become highly relevant for retributivists,[44] a conclusion that runs counter to their professed position. Indeed, it

---

severe punishment, but whether such punishment is ever imposed is a matter of indifference, then this aspect of our argument would be irrelevant. We do not understand, however, the reasoning on which this particular mixed retributive theory rests. As a leading retributivist states:

> [T]he retributive theory in any except emaciated forms implies both that punishment may be useless but just and that punishment may be obligatory but useless. . . . There seems to be something very unsatisfactory about the common retributionist's reply that just punishment is obligatory "when it is useful," for this is according to the dictates of justice a very negative role, a role of a much more negative character than is accorded to the demands of justice elsewhere. The duties of justice are typically more positive than merely abstaining from acts of injustice. (McCloskey 1967, 109–10)

See also Sprigge (1965, 267–68): "[I]t seems clear that on any reasonable definition of Justice, it is something which there is a positive duty to promote, and not something which it is merely morally permissible to promote. It would be odd if this did not extend to just punishment."

42. In addition, retributivists who eschew consequences ignore the frequency with which punishment is mistakenly imposed on the innocent, as we discuss in subsection C.4.

43. See Moore (1993b), giving an account of retributivism that he argues is consistent with consequentialist or deontological views. But see Dolinko (1997), challenging Moore's claim that a consequentialist theory of retributivism is tenable.

44. This observation reinforces the point that a more complete theory of retributive justice would entail an elaborate consequentialist analysis that would in many ways be similar in structure to the analysis required under welfare economics. See note 36.

would be ironic for deterrence to be of central importance to the very group that, since the days of Bentham, has vigorously attacked utilitarians and other consequentialists because of their attention to deterrence.

Finally, we elaborate on our prior observation that most modern writers (especially legal policy analysts) who support retributive conceptions of fairness do not view them as absolute; instead, they espouse mixed views that combine concerns about fairness and concerns about individuals' well-being. In particular, few writers would argue that the amount of harm that criminals cause and the cost of operating the legal system (police, courts, prisons) are without importance.[45]

Mixed views take many forms.[46] Most simply, one could engage in bal-

45. As Hart states:

> [M]ost contemporary forms of retributive theory recognize that any theory of punishment purporting to be relevant to a modern system of criminal law must allot an important place to the Utilitarian conception that the institution of criminal punishment is to be justified as a method of preventing harmful crime, even if the mechanism of prevention is fear rather than the reinforcement of moral inhibition. (Hart 1968a, 235–36)

46. Whether describing the theory that is implicit in the existing legal system, that is generally held in the population, or that is normatively compelling independently of current practice or popular understanding, writers have presented many such mixed views, although often not specifying their character. See, for example, Bonnie et al. (1997, 30), stating that "our criminal process may be fairly characterized as a 'mixed' system in that lawmakers draw on both retributive and utilitarian principles to justify criminal punishment," and that "the optimal system . . . may be one in which retributive thinking dominates some phases . . . while utilitarian thinking dominates others"; Bradley ([1876] 1927, 27), stating, in the course of describing common people's views, that "[h]aving once the right to punish, we may modify the punishment according to the useful and the pleasant"; Fletcher (1978, 418), noting "numerous efforts to combine these distinct rationalia in an eclectic justification for imposing sanctions in the name both of [retributive] justice and of social protection"; ibid., suggesting that the Model Penal Code embraces a mixed view; LaFave and Scott (1986, 22–29), describing generally accepted views; Nozick (1981, 719 n.84): "Is [carrying out punishment] important enough to let the heavens fall, or does it merely get some weight in a utilitarian-like calculation? Neither of these positions seems appropriate. . . ."; Packer (1968, 62–70), stating that prevention is the purpose of punishment, subject to limits set by retributivism; Armstrong (1961, 486): "There is . . . no reason, having got some idea of the permissible limits of a man's punishment from Retributive considerations, why we should not be guided in our choice of the form of the penalty by Deterrent and Reformatory considerations."; ibid. (487): "For a variety of reasons (amongst them the hope of reforming the criminal) the appropriate authority may choose to punish a man less than it is entitled to, but it is never just to punish a man more than he deserves."; Byrd (1989), arguing that Kant in fact endorsed a mixed view of punishment, wherein the benefit of deterrence justifies punishment and retributive justice serves to limit its magnitude; Crocker (1992), defending the view that retributive theory should provide upper

ancing, according positive weight to both retributive principles and factors relevant to individuals' well-being in determining punishment (and law enforcement policy more generally). Alternatively, one could view retributive theory as providing a constraint on the use of punishment to pursue other objectives, notably the promotion of individuals' well-being. Or one might believe that different theories each have their own place—for example, the general social institution of punishment, embodied in legislation, may be justified on the basis of deterrence, incapacitation, and other factors pertinent to individuals' well-being, whereas the actual application of punishment by judges may be guided by retributive principles.[47] Whatever the mixed

---

and lower limits on punishment, whereas utilitarian considerations should guide the choice within those limits; Ezorsky (1972, xi), stating that, from the perspective of teleological retributivist philosophers, "[j]ustice is not served by the infliction of deserved suffering for its own sake[, but] justice is served if teleological [consequentialist] aims are held in check by principles of justice, e.g., that the suffering of punishment should not exceed the offender's desert"; Gendin (1971, 8), stating that the "retributive principle does not insist that justice must prevail at all costs"; Greenawalt (1983, 354–55), discussing the view that "someone should never be punished more severely than could be justified both by utilitarian objectives and by the degree of his wrongdoing," and seeming to endorse a similar but more flexible mixed view; Lyons (1969, 651), stating that a "more moderate 'retributive' position involves suggesting (as Hart and others do) that nonutilitarian principles place limits on the moral acceptability of useful institutions," and suggesting that such a view is held by some leading retributivists; McCloskey (1965, 251–52): "Sometimes it is morally permissible and obligatory to override the dictates of justice. The retributive theory is a theory about justice in punishment and tells only part of the whole story about the morality of punishment."; ibid. (251): "[U]njust punishments may, in extreme circumstances, become permissible, but this would only be so if a grave evil has to be perpetrated to achieve a very considerable good."; ibid. (261): "Production of the greatest good is obviously a relevant consideration when determining which punishment may properly be inflicted. . . ."; McCloskey (1967, 91–92): "To be morally justified, unjust punishment must not simply be useful; rather, the good it achieves must be so great that it outweighs the evil of the injustice involved." (emphasis omitted); Murphy (1987, 523), describing a view under which punishment according to desert is not the primary aim of punishment, but a constraint on the pursuit of other goals, such as deterrence; and Wertheimer (1975, 403–04): "[E]ven those philosophers who stroll down the winding paths of a theory of happiness also generally pay homage to some version of retributivism. It is often argued that punishment should somehow be commensurate with the crime, should 'fit the crime,' or should (at least) not exceed the punishment that is deserved, that is, commensurate with the crime." See also note 47, elaborating on the nature of mixed views of punishment. Compare Sentencing Reform Act (1984, §994(c)(4)–(5)), stating the statutory purpose of the Sentencing Reform Act of 1984 as providing just punishment as well as serving instrumental objectives.

47. We note that those writers who describe or hold many of these mixed views do not state how much weight should be given to each normative approach or how in principle to go about determining such weights. This aspect of incompleteness seems to be recognized, although such recognition has not led to further analysis of the question. The exceptions are those analysts who specify a particular role for each normative approach. For example, one

theory may be, however, it will be subject to the preceding criticisms—and

---

approach endorses applying whichever punishment is lower, that permitted under retributive theory or that optimal under some consequentialist approach. The reason that one would mix two unrelated normative theories in this manner, rather than compromising in some way between the punishments that are ideal under each theory, is not clear.

To illustrate the problems that arise with some mixed views, we elaborate on the mixed view that holds that the legislature, in creating a system of punishment, should be guided by welfare, whereas judges, when meting out punishment, should follow retributive principles. In addition to being endorsed in some of the references in note 46, this kind of view is of the type described by Hart. See Hart (1968b, 9), suggesting, without necessarily endorsing, the idea that deterrence and other utilitarian objectives may constitute the general justifying aim of punishment, whereas retributive justice may be the appropriate guide for the distribution of punishment. A similar interpretation is also sometimes given to Rawls. See Rawls (1955, 7): "The decision whether or not to use law . . . and what penalties to assign may be settled by utilitarian arguments; but if one decides to have laws then one has decided on something whose working in particular cases is retributive in form." Our further reference to Rawls, below, will raise some question about the accuracy of this characterization. See also our discussion of Mabbott's views in note 12.

This mixed view seems difficult to defend. First, it is hard to understand exactly what the view means. On one hand, if judges' following retributivism implies that they can ignore the rules established by the legislature, then we do not have a mixed system: the legislation is irrelevant and the system is purely retributive. On the other hand, if legislation must be obeyed, and if it tells judges what to do, there seems to be little room for retributivism. Indeed, if the legislature allows no discretion, such as by enacting a precise sentence for each offense, retributivism would play no role. Similarly, one can imagine a legislature that allows discretion but specifically provides that it is to be exercised to promote welfare. Perhaps theorists imagine merely that judges are to apply the legislature's welfarist rules in an even-handed fashion, but this hardly entails a departure from welfarism. See Hare (1981, 162), observing that rules governing the imposition of punishment may appear deontological even when they are selected entirely on utilitarian grounds; Bedau (1977, 59): "'Because we meant what we said,' therefore, is a kind of further reason for punishing those eligible for punishment. Is it a retributive reason? I think not."; and Wasserstrom (1977, 188): "Retributivism is reduced [under this mixed view] to a special instance of the general case for having a system follow and apply its own rules whatever they happen to be." Compare subsection VIII.C.2, discussing how the requirement of equal treatment under legal rules is implied by welfarism.

Second, the view appears to be illogical at the most basic level. If one principle—be it welfarism or retributivism—is supposed to be ethically attractive, why is that principle not always our ethical guide? How can our ethical objective change just because we happen to be discussing the application of punishment by judges instead of the determination of laws (including those that set punishments) by legislatures? Compare Dolinko (1991, 541): "And to split off, as Hart does, the question of who may be punished from both definition and 'general justifying aim' suggests that we can decide what punishment is and why we engage in it without knowing who is supposed to receive punishment—which seems preposterous." It is true, of course, that we may want to limit the decisionmaking power of judges—because they may not share society's ethical objectives, because they lack expertise, or because we may wish to constrain their opportunities to abuse their discretion—but this need is a different

our main argument in section C will apply—to the extent that the mixed theory accords some importance to a retributive conception of fairness.

C. Welfare Economics versus Fairness and Law Enforcement

From the general description of the two approaches above, it is clear that there are real differences between the two types of normative analysis of legal rules regarding punishment. Rather than undertake an exhaustive comparison of the two approaches, we will focus, as indicated above, on the conflict between welfare economics and notions of fair punishment in a setting in-

---

point, one about how to attain our ethical objectives in the face of constraints. See subsections V.C.2 and VIII.A.2. For arguments that one might, wholly within a utilitarian justification for the practice of punishment, choose to adopt a retributive view regarding punishment in particular cases, see Rawls (1955, 4–13), and Wertheimer (1976), arguing that the utilitarian justification of punishment at the legislative level requires that retributive theory govern the imposition of punishment because deterrence is accomplished only if there is a credible commitment to punish, which exists under a retributive, backward-looking theory but not necessarily under a utilitarian, forward-looking theory. See also Moore (1993b, 17), suggesting that a purely utilitarian view of punishment might still favor adopting facially non-utilitarian rules for its implementation, and likewise for a purely retributive view.

Third, suppose that we take the view at face value and assume that the legislature is to follow welfarist goals and judges are to follow retributive goals. Then it is possible that we would find ourselves with a justice system that is inferior with regard to both systems of evaluation. Suppose that the welfarist legislature adopts a two-year prison sentence for auto thieves, the sentence being rather high because auto theft is difficult to detect. The retributivist judiciary may refuse to convict because this sentence is unfairly high (perhaps the just punishment is deemed to be six months). The result is a de facto system of no punishment, which may be worse than any number of compromise systems, consistently employed, in terms of both welfare and retribution. (Of course, a sophisticated welfarist legislature may anticipate judges' retributivist behavior and thus enact a system that compromises between welfarism and retributivism in the first place by, say, enacting a one-year sentence, which, although failing to optimize deterrence, does achieve some deterrence at tolerable cost, and which, although not entirely fair, might be deemed more fair by retributivist judges than letting auto thieves go scot-free. The mixed view implicit in such a result would be different from that suggested by the philosophers who have discussed it: essentially, the system is one in which legislators maximize welfare subject to the constraint that, if they deviate too much from what retributive theory requires, the legislated scheme of punishment will be nullified.)

In any event, we note that most policy analysts who study crime either do not articulate any particular mixed view or seem to adopt the simple mixed view that both fairness and standard social welfare factors count in the normative calculus, without distinguishing between the legislature and judiciary in terms of the appropriate normative theory that should be employed.

volving the deterrence of crime. Deterrence is the subject with which most of the writing comparing the two approaches has been concerned. By examining cases involving deterrence, we obtain a fairly good idea of the arguments that apply to the comparison of welfare economics and fairness in the law enforcement context. We defer until subsection D.2 our consideration of the possibilities that individuals may have a taste for satisfaction of retributive principles of punishment and that punishment may affect social norms that influence compliance with the law, points mentioned in our sketch of welfare economics in section A.

1. Fair Punishment and Deterrence in a Paradigm Case

(a) Description. Suppose that an act causes harm of 100 and that the gains to the people who commit it are less than that amount. Suppose as well that the probability that a person committing the act will be punished is 25 percent and that imposing a sanction involves a public cost of 2 per unit of sanction, in addition to a cost of 1 per unit of sanction borne by a sanctioned individual.[48] Finally, assume that the fair sanction is 100, that is, equal to the harm. (We make this assumption only for concreteness. We do not mean to limit our analysis to any particular retributive view about the proper proportion between the sanction and the gravity of the act; it will be apparent that the character of our analysis would be the same if a different sanction were viewed as the fair sanction.[49])

(b) Behavior of Individuals under Different Sanctions. Under the fair sanction of 100, the expected sanction is 25,[50] so that all individuals who obtain a benefit exceeding 25 will commit the act.[51] Suppose that there are 1,000 such

---

48. For convenience, we ignore the cost involved (to hire police and so forth) in achieving a probability of imposing punishment of 25 percent; because this cost will be held constant in our analysis, it will not affect any of the comparisons that we consider.

49. In particular, for any fair sanction under 400, the argument would be the same; only the numbers of violators and the costs of imposing the fair sanction would be different. If the fair sanction were deemed to be greater than or equal to 400 (say, 500), it will be evident that we could simply have chosen an example in which the probability of detection was lower (say, 10 percent), and our arguments and conclusions would be the same.

50. As we discuss in note 53, we assume that potential criminals are risk neutral with respect to sanctions.

51. Any disutility individuals may suffer from knowing that they are breaking a law can be understood as reducing their benefit from committing the harmful act, or, for individuals who would not contemplate violating the law, as eliminating their benefit (or making it negative). Compare Kornhauser (1999), discussing the idea that some individuals may, out of

individuals. Because 25 percent of these 1,000 individuals will be detected and punished, 250 individuals will be punished. Each punished individual will experience disutility of 100, and each imposition of punishment will result in the state bearing a cost of 200.

The higher the sanction, the fewer the number of individuals who will commit the harmful act.[52] In particular, if the sanction equals 400, the expected sanction will be 100, and no individual will commit the act.[53]

(c) Choice of Sanction Using Welfare Economics. The best sanction under welfare economics is 400, for if the sanction is 400, all individuals are deterred from committing the harmful act. That means not only that no harm is done, but also that, because no individuals are punished, no public costs of imposing sanctions are incurred. In addition, because no individuals actually are punished, none suffer disutility from punishment.

Suppose instead that the fair sanction of 100 is employed. Then there will be two costs that do not arise with the higher sanction of 400. First, 1,000 crimes will be committed, each causing harm of 100, resulting in a

---

obligation, follow the law, without making a cost-benefit decision based on the benefit of violation and expected sanction cost.

52. In making this statement and in offering particular numerical examples below, we do not mean to adopt any particular position about the extent to which sanctions do in fact deter the commission of acts subject to the sanctions. Our consideration of deterrence in our examples is for conceptual purposes. We begin with an extreme case, in which all acts are deterred, because it is the simplest case in which to see the contrast between the competing theories. In subsection 3, we consider the more realistic case in which deterrence is incomplete, and, in subsection 4, we introduce the possibility that sanctions are sometimes erroneously imposed on innocent people. It should be kept in mind that, in settings in which the only possible benefit to individuals' well-being from raising sanctions is deterrence, any welfare economic endorsement of sanctions higher than those favored under the retributive view is contingent on whether sufficient further deterrence will occur.

53. No individuals will commit the act because we have assumed that the benefits they would obtain from the act are less than 100. Our discussion implicitly assumes that individuals treat a 25 percent chance of being subject to a sanction of 400 as equivalent to a certain sanction of 100; if this were not the case, say, because individuals are averse to risk, then some sanction lower than 400 would be sufficient to deter everyone (or if individuals view risky sanctions less negatively than certain sanctions with the same expected value, some sanction higher than 400 would be necessary to deter everyone). We also note that, even under our assumption, it is possible that a sanction lower than 400 may suffice to deter everyone, as long as no one receives benefits that are very high (near 100). Finally, it is also true that a sanction greater than 400 would work equally well in this example (although when we introduce the possibility in later subsections that not everyone will be deterred or that some individuals might be punished by mistake, it will be desirable to use low sanctions rather than high ones, other things being equal).

total harm of 100,000. (To be sure, those committing the crimes will receive some benefit, but their benefits are less than the harm due to their crimes.[54]) Second, punishment of 100 will be imposed on 250 individuals. Because its members will have to pay taxes to finance the imposition of sanctions, society will suffer losses of 200 per individual punished, and each individual who is sanctioned will suffer a cost of 100, making total costs equal to 300 per individual punished. Hence, the total social costs of punishment will be 75,000. Compared to the total cost of 0 under a sanction of 400, it is clear that the sanction of 100 is inferior.

(d) *Choice of Sanction Using Notions of Fairness.* As already stated, the fair sanction is 100.

(e) *Why the Choice of Sanction Should Be Based Only on Individuals' Well-Being.* We have just shown that the retributive notion of fair punishment conflicts with welfare economics in our example. In particular, the pursuit of retributive justice leads to individuals suffering harm from a significant amount of crime rather than none and to society incurring significant costs of imposing punishment rather than none. This example suggests that the retributive con-

---

54. Thus, their commission of the crime lowers social welfare. More generally, we are assuming that the acts that we call crimes are socially undesirable because the social benefits that accrue when they are committed are outweighed by the social costs (the numbers in the text could be interpreted as representing units of social welfare). Thus, we are not considering cases in which a "crime" involves, say, a lost hiker who, because he is starving to death, breaks into a vacant cabin in the wilderness to take some food (a case in which the actor may well be excused under many systems, including one based on welfare economics). In addition, we are assuming that there are no social benefits from improving the distribution of income through criminal activity—or at least none that cannot better be provided through more direct means, such as through the income tax and transfer programs. (Relatedly, criminals who are caught may, due to the sanction they receive, be worse off than others, including criminals who escape detection; this possibility might make it optimal to employ somewhat lower sanctions than otherwise.)

Another point is that some may not wish to credit criminals' gains as part of social welfare. If one stipulates that criminals' gains should not be counted, it will become apparent that our conclusions would not be altered in an essential way. Indeed, our conclusions are reinforced, for crimes become socially worse, and thus socially more desirable to deter, when criminals' gains are not counted. As we discuss below, retributivists can be understood as implicitly viewing adverse effects on criminals—in particular, adverse effects from punishment—as counting more than adverse effects on noncriminals who suffer harm from crime. This observation is ironic in light of some retributivists' criticism of utilitarianism for counting the suffering of criminals as on a par with that of victims. See, for example, Lyons (1969, 649). See also subsection VIII.B.3, discussing the trumping of objectionable preferences.

ception of fairness is seriously flawed. Indeed, were we to modify our example in certain ways, it would be the case that—as in chapters III–V—advancing this notion of fairness would result in literally everyone being made worse off.[55]

Moreover, we stress that this conflict arises not only if an analyst chooses sanctions solely by reference to retributive principles, but also if the analyst holds a mixed view that gives weight to both fairness and welfare.[56] Suppose, for example, that an analyst compromises between the welfare-optimal sanction of 400 and the purely fair sanction of 100, choosing a sanction of 250.

55. As we emphasize below, the only winners under the regime of fair punishment are potential criminals who have high benefits from crime (high enough so as not to be deterred by the fair sanction of 100). Now, instead of postulating that particular individuals are initially endowed with atypically high benefits from committing crime, we could consider a symmetric setting in which opportunities for such atypically high benefits will be experienced randomly (with equal probability) by everyone in the population. For example, imagine that each person is equally likely to happen on a briefly unattended bag of cash next to an armored car. Then, ex ante, every individual experiences the same expected costs and benefits under any level of the sanction, and thus they will all be better off under the sanction that minimizes aggregate costs from crime. In our example, that is clearly the sanction of 400; everyone will expect to be worse off under the regime in which the sanction is 100. More generally, whatever is the best sanction under welfare economics will, by definition, be that which maximizes individuals' well-being. Therefore, any deviation that results from giving some weight to a notion of fairness will result in everyone being worse off in this sort of symmetric setting. See generally subsections II.C.1 and III.C.1(e)(iii), discussing this point more generally.

The reason that we do not present a symmetric case in the text—which is often our practice elsewhere in this book—is that it is conventional in discussing law enforcement to view only certain individuals as likely criminals (individuals who are usually thought to be unlike those performing the analysis and voting for or implementing the policy). But, as we elaborate in subsections II.C.1, III.C.1(e)(iii), and VIII.C.1, examining symmetric cases from an ex ante perspective is probably the most compelling perspective to adopt (and it is one under which everyone is necessarily made worse off by any deviation from the prescriptions of welfare economics). In asymmetric cases such as the one considered in the text here, the only individuals who, ex ante, will prefer different sanctions from those optimal under welfare economics are potential criminals who stand to gain personally from their crimes but would find crime unattractive if the level of punishment were sufficiently high.

56. Our point is also more general than our particular example suggests in that, whenever the probability of imposition of sanctions is less than one (as it usually is, in fact; see, for example, Robinson and Darley (1997, 461 table 1), giving statistics), the fair sanction equal to the harm done will not deter bad acts that would be deterred by higher sanctions.

Of course, if the fair sanction exceeds harm, deterrence will be greater, but there will still be a problem when the probability of imposing sanctions is sufficiently low (which is often the case, see ibid., though, of course, less often than the probability simply being less than one). We also note that when the probability is fairly high, a fair sanction significantly in excess of harm can cause other problems (such as in our variation in subsection 4, in which some innocent individuals are punished by mistake).

Then, everything we said about the fair sanction of 100 will continue to be true, although to a lesser extent. The number of undeterred harmful acts might be 200 rather than 1,000, so the needless harm and avoidable costs of imposing sanctions will each be correspondingly lower, but the basic point remains: giving weight to the retributive notion of fairness will be detrimental, to an extent that increases with the weight accorded to fairness.

(i) *Effects on the Well-Being of Different Groups.* Now let us examine in more detail the logic of our claim that exclusive weight should be given to effects on individuals' well-being and attempt to understand better the essence of retributive justice.[57] First, it is useful to compare the well-being of different groups of individuals under the fair sanction and under the sanction chosen under welfare economics. There are three groups of interest in the present setting: noncriminals, criminals who are caught when the sanction is fair, and criminals who are not caught when the sanction is fair. Members of the first group, noncriminals, are worse off when the sanction is fair. When the sanction of 100 is used instead of the sanction of 400, noncriminals as a group suffer harm of 100,000 from the 1,000 offenses that could have been prevented, and they pay 50,000 in taxes to cover the social cost of punishing the 250 criminals who are caught.[58] Both of these costs are avoided entirely when the sanction is 400. The second group, criminals who are caught, are also worse off when the sanction is fair. When the sanction is 100 and they are caught, they suffer a sanction of 100, which by assumption exceeds their benefit from committing the crime. By contrast, if the sanction is 400, they are deterred, so they suffer no sanctions.[59] Members of the third group, criminals who are not caught, are better off when the sanction is fair, because when the sanction is 100 they obtain gains from their crimes and suffer no sanction, but when the sanction is 400 they obtain no gains because they are deterred.

In other words, the actual consequence of fair punishment is to make all individuals worse off except for the criminals who are not caught. Thus, to justify the fair sanction, a proponent must provide reasons why it is so-

57. Though we will use the figures from our original example, it should be clear from the preceding paragraph that the qualitative nature of the analysis would be the same as long as some weight were given to fairness in setting the sanction.

58. Actually, a small proportion of these costs will be borne by the 1,000 criminals, but this fact does not affect the basic point.

59. This second group is worse off only from an ex post perspective. As we explain below, from an ex ante perspective, the second and third groups are indistinguishable, and they are better off under a fair sanction of 100 because this sanction is sufficiently low to preserve the expected profitability of their wrongful acts.

cially better to make noncriminals and criminals who are caught worse off in order to improve the situation of criminals who go scot-free. This difficulty in justifying fair punishment is basic, for it arises whenever deterrence is cost-effective but is not accomplished by the fair sanction. Moreover, this fundamental problem with the retributive conception of fairness arises even if the analyst applies a mixed view, under which weight is also given to welfare in setting sanctions. As long as any weight is given to the conception of fair punishment and, accordingly, a lower sanction is employed in this setting, the underlying question remains: Why should it be deemed socially desirable to make all noncriminals worse off in order to provide a smaller benefit to criminals by preserving the profitability of some crimes?[60] This question seems all the more perplexing when one considers that the retributive theory that requires punishment to be set at a level that preserves the profitability of these crimes is simultaneously a theory that condemns them as morally wrong.[61]

The foregoing example and discussion make concrete the true nature of the retributive theory presented in section B. Under this theory, the harm caused by criminals to innocent people and the social costs of imposing punishment are implicitly ignored or, at least, are deemed to be less important than the smaller (possibly much smaller) gains to a subgroup of criminals.[62] Or, as in the case of other fairness theories, it might be more appropriate to characterize retributive justice as a notion under which all such considerations are simply irrelevant. Fair punishment is an end in itself, and one that takes precedence over all other ends (or, under mixed views, fair punishment is at least taken to be independently significant). But what is that end? That is, what is the point of fair punishment in the present context?[63] In

---

60. We also remind the reader that, were we to consider a symmetric setting, giving any weight to a notion of fairness would result in literally everyone being made worse off. See note 55.

61. See subsection B.2.

62. Compare Benn (1958, 329): "[The criminal] must count 'for no more than one.' While we must not lose sight of his welfare altogether, we are not bound to treat him as our sole legitimate concern."

63. Retributive theory holds that criminals—despite having violated society's rules by committing wrongful acts—deserve only a particular, fair level of punishment. That is, even though criminals are understood to have no right to commit their crimes in the first place, they simultaneously are understood to have a right not to be punished by more than the fair amount if they do. The question we are pursuing in the text is *why* such a right should be deemed to exist when its only consequence is to preserve the opportunity for some individuals to benefit through criminal acts at a greater cost to all other (innocent) individuals in society. To put the point another way, the question is why a sanction that preserves the profitability

order to determine if any plausible answer to this basic question can be found, we now examine our example from another perspective and then consider the literature on retributive justice.

(ii) Actual Imposition of Unfair Punishment under the Two Approaches. Given that a central requirement of the retributive view is that unfair punishment not be imposed, we now consider more closely the difference between applying a sanction of 100 and applying a sanction of 400 from the perspective of the fair treatment of criminals (as opposed to the well-being of all individuals).[64]

First, if society employs the sanction of 400 that is optimal under welfare economics rather than the fair one of 100, will any criminals be unfairly punished? The answer is no. For when the sanction is 400, every potential criminal is deterred, so that no one suffers the unfair sanction of 400. In other words, by ignoring deterrence, the fairness view fails to consider that under the unfair sanction of 400 there are no actual instances of unfairness because sanctions are never in fact imposed. (We discuss situations in which the high sanction will sometimes turn out to be imposed in subsections 3 and 4, below, where we explain that the qualitative character of our conclusion does not change.)

Note as well that the only real sense in which potential criminals are treated poorly when the sanction is 400 is that they are deterred from committing a crime that they would find it in their self-interest to commit were they under the regime with the fair punishment. But that potential criminals are discouraged from committing wrongful acts can hardly qualify as an injustice to them.[65] Retributivists do not focus on the fact that the manner in which their notion of fairness may protect wrongdoers is by preserving the profitability of their wrongful conduct.

---

of a wrongful act should be deemed more fair than a sanction that eliminates its profitability. The literature—as we note in section B and discuss further below—does not supply a plausible reason, and we do not see how one could be grounded in this basic feature of retributive theory.

64. The arguments we are about to make are examples of the point stressed in subsection B.2 that retributivists tend not to take into account how punishment affects the number of instances of unfair punishment.

65. This characterization may seem sharp, but it is in a sense an understatement in the setting under consideration. After all, the only other effects of pursuing fairness are to harm innocent individuals and to make them pay additional taxes to finance the punishment of undeterred criminals. These concerns, which seem to be ignored under the retributive conception of fairness, hardly lend appeal to the notion. See also note 55, showing that, in a symmetric setting, everyone is worse off with fair punishment.

Second, if the sanction is set at the fair level of 100, is it really true that criminals are fairly treated? The answer in our example is that only a minority of them are. Under the sanction of 100, 250 criminals do suffer the fair sanction of 100. It is also true, however, that 750 criminals escape punishment. This result, of course, is unfair: When a person commits a wrong and ought to suffer a sanction of 100 but suffers none, the situation is unjust under the retributive notion, which holds that justice requires the punishment of those who commit wrongful acts.[66] It is peculiar, then, for retributivists to insist that the sanction should not exceed the fair ideal of 100 regardless of how much unfairness results with regard to those who go scot-free.[67] Recall, moreover, that under the unfair sanction of 400, no one, rather than 750 people, receives unfair treatment. Therefore, when one considers the unfairness surrounding the punishment of all the criminals who commit the wrongful act when the sanction is 100, one should be troubled. The fairness view, on its own terms, seems erroneously constrained as it only considers the 250 individuals who are caught and ignores the 750 who are not.[68]

66. See notes 9, 41, 68.

67. Note that the fairness view that the sanction should be 100 seemingly applies no matter how many people would escape sanctions, and thus receive unfairly little—namely 0—punishment for their wrongs. The view would hold, for instance, if only 1 person would be caught and 1 million would escape, or, apparently, if none would be caught and all would escape.

68. We do not think that a retributivist could reasonably argue that there is no injustice involved when criminals go scot-free because society had no immediate opportunity to punish them. Such a position seems prima facie unappealing given the purported rationale for the retributive view because, whether a criminal escapes or is caught but not punished, he has committed a wrong and has not experienced punishment.

Moreover, society exercises control over the probability of capture. This leads to two observations. On one hand, it means that if society relaxed its efforts to catch criminals, more would escape, and in principle all would escape punishment if society made no effort to capture them. Thus, the view that fairness comes into play only with respect to the criminals who are in fact captured leads to the reductio ad absurdum that a system of justice in which no criminals are caught would be perfectly fair, and all that matters is that the punishment on the books is fair. Indeed, when one allows for mistakes in applying actual punishment, this regime of complete nonenforcement is the only scheme of punishment that would be entirely fair. On the other hand, because society can increase its ability to catch criminals by devoting resources to that task, it is evident that, stepping back to the social decision about enforcement effort, the failure to punish more criminals because they are not caught may be considered failure to punish when society really does have an opportunity to punish.

Thus, the argument that no unfairness results when criminals escape capture and therefore are not punished is difficult to maintain under retributive theory. See also notes 9 and 41, discussing further whether the retributive view requires or merely authorizes the imposition of punishment. To our knowledge, this issue is not addressed directly in the literature on retributive theory, so we cannot be sure how retributivists in fact would deal with the matter.

(iii) Comments on the Literature. When we examine the literature on fair punishment, we do not find any analysis that addresses the difficulties that we have just described. As we explain in subsection B.1, retributive theorists usually speak of the underlying justification for punishment in essentially conclusory terms, if they address it at all. Even though much of this literature is concerned with the possibility of excessive punishment and is critical of attention to deterrence—that is, it purports to be concerned primarily with the case in which one should, under retributive theory, sacrifice deterrence to avoid unfairly high punishment—it does not consider in a sustained way the simple type of situation that we examine here, which is a natural setting in which to consider the conflict between fair punishment and deterrence.[69] It seems that retributivists have not appreciated the direct implications of their own theory.[70] If they did,

69. Although raising sanctions sufficiently above the fair level achieves complete deterrence in the example under consideration—so that there never is any problem with the actual imposition of excessive punishment—our conclusions still have force (and are sometimes even stronger) in variations of the paradigm case in which punishment is in fact imposed, as we discuss in subsections 3 and 4.

70. A few commentators have noted that, due to low probabilities of punishment, the insistence that punishment not exceed the level that is proportionate to the crime may result in the sorts of effects that we identify, which, even under retributive theories, would be viewed as involving injustice and thus be problematic. See Goldman (1979, article entitled "The Paradox of Punishment"), referring, among other things, to deterrable crimes that violate people's rights, and observing that higher punishments may minimize violations of rights, but emphasizing that rights may not simply be aggregated under retributive theory; and Wertheimer (1975). In response to this problem, Alexander argues that criminals are not treated unjustly if they are on notice that punishment may be high, because their decision to engage in wrongful acts waives any rights they might have to better treatment. Furthermore, he claims that allowing such waiver is appropriate in respecting criminals' autonomy. See L. Alexander (1980, 208–19). Goldman and Wertheimer reject this way of addressing the problem because they recognize that it eliminates any role for retributive theory in determining the just level of punishment. See Goldman (1979, 55): "In general, having warned someone that he would be treated unjustly is no justification for then doing so. . . ."; and Wertheimer (1975, 415–16). Indeed, Alexander states this conclusion explicitly. See L. Alexander (1980, 214) (emphasis omitted): "When 'punishment' of criminals is in pursuance of the enterprise of prevention, it does not conflict with but rather supersedes the enterprise of retribution and the latter's principle of proportionality." He also describes Goldman's argument as amounting to mere assertion. See ibid. (221–22 n.18). But Alexander does not explain what is left of retributive theory. In the end, Goldman and Wertheimer believe that they have identified an important problem within retributive theory, but have not yet discovered a solution. See Goldman (1979, 57–58), inquiring into possible ways out of the dilemma, such as raising deterrence in other ways and attacking the underlying causes of crime, but concluding that "the moral problem defined here would remain, though perhaps in less acute form"; and Wertheimer (1975, 421), concluding his article with the statement: "I trust that to demonstrate the intransigence of the obstacles to the development of an adequate theory of penalties represents a form of philosophical progress." *(continued)*

we are uncertain whether they would wish to adhere to their beliefs about fair punishment, implying such conclusions as that in our example—that it is a more just state of affairs for 1,000 crimes to be committed and for 750 criminals to escape punishment than for no crimes to be committed and for no one to escape punishment or to be unfairly punished. (As suggested by our earlier discussion, this question also must be addressed by those who hold a mixed view, under which the same sort of result is favored, only to a lesser extent.)

We should note that we do see one way that the literature on retributive conceptions of fairness can be at least partially reconciled with the conclusions of welfare economics, thus minimizing both the perverse effects with regard to individuals' well-being and the implications that seem unjust even on retributivists' own terms. In prior writing, retributivists have adopted an ex post perspective: They take the commission of a crime as a given,[71] and they insist that punishment should, at the time that sanctions are to be imposed, be set equal to the harm done (or bear some appropriate proportion to it). Suppose, however, that retributivists were to take an ex ante perspective and to ask what level of sanction would result in an *expected* punishment equal to the gravity of an offense. Arguably, this perspective is consistent with the spirit of retributivist thought because it imposes on every wrongdoer an expected punishment equal to the punishment that is deemed to fit the wrongful act in question.[72] Were retributivists to adopt this approach, they

---

Wertheimer notes the absurdity of the proportionality requirement for difficult-to-detect property crimes. See Wertheimer (1975, 420), noting that *lex talionis* would allow a television thief to retain all the stolen television sets from crimes that were not detected, because it would only punish the criminal by taking away a single television set for each crime that was detected. Furthermore, he observes that the original principle of *lex talionis* seems to have been abandoned in the Bible for such cases: "'If a man shall steal an ox or a sheep, and kill it, or sell it, he shall restore five oxen for an ox, and four sheep for a sheep.'" Ibid., quoting *Exodus* 22:1.

71. In addition, as our discussion reveals, they also implicitly assume that the criminal is caught, or restrict their analysis to those who are caught, ignoring those who escape.

72. Indeed, one presumes that the potential criminal, when contemplating whether to commit a crime, takes an ex ante view that accounts for the probability of punishment. Furthermore, because the perspective of the criminal is what many retributivists emphasize, see, for example, Pincoffs (1966, chapter 1), one might argue that the ex ante view of punishment is entirely appropriate. Nevertheless, the suggestion that punishment should be more severe when its imposition is less than certain is generally understood to be in "flat opposition to retributivism." Ibid. (19). See Bedau (1977, 53): "[A] retributive theory is necessarily backward-looking in its orientation to punishment."; and Wertheimer (1975, 405), stating that "the appropriate severity of punishment is always to be determined by looking backward to the characteristics of the criminal act and/or the criminal," addressing punishments that are scaled up to reflect the probability of being caught, and finding such punishments to be contrary to retributive theory.

would find that the fair punishment would often comport with the punishment that is best under welfare economics. In our example, for instance, the regime with an actual punishment of 400 and a probability of sanctions of 25 percent would be considered fair because the expected punishment, which is 100, fits the crime. Moreover, from this ex ante perspective, the regime with an actual punishment of 100 would not be considered fair, but rather unfair, as it produces an expected punishment of only 25. Thus, in our example, such an ex ante retributive view would be aligned with welfare economics. However, the ex ante retributive view is, as we said, inconsistent with the perspective adopted by retributivists and, in any case, would not eliminate, but only reduce, the conflict between fairness and welfare economics.[73]

Finally, we observe that the notion that punishment should be proportional to the gravity of an offense does make some sense as a crude proxy principle if the purpose of the legal system is to promote individuals' well-being. All else being equal, greater harms tend to warrant greater sanctions. The reason is that the social value of any deterrence (or incapacitation or rehabilitation) achieved through punishment is greater when the harm is greater; hence, when harm is greater, it will usually make sense for society to incur greater costs of punishment in order to prevent harm.[74] To reinforce

73. For instance, under welfare economics, the optimal punishment might be lower than the expected harm, possibly zero, because of the high costs of imposing punishment, whereas the ex ante fairness perspective would suggest that punishment always equal expected harm. Consider an example in which a wrongful act is not very harmful and would not be committed by many individuals in the absence of legal sanctions, but most of those who would commit the act are not deterrable (see our discussion of undeterrable individuals in subsection 3). The ex ante retributive view would insist that expected punishment equal the harm caused. Given our assumptions, this sanction—in contrast to no sanction at all—may well make everyone worse off. Innocent individuals suffer more from having to pay taxes to fund the punishment scheme than they would have suffered from any harm that it deters (which, recall, was negligible), and the small group of prospective (undeterrable) criminals is, of course, also worse off. Compare Ten (1991, 369), discussing a case in which imposing the level of punishment required by retributive theory causes an increase in crime and asking: "For whose benefit is punishment to be instituted? Surely not for the benefit of law-abiding citizens who run an increased risk of being victims of crime. Why should innocent people suffer for the sake of dispensing retributive justice?"

74. In commenting on Ross's belief that utilitarianism is unable to account for a requirement that punishment be proportional to the offense, Rawls points out that utilitarians' arguments about the proper level of punishment do tend to imply proportionality. See Rawls (1955, 12–13 n.14). Indeed, Bentham himself spoke in the language of proportionality. See Bentham ([1781] 1988, 70): "In proportion as an act tends to disturb that happiness, in proportion as the tendency of it is pernicious, will be the demand it creates for punishment." Rawls does not, however, emphasize those of Bentham's arguments, such as the need to raise

this conclusion, consider a world wherein the level of punishment is unrelated to the magnitude of harm. In particular, suppose that some very harmful acts are subject to low sanctions and some acts causing little harm are subject to very high sanctions. Then, the more harmful acts will be inadequately deterred, and the less harmful acts will be excessively deterred (in the sense of greater deterrence than is justified by the costs of achieving it).[75]

However, setting the punishment in proportion to the gravity of an offense is only a crude proxy device, rather than a sound ultimate standard, for determining punishment for the obvious reason that the gravity of an offense is but one factor relevant to setting punishment so as to promote individuals' well-being. We have emphasized that the probability of detecting and punishing a type of act is important as well.[76] Discussion of our next topic reinforces this conclusion.

2. Variation of the Paradigm Case: Different Crimes

For simplicity, we focus above on a case involving one type of crime. The principle of fairness that punishment be proportional to the wrongfulness of a crime not only implies what the punishment should be for a particular type of crime, but also implies that the magnitude of punishment should increase with the gravity of wrongdoing as between different crimes. This aspect of proportionality and fair punishment raises essentially the same conflict with welfare economics as that which we have just examined.

To illustrate, let us modify our example from the last subsection and suppose that there is a second type of crime, that it results in double the harm, 200, and that—unlike the first type of crime—it would be detected

---

sanctions when the probability of punishment is low, that may lead to violations of proportionality. See Bentham ([1781] 1988, 183–84). Yet Bentham himself was explicit about the relationship between the principle of proportionality and complicating factors. See, for example, ibid. (178–79), stating that "the rules or canons by which the proportion of punishments to offences is to be governed" must be subservient to the objects of punishment: preventing all offenses, preventing the worst offenses, keeping down the mischief of offenses, and minimizing costs.

75. Another reason for punishment to rise with the gravity of the act—sometimes called "marginal deterrence"—is that, if a person is not deterred from committing a wrongful act, we would at least like to furnish him with a reason to do less harm rather than more. For example, we would like a person who kidnaps someone not to kill the kidnap victim. If the sanction for kidnapping alone is lower than that for kidnapping plus murdering the kidnap victim, the kidnapper will have an incentive to refrain from murdering his victim. See, for example, Bentham ([1781] 1988, 178, 181) and Stigler (1970, 533).

76. Another significant factor is the extent to which raising sanctions deters crime, a point we note in subsection 3.

and punished with certainty. The fair punishment for this act we suppose to be 200, equal to the harm from the act (just as we assumed that the fair punishment for the act that caused harm of 100 was 100). But this punishment happens also to be the welfare-maximizing punishment for the act: When the sanction is 200, all crimes will be deterred because the sanction is certain;[77] moreover, as all crimes will be deterred, no punishment will actually be imposed.

Employing the fair punishment for each act does result in proportionality with regard to the two acts: The ratio of the gravity of the offenses (two to one) equals that of the punishments. The welfare-maximizing punishments for the two crimes are not, however, in proportion to their harmfulness: The best punishment for the crime that causes harm of 100 is 400, whereas the best punishment for the crime that causes harm of 200 is only 200; hence, the crime that causes twice the harm results in half the punishment. Thus, welfare-maximizing punishments may violate the principle of proportionality as it applies to different crimes.

Suppose that society adheres to the principle of proportionality, applying a sanction of 100 to the crime that causes harm of 100 and a sanction of 200 to the crime that causes harm of 200.[78] Then, the analysis would be precisely the same as in the preceding subsection with regard to the lower-harm crime: Innocent individuals are often victimized, society spends significant resources on punishment, and the only individuals who gain are criminals who commit this type of crime and escape sanctions. For the crime causing harm of 200, the fair sanction is the same as the one that best promotes individuals' well-being, so nothing further need be said.

The consideration of different crimes, each of which may be associated with a different probability of punishment, further illustrates the manner in which fair sanctions may differ from those that promote welfare. The underlying analysis is essentially the same as that when we consider a single act.[79]

---

77. As before, we assume that individuals' benefits are less than the harm.

78. Another way that society could maintain proportionality between the punishments for the two acts would be to apply the welfare-maximizing sanction of 400 to the first act and a sanction of 800 to the second act. Of course, neither punishment would fit the crime. Moreover, this scheme may not maximize welfare because the high punishment for the second act (800 rather than 200) will generate additional social costs in some situations, such as when not all individuals can plausibly be deterred or when there are inevitable mistakes in applying punishment. See subsections 3 and 4.

79. We just replicate the analysis of a single act for each of the acts. Other complications arise when there are multiple crimes that may be committed—such as those involving marginal deterrence, see note 75, and the fact that, when one also considers how the probability of detection is set, there may be interdependencies among offenses (raising the probability

Likewise, our earlier point about adopting an ex ante retributivist perspective applies here as well: Expected sanctions under the welfare-maximizing regime, which are 100 and 200 (rather than 400 and 200), comport with proportionality, whereas the expected sanctions when punishment is fair, which are 25 and 200 (rather than 100 and 200), do not. In addition, our earlier point about retributive conceptions of fairness serving as a crude proxy for advancing social welfare continues to be true: All else being equal, punishment generally should be greater for more harmful acts; thus, if the probabilities of punishment for the two acts were the same, the welfare-maximizing sanctions would rise proportionally with the harm.[80]

Much of the literature on retributive justice addresses the principle of proportionality, but most does not confront the points that we consider here. A few writers, however, have recognized the conundrums posed for retributive conceptions of fairness by the possibility that the probability of apprehension may vary among acts, but they do not present solutions within retributive theory; nor do they take up directly the subject of whether retributive justice or a concern for individuals' well-being should provide the basis for setting levels of punishment.[81]

3. Variation of the Paradigm Case: Imperfect Deterrence

Here we show that our basic analysis and conclusions hold when we consider a more realistic and complex setting in which deterrence is imperfect and, accordingly, some individuals will suffer sanctions even when the sanction for a crime is set at the level that is best under welfare economics. Perfect deterrence generally will not be achieved because, among other factors, some actors may regard the probability of capture as very low, may not find the prospect of punishment very distasteful, or may act in the heat of the moment to pursue a high perceived gain.[82]

We can modify our initial example from subsection 1 to illustrate the possibility of imperfect deterrence. Assume that it continues to be true that

---

of catching speeders may raise the probability of detecting drunk drivers because the same patrolling officers may observe both offenses). But the fundamental nature of the conflict between fairness and welfare economics is unaffected.

80. The probability of apprehension is not the only factor ignored by the standard retributive view. As we noted previously, there are other factors that may vary, in which case sanctions proportionate to harm may no longer be welfare maximizing.

81. See note 70, discussing the literature.

82. Also, for various reasons, it may not be feasible or desirable to set sanctions and the probability of punishment sufficiently high to deter all potential offenders, even in the absence of the complications identified in the text.

1,000 individuals are not deterred by the fair penalty of 100,[83] and suppose further that some of them, say 40 individuals, are essentially undeterrable.[84] This variation does not change the situation under the fair penalty of 100: The costs of imposing sanctions (borne by society and by criminals) would continue to be 75,000, and harm, 100,000 (minus the lesser benefits to the criminals themselves).

When the sanction is 400, however, not all criminals will be deterred as they were before. Now, 40 individuals will be undeterred, and they will cause harm of 4,000 (and receive benefits of a lesser amount). In addition, of these 40 people, 25 percent, or 10, will be caught; because each will suffer the sanction of 400, additional costs of 12,000 will be borne (800 by society to punish each person and 400 by each person, for a sum of 1,200 per person).

It should be clear that the evaluation of the legal rules is essentially the same as before, with the sanction of 400 being superior to the fair sanction of 100. Although the sanction of 400 no longer completely deters, and thus involves total social costs of 16,000, it is still greatly preferable to the sanction of 100, which involves costs of 175,000.[85]

As we did in the paradigm case, we can also consider the well-being of different groups of people under each of the two sanctions. Noncriminals are worse off when the sanction is fair because they suffer harm from 1,000 offenses rather than from only 40 and have to pay taxes sufficient to support punishment of 250 individuals rather than of only 10. Criminals who would be deterred by the sanction of 400 but are not deterred by the sanction of 100 and are caught are also made worse off by the sanction of 100. Criminals who are not caught are, as before, beneficiaries of the fair sanction. Additional beneficiaries now are the criminals who would not be deterred by either sanction, for they suffer a sanction of 100 rather than 400. Yet it seems hard to justify deeming the improvement in the position of these two groups of criminals—those who have the luck to get away with their crimes and those who do not react to the threat of punishment—to be socially more important than the substantially greater loss suffered by noncriminals and by the potential criminals who would be deterred by the sanction of 400.

We also emphasize that the familiar criticism of consequentialist analysis

83. We make this assumption for simplicity; implicitly, we are imagining that the undeterrable individuals substitute for individuals who would have been deterred in our original example, but only by the higher sanction of 400.

84. For instance, these individuals might mistakenly perceive the probability of sanctions to be zero.

85. Details concerning the benefits to criminals, which provide a partial offset to the harm from crime but do not affect our conclusions, will not be repeated here. See note 54.

of sanctions—that it views individuals who are punished merely as a means to the end of deterrence[86]—is incorrect, or at least is very misleading. The

86. In a classic expression of this criticism, Kant states:

> Punishment by a court . . . can never be inflicted merely as a means to promote some other good for the criminal himself or for civil society. It must always be inflicted upon him only *because he has committed a crime*. For a human being can never be treated merely as a means to the purposes of another. . . . The law of punishment is a categorical imperative, and woe to him who crawls through the windings of eudaemonism [looking for some advantage to be gained by manipulating the magnitude of punishment]. (Kant [1797] 1996, 105)

See also Armstrong (1961, 484): "If we fix the penalty on a Deterrent principle (*i.e.* What penalty given to this criminal, or class of criminal, will effectively deter others from imitating his crime?) we are using him as a mere means to somebody else's end, and surely Kant was right when he objected to that!"; Benn (1967, 31), noting the criticism that utilitarians need to treat human beings "not as a mere instrument for the promotion of the interests of others"; Dolinko (1992, 1642–45), describing leading retributivists' views; and Greenawalt (1983, 353): "The most fundamental objection [to utilitarianism] is to treating the criminal as a means to satisfy social purposes rather than as an end in himself."

Kant's famous dictum that people (including criminals) should not be used as mere means to ends (their own ends or those of others) has gained wide appeal but, on closer examination, we find it troubling, particularly as it is often applied. We sketch here the reasons that we do not find the Kantian position to raise problems for our argument. First, it is often forgotten that Kant's statement is that people should not be used *merely* as a means to other ends. This qualification is important, for otherwise—if people should not be used at all as means to other ends—one could not employ a worker (say, to build a needed hospital), buy a product or service produced by another, or engage in most other productive activity; indeed, one could not exert effort to grow food even for oneself (given that Kant's imperative also requires that we not use ourselves for our own ends). Thus, the qualification that people should be treated not *merely* as a means but *also* at the same time as an end, seems crucial. See Kant ([1785] 1997, 37): "Now I say that the human being . . . *exists* as an end in itself, *not merely as a means* to be used by this or that will at its discretion; instead he must in all his actions, whether directed to himself or also to other rational beings, always be regarded *at the same time as an end*." (emphasis in original); ibid. (38), restating his injunction in similar language. Once formulated in this manner, the familiar criticism of using criminals as a mere means is no longer applicable to welfare economics (or to most other consequentialist approaches) because, as we explain in the text, the criminal himself is considered important in his own right, in terms of his own well-being, in the assessment of appropriate punishment. See, for example, Hare (1997, chapter 8, entitled "Could Kant Have Been a Utilitarian?"), and Benn (1958, 329): "To look to the consequences does not entail treating the criminal merely as a means to a social end, as critics have asserted; for in weighing advantages and disadvantages, the criminal, too, must 'count for one.' But equally, he must count 'for no more than one'." Dolinko offers a related perspective:

> We would also benefit from admitting frankly, as deterrence theorists, that punishing criminals is a dirty business but the lesser of two evils and thus a sad necessity,

suffering of those who are punished is certainly included in the welfare economic calculus. As has been seen, we tally as a social cost the pain experienced by those who suffer sanctions. Furthermore, this cost is placed on the
same plane as other elements of our evaluation; in particular, criminals'

---

not a noble and uplifting enterprise that attests to the richness and depth of our
moral character. Indeed, I think one could argue that it is the deterrence theorists,
with their utilitarian outlook, who truly "respect" the criminal by acknowledging
that inflicting pain on him is, in itself, *bad,* and not to be done unless it can be
outweighed by its good consequences. (Dolinko 1992, 1656)

See also note 12 in chapter VII, addressing the meaning of respecting "the distinction between
persons."

Second, if this qualification to Kant's maxim is not considered to be sufficient to make
the maxim essentially irrelevant to welfare economics, then it would seem to raise similar
problems for retributive theory. Most attempts under this theory to deny that the criminal
is being used as a mere means have proved to be problematic. Some retributivists seek to
justify punishment as aiding the criminal, but most commentators agree that punishment
does not inevitably benefit a convict, and many suspect that incarceration typically has the
opposite effect. Arguments such as Hegel's that punishment is, in some mystical or metaphori-
cal sense, right for the criminal, see note 11, are difficult to justify and have not gained wide
endorsement even from retributivists. Nothing in the basic command of retributive theory,
that individuals be punished if but only if they have committed a wrongful act, makes their
punishment other than the means to some end. The end may be justice, restoring moral
balance, or some other intangible goal, but it is no less an end. Literally the only way for
punishment to be other than the means to some end is to insist that there is no point to
punishment whatsoever, which hardly seems to capture the thrust of retributive writing. Compare Hume ([1751] 1998, 194): "It appears, that there never was any quality recommended
by any one, as a virtue or moral excellence, but on account of its being *useful,* or *agreeable*
to a man *himself,* or to *others.* For what other reason can ever be assigned for praise or approbation? Or where would be the sense of extolling a *good* character or action, which, at the same
time, is allowed to be *good for nothing?*"; Sidgwick (1907, 394): "It would be a palpable and
violent paradox to set before the right-seeking mind no end except this right-seeking itself. . . ."; and Harsanyi (1958), stating that, for there to be a moral reason to act, there must
as a matter of logic and definition be a presumed purpose.

Third, we doubt that retributivists would insist in a general way that criminals never be
used merely as a means. For example, we doubt that they would say that I could not push
someone who was about to stab me (or someone else) with a knife—bearing in mind that
my pushing surely would be done solely as a means to an end.

Although retributivists often invoke Kant's "means/end" formulation, we have not seen
in this literature a careful discussion of the issues that we raise here. See also Davis (1984b),
stating that philosophers have had difficulty identifying what counts as "using persons" in a
manner that is morally objectionable, observing that, often, they appeal to commonsense
notions, but these notions provide little assistance in defining objectionable "use," and even
less in providing a moral justification for the importance of the concept; and note 106, discussing difficulties with the "doctrine of double effect," one formulation of which involves
attempting to distinguish when people are used as a means from when they are not.

suffering on account of sanctions is treated in the same manner as victims' suffering on account of criminals' wrongful acts. Indeed, under a welfare economic analysis, if the cost of imposing sanctions on criminals is sufficiently large, it may be appropriate to employ a lower sanction—possibly one even lower than the "fair" punishment. This will be true when the savings in punishment costs (which include both the costs borne by those who are punished and the costs borne by society in punishing them) exceed any deterrence benefits.[87]

Retributive analysis differs from analysis under welfare economics, not because the concept of social welfare fails to reflect the suffering of criminals, but rather because retributive notions of fairness implicitly accord far greater weight to the suffering of criminals than to the harm they cause to others.[88] In our example in this subsection, retributivists implicitly place much greater weight on the fact that 10 criminals suffer an excessive punishment of 400 (of which only 300 is unfair, so that the total unfairly applied punishment is 3,000) than they place on the 960 additional instances in which harm is sustained by innocent people (implying 96,000 more harm in aggregate) and the extra costs due to imprisoning 240 more individuals (generating 72,000 in additional costs).[89] An extreme instance of weighting the suffering of criminals over that of the rest of society occurs in our paradigm case, as previously noted. There, the high sanction of 400 achieved complete deterrence, so that the suffering of criminals from the imposition of sanctions was nonexistent, only notional. Yet retributive theories favor the fair punishment of 100 and implicitly ignore the harm done to 1,000 victims and the resulting costs of punishment.[90]

87. For example, if we reduced the sanction from 400 to 390, deterrence might not decrease at all, whereas we would achieve a savings because a lower sanction would be imposed on the 10 individuals who ultimately are sanctioned. Thus, it would be desirable under welfare economics to lower the sanction (at least) to 390. Moreover, if undeterrables are sufficiently numerous and the deterrent effect of high penalties is small, a lower sanction than the fair sanction would be best from the perspective of welfare. Compare note 73, presenting another instance in which the optimal sanction is less than the fair sanction. In this case, insistence on fair punishment may well be to the detriment of both criminals and innocent individuals (who may have to pay more to imprison primarily undeterrable individuals than the amount of any benefit they receive from reduced crime).

88. See Benn (1958, 329), stating that the criminal should count for one but only for one.

89. As we discuss in subsection C.1(e)(ii), the retributivists also implicitly ignore that 750 criminals—those who go scot-free—do not receive fair punishment under the supposedly fair sanction of 100, whereas only 30 criminals escape punishment under the supposedly unfair sanction of 400.

90. The literature on retributive justice emphasizes the desire to be fair to those who are punished, but does not explain why these criminals' situations should be the focus when assessing the overall justice of the state of affairs, and, correspondingly, why the situation of those who are not criminals and who might suffer harm should be ignored.

As before, we also find that the ex ante view is instructive: As we note in subsection 1, the main effect of the retributive view is to preserve the profitability of crime to some potential criminals at a greater expense to their victims and to all who must finance the costs of punishment. It is not clear how this treatment respects the dictum not to use people merely as a means to others' ends, for it could be said that everyone else in society is thus used by criminals when fair punishment is insisted on.[91]

4. Variation of the Paradigm Case: Punishment of the Innocent

We now consider issues raised by the prospect that innocent individuals might be punished. This possibility is very real, of course, due to the inevitable errors that are made by the police in apprehending alleged criminals and by the legal system in verifying their guilt. We now explain why this possibility does not change the essential nature of our analysis or our conclusions about retributive justice and welfare economics. Indeed, it may well lead to an even stronger case against choosing the level of punishment favored under retributive notions of fairness than exists in the paradigm case, in which we assume that innocent individuals are never punished. We also discuss retributivist criticism of consequentialism with regard to punishment of the innocent.

(a) Analysis of a Basic Situation. Consider a variation of our paradigm case in which we suppose that one innocent person is mistakenly punished for every ten guilty people who are punished. In other words, mistakes in the administration of justice result in a certain proportion of innocent people being ensnared along with the guilty. Now recall that when the fair sanction of 100 is imposed, 1,000 people commit the offense and 250 of them are caught and punished. Hence, our new assumption means that along with these 250 guilty people, 25 innocent people are also punished. If instead the sanction is 400, then there is complete deterrence—no one commits the offense, so there are no crimes to be investigated and prosecuted, and thus no one is punished. In particular, this outcome implies that no innocent people are mistakenly punished.

Hence, the superiority of the sanction of 400 over the fair sanction of 100 is even greater than before, due to the enhanced value of deterrence: Not only does deterrence reduce the amount of harm done, but deterrence

---

91. A few retributivists have acknowledged this problem with their theory but have not offered a solution. One writer (L. Alexander, discussed in note 70) suggests that we view the criminal as having waived his rights when he chooses to commit a crime, a voluntary choice that we should respect. Of course, crime victims do not have this same choice; hence, there seems to be a stronger sense in which, from this Kantian perspective, the victims are being used as a mere means, independently of the course they would will for themselves.

also reduces the number of innocent people who are mistakenly punished. Deterrence produces this additional benefit because it reduces the number of offenses and thus the number of investigations, some of which lead to mistaken convictions of innocent people.

Consider, as we do in subsection 1, how the two different levels of punishment affect different groups of people. First, under the fair punishment, there is more crime and thus there are more victims: 1,000 harmful acts as opposed to zero. Second, under the fair punishment, there are more erroneously punished people than under the punishment of 400: 25 innocent people are mistakenly sanctioned instead of none. Third, there is more punishment meted out, and thus greater social costs incurred, when the punishment is fair: 275 people are punished rather than none. It would be peculiar to maintain that the situation is more just under the fair punishment— which, as we have just stated, results in more harm, more punishment of the innocent, and more punishment overall—than under the welfare-maximizing punishment of 400. And it would be especially peculiar to suggest that the retributive conception of fairness should be favored out of a special concern to avoid punishment of the innocent when insisting on the level of punishment deemed to be fair under retributive theory is precisely the cause of many innocent people being punished.

Another way of expressing the superiority of a sanction of 400 to the fair sanction of 100 is to observe that, ex ante, noncriminals would unanimously prefer to be subject to the sanction of 400. The reason is that then they would never suffer harm, never have to pay for the imposition of sanctions, and never face a risk of mistakenly bearing sanctions, whereas if the sanction were 100, they would suffer harm, have to pay for the imposition of sanctions, and face a risk of bearing sanctions. As in our prior subsections, the only individuals who benefit from a regime in which there is fair punishment are potential criminals who expect to profit from criminal acts that would be rendered unprofitable if punishment were set higher. The only difference from our prior examples is that they now benefit not only at the expense of victims of crime and taxpayers, but also at the expense of innocent people who are punished by mistake.

Although in this simple example no individuals are mistakenly punished when the optimal sanction of 400 is employed, in general that will not be so; some innocent people will be punished when optimal sanctions are used. But the general tendency of deterrence to reduce the punishment of the innocent remains. For example, if we consider the variation in subsection 3 in which 40 individuals are not deterred when the sanction is 400 and 25 percent of them, 10 in all, are punished, then it would be the case that 1 innocent person would be punished, which compares favorably with the 25 innocent people who are punished when the fair sanction of 100 is employed.

(If an even greater number of individuals were undeterred under the higher sanction, more innocent people would be punished under it. It would remain true, however, that to the extent that the higher sanction does deter more crime, fewer innocent people will be punished as a result.)

In sum, introducing the possibility that innocent people will be punished reinforces the appeal of assessing law enforcement policy under welfare economics. We also observe that, as in our prior discussions of retributive conceptions of fairness, our reasoning applies to mixed views under which weight is also given to effects on individuals' well-being. Recall our example in which a mixed view led one to choose a sanction of 250—a compromise between a welfare-optimal sanction of 400 and the fair sanction of 100—and the result was that 200 crimes occurred. Because the punishment rate was 25 percent, 50 criminals would be punished. In the present setting, such a regime would result in the punishment of 5 innocent individuals. Thus, as long as some weight is placed on retributive justice when setting sanctions, mixed views produce each of the detrimental effects of retributive justice.

We further note that the prospect of punishing innocent people, even though it does not upset (but actually strengthens) the argument for applying the sanction that previously seemed best under welfare economics, may nevertheless call for some adjustments to punishment policy. That is, if one follows the prescriptions of welfare economics, society may be able to achieve a better outcome than that in our example. First, although the sanction of 400 is clearly superior to the fair sanction of 100, a different sanction may be even better; in particular, it may be that a lower sanction should be employed. For instance, if a moderate reduction in sanctions would barely dilute deterrence, there would be little loss from lowering the sanction but there would be a gain in that punishment costs with regard to the innocent persons who are mistakenly punished would be reduced. (This point obviously applies only in the realistic variation in which not everyone is deterred.) Second, when there is a problem with punishing the innocent, greater social resources should be spent increasing the accuracy of the legal system, thereby reducing the rate at which innocent people are punished. (In contrast, as we note in subsection B.2, it is unclear under the retributive theory of fair punishment whether the number of unfair outcomes matters at all. Furthermore, if it does matter, the theory does not tell us how to decide what level of social resources should be devoted to addressing the problem.)

It is worth emphasizing that, under welfare economics, the preceding points assume greater significance when the costs of punishing the innocent are higher than those of punishing the guilty, and indeed that seems to be the case. First, innocent people who are punished suffer the ordinary disutility of punishment and, quite possibly, an additional cost because they know they are being punished wrongly. Likewise, friends and relatives may also suffer more on this account.[92] Second, the population at large may suffer out of sympathy for the plight of the innocent and also may experience anxiety due to the possibility that they themselves might be wrongly convicted.[93] Third, deterrence is diluted by punishing the innocent.[94]

We can thus see that, under welfare economics, the prospect of punishing the innocent is taken very seriously, and punishment of the innocent is understood to be more costly than punishment of the guilty (which not only does not result in the aforementioned costs but also tends directly to reduce crime, through deterrence and incapacitation). Thus, an analyst employing welfare economics acts with a heavy heart when proposing a system of punishment that may involve any punishment of the innocent.[95]

(b) Comments on the Literature. Retributivists, as we have indicated, suggest that the issue of punishment of the innocent leads to an important (and some think decisive) criticism of consequentialist approaches such as welfare economics.[96] Their argument essentially involves two components. First, (some) retributivists hold that punishment of the innocent is absolutely impermissi-

92. See, for example, Sprigge (1965, 278–79).

93. Compounding this fear is the fact that systems in which punishment of the innocent can more readily occur by accident will also tend to be systems in which abuse is more likely, such as by the prosecution of political opponents. The problem of abuse also helps to explain why it is likely to be valuable to have a strong social norm against punishing the innocent. See note 112.

94. Deterrence depends on the incremental penalty for wrongdoing, and punishing the innocent reduces the benefit of avoiding wrongdoing and thus makes wrongdoing itself relatively more attractive. It also seems plausible that a higher rate of punishment of the innocent will often go hand in hand with a lower rate of punishment of the guilty.

95. Compare Smart (1965, 347–48), emphasizing that when a utilitarian favors what seems to be unjust punishment, misery results and is justified only as the lesser of two evils. This problem is not, of course, unique to punishment. A person who recommends that a badly needed hospital be built must recognize that such projects entail serious risks of construction accidents, in which some innocent people might be seriously injured or die.

96. In particular, retributivists usually challenge those who favor deterrence (which is not itself a justificatory theory but rather a particular effect of punishment that is important under most consequentialist theories) or utilitarians in particular. See, for example, Pincoffs (1966, 34), stating that punishment of the innocent "is so unwelcome that it constitutes one of the strongest arguments against the utilitarian theories of ethics in general"; Benn (1967, 31): "The dilemma of utilitarianism . . . is that it justifies punishing innocent people. . . ."; Greenawalt (1983, 353): "[T]he most damaging aspect of the attack is that utilitarianism admits the possibility of justified punishment of the innocent."; Philips (1985, 389), noting that the point that utilitarianism would sometimes allow punishment of the innocent "is often taken to be a sufficient refutation of Utilitarian theories of punishment and of Utilitarianism in general"; and Wertheimer (1977, 45), stating that the "classic objection to utilitarian theories of punishment is that they would justify the intentional punishment of the innocent."

ble.[97] Second, they note that consequentialist approaches can, in principle, endorse regimes that involve some punishment of the innocent, because consequentialists are willing to make tradeoffs. Therefore, retributivists conclude, consequentialist approaches must be rejected.

In light of our preceding analysis, it is apparent that this argument is highly problematic even on its own terms. The reason is that retributivists advancing the argument have failed to consider whether the second step of the argument applies to retributivism as well as to consequentialism. As we have just seen, in any realistic situation—in which some punishment of the innocent is unavoidable—retributivist punishment will in fact involve punishing the innocent. Indeed, in plausible cases, more innocent people are punished under fair sanctions than when sanctions are set at levels favored under welfare economics.[98]

Given that punishment of the innocent is inevitable, retributivist theorists have two choices. One is that they can insist on their first point, that punishment of the innocent is absolutely impermissible. The immediate implication is that, in the actual world in which we live, any legal system that metes out punishment must be rejected because it will sometimes result in punishment of the innocent. This ramification of the commonly expressed retributivist argument does not seem to have been noticed by most retributivists.[99] Moreover, abandonment of punishment would be greatly at odds

97. See, for example, Philips (1985, 389): "It is widely held by moral philosophers that it is always wrong to punish the innocent."

98. Ezorsky has remarked—in a hypothetical example involving a "crime cure pill"—that there could exist a world in which there would be less punishment of the innocent under utilitarianism than under retributivism. See Ezorsky (1972, xviii–xix). But, to our knowledge, it has not been recognized that retributivism may well result in more punishment of the innocent in the paradigmatic (and realistic) case in which fair punishment under retributive justice comes at some cost in terms of deterrence, indeed, in precisely the case that retributivists have long emphasized in their general discussions of competing justifications of punishment. In fact, very few even raise the possibility that the retributive justification for having any punishment at all involves some punishment of the innocent. For exceptions, see the sources cited in note 99.

99. The problem has not, however, gone unrecognized by all commentators:

> Remember these philosophers emphasize that only the guilty may be punished. But no infallible method for determining guilt has ever been devised. Indeed, it is a virtual certainty that honest, reasonable jurors have convicted defendants who appeared guilty but were, in fact, innocent. Thus, as it turns out, the price of a system which punishes the guilty is sacrifice of some innocents. Unless retributivists avoid punishing the guilty, they will be unable to avoid punishing the innocent. (Ezorsky 1972, xviii)

See, for example, Dolinko (1992, 1632–34); Philips (1985, 389): "It is rarely if ever recognized that every criminal justice system will punish some innocent persons."; ibid. (389): "If rights

with a major tenet of retributive theory, which requires punishment as a matter of desert, thereby obligating the state to operate a system that imposes punishment.[100] In other words, retributivists who believe that schemes of punishment can never countenance punishment of the innocent must defend a regime that is tantamount to anarchy and must abandon the central tenet of retributive theory that wrongdoers be punished.

We do not believe, however, that retributivists are forced to go this route, and we suspect that, if the foregoing implications were appreciated, most would take a second path: They would continue to adhere to the core of retributive theory, which demands punishment, but they would relax the requirement that punishment of the innocent may never be permitted.[101] Once this step is taken, however, retributivists would have to make tradeoffs. Different levels of punishment, as we have explained, affect how many innocent people will be punished. Thus, retributivists could no longer maintain that the ideal punishment is the one that best fits the crime, because that level of punishment might entail greater punishment of the innocent than would a higher level. The modified retributivist approach therefore involves a considerable departure from what is generally understood to be the retributive view.[102] More importantly, the departure is one in which the analyst must trade off avoiding punishment of the innocent against other aspects of desirable punishment—whereas the willingness to make this tradeoff was precisely the retributivists' original objection to consequentialism.

It should now be apparent that the difference between retributive theories and consequentialist approaches such as welfare economics with regard to punishment of the innocent is not the one that has been commonly sup-

---

are always trumps, justice requires disbanding the entire criminal justice system."; and Schedler (1980), arguing that retributivists cannot consistently condemn punishment that singles out an innocent person without also condemning all legal punishment. See also L. Alexander (1983), arguing that this problem is not limited to the imposition of capital punishment.

100. For further discussion of variations in the literature on this point and of whether there is a plausible retributivist position under which punishment is not affirmatively called for, see notes 9, 41, and 68.

101. See, for example, L. Alexander (1983), advocating such an approach in order to avoid the implication of stronger retributive theories that no system of punishment could be justified, on account of its inevitable fallibility.

102. We emphasize, as we do in our discussion in subsection B.2, that the need to modify the standard retributive view is *not* an argument that one should compromise in some way between the dictates of retributive justice and a concern for individuals' well-being. Rather, the argument at this point is wholly *within* the retributive theory of justice, as it accepts retributivists' expressed concern about punishment of the innocent as well as their belief that punishment must fit the crime. Admitting only these two elements (while still ignoring individuals' well-being) is sufficient to require making tradeoffs of the sort we describe in the text.

posed, namely, that the former is unwilling to make tradeoffs with regard to punishing the innocent but the latter is willing to do so. Rather, both theories make qualitatively similar tradeoffs. The main difference—and an important one—is what the theories value on the other side of the tradeoff. Under welfare economics, some punishment of the innocent may be tolerated in order to reduce the harm to other innocent individuals caused by wrongful acts. Under retributive theory, some punishment of the innocent may be tolerated in order to approximate more closely an ideal state in which wrongdoers receive fitting punishments. It is this difference that has been our focus throughout section C, and with regard to which we have argued that the welfare economic approach is superior. We also remind the reader that, under welfare economics, any punishment of the innocent that does occur is regarded as a serious cost.[103]

Before concluding our discussion of retributive theorists' concern with punishment of the innocent, we wish to comment on the particular way that their argument usually is expressed. It typically relates to a hypothetical example of the following sort. It is imagined that there is about to be a riot that will cause many deaths because the population is in an uproar about an unsolved crime. Then it is asked whether it would be permissible for the government (through a police officer or a prosecutor) to frame some innocent person in order to avoid the riot, thereby preventing the much greater harm that the riot would create. Retributivists suggest that, yes, such punishment would be permissible under consequentialist theories but, no, it would not be permissible under retributive theories because they oppose all punishment of the innocent. Then it is stated, or left to the reader to see, that this

---

103. Retributive theory may well differ with respect to how the cost of punishing the innocent is measured. Of course, once tradeoffs are admitted, this cost must be measured in some manner. Because retributive theory has not been articulated along the dimension that we are exploring here, we do not know how much negative value would be deemed to attach to punishment of the innocent—that is, how much of it a retributivist would, on reflection, tolerate in order to make punishment more closely fit the crime.

We might suppose that moderate retributivists hold the view that punishment of the innocent may be countenanced, but that their punishment should count more heavily than punishment of the guilty. A possible example is Ross (1929, 205), although he is not explicit about his view on the matter. But welfare economics also places relatively more weight on punishment of the innocent, as we explain in subsection (a). Furthermore, retributivism and welfare economics value the benefits of punishment differently; we cannot determine how much retributivists value the benefits, and, in particular, whether retributivists value them more or less than welfare economics does. Accordingly, it is not possible to say which approach values punishment of the innocent relatively more than the other, and how any valuation difference might vary by context. Compare note 105, indicating that it is not obvious whether the weight given to punishment of the innocent by our intuitions is more or less than the weight given under welfare economics.

contrast is a blow against consequentialist theories because punishing an innocent person grates against our moral intuition.[104]

We have several reactions to such an example.[105] Initially, we find it odd for the retributivist literature to focus on such fanciful hypothetical examples to generate a scenario in which an innocent person might be punished when every actual legal system results in the punishment of some innocent people on a regular basis. As we have explained, when this much more important case of punishing the innocent is considered, the retributivists' argument fails: It either insists that the legal system should be eliminated or the argument must be modified to allow trading off punishment of the

---

104. See, for example, Carritt (1947, 65), using the example of hanging an innocent man when a type of serious crime becomes common and real perpetrators cannot be caught; Hart (1968b, 5–6): "[T]he stock 'retributive' argument is: If [beneficial consequences constitute] the justification of punishment, why not apply it, when it pays to do so, to those innocent of any crime, chosen at random, or to the wife and children of the offender?"; ibid. (11–12): "[In t]he standard example . . . [i]t is supposed that in order to avert some social catastrophe officials of the system fabricate evidence on which [an innocent person] is charged, tried, convicted and sent to prison or death."; Pincoffs (1966, 33–34), describing the argument about punishing the innocent in the traditional debate between retributivists and utilitarians; McCloskey (1965, 255–59), using many variations of this example; and Ross (1929, 205), referring to such a situation.

105. In addition to the arguments presented in the text, there is also a serious difficulty simply in understanding what most retributivists argue. Because, as we explain in subsection B.2, most retributivists in fact hold mixed views under which deviating from fair punishment may be justified by reference to its consequences, this type of example does not really present even a prima facie argument in favor of their theories. The reason is that there is no basis for retributivists' implicit assumption that their own theories, when properly applied, would not approve the punishment of an innocent person in the hypothesized example. Indeed, under most mixed views, such punishment would be deemed proper as long as the benefits were sufficiently high. McCloskey exemplifies this inconsistency. In the same article, he both presents a mixed view (see McCloskey (1965, 251): "[U]njust punishments may, in extreme circumstances, become permissible . . . if a grave evil has to be perpetrated to achieve a very considerable good."), and also argues that utilitarianism is fatally flawed because it would justify framing an innocent person in the extreme case in which this would save others' lives. See ibid. (255–59). See also Sprigge (1965, 270). One might argue that retributive theory still is qualitatively different because it would accord special weight against punishing the innocent in this sort of example on the ground that such punishment is unjust, whereas there is no such special weight against punishing the innocent when welfare is the sole basis for analysis. But the latter part of this argument is wrong because, when welfare is the criterion, there is, as noted, substantial weight placed on avoiding punishment of the innocent generally and, as we explore in the text below, there are additional reasons that punishing the innocent in the setting of the hypothetical example would tend to reduce welfare. Hence, the suggestion that retributive theory (in the mixed form that most advance) is in close accord with our intuition, whereas consequentialist approaches differ substantially from our intuition, is not supported in the first place. See also note 103, discussing the relative weight accorded to punishment of the innocent under retributive theory and under welfare economics.

innocent with other objectives.[106] Moreover, as our previous examples

106. See sources cited in note 99, and Wertheimer (1977, 45): "[W]hatever the importance of [intentional punishment of the innocent] as a counter-example to utilitarianism, [such punishments] are of less general relevance to a theory of punishment than the unintentional punishment of the innocent, or what I shall refer to as *punishment mistakes.*" See also Philips (1985, 390), making an analogous argument with respect to the police, who are explicitly authorized to arrest and put into jail individuals who are merely suspects and thus are assumed by the system to include some innocent people.

Some retributivists might seek to distinguish the state's framing an innocent person, characterized as an act in which the innocent are punished *intentionally,* from the state's adopting a system in which innocent people are punished *incidentally.*

> Every practical system of punishment must admit the possibility that mistakes will lead to innocent persons being punished, but knowingly to punish an innocent person is to violate an independent moral norm. Wrongdoing alone may not be a sufficient basis to justify punishment, but the wrongful act creates a right of society to punish that does not exist with innocent persons. (Greenawalt 1983, 355)

See, for example, L. Alexander (1983, 245), observing that "if knowingly risking punishing the innocent is morally equivalent to knowingly punishing the innocent, *we can never punish anyone,*" but arguing that it is a mistake to equate the two because deliberately framing an innocent person is morally worse than mistakenly convicting an innocent person—relying on Dworkin's essay, discussed below in this note. But see Philips (1985), criticizing this type of argument by suggesting that there is little moral distinction between directly punishing an innocent person and adopting a system that we know will result in punishment of the innocent. This sort of distinction is often discussed under the rubric of the "doctrine of double effect," following Aquinas. The second, or "double" effect from an action refers to a bad consequence, produced as a side-effect, that would be improper for the agent to pursue directly but may, under this doctrine, be caused indirectly. Recent discussions of this and related notions include Kamm (1996), Quinn (1993), Bennett (1981), and G. Dworkin (1987). See also Davis (1984a), identifying the origins of the doctrine in theological ethics and, particularly, in the Catholic tradition, and presenting and criticizing representative arguments; and Foot (1967), arguing that the act/omission distinction better accords with existing moral beliefs than does the doctrine of double effect. In the present context, the import of accepting such a distinction would be that the punishment of innocent people that accompanies the operation of an ordinary legal system would be allowable (a permissible double effect), whereas the state's punishing an innocent individual in the example in the text would remain improper.

Initially, we observe that our subsequent discussion in the text suggests that this distinction is substantially inaccurate in the present setting. Even in the critics' favored hypothetical example, the state as an abstract entity does not punish; rather it is an individual police officer or prosecutor who takes it upon himself to frame the innocent person. But this is exactly how innocent people are sometimes punished in real legal systems. Thus, even if the distinction is coherent and convincing, it does not seem to provide any support for the retributivists' position.

With regard to the merits of the distinction itself, a large literature (some of it cited above) has developed, and we obviously cannot explore it in depth here. Nevertheless, it is worth noting two difficulties that have been identified. The first difficulty is conceptual: Philosophers have had great trouble formally stating the distinction in a coherent manner. The second problem is substantive: Normative arguments justifying the moral relevance of the distinction (if they go beyond appeals to intuitions that themselves cannot be grounded) have been found

illustrate, the level of punishment chosen under welfare economics may

---

lacking or inadequate. See, for example, Dolinko (1992, 1633–34), discussing problems with distinctions associated with the doctrine of double effect in the context of punishing the innocent. Both of these points can be understood by examining the distinction more carefully.

The relevant distinction is often stated as the difference between, on one hand, intending (or, as some say, willing) a consequence in the sense that the result itself is desired and, on the other hand, wishing for something else but knowingly causing the undesirable consequence as an unavoidable by-product. But, of course, the consequentialist who, in the hypothetical example, might ultimately believe that it is better to punish an innocent person no more desires this outcome than the retributivist who favors a criminal justice system that inevitably results in the punishment of some innocent people. Compare Sidgwick (1907, 202), suggesting that "intention" should be taken to include all foreseen undesirable consequences because responsibility should be understood to exist for such consequences whenever clearly chosen or willed. Moreover, determining whether a harmful outcome is part of what is "intended" depends on how the actor's intention is characterized. (Does one intend to kill a bystander in order to prevent a greater wrong, or does one intend to prevent the greater wrong, which has the unavoidable by-product of killing the bystander?) Likewise, what is deemed necessary or incidental depends on arbitrary statements of the actual facts. (In a common example, it is said that bombing a military target is acceptable when it is known that civilians nearby will be killed, because their presence is unnecessary to the outcome, whereas bombing the same civilians to decrease enemy morale is unacceptable. But one could as easily assume that there are in principle many sorts of bombings or other acts that would decrease morale, and it just so happens that only the bombing of civilians happens to be feasible at the moment.)

Alternatively, as Greenawalt suggests in the above passage, perhaps the distinction depends on whether the innocent are punished knowingly (or, perhaps, with foresight). But the retributivist who creates a legal system knows—unless there is stunning willful ignorance—that there is a 99.9999 percent chance that some innocent people will be punished. See Schedler (1980, 188), stating that because officials are aware of the fallibility of humans, "they cannot truly say that they believe all persons convicted under the system are really guilty"; they may "say that they do not know how many innocent people are condemned to such fates." And even one who singles out a particular innocent person for punishment may end up punishing an innocent person somewhat less often than do real legal systems because the person singled out might escape, die of natural causes before punishment is meted out, and so forth. Moreover, the fact that the probability of punishing an innocent person is less than 100 percent in an ordinary legal system can hardly be decisive: Would it be better to adopt a regime that would with certainty mistakenly punish one, but only one, innocent person or a regime that almost certainly would punish hundreds, but in which there was an infinitesimal chance that society would be lucky and none would be punished?

Relatedly, it might be suggested that not knowing the identity of the prospective innocent victims when creating a fallible legal system distinguishes that act from "singling out" an individual of known identity. The basis for this distinction, however, is difficult to understand because the actual identity of the victim is presumably irrelevant; that is, once one knows the identity of the person, what is morally correct is presumed to be the same whichever member of the population it turns out to be. Compare Dolinko (1992, 1632), stating that a terrorist's ignorance of the identity of his prospective victims is irrelevant in assessing the wrongfulness of his act. Also, one can ask whether the retributivist's argument would be inapplicable if

well result in fewer innocent people being punished than when the level of

---

those singling out the victim covered the victim's head so as not to learn his or her identity.

Another distinction made in the literature involves whether or not one "aims" at a particular target. But it is hard to understand what is meant if not one of the preceding distinctions—that is, if aiming does not mean something like intending, wishing, knowing, or foreseeing, what does it mean?

Dworkin offers another attempt to distinguish between adopting a regime in which innocents are sometimes punished and framing an innocent person. See R. Dworkin (1985, 85). On one hand, he says that the former is acceptable "because each citizen is antecedently equally likely to be drawn into the criminal process though innocent, and equally likely to benefit." Ibid. On the other hand, he describes framing as "a case of a fresh political decision that does not treat [the citizen] as an equal . . . and that is true even when he is selected by lot." Ibid. It seems that these two arguments contradict one another, for in the sorts of cases hypothesized, the decision to adopt the lottery is precisely one in which each citizen is "equally likely to be drawn into the criminal process though innocent" (in fact, when an explicit lottery is used, equal likelihood is guaranteed rather than merely approximated) and in which each is "equally likely to benefit" in the hypothesized manner. Nor do we see how the same political decision that would satisfy his principle suddenly violates it if the decision is "fresh." (In any event, one could just change the example so that the authorization for framing the innocent in certain settings was made in advance, rather than at the moment the case arose.) Moreover, as we state earlier in this note, one of the ways that innocent people are convicted in actual legal systems (as a consequence of implementing imperfect regimes ex ante, in which there are limits to the resources spent to avoid error, which Dworkin explicitly condones) is precisely through police or prosecutors sometimes framing an innocent person when they think it would produce desirable results. See also Schedler (1980, 188), arguing that the fact that officials do not select particular innocent people is morally irrelevant and noting that such a system could be designed so that the numbers and identities of innocents singled out would not become known to the officials who set up the system, but stating that this ignorance could hardly make those officials' actions more just. Dworkin also argues that "[f]raming would lose its point if there were a public commitment to frame people meeting a certain public test," R. Dworkin (1985, 85), but this argument is precisely one of the standard responses of consequentialists to the retributivists' hypotheticals, as we discuss in the text to follow. Accepting this point, it is only those instances of framing that arise without explicit approval that raise any possibility of disagreement between the two approaches, but we have already explained why that case is equally problematic for retributivists.

Consistent with the above discussion, some commentators have doubted whether it is even possible to express the posited distinction in a meaningful way. See, for example, Davis (1984a), identifying two main approaches to defining notions of intention, causation, and using as a means that seem implicit in proponents' arguments, but showing that either approach, if followed consistently, fails to distinguish the standard cases that the doctrine of double effect purports to distinguish. But even if the necessary distinction could be stated, there remains the question of the basis for deeming the distinction to be morally relevant.

The normative basis for the proposed distinction has been called into question. See, for example, Bennett (1966). Ultimately, proponents seem to rest their conclusions on intuitions, without examining their origins, foundations, or applicability to the particular context, as we discuss in the text to follow and in note 112. A particular shortcoming is that many of the intuitions in question, and the distinctions they support, are related to social norms that have

punishment is set at a fair level according to a theory of retributive justice.[107]

---

welfare-promoting functions, which suggests that the intuitions are not appropriate grounds for employing evaluative principles that are independent of, and in conflict with, welfare. See notes 108 and 121 in chapter II, discussing general problems with intuitionist moral philosophy in this regard, and subsection D.2, examining the unreliability of intuitions regarding retributive theory in particular. See also Baron (1993, chapter 7), advancing similar arguments with regard to philosophical treatments of the act-omission distinction, and emphasizing that applications of the distinction that conflict with consequentialist judgments may reflect overgeneralization of intuitions, in the same manner that other cognitive heuristics are commonly misapplied.

To assess further the normative basis for the distinction, it is useful to examine its application to the types of problems that are meant to be addressed. Thus, for example, is it acceptable for police snipers, when confronted with a terrorist about to detonate a large bomb, to aim and then shoot at the terrorist, knowing that some bystanders will be shot, but not to aim "at" a small group of bystanders when the terrorist is known to be hiding behind them, even if everyone knows that the distribution of death will be the same? If this proposed moral distinction is recognized, does it depend on whether police snipers find that they are more accurate when they imagine themselves as aiming *at* the bystanders or imagine that they are aiming *through* them, as if they were not there, at the terrorist whom they cannot see? Must the officer in charge first ask each sniper what he is thinking? Compare Glover (1977), noting the arbitrariness in applying the doctrine of double effect in attempting to decide whether bad consequences that might be permissible should be included in the definition of the act, in which case they would be impermissible. It is difficult to see what could be the moral justification for making the permissibility of the police snipers' actions turn on the answers to such elusive questions.

We also find it helpful to consider an example of ordinary social decisionmaking outside the punishment context. Suppose there is a great need to build a hospital, but that inevitably at least one worker will die in a construction accident. One presumes that most everyone who adheres to the kind of theory that we are examining would endorse building the hospital in such a situation. It would be said that the death of the worker is an incidental cost rather than an instance of direct sacrifice. Suppose, however, that the leader of the polity had available a button and that just before the worker was about to die, time stood still for a moment; if the button was pushed, the worker would die and the project would proceed to completion, but if it was not pushed, the work done to date would disintegrate, and construction would have to begin anew. (And, if further attempts were made to build the hospital, the cycle would be repeated.) Now, pushing the button is a direct act that sacrifices the worker, which is impermissible; but failing to push the button is to reject the decision to build the needed hospital, which also is untenable. Put another way, if the original distinction is coherent and morally decisive, then many ordinary activities, such as building hospitals, are morally impermissible. It would seem that the only alternative lesson to draw from such examples is that changes in the technology of such things as push-buttons or in other factors that one would have thought to be entirely arbitrary as a matter of morality are in fact of potentially crucial moral significance under the doctrines proffered by certain deontological philosophers, a result that would seem to require some defense.

107. The present discussion presents another instance of the inherent difficulty of ignoring consequences, even under a purportedly nonconsequentialist theory like retributiv-

In addition, when we examine the retributivists' hypothetical example, serious problems become apparent. As many commentators have explained, consequentialist approaches would most likely oppose punishment of the innocent person in the type of example in question. First, such punishment would fail in its purpose and have serious adverse consequences if word got out, which is likely. Second, on average and over the long run, a system that authorized secret frame-ups would likely misfire more often than it would succeed.[108] Thus, in the actual world, in those we have studied, and in those we can most plausibly imagine, retributivists err in suggesting that consequentialist analysis is at odds with our intuitions about the right result in their hypothetical case of singling out for punishment a person known to be innocent.

To circumvent this response, some retributivists insist on considering admittedly farfetched cases in which, in essence, there is a perfectly functioning and reliable secret police that never abuses its power.[109] At this point,

---

ism. See subsection B.2. Here, a large body of retributivist scholarship appears to have overlooked the fact that paying attention to deterrence—which retributivists eschew—leads one to recognize that reductions in crime result in reductions in the rate at which punishment must be imposed, which in turn involves a reduction in the rate at which innocents are punished by mistake. If consequences are truly to be ignored, the position of retributivists with regard to punishing the innocent is essentially that retributive justice entails two propositions. First, those who create a system of punishment must formally proclaim that their system never punishes the innocent even if that system is fully understood to punish the innocent, perhaps often. Second, it is unjust to adopt a system that results in less punishment of the innocent—or even none (as in our initial example)—if those presenting the rationale for that system do not formally (and disingenuously) proclaim that the innocent must never be punished.

108. See, for example, Pincoffs (1966, 34–36); Hardin (1986, 63–67); Rawls (1955, 8), discussing the longstanding utilitarian argument—advanced by Bentham—against giving officials the "discretionary power to inflict penalties whenever [they think] it for the benefit of society"; ibid. (9–13), discussing how a type of rule utilitarianism allows one to avoid standard criticisms such as that involving punishment of the innocent and concluding: "If one pictures how such an institution [for selectively punishing the innocent] would actually work, and the enormous risks involved in it, it seems clear that it would serve no useful purpose. A utilitarian justification for this institution is most unlikely."; and Sprigge (1965, 275–79). Other points may be mentioned as well. For example, such a policy might be upsetting to people, and it might undermine certain important social norms. See Hampton (1984, 230), stating that punishment of the innocent would undermine the moral lesson of punishment; Hare (1986, 220), noting the prospect of great long-run harm from the breakdown of public confidence in judicial procedures; ibid.: "In the real world, as opposed to the examples provided by philosophers with axes to grind, it is rather obvious that the principles of retributive justice in which we all believe [strongly tend to promote well-being]."; and subsection D.2.

109. There is an obvious tension here. On one hand, it must be supposed that the action is secret and not recognized in any official, public manner. On the other hand, if the action

however, the retributivists face a different problem, one that is related to the fact that they usually do not make an affirmative argument against punishment of the innocent (as is done under consequentialist approaches) but rather rely on readers' intuitions to support the view that punishment of the innocent in this setting seems wrong. The difficulty is that our intuitions—whatever their source[110] (short of divine revelation that is precisely tailored to all conceivable circumstances)—reflect the situations that we ordinarily confront and have experienced. In this instance, the prospect of secret state operatives framing an innocent person is naturally, even if not consciously, associated with such practices as giving unchecked power to government officials, engaging in mass deception of the public, subverting the legal process, encouraging vigilantism, and so forth. That is, the example brings to

---

is secret and lacking in official authorization, the further assumption that we can be confident that there would be no abuse is implausible. Moreover, as we explore in the text below, it is not clear that retributivists would insist on their objection if the action did not have official approval (for, if they did object, they would again find that they had to oppose the existence of any real system of punishment).

In discussing the use of such examples to buttress retributive theory, McCloskey explains: "With each example a critic such as Sprigge can point to the complexity of the relevant factors, and I can reply by writing in more and more details" such that a utilitarian would in fact favor the outcome that seems contrary to moral intuition. McCloskey (1967, 97). Aside from the argument that follows in the text, there are additional difficulties with McCloskey's reasoning. First, his appeal to intuition insists only that the injustice regarding the innocent person should count. But under a utilitarian approach—or under welfare economics more generally—there are many negative aspects of punishing an innocent person that already count, very heavily, as we discuss in subsection (a). Hence, it is necessary to identify an independent notion of justice, not already captured in such analysis and based on factors irrelevant to anyone's well-being, including that of the innocent person. Moreover, as we suggest throughout, people may have a taste for a notion of fairness, and in subsection D.2 we suggest that this is the case with respect to aspects of retributive justice. When McCloskey and others appeal to the feelings and reactions of the ordinary observer, it is entirely possible that such feelings are precisely the manifestation of the observer's taste for a notion of fairness. This possibility, which McCloskey does not consider, undermines his only ground for concluding that some weight should be given to an independent conception of justice. See also Hart (1968b, 12), asserting that in extreme cases we may have to resort to such measures as punishing the innocent as an expedient, but in doing so "[w]e should be conscious of choosing the lesser of two evils, and this would be inexplicable if the principle sacrificed to utility were itself only a requirement of utility"—but not explaining why it is impossible for there to be two evils, both concerned with the same general phenomenon, such as well-being, and also failing to acknowledge that, focusing only on well-being, there are a range of different respects in which punishing the innocent is undesirable.

110. See section D, exploring the likely source of our intuitions concerning retribution and explaining why it undermines the case for giving independent weight to retributive justice.

mind a flood of undesirable historical experiences and plausible horrors. The retributivist asks us to consult our intuitions on the subject, intuitions that undoubtedly are based on just these effects, but then the retributivist tells us to ignore them—as though our minds, when absorbing what is usually a single sentence of abstract prose, can instantly re-channel partly subconscious intuitions that we have developed over a lifetime.[111] Plainly, our intuitions are unlikely to be reliable guides in extremely unrealistic hypothetical situations that diverge in highly relevant respects from the contexts in which our intuitions were formed.[112]

111. See, for example, Sprigge (1965, 274): "If one finds oneself still half-inclined to call such punishment wrong, it may well be because one does not really succeed in envisaging the situation just as described, but surrounds it with those circumstances of real life which would in fact create a greater probability of unhappiness in its consequences than happiness."

112. See, for example, Baron (1993, 12): "[O]ur intuitive rules often conflict with the conclusions we reach when we consider highly hypothetical cases for which our rules were not intended, such as those put forward by anti-utilitarian philosophers."; Binmore (1998, 257): "[O]ne can learn a great deal about the mechanics of moral algorithms by triggering them under pathological circumstances—but only if one does not make the mistake of supposing that the moral rules have been designed to cope with pathological problems."; ibid. (450): "If a moral problem is sufficiently outlandish, it will have occurred so infrequently in our evolutionary history that it would be amazing if our moral intuitions were adapted to solving it in a way that made any sense."; R. Posner (1998, 1675): "[W]e can have no settled or reliable intuitions regarding the stranger case, because the case is outside our empirical experience; it belongs to science-fiction."; and Sprigge (1965, 272–75), addressing the problem of fanciful hypothetical examples in the context of punishing the innocent. See also notes 108 and 121 in chapter II, further elaborating on appeals to intuition.

Another point to note is that a well-socialized, moral (in the sense of common morality, see section II.D on social norms) person would have great compunction about framing an innocent person. See Smart (1965, 348): "[T]he possibility that one ought to commit injustice will be felt to be acutely unsatisfactory by someone who has had a normal civilized upbringing."; Sprigge (1965, 274): "[T]he utilitarian shares . . . in the unease produced by these examples. Although he may admit that in such a situation punishment of the innocent would be right, he still regards favourably the distaste which is aroused at the idea of its being called right."; and ibid. (279–80). Precisely because singling out an innocent person for punishment will rarely be desirable, whereas taking advantage of innocent people, say, for personal gain, will often appear attractive, society benefits from strongly inculcating social norms against taking advantage of innocent people. See ibid. (281), indicating that an action may serve as a bad example, encouraging similar acts in other situations in which those acts are not justified; and Smart (1973, 71–73), discussing the value, from a utilitarian perspective, of members of society holding views that make it difficult for them to countenance punishing the innocent. Moreover, we may suppose that readers and authors are such well-socialized people. Hence, it runs deeply against our grain to behave in the manner that might be optimal in the highly unusual setting that retributivists posit.

But, as we have discussed previously, see subsection II.D.2, it is a logical mistake to infer

As a result, if one seeks to understand punishment in the hypothetical example, one must analyze the posited situation explicitly. It seems appropriate to ask what sort of legal regime citizens would favor before such circumstances arose.[113] Would they reject a regime that, with extremely small probability, would single them out for punishment but, with much greater probability, would save them from harm (caused when some fellow citizens single them out as a target of random violence during a riot)? Clearly, all would expect to be better off under such a regime—that is, if in fact it operated (unrealistically) as retributivists suppose in their hypotheticals.

It is useful to reflect on this reasoning and the hypothesized situation

---

from such instincts that the behavior that feels troubling to us is in fact socially undesirable. This kind of point has been developed at length in Hare (1981, chapter 8). See also note 108 in chapter II, offering reasons that intuitions are unreliable guides in moral analysis; section D, discussing the origin of retributive principles, which further suggests why our intuitions on law enforcement should not be taken as reliable indicators of the principles that should be used for policy assessment; and note 121 in chapter II, providing additional references. We should keep in mind that it is entirely possible that an instinct or intuition about how to behave is, on moral grounds, a good one for everyone to have while, at the same time, the behavior most consistent with that feeling would turn out to be morally undesirable in a particular case (especially in an atypical case). See Sidgwick (1907, 493): "[T]he Utilitarian . . . may without inconsistency admire the Disposition or Motive if it is of a kind which it is generally desirable to encourage, even while he disapproves of the conduct to which it has led in any particular case." This distinction relates to our discussion in note 121 in chapter II of the difference between rules of common morality and principles appropriately employed to assess the desirability of such rules.

The point that moral intuitions are unreliable in unfamiliar contexts has repeatedly been advanced yet has met with little response from retributivists. An exception is McCloskey, who in addressing Sprigge's criticism argues:

> [I]t is not true that moral attitudes have developed only in respect of the physical world as we know it. They have long been applied to gods who inhabit worlds of varying sorts—and this without any sense of strain or awkwardness in those who have pressed the moral judgments. That Christians acknowledge the problem of evil to be such a real problem shows that moral attitudes are not based simply on a consideration of the physical world peopled by moral agents with the sorts of human natures we know them to have. That we can enter into a serious moral appraisal of Christ's reported use of his miraculous powers further confirms this. (McCloskey 1967, 93–94)

This reply, however, seems merely to show that there are other settings in which people have attempted to apply their moral intuitions beyond their range of experience. His observation therefore is not responsive to the argument that such applications are unreliable and does not indicate why intuition is superior to explicit analysis.

113. For elaboration of why this is the correct way to put the question, see subsection VIII.C.1.

in the context of punishment of the innocent that actually occurs under even the most well-run legal systems. Citizens do choose to be governed by regimes that sometimes punish the innocent rather than to live in anarchy, and, as we have already discussed, we doubt that retributivists could find this choice to be morally incorrect.[114] Moreover, it is worth emphasizing that punishment of the innocent in our existing legal system no doubt occasionally involves precisely such instances in which a police officer or prosecutor frames someone, believing that the outcome will benefit society. Therefore, if retributivists are ever to accept real systems of punishment, they will have accepted regimes in which innocent individuals are occasionally singled out for punishment.[115]

In summary, consideration of the problem of the punishment of innocents reinforces the point that setting sanctions based on retributive conceptions of fairness can lead us to favor undesirable policies. Further analysis of the retributive position reveals that its actual implications for treatment of the innocent are quite different from (and in plausible instances, opposite to) those that retributivists usually suppose and that, however one may attempt to revise retributive theory, it does not provide a basis for deviating from policies that best promote individuals' well-being. We now take up the question of how it can be that retributive principles seem so attractive despite their providing a poor foundation for the evaluation of legal policy.

D. The Appeal of Notions of Fairness and Its Implications

Our preceding analysis, which suggests that retributive notions should not be viewed as independent evaluative principles to be used in guiding legal policy, raises the question of why the retributive conception of fair punishment has such appeal both to the population at large and to legal scholars

---

114. Furthermore, some specific law enforcement policies, such as authorized high-speed chases and police officers' use of firearms, on some occasions will injure or kill innocent bystanders, but nevertheless the policies are regarded as desirable by citizens (even if the practices are sometimes overused or abused).

Separately, we note that acts of rioting are themselves wrongs, so that the regime in which an innocent person may be framed that the retributivists find objectionable is a regime that produces a world in which there is less wrongful activity from a retributive view—a point we raise in subsections B.2 and C.1, and one that retributivists have not addressed directly.

115. On retributivists' attempts to distinguish punishment of the innocent in real legal systems (which they must accept) from punishment of the innocent in unusual hypothetical examples (which they condemn), see note 106.

and philosophers who have inquired into the justifications for punishment. In this section, we suggest that an important part of the explanation may be that notions of retributive justice are associated with internalized social norms about wrongful conduct and punishment. In subsection 1, we discuss retribution as a social norm, focusing on the possible origins and functions of our instincts and intuitions about punishment, including the element of proportionality. In subsection 2, we draw out the implications of these ideas for the analysis of legal policy. Then, in subsection 3, we comment on an additional aspect of notions of fair punishment that may help to explain their attractiveness, namely, their ex post character.

1. The Origins and Functions of Notions of Fairness

Retributive principles obviously are widely held.[116] Here we inquire into the origins and functions of these principles. We admit at the outset that many aspects of the argument that follows are speculative. Nevertheless, we pursue this line of inquiry in the hope of illuminating the possible sources of our instincts and intuitions about just punishment.

Norms of retribution probably guided human behavior long before the emergence of the modern state, with its law enforcement apparatus, and long before the development of explicit rationalizations for the imposition of punishment. In primitive settings, the problem of aggression by others must have been significant. Retaliation—and, importantly, the threat thereof—was probably an important means of protecting against aggression. Punishment of wrongdoers was, one suspects, necessary for survival.[117]

---

116. As Hare observes:

> We find ordinary people, including ordinary judges, legislators, policemen, etc., firmly wedded (at least we hope so) to a set of principles of retributive justice. By "firmly wedded" I mean not merely that they have moral opinions in the sense of being ready to express them when asked. I mean that they have what are called "consciences": if they feel tempted to break these principles, they at once experience a strong feeling of repugnance; if others break them, they experience feelings of what Sir Stuart Hampshire calls "outrage or shock." (Hare 1986, 218)

See, for example, Burgh (1982, 195): "When most experience wrongdoing, especially as the object of wrongdoing, their immediate, intuitive response is that the wrongdoer deserves to suffer. I take this to be unquestionable fact."

117. See, for example, Daly and Wilson (1988, 256): "From the perspective of evolutionary psychology, this almost mystical and seemingly irreducible sort of moral imperative is the output of a mental mechanism with a straightforward adaptive function: to reckon justice and administer punishment by a calculus which ensures that violators reap no advantage from their misdeeds."; Sidgwick (1907, 427): "[T]he corresponding feeling of revenge was for

A difficulty with retribution concerns an actor's incentive to carry out a retributive act once an aggressor's intrusion is complete.[118] Retaliation is costly: The actor must divert effort from directly productive activity, and seeking revenge is dangerous. Therefore, after an aggressor's intrusion, the actor's self-interest may dictate that he ignore it. But a pattern of failing to retaliate would be problematic, for individuals or groups known to behave in such a manner would become targets for predation. Hence, it would have been beneficial for individuals to develop a strong taste for vengeance—a taste sufficient to induce retaliation even when there was significant risk and no immediate gain—thereby producing a reputation for seeking retribution.[119] Such a desire for retribution would likely develop not only through learning and socialization but also through natural selection. That is, instincts concerning retribution probably have a biological foundation and constitute part of our essential makeup.[120] This point is supported by the fact that other animal species exhibit similar behavior.[121]

---

centuries the one bulwark against social anarchy. . . ."; R. Posner (1980b, 75–76); and Vidmar (2000, 3): "Anthropologists have argued that [retribution and revenge] are the [principal] means of social control in 'pre-law' societies as diverse as the pre-colonial tribes of New Guinea, the Dafla hill people of India, African Bushmen and American Indians." Posner also explores the evolution of primitive societies away from simple norms of retaliation on account of the costs of such punishment (discussed later in this subsection). See R. Posner (1980c, 42–52), discussing tort and criminal law.

118. The actor's incentive is straightforward when he is acting in self-defense during an intrusion.

119. See, for example, Daly and Wilson (1988, 229–31), Frank (1988, chapters 3–4), and R. Posner (1980b, 77–78): "My point here is only that the avenger must derive utility from his act in order to be motivated to do it in the absence of compensation."

120. See, for example, Trivers (1971, 49), Hirshleifer (1978, 334), and Romer (1996, 204–06). See also Romer (1996, 204–05), suggesting that individuals may also have developed a hardwired taste for punishment because such a habit may be superior to individuals' determining the benefits of retaliation through strategic calculation. Commonalities in retributive behavior across cultures and over time support this view. See Daly and Wilson (1988, chapters 10–11), and ibid. (226) (emphasis in original): "*Lethal retribution is an ancient and cross-culturally universal recourse of those subjected to abuse.*"

121. See, for example, Mill ([1861] 1998, 95): "It is natural to resent, and to repel or retaliate. . . . The origin of this sentiment it is not necessary here to discuss. Whether it be an instinct or a result of intelligence, it is, we know, common to all animal nature; for *every animal tries to hurt those who have hurt. . . .*"; Mackie (1991, 683): "[W]hat look like the same or similar tendencies are not difficult to detect in some non-human animals. Nor is there the slightest difficulty in understanding how such instinctive patterns of behaviour, and feelings that harmonize with that behaviour, could have developed by an evolutionary process of biological natural selection."; and Romer (1996, 211), citing evidence of a taste for revenge in the behavior of nonhuman primates, as well as evidence that humans display retributive behavior

In our discussion of the retributive theory of fair punishment, we emphasize the aspect of the theory holding that punishment should be proportional to the offense. We now observe that the social norm of retribution presently under discussion follows this proportionality principle. It is easy to see that this feature also probably served important functions. Limiting punishment to the severity of the transgression tends to conserve resources devoted to retaliation.[122] Relatedly, because there were probably numerous minor altercations, victims would have expended excessive effort if reactions were not modest in such cases. But if serious intrusions were met with the same limited responses as small infractions, the main purpose of retribution—warding off significant aggression—would have been compromised. Finally, the problem of escalating retaliation creates a need for graded responses.[123] (We note that the "tit-for-tat" strategy, which has been discussed as a way of avoiding confrontational outcomes,[124] corresponds well to the rule of *lex talionis* or, more broadly, to the idea that punishment should reflect the gravity of the offense.[125]) It bears emphasis that the principle that punishment should be limited to the seriousness of the intrusion must be ingrained in us given that a strong desire for vengeance is part of our make-up, for it is necessary for people to maintain self-control when responding, in the heat of passion, to others' aggression. If one's inner restraint is not

---

across cultures and in ancient times. Compare Waal (1982, 205–07), noting that chimpanzees' reciprocal behavior includes punishment of those who violate understood social rules.

122. Because retaliation is costly, greater retaliation will tend to be functional when the benefits of retaliation are greater, and this in turn will be true when the harm to be avoided is greater.

123. See, for example, Baron (1994a, 7): "The retributive rule of punishment, 'an eye for an eye,' was originally a reform, an improvement over the kind of moral system that led to escalating feuds."; and R. Posner (1980b, 82), describing the proportionality limitation on retaliation as a mechanism for avoiding the "endless cycle of injury, retaliation, and counter-retaliation—a costly system for controlling aggression."

124. See, for example, Axelrod and Hamilton (1981) and Axelrod (1984). See also Binmore (1998, 313–19), discussing respects in which the evolutionary superiority of the tit-for-tat strategy has been overstated in the literature.

125. This theme is developed by Daly and Wilson, who survey relevant anthropological studies. See Daly and Wilson (1988, chapter 10); ibid. (232): "So excess in revenge is a constant temptation and a not infrequent reality. 'An eye for an eye' is not so much the articulation of the revenge motive as it is a *moral injunction* to equity—an attempt to *contain* revenge." (emphasis in original); ibid. (233): "[A] precise equity in revenge may often be in the best interests of the avenger himself."; and ibid. (235): "It follows that the powerful positive effect associated with measured retaliation . . . may well represent the human psyche's evolved response to the fundamental cost-benefit structure of enduring social relations among potential rivals."

substantial and automatic, retaliation would often get out of hand; a serious mistake could be highly damaging, even fatal. In all, limiting retribution to the extent of the transgression seems likely to have been an important aspect of the overall scheme of retributive behavior, and there is reason to believe that it too has a biological foundation.[126]

In contemporary society, with a modern state that has a formal monopoly on the police power and, accordingly, has sole responsibility for enforcing the criminal law, the need for individuals to have a strong (albeit controlled) desire for vengeance in order to exact retribution is different from and more limited than it once was.[127] The powerful impulse for direct and immediate revenge against physical aggression is one that society now seeks to subdue because continued vengeful activity is likely to produce more unwanted violence than accompanies the use of formal law enforcement. Thus, individuals are taught not to take the law into their own hands, to reject vigilante justice.[128] Social norms tend to change slowly, however, especially when they have a biological foundation; hence, we would expect significant vestiges of our original retributive impulse to remain.[129]

---

126. Evidence suggesting a biological foundation for the proportionality limitation is provided by the existence of similar behavior among nonhuman primates. See, for example, Wilson (1980, 275), identifying as a feature common among primates the "scaling in the intensity of responses, especially during aggressive interactions." Compare Waal (1982, 205–07), describing reciprocal behavior among chimpanzees, who follow the basic rule of "an eye for an eye, a tooth for a tooth."

We further note that, to be successful, social norms about retribution will tend to pervade the relevant society, so that more than just the victim will mobilize against aggressors. See, for example, R. Posner (1980b, 76–77; 1980c, 43–45). Moreover, there are various second-order behaviors that reinforce the primary social norms. Thus, an individual will tend to derive satisfaction when others engage in retribution, and he will be angry when others do not do their part. Similarly, an individual will be anxious when the response is too weak and disturbed when it is excessive. Such generalized attitudes are particularly likely to spill over into thinking about formal punishment, as we discuss in subsection 2. See generally Daly and Wilson (1988, chapter 10).

127. Other developments, such as using tort law to exact compensation from injurers rather than punishing them (through direct retaliation or the state apparatus), have also reduced the functional value of victims' seeking retribution directly from their injurers. See R. Posner (1980c, 43).

128. Of course, in civil matters, individuals must take the law into their own hands to an extent—by bringing lawsuits—if they wish legal redress, and, as noted in the text to follow, they must stand up for themselves in a wide range of settings. The maxim of not taking the law into one's own hands is, therefore, understood to be limited primarily to physical responses, although even in this regard there is permission for some self-defense.

129. An additional reason to believe that preexisting retributive norms continue to influence us is that the shift to the modern state with its monopoly on the police power was gradual

Moreover, the retributive urge, even if in a less aggressive form, continues to play an important role with respect to law enforcement and other aspects of human behavior. Notably, the desire for retribution often leads individuals to cooperate with law enforcement authorities when they otherwise would not do so (stepping forward as a witness, for example, can be time-consuming and sometimes dangerous).[130] In addition, social norms about punishment are related to, and reinforce, feelings about wrongful action; accordingly, they may enhance compliance with the law. Finally, there are many areas of social interaction that are largely unregulated by the state, so individuals need the instinctive capacity to stand up for themselves to avoid being taken advantage of in various respects. As a result, even if a society could remake its members instantaneously and transform its cultural norms overnight, it would not be advisable to erase all traces of our desire for retribution.

There also exists a direct process of norm inculcation that is important even in our current social condition, a process that supplements the previously described sources of retributive instincts. Parents, teachers, and other authorities teach retributive principles to children, and, as adults, we all act in ways that reinforce these commonly held norms.[131] Children begin to learn at a very early age the difference between right and wrong, and some of this learning is accomplished through the imposition of punishment in general accord with retributive principles.[132] Over time, certain norms of behavior

---

and did not reach its current form until recently in history. In particular, during the long transition from primitive society to the modern state, it appears that there was a significant period during which there was a substantial overlap in functions, with the social norm of retribution continuing to play a significant direct role (independent of state apparatus) in maintaining order. And it was not that long ago in our history that victims played a much more direct role in bringing criminals to justice. See, for example, Stephen (1883, vol. 1, chapter 8).

130. See, for example, R. Posner (1980b, 81). Compare Sidgwick (1907, 427), suggesting that the feeling of revenge that was once necessary to avoid anarchy "is even now one of the chief restraints to crime."

131. In the text to follow, we elaborate on this process as it regards children. With respect to adults, many mechanisms operate, such as expressions of disapprobation in response to misbehavior, severance of relations, editorials on the state of society in the news media, and so forth.

132. We learn these lessons during our childhood by actually experiencing punishment according to retributive principles, by witnessing punishment applied to others (such as siblings and classmates) according to the principles, and by having the principles of punishment announced to us (often at the time punishment is imposed). See, for example, Benn (1967, 30): "Moreover, in the family and the school punishment is often used to reinforce moral condemnation as part of the process of moral education."; and Greenawalt (1983, 351): "For

and of punishment become ingrained. These norms tend to be taught for many reasons. In the short run, there is direct self-interest; parents and teachers, for example, need to maintain order.[133] In the long run, these same individuals wish to prepare children for their lives as adults, not only so they will stay out of trouble, but also so they will watch out for their own interests in a world where others may act opportunistically. In addition, the norms may be taught without conscious reflection, either by example or even through explicit instruction whereby individuals simply teach those principles of right and wrong that seem natural to them.

In these settings in which retributive ideas are inculcated, the proportionality principle will be important for several reasons. First, parents and others find the imposition of punishment costly, especially because they care directly about the well-being of those being punished and thus do not like imposing punishment. Hence, minimizing the amount of punishment is important. However, they will be reluctant to impose light punishment for serious misbehavior because the cost of failing adequately to deter such activity will be great. Second, the proportionality principle enhances the tutelary function of punishment.[134] Children will not always be able to control themselves, and they will not remember all lessons equally well. Thus, differential responses are useful in ensuring that the most important violations will not be repeated, without giving up entirely on efforts to control lesser misdeeds.[135] Third, because children are being prepared for life in the adult

---

young children, the line may be very thin between believing that behavior is wrong and fearing punishment."

133. For example, adults punish children for doing harm because a child's fear of being punished will reduce the frequency of events that adults dislike: mundane harms (such as from spilling food or knocking over breakable objects), injuries from altercations, losses of temper, and so forth. Moreover, there may be a concern that children would otherwise seriously harm younger siblings. See, for example, Kagan (1984, 131).

134. Compare Brandt (1979, 288), noting that the intensity of young children's feelings of guilt is often a function of how much damage their wrongdoing causes, and Waldron (1992, 31), suggesting that criminal punishment that follows *lex talionis* may be functional for adults because "the vivid lesson conveyed by 'turning the tables' on the offender is the quickest route to awareness of wrong-doing and repentance."

135. For related reasons, it is also generally the case that children are punished only when they misbehave, rather than whenever harm has occurred. (This point, which is relevant to the fact that criminal punishment is usually not based on strict liability for causing harm, bears only indirectly on our discussion of the level of sanctions.) One reason for thus limiting the use of punishment derives from the fact that parents dislike punishing their children. Therefore, other things being equal, it makes sense for parents to create incentives for good behavior in a way that minimizes the actual use of punishment; this result is accomplished by using a fault principle rather than strict liability. Second, the tutelary function of punishment is

world, it is valuable for them to understand that they must keep the extent of punishment in check, for otherwise they may induce escalating retaliation. And, as noted above, the developed internal need to restrain oneself needs to be strong, for it must overcome the competing taste for vengeance, often in the heat of passion. We would expect this socialization process, like the evolutionary process described previously, to exert a strong influence on the attitudes and behavior of all well-socialized individuals, whose intuitions will thus reflect retributive principles of punishment.

2. Implications for the Role of Notions of Fairness in Legal Policy Analysis

The foregoing discussion suggests that we all will have intuitions and instincts about the practice of punishment, and that these will correspond to the general contours of retributive theory. In particular, it has been suggested that the proportionality requirement must be internalized to help counterbalance the retaliatory urge, in which case the proportionality requirement would be embedded in our psychology. If this characterization of our dispositions is correct, it would not be surprising that everyone, including philosophers and legal scholars, would be inclined to find the retributive conception of fair punishment intuitively appealing.[136]

---

better served by restricting punishment to those occasions on which the behavior of the child was faulty, because children will more readily understand which behaviors they are expected to modify. Compare subsection III.E.1, making an analogous point concerning the appeal of the fault principle as an aspect of social norms in the tort setting.

136. The suggestion that moral intuitions about retributive punishment have their origins in human emotions, themselves a product of biological and social evolution, has been advanced by Mackie:

> I suggest that we can find a biological explanation for the tendency to feel nonmoral resentment of injuries and gratitude for benefits, and a sociological explanation for the development, out of these, of their moral counterparts.
>
> . . . For both [psychological and genetic] reasons there will then be some selective pressure in favor of the tendency to retaliate. . . .
>
> Initially what is thus explained is retributive behavior, but in creatures that have the capacity for emotion this will naturally be accompanied by the development of retributive emotions directed towards the sources of injury or help. . . .
>
> From cooperation in resentment to moral disapproval or indignation is a further step, but not an enormous one. . . .
>
> . . . .
>
> We can, then, describe a possible course of evolution by which retributive behavior and emotions, cooperative resentment, and the disinterested moral sentiments could have developed in turn. (Mackie 1982b, 8–9) *(continued)*

Nevertheless, the analysis of retribution as a social norm does not provide any basis for viewing retributive justice as an independent evaluative principle for use in the design of legal institutions, rather than relying exclusively on welfare economics. Indeed, if the underlying purpose of social norms involving retribution concerns the advancement of individuals' well-being,[137] it would make no sense, in the name of retributive principles, to pursue policies that reduce well-being.[138]

This conclusion is reinforced by a comparison of the context in which retributive principles have emerged as social norms with the setting of formal law enforcement.[139] On one hand, we suggest that retributive principles have as their purpose the control of wrongdoing, so there is reason to believe that following them when setting law enforcement policy would tend to be functional; that is, retributive principles will to an extent serve as a proxy

---

See, for example, Mackie (1991). A competing view (that we find obscure) is offered by Moore. See Moore (1993b, 44): "The moral fact of the matter often causes our moral beliefs through the intermediate causing of our emotional responses." See also ibid. (38), stating that the best explanation for our reactions to "Kant-like thought experiments is that those reactions are caused by the existing moral qualities of wrongness and of culpability, the combination of which I call *desert.*"

137. See, for example, Daly and Wilson (1988, 251): "Effective deterrence is the ultimate function behind the human passion for measured retributive justice—it is the reason why that passion evolved. But our passion for evening the score has thus become an entity in its own right, an evolved aspect of the human mind. Our desire for justice fundamentally entails a desire for revenge."; and Mackie (1982b, 9), stating, with regard to retributive moral views, that "[t]hese utilitarian 'ends' are the results for which moral resentment, and its nonmoral forerunners, have been selected and encouraged by genetic and social evolutionary mechanisms."

138. It is particularly ironic that norms that have evolved, whether socially or biologically, for the purpose of deterrence have been taken by philosophers, in addressing the problem of choosing the level of punishment imposed by the legal system, to constitute principles that are directly opposed to concerns about deterrence.

139. This comparison relates to the general distinction that we discuss in subsection II.D.2, and especially to the point we emphasize in note 121 in chapter II, that moral theories are often directed toward behavior in everyday life, which may differ qualitatively from the context of the formal legal system. In comparing blame, a form of social disapprobation, with punishment imposed by the state, Benn argues as follows:

> We do not punish men because they are morally guilty, nor must we *necessarily* refrain because they are morally guiltless, nor mitigate the punishment in the same degree for all the same reasons that we mitigate blame. This is not to say that the justifications sought are not *moral* justifications; it is simply that they must be made in the light of criteria different from those governing blame, since however close the analogy may be between the two techniques of control, there are still significant differences between them. (Benn 1958, 341)

device for promoting individuals' well-being. Indeed, we note in subsections C.1 and C.2 that this is the case with the requirement of proportionality.

On the other hand, the contexts are different in important respects, and it is recognized that well-developed tastes concerning vengeance may often be inappropriate in our current social situation with regard to punishing criminals.[140] In particular, the methods of detecting wrongdoing and of meting out punishment are different in the setting of evolved social norms of retribution and that of modern, formal law enforcement by the state. Long ago, much retribution was probably carried out immediately, in warding off aggressors. In face-to-face settings with an adversary, the probability of punishment was high, approaching certainty.[141] Likewise, in many settings in the family or in school, a high proportion of infractions will be detected directly by those who impose punishment.[142] By contrast, the means of detection and punishment in the formal legal system are indirect. Policing and

140. See generally R. Posner (1980b). Posner's conclusion is that, aside from any benefit of satisfying tastes per se, a taste for "retribution is an important component of a system of private law enforcement but has only a small role to play in a system of public enforcement." Ibid. (75). As we discuss later in this subsection, retributivists often dissociate their position from dependence on individuals' tastes regarding punishment.

Another reason, besides differences in contexts, that the social norm of retribution may not be a good proxy device for designing law enforcement policy is that the relationship between retribution and deterrence is imperfect to begin with.

> Such a tendency [for people to favor retribution as the basis of punishment] could result from overgeneralization of a deterrence rule. It may be easier for people—in the course of development—to understand punishment in terms of rules of retribution than in terms of deterrence. Those who do understand the deterrence rationale generally make the same judgments—because deterrence and retribution principles usually agree—so opportunities for social learning are limited. (Baron 1994a, 5)

141. Additional aspects of primitive societies contributed to the high probability of punishment. See R. Posner (1980c, 43–48), describing factors contributing to a high probability, and R. Posner (1980b, 81), arguing that, in primitive societies, the probability of apprehension and punishment approached one. See also ibid. (83): "But retributive justice is not functional when those conditions are not fulfilled—when enforcement is not private and probabilities of detection and punishment are not high. . . ."

142. Of course, this is not always the case, and one suspects that punishment of infractions that are generally difficult to detect, are deliberately hidden from view, or are indicative of likely prior, undetected violations will be punished more harshly on that account. For example, if a parent finds cigarettes hidden in a drawer, the punishment might be more severe than for the act of smoking a single cigarette. Similarly, a parent is likely to impose more serious punishment on a child who hides the fact that he is not completing homework assignments than on one who informs his parents of that fact.

prosecution are largely carried out by third parties, who must rely on others to supply information or must employ additional agents to monitor, audit, or investigate.[143] Other differences are that, through its greater economies of scale, the state can fine-tune its enforcement apparatus, whereas social norms that are inculcated in children and must apply to a range of settings tend to be more simple and general;[144] through its legal institutions, the state may be able to make the commitments necessary to ensure deterrence that an individual may not credibly be able to make; and through its monopoly on the police power, the state can control the problem of escalating retaliation.

All of these differences suggest that the law enforcement policies that may be best for the modern state will sometimes differ from those suggested by our retributive notions that emerged long ago or that are taught to children today. In particular, many of these differences suggest that the state may often find that the probability of detection for some offenses will be low. (A higher probability may be almost impossible to produce or may be very costly, in terms of required resources and the degree of intrusiveness involved.) Indeed, this problem arises with respect to many offenses.[145] Thus, it may often be desirable to employ higher punishments than those called for under the proportionality principle. In such settings, following retributive principles in designing law enforcement policy will not be a very good proxy indicator of what best promotes individuals' well-being.[146] Furthermore, un-

143. Interestingly, the use of juries in the distant past blurred this difference. When there was a crime, often in a small community with a substantial network of shared information, the jurors consisted of those in the vicinity who were familiar with the involved individuals and events or in a good position to find out about them. See, for example, Green (1988). In contrast, today we ensure that jurors have no such connections, and they may not investigate on their own.

144. The acknowledged need for basic rules to be simple and thus sometimes overinclusive or underinclusive casts in a different light retributivists' arguments to the effect that they can construct instances in which consequentialist prescriptions are inconsistent with common intuitions. It would, in fact, be surprising if any valid normative theory never conflicted with our intuitions, which are grounded in simple principles that constitute social norms such as that concerning retribution. We further discuss the problem of retributivists' reliance on intuitions in the text below.

145. See, for example, Robinson and Darley (1997, 461 table 1), indicating that some important categories of crime have probabilities of punishment of no more than one or two percent.

146. As suggested previously, given the slow rate at which social norms (especially ones with a biological foundation) change, we might expect persistence of this divergence between our intuitions and instincts, on one hand, and what is, after careful analysis, truly most conducive to individuals' well-being, on the other hand. Moreover, efforts in modern states to sublimate the taste for retribution may have the side effect of producing even stronger intuitions

derstanding the origins and functions of retribution as a social norm makes clear that there is no good reason for treating our intuitions about retribution as if they constituted an independent basis for assessing law enforcement policy.

Even though the retributive conception of fair punishment should not be taken as an independent evaluative principle, the existence of social norms about retribution is relevant to the assessment of legal rules under welfare economics. First, as our discussion in subsection 1 indicates, we should expect individuals to have a taste for punishing wrongdoers as well as a taste for having punishment fit the crime. To this extent, retributive principles are relevant in designing law enforcement policy.[147] For example, it may make sense to devote additional resources (more than would be justified by deterrence and incapacitation benefits) to capturing those who commit well publicized heinous crimes; otherwise, individuals' tastes for retribution would be unsatisfied.[148] Similarly, it may not be desirable to employ as high a level of punishment as otherwise might seem best if most of the population would find such a disproportionate punishment upsetting; perhaps in light of individuals' tastes, the optimal punishment would reflect a compromise. We emphasize, however, that the appropriateness of such adjustments to law enforcement policy would depend entirely on the empirical question of the strength of individuals' actual tastes.[149] (Some of these tastes have proba-

---

against high punishments. Nevertheless, citizens in a modern state have come to expect differences between their intuitions and instincts and what makes for good policy; that is, there is a tendency to compartmentalize, to defer to elected representatives and experts, and so forth. See section VII.C. For example, the maxim that one should not take the law into one's own hands distinguishes the role of the individual and that of the state with regard to punishment. In addition, children learn quickly that there is a difference between how they are expected to treat peers who may do wrong and how parents, teachers, or other authorities deal with adult transgressors.

147. See, for example, Polinsky and Shavell (2000), and Wittman (1974), presenting a formal economic analysis of punishment that incorporates people's tastes for retribution.

148. In addition, one might think it particularly important, in terms of individuals' welfare, to capture and punish such criminals because of the anxiety the population would otherwise feel about being victimized in the future. It is not clear, however, the extent to which these are distinct feelings, for an evolved sense of anxiety from failing to exact retribution may well be an aspect of the set of tastes that induce individuals to seek vengeance. In any event, all such feelings, considered as tastes, would be relevant under welfare economics.

149. Our conjecture is that, for many violations of the law, individuals will not have strong independent tastes regarding the level of punishment. Thus, for regulatory offenses, there may be no deep feeling about what punishment is best because these offenses may not have a natural analogue to a common crime and may differ qualitatively from the sorts of wrongs committed by children. In addition, there may be a fair amount of leeway in prefer-

bly been sublimated through modern socialization,[150] although this change
in tastes may also suggest a preference for less harsh punishments.[151])

As we have emphasized since subsections II.A.1 and II.D.2, the empirical
question about the strength of individuals' tastes is distinct from the question
whether a notion of fairness such as retributive justice should serve as an
independent principle for evaluation—independent of individuals' well-
being and thus of their tastes for retribution.[152] Perhaps because of the close
alignment between the contours of individuals' tastes for retribution (often

---

ences, so individuals may not strongly differentiate between a fine of $5 or $25 for a parking
meter violation, or between a sentence of three months or fifteen months for car theft. Furthermore, individuals' tastes would be relatively unimportant in determining how sanctions should
be set if, in the long run, tastes change as sanctions change. There will be cases, however, in
which tastes are likely to be strong. See generally Glaeser and Sacerdote (2000), finding that
sentences for murder vary with victim characteristics in a manner suggesting that sentencing
reflects, in part, a taste for vengeance. A 90-day sentence or a $1,000 fine for murder or for
rape would undoubtedly cause great upset among the population. Likewise, life imprisonment
for littering would be widely regarded with extreme distaste.

Another factor is that, as we discuss in note 146, individuals in modern societies compartmentalize their thinking to an extent, and perhaps also their tastes, so they may have stronger
tastes about the propriety of various types of retributive behavior among friends or at work
than about sanctions imposed by the government.

150. See generally Gorecki (1983, chapter 5), discussing factors that lead the criminal
law to be less harsh over time. A manifestation of this phenomenon concerns the abolition
of capital punishment in many societies, wherein the pattern of abolition seems roughly to
match those factors that would be associated with a general attempt to reduce the taste for
vengeance through socialization. For example, societies that are most likely to have abolished
capital punishment seem to be those that are more developed economically and legally; those
that have democratic governments and thus, one might suppose, a higher perceived legitimacy
of the formal legal system; and those that suffer less from uncontrolled crime, so citizens feel
less of a need for self-protection. Indeed, abolition of capital punishment may be part of that
process of decreasing the taste for vengeance through socialization. For further discussion,
see note 161 and subsection VIII.B.2.

151. For example, a wide range of offenses were once subject to capital punishment, but
the list has greatly narrowed (even where capital punishment has not been abolished) and
the current penalties for many of the same offenses are appreciably less than life imprisonment.
See Gorecki (1983, chapter 6), discussing the history in the United States. (Of course, other
factors may help to explain this change, such as the increasing cost of incarceration and the
greater opportunity cost, and thus higher deterrent effect, of short periods of incarceration.)
However, it appears that popular opinion views the current treatment of criminals by the
courts as too lenient overall rather than as too harsh. See, for example, Tyler (1997, 872).

152. Compare Robinson and Darley (1997, 456), noting that, under their utilitarian-
based argument for punishments based on desert, the relevant indicator of the deserved level
of punishment is community sentiment, not philosophers' theories; thus describing their approach as "heretical" and one that some philosophers "will find . . . repugnant."

phrased as tastes for vengeance or revenge) and retributive theories of punishment, proponents of retributive justice have long been at pains to insist
that their theories are distinct from individuals' tastes for retribution.[153] Re-

153. See, for example, Fletcher (1978, 417), stating that retribution "is obviously not to
be identified with vengeance or revenge, any more than love is to be identified with lust";
Moore (1984, 235): "Retributivism is quite distinct from a view that urges that punishment
is justified because a majority of citizens feel that offenders should be punished. . . . What a
populace may think or feel about vengeance on an offender is one thing; what treatment an
offender deserves is another."; Moore (1987, 180–81), claiming that retributivism is not the
view that punishment should satisfy desires for vengeance; and Murphy and Coleman (1990,
120): "Kant is concerned to defend a theory of punishment that is generally called *retributivism*,
and Kant (with all other sensible retributivists) would stress that a commitment to retribution
is quite different from a commitment to such unattractive things as revenge or vindictiveness."
Some legal scholars, however, explicitly combine the ideas as if they were indistinguishable.
See, for example, LaFave and Scott (1986, 25), stating that the theory of retribution is "also
called *revenge* or *retaliation*"; ibid. (26, quoting Wood (1938, 636)): "Typical of the criticism
is that this theory [of retribution] 'is a form of retaliation, and as such, is morally indefensible.'"
Nozick, in his essay on retribution, discusses at some length the distinction between retribution
and revenge. See Nozick (1981, 366–70). He states that the retributive view "strikes some people
as a primitive view, expressive only of the thirst for revenge." Ibid. (366). He proceeds to list
a number of differences between the two (some of which are inapt if one considers the general
social norm of retribution described in subsection 1, which embraces proportionality and is
not necessarily limited to acts by a victim in direct response to one who has caused him injury).
He further notes that simply because one can distinguish the two notions does not show why
retributive theory is justified or why the two notions are so often confused.

Pincoffs offers an extended discussion of retributivists' difficulty in dealing with the problem of distinguishing their justification for punishment from revenge. He begins by asking:
"And has the retributivist cleared himself of the charge, sure to arise, that the theory is but
a cover for a much less commendable motive than respect for justice: elegant draping for
naked revenge?" Pincoffs (1966, 16).

> Retributivists are often, and in a variety of ways, accused of wishing to have
> revenge upon the criminal. . . . It is that since the retributivist explicitly ignores
> the consideration of the question whether any good consequences may be expected
> from punishment, and yet insists on the right to punish where a crime has been
> committed, his position is morally indistinguishable from that of a man who simply
> insists on revenge for crime.
>
>   . . . .
>
> To give as one's *reason* for inflicting pain or deprivation on a man that he has
> done a certain thing is an all too familiar way of talking. This is the language of
> revenge. . . . The suspicion is confirmed that retributivism is revenge-taking in
> disguise when we note how naturally revenge-taking assumes the form of the "Prin-
> ciple of equality": ambush the ambusher, blackball the blackballer. (Ibid., 43, 45)

See also ibid. (45): "The mystic connection which Hegel sees between crime and punishment
has very real historical and emotional roots."; and ibid. (46), discussing those who trace the
origin of criminal law to simple retaliation and psychiatrists who "are convinced that the *real*

tributivists seem to believe that their theories would have few adherents if the theories were understood merely as philosophers' abstract restatements of individuals' tastes for vengeance.[154] Indeed, because modern societies have sought to cabin tastes for retribution, it has been important for retributivists, who hope to persuade a contemporary, highly educated audience, to distinguish their views from individuals' tastes for seeing that criminals are punished.

Although retributivists are correct that a taste for retribution is qualitatively different from retribution as an independent evaluative principle, they have not provided satisfactory reasons to believe that we should regard retributive theory as other than a philosophized version of tastes for retribution. First, the degree of alignment between their theory—especially the core elements that are endorsed by most retributivists (notably, that wrongdoing and only wrongdoing should be subject to punishment and that punishment should be in proportion to wrongdoing)—and tastes for retribution seems too close to be due merely to chance. Second, their theory—which many

---

reason for punishment is the desire for revenge." Pincoffs states that he wants to examine how "traditional retributivists could meet the revenge argument: 'could,' because I have not found an explicit defense of the traditional view." Ibid.

> But the retributivist has not yet met the gravamen of the revenge argument. It is that the very theorizing about justice, freedom, and human dignity is what lies on the surface: that these are but glosses over the demand for revenge. . . . The retributivist has been challenged to produce a criterion by means of which we can say that A is punishing from motives of justice, but that B is punishing from motives of revenge. How are we to distinguish Solomon from Hatfield [when he takes revenge against McCoy], if both can speak the language of theory? (Ibid., 47)

See also ibid. (46): "[A]rguments about the origin and emotional basis of retributivism prove nothing about the validity of that position." Similar views have been expressed by others. See, for example, Holmes (1881, 40): "[I]t has never ceased to be one object of punishment to satisfy the desire for vengeance."; and ibid. (45): "The feeling of fitness [of punishment for wrongdoing] seems to me to be only vengeance in disguise. . . ." See also Crocker (1992, 1060 n.1), noting that some theorists have supported the association between retribution and revenge, but that if this is what retribution amounts to, "it would be no more than a wrinkle on the utilitarian prune."

154. See, for example, Crocker (1992, 1060): "In the public mind 'retribution' is synonymous with 'revenge.' As such, it is plausibly contended, retribution is something that an enlightened and humane criminal justice system can well do without. It belongs, along with whipping and the cutting off of hands, to the barbaric past."; Murphy (1991, 352–53): "We prefer to talk highmindedly of our reluctantly advocating punishment of criminals . . . and tend to think that it is only primitives who would actually *hate* criminals and want them to suffer. . . . Good people are above such passions or at least they try to be."; and sources cited in note 153.

have insisted (at least since Kant) is a distinct product of human reason—
is one that deems to be the essence of just punishment the same pattern of
behavior that, as we note in subsection 1, is engaged in by other animal
species and was probably followed by humans in primitive societies long
before the development of most notions of contemporary moral philosophy.
This coincidence appears to be even more troubling for the belief that views
about just punishment are distinct from tastes for retribution; the alignment
makes it difficult to imagine a plausible competing hypothesis that could
explain human intuitions and instincts about punishment over the course
of history as well as the behavior of other animal species. Third, as we discuss
in subsection B.1, most retributivists offer little direct argument to justify
their theory; rather, they take the matter of justification as largely self-evident
or, relatedly, invoke the views or feelings of ordinary people by explicitly
calling on our moral intuitions and instincts.[155] But there is every reason to

---

155. See generally note 108 in chapter II, discussing the problematic nature of fairness
notions that draw on intuition and instinct, and subsection VI.C.4(b) and note 112, discussing
the unreliability of appeals to instinct in retributivists' arguments about punishing the innocent.

Retributive theorists commonly appeal to moral intuitions and instincts to support their
theories. Ross, in one of the leading twentieth-century essays advancing the retributive view,
refers to the "plain men" who would "revolt" against or "feel the injustice" of a theory that
led to certain outcomes. Ross (1929, 205). Ross even refers to the retributive view, which he
supports, as intuitionistic and criticizes consequentialist approaches as "not the true intuitionistic view." Ibid. (206). He later suggests that many people no longer have a sense of the duty
of retribution, see ibid. (209), but goes on to conclude by referring to "the moral satisfaction
that is felt by the community when the guilty are punished, and the moral indignation that
is felt when the guilty are not punished, and still more when the innocent are." Ibid. (211).
This sense that retributive theory involves an attempt to identify the principles that best describe existing views or intuitions—rather than to present an affirmatively justified normative
framework—is reinforced by Wasserstrom, who states that the main point of retributive theory "is, essentially, that there are some important facts that need explaining and that neither
rehabilitative nor deterrent theories can explain; namely, that there are cases in which punishment seems appropriate and in which appeals either to the aim of deterrence or rehabilitation
appear to be quite beside the point." Wasserstrom (1977, 188). See also Ezorsky (1972, xxi),
describing the teleological retributivist view as a better statement of common morality than
utilitarianism. Wasserstrom concludes his discussion of retributivism and intuitions as follows:

> It seems no more or less illuminating than to speak of punishment for rape as
> deserved because of the seriousness of the wrong. It is to return, perhaps, to the very
> plausible intuition with which retributivism begins—that serious crime deserves to
> be punished—but it is not to give a wholly clear or distinct reason for moving
> beyond that intuition. We do not, I think, yet have in retributivism a set of moral
> arguments sufficiently sound, convincing, and worked out upon which to rest the
> justifiability of punishment. (Wasserstrom 1977, 194)   *(continued)*

believe that these intuitions and instincts are the products of evolution and

---

Greenawalt offers the following explanation:

> Why should wrongdoers be punished? Most people might respond simply that they deserve it or that they should suffer in return for the harm they have done. Such feelings are deeply ingrained, at least in many cultures, and are often supported by notions of divine punishment for those who disobey God's laws. A simple retributivist justification provides a philosophical account corresponding to these feelings. . . . (Greenawalt 1983, 347)

McCloskey discusses challenges to his own reliance on intuition in the following terms:

> The metaethic presupposed by my argument is an intuitionist one, but, as I have noted elsewhere and as a critic such as J. J. C. Smart has noted, my appeals to moral insights are readily reinterpreted as appeals to moral feelings and attitudes which are relevant considerations for those who hold emotivist, prescriptivist, and such metaethical theories, although I should, of course, wish to insist that they are more and other than this. (McCloskey 1967, 91)

See ibid. (105): "My own view is that all are committed to some sort of intuitionist view, or at least practice, in the area of justice, in determining what are relevant differences" pertaining to the punishment that a person deserves. He elaborates further in another article on the subject:

> Utilitarians frequently wish to dismiss such appeals to our moral consciousness as amounting to an uncritical acceptance of our emotional responses. Obviously they are not that. Our uncritical moral consciousness gives answers which we do not accept as defensible after critical reflection, and it is the judgements which we accept after critical reflection which are being appealed to here. (McCloskey 1965, 252)

Thus, McCloskey insists that he is drawing on intuitions rather than feelings or emotions, but he does not address the source of these intuitions, the sense in which they are distinct from tastes, or the basis for deeming them to be a valid source of insight. That is, he offers no criteria or system for critical reflection that could tell us when our intuitions should be trusted and when they should not. See also Hare (1986, 218), stating, in the course of referring to ordinary people's feelings concerning retribution, that: "We can if we wish dignify these experiences by the name of 'moral intuitions.'"; and Moore (1987, 189–90, 201–02), suggesting that emotions, not intuitions, should be our source of moral insight. This stance is problematic, particularly in light of the issues raised in the text (some of which, it should be noted, were suggested by Mill and other utilitarians writing long before McCloskey and most other retributivists whom we cite, which makes their failure to confront these challenges especially troubling). See also note 156. Finally, we observe that the heavy use of intuition in arguments about proper punishment is not confined to more philosophical treatments, but can also be found in applied works by legal scholars who examine particular legal doctrines as well as general principles of punishment. See, for example, Crocker (1992, 1066, 1073), indicating the essential role of moral intuition in applying principles of just punishment; and ibid. (1083, 1088, 1091), invoking moral intuition in assessing particular factors pertaining to the level of punishment.

It also should be noted that intuitions about "punishment" are not limited to the realm of punishment through formal government processes, but extend also to parents' and teachers' punishment of children, informal modes of punishment in social and business settings, behav-

the socialization processes described in subsection 1, which in turn give rise to tastes for punishment of a retributive sort.[156] Thus, despite the retributivists' protests, we submit that there is a good case for believing that the appeal of the retributive conception of fair punishment can be explained in the manner that we have suggested.

The preceding discussion of individuals' tastes for retribution began with the point that, under welfare economics, punishment should be adjusted to take account of individuals' preferences. The origins and functions of retribution as a social norm may also be relevant under welfare economics in a second manner, concerning the possible feedback effect of the law (here, policies concerning punishment) on social norms. To illustrate,[157] suppose

---

ior in international relations, and so forth. Most retributivist writers clearly have in mind only government-imposed punishment, but do not clearly distinguish the other punishment contexts in their arguments. (One problem that thus arises concerns the incompleteness of retributive theories with respect to defining which wrongful acts should be subject to legal punishment, as we discuss in subsection B.2.) For present purposes, it is clear that our intuitions and instincts about punishment arise in other contexts and are not limited in their application to formal law enforcement settings. Nevertheless, it is these highly generalized intuitions on which retributivists draw in order to determine what constitutes a just level of criminal punishment. In addition, as we note in the text, there are systematic differences between the two contexts that give us reason to believe that, even if intuitions provide a valid basis for inferring moral truth, it would be moral truth about how parents should treat children or how adults should treat each other, not necessarily about how governments should treat citizens.

156. See, for example, Daly and Wilson (1988, 256): "From the perspective of evolutionary psychology, the retributivist may be said to consult evolved moral/cognitive/emotional mechanisms to apprehend what *feels just*. Utilitarian considerations are then relevant to the task of explaining why such mental mechanisms have evolved." (Emphasis in original.) Retributivists might argue that their reflections and analysis have made them immune from their own human nature and socialization. We do not doubt that reason can play a significant role in analyzing normative principles. Indeed, our entire enterprise reflects such a view. Nevertheless, when retributivists fail to support their positions with explicit reasoning and instead appeal directly to intuitions and instincts (which are the same ones held by the general population, who cannot be presumed to have engaged in special reflection and analysis), one should be suspicious of their argument, particularly given what we know about the origins of those intuitions and instincts.

Some religions posit that certain, or all, individuals have direct access to divine revelation, in which case individuals' moral intuitions and instincts would have a claim to validity. We do not, however, understand most retributivists as grounding their theories in these terms. But there do seem to be exceptions. See note 12, quoting a statement from Pope Pius XII, whose views seem similar to those of leading retributivists. See also note 136, quoting Moore's explanation of the source of our moral beliefs.

157. Other factors pertaining to criminal punishment—less relevant to our discussion of the proportionality principle—have also been suggested as affecting public acceptance of criminal law. See, for example, Kadish (1967).

that society does not spend significant resources to pursue and punish those who commit a certain crime because the necessary expenditures would not directly be cost-effective. Such a policy may nevertheless reduce welfare if the resulting failure to mete out the punishment that individuals feel to be warranted causes a reduction in the perceived legitimacy of the legal system, thereby eroding social norms that produce voluntary compliance with the law and cooperation with legal authorities.[158] Likewise, punishments perceived as unduly harsh or lenient might undermine legitimacy as well as send misleading signals about right and wrong (and, in particular, about degrees of right and wrong).[159] As we discuss in subsections V.C.2 and VIII.A.3, such concerns are relevant to the effectiveness of the legal system and thus ultimately to individuals' well-being.[160] Under welfare economics, one would attempt to design the legal system in a manner that reinforces social norms serving valuable functions and that erodes social norms resulting in overly aggressive or otherwise counterproductive behavior.[161] We

158. See, for example, Bentham ([1781] 1988, 198–99): "When the people are satisfied with the law, they voluntarily lend their assistance in the execution: when they are dissatisfied, they will naturally withhold that assistance. . . ."; and Greenawalt (1983, 359): "The idea is that since people naturally think in retributive terms, they will be disenchanted and eventually less law-abiding if the law does not recognize that offenders should receive the punishment they 'deserve.' Although love for one's enemies may be a moral ideal, perhaps most people cannot feel strongly committed to a moral code without also wanting to see those who break that code punished." See also Daly and Wilson (1988, 246): "People are *relieved* to relinquish the duty of vengeance, but only if they can trust the machinery of the state to punish their enemies in their behalf, and thus to deter future wrongs."; and Wilson and Herrnstein (1985, chapter 19), arguing that levels of punishment should not deviate significantly from the retributive proportionality principle because excessively lax punishment risks vigilantism and excessively harsh punishment risks revolt.

159. See Hart (1968b, 25): "[F]or where the legal gradation of crimes expressed in the relative severity of penalties diverges sharply from this rough scale, there is a risk of either confusing common morality or flouting it and bringing the law into contempt." As mentioned in note 6, Robinson and Darley advocate—on entirely utilitarian grounds—that punishment be based on the popular understanding of desert for just this reason. See also Arenella (1992), emphasizing the tension between the criminal law's notion of culpability, which is broad in order to control dangerous activity, and morality's narrower notion of culpability, which the criminal law should respect in order for the legal system to be perceived as legitimate; Dan-Cohen (1984), exploring aspects of the criminal law that seem to send one signal to the general public—perhaps a harsh one, in accord with social norms concerning an act—and a different message to those who apply the law—such as permitting judicial leniency when it appears that punishment would not in fact be desirable in a particular type of case; and Kahan (1997), discussing the effect of punishment on social norms.

160. See generally Robinson and Darley (1995, 1997).

161. See generally Andenaes (1974, 59–60), emphasizing this function of punishment and giving as an example the effect of mandatory prison sentences on social norms toward

note, moreover, that the possible feedback effect of punishment on social norms may help to explain the appeal of retributive theory. After all, this theory favors punishment that is understood to be deserved in light of the wrongfulness of the act, and it seems plausible that such punishment—as we discuss in subsection 1 when addressing the inculcation of social norms—would tend to be functional in sending the right messages about proper behavior.[162]

In sum, social norms involving retribution are undoubtedly of some importance under welfare economics in assessing law enforcement policy, both because they manifest themselves as tastes and because they influence individuals' behavior (including compliance with the law and cooperation with law enforcement authorities). But the relevance of retribution as a social norm under welfare economics is entirely different from—and provides no warrant for—viewing retributive conceptions of fair punishment as independent evaluative principles, to be pursued at the expense of individuals' well-being.

---

drunk driving, and Dau-Schmidt (1990, 24–37), discussing the respects in which existing criminal law may shape preferences in useful ways.

Analysis of the effects of law enforcement policy on social norms and legitimacy is complicated. Maintaining an ineffective law for symbolic purposes may also send a negative message, that the legal system is not serious or is hypocritical. If the legal system is viewed in this manner, individuals may be less compliant with the law, less cooperative with authorities, and more inclined to engage in vigilantism. Furthermore, some laws may send multiple and even opposing messages about right and wrong. For example, a decision to impose capital punishment sends (at least) two messages: first, that taking life is viewed as a particularly serious wrong—so much so that the state is willing itself to engage in a most distasteful practice—and second, that taking life is not always so terribly wrong, as evidenced by the state's willingness to do so when it suits its purposes. See also note 150, discussing tastes for vengeance and the use of capital punishment, and subsection VIII.B.2, discussing the possible effect of the law on preferences. It is surely a complicated task to determine even the direction, much less the magnitude, of such feedback effects of the law on social norms, but it is important that the task be undertaken when the phenomenon may be significant. It is possible, for example, that these effects of capital punishment are as or more important than its immediate deterrent effects.

162. As we emphasize in our preceding discussion of tastes for retribution, however, the relevant notion of desert for present purposes depends on popular understanding, not philosophers' theories, which may depart from commonly held views in society. See also Robinson and Darley (1997), cited in note 152, regarding this distinction. We also note that this functionalist view of punishment, although it may seem similar to retributive theory, is actually quite distinct from it. See, for example, Moore (1987, 181): "Nor is retributivism to be confused with denunciatory theories of punishment [which are forms of] utilitarian theory. . . ."

3. Remark on the Ex Post Character of Notions of Fairness

Having now explored how social norms concerning retribution may underlie the appeal of the retributive theory of punishment, we remark on another aspect of retributive theory that may help us to understand its attractiveness, namely, its ex post character. As we discuss in subsection II.B.2(c), many notions of fairness lead one to adopt an ex post perspective, in which one focuses on particular outcomes (to the exclusion of other, potentially more frequent outcomes) and one tends to ignore the effects of legal rules on individuals' ex ante behavior. As we have already discussed in this chapter, the retributive theory of fair punishment has these features. We note in subsections C.1 and C.2 that punishments may seem fair ex post when one confines attention to those wrongdoers who are caught, whereas for many crimes most perpetrators go scot-free and hence do not receive fair punishment. Moreover, when one adopts an ex ante perspective—which is the outlook of the potential criminal when deciding whether to commit a crime—it is the (expected) punishments that tend to be favored under welfare economics that are proportional to the offense, not those deemed fair under retributive theory. In addition, as we observe in subsection C.4, using retributive theory as a guide to setting punishment may lead to more punishment of the innocent when one takes into account the ex ante effect of punishment on behavior, even though this outcome is undesirable not only on welfare economic grounds but also, it would seem, under retributive theory itself.[163] Overall, most factors that explain why the fair level of punishment under retributive theory differs from the level of punishment favored under welfare economics are ones whose significance under welfare economics is attributable to its more encompassing perspective. Notably, welfare economics pays attention to criminals who escape as well as criminals who are apprehended, and relatedly, takes account of how punishment affects potential criminals' behavior—factors that tend to be downplayed or ignored under retributive theory's ex post view.

In our initial discussion of the subject, we suggest that the inclination to adopt an ex post perspective can be understood by reference to well-known cognitive biases. Thus, when a criminal is apprehended and convicted, it is the proper punishment for this individual that seems most relevant, not how punishment should be set in light of the fact that there are many more unapprehended criminals who are not now, and never will be, before us for sentencing. Similarly, we are not inclined to focus on the crimi-

---

163. We note the same phenomenon in our internal critique of retributive justice in subsection B.2.

nal's initial choice and how it might have been affected by the punishment that would be applied, taking into account the probability of apprehension, for that choice has already been made and the criminal before us has already been caught.

That such an ex post perspective seems natural when we form impressions of a situation helps to explain why notions of fairness that embody this perspective seem congenial to us. These deficiencies in our intuitive thought processes, however, do not provide justification for viewing intuitively attractive notions of fairness, such as the proportionality requirement of retributive justice, as independent evaluative principles. This conclusion is reinforced by the fact that the alternative is to employ welfare economics, a system of assessment that does not suffer from these limitations but instead takes a more inclusive perspective in order to consider all of the effects of legal rules that may bear on individuals' well-being.

E. The Extent to Which the Use of Notions of Fairness Has Led Us Astray

In this section, we inquire briefly into the extent to which reliance on principles of fairness concerning punishment has led society to make unwise decisions concerning law enforcement policy. We suggest that the existing system of punishment follows neither retributive theory nor welfare economics very closely. Nevertheless, we identify a number of respects in which the retributive conception of fairness does seem to be given real weight, with possibly significant adverse consequences.

Under the retributive conception of fairness, punishment should fit or, according to some, should be equal to the gravity of the offense. However, actual punishment is substantially higher than retributive principles would seem to require or permit when there is a low probability of apprehension, such as there is for many common categories of crime, for which the probability often is only one or two percent.[164] In discussing society's practice with

---

164. Robinson and Darley report that the average rate of conviction for all offenses listed is 1.5%. The particulars are: motor-vehicle theft, 1.1%; larceny-theft, 0.9%; burglary, 2.1%; assault, 1.1%; robbery, 4.2%; rape, 14.0%; murder and non-negligent manslaughter, 47%. Robinson and Darley (1997, 461 table 1). (The average is so low despite the latter figures because there are many more offenses in the categories with low conviction rates.) Low probabilities of apprehension are not a unique feature either of the current times or of the United States legal system. See, for example, Paley ([1785] 1825, 371), describing the practices of eighteenth-century England and other governments.

regard to the retributive theory of punishment in contexts in which the probability is low, one commentator remarks that, "[e]specially in regard to crimes against property, punishments by imprisonment are far more severe, on the average, than the harm caused to victims of these crimes."[165] He offers the example of theft of a few thousand dollars, which might be punished by years of imprisonment, and concludes: "The disproportion between violated or deprived rights of the victims and those of the criminals in these crimes is obvious."[166] For very minor offenses as well, like parking violations, penalties are often very disproportionate to the offense. For example, a person who fails to put $0.25 in a parking meter may be fined $15.00, a ratio of fine to offense of 60 to 1. In contrast, for murder the ratio obviously never exceeds 1 to 1, and, for many categories of murder and manslaughter, the penalty is neither life imprisonment without parole nor capital punishment. Thus, it is fair to say that penalties are not, even approximately, in any particular proportion to the underlying offense (much less a proportion of one).[167]

Nor is it the case that punishments are set as they would be under welfare economics.[168] The validity of this claim is suggested by the nature of academic analysis and public discourse about punishment. To be sure, the instrumental goal of controlling crime often receives much attention, but in many contexts incapacitation is emphasized and deterrence is ignored, and assessments of punishment do not explicitly compare the costs and benefits of different policies. In addition, notions of fair punishment are frequently invoked, and these references do not seem simply to refer to individuals' tastes about punishment. Indeed, fairness arguments often are advanced in opposition to public opinion. Because both explicit analysis and general discourse

165. Goldman (1979, 49).

166. Ibid. For sentencing data, see note 169.

167. The practice of increasing the level of punishment for categories of crime for which detection is more difficult has a long history. As Wertheimer has noted, even the Bible, which states the general rule of *lex talionis,* deems a proportion greater than one appropriate for property crimes. See note 70.

168. See, for example, 28 U.S.C. §994(c)(4)–(5), stating the purpose of the Sentencing Reform Act of 1984, creating the U.S. Sentencing Commission, as providing just punishment, in addition to achieving instrumental objectives. Nevertheless, patterns of punishment often do reflect welfare economic considerations. See, for example, Glaeser and Sacerdote (2000), finding evidence that sentences actually imposed for murder do vary with the expected apprehension rate, likely responsiveness of behavior to punishment, and expected recidivism rates, consistent with the view that punishment is designed to deter and incapacitate, but also finding that punishments reflect victim characteristics in a manner that corresponds to the level of sympathy that citizens might display for different victims.

do not reflect systematic welfare economic thinking and instead give weight to fairness, there is reason to suspect that our system of punishment often may fail to promote individuals' well-being to the fullest possible extent.

A brief examination of some particular aspects of actual punishment policy indicates that such failures do seem to arise. Consider first whether the level of sanctions for certain offenses is sufficiently high. As noted, the probability of conviction for many offenses is only one or two percent. Even though penalties usually exceed the harm caused, they do not do so by an amount that would seem to be necessary to achieve deterrence objectives.[169] For example, in the case of motor-vehicle theft, even though imposed sanctions exceed a year (which does seem disproportionate to the offense), the expected sanction is under a week, which is probably less than many potential offenders' expected gain.[170] Another example is income tax evasion. The probability of an audit for many groups is under one percent, yet the standard penalty (short of proof of criminal fraud, a difficult standard to meet) does not even require the taxpayer to return twice the amount of taxes that were avoided.[171] Thus, it is not very surprising that, outside of areas with electronic reporting (which ensures a very high probability of detection even without a standard audit), the rate of noncompliance in the United States is often over twenty-five percent and the estimated tax gap approaches $100 billion per year.[172] Higher penalties for tax evasion—and even stiffer prison

169. Robinson and Darley indicate that the federal/state sentences imposed (with time served in months in parentheses and with average rates of conviction in brackets) for less serious crime categories are as follows: motor-vehicle theft, 28/33 (21/13) [1.1%]; larceny-theft, 19/33 (16/14) [0.9%]; burglary, 34/61 (26/22) [2.1%]; assault, 35/52 (42/23) [1.1%]. Robinson and Darley (1997, 461 table 1). Thus, expected sanctions for these crimes are less than one month.

170. Because the average time served for motor vehicle theft is in the range of 13 to 21 months, ibid., or about 56 to 91 weeks, and the probability of conviction is 1.1%, the expected sanction is under a week.

171. In 1995 the average audit rate for individual returns was 1.7%, and the civil penalty for underpayment of taxes ordinarily is calculated as 20% of the underpayment that results from wrongful conduct. See Andreoni, Erard, and Feinstein (1998, 820). Thus, for every dollar of underpayment, the expected payment, including the underpayment and the civil penalty, is only about 2¢ (0.017 × $1.20). Since 1995, the audit rate has fallen below 1 percent, making the problem of underdeterrence even greater. See Internal Revenue Service (2000b). However, supplemental deterrence is provided by the possibility of prosecution for criminal fraud, although there are few convictions, typically just under 2000 per year. See Internal Revenue Service (2000a).

172. See, for example, Internal Revenue Service (1996, 5 table 1), presenting estimates of the federal personal income tax collection gap for tax year 1992 that range from $93.2 to $95.3 billion; ibid. (8 table 3), indicating that the portion misreported averages about

terms for property crimes—seem to fall beyond the bounds of fairness for many people, which may help explain why less stringent punishment is employed instead.[173] It is possible that individuals have very strong tastes about these matters or that using higher penalties would send confusing signals about right and wrong or undermine the legitimacy of the legal system, in which case our analysis in subsection D.2 would indicate that higher penalties would not best promote welfare after all.[174] But, as analysts have not done the necessary work to assess these or other factors properly, we hardly can be confident that this is the case.

A related problem is that society may be forgoing the opportunity to economize on or usefully reallocate enforcement resources because of misguided concerns about fair punishment. To take a mundane but important example, suppose that we reduce enforcement expenditures on illegal parking by half. This reduction would free a great deal of policing resources that could be used elsewhere, such as for controlling violent crime.[175] We could reduce enforcement expenditures on illegal parking without affecting the number of parking violations if we were to raise the typical parking fine, say, from $20 to $40. But such a high fine might be considered unfair, in which case a large potential gain is sacrificed. Again, it is possible that people would have strong tastes about any increase in the sanctions for parking violations, but if one reflects on the likely truth of the matter, it seems that people would not feel so strongly and thus, if the gains in enforcement resources were truly substantial, they would not find such a policy change

---

30 percent for business income, in contrast to about 1 percent for wages, 2 percent for interest, and 8 percent for dividends.

173. Another strategy to address underdeterrence would be to increase greatly the detection rate, but this strategy would be very costly. For example, a very high tax audit rate (well in excess of 50 percent at given penalty levels if evasion were to be made unprofitable) would be extremely expensive in terms of audit resources, taxpayers' time, and the perceived intrusion involved. These costs probably help to explain the opposition to providing significantly more audit resources to the IRS.

174. Opposition to higher sanctions may reflect a misunderstanding of how sanctions should be set rather than a strong taste for lower sanctions. See generally section VII.C, discussing the possibility that citizens may not understand which laws are best. For example, if asked what was the appropriate punishment for some offense, most people might well offer an answer that did not reflect its probability of apprehension—and, in particular, the reality that it may be only one or two percent. But if the same people were asked (after the relevant theory was fully explained) whether a higher sanction, one designed to raise the *expected* punishment closer to the level of harm caused by the offense, was appropriate, they might well agree.

175. For example, New York City's Parking Enforcement District has just over 2000 enforcement personnel. Parking Enforcement District (2000).

inappropriate.[176] In any event, in this and other contexts, society may be ignoring valuable strategies because they are deemed out of bounds on account of their perceived unfairness.

Another concern is that following the principles of retributive theory might lead society to set punishment higher than is best from the standpoint of individuals' well-being.[177] For example, consider the recent popularity of "three-strikes-and-you're-out" policies, under which an individual who is convicted for a third time of committing even fairly minor crimes receives a sentence of life imprisonment.[178] Although such policies obviously reflect a desire to decrease crime, they also seem to be fueled by concerns about retribution, which are particularly sharp, many believe, because multiple recidivists have so clearly rejected society's norms and institutions.[179] One should consider, however, that very high sanctions are not necessary to deter most individuals who can plausibly be deterred, especially from committing relatively minor offenses. Thus, it may be that the main impact of three-strikes policies is to impose very costly additional sanctions on groups who essentially are undeterrable (a practice that our analysis in subsection C.3 indicates would tend to reduce welfare).[180] It is true that long incarceration

176. There are limits to the potential to save resources in this manner. For example, a fine of $1,000 for a parking meter violation would be viewed as outrageous, and, even if it ultimately could be justified, it probably would be difficult to communicate the reasoning effectively to an irate citizenry. Furthermore, even without regard to tastes, such high fines would be problematic under welfare economics, due to individuals' risk aversion, increased expenditures devoted to contesting tickets, and increased incentives for corruption that would exist with such high fines in this setting. It seems doubtful, however, that such factors are very significant in the range of fines considered in the text.

177. Dolinko offers this explanation for many recent trends in punishment policy that he believes to be unwise. See Dolinko (1991, 559; 1992, 1652–54). Although his evidence on the cause of the trends is not convincing in our view, and although he does not directly argue for his claim about the undesirability of the trends, his discussions do raise the question whether growing attention to retributivism may lead society irrationally to adopt unduly harsh punishment.

178. See, for example, Tonry (1996, 3–4) and Kessler and Levitt (1999, 350–52). We note, however, that many three-strikes laws are narrower or are not applied as vigorously as one might expect from the rhetoric that often is used to describe them. See, for example, Kessler and Levitt (1999, 360).

179. See, for example, Greenwood et al. (1996, 54), surveying standard arguments for three-strikes laws, including the view that "[i]t is the 'right thing to do' [because] justice demands that those who repeatedly cause injury and loss to others have their freedom revoked."

180. See, for example, Tonry (1996, 134–35). With regard to those who are deterrable, there is the problem that three-strikes rules may reduce marginal deterrence; for example, a two-time offender may face life imprisonment for the next offense regardless of its severity.

may yield crime reduction benefits through incapacitation, but criminal activity tends to drop off substantially with age, so there may be little benefit in this respect as well.[181] As with our prior examples, we are not claiming that existing policies are definitely erroneous. We do suggest, however, that there is a basis for concern in light of analysis that gives attention to fairness while downplaying or ignoring important factors pertinent to individuals' well-being and given the existence of various particular policies that seem questionable. Thus, it is important to society for legal policy analysis to be redirected along the lines of welfare economics.

181. See, for example, Tonry (1996, 138, 191–92), Blumstein (1983), and Kessler and Levitt (1999, 345–46).

PART THREE

EXTENSIONS

CHAPTER VII

On the Use of Notions of Fairness
and Welfare Economics by Different
Types of Actors

In chapters III–VI, we attempt to show that the framework of welfare economics is compelling and that notions of fairness should not be given independent weight in the evaluation of legal policy. In this chapter, we explore the implications of our thesis for three different types of actors: ordinary individuals, who must make decisions in their everyday lives; legal academics and other policy analysts (our primary audience), on whom society relies for expert guidance in designing legal rules and institutions; and government decisionmakers, who need the advice of experts but also must be held accountable to ordinary individuals for the policy decisions that they reach.

As we discuss in section A, many notions of fairness that are internalized in individuals serve the function of curbing opportunistic behavior that might result if individuals were to calculate what is in their own self-interest. In addition, ordinary individuals cannot be expected to employ rigorous analysis in making decisions in their daily lives; for such individuals, notions of fairness function as proxy devices that substitute for explicit analysis. Hence, it tends to be socially desirable for individuals to be guided by notions of fairness.

As we first describe in section II.D, however, these justifications for ordinary individuals' making decisions based on notions of fairness do not apply to legal academics.[1] In section B, we consider why notions of fairness nevertheless seem to hold so much appeal to those who analyze legal policies. Furthermore, we elaborate on why it is important for legal academics to

---

1. We refer only to their work as academics. Even in that domain, however, there are exceptions. Notably, a strong norm of scholarly integrity is probably socially useful in the academic community.

make explicit use of welfare economics rather than to employ fairness-based analysis.

In section C, we briefly explore the somewhat more complicated role of government decisionmakers—legislators, regulators, and judges—who occupy an intermediate position, standing between the experts and ordinary citizens. We believe that government decisionmakers should generally be guided by the proper normative framework, which we have argued is that of welfare economics. We recognize, however, that they sometimes may need to make adjustments in light of the limited understanding of the people whom they represent and to whom they are accountable.

A. Ordinary Individuals

As we discuss in section II.D and illustrate in chapters III–VI, notions of fairness correspond to social norms that are useful in guiding ordinary individuals in their everyday lives. We identified two main functions of social norms. First, the inculcation of social norms may lead individuals to behave more in society's interest by avoiding opportunistic, self-interested behavior. Second, social norms may serve as rules of thumb for countless decisions for which careful calculation would be wasteful because the stakes are insufficient to warrant the required effort. To fulfill both functions, we emphasized, social norms must be ingrained to the extent that individuals would tend to conform their behavior to them without real reflection. Were individuals consciously to assess the consequences of their behavior, they might act in their self-interest, defeating the first function of the norms. And considered appraisal of decisions would, by definition, compromise the second purpose of the norms as well, for then calculation costs would be incurred.

This use of social norms by individuals in the course of everyday life thus makes good sense. Of course, it is true that following social norms, rules of sorts, will sometimes lead individuals to behave in other than an ideal manner, but such consequences are unavoidable. Moreover, some social norms may be detrimental or, at a minimum, may benefit from further calibration.[2] In all, however, it seems clear that social norms can and do serve useful functions in channeling behavior in ways that promote individuals' well-being; furthermore, welfare economics encompasses this aspect of social norms.

The foregoing points make clear that our criticism of the use of notions

---

2. See note 92 in chapter II. Thus, our endorsement of social norms in the domain of everyday life should not be understood as ruling out the possible desirability of their refinement or even significant reform through the efforts of educational and other social institutions.

of fairness is not relevant to the behavior of ordinary individuals in realms governed by social norms. Our critique concerns the importantly different setting of legal policy analysis. It is in that context that we argue that the use of notions of fairness, which usually correspond to social norms, is inappropriate.[3] The allure and resilience of notions of fairness to policy analysts has been unfortunate in this regard, as we now discuss more fully.[4]

B. Legal Academics

In this section, we consider why legal academics (and other legal policy analysts) rely heavily on notions of fairness and elaborate on why we believe this practice generally to be counterproductive. We close by reminding the reader of the ways in which notions of fairness may be relevant under welfare economics, even though they should not serve as ultimate criteria for policy assessment.

1. The Appeal of Notions of Fairness to Legal Academics

We have argued that, in the wide range of legal contexts that we have examined, legal policy analysis should be guided exclusively by welfare economics, and thus that no weight should be given to notions of fairness as independent evaluative principles. If our argument is correct, it raises the question why legal academics so often choose to invoke notions of fairness and related concepts. We have a number of conjectures that may help to answer the question. Although our ideas in this regard might be described as involving speculative sociology, we believe that there is some value in reflecting on the roots of current normative discourse in the legal academy.

Before discussing reasons that use of notions of fairness may be attractive to legal academics, we observe that the alternative of employing normative

3. There is, as we discuss in section C, an important case of overlap, namely, when ordinary individuals act in their role as voters or otherwise participate in the formulation of public policy. In these settings, we believe that individuals should and already do to some extent adopt a somewhat different perspective from that they take in everyday life, and, in particular, one that more comports with a welfare economic approach.

4. Our argument about the difference between the norms appropriate for individuals in ordinary life and the principles that should guide legal policy analysis is analogous to the distinction between levels of moral thought that we discuss in note 121 in chapter II. Indeed, the distinction between levels of moral thought has primarily been employed as a device both for better understanding the operation of social norms that guide the behavior of ordinary individuals and for providing a perspective from which one can critically assess the content of prevailing social norms.

economic analysis has seemed problematic to many of them.[5] We suspect
that they have often found normative economic analysis inadequate because
of a belief that it excludes important considerations. However, as we explain
at some length in section II.A and illustrate throughout chapters III–VI, the
welfare economic framework is significantly more encompassing than what
is generally understood to be the normative economic approach to assessing
legal policy. (As just one example, welfare economics considers effects on the
distribution of income to be important.[6]) Nevertheless, the welfare economic
approach that we present in this book is not well understood in legal academia because to date there has been no sustained attempt, even among law
and economics scholars, to present welfare economics in a systematic manner. Thus, the appeal of using notions of fairness may in part stem from a
misunderstanding about the nature of the alternative.[7]

We now turn to affirmative reasons that the use of notions of fairness
may be attractive to legal policy analysts.[8] First, as we discuss throughout the
book, notions of fairness tend to have intuitive appeal to analysts (including
ourselves) because they correspond to internalized social norms. The explanation, recall, is that analysts themselves are members of society and thus

5. Recall that we define notions of fairness to encompass all bases for evaluation other
than welfare economics. See subsection II.B.1. Thus, in the context of our argument, welfare
economics is by definition the only alternative to using notions of fairness. Yet, as we discuss
in the text to follow, normative economic analysis is not generally understood in legal academia
to mean welfare economics, as we describe that normative framework in this book.

6. As we point out in note 41 in chapter II, certain arguments by Richard Posner favoring
wealth maximization were criticized by economists (as well as by philosophers and legal academics) for ignoring concerns about the distribution of income.

7. This diagnosis seems particularly apt when a notion of fairness is embraced because
it incorporates an aspect of well-being or a concern about income distribution that one thinks
is missing from an economic evaluation. For example, in subsection V.C.2 we note that certain
issues involving legal procedure that are often expressed using the rubrics of fairness and
justice, such as concerns about abuse of power and the legitimacy of the legal system, are not
thought to be included in a normative economic assessment; but since these concerns are
related to individuals' well-being, they are in fact incorporated in a welfare economic analysis.
In such an instance, one might ask why it matters whether the analyst continues to use the
notion of fairness or engages in welfare economic analysis. As we elaborate in subsection 2,
we believe that there is value in using welfare economics explicitly because doing so helps the
analyst keep ultimate objectives clearly in mind. If one really is concerned about individuals'
well-being, then one should assess legal rules directly in terms of how they affect well-being.
If one instead employs notions of fairness as proxy indicators of well-being, one runs the risk
that the notions will take on lives of their own, so that one ends up pursuing notions of
fairness even when they will reduce well-being. Our discussions throughout chapters III–VI
suggest that this danger is substantial.

8. Given the speculative nature of this subsection, we do not assume that our list of
reasons is exhaustive.

have had social norms involving notions of fairness inculcated in them from an early age;[9] principles of fairness govern our interactions from the beginning of childhood and are the central element of normative discourse in everyday life. Moreover, we have explained that it is in the nature of social norms and the process of their transmission to small children that the norms come to be understood as having intrinsic importance. The implication is that notions of fairness can be expected to have a strong hold on the mind of any well-socialized individual when that individual engages in legal policy analysis, particularly in light of the similarities that exist in the behavior that is regulated in everyday life and in the legal context—behavior that may harm others.[10]

Second, we frequently emphasize that many notions of fairness involve the adoption of an ex post perspective, which tends to be attractive because it focuses on the most salient features of a situation.[11] Our analysis suggests that familiar cognitive biases incline everyone, including academics, to employ such an approach, even though it leads one to downplay important aspects of the problems at hand, aspects that are incorporated under welfare economics because they affect individuals' well-being.

Third, legal academics who advance arguments under the rubric of fairness often are able to assume the mantle of moral superiority in discourse with other academics.[12] In part, this is due to the correspondence between

9. As we note in subsection II.D.1, some scholars suggest that certain social norms are innate rather than inculcated (see, for example, note 94 in chapter II; see also subsection VI.D.1, discussing social norms concerning retribution), but our point obviously holds in this case as well.

10. See subsection II.D.2.

11. See subsection II.B.2(c).

12. For example, it seems to be almost a standard in contemporary moral philosophy— at least those parts of the field most familiar to legal academics—that the "right" (which is associated with notions of fairness) is normatively prior to (superior to) the "good" (of which one conception is welfare economics). See, for example, R. Dworkin (1977) and Rawls (1971, 1988). It appears to be the case that analysts who employ the language of rights (fairness, justice) are themselves regarded as morally superior to their peers who are wholly concerned with the good. There is an irony in this state of affairs because the "good" includes *everything* related to individuals' well-being, a basic fact that is rarely made clear. Moreover, much of this general philosophical writing (like the scholarship, criticized in chapters III–VI, addressed to particular notions of fairness), as well as typical legal academic discussions of the matter, makes little direct effort to defend placing greater weight on even the slightest advance in the right over unlimited costs to the well-being of everyone (including purported beneficiaries of greater protection of rights). The alleged supremacy of the right over the good has a long history, and the prevalence of the view seems to have motivated some of Mill's writing. See Mill ([1861] 1998, 102–03), discussing "the difference between the Just and the Expedient" and the related belief "that justice is a more sacred thing than policy," and explaining the view in terms of a two-level theory; and ibid. (107), exploring further the sentiment that

notions of fairness and norms of common morality that have been instilled in everyone. The moral overtones of the debate between analysts who use

---

justice is more important than expediency by making reference to social norms that advance welfare. However, Mill's arguments (and those of others) seem to have been largely ignored by twentieth-century scholars. See note 121 in chapter II, presenting the foregoing point and discussing two-level theories more generally. See also Hare (1981, chapter 9), critically examining typical philosophical arguments concerned with rights and justice, and ibid. (154–56), stating that "[w]e are very reasonably told [by Dworkin] that we should 'take rights seriously,' [and if] we take them seriously enough to inquire what they are and what their status is, we shall discover that they are, indeed, an immensely important element in our moral thinking," but arguing that the special status of rights is properly established by two-level utilitarian thinking, not by prevailing intuitionist theories that proclaim rights to be trumps.

The aura of moral superiority surrounding proponents of notions of fairness may also be supported by another common misinterpretation concerning welfare economics (and utilitarianism, and consequentialism more generally): "It is both the essence of consequentialism and the trouble with it that it treats The Good, rather than people, as the source of normative claims." Korsgaard (1996, 301). Such characterizations give the impression that analysts who use welfare economics (or other consequentialist approaches) are individuals who lack a basic concern for humanity. Yet it should be clear from section II.A that the opposite is true. The very definition of welfare economics (and, on this issue, the same is true of utilitarianism, the most commonly advanced form of consequentialism) is that what counts as "The Good" is precisely that which is valuable to people. Essentially the same point was expressed by the early utilitarians. See, for example, Bentham ([1781] 1988, 3): "The community is a fictitious *body,* composed of the individual persons who are considered as constituting as it were its *members.* The interest of the community then is, what?—the sum of the interests of the several members who compose it."; and Mill ([1861] 1998, 82–83), emphasizing that the principle of utility does not mean that pleasures or exemptions from pain should be understood as a "means to a collective something termed happiness, and to be desired on that account." Perhaps because economists often use "wealth," "efficiency," and other shorthand expressions and proxy objectives, see subsection II.A.3, this point about the basic nature of welfare economics is not more generally understood. Moreover, as we discuss in section II.B, notions of fairness are principles of evaluation that by their very nature depart from individuals' well-being and consider other factors to be of independent normative significance. Hence, by definition, such notions are not ones that make people—or, at least, their well-being, which includes everything that is important to them—the source of normative claims.

A similar issue arises with an often-quoted statement of Rawls that "[u]tilitarianism does not take seriously the distinction between persons." Rawls (1971, 27). This assertion is discussed by Hare, who emphasizes that utilitarians are aware that distinct persons are involved, so the only meaning that can be given to the familiar objection of failing to "take seriously the distinction between persons" is to understand it as a criticism of the equal treatment of persons required by utilitarianism. See Hare (1997, 151–52). Hare further explains how, as Mill had suggested, Kant's views seem to require precisely the treatment of people dictated by utilitarianism, for to treat others' ends as my own ends requires that I not "distinguish between different people, but, as justice demands, [give] equal weight to their and my equal interests." Ibid. See also Hare (1989a), discussing Mackie's more nuanced version of Rawls's criticism.

notions of fairness and those who employ a normative economic approach reflect the fact that most of the audience—other legal academics, judges, law clerks, students, readers of op-ed pieces, friends—share a common background in which notions of fairness and justice are seen as having moral force.[13] Moreover, most of this audience is not trained in policy analysis.[14]

This state of affairs is reinforced by a related point: The alternative to employing notions of fairness is perceived as involving a calculating, cold-hearted approach that seems foreign to our moral intuitions.[15] It appears to some that normative economic analysts care only about numbers, whereas analysts who endorse notions of fairness, by virtue of this very practice, act in a moral manner.[16] But, as we have emphasized, this view represents a basic misunderstanding of welfare economics, the defining feature of which is an exclusive concern with individuals' well-being. That is, the statistics of

---

13. Furthermore, as suggested by our discussion of the operation of social norms in subsection II.D.1, individuals—whether through socialization or evolution—develop automatic negative reactions to norm violations by others, which suggests that individuals will reflexively express disapproval toward those who speak, write, or otherwise display attitudes that appear to be in tension with governing norms. Thus, when welfare economics seems to conflict with notions of fairness that correspond to social norms, the natural human reaction is not to side with notions of fairness in an academically objective and detached manner, but rather to react with emotion. In academic interchange, we believe that this phenomenon manifests itself in a reluctance to question the prevailing normative views and in a tendency to be dismissive toward those who do express doubts and to regard them as ignorant or amoral. In this respect, attitudes about notions of fairness, even if derived from tastes associated with social norms, see note 117 in chapter II, have a different character from most other types of tastes when there is disagreement. Were food scientists to debate about the taste that people do or should display for rhubarb, their reactions to colleagues who challenge dominant views would be quite different from the typical responses to analysts who challenge the foundations of prevailing notions of fairness.

14. In addition, the bulk of legal academic work is published in journals for which the selection of articles is undertaken by student editors, who typically have only a few years of legal training and no formal academic training or experience, rather than by leading experts with substantial training and experience within a discipline. And, as suggested by the text, these students, like everyone else, have been exposed to and inculcated with notions of fairness and thus will naturally find attractive submissions that employ those notions rather than welfare economics. This situation further increases the incentives for legal academics to appeal to notions of fairness in their writing.

15. One may recall from subsection II.D.1 that social norms (common morality) tend to be such that calculation and reflective analysis are discouraged.

16. Compare R. Posner (1998, 1657): "And moral discourse may to a considerable extent be a mystification rooted in a desire to feel good about ourselves—to feel that we are more than just monkeys with big brains, that we are special enough for God to take a particular interest in us."

the seemingly cold-hearted analyst measure such matters as how many people are hurt or helped, and to what extent, by different legal rules[17]—matters
that, as we have explained, often are ignored or are addressed only indirectly
when analysis is based on popular notions of fairness.[18]

A fourth explanation for the use of notions of fairness by legal academics
is that they are often best able to influence policy by employing the form
of discourse that is congenial to the most common set of legal decisionmakers that they address, namely, judges. Judges have largely the same background, training, and inclinations as legal academics, so notions of fairness
will seem attractive to them as well. In addition, judges are not, in the ordinary course of their work, systematically exposed to detailed policy analysis
from experts.[19]

A fifth factor explaining the use of notions of fairness by legal academics
is that the notions often allow analysts to reach definite conclusions, a result
that is psychologically pleasing and also makes it possible to recommend
policies with greater assurance.[20] The main reason that the use of notions
of fairness often leads to more confident conclusions is that the implications
of the notions do not depend on the effects of a legal rule on behavior, its
administrative costs, and so forth[21]—all of which may be difficult to deter-

17. See also subsection II.A.3, discussing the relationship between the welfare economic
concern with well-being and the concepts of wealth maximization and efficiency.

18. A real irony is involved here. On one hand, welfare economics is concerned entirely
with individuals' well-being—virtually the definition of humanitarianism—whereas notions
of fairness are concerned only partly (and, some aver, not at all) with well-being. On the
other hand, it seems that many people are inclined to view normative economic analysis as
cold-hearted, while viewing fairness-based normative analysis as humanitarian. (For a discussion of the view that the technical work required of analysts will make them cold-hearted,
see note 116 in chapter VIII.)

19. Furthermore, the most common work experience of legal academics, outside the
academy, is as clerks to judges (and not as assistants to regulators or legislators). Also, when
legal academics address the judiciary, they need not be concerned with persuading intermediaries such as expert staffs, lobbyists, or political organizations; they may focus on the judges
themselves or on their law clerks, who are former students of the legal academics.

20. Greater assurance in recommending policies may not translate into greater success.
The relevant audience may adhere to notions of fairness that differ from the analysts' preferred
notions; nevertheless, analysts most interested in being influential might be inclined to base
their assessments on the notions that are endorsed by the relevant audience. In addition, there
remains room for controversy among analysts about the correct notions of fairness to employ,
although many groups at particular points in time may experience an approximate consensus.

21. As we discuss in subsection II.D.1, it is important that social norms (which correspond to notions of fairness) be relatively simple and easy to apply—without undertaking
much, if any, explicit analysis and thus not attending to the particular and possibly subtle

mine, thereby rendering conclusions under welfare economics less certain. (This "shortcoming" of welfare economics is, of course, an essential feature of a framework designed to assess, in a complex world, the actual effects of legal rules on individuals' well-being.[22])

In sum, legal academics are naturally drawn to notions of fairness, and using the notions appears to have the benefit of increasing legal academics' influence. As we elaborate in the next subsection, however, legal academics must employ welfare economics in their policy analysis if they truly are going to be in a position to improve government decisionmakers' choices of legal rules, measured against the benchmark of individuals' well-being.

2. Why Legal Academics Should Be Guided by Welfare Economics

Throughout this book, we argue that the assessment of legal rules should be based on welfare economics, under which exclusive attention is given to the effects of legal rules on individuals' well-being. Here, we presume this argument to be correct and consider its implications for the work of legal academics in particular.[23]

Initially, we observe that it is important that there exists a substantial group of experts who engage in normative (and positive) economic analysis of legal rules. As with most other forms of expert policy analysis (say, of drug safety, highway design, or military preparedness), ordinary individuals in their capacity as citizens are, understandably, unable to engage in refined legal policy analysis. In addition, government decisionmakers are often too busy and sometimes not sufficiently trained to perform the required analysis themselves. Therefore, we suggest, the social responsibility to provide proper expert advice about the design of legal rules and institutions will often rest with legal academics.[24]

---

features of a situation. Moreover, as we note previously in this subsection, such limitations on the inquiry may in part be a by-product of the attraction to the ex post perspective entailed by many notions of fairness.

22. Nevertheless, the potential uncertainty of economic analysis in this respect is often explicitly identified as a defect. For further discussion of this issue, see subsection VIII.D.4(a).

23. We do not mean to suggest that there are no other important functions of legal academics (such as understanding and teaching the content of legal doctrines or of transactions in which lawyers take part), but rather that a significant group of legal academics should and do engage in policy analysis and that this analysis should be based explicitly on welfare economics.

24. The only plausible alternative is that the work should be done primarily by social scientists in schools of arts and sciences or in think tanks. But if legal academics are to engage in policy analysis, then in producing their own analysis or in translating the work of social scientists for government decisionmakers, they must employ the proper normative frame-

We do not discharge our responsibility as legal policy experts if we allow ourselves to be guided by simple norms designed for everyday life, if we restrict the sophistication of our academic analysis to ensure that it is fully accessible to those with little welfare economic expertise, and if we resist being viewed as engaged in a sometimes technical enterprise.[25] Relatedly, we are unlikely to invest the effort to undertake the empirical work that is necessary to determine the actual effects of legal policies if we are strongly influenced by notions of fairness whose nonconsequentialist character denies or diminishes the relevance of such effects for legal policymaking.

Moreover, we contend that undertaking welfare economic analysis in an explicit manner is the best way to practice welfare economics, which is to say, it is the best way to determine which legal rules in fact are most likely to improve the well-being of members of society. To many, this claim may seem obvious, for the best way to achieve an objective is usually to aim for it directly rather than to engage in a qualitatively different enterprise. Nevertheless, some suggest that pursuing notions of fairness—not as principles important in their own right, but merely as a means to the end of identifying legal rules that increase welfare—may be attractive in light of two facts: First, notions of fairness often align with welfare, and second, explicit welfare economic analysis is difficult, both because the analytical work is complex and because empirical knowledge is often limited.

In the context of legal policy analysis, this latter view should carry very little weight. First, notions of fairness, usually corresponding to social norms, tend to be simple in structure, and they are designed to function in the qualitatively different environment of everyday life. As we discuss in subsec-

---

work. Moreover, there are good reasons for much legal policy research to be undertaken by legal academics and not just by scholars elsewhere in the academy. First, legal academics are closer to the law, lawyers, and legal institutions and thus have a comparative advantage in studying them. Second, government officials and the public look to the legal academy for guidance, not only because of this comparative advantage, but also because legal academics now offer such advice and other sources of advice are insufficient. Third, it is socially valuable for lawyers—who will often present arguments and analysis to government officials and who will sometimes be the officials themselves—to be exposed to proper methods of policy analysis during their training.

25. We suggest that legal academics have a further responsibility concerning the communication of ideas to policymakers and the public. An implication of our analysis in subsection 1 is that it would be easy to present appealing but misleading critiques of the normative economic approach that appeal to contrary fairness notions. Legal academic commentators need to develop ways to present clearly and comprehensibly what can be subtle, technical, or counterintuitive aspects of welfare economic analysis in order to prevent others from being misguided by such criticism.

tion II.D.1, some social norms are explicitly rationalized as rules of thumb to be used when the stakes are low, when there is little time for calculation, and when the decisionmaker is not trained to undertake proper analysis. Moreover, one of the most important functions of social norms—including most that correspond to the notions of fairness that are widely used in legal policy analysis—is to restrain individuals from doing what otherwise would make sense to them, thus preventing them from opportunistically pursuing their self-interest at the expense of others. To accomplish these objectives, the norms lead individuals to refrain from explicit assessment of decisions and their consequences. But notions that are intended to cabin analysis are notions that should not be employed in the context of academic policy evaluation, as we discuss further in a moment.

Perhaps the most important limitation on the use of notions of fairness for policy analysis stems from the fact that the contexts of informal regulation of everyday life and formal legal regulation are so different. We have, for example, identified differences in the sanctions employed, methods of detecting violations, availability of information, motives of agents involved in enforcement, and other factors that imply that different rules may be more suitable in the formal legal setting.[26] Once the social norms that correspond to most notions of fairness are well understood, it is evident that following notions of fairness when designing legal rules will often lead us to incorrect conclusions.

Second, we have compared analysis based on leading notions of fairness to that based on welfare economics in a wide range of legal contexts, in chapters III–VI, and we have repeatedly found that rules grounded in notions of fairness may indeed be misguided. Often, it is clear that a notion of fairness omits important factors, such as the administrative costs of operating the legal system or the deterrent effect of different legal rules. Once an omitted factor is identified, it makes little sense for analysts to continue pursuing the notion of fairness on the ground that following notions of fairness sometimes will lead us to select the same legal rules as we would choose under welfare economics. We also observe that the relative ease of applying notions of fairness, compared with careful analysis under welfare economics, is closely related to this shortcoming of fairness-based analysis. A complete welfare economic analysis may be difficult because the actual circumstances are complex and important facts are not known with confi-

---

26. See, for example, subsection II.D.2. Another relevant factor is that social norms evolve slowly, and thus norms that are no longer useful may not yet have been displaced. See note 92 in chapter II.

dence. Analysis based on a notion of fairness can allow an analyst to avoid these difficulties only because such analysis ignores complicating factors or favors one legal rule over another without regard to facts concerning its actual effects. Fairness-based analysis may seem less problematic, but only because its deficiencies remain hidden.

Third, we believe that the argument for making substantial instrumental use of notions of fairness reflects a misunderstanding of the enterprise of academic policy analysis. If analysts had to make policy recommendations on very short notice, then their use of common notions of fairness might be sensible, for analysts would not have the time to undertake meaningful investigation. But this is patently not the situation of analysts in the academy. Academics study problems, such as choosing among tort rules or setting levels of punishments, over the years. Their work is undertaken collaboratively by dozens or hundreds of scholars, each building, usually incrementally and sometimes critically, on the work of others.[27]

Therefore, with regard to our primary audience of legal academics and other serious analysts of legal rules, the question is how best to conduct this enterprise over time, which is to say, how to design a research agenda. Such an agenda includes preliminary fact gathering and analysis, followed by an ongoing process of refinement and reformulation of hypotheses combined with empirical tests. The process exploits a well-recognized and important synergy between theoretical and empirical work: The latter tests the hypotheses of the former, and the former builds or modifies its models and chooses its avenues of research in light of the facts identified by the latter. In this setting, it is clear that the overall research program should be formulated by direct reference to the actual objective one seeks to pursue, the advancement of individuals' well-being. Notions of fairness that limit the scope of analysis, that do not suggest the full path of inquiry, and that systematically diverge from the real goal will not provide sound guidance.[28]

27. Baron emphasizes that the value to individuals, in the setting of everyday life, of rules of common morality that entail simplification because of human limitations does

> not imply that [these] simpler rules are more adequate as normative standards than full consequentialist analyses.
>
> Moreover, some decisions are so important that the cost of thorough thinking and discussion pales by comparison to the cost of erroneous choices. . . . In these matters, the thinking is often done by groups of people engaged in serious debate, not by individuals. Thus, there is more protection from error, and the effort is more likely to pay off. (Baron 1994a, 8)

28. Relatedly, Posner argues that legal academic work would be more socially useful if it shifted emphasis from what he refers to as academic moralism to explicit social scientific

It is useful to contrast two instrumental uses of notions of fairness by legal policy analysts. One use, which we believe to be valuable, draws on our intuitions and instincts about notions of fairness as heuristics or diagnostics. Notions of fairness are like other intuitions and instincts: They may suggest a tentative answer to questions, motivate inquiry in useful directions, and serve as a check against the tendency to accept too readily new and intriguing yet untested ideas. Thus, when a particular result seems fair or unfair to us, we should, for purposes of analysis, entertain the working hypothesis that there may well be something behind our feelings.[29] We should then explore the problem, both analytically and empirically, and also reflect on our notion of fairness, such as by trying to determine its origin—perhaps in a social norm that serves an identifiable purpose. In some instances, we will thereby identify important considerations that we might otherwise have omitted from our analysis. At other times, we will find ourselves replicating analysis that we have already undertaken. But there also will be occasions, as we repeatedly illustrate in chapters III–VI, when we will find our notion of fairness to be misleading. As we note above, a common phenomenon is that the notion of fairness reflects one important factor in a situation but ignores others, such as the administrative costs of the legal system or variations in the rates of detection of different offenses.

Alternatively, analysts might make substantial instrumental use of notions of fairness. Our argument against this approach can be summarized as follows. First, if one substitutes analysis based on notions of fairness for

---

investigation of the effects of the legal system. See, for example, R. Posner (1999, viii), advocating the use of "analytic methods, empirical techniques, and findings of the social sciences"; and ibid. (xiii): "Too large a fraction [of the intellectual resources that are invested in law] is going to the articulation and elaboration of abstract normative theories and too small a one to the development and application of social scientific theories and to the collection of data about how the legal system actually operates and with what costs and other consequences."

29. See, for example, Hare (1971, 128): "[V]ery often, many heads are better than one, and many ordinary men in the course of generations may have seen aspects of the question which in our relatively brief experience we have ignored."; ibid. (134), suggesting that the opinions of ordinary men "do not supply an argument; but they make us look for one"; Harsanyi (1995, 331): "No doubt, our moral intuitions can have a useful *heuristic role* in ethics, even in utilitarian ethics, because they may call our attention to some moral problems we might otherwise have overlooked. But they cannot replace our *rational judgment* on how to resolve these moral problems in the best interest of the people affected."; Mirrlees (1982, 75), stating that the fact that a properly derived conclusion is contrary to instinct is "a good reason to check the argument, particularly for omitted considerations; not a reason for rejection"; and Smart (1973, 37). Compare Stigler (1972, 5), suggesting that most people's conceptions of justice are not broad or definite enough to solve policy problems, and that injustice suggests a need for change more than it suggests the method or direction of change.

the explicit analysis called for by welfare economics, one will not be able to distinguish among the different types of situations described in the preceding paragraph, so one will never know when our intuitions in fact lead us astray.[30] Second, if one does undertake the proper analysis and finds that the notion of fairness is incomplete or otherwise deficient, there is no reason at that point to continue to be guided by fairness notions just because they sometimes (notably, other times) serve the instrumental function of helping to identify which legal rule is best. Any instrumental gain from using the notion of fairness to suggest a path of investigation will have been exhausted. Thus, although there are reasons for legal academics to draw insight from intuitions about which legal rules seem fair, there is no ongoing or independent role for analysis based on notions of fairness, presuming that ultimately one is convinced that we should choose those legal rules that best advance individuals' well-being.

3. Reminder of the Ways in Which Notions of Fairness Are Relevant for Legal Policy Analysis under Welfare Economics

We have argued that legal rules should be assessed under welfare economics, wherein exclusive attention is paid to the manner in which the rules affect individuals' well-being. In this subsection, we briefly remind the reader of various ways in which notions of fairness remain relevant for legal policy analysis under the framework of welfare economics, though not as independent principles for evaluating legal rules.

First, as we have just discussed, notions of fairness sometimes help to identify rules that advance welfare and thus, to an extent, may be useful in suggesting avenues for analysis. Second, when individuals have a taste for a notion of fairness—that is, they feel better off when a legal rule reflects their preferred fairness notion—a welfare economic approach accords weight to the notion of fairness, just as it would any other taste, to a degree that reflects

---

30. One of our main points in subsection II.D.2 is that notions of fairness correspond to social norms that may well be functional in the contexts of ordinary life for which they were designed, but may be unsuitable in the qualitatively different setting of designing rules for the formal legal system. In a sense, therefore, many arguments about legal policy that are based on notions of fairness can be understood implicitly as involving reasoning by analogy. Such reasoning can be illuminating, but, for familiar reasons, it is often unreliable. See, for example, Baron (1994a, 1998), analyzing the problem of overgeneralizing moral rules in making policy decisions; R. Posner (1998, 1660–61 n.38): "Generalization (less grandly, pattern recognition) seems to be an innate and very valuable, but of course fallible, capacity of the human animal."; and ibid. (1675): "Analogies stimulate inquiry; they do not justify conclusions."

the strength of that taste.[31] Third, notions of fairness often correspond to social norms that regulate individuals' behavior in everyday life; if a legal rule might reinforce or undermine such social norms, this effect would factor into an assessment of the rule's desirability.

To illustrate these points, we recall our discussion in chapter VI of the notion of fairness that the punishment should fit the crime, which is to say that penalties should be proportional to the gravity of offenses. This notion of fairness might be relevant to welfare economic analysis for each of the reasons just mentioned. First, punishment that fits the crime implies more severe punishments for more serious offenses, which tends to make sense in terms of deterrence and incapacitation because, the more harmful the crime, the greater the benefit of reducing its incidence. Second, individuals may be upset if punishments depart significantly from the principle of proportionality; hence, their well-being might be reduced if the principle is ignored in the analysis. Third, as we explain, the proportionality principle corresponds to a social norm that usefully regulates the degree of social sanctions and also strengthens general understandings of right and wrong; perhaps significant violations of the principle when setting criminal sanctions would lead to some erosion of this presumably valuable social norm.[32]

Nevertheless, the foregoing hardly implies that criminal punishments should closely adhere to proportionality. For example, if the proportional punishment for automobile theft were imposed, it might be that, on account

---

31. We emphasize, as we discuss in subsection II.A.1, and throughout the book, that tastes for notions of fairness are qualitatively distinct from notions of fairness used as independent evaluative principles. Moreover, as we explain in note 13 in chapter II, most legal academics and philosophers who advance notions of fairness do not understand themselves to be referring to individuals' tastes. Finally, when it comes to the empirical question of determining what fairness-related tastes individuals have and how much they value satisfying those tastes as compared to other tastes, we observe that our empirical hunches as academics are unlikely to be reliable guides. First, the aesthetic preferences of individuals who choose an academic life are probably atypical. In particular, we probably have greater intrinsic interest in certain matters, which induces us to study them even though the compensation is below that of available alternative occupations. Second, we are undoubtedly influenced by the very process of study. Hence, we are far more aware of what rules exist and what alternatives are possible, and we may cultivate tastes about rules and institutions through intensive, prolonged examination of them. One conjecture is that most of these observations are particularly applicable to philosophers and others who specialize in the elaboration of notions of fairness. In addition, these points may have some relevance for individuals who choose to devote significant parts of their careers to government service (especially at the highest levels, where there is greater responsibility and discretion with regard to policymaking).

32. See subsection VI.D.2.

of the low likelihood of punishment for the crime, automobile theft would become rampant and huge social losses would follow. Many would not buy cars; others would curtail their use of cars and make substantial expenditures to prevent theft. In this case, the proportionality notion is arguably not a good means of determining the best level of punishment. Moreover, disproportionately high penalties for automobile theft, such as those typically imposed,[33] probably have neither caused great displeasure among our citizens nor seriously corrupted social norms. This example illustrates that, in spite of the various ways in which notions of fairness may be important under welfare economics, analysis based on an explicit assessment of all the effects of legal rules on individuals' well-being will often lead one to conclusions different from those that one would reach if one asked which rule most closely reflected a notion of fairness.

C. Government Decisionmakers

Legal policy decisions are generally made by government officials—legislators, regulators, judges—who occupy an intermediate position between the citizens they serve and legal academics and other policy analysts who, in principle, supply expert advice.[34] We focus here on problems that may arise due to the fact that the language and content of the expert advice that government actors receive may not always be readily understood by constituents. Particularly when policies have subtle or counterintuitive effects, citizens may not easily accept the rationale of the recommended policies, which may conflict with familiar notions of fairness.

Before proceeding, let us note the existence of important differences among government decisionmakers in their expertise, available time, modes of operation, delegated powers, and political accountability. One consequence of these factors is that many government officials have little of the policymaking authority under discussion. An auditor who works for the Internal Revenue Service is not authorized to make tax policy, either in general or in the case of a particular taxpayer under audit; such authority rests in Congress and, to a lesser degree, through delegation, is vested in various other officials in the Internal Revenue Service and the Department of the

---

33. See section VI.E and note 169 in chapter VI.

34. Some legal policy decisions are made directly by citizens through referenda. In such instances, there are often groups—political parties, organizations representing particular interests, or self-appointed concerned citizens (sometimes including legal academics)—who serve some of the intermediary functions that we discuss in this section.

Treasury. It is the latter groups with whom we are concerned here. Another case is that of judges, who have some policymaking discretion, although they are also constrained by rules of procedure, statutes, precedent, and the Constitution. The extent to which judges should employ welfare economics or other decisionmaking techniques obviously depends on the nature of the authority they have been delegated and other factors that are outside the scope of our inquiry.[35] For the remainder of our discussion, we consider the position of those government decisionmakers who do have substantial policymaking discretion, and we examine some of the common issues they face in making and communicating their decisions that are based on welfare economic analysis.[36]

One strategy for addressing citizens' limited capacities to comprehend policy analysis is for political actors to use familiar language—such as the language of fairness—in public statements (including, possibly, court opinions[37]) when explaining their decisions. On one hand, this strategy often will be easy to employ, for there are sufficiently many notions of fairness perti-

35. What authority they should be delegated by a legislature or in a constitution is itself a question that can and should be analyzed under welfare economics, as suggested by our discussions in subsections V.C.2 and VIII.A.2. We also note that courts might not be delegated the authority to undertake extensive welfare economic analysis on their own (in the manner we suggest in subsection B.2 that analysis should be undertaken, over long periods of time by expert policy analysts), but they might nevertheless be directed to perform simplified versions of the analysis or to make use of such analysis performed by others. Furthermore, if it is determined that courts should be restrained in their use of welfare economics, it does not follow that they should rely on notions of fairness instead; nor do we know which particular notions among the many conflicting ones judges should consult even if notions of fairness are deemed authoritative. When a notion of fairness serves as a good proxy for promoting welfare, however, it is more plausible that a court should be instructed to employ the notion of fairness, at least as a rule of thumb.

36. It follows from the preceding discussion of institutional differences that the existence of common issues does not imply that their appropriate resolution is the same for different types of government decisionmakers. For example, the situation of a specialized regulator who is accountable mainly to the corresponding congressional committees may differ from that of a legislator who reports directly to a group of citizens.

37. Some seem to believe that court opinions and other official statements of legal policy should employ language that can be understood by the masses. Of course, most individuals would never read or understand most such pronouncements even if their authors avoided technical language, whether legal or economic. The dominant audiences for court opinions are judges, lawyers, academics, other compilers of legal doctrine and critics thereof, and—in some areas of the law (regulation of abortion, not details of bankruptcy rules)—the media. It is not obvious that these groups should find it more difficult to understand basic (and even some more sophisticated) principles of economic analysis—positive and normative—than to understand often arcane legal language and rules.

nent to most issues that a favored policy can usually be justified by reference to some notion of fairness. In addition, because notions of fairness often serve as proxy indicators of elements of a welfare economic analysis, it will sometimes be possible to identify a fairness argument that captures the essence of an important factor under welfare economics. On the other hand, precisely because there are so many notions of fairness and because they tend to be broad and incompletely defined, the language of fairness may not communicate the justifications for policy choices very well. Given that statements will be subject to different and conflicting interpretations by the audience, it will be difficult to sort out the arguments. Further complications will arise when others, who disagree, themselves invoke competing notions of fairness. (Consider the argument that strict liability is fair because innocent victims deserve compensation, which can readily be met with the response that the negligence rule is fair because it is improper to punish individuals who have done nothing wrong.)

It may be largely unnecessary, however, to resort to the language of fairness in order to communicate the basis for conclusions reached under welfare economics. Much economic reasoning is, at root, easy to explain. If government officials tell citizens that a new rule is favored because it deters harmful behavior or saves administrative resources, the citizens will be able to understand these rationales. Thus, we suspect that it would often be best for government decisionmakers to speak directly about the actual effects of competing policies on individuals' well-being (without necessarily resorting to the formal language of economics).[38] For example, decisionmakers can explain that the overly generous provision of insurance without co-payments may induce overuse of services, without any need to use the term "moral hazard."

Although we believe the problem of communication of welfare economic justifications to be less serious than many suppose, there will sometimes be a significant conflict between the policy that decisionmakers, based on advice from legal policy analysts, understand to be best and the policy that ordinary citizens think is fair.[39] Should political officials, who are supposed to

38. Compare Schelling (1981, 42): "[W]hatever I know as an economist that can help, in the analysis of interacting behaviors in the market and in identifying where the ethical issues are, I can probably communicate it if you have an hour or two. You needn't just take my word on it, and you needn't think it inaccessible."

39. Sometimes the opposite is the case; citizens might demand greater attention to costs and benefits—such as litigation costs in the tort context or benefits of crime control with regard to law enforcement—while various legal academics might advocate downplaying considerations of welfare in order that legal rules may better reflect their own preferred notions of fairness.

be accountable, do what they think will actually benefit citizens, or should they do what their constituents mistakenly believe to be appropriate?[40]

With regard to such a problem, we offer three observations. First, the problem has nothing in particular to do with economic analysis, whether positive or normative, or with what are generally viewed as legal rules. Thus, a government official might be confronted with two competing designs for a new highway, one that engineers have demonstrated to be safer and another that the public thinks to be safer. Then one must ask whether the official should adopt the design that saves more lives or the one that uninformed citizens mistakenly think is superior.

Second, however one should resolve such conflicts, it is essential that government decisionmakers receive good advice in the first place. Even if they will not always automatically choose the safest highway design, surely those responsible for the decision should learn from experts which design is actually safer and by how much. After all, one hopes that government officials will usually follow such advice, and, when deciding whether to deviate, they will wish to know the costs: Just how much less safe is the more popular design? (Indeed, such decisions by government officials can themselves be analyzed using welfare economics, just as can other institutional issues, as we discuss in section VIII.A.) Analysts should not abandon their task and instead deliver opinions that will be perceived as attractive even though they are not well founded. If compromises are to be made on account of public misunderstanding, such decisions should be left to those who are publicly accountable, not to engineers, scientists, or legal policy analysts. The duty of analysts is to teach, write, and speak publicly about the virtues of sound analysis, even at the expense of their own popularity, particularly in cases in which such analysis may strike a less expert audience as troubling because its rationale is counterintuitive.[41]

---

40. Compare E. Posner (1998, 1207–13), discussing the analogous problem of the government's need to make tradeoffs when citizens purport to believe that competing factors are incommensurable.

As we explain in subsections II.A.1 and II.D.2, and elaborate in subsection VIII.B.4, to the extent that individuals actually have a taste for fairness—or for any other characteristic of a policy—that taste would presumptively be included in assessing which policy best advances social welfare. Thus, the conflict presented in the text concerns a case in which citizens mistakenly believe that one policy is better when they either do not have any independent taste for the favored policy (which we think would often be the case) or do not have a sufficiently strong taste for that policy so as to exceed the other, unappreciated benefits of the competing policy.

41. As one commentator remarks:

[Legal academics] could in appropriate circumstances adopt a view of professionalism closer to that of economists. This would mean confining themselves to present-

Third, the actual need for compromise between doing what will improve individuals' well-being and doing what individuals mistakenly believe to be best can readily be overstated. Often, no real conflict will exist. Many legal rules and features of institutional design are unlikely to be perceived by ordinary individuals in any event.[42] In addition, citizens often expect government

---

ing the advantages and disadvantages of available choices as honestly as possible and then deferring to other decisionmakers. In private contexts this would be entirely consistent with lawyers' traditional obligations to their clients. In public contexts, though, it would require lawyers to place less emphasis on their roles as advocates and participating decisionmakers, and to view the government—or the public— as their client. (Katz 1996, 2266)

Our point is not that legal academics have no responsibility for their actions. To the contrary, they have, for the reasons we discuss, a responsibility to provide undistorted advice to government officials. Although one can construct scenarios in which government officials are sufficiently corrupt or evil that they should not be advised honestly, we doubt that most contemporary legal academics typically find themselves in a position in which they would be justified in behaving in a manner that is not designed accurately to inform government officials and the rest of society.

A more plausible case can be made in favor of legal and other policy analysts concentrating their efforts in a manner that offsets certain asymmetries in the political process. For example, if a well-organized special interest group is able to fund experts to present analyses favorable to one side of a question, it may be appropriate for some academic policy analysts to concentrate on the other side of the question because that is where they are more likely to make a real contribution to understanding. We are very reluctant, however, to take this point further, to the extent of justifying the provision of false information—whether through dishonest research or through analysis and argument that relies on misleading principles of assessment (which we consider notions of fairness to be, when they conflict with welfare economics)—on the ground that such a strategy is necessary to counterbalance forces on the opposite side of an issue. Our conjecture is that the long-run costs of this type of behavior are likely to be very high, involving loss of credibility by the few relatively disinterested expert sources of policy advice. (The reader should recognize that we are making the familiar sort of argument that following a general rule or principle uniformly may be in the long-run interest of society, even if deviations in a particular case might seem justifiable. Compare subsection II.D.1, discussing social norms that operate as rules that, among other things, may prevent miscalculation that arises from case-by-case decisionmaking, which may be distorted by self-interest, pressures of the situation at hand, or other factors; subsection V.C.2, describing the role of legal procedures in limiting the potential for abuse; and subsection VIII.A.2, noting the use of rules to prevent abuse of power by government officials.)

42. See, for example, Sunstein (1996a, 2050): "Statute books are rarely read and are barely intelligible when they are read. The same is even more emphatically true for the *Federal Register*. Supreme Court decisions are at best filtered through newspapers and magazines." In addition, some laws may be perceived in one way by citizens but be interpreted differently by the government officials who apply them. See, for example, Dan-Cohen (1984), discussing this phenomenon with respect to the criminal law.

officials to act based on superior, expert knowledge rather than in response to opinion polls. Sometimes this delegation is explicit, as in the case of the FDA. More commonly, the delegation is implicit; citizens expect government agencies, legislative committees with expert staffs, and even judges to pay substantial attention to expert advice rather than simply to enact whatever rule or regulation would likely be favored by a group of citizens chatting over a few beers.[43] Furthermore, citizens to some extent probably appreciate the distinction between the notions of fairness—the social norms—that are appropriate in guiding everyday interactions and the methods of analysis that should guide the design of legal rules and institutions to govern a complex economy and society. For example, citizens may not expect to understand the analysis used to determine rules for intricate commercial transactions, and they may not be at all surprised to learn that these rules may deviate in certain respects from the principles of fairness that guide their interactions with neighbors.[44] Finally, government decisionmakers should not overlook the possibility of educating their constituents, particularly over the long run, especially if they will receive the constructive assistance of legal policy analysts.[45]

43. See, for example, Brandt (1979, 324–25), stating that the principles for the optimal tax and transfer scheme are too complex to teach people as part of the moral code but that such effort is unnecessary because "[t]hose persons charged with implementing the code will know what to do."

44. See also note 146 in chapter VI, discussing the tendency of individuals to compartmentalize views about ideal government policy and about appropriate individual behavior.

45. Compare Bentham ([1781] 1988, 199), suggesting that popular discontent with sound punishment policy arises only when people are under the hold of "some prejudice or other, which it is the business of the legislator to endeavour to correct"; Calabresi (1970, 295), stating that the public cannot change its feelings immediately and that traditional moral attitudes are difficult to change, but that if proofs are strong, attitudes will eventually change; and Sunstein (1997), arguing that some reasons that the public is concerned about particular types of death reflect confusion and suggesting that public opinion should be educated rather than followed when setting regulatory policy. As we discuss in subsection VIII.B.2, sometimes laws themselves may have an educative function. To the extent that they do, if legal policy follows the prescriptions of welfare economics, citizens who do not initially appreciate the desirability of laws that in fact benefit them will be more likely to accept such laws over time.

The analysis is more complicated when one wishes to enforce individually irrational but socially productive social norms, see subsection II.D.1, such as a norm of retribution that leads individuals to make personal sacrifices to assist in the apprehension of criminals. See subsection VI.D.1. In this case, if government officials successfully explain their purpose, they might undermine the norm-inculcating effect. Compare L. Alexander and Sherwin (1994), discussing the problem of a ruling authority that wants its subjects, without having the discretion to make their own exceptions, to follow rules that the authority knows are sometimes overinclusive or underinclusive and hence may command individuals to behave wrongly.

In spite of the preceding arguments, the problem that government officials must mediate between experts and constituents is real. Although we do not have any special solution to offer, we do wish to reemphasize two points. First, the problem has nothing in particular to do with the use of welfare economics or the domain of legal rules. Second, the primary audience for this book—the group who we believe should employ welfare economics exclusively—is not government decisionmakers, but rather legal academics and other analysts who engage in systematic assessment of the desirability of legal policies.

CHAPTER VIII

Comments on the Breadth and Soundness of Welfare Economics

A number of questions and criticisms are commonly raised about normative economic analysis of law. Although we address many of them in section II.A or implicitly in chapters III–VI, it is useful to consider some of the more prominent ones in greater depth because our comments relate to our general thesis about the virtue of welfare economics. In section A, we examine how welfare economics deals with a variety of concerns about the design of legal institutions that are often expressed under the rubric of fairness. In section B, we explain how analysis under welfare economics deals with problems related to the idea that legal policy should be based on individuals' preferences, and we consider further the possibility that individuals' preferences may include a taste for notions of fairness. In section C, we discuss whether welfare economics properly takes into account bad luck and inequality. Finally, in section D, we offer remarks about other asserted difficulties associated with economic analysis of legal policy.

The generality of welfare economics is a theme that we emphasize throughout this chapter. Much skepticism about the normative economic approach appears to reflect a belief that it is too narrow to capture certain matters that are of concern to individuals and society. This belief, however, fails to recognize the true nature of welfare economics that we elaborate in section II.A. To the extent that anything is actually important to individuals, welfare economics encompasses it by definition: Everything that is thought to be socially relevant because it has value to members of society is included in the measure of social welfare. To be sure, some factors influencing individuals' well-being may be difficult to analyze or to quantify, but this problem is not a shortcoming of the welfare economic framework; rather, it is intrinsic to the assessment of individuals' well-being, which is an unavoidably complex undertaking. Moreover, in the face of such a challenge, it would obviously be a mistake to substitute some other criterion for evaluation, such as a notion of fairness, on the ground that it is difficult to ascertain how best to achieve the objective that we truly wish to pursue. After all, making other criteria the basis for policy assessment will turn out to be easier than a welfare economic analysis only if the alternatives ignore real complexities concerning the effects of legal rules on individuals' well-being.[1]

A. Design of Legal Institutions

Some writers suggest that normative economic analysis of law fails to recognize important concerns regarding the design of legal institutions.[2] Moreover, certain notions of fairness, particularly those relating to legal procedure, address such matters and thus might be seen to gain appeal by remedying a deficiency in the economic approach. In this section, we consider the manner in which welfare economics in fact incorporates a number of considerations involving legal institutions. Our primary message is that institutional concerns are properly addressed by welfare economics because it encompasses all respects in which legal rules and institutions may affect individuals' well-being.[3]

---

1. Indeed, in chapters III–VI we often suggest that notions of fairness tend to favor different policies from those recommended under welfare economics precisely when the notions are insensitive to important factors that are included in a welfare economic analysis. See also subsection VII.B.1, suggesting that an aspect of the appeal of notions of fairness to legal academics may be their ease of application, which is due to their ignoring relevant complexities in the world.

2. See, for example, Tribe (1985), suggesting that such concerns as the need to constrain government actors for fear of abuse of power—see subsection 2—are outside of a normative economic approach. This criticism is somewhat surprising given that the classical utilitarians, viewed by many as among the first to engage in what has evolved into modern normative economic analysis, were explicitly concerned with issues of abuse of power. See, for example, Bentham ([1822–1823] 1990), and Mill ([1861] 1998, 93): "We should be glad to see just conduct enforced and injustice repressed, even in the minutest details, if we were not, with reason, afraid of trusting the magistrate with so unlimited an amount of power over individuals."

3. We offer two observations about economic analysis in this regard. First, economic analysis of legal policy often sets aside issues of institutional design in order to focus on other factors. But, as we explain in subsection II.A.3, this approach to analysis helps to advance understanding; the use of the method should not be misunderstood as reflecting a belief that institutional concerns are unimportant or somehow outside the scope of welfare economics. (continued)

1. Accuracy

As we illustrate in section V.B, a number of procedures and institutions that are favored on grounds of fairness—for example, the right to a hearing, a day in court, or an unbiased adjudicator—are means to enhance the accuracy of the legal system. Other arguments relying on ideas of fairness—such as the objection to simple "rules" that are sometimes overinclusive or underinclusive (in contrast to more open-ended "standards")—suggest even more directly that accuracy is at stake. As we explore above, however, the accuracy of the legal system is often relevant to individuals' well-being, and the subject of accuracy is thus, unsurprisingly, amenable to welfare economic analysis.[4]

Of course, welfare economics does not simply favor more accuracy; instead it takes account of the cost of accuracy and the extent to which greater accuracy actually promotes individuals' well-being, which varies greatly by context. This approach contrasts with notions of fairness that favor greater procedural refinement regardless of its contribution to accuracy, the benefit from greater accuracy in a particular context, or the cost of achieving it. The welfare economic approach also differs from more moderate notions of fairness that favor accuracy-promoting procedures to a point but that do not provide any basis for determining when and to what extent such procedures are desirable.[5]

Second, the requisite positive analysis of institutional issues—which involves predicting the behavior of legislators, regulators, judges, and other government actors—may require techniques that are somewhat different from those that are used to analyze the behavior of private actors in the marketplace. Predicting the behavior of government officials and institutions, however, has become the subject of a growing body of literature in the field variously described as public choice theory, rational choice theory, positive political theory, and political economy. Seminal modern works include Downs (1957), Buchanan and Tullock (1962), Olson (1965), and Niskanen (1971). More recent works, collections, and surveys include Mueller (1989, 1997), Ordeshook (1986), Alt and Shepsle (1990), and Buchanan, Tollison, and Tullock (1980). Work in this field is less developed than that concerning the economics of market behavior, reflecting the shorter time of intense study and perhaps the greater inherent difficulty of analyzing government behavior. In any event, the correct overall approach is clear in principle: Under the appropriate normative framework—welfare economics—the relevant *positive* analysis includes any pertinent branch of the social sciences, not just certain familiar aspects of positive economics. See subsection D.5, further discussing the relevance of other social sciences to welfare economic analysis.

4. In addition to the references in section V.B on the economic analysis of accuracy in adjudication, see those cited in Kaplow (1998), and Kaplow (2000), discussing the precision of legal rules and other matters pertaining to the choice between rules and standards.

5. See subsections V.B.2 and V.B.3(e).

2. Controlling Government Officials' Behavior

Calls for fair procedures and institutions may also reflect concerns about the problem of controlling government officials' behavior, particularly their exercise of discretion.[6] Society desires judges and juries to be bound by the law, agencies to implement statutes faithfully, government officials to make decisions on the merits rather than on the basis of political bias or private financial interest, and all actors to apply effort rather than to shirk their duties. Indeed, standard lay definitions of fairness refer explicitly to some of these concepts.[7]

The desire to control government officials' behavior, like the concern for accuracy, is properly addressed using welfare economics.[8] Indeed, this general problem is the subject of a substantial body of economic scholarship and has parallels with issues considered in the economic analysis of corporate law, particularly the control of the behavior of agents (managers rather than government officials) for the benefit of principals (shareholders rather than citizens).[9] It is true that applying the economic approach to the control of government officials and institutions may require somewhat different analysis from that employed in traditional market settings,[10] and the costs of abuse of discretion may have a different character in the public context. Nevertheless, the overall orientation is the same: Higher-quality legal institutions are not defined in a vacuum or viewed as a good in themselves, but are understood as a means to better decisions that, in turn, promote individuals' wellbeing. We also observe that promoting individuals' well-being embraces the notion, which underlies many constitutional provisions,[11] that it might be

6. See sources cited in note 2, and in note 154 in chapter V.

7. See, for example, *Merriam-Webster's Collegiate Dictionary* (10th ed. 1993), defining "fair" as, among other things, "marked by impartiality and honesty: free from self-interest, prejudice, or favoritism," and "conforming with the established rules."

8. See subsection V.C.2.

9. See, for example, Pratt and Zeckhauser (1985), Shleifer and Vishny (1997), and Stiglitz (1987). We also note that tools similar to those used to constrain government institutions— including mandatory corporate rules and provisions in corporate charters or bond covenants that are difficult to amend—are utilized in this sphere.

10. See note 3.

11. Although often couched in the language of fairness, concerns about abuse by government officials seem to be a central motivation underlying many constitutional provisions. See, for example, Stanley v. Illinois, 405 U.S. 645, 656 (1972), stating that the Bill of Rights was designed to protect citizens from overbearing government officials, and Schauer (1991a). See also sources cited in note 154 in chapter V. Tribe argues that there must be some independent principles behind the constitutional constraints, see Tribe (1985, 620), but he fails to explain why the more straightforward and familiar interpretation offered here does not better explain the purpose of these provisions. That is, one might prohibit government officials from employing certain means not because those means are evil per se, but rather because of the fear that those means may too often be abused.

best in the long run to restrain some institutions from making certain types of decisions on the ground that, if given sufficient discretion, power might be abused to such an extent that society would likely be worse off.[12]

Our impression is that many notions of fairness involving institutional design possess appeal because they are concerned with limiting the abuse of power. Yet, because policy analysts who use these notions of fairness do not explicitly link them to their underlying purposes, such notions may fail to illuminate the proper path of analysis or to indicate how to make a final evaluation when other considerations are also relevant.

3. Legitimacy of Legal Institutions

In choosing legal rules and in designing legal institutions, concerns for fairness may be relevant because they bear on the perceived legitimacy of the legal system[13]—that is, the extent to which citizens accept, as valid and proper, existing legal rules and the acts of legal authorities such as judges and the police. The degree of perceived legitimacy, in turn, may affect the extent to which individuals voluntarily comply with the law and otherwise cooperate with law enforcement officials and courts (such as by supplying information that will assist in criminal prosecutions).[14] These functional benefits of legitimacy are obviously relevant to individuals' well-being and thus

12. See, for example, sources cited in note 2, and in note 154 in chapter V. For example, it is commonly suggested that restricting officials' tasks to the application of clear rules rather than permitting them to consider all relevant factors may reduce their opportunity to make decisions on improper grounds, because deviation from their assigned tasks will be easier to detect. See, for example, Schauer (1991b, 150–52). Thus, mandatory sentencing guidelines or damages tables may reduce the opportunity for prejudice to influence sanctions.

The use of rules that may, in some cases, deviate from welfare maximization, in order to control agents' discretion, is analogous to the use of social norms (such as notions of fairness) that may deviate from welfare maximization to guide decisions of ordinary individuals in everyday life. See section II.D. Indeed, an important argument supporting the use of social norms to guide and constrain individuals' behavior in place of case-specific evaluation is that, under stress, individuals may succumb to temptation; similarly, a significant justification for some constitutional provisions is that, in socially tense times, the government may be inclined to undervalue or ignore important interests, such as the well-being of a minority group. (We also observe that concerns about shaping or trumping individuals' preferences, see section B, which some advocate should be given greater attention by legal policymakers, are similar to concerns about mischievous speech and despised religions that we sometimes constrain government officials from acting on. See note 44.)

13. See sources cited in note 161 in chapter V.

14. Consider, for example, our discussion in subsection VI.D.2 of how legitimacy may be affected by the setting of punishment. The instrumental function of legitimacy is associated with Weber ([1922] 1947, 124–32).

would be included in a complete welfare economic analysis.[15] This approach
to legitimacy contrasts with the sort of notion that we reject, under which
legitimacy would be deemed important for reasons unrelated to its functional aspects and thus would stand as an independent principle to be used
in choosing legal rules, at the expense of individuals' well-being.[16]

It is unclear, in any event, how often perceptions of legitimacy are important in the evaluation of particular legal rules. Many rules probably have
no appreciable effect on perceived legitimacy, either because most individuals are unaware of the rules or because most have no developed sense that
one or another legal rule is more legitimate.[17] Also, it seems risky to depart
from otherwise sound legal policy on the ground that most citizens will, in
the long run, find some unsound policy to be substantially more legitimate.[18]

4. Administrative Costs

Given the high costs of litigation, of enforcing regulations, and of other aspects of the legal system, attention to administrative costs is usually understood to be important. In contrast to the other concerns that we consider
in this section, it is generally appreciated that normative economic analysis
takes such costs into account. And, in fact, administrative costs are featured
in many of the specific legal contexts that we examine in chapters III–VI.
Such costs may affect the choice between rules (strict liability versus negligence), the details of particular rules (the accuracy with which damages are
estimated), and basic features of institutional design (whether to permit private lawsuits in the first place). Moreover, a virtue of welfare economics is
that it highlights these costs and makes recommendations that are contingent
on their significance, whereas many notions of fairness appear to be insensitive to administrative costs. Indeed, some would regard selecting rules on
the basis of differences in administrative costs as the antithesis of choosing
rules on grounds of fairness.

15. See subsection V.C.2.

16. A caveat, which we discuss in subsections II.A.1 and II.D.2, and in subsection B.4,
involves instances in which individuals have a taste for notions of fairness. It is indeed possible
that individuals will feel better off if they live in a regime that they find to be more legitimate
than another, independently of any functional benefits the first regime may have.

17. See, for example, subsection V.C.2. See also Hyde (1983, 408–09), describing the
limited public awareness even of most actions of the Supreme Court. Legal policy elites who
make predictions on these matters need to collect empirical evidence rather than rely on their
own impressions because they may be out of touch with ordinary citizens. For example, many
criminal justice reforms that advocates believed were necessary to enhance legitimacy may
have led most citizens to perceive the system as less legitimate.

18. See also section VII.C, addressing how government officials should act in a situation
in which individuals do not appreciate the benefits of a superior policy.

B. Preferences and Individuals' Well-Being

Because under welfare economics social welfare is presumed to be a function of individuals' well-being, we have emphasized that understanding the meaning and breadth of the concept of individuals' well-being is of central importance.[19] Here, we consider three respects in which relying on individuals' existing preferences, as revealed by their behavior, for the purpose of assessing their well-being is thought to be problematic by some commentators. In subsection 1, we consider instances in which individuals' imperfect information about various goods or experiences and other limitations affect their actual well-being. In subsection 2, we examine the possibility that changes in the law itself influence individuals' preferences. Then, in subsection 3, we address the view that some individual preferences (bigotry, sadism) should be ignored on the ground that they are objectionable. In each subsection, we suggest that the proper approach is to continue to view social welfare as an aggregation of individuals' well-being; the only complication is that it may be more difficult to assess how particular legal rules affect individuals' well-being.[20] (Throughout this section, we elaborate and defend the welfare economic conception of well-being; we note, however, that much of our analysis in this book would remain applicable if other conceptions of well-being were endorsed instead.[21])

In subsection 4, we turn to another subject concerning preferences, examining in more depth the possibility that individuals may have tastes for some notions of fairness.[22] We assess the relevance of such tastes for the evaluation of legal policy and discuss why notions of fairness cannot be reconciled with welfare economics merely by imputing tastes for notions of fairness to individuals.

---

19. See subsection II.A.1.

20. Suppose that one were to conclude that, for purposes of considering some legal reform, individuals' preferences implied by their current market choices are X, but the preferences that would indicate their actual well-being are Y. One would still seek to enhance individuals' well-being, now assessed by reference to Y (rather than citing the problems with relying on X as grounds for adopting legal rules without regard to individuals' well-being, once properly understood). Compare Adler and E. Posner (1999), offering a qualified defense on welfarist grounds of cost-benefit analysis, which does not assume that individuals' well-being is reflected in individuals' preferences. For readers who are concerned that this formulation admits anything, including the notions of fairness that we criticize, see subsection 4.

21. See note 14 in chapter II.

22. We initially discuss this subject in subsections II.A.1 and II.D.2 and offer examples in chapters III–VI.

1. Imperfect Information and Other Limitations on Individuals' Decisionmaking

Individuals' decisions may reflect imperfect information—that is, limited or erroneous data about the world—as well as a whole range of shortcomings that may prevent individuals from promoting their well-being. These deficiencies include an inability to process available information, "wishful thinking," myopia, and so forth.[23]

Some suggest that the normative economic approach improperly credits individuals' expressed preferences in spite of these aforementioned infirmities, but this characterization is inapplicable to proper welfare economic analysis.[24] The reason is that, when such imperfections are present, individu-

23. See, for example, Kelman (1987, 126–41), Kahneman (1994), Kahneman and Varey (1991), Kronman (1983), and sources cited in note 25. Compare Berridge (1996), exploring neurological differences in sources of pleasure and of motivation. A wide range of possible defects in individuals' decisionmaking can be understood as reflecting problems of imperfect information. Consider addiction: If individuals, before developing a habit, understood the difficulty of breaking it and the costs and benefits of engaging in it and were able to process this information at the outset, there would be no clear basis for failing to respect their choice (although in actuality we may be concerned that many people lack the necessary information and cognitive abilities). See, for example, Becker (1992) and Stigler and Becker (1977, 80–81). To illustrate this point, consider someone who sets out to cultivate a taste for classical music, knowing from the experience of others that, once he develops a sufficient appreciation, he will find it disturbing not to have continued access to the music.

24. See, for example, Kelman (1979a; 1987, 126–37). Although at various times (particularly in the middle of the twentieth century) economists focused attention on individuals' preferences as revealed by their behavior, such an emphasis is hardly inherent in the economic approach. See, for example, Harsanyi (1955, 311 n.7), stating that normative analysis should be based on individuals' rational, fully informed preferences, rather than their revealed preferences, when the two differ; and Mirrlees (1982, 64–65), stating that policy assessments should account at least for errors of foresight and memory and should also consider the possibility that people may not know what is good for them, and further noting that Sen might view such modifications as outside the social welfare framework because non-utility information is used, but arguing that the term "utility" seems appropriate for referring to a person's actual well-being. See also Baron (1993, 25–27, 35–39; 1996, 174–76); Sidgwick (1907, 111), stating that what is desirable for individuals should be understood "supposing the desirer to possess a perfect forecast, emotional as well as intellectual, of the state of attainment or fruition"; ibid. (111–12): "[A] man's future good on the whole is what he would now desire and seek on the whole if all the consequences of all the different lines of conduct open to him were accurately foreseen and adequately realised in imagination at the present point of time."; Sunstein (1986, 1150 n.78): "Utilitarian theories need not, however, take existing preferences as exogenous."; and Zamir (1998, 233–54), emphasizing that normative economic analysis is based on informed rather than actual preferences. We also note that some of the more subtle and complex problems concerning preferences received attention from economists for quite some time. See, for example, Stigler and Becker (1977), Strotz (1955–1956), and sources cited in note 30.

als' actions may fail to advance their own well-being, and welfare economic evaluation depends directly on individuals' well-being. Therefore, proper welfare economic analysis takes these imperfections into account.

We now outline how these limitations are analyzed under welfare economics.[25] First, individuals sometimes are aware of their own limitations and act accordingly (for example, by paying more for products that come with warranties or by acquiring expert advice). In this case, legal policy need not be concerned with limitations on individuals' decisionmaking.[26] Second, when individuals are uninformed and unable to overcome their deficiencies on their own, it may be sufficient for the government simply to supply better information.[27] However, cognitive impediments may prevent individuals from acting rationally, and there are limits to the amount of information that any individual can absorb.[28] Third, when individuals' decisionmaking capacity is inherently limited, different legal rules may be appropriate. For example, in cases in which individuals underestimate product risks, there may be an argument for strict products liability[29] or regulation of product access (such as in the case of prescription drugs).

An interesting case of imperfect information arises when individuals are not fully informed about their own preferences.[30] For example, it might be

25. See, for example, Trebilcock (1993, chapter 7), Sunstein (1986), and Zamir (1998, 254–84). Crafting government policy to account for individuals' shortcomings is often described as involving "paternalism," which to some is a heavily loaded term. See, for example, Shapiro (1988, 519), describing the negative view toward paternalism. However, such government action need not be viewed in this manner. See Sunstein (1986, 1166), stating that intervention motivated by the absence of information and related cognitive errors is "in a sense . . . not a straightforward rejection of private preferences at all."

The discussion in the text abstracts from institutional concerns, such as the extent to which it is appropriate to permit certain types of government actors to make decisions on paternalistic grounds. The view that the government should not act paternalistically because permitting it to do so will be more likely to reduce overall well-being is, of course, familiar from Mill's *On Liberty*. See Mill (1859, chapter 4). See also Shapiro (1988), suggesting that courts should be less willing than legislatures to entertain paternalistic grounds for decisions, and note 12, observing that it may be desirable to restrain the government to prevent abuses of power.

26. See, for example, Burrows (1993, 559), suggesting that a necessary condition for government intervention should be that the government can identify limitations that individuals do not otherwise recognize.

27. Much information is, of course, provided in the marketplace. Because of public goods problems, however, government provision or subsidy is sometimes desirable.

28. See, for example, Magat and Viscusi (1992) and Viscusi and Magat (1987).

29. See, for example, Shavell (1980b, 14–17) and Spence (1977).

30. See generally Cyert and De Groot (1975), moving from the idea that individuals may learn probabilities—information—over time to the idea that individuals may learn about their own utility functions over time, and Weizsäcker (1971), discussing changes in tastes and imperfect information about future preferences.

suggested that if person *A* would only try skydiving or some exotic cuisine, he would enjoy it; but he is unwilling to do so. Although some view this situation as presenting a distinct problem, it is qualitatively indistinguishable from the preceding one.[31] Individuals may perceive that their own experience is limited and make adjustments, such as by inquiring of others with differing experiences. Government provision of information is also a possibility. With regard to whether different policies should be adopted on account of individuals' limited experiences, we note that it often will be difficult for a government decisionmaker to know with confidence that the *A*s of the world would in fact like something else better. Indeed, the best evidence of what the *A*s would like, aside from their own expressed preferences, would be the experiences of similarly situated individuals, but then the *A*s would probably know about those experiences and be in a better position to determine whose experiences were relevant to their own situation.[32] Sometimes, however, the gov-

31. The problem of imperfect information about preferences can also be characterized as one in which the individual knows his preferences but is imperfectly informed about how something new would satisfy them. We do not see more than a semantic difference between these formulations, though the latter has the benefit of emphasizing the similarity with the more familiar settings that we discuss in the preceding paragraph. More broadly, similar concerns—as well as some of the issues explored in subsection 2—arise from possible changes in tastes, which themselves may be understood as involving stable tastes but changed circumstances or new information. See, for example, Stigler and Becker (1977).

32. See, for example, Bentham ([1781] 1988, 319–21), identifying the problem that a person may not know himself well, but questioning how the legislator can know more; and observing that it may be possible to determine people's true ends when most others behave in the same way but warning of the danger that legislators will go too far; Mill (1859, 137): "[W]ith respect to his own feelings and circumstances, the most ordinary man or woman has means of knowledge immeasurably surpassing those that can be possessed by any one else. The interference of society to overrule his judgement and purposes in what only regards himself, must be grounded on general presumptions; which may be altogether wrong, and even if right, are as likely as not to be misapplied to individual cases. . . ."; and Weizsäcker (1971, 363): "There is an obvious criticism against this argument. We have endowed the government with the knowledge of the whole preference structure of the individual, which, as his behavior shows, he does not know himself. No wonder that the government should do better than the individual."

This question of the informational basis for paternalistic intervention has occupied some legal commentators. Kennedy, for example, makes clear the need for the intervening actor to have sufficient information about the intended beneficiaries (leading him to distinguish paternalism by individual actors with intimate knowledge of another's situation, which he finds not particularly difficult to justify, from paternalism by government officials, which he finds more difficult to support, though still justified to an extent). See Kennedy (1982, 624–49). Because of this limitation, some have been critical of Kennedy's defense of paternalism. See, for example, Kelman (1987, 139–41). West argues that judges (unlike legislators) are in

ernment may have access to superior information—regarding, for example, the outcomes of low-probability events that most individuals would not find worthwhile to evaluate carefully—in which case legal policy decisions should reflect this fact. For example, if it is discovered that individuals are able to adapt to certain physical disabilities more or less readily than is commonly supposed, the valuations employed in measuring tort damages or in performing cost-benefit analysis (for example, of highway safety improvements) should reflect actual harm rather than victims' uninformed ex ante estimates.

Each of these points, of course, is relevant if the aim of legal policymaking is to maximize social welfare, understood as a function of individuals' well-being. The only difference from much of the analysis in this book is that the empirical inquiry becomes more difficult when individuals' choices in the marketplace or in other settings are not reliable indicators of their actual well-being. This challenge, however, provides no ground for avoiding the necessary analysis of how legal policies affect individuals' well-being or for substituting some other inquiry that evades the relevant question.

2. *The Effect of the Law on Preferences*

A second problem with simply taking individuals' preferences as given when analyzing legal rules is that legal rules themselves may affect preferences. In particular, some commentators suggest that, because the law does influence individuals' preferences, it should be employed to shape them in a desirable manner.[33] (Some "paternalistic" arguments have this charac-

---

a position to know parties intimately and thus to make sound paternalistic judgments. See West (1990). We, however, are skeptical that courts often know parties intimately, particularly appellate courts, which may never even meet the parties. Moreover, the relevant legal decisions are often of general application, so even intimate knowledge of a single party's situation provides little basis for choosing between competing legal rules.

33. Economists and philosophers, among others, advance this view. For example, Harsanyi states:

> The modern methods of propaganda and education offer a powerful tool for producing substantial changes in people's tastes at relatively low costs. For this reason, to-day the *Economic Problem* of a community—whether of a highly industrialised community or of an industrially backward one—does not consist merely in finding the best uses for its scarce resources so as to gratify people's actual wants to the highest possible degree. Rather, it includes also the question of how these scarce resources should be divided between productive operations for *satisfying* people's actual wants and measures for *changing* these wants. (Harsanyi 1953–1954, 213)

See, for example, Hare (1988, 245–46).

This prospect is similar to the one that we discuss in the preceding subsection, where we consider the possibility that exposing individuals to new experiences—ones they would

ter.[34]) Thus, an analyst might argue in favor of a legal reform that is contrary to individuals' current preferences—individuals would be made worse off if their preferences were taken as given—but that will produce a change in preferences such that, under the new preferences, individuals will ultimately be better off. Likewise, an analyst might argue against a legal reform that might otherwise seem desirable if it would have an adverse effect on preferences.

Because welfare economics is concerned with all respects in which legal policies affect individuals' well-being, the possible effect of the law on individuals' preferences is relevant under welfare economics. In elaborating this

---

not voluntarily select—would increase their well-being. In our prior discussion, we wrote as if individuals might thereby acquire information that changes their views regarding which experiences best satisfy their existing preferences. In contrast, in this subsection we follow the relevant literature by describing information or events as causing a change in their preferences. As we indicate in note 31, this difference in characterization seems to be purely semantic. There is, however, some difference in the facts that are often imagined to exist in the two settings. Previously, we supposed that there was an information problem of the sort that would quickly be overcome through exposure to new experiences, whereas here we do not. Also, here we do not assume that individuals' preferences will change completely. Instead, they may become sufficiently muted so as to change the welfare balance, or subsequent generations may develop different preferences (perhaps as a result of symbolic effects of the law). Another manner in which social welfare may be affected by a change in preferences brought about by legal reform—independently of any direct benefit or cost to the affected individuals—is that the reform may lead individuals to behave differently, in a manner that raises others' well-being.

34. That is, some arguments are premised on the view that the individual whose preference is disregarded will be better off as a consequence (whereas in the text we are also admitting cases in which that individual may not be better off but society as a whole will be better off, which arise when the gain to others, perhaps on account of different behavior by the individual, more than offsets any harm to the individual). For discussions of paternalism, see Sartorius (1983).

Some analysts (for example, those who favor trumping preferences in the manner we discuss in subsection 3) argue that a legal change is justified with regard to effects on the individual even though individuals' preferences are not expected to change such that the individual is ultimately better off when evaluated with regard to the changed preferences. We do not see a paternalistic (or any other) justification for such a claim because we find it difficult to understand how the intervention can be viewed as for the individual's "own good." See, for example, Mirrlees (1982, 69): "It cannot be wrong in principle to try to get someone to do what would be better for him even though he does not recognise it: but there must be some basis for saying that, with full understanding, he would come to accept the rightness of the altered utility function, or, rather, of the underlying preferences." See also subsection 4, addressing the idea of stipulating that individuals have a taste for fairness that they do not have and will never come to have.

point, it is useful to distinguish between the positive and normative aspects of the analysis.

The positive questions are whether and how preferences will in fact change over time. The suggestion is often made that, if the law symbolically denounces some preferences or reinforces others by appearing to embody certain viewpoints, individuals will come to adopt different preferences and, in turn, to behave differently.[35] For example, social norms—which, as we discuss in section II.D, influence individuals' behavior and tend to have the character of tastes—may be influenced by whether they are reinforced by or in tension with prevailing legal rules.

This possible effect of the law on behavior and ultimately on individuals' well-being can, in principle, be assessed just as one assesses other possible effects of the law. As in the case of the legitimacy of the legal system (discussed in subsection A.3), our conjecture is that typically the law does little

---

35. See subsections II.D.2 and VI.D.2. See also Kornhauser (1989, 42–49), discussing how individuals may be motivated to act in conformity with the law because they may develop preferences that align with the law's requirements; Sunstein (1986); and Sunstein (1996b), suggesting that the government has, and should have, a significant role in norm management, including through the use of law. Compare Sunstein (1996a), criticizing the use of the law for "expressive" purposes—that is, using legal reform to make a statement for its own sake—without regard to the law's effect on social norms or in spite of possible negative effects.

Changes in preferences and behavior are produced not only by laws' symbolic effects, but also because laws may directly change people's experiences, which in turn can influence people's preferences and behavior. See, for example, Trebilcock (1993, 196), citing evidence that immigration in Canada reduced discriminatory attitudes of residents. See also Gintis (1972).

A different but related view is that the process of considering which laws to adopt may itself affect preferences. See, for example, Elster (1983, 35): "Much more important—in theory and for practice—is the idea that the central concern of politics should be the *transformation of preferences* rather than their aggregation. On this view the core of the political process is the public and rational discussion about the common good, not the isolated act of voting according to private preferences." See also Tribe (1973), suggesting that many important policy decisions involve deliberation about our values, and Tribe (1974), arguing that the process of considering means is an act that clarifies our ends. For the reasons that we provide in the text, this view seems largely inapplicable for a substantial range of lawmaking. When it is relevant, it is not clear how much this view differs from the simple idea that, in order to make decisions (about society's laws or anything else), it is first necessary to collect and assess information and reflect on what one values. A separate point is that legal change has an added benefit of forcing more frequent deliberations, but this justification assumes both that legal change is a prerequisite to deliberation and that the spillover effects of deliberation are sufficiently positive that one may prefer more frequently changed or different legal regimes than would otherwise be desirable, simply to stimulate discussion.

to change social norms. Most individuals are unaware of the rules, and even individuals advised in light of such laws (for instance, agents in corporations) will not be influenced, due to the filtration of the law through lawyers and other intermediaries.[36] In addition, many rules (for example, detailed rules of commercial transactions) may not have any obvious connection in the minds of ordinary individuals to the deeply held views that are embodied in social norms. Finally, there are undoubtedly limits on the extent to which even legal rules that are clearly understood to relate to social norms will influence those norms.[37]

In some spheres, however, symbolic effects and resulting changes in social norms are plausible. The use of capital punishment, for example, may affect society through its influence on individuals' perceptions of the sanctity of life.[38] And unusually noteworthy Supreme Court decisions like Brown v. Board of Education, or statutes like the Civil Rights Act of 1964, may have a significant long-run impact on the next generation's attitudes about discrimination.[39]

The normative question is whether changes in preferences, assuming that they will occur, are desirable. Here, we emphasize that it is important that this question be answered explicitly; it should not merely be assumed that such changes are advantageous.[40] We suggest that the only sensi-

36. See, for example, note 42 in chapter VII, quoting Sunstein. See also Sunstein (1996b, 965), identifying a need for empirical work on whether and when laws do affect social norms.

37. This observation seems true generally, as social norms tend to evolve quite slowly, and it is particularly true of social norms that have a biological foundation.

38. It is not obvious, however, whether this effect would be positive or negative, as we suggest in note 161 in chapter VI. Many advocates of capital punishment believe that it constitutes a strong governmental affirmation of the value of life, whereas many abolitionists believe that the willingness of the state itself to take life—even a murderer's life—detracts from the sanctity of life. In this instance, psychological and sociological inquiry may illuminate the debate, but no ready answers are available. We note too that, if capital punishment is imposed infrequently, this symbolic effect—in whichever direction—may be more important than any direct deterrent effect or differential cost of implementation.

39. To emphasize our point that this possibility is encompassed by a complete welfare economic analysis, we note that economists are among those who mention that laws and experiences may affect individuals' attitudes regarding discrimination. See, for example, Becker (1996, 19) and Frank (1985, 122–23). It has, however, been suggested that such effects are not likely to be frequent. See Eisgruber (1992), exploring the Supreme Court's educative function, and suggesting that the Court will use it only occasionally.

40. Often analysts simply suppose that a change in preferences would be desirable. That certain preferences are good and others are bad may seem obvious within some community of discourse (say, among a small group of philosophers), but its members may differ in relevant respects from most individuals in society. Those who have more education and, often, more

ble way to address the question is to determine whether, as a result of a change in preferences, individuals would actually be better off.

Let us consider some cases in which it seems that changes in preferences would be desirable. If we could induce individuals to adopt less extravagant tastes or to come to enjoy more healthful foods, then they could achieve a given level of satisfaction at lower cost, thereby making available additional resources that all could enjoy.[41] Alternatively, and perhaps more relevant for some legal reforms, if we could induce individuals to respect the law, they might engage in fewer harmful acts. Or, returning to the subject of antidiscrimination law, if legal reform resulted in individuals becoming less bigoted over time, we would be able to make society better off.[42] In particular, individuals who are not bigoted may be less likely to engage in certain activities that harm others. In addition, society would be able to satisfy the preferences of the former bigots without simultaneously having to harm those who are members of a presently disliked group.[43]

---

income and more time for contemplative activity—particularly those who have self-selected atypical professions (notably, the small portion of lawyers who choose to become academics)—will often have different preferences, or, at a minimum, will prefer very different things given their different circumstances. It is easy, but dangerous, for such a group simply to impose its notion of the good life on others on the assumption that the others will change their tastes and that, if they do, they will then be better off in a meaningful way. We discuss this problem further in subsection 3 on trumping objectionable preferences, and in subsection 4 with regard to tastes for notions of fairness.

41. These possibilities suggest a rationale for the argument sometimes expressed, see note 46, that society should not give weight to expensive tastes that individuals choose to develop. (If individuals who cultivate such tastes receive a greater allocation as a result—as is commonly supposed by many commentators, but only follows under welfare economics for certain forms of the social welfare function and if the government can identify those with such tastes—there would exist perverse incentives with regard to preference development.)

42. Even if such attitudes are largely immutable once entrenched, the next generation may be less bigoted.

43. The illustrations in the text suggest that, when laws change preferences, there can be two types of effects on individuals' well-being. First, different preferences may lead individuals to behave differently, which in turn will affect well-being. Second, for any given behavior, when preferences change, well-being will tend to be different because the affected individuals will evaluate a given state of affairs in a new light. We also note that, unlike the example in the text, it is not necessary that both factors point in the same direction. For example, if a law results in individuals experiencing feelings of guilt in certain settings, such feelings might induce some individuals to refrain from harmful behavior. But when the feelings are not sufficiently strong to deter such behavior, individuals may be worse off on account of experiencing such feelings. Relatedly, symbolic laws may raise expectations for changes in behavior that are not forthcoming, resulting in disappointment. More broadly, symbolic laws that have little direct effect may breed disrespect for other laws.

This argument, we emphasize, is one that falls within the framework of welfare economics because it is concerned with individuals' well-being. When a policy is evaluated in the manner just described, individuals' actual preferences are used: their preexisting ones for as long as they remain in existence and their new ones after their preferences have changed. The suggestion is that the long-run strategy designed to change preferences may make society as a whole, over time, better off.[44] As we elaborate in the next two subsections, however, it is not appropriate under welfare economics to use the law to shape preferences when individuals' actual well-being will not be improved as a result, but rather the analyst wishes to impose on society his or her own view concerning what other people's preferences "ought" to be.

3. Trumping Objectionable Preferences

A number of commentators (including some economists[45]) have suggested that certain preferences that underlie even entirely informed and rational behavior should be trumped—that is, given no weight in the evaluation of social policy. Such a view is most often advanced with regard to malevolent preferences, such as those reflecting bigotry or sadism.[46] In this subsection,

44. See, for example, Becker (1996, 20). Because of concerns about potential abuse of power, many suggest that government institutions should not be free to pursue otherwise undesirable policies based on officials' beliefs that reform will change preferences for the better. See, for example, Trebilcock (1993, 157–58); Brock (1983, 255): "[R]estrictions on paternalism based on empirical considerations of these sorts, which might not too misleadingly be lumped under a general 'potential for abuse' rubric, are especially important for the issue of paternalism, and are especially significant considerations in the formation of most persons' considered moral judgments regarding paternalism."; G. Dworkin (1983, 33): "However, rational people who know something about the resources of ignorance, ill-will, and stupidity available to the lawmakers of a society . . . will be concerned to limit such intervention to a minimum."; and note 12. See also Dan-Cohen (1984), discussing instances in which the criminal law is understood by the general public to send one command—perhaps one in accord with social norms about right and wrong—while simultaneously creating a different rule concerning how government officials apply the law—such as to provide more lenient punishment than apparently commanded when harsher punishment would be undesirable.

45. See, for example, Harsanyi (1977, 62), Harsanyi (1988, 96–98), and Hammond (1982a, 1499).

46. See, for example, sources cited in note 45, and note 60, discussing Williams's views. Yet another view, associated with Dworkin, is that differences among individuals' preferences should largely be ignored—an approach that is tantamount to ignoring all actual preferences and substituting some external view of "natural" or appropriate preferences—because individuals are themselves responsible for those differences. See R. Dworkin (1981a). See also Rakowski (1991, chapter 2); Roemer (1996, chapters 7–8), modifying Dworkin's view to distinguish preferences that are the product of one's environment; and note 27 in chapter II, discussing Rawls's and Sen's constructs that appear to be independent of individuals' actual preferences. We find it difficult to identify the rationale for ignoring the particularities of individuals'

we discuss why the arguments that are usually presented against crediting objectionable preferences are problematic. We then explain how one can, nevertheless, employ the framework of welfare economics to analyze objectionable preferences and to understand our intuition that social policy should not be designed to satisfy such preferences.[47]

To trump preferences is, in essence, to redefine individuals' well-being in a manner that substitutes some other preferences—ones that are cleansed,

---

preferences on these grounds. In fact, many preferences held by individuals are not "chosen" in any sense, so it is not clear why individuals should be "responsible" for them. Much of Roemer's analysis of Dworkin's view is concerned with this point, but Roemer does not explain why there is anything left to assess once such preferences are excepted from Dworkin's principle. Dworkin permits an exception for "weakness of will," also without explaining what, if anything, remains covered by his approach once such an exception is allowed. R. Dworkin (1981a, 219). (We note that Elster, who once had expressed a position similar to Dworkin's, has subsequently taken a much more qualified view. See Elster (1983, vii): "To some extent [this book] also corrects what I now see as an overly enthusiastic application of the idea that men can choose their own character. The chapter on states that are essentially by-products suggests that there are limits to what may be achieved by character planning. There is hubris in the view that one can be the master of one's soul.")

It appears that much of the motivation for the view of Dworkin and others reflects a concern about the social cost of accommodating individuals who have expensive tastes, which seems to refer to individuals who require more resources than others to reach a given level of satisfaction. Yet the most apparent "expensive tastes" for which societies often provide compensation arise from physical handicap, and Dworkin expressly approves of responding to such tastes. With respect to preferences that individuals consciously cultivate, Dworkin and others seem to be particularly worried about cases in which individuals decide to cultivate expensive tastes. Developing the types of expensive tastes under consideration would, however, make those individuals worse off if society did not provide compensation on account of their tastes being more expensive to satisfy than those of others, and society does not generally compensate us for such tastes. Thus, it seems that these are not the types of preferences individuals would typically choose to cultivate. (An exception to the analysis, although of a different sort, arises when individuals are mistaken—perhaps they unwittingly become addicted to harmful substances—or are subject to undue influence. See subsection 1.) Nor, under welfare economics, would one adopt social policies that provide compensation for such expensive tastes, precisely because the prospect of such compensation would lead individuals to develop tastes that required more resources to satisfy and thus would tend to reduce overall well-being.

47. Furthermore, we observe that the resolution of this issue of the role of objectionable preferences in well-being and social welfare is largely independent of most of our analysis in this book. Notably, it remains true that any notion of fairness will, in some instances, reduce everyone's well-being, however one chooses to interpret that concept. Moreover, the notions of fairness generally employed in the areas of law that we examine, and our criticisms of them, are largely unrelated to the subject of objectionable preferences. (The main exception is that, in our discussion of law enforcement, we credit gains to criminals from committing offenses in our assessment of social welfare; we explain, however, that excluding such gains would merely reinforce our criticism of retributive justice, the notion of fairness under consideration. See note 54 in chapter VI.)

so to speak—for individuals' actual preferences. Having done this, an analyst can proceed to determine how different policies affect individuals' well-being, thus reconstructed.[48] But such an approach is troubling from the perspective of welfare economics because the moral force and appeal of welfare economics lies in promoting the actual well-being of people, not in advancing some hypothetical notion of satisfaction that is distinct from that of the individuals who are the object of our concern. Furthermore, employing a cleansed version of preferences rather than actual preferences may lead one to favor policies that make everyone worse off, just as when a notion of fairness is pursued at the expense of individuals' well-being.[49]

48. We note that it is not clear how one could accomplish the project of revising individuals' preferences because preferences for different factors (here, some permissible and some not) may be interdependent. Consider, for example, a sadist, who may have an entirely different lifestyle from others, wearing different clothes, having different friends, and so forth. That is, being a sadistic person may entail a plethora of different preferences, related in various ways and degrees to the individual's sadistic nature. Supposing such an individual not to have sadistic preferences is not merely to imagine that the person would no longer purchase some good, but rather is to hypothesize that he would become an entirely different person. And the theory hardly tells us what other person we should conceive.

Redefining preferences can also have paradoxical implications. For example, if we are unable to prohibit satisfaction of an objectionable preference, then individuals with objectionable preferences may be deemed to be worse off than otherwise. (Because we ignore a positive source of their satisfaction, their total well-being, based only on their other, acceptable sources of satisfaction, will be lower.) Under a number of theories of distributive justice (including many that the analysts who advocate censoring preferences seem to favor), however, the resulting decline in deemed well-being of these individuals would call for giving them a greater share of wealth than otherwise. (Thus, if sadists could be identified, they might be eligible for tax credits to compensate them for the income they spend on sadistic pleasure, which does not count in the welfare calculus.) Moreover, this treatment may lead them to engage in their objectionable activity to an even greater extent, supposing that the level of the activity responds positively to their level of income.

49. Consider the case in which all individuals have the same malevolent preferences and satisfying them involves a uniform harm to everyone. In such circumstances, it will always be true that, whenever an analysis based on those preferences favors a policy that satisfies such preferences, all individuals will be made better off. For concreteness, consider a group of individuals who each, on occasion, plays practical jokes on the others. Suppose further that individuals who are the butt of a particular practical joke are, on that isolated occasion, somewhat worse off, but that everyone in the group prefers living in an environment in which such behavior is permitted. In such a situation, prohibition of practical jokes would make everyone worse off: Each individual's gain in the occasional case in which he is protected against a joke is less than what he loses in all the other cases in which he no longer benefits from jokes played on others. Of course, this context of practical jokes is hardly the sort contemplated by commentators or, as we discuss in the text to follow, one that is likely to arise, as a practical matter, with regard to the more extreme forms of malevolent preferences that

Moreover, many analysts who do not endorse welfare economics should nevertheless regard the overriding of certain preferences as presumptively inappropriate. The idea of an analyst substituting his or her own conception

---

analysts have considered. That analysts usually pose situations in which negative overall results for individuals' well-being seem likely, rather than the benign situation described in this note, suggests that the broad categories used by analysts and the abstract arguments employed to justify wholesale condemnation may both be off the mark. In contrast, our focus on how different sorts of preferences have different types of effects on welfare in different circumstances both helps to explain widely held views on the subject and serves to justify failing to satisfy certain preferences in particular instances.

The possibility that trumping preferences will make everyone worse off is much more general than is suggested by the foregoing example of practical jokes. This conclusion follows from the proof in Kaplow and Shavell (2001) that any notion of fairness not based solely on individuals' well-being sometimes violates the Pareto principle. To illustrate the argument, consider a case in which sadists spend money to produce and watch movies depicting sadistic acts. A policy that prohibits such expenditures will make sadists worse off, given the amount of resources at their disposal. Suppose that the prohibition is replaced by a tax that absorbs a portion of sadists' benefits from their movies, with the proceeds distributed pro rata to all individuals. Then everyone will be better off. Now, this example also is unlike those ordinarily given by proponents of preference censoring because they imagine that objectionable preferences are satisfied by acts that harm third parties. This observation further reinforces our argument in the text that negative welfare effects underlie objections to preferences. Moreover, one can still construct examples in which preference censoring leaves everyone worse off, even with negative welfare effects on others, by introducing appropriate redistribution along with the policy that permits objectionable preferences to be satisfied. (Indeed, in our example of practical jokes, there is a negative welfare effect on others; no redistribution was necessary to show that permitting satisfaction of such preferences benefitted everyone because we considered a symmetric case.) This possibility of making everyone worse off when preferences are censored will exist except when the adoption of policies that discourage satisfaction of objectionable preferences actually raises total welfare—which, as discussed in the text, is a likely case for some preferences—but in that case welfare economics would favor the policy.

The only sort of censorship of objectionable preferences that would not necessarily raise the possibility of making everyone worse off would involve limiting the censorship to purely distributive judgments. This conclusion is an implication of the analysis in Kaplow and Shavell (2001). Thus, for example, if one gave more resources to Jill and less to Bill because Bill's preferences were objectionable and Jill's were not, there would be no conflict with the Pareto principle. Even in this case, however, a conflict would arise if one modified the example slightly. For example, if Bill could "change" his preferences with an expenditure—perhaps on therapy—then he could influence his distributive share. In such a case, our proof would again apply, and in fact it is not difficult to construct cases in which a policy of ignoring certain preferences could, through leading to expenditures that do not ultimately raise anyone's well-being, make everyone worse off. Thus, although it might have seemed obvious that the desire to ignore certain objectionable preferences was inherently beneficial at least to an identified class of potential victims, the idea (as conventionally articulated) actually is in fundamental conflict with a concern for individuals' well-being.

of what individuals should value for the actual views of the individuals themselves conflicts with individuals' basic autonomy and freedom. Given this
inherently problematic character of the censoring of preferences, it is insufficient for the analyst simply to announce that some preferences should be
trumped.[50] Rather, it is necessary for the analyst to adduce and justify a
principle for identifying which preferences are to be ignored and which are
to be respected. We now consider what such a principle might be.

Generalizing from the sorts of examples usually offered, which involve
malevolence, one might think that the objectionable class of preferences are
those preferences that, when satisfied, result in other individuals suffering
in some regard. But this class of preferences is obviously overinclusive. For
example, the satisfaction of our preferences to watch ballet or sporting events
often requires performers to exert strenuous effort and sometimes to experi-

---

50. For example, when Trebilcock critically reviews the legal academic literature on the
subject and offers his own views, he seems to give a qualified endorsement to the possibility
of trumping some preferences, but he neither identifies a foundation for his views in the
literature nor offers his own scheme for determining which preferences are problematic. See
Trebilcock (1993, chapter 7). Similarly, Elster would eliminate improper preferences in defining which of individuals' preferences are "autonomous," but his method of determining which
preferences are objectionable seems to be entirely ad hoc. See, for example, Elster (1983,
chapter 1, especially pages 20–24). We also find it hard to understand how Elster can regard
the rejection of a subset of an individual's own preferences as a central aspect of defining or
respecting that person's autonomy. Clearly, the motivation must lie elsewhere, but he does
not tell us where. This shortcoming is analogous to the general difficulty with objectivist
theories of welfare:

> Although it is easy to find philosophers who count themselves as objectivists about
> welfare, it is surprising how few of them have anything like a genuine theory to
> offer. Recall the distinction . . . between the nature of welfare and its sources. We
> are seeking an explication of the former, not merely a list or inventory of the latter.
> Yet such a list is all that most objectivists give us. (Sumner 1996, 45)

Some suggest that existing preferences should not be respected because they are socially
determined. The idea appears to be that an aspect of a person's reality—the preferences they
actually have—should be treated as if it is nonexistent on the ground that it stems from social
conditions. But such reasoning involves a non sequitur. (By similar logic, society should ignore
diseases that people actually have if their contracting the disease were attributable to social
conditions.) There may be grounds for changing social conditions in the future, but there is
no basis for ignoring the preferences that in fact exist. The argument for satisfying preferences
is that *they are the individual's, whatever their origin.* Compare Becker (1996, 20–22), explaining that an individual who has acquired certain preferences through socialization, but
wishes that he had not acquired them, would be worse off if he acted on his desired preferences
rather than on his actual ones; and Trebilcock (1993, 155), noting Hayek's critique of Gal-
braith's discussion of social influences on preferences.

ence pain. Indeed, making use of any good or service that requires labor to produce will tend to involve some others' suffering disutility. So will other sorts of ordinary economic activity, such as placing the highest bid for a house or a painting, which will generally leave the next-highest bidder worse off.[51]

Because the aforementioned class of preferences is clearly too broad, it must be narrowed in some manner. Again, drawing on the typical examples of objectionable preferences, we might restrict the class to preferences the satisfaction of which not only results in others suffering, but also for which the reduction in others' well-being is itself the source of satisfaction. But this class of preferences seems too limited because it may well exclude many of the preferences that are generally regarded as troublesome. For example, the preferences of rapists would not be included in the class under consideration, and thus would not be censored, if the rapists derive their pleasure from how the experience feels to themselves or from their exercising power over others rather than from the actual reduction in their victims' well-being that results from their acts.[52]

The literature on the subject of objectionable preferences adopts a somewhat different approach from that just described, under which all "other-regarding" preferences are deemed to be objectionable.[53] Unfortunately, the

51. Even deciding to purchase an apple would, in a small market, have some negative effect on other prospective purchasers of apples by slightly bidding up the price.

We note that the examples in the text generally involve voluntary transactions, whereas common examples in the literature on trumping preferences involve the use of force. This difference should not matter, however, because the objection under consideration is directed at crediting the satisfaction of particular types of preferences, not the manner in which a particular preference is satisfied. For example, the fact that some people steal food or other objects does not make the preference for such goods objectionable per se.

52. In fact, it seems entirely plausible that many rapists are indifferent to the plight of their victims per se. They probably do not know and may not care, for example, whether their victims are seriously traumatized by the event or are able to get on with their lives.

Moreover, however one refines the definition of what types of preferences are to be deemed objectionable under this approach, it seems that whether rapists' preferences are credited or censored will depend on the subtleties of the precise nature of their preferences. Yet we doubt that our negative intuitive reaction against crediting rapists' preferences—or any ultimate rationale for our negative view—should depend on such particulars. As we indicate in the text to follow, under welfare economics, the proper analysis does not so depend. We also note that there is no apparent way to be sure to include all (or most) versions of rapists' preferences without also sweeping in many ordinary preferences of the type described in the preceding paragraph.

53. See, for example, Nozick (1974, 245). See also Harsanyi (1977, 62; 1988, 96–98), Rakowski (1991, 26–29), R. Dworkin (1981a), and Hampton (1992, 671).

literature is not very clear about the meaning of this term (or related ones). It seems that the concept refers to any preferences that concern or involve the activity or thoughts of other individuals. This definition, however, is seriously overinclusive because it encompasses preferences for watching ballet or other performances (as does the first definition of objectionable preferences that we consider) as well as preferences for conversation, companionship, and indeed, virtually all forms of human interaction.[54]

The category of other-regarding preferences under discussion suffers from an additional sort of overbreadth, namely that trumping all other-regarding preferences would render irrelevant the care and concern that individuals have for others—friends, family, and sometimes even society at large. According to this view, one should favor social policies that discourage or even prohibit individuals from making sacrifices to benefit their children or from entering the less financially remunerative helping professions.[55]

54. To argue that all other-regarding preferences, in the manner defined in the text, should be censored seems tantamount to endorsing the view that people should have preferences only for other *things* and not for other people—a particularly narrow sort of materialism. For example, preferences regarding the viewing of mountains, paintings, and stars would not be rejected. Or would they, because these preferences involve regarding something that is "other" than oneself? That is, one could define other-regarding preferences as including literally everything that is not inwardly focused. This view would be even more puzzling, and we are unable to discern a rationale for demanding that all individuals in society conform their lives to it. Compare Griffin (1986, 24): "[I]t is impossible to separate self-regarding and other-regarding desires. Each of us wants certain pure states of himself (e.g. to be free from pain); but we also want our lives to have some point, and this desired state can be hard to separate from states of others."

There is another curious feature of the commonly stated distinction: Even though some suggest that society should not count an individual's preference regarding what he observes of another's behavior, most agree that society should be concerned about the satisfaction of an individual's preference that is influenced by the tangible effects of another's behavior. Thus, if my neighbor's activity is noxious to me in the form of pollution (smoke belched into my yard by my neighbor's barbeque), then my negative preference regarding that phenomenon is credited. Although the distinction between tangible and psychic externalities may make sense as a matter of policy, for reasons that could be adduced, it is difficult to understand the distinction as a matter of first principle. After all, everything that affects someone's well-being is ultimately perceived by the senses and mediated in the human brain; it is unclear what is the a priori normative basis for expressing concerns about certain triggers of particular neurons over others. (Nor can one avoid this problem by positing that the neighbor has a right to do one activity but not the other, because what rights the neighbor should be deemed to have is the very question to be decided.)

55. To explain this implication, individuals behaving in such ways incur costs in order to obtain what they perceive as benefits; hence, if society were to ignore these benefits (and all the more so if such private benefits were viewed as social costs), such individuals would

One could amend the concept of other-regarding preferences to include only negative other-regarding preferences, but problems would remain.[56] The concept would still encompass many ordinary preferences—basically, negative analogues to the preferences described previously (for example, a desire to avoid people one finds annoying). In addition, even negative views of third parties' actions that do not directly impinge on an individual are not necessarily undesirable. Consider, for example, our distaste for individuals who commit wrongful acts, which is commonly expressed as disapprobation. The anticipation of such disapprobation often deters individuals from improper behavior.[57] Yet, if one must censor other-regarding preferences

---

be seen as undertaking acts that are socially undesirable. To offer another example indicating the perverse implications of the view, consider the difference between an opera singer who performs for the money and one who would not be induced to perform by money alone but chooses to perform because of the pleasure of pleasing an audience; under the posited theory, the latter singer should not be permitted to perform.

Some analysts who address altruistic preferences oppose giving them weight, on the ground that to do so unfairly favors individuals who are the objects of others' altruism. See, for example, Hampton (1992, 671) and Harsanyi (1988, 98). But this view, as just explained, prohibits activities in which individuals voluntarily confer benefits on others—and, given their positive other-regarding preferences, on themselves as well—at no one's expense. It is clear that everyone might be worse off if policies embodied such a view. For example, if all parents show altruism toward their children or if all individuals are willing to take efforts to warn others of an impending natural disaster, policies prohibiting the satisfaction of altruistic preferences will be to everyone's detriment. See also note 64, identifying additional benefits to cultivating altruistic preferences. Also, it does not seem to be recognized that, if one were consistently to ignore types of preferences on the ground that respecting them advantaged some individuals over others, many ordinary preferences would have to be trumped. For example, a preference for music advantages individuals born with musical talent because they are able to command a higher wage; a preference for reading novels advantages those with literary talent; a preference for wood furniture benefits those who own timber; and so forth. Indeed, the satisfaction of virtually any taste has third-party effects that result in relative advantages and disadvantages to other people. (Moreover, if the same logic were applied to social policies generally, and not just a social policy of crediting certain preferences, virtually every law would be impermissible because it benefits some at the expense of others.)

56. To clarify, negative other-regarding preferences in some respects are broader than the first classification we consider (preferences the satisfaction of which results in harm to others) because it is not required that others actually are harmed. In other respects, negative other-regarding preferences are narrower because it is required that there be a negative view of others. Regarding the merits of this definition of the class of objectionable preferences, it would be necessary to offer rationales (not related to those underlying welfare economics) for defining the forbidden category of preferences specifically in terms of whether they are other regarding—rather than, say, as preferences the satisfaction of which harms others—and then to admit some but to exclude others.

57. See, for example, subsection II.D.1.

and root out their manifestations, then it seems necessary to destroy the entire system of social norms that regulates behavior, a system generally viewed as essential to the functioning of society.[58]

The foregoing discussion suggests that attempts to define objectionable preferences by reference to preferences that result in harm to others, preferences for others to suffer, other-regarding preferences, or any related classifications are not likely to be successful. These attempts to define the set of preferences that are objectionable encompass too wide or too narrow a class relative to the apparent intention of commentators. But this result should not be surprising. The broadly accepted view that some preferences should be trumped is not based directly on any general principle. Rather, it is largely motivated by particular, provocative examples, such as ones involving rapists, bigots, or sadists. Attempts in the literature to define which preferences should be viewed as problematic have been incomplete, and many relevant cases have not been considered. On examination, it seems that looking at particular characteristics of certain underlying tastes is in itself insufficient to separate seemingly objectionable preferences from many others that are naturally viewed as neutral or even laudable. Furthermore, the literature that favors ignoring certain types of preferences does not provide a general affirmative justification for so doing.[59]

---

58. To consider another example related to our discussion of law enforcement and retributive justice, the desire that criminals receive just punishment may reinforce internal restraints against harming others and may lead individuals to assist authorities in apprehending criminals. Most acts that aid authorities in identifying, capturing, and prosecuting criminals will be costly to individuals, so these individuals will not be inclined to offer assistance unless they derive some satisfaction from seeing criminals brought to justice. See section VI.D. Sidgwick acknowledges that resentment may play a valuable role in discouraging undesirable behavior, but he also offers a cautionary note (which parallels one of our welfare economic arguments in the text to follow):

> [P]ersonal ill-will is a very dangerous means to the general happiness: for its direct end is the exact opposite of happiness; and though the realisation of this end may in certain cases be the least of two evils, still the impulse if encouraged is likely to prompt to the infliction of pain beyond the limits of just punishment, and to have an injurious reaction on the character of the angry person. (Sidgwick 1907, 449)

59. See, for example, Hare (1988, 246–47) and Ng (1999, 203–04). Although the view that other-regarding preferences should be trumped has received a good deal of attention and support, the literature does not confront the problems that we identify here. Analysts tend to focus primarily on bigotry, sadism, and the like, and then they present a doctrine that sweeps in many preferences that one suspects they would not wish to censor when making social decisions. Defense of the doctrine seems to rely primarily on the reader's intuitive distaste for satisfying the particular other-regarding preferences under discussion.

In spite of what appears to be an inability to identify a principle that indicates which, if any, preferences should be deemed objectionable and to articulate a supporting rationale, it is nevertheless true that most of us are greatly troubled by crediting certain preferences commonly mentioned in the literature, such as the bigot's or the sadist's. We now examine how the framework of welfare economics helps illuminate the source of our instincts and intuitions about these unsettling cases. More importantly, we suggest that the framework of welfare economics offers a sound approach to identifying what sorts of preferences are problematic in which circumstances and to determining what sorts of social policies might accordingly be desirable.

Under a welfare economic analysis, any actual preference is given weight because it reflects an individual's actual well-being; there is no a priori basis under welfare economics for ignoring certain preferences. Nevertheless, a complete welfare economic analysis of many of the preferences that are generally believed to be objectionable will not ordinarily lead one to favor policies that satisfy such preferences. The reason is that the detrimental effects of so doing—reductions in other individuals' well-being and often, in the long run, the well-being of those with the objectionable preferences—will tend to outweigh the benefits of satisfying such preferences.[60] Indeed, it is

60. See, for example, Baron (1994b, 34): "[T]he principle of neglecting evil desires is a good *prescriptive* one. Only rarely, outside of fantastic hypothetical cases, does this principle go against utility maximization, and we ought to lack confidence in our ability to recognize these cases." Compare Sunstein (1986, 1139), referring to "arguments [that] are not paternalistic in the ordinary sense; they attempt instead to isolate particular defects in private preference structures that lead to gains—in terms of welfare, autonomy, or both—from collective action." There is a long history of using economic analysis to assess which preferences (utility functions) are more desirable for individuals to have. See, for example, Harsanyi (1953–1954) and Weisbrod (1977). More recently, this view has been advanced in Burrows (1993, 1995). Brock, who is critical of consequentialism in many respects, argues that it handles issues involving paternalism well. See Brock (1983, 237).

Some writers, such as Williams, are critical of consequentialists' view that effects on the individual or on society explain our attitude about objectionable preferences and certain of our other intuitions. See Williams (1973, 100–05). Yet these critics typically do not explain what value is served by not crediting objectionable preferences. (Williams himself refers to individuals' "integrity" in explicating what preferences are objectionable, see ibid., 108–18, but he does not give it independent content or justify according it independent normative significance.) Moreover, because critics refer to circumstances in which welfare effects typically do arise, their appeals to intuition in these contexts to support welfare-independent notions are suspect. For example, as Smart explains:

> Our repugnance to the sadist arises, naturally enough, because in our universe sadists invariably do harm. . . . Normally when we call a thing 'bad' we mean indifferently to express a dislike for it in itself or to express a dislike for what it leads to. . . .

this conclusion regarding the adverse effects on individuals' well-being that ultimately provides the rationale under welfare economics for deeming some preferences to be objectionable.[61] We now suggest two reasons that satisfying

---

[B]ut when a state of mind is always, or almost always, extrinsically bad, it is easy for us to confuse an extrinsic distaste for it with an intrinsic one. If we allow for this, it does not seem so absurd to hold that there are no pleasures which are intrinsically bad. Pleasures are bad only because they cause harm to the person who has them or to other people. (Smart 1973, 25–26)

See also Hare (1981, 140–46), identifying the value of encouraging condemnation of evil desires so as to discourage them, which "will maximize preference-satisfaction as a whole in the long term, even when preference-satisfaction is assessed in an impartial and content-indifferent way"; Hare (1988, 246–47) (same); and subsection VI.C.4(b), discussing the intuitive revulsion to punishing the innocent. Munzer argues that Hare's welfare-based argument concerning when preferences should be changed does not go far enough, because there will remain some objectionable preferences that the argument does not capture. See Munzer (1984, 749–53), reviewing Hare's *Moral Thinking* (1981). Yet Munzer does not suggest what criteria one might employ, other than intuition, for determining what preferences are objectionable. Additionally, in accordance with our preceding discussion, he relies on an example that strikes us as involving welfare-reducing tastes, but he asserts that our intuitive aversion to the preference in question is independent of this fact.

61. It is often thought to be a problematic feature of welfarist (or, more broadly, consequentialist) analysis that its conclusions are not absolute, but instead are contingent—here, on what will in fact best promote individuals' well-being (as well as on distributive judgments concerning how one aggregates the well-being of the sadist, his victim, and onlookers, see subsections II.A.2 and II.A.3). Such an objection should, however, be considered in light of examples in which it is plausible that individuals would be made better off—indeed, in which everyone might be better off—as a consequence of taking into account negative other-regarding preferences. See note 49. In addition, with regard to explaining our intuitions on the subject of objectionable tastes, it is worth reflecting on the fact that virtually all arguments on the subject make reference to tastes and to situations in which the net welfare effects of satisfying the objectionable preference are indeed negative. See note 60, quoting Smart.

Furthermore, the objection that the conclusions are contingent on the actual effects of policies presumes that there exists a viable alternative formulation under which conclusions are absolutely uncontingent. As our prior discussion in the text suggests, however, there is no other plausible way to determine in a vacuum which preferences should be deemed objectionable. In any event, it is difficult to imagine what would be the source of such absolute conclusions, unless instinct and intuition are to be viewed as infallible revelation, beyond human criticism (and beyond the sort of alternative explanation that we offer in the text). Also, as is apparent from our discussions elsewhere, the implications of such absolute views are unacceptable and are not, on reflection, likely to be endorsed by many analysts. In particular, if a principle is truly absolute, it will by definition be better to satisfy it even if doing so greatly reduces the well-being of everyone (including any individuals who are purported beneficiaries of the principles). (To take an example, suppose that one objects absolutely to torture, which satisfies the torturer's sadistic preference. Suppose, furthermore, that eliminating torture would make everyone worse off, including the torturer's victim. Perhaps the torturer, when satisfied, is fabulously productive, generating great social benefits or tax revenues, some of

certain types of preferences may be counterproductive in terms of the overall well-being of members of society and explore how these reasons relate to our intuitions about particular preferences that seem to be objectionable.[62]

The first reason involves externalities: Other parties may be made worse off as a result of the satisfaction of certain preferences. For example, a sadist may derive pleasure from torturing individuals, but those tortured are harmed and the general population may be made worse off knowing that torture has occurred, in which case social welfare will very likely fall on account of the sadist's action. This argument, of course, does not really involve trumping sadistic preferences; rather, given everyone's preferences, the gain to the sadist will, in most cases ordinarily imagined, be greatly exceeded by the aggregate utility loss to others.

We observe that this general point about externalities distinguishes the other-regarding preferences, like sadism, that most commentators find objectionable from the other-regarding preferences, like ordinary altruism, that are generally regarded as valuable. When the latter types of preferences are satisfied, other individuals do not tend to suffer; indeed, they may derive positive utility as a result. Likewise, this point distinguishes certain negative other-regarding preferences that are not ordinarily considered objectionable. For example, the disapprobation that is bestowed on individuals who act wrongfully reflects a negative preference of onlookers; but disdain for, say, burglars or cheaters is not seen as inappropriate. Furthermore, the prospect of disapprobation discourages wrongful behavior; hence, the presence of such preferences results in a positive externality (consisting of benefits to those who would otherwise be victims of wrongful acts).

The second reason that satisfying certain preferences may reduce social

which can be given to the victim; perhaps the victim is tortured quite briefly, is not very sensitive to pain, and will have no memory of the experience. Moreover, preventing the act of torture may be very costly, even dangerous, carrying a risk of greater injury to the victim. Are we still absolutely sure of the intuition that torture is always bad, whatever the consequences? What if we posited further that the victim does not view the procedure as painful at all, but rather as entertaining? Can we even define "torture" independently of its effects on well-being? We should recognize that our intuitions about torture almost surely are not based on such abstract hypotheticals, but rather on those instances of torture of which we are aware, from history or fiction. We also should recognize that our minds operate in a manner that uses generalizations that, by their nature, do not methodically keep track of the background conditions that generated our intuitions in the first place.)

62. Just as in subsections 1 and 2, we merely intend to sketch some of the appropriate components of a welfare economic analysis, without indicating the extent to which it makes sense to empower various government institutions to enact laws based on these considerations or to inculcate various attitudes through other means, such as in educational and religious institutions or in the context of the family.

welfare is that the alternative of adopting policies contrary to the current preferences of some individuals may change those preferences, and, over the long run, social welfare may rise as a result.[63] This phenomenon is precisely the one that we examine in subsection 2. As we explain there, the argument (like the preceding one involving externalities) does not actually entail trumping preferences. Rather, individuals' current preferences are not decisive if any short-run welfare loss from not satisfying them is outweighed by future welfare gains—evaluated by reference to the different, unobjectionable preferences one ultimately expects individuals to adopt. (Recall the example involving anti-discrimination laws.)

We further suggest that this argument, like the point about externalities, allows us to identify which of many types of preferences should be viewed as objectionable (they would often be the commonly cited negative other-regarding preferences) and to do so in a manner roughly consistent with our intuitions.[64] It therefore appears that familiar arguments about censoring certain preferences may largely reflect welfare-oriented thinking after all.[65]

63. See, for example, Baron (1994b, 34): "[T]aking a desire into account affects its strength in those who have it now and in those who might develop it in the future. . . . When we ignore a desire, we discourage its development."

64. This explanation seems to hold true with regard to certain types of negative other-regarding preferences, as we explain above. See, for example, Hare (1989b, 243), describing the utilitarian basis for discouraging and suppressing envy, jealousy, and ill will because of their harmful effects and stating: "What received opinion is condemning is the vice, i.e. the bad *habit of mind* or disposition; and this is to be condemned if it is a bad thing *in general* to encourage, which is indeed so in the case of these dispositions." Likewise, cultivating stronger positive other-regarding preferences (which, as noted, seems to accord with our intuitions) tends to be socially valuable because individuals are more likely to help and less likely to hurt others and because a given amount of resources will do more to enhance social welfare (for example, improving the lot of one individual will also improve the welfare of those who have altruistic feelings about him). See, for example, Kaplow (1995). But see Bernheim and Stark (1988), noting qualifications.

65. We do not mean to suggest that the merit of the welfare economic approach should be determined by whether its prescriptions accord with intuition. See note 61. See also notes 108 and 121 in chapter II, discussing the role of intuitions in normative analysis more generally. Rather, we merely suggest that current intuitions about objectionable preferences, which have not been well grounded in the existing literature that invokes them, may be explained in large part on functionalist grounds concerning individuals' well-being. Nor do we suggest that a welfare economic analysis perfectly accords with intuition, which would be impossible in any event since our intuitions are imprecise and conflicting. Intuitive views about notions of fairness, often reflected in what we refer to as social norms, have a general tendency to promote welfare in the context of everyday interaction, but will sometimes lead policy analysts astray in the qualitatively different context of designing the legal system. On these and related points more generally, see section II.D.

Indeed, the fact that most of us cringe at the prospect of crediting certain preferences that others might have is itself a kind of other-regarding preference. However, it is one that can be understood to have a positive result: Expressing such attitudes and inculcating them in others tends to contribute to a socialization process that produces a community of individuals who are less likely to engage in harmful behavior toward others and who are more likely to find opportunities for mutually beneficial interactions. Such considerations, we submit, may underlie commonly expressed views about objectionable preferences. More importantly, the fact that negative attitudes about such preferences tend to contribute to the well-being of individuals in society, rather than to make people worse off, provides a justification—a welfare economic justification—for such attitudes, whatever their origin.

4. Tastes for Notions of Fairness

Of particular relevance to our analysis is the possibility that individuals have tastes for legal rules that comport with some personally held notions of fairness. We here consider at somewhat greater length than before how this possibility should be taken into account under welfare economics. We also address briefly the idea that individuals' well-being should be deemed to incorporate tastes for particular notions of fairness regardless of individuals' actual preferences.

As we discuss previously,[66] if individuals in fact have tastes for notions of fairness—that is, if they feel better off when laws that exist or events that they observe are in accord with what they consider to be fair—then analysis under welfare economics will take such tastes into account when measuring individuals' well-being, just as it will take any other tastes into account. The importance of fairness on this ground therefore depends on whether individuals actually possess preferences for notions of fairness and on the strength of any such preferences. These are empirical questions, best answered by statisticians and opinion researchers; they are not questions that can be answered by philosophical inquiry.[67]

However, it may be difficult to measure individuals' tastes with regard to the fairness of legal rules. There usually do not exist market transactions

66. See, in particular, subsections II.A.1 and II.D.2.

67. Compare Katz (1996, 2266), stating that, if legal academics were to move away from being advocates or decisionmakers and instead view the public or the government as their clients, this perspective would, "if taken seriously, require the sorts of tasks that private lawyers undertake in regard to their clients; in particular, it would mean consulting the public and paying attention to its actual views."

that would provide a basis for quantifying individuals' tastes for notions of fairness in the manner that their taste, say, for apples can be inferred from the market price. (It is, nevertheless, sometimes possible to use market data to make inferences about tastes for notions of fairness. For example, one might learn about individuals' preferences for legal procedures from their choices among modes of dispute resolution when making contractual arrangements.[68]) Moreover, opinion research will often have limited value. The unreliability of polling information is suggested by the sensitivity of responses to modest changes in the wording of the questions posed and by other factors.[69]

Another difficulty in ascertaining individuals' tastes is that their opinions concerning which legal rules and procedures are fair may reflect their views about which schemes are best for society rather than a direct taste, say, for a particular legal doctrine.[70] For example, an individual who thinks that cur-

68. See subsection V.C.1.

69. Compare Harris and Joyce (1980), finding that whether allocations should provide equal outcomes or rewards reflecting differential effort depended on whether participants were asked to allocate costs or final rewards; Kahneman, Knetsch, and Thaler (1987, 113–14), suggesting that assessments of the fairness of economic actors' behavior is affected by the manner in which the reference transaction is framed; and Kahneman and Varey (1991, 151), suggesting that endowment effects may be due to framing. See generally Baron (1997), summarizing biases in individuals' responses to surveys concerning their valuations of public goods and policies, and Fischhoff, Welch, and Frederick (1999), surveying the difficulties in research design resulting from respondents' tendencies to interpret questions in a manner that differs from researchers' intended meaning. Furthermore, one suspects that individuals often have not thought very hard about the issues that are relevant to legal policy and thus may not be in a position to give reliable answers.

In addition, responses to surveys may not reflect actual behavior. For example, studies comparing subjects' expressed willingness to pay with what they are actually willing to pay find large discrepancies. See, for example, Cummings, Harrison, and Rutström (1995) and Neill et al. (1994). Differing views have been presented on the usefulness of contingent value surveys. See, for example, Diamond and Hausman (1994); Frederick and Fischhoff (1998); Hanemann (1994); and Kahneman and Knetsch (1992), presenting evidence that valuations obtained in surveys are not evidence of willingness to pay for the public goods in question, but rather reflect the moral satisfaction derived from being willing to give. In addition, there is the familiar problem that individuals' answers to surveys may reflect attempts to please the questioner or to present themselves in a positive light rather than to reveal what they actually believe.

Finally, as we indicate in subsection 1, there are settings in which, even if individuals' behavior could be observed, inferences concerning individuals' actual preferences could be misleading because individuals may be misinformed or otherwise unable to make good decisions.

70. Legal academics, in contrast, may have aesthetic preferences concerning legal doctrines. For example, those who study rules of jurisdiction for decades may find certain rules

rent medical malpractice liability is unfairly onerous may not feel worse off directly as a result of the rule's existence but may merely believe that the current regime is unwise because it raises medical costs. Moreover, as we note in subsection 2, individuals may be unaware of the content of most legal rules, in which case their well-being is unlikely to be affected by any tastes concerning the fairness of such rules.[71]

When individuals do appear to have a taste for a particular legal regime on grounds of fairness, there remains the question whether it is always best for society to attempt to satisfy this preference, in light of the issues that we address in subsections 1–3. Because most individuals know little about the effects of legal rules and procedures, such a preference may be mistaken, particularly when they favor a rule that in fact reduces social welfare. Indeed, it would not be surprising if most individuals who perceive one rule to be more fair than another believe that the preferred rule really does promote individuals' well-being, assessed without regard to any personal tastes they may have about its fairness. Suppose that individuals believe that medical malpractice liability is unjust because they have heard from unrepresentative press accounts that jury findings are arbitrary and that liability results in wasteful defensive medical practice. However, suppose further that this liability actually provides good incentives for proper precautions, including the disciplining of careless physicians. If such misinformed individuals were confronted with two rules and then learned that the one they initially thought was fair actually reduced individuals' well-being, they might well change their minds about which rule was more fair. In that case, it might be worth trying to educate individuals because society could then adopt the rule that in other respects advances individuals' well-being without generating displeasure on account of perceived unfairness.[72] Alternatively, if one

---

or court interpretations to be in harmony with what they see as the underlying structure of the doctrine in the field, and they may have developed a taste for the perceived orderliness of the law. We are, however, skeptical that most individuals have such tastes to any significant degree.

71. It is entirely possible for legal rules to have significant effects on many individuals' well-being even though these individuals are unaware of the rules, such as when a law regulates the behavior of corporations, which, in turn, make decisions about research, production, pricing, employment, and so forth. In addition, as we note in subsection V.C.1, many rules of procedure will have little direct impact on most individuals' perceptions of the fairness of the legal system because non-litigants will never hear about them and litigants often settle. Furthermore, participation through lawyers will often mitigate or eliminate the channel by which individuals' tastes about procedural rules would otherwise come into play.

72. A simple survey by Ng suggests the potential for education to affect individuals' views about what is fair. He asked a group of individuals whether it was fair for a busy restaurant to impose a surcharge for Saturday night reservations. Just under thirty percent of the partici-

believes that individuals' views about what rule is fair will change over the long run to be in accord with what the law actually is, one may adopt the rule that best promotes individuals' well-being without regard to their apparent tastes about fairness because one could predict that those tastes would change in an accommodating manner. We caution, however, that sometimes such changes in understanding could be detrimental on other grounds; in particular, the preexisting view may reflect an inculcated social norm that serves to counter people's tendency to behave opportunistically.[73]

The foregoing discussion of individuals' actual tastes concerning fairness involves the determination of the effects of legal rules on individuals' well-being. We conclude by considering briefly whether an analyst could plausibly argue that, even if individuals do not have a taste for some favored notion of fairness, they *should* have one.[74] We believe that this argument cannot be

---

pants believed it fair or acceptable, but after being presented with a one-paragraph explanation of the allocative benefits of imposing such a fee, that percentage rose to fifty percent. See Ng (1988, 230–31). A similar view is suggested by a series of surveys undertaken by Baron. One involved a notion of fairness concerned with compensation of victims (when misfortune was caused by a person versus by nature). Another concerned the distinction between acts and omissions. In both instances, "debiasing" instructions led a significant number of individuals to shift away from their initial normative and emotional attachment to notions of fairness in favor of a consequentialist approach. See Baron (1992).

73. For example, our discussion in section II.D indicates that society may benefit if individuals cultivate a taste that changes what they deem to be in their interest, such as when individuals develop feelings of guilt that make them more reluctant to engage in conduct that harms others. However, such social norms can have counterproductive effects when applied to the formation of social policy. That is, a policy may be socially optimal and yet create effects that trigger negative feelings of guilt. This outcome is possible because inculcated social norms need to be simple and few in number and thus can only serve as a proxy indicator of what is in the social interest. Also, as we explain above, the difference between the context in which social norms ordinarily operate and that of policymaking suggests that norms suited to the former may lead us astray in the latter. If such a seemingly desirable policy ultimately caused feelings of guilt to erode generally (rather than merely eroding the norm in the specific setting in which it clashed with the otherwise sensible policy), society might be worse off as a consequence of unleashing the opportunistic, self-interested behavior that those feelings of guilt formerly curbed. This point is pertinent to our discussion in subsection 2 about using the law to shape preferences and seems related to some concerns, which we note in subsection D.3, that have been raised about allowing markets to operate in certain realms, such as adoption.

74. Indeed, one could argue that such an approach would allow fairness-minded analysts to reconcile their position with welfare economics, which gives exclusive attention to individuals' well-being: If one were to assume that individuals have a sufficient taste for a notion of fairness, there would be no conflict between promoting a notion of fairness and promoting well-being. Such a reconciliation, however, would be merely semantic. Because the resulting view would be misleading on account of the manner in which it blurs two clearly distinct notions of the proper goals of social policy—as our analysis in chapters II–VI shows—such

sustained; there is no sound justification for imputing an analyst's tastes to citizens at large. Although one might argue that if individuals "tried on" a notion of fairness they would like it[75]—either immediately or over time—there is no particular reason to expect such a prediction to be true. Why should certain notions of fairness—rather than other (even opposing) notions of fairness or tastes unrelated to fairness—be especially appealing as a new taste that individuals should be induced or forced to adopt for themselves?[76] Nor is it usually the case (as it might be in some instances of negative other-regarding preferences considered in subsection 3) that individuals' well-being would be directly enhanced if they had different tastes. Although people might be better off if they could learn not to hate others, it is difficult to understand how people would be made better off by adopting a taste for a rule that, while promoting some notion of fairness, actually makes them worse off.[77]

In sum, treating individuals as if they have tastes for notions of fairness, even when they do not, is an untenable approach. It deprives the concept

---

an interpretation should not be favored. See generally Sumner (1996), arguing that an account of well-being needs to be descriptively accurate and emphasizing the distinction between the role well-being should play in moral theory and whether a particular moral theory is really about individuals' well-being.

75. Even if one were successful in convincing all individuals to adopt a preference for some notions of fairness, there would remain the question of the strength of the new preference. If the preference had little strength, the whole matter would be of little importance. If the preference were strong, then adopting it would mean that individuals were willing to make a significant sacrifice in their well-being, evaluated as it would be in the absence of the imputed taste for fairness. Thus, the rarely addressed question of the appropriate strength of notions of fairness is a matter of great consequence in assessing them.

76. Compare Hare (1963, 114): "The extreme sort of Fascist is a fanatic who not merely wants something for himself, but thinks that it ought to be brought into existence universally, whether or not anybody else, or even he himself if his tastes change, wants it." Mill, in addressing the problem of a majority of the public imposing its views on the minority, states:

> In its interferences with personal conduct it is seldom thinking of anything but the enormity of acting or feeling differently from itself; and this standard of judgement, thinly disguised, is held up to all mankind as the dictate of religion and philosophy, by nine-tenths of all moralists and speculative writers. These teach that things are right because they are right; because we feel them to be so. (Mill 1859, 151)

He proceeds to warn of the universal human propensity "to extend the bounds of what may be called moral police." Ibid. (152).

77. If individuals were to adopt the fairness taste for the rule and if it were sufficiently strong to swing the balance, the overall change would be desirable. But if individuals' tastes are so malleable, it would make more sense for them to adopt equally strong tastes in favor of rules that, in other respects, made them better off rather than worse off. That is, they should develop tastes for rules favored under welfare economics.

of individuals' well-being of its moral force, which is grounded in the actual situations of real individuals.[78] Hence, it is not surprising that notions of fairness are almost never explicitly cast as claims about what people's tastes are[79] or should become,[80] although some fairness theories seem implicitly to be of the latter type.[81]

C. Bad Luck and Inequality

In subsection 1, we elaborate on why our arguments that depend on an ex ante perspective are compelling despite the suggestion that an ex post evalua-

---

78. In discussing rationales for utilitarianism motivated by the desire to enhance individuals' well-being, Harsanyi notes the possibility of reinterpreting preferences as those which individuals ought to have, even if they do not, but he stresses that this "interpretation would, of course, deprive the postulates of most of their individualistic meaning." Harsanyi (1955, 311 n.7). He further observes:

> Moral philosophy can point out the fact of fundamental importance that in ultimate analysis all non-humanistic codes of behaviour are merely expressions of contingent personal preferences . . . whereas the code of impartially sympathetic humanism is the only one which by definition gives the same equal weight to the preferences of any other person as well. . . .
> . . . The only important thing is that this fundamental difference between humanistic and non-humanistic standards of behaviour should be brought out in full relief for the information of those people who have to choose between them. (Harsanyi 1958, 316)

See also subsection 3, offering a similar argument about the lack of moral foundation for trumping preferences simply because an analyst deems them objectionable.

79. See note 13 in chapter II.

80. After all, there are many different analysts, of fairness and of other matters, many of whom have different tastes, both regarding fairness and other things. Hence, the fairness advocate's argument that we are considering is tantamount to a claim that other individuals—literally all members of society—should have different tastes: Namely, they should all have the advocate's *own* (presumably enlightened) tastes. Compare Harsanyi (1975, 328), arguing that, "at a deeper level of philosophical analysis," an approach is "highly *irrational*" if it involves an individual making a social judgment imposing "his own political preferences on the members of society."

81. Indeed, we often find it difficult to determine any other basis for some fairness theorists' claims that the world should be ordered consistently with their own views. For example, the idea that the analyst's preferences should be substituted for individuals' actual preferences seems hard to distinguish from the arguments of philosophers who take an "objective" or "ideal" view about preferences. See generally Sumner (1996, chapters 2–3), contrasting subjective and objective theories of well-being and arguing that objective theories are not really

tion is appropriately more sensitive to individuals who turn out to have bad luck. In subsection 2, we examine various respects in which problems of inequality are addressed under welfare economics, emphasizing the notion of equal treatment under the law. (We do not address here the general degree of equality in the distribution of income or well-being because the manner in which this subject is included under welfare economics is explained in subsections II.A.2 and II.A.3.)

1. Bad Luck: Ex Ante versus Ex Post Evaluation

Our examination of notions of fairness in chapters III–VI shows that they typically exhibit an ex post perspective, often focusing on the situation of an individual who suffered bad luck. For example, under some notions of fairness in the tort context, the concern is that victims of accidents receive compensation, and under a leading fairness notion in contract law, the concern is that promisees who rely on promises and then become victims of breach obtain compensation.[82]

As we discuss initially in subsection II.B.2(c), the welfare economic view, by incorporating an ex ante perspective, encompasses a range of considerations that is broader than the ex post perspective in two respects. First, the ex post perspective tends to focus on salient and often atypical outcomes. (An accident or a breach of contract is not the ordinary outcome of most acts that might cause accidents or of most contracts.) A comprehensive evaluation of a legal rule, however, requires considering all possible outcomes an individual might experience, not just a particular one that may involve bad luck. Indeed, a standard welfare economic evaluation of a rule weights all possibilities by their probabilities precisely to avoid granting excessive weight to a particular subset of outcomes. Second, welfare economics takes into account the fact that the choice of legal rules may affect how individuals behave at the outset, which often has an important influence on individuals' well-being. (Stiffer requirements of compensation may deter accidents; onerous contract remedies may discourage individuals from entering into contracts and, when they do enter contracts, will affect contract terms, notably,

---

about individuals' well-being, as that concept is generally understood; and subsection 3, discussing the trumping of preferences that analysts find objectionable.

82. Similarly, notions of fairness with regard to legal procedure focus on the perspective of individuals after they have become victims, considering their rights to sue for redress or to receive accurate compensation. With regard to law enforcement, the notion that the punishment should fit the crime is ordinarily applied ex post and thus is concerned with individuals who have chosen to commit crimes and who are unlucky enough to get caught and convicted.

the price.) Hence, when one adopts an ex post perspective, one often ignores important effects of legal rules.[83]

To illustrate how the analysis differs when it is not limited to an ex post perspective, recall our discussion of reciprocal accidents involving uncertain harm.[84] We showed that a rule of no liability would sometimes be preferable to both strict liability and the negligence rule, namely, when imposing liability involves administrative costs and taking precautions is not worthwhile. Indeed, we emphasized the fact that, ex ante, all individuals are better off without liability in certain settings. That is, we showed that before individuals learn the position they will occupy—in particular, whether they will turn out to cause an accident or be injured in one—all are made better off by the same legal rule. Moreover, we demonstrated that this was so in a wide range of contexts: when individuals are risk neutral, so that there is no value to any protection against risk that compensation may provide; when individuals are risk averse but are insured; and when risk-averse individuals remain uninsured but the cost of providing implicit insurance through the tort system exceeds the value to them of protection against risk.[85]

Of course, even in many instances in which individuals would prefer ex ante to be governed by a particular rule, some will prefer that the rule is otherwise ex post. Thus, in the foregoing illustration, even if all would oppose strict liability at the outset, those who subsequently become accident victims would then prefer strict liability because it would compensate them. But if one were to adopt a regime of strict liability in order to compensate those who actually suffer bad luck, every individual would be worse off ex ante.

We suspect that many readers will find it self-evident that, in the sorts of situations we consider, the ex ante perspective is correct.[86] Yet, as we note

83. In our prior discussion, we also suggest an explanation, in terms of cognitive biases, for why an ex post perspective seems attractive despite these shortcomings.

84. See subsection III.D.1.

85. As the latter case should make clear, if the idea that ex post "bad luck" calls for compensation is interpreted to refer to the value to individuals of protection against risk, then by definition there will be no conflict between paying attention to this idea and focusing exclusively on individuals' well-being ex ante because proper ex ante analysis already fully incorporates this concern. See section III.D.

86. Ex ante perspectives of some form are endorsed by scholars who in other respects have a range of viewpoints. See, for example, Fried (1970, 204); Rakowski (1991, chapters 3–4, 6); ibid. (253), employing an ex ante perspective to apply his notion of corrective justice to nuisance law; Rawls (1971, 17); R. Dworkin (1981b); and Harsanyi (1953). See also Hare (1981, 154), noting the commonality between groundings for rights, such as Dworkin's invocation of "equal concern and respect," Bentham's principle that " '[e]verybody [is] to count for

throughout this book, many notions of fairness seem to be premised on the view that the ex post perspective is appropriate. In light of what we have already said, it seems difficult to maintain such a view. Indeed, in all situations in which individuals are symmetrically situated ex ante (a possibility that is in principle in the domain of virtually any notion of fairness), relying on an ex post view, when it differs from the ex ante perspective, always entails favoring a legal policy under which everyone is worse off ex ante.[87] Thus, if individuals are allowed to choose which rule should govern them, before learning whether they will be lucky or unlucky, they will unanimously choose a rule different from the one favored under notions of fairness.

To make this point more concrete, we consider two particular settings. The first involves two individuals who might enter into a contract, such as the one that we examine in section IV.C. Suppose Jack finds it in his interest to agree to produce a cabinet for Jill in return for a fixed price that she pays at the outset. Jack stands to gain because his expected production cost is

---

one, nobody for more than one,'" and other such principles, all variants of his own notion of "universalizability"; and Hare (1973b, 154–155), suggesting that an ideal-observer theory, rational-contractor theories such as Rawls's, and others must, on certain interpretations, "yield the same results." Yet the implications of consistently adhering to the ex ante perspective are not always endorsed, even by some of these writers and their many followers. This point should be apparent from our arguments in chapters III–VI, which show how adopting this perspective leads to the view that the exclusive basis for assessing legal policy should be consideration of individuals' well-being, not notions of fairness—some of which are favored by analysts who otherwise seem to endorse this general ex ante perspective.

Although the ex ante perspective is widely endorsed and, as we argue in the text to follow, is compelling in the present setting, we wish to emphasize that most of our argument in this book does not depend on adopting an ex ante perspective instead of an ex post perspective. The reason is that most of our analysis can be shown to apply to cases in which there is no difference between what is anticipated ex ante and what in fact occurs ex post. First, we often consider cases involving no uncertainty, so that the result ex post is identical to that expected ex ante. See section III.C, analyzing torts, and section V.A, analyzing legal procedure—in particular, the ability to bring suit. Second, when we consider cases involving uncertainty, we could usually have modified our examples to pose cases involving certainty. (For example, instead of considering a contract in which there is, ex ante, a 90 percent chance that the cost of producing a single item will be low and a 10 percent chance that the cost will be high, we could as well have considered a contract in which ten items will be produced and it is certain that nine will turn out to have a low production cost and one will turn out to have a high production cost. Then, the ex ante prediction would precisely equal the ex post result.) Indeed, as we discuss in note 95, the possibility of linking the ex ante and ex post views in such a manner is quite general. Accordingly, even analysts who conclude, contrary to our arguments and those of others, that the ex post view is compelling will still need to confront most of the arguments that we present.

87. See subsections II.C.1 and III.C.1(e)(iii).

below the contract price (and he is risk neutral, so only the expected cost matters to him). But it is possible that the cost will be higher than the price. Jill values the cabinet greatly and intends to make substantial reliance expenditures in the meantime. Now, if it turns out that Jack's production cost does exceed the price, Jack should have no ground for complaint and, in particular, should not be excused from the contract on this account. To be sure, Jack's ex post preference—that is, his wish, taking advantage of hindsight—is that he had never entered the contract. But if legal policy were predicated on such preferences, the Jacks (and Jills) of the world may not find it worthwhile to enter into such contracts, a result that would be to everyone's detriment.

Second, although it is less conventional than the setting just discussed, consider the difference between the ex ante and ex post perspectives with regard to actions that an individual takes that affect only himself. Suppose that Jack chooses to go to the beach when there is a ten percent chance of rain. If Jack is to be protected against ever being rained on while at the beach—that is, against the possibility of being a loser ex post—beaches may have to be closed. But this regime would not promote Jack's well-being (assuming, as we are, that Jack is aware of the possibilities and still prefers to take his chances). In sum, individuals and groups will wish their affairs to be governed by ex ante analysis rather than having their generally beneficial actions thwarted by restrictions that prevent them from sometimes experiencing bad luck ex post.[88]

The foregoing discussion considers individuals' well-being. Similar logic that focuses instead on the notion of consent likewise favors the ex ante perspective. In this regard, we observe that there is a close relationship be-

88. See, for example, Myerson (1981, 890): "[T]iming would never be a cause for dispute, because all individuals would agree that earlier (planned-ahead) choices yield better expected outcomes." Even many egalitarians favor allowing individuals to subject themselves to gambles that could leave them worse off. See, for example, R. Dworkin (1981b, 292–304).

We remind the reader that a fully ex ante perspective already incorporates individuals' concern about exposure to risk. Indeed, a willingness to upset ex ante arrangements in order to protect individuals from being losers ex post can destroy insurance arrangements. The reason is that individuals who procure insurance and suffer no loss will be worse off ex post because they agreed to pay a premium. If one attempted to correct this ex post reduction in well-being, one would have to require that insurance companies return the premiums paid by individuals who did not suffer any losses. This requirement would obviously make it infeasible to offer insurance.

A qualification to the ex ante perspective concerns possible problems with information and preferences of the sort we consider in subsection B.1. As we explain there, the proper procedure is to take any such problems into account directly within the framework of welfare economics, not to substitute some other, inappropriate method.

tween arguments based on consent and endorsement of an ex ante perspective. After all, the standard structure of consent arguments is that, once individuals have agreed—ex ante—to some treatment governing their prospective acts, they are bound to such agreements even when after the fact—ex post—they would benefit from a different rule.

First, there may be actual consent, such as when individuals vote to adopt a regime before accidents occur or when they enter into contracts. One might also invoke imputed consent, such as when duly elected government officials have adopted a regime on behalf of their constituents.

Second, implied consent (such as to a "hypothetical contract") provides a strong argument for the ex ante view. If individuals actually do make a contract with full information and no infirmities, virtually all normative approaches to law would honor their agreement.[89] If it is impossible or too costly to enter a contract but we know what contractual provision the parties would have adopted, similar analysis supports enforcing the implied contract.[90] Some object that hypothetical consent is not actual consent—and it is not—but this point does not upset our conclusion.[91] If, for example, individuals would unanimously[92] prefer regime A to regime B if there were a referendum, we do not understand how it can be argued that, on occasions when no vote is possible and thus the government officials themselves must decide between A and B, they may pick B. That is, the move from the lack of actual consent to the adoption of a decision known to be contrary to the dictates of unanimous hypothetical consent involves a non sequitur.[93]

89. For an extensive discussion of this perspective that is generally supportive of enforcing such hypothetical contracts, see Charny (1991).

90. See subsection IV.C.2(e).

91. See, for example, Hampton (1992, 675–76), stating that the moral force of the Kantian notion of social contract does not derive from our concern for hypothetical consent itself, but rather arises because the process by which individuals would reach hypothetical agreement is morally revealing. See generally Hare (1981, 112–16), arguing that universal moral principles should be understood as applicable to, and thus may be assessed by reference to, hypothetical cases.

92. The logic of the argument in the text does not depend on unanimity; one could substitute any voting rule deemed to be appropriate.

93. The primary problems with hypothetical consent of this sort concern imperfect information (actual consent ordinarily gives us more confidence about what people in fact prefer) and the possibility that agents empowered to act based on hypothetical consent might abuse their power. See subsection A.2. On these grounds, we might, for example, wish to constrain judges or agencies from modifying laws enacted by legislatures or through referenda. Still, it hardly follows that agents who must make a legal decision should ignore what individuals would have consented to, if asked, and instead make choices that the best information indicates would be unanimously opposed if individuals actually were permitted to choose. Compare note 96 in chapter IV, criticizing Barnett's consent theory of contract law.

Finally, the ex ante view possesses normative appeal independent of actual or hypothetical consent, from the perspective of a just social contract. To the extent that a normative view is to embody a disinterested rather than a self-interested perspective about what is socially desirable, it is necessary that decisions be made without regard to how particular outcomes will affect particular individuals. This view is familiar from centuries of arguments that appeal to the Golden Rule, a categorical imperative, a just social contract, and an impartial observer, as well as from more recent appeals to an original position or a veil of ignorance.[94]

We do not see a persuasive affirmative argument for an ex post view that would trump policies that maximize individuals' well-being ex ante— policies that have in fact received individuals' consent or that would receive it. Under a just regime, some individuals who are unlucky or who behave badly may accordingly be worse off ex post. As a consequence, their self-interest may lead them subsequently to prefer some other regime. But this

---

94. See, for example, Hare (1997, 26), describing the relationship between Kant's categorical imperative and impartiality; Hare (1986, 219), describing the similarity between the role of equality in critical utilitarian theory, which entails impartially giving equal weight to everyone, and various formulations by Kant, which also emphasize impartiality; Kant ([1785] 1997, 15): "*I ought never to act except in such a way that I could also will that my maxim should become a universal law.*" (emphasis in original); Korsgaard (1996, 100–01), interpreting Kant's categorical imperative as rejecting a self-interested perspective; Mill ([1861] 1998, 64), relating the requirement of being a "strictly impartial . . . disinterested and benevolent spectator" to "the golden rule of Jesus of Nazareth" and to utilitarian morality's requirement of universal benevolence; Sidgwick (1907, xix) (preface to 6th edition), endorsing Kant's view that principles should be universal, one of the formulations of the categorical imperative, although not accepting Kant's metaphysical argument for it; ibid. (507): "I find that I undoubtedly seem to perceive, as clearly and certainly as I see any axiom in Arithmetic or Geometry, that it is 'right' and 'reasonable' for me to treat others as I should think that I myself ought to be treated under similar conditions. . . ."; Singer (1981, 135–36), stating that "[t]he idea of an impartial standard for ethics has been expressed by the leading thinkers of the major ethical and religious traditions" and providing references to Judaism, Jesus, Confucius, Indian thought, and Stoic philosophers of the Roman Empire; Smith ([1790] 1976, 135): "We must view [conflicting interests] from the place and with the eyes of a third person, who has no particular connexion with either, and who judges with impartiality between us." See also Wiggins (1998), referring to Confucius and Leibniz, among others, who expressed such views. The original position and veil of ignorance are usually attributed to Rawls (1971), although Harsanyi and Vickrey pressed this view earlier. See Harsanyi (1953) and Vickrey (1945, 329). (Rawls's original position is distinctive in various respects, see, for example, Rawls (1980, 549–50), but the idea that such a construct allows one to remove self-interest is common.) We further note that the perspective of a fully informed, rational, disinterested observer is in many respects equivalent to taking an ex ante view. See, for example, Harsanyi (1955; 1977, chapter 4). See also note 86, noting a range of philosophers who adopt an ex ante perspective, among them Hare, who emphasizes the relationship among different formulations that implement the idea of impartiality.

is equally true of those who enter contracts that turn out to be disadvantageous, who consciously break society's rules, such as by committing crimes, or who simply undertake risks that affect only themselves and turn out to be unlucky. Welfare economics, which takes full account of all possible outcomes, including those that are unfortunate for an individual, gives due attention to bad luck. In contrast, notions of fairness that reflect an ex post perspective, from which one would upset the outcomes of such analysis (including in cases in which all individuals would have opposed the supposedly fair policy), lack foundation.[95]

95. An additional, less typical, argument for the ex ante view is based on a type of logical consistency. The first step of the argument states its domain: In some settings (including many that we have examined), there seems to be consensus on which is the correct view from an ex ante perspective, but room for disagreement about which view is correct from an ex post perspective. Second, suppose that sometimes the ex ante and ex post situations are identical in all relevant respects. (We illustrate this possibility below.) It follows that, in those situations, the ex ante view must govern, if one is to be consistent (and given the first premise). Third, making a further application of the logical consistency requirement, because we know that the ex ante view is correct in some ex post situations and because consistency within the ex post view requires that the same ex post view be adopted in all settings in the relevant domain, it follows that the ex ante view must be the correct ex post view as well.

To demonstrate this claim, we still must illustrate how the second step works. Suppose, for example, that it is within the domain of the evaluative principle to assess a case in which, ex ante, it is expected that one in ten identically situated individuals will be a loser, while the other nine will gain, and the net result is deemed to be desirable because all individuals are better off ex ante. Suppose further that this is exactly what happens—that is, ex post, nine individuals in fact gain and only one in fact loses. Since what happens ex post is exactly what was predicted to happen ex ante, the two situations must be evaluated in the same manner. It will not do to say that regime A is normatively superior to regime B and then, a moment later, after learning the actual outcome of implementing regime A, to argue that regime B is (was?) normatively superior—particularly when the actual outcome coincides with the expected outcome (that is, when hindsight does not differ from foresight). If one did hold such an inconsistent view, no equilibrium assessment would be possible in a world in which the analyst had the power to reverse policies and start anew. Ex ante, one would adopt regime A. Once it was in place and had its predicted effect, one would switch to regime B, thereby repealing A. But then one would be back to where one started, and, by assumption, one would choose to enact A once again, and so on, ad infinitum. Therefore, when the ex ante view yields an unambiguous conclusion—such as when all individuals are better off under one legal rule than under another—it follows that the initial judgment should not be upset by analysis of the corresponding ex post situation (which may, at first, seem ambiguous). Compare Baron (1993, 27–29), arguing that, when a normative assessment is clear under the assumption that we do not know the identities of gainers and losers, there is no basis for changing the normative assessment if we learn those identities. (We observe that it has been demonstrated that this sort of consistency between ex ante and ex post evaluations requires, in cases involving uncertainty such as the one we are now examining, that the social welfare function be linear in individuals' utilities—that is, utilitarian. See, for example, Hammond (1983), Myerson (1981), and Ng (1981a, 244–45).) *(continued)*

2. Equality and Equal Treatment

As we state in subsection II.B.1, we use the term "fairness" to encompass any evaluative principle that is not exclusively concerned with promoting individuals' well-being. As a result, when we argue that all notions of fairness are uncompelling, it might appear that we are also casting doubt on various equality-based principles.[96] In this subsection, we address the relevance of aspects of equality under welfare economics.

First, as we explain at some length in subsections II.A.2 and II.A.3, many concerns about the distribution of income or well-being—economic equality—are directly incorporated under welfare economics. Second, to the extent that people have a taste for some notion of equality (in the sense that they feel better off when the notion is reflected in the law), this taste will be credited in assessing individuals' well-being and thus in determining social welfare.[97] Third, the value judgment that all individuals should be given equal weight in determining social welfare is ordinarily embraced under welfare economics.[98] Thus, much of what is thought to be important with regard to equality is already included in the welfare economic approach.

One might attempt to defend the ex post view in the preceding example or more generally by considering possible grounds for regretting the ex ante choice, but these considerations do not affect our basic claim. First, society might simply suffer from bad luck. (For example, the annual picnic may have been rained out, even though the weather forecast was favorable.) One would then wish that a different choice had been made, but this does not constitute a criticism of the original policy choice if it took into account all possible outcomes and their associated probabilities. Second, society might have made a mistake in choosing A initially. (For example, if someone had bothered to check the weather forecast, it would have been obvious that the picnic should have been postponed from time A to time B.) Then, B would have been the ideal ex ante policy, but this case does not generate an argument against the ex ante perspective. Third, sometimes the optimal regime is in fact *conditional* on what subsequently materializes. (For example, choose time A, but if the weather looks bad the night before, reschedule to time B.) In that case, an unconditional choice of A might not be superior ex ante, but neither would an unconditional choice of B. Rather, one would say that A is superior in event X but B is superior in event Y. This condition can be specified ex ante, in the sense that other options (including an uncontingent commitment either to A or to B) may be ruled out, and, once X or Y happens, the choice will be determined.

96. Standard dictionary definitions of fairness refer to the absence of arbitrary, discriminatory, or biased treatment. See, for example, note 7.

97. See subsections II.A.1 and II.A.3.

98. We discuss the symmetry requirement in subsection II.A.2. As we note there, the requirement is almost uniformly endorsed, although, of course, it does not follow simply from the insistence that evaluation be based exclusively on individuals' well-being. At a minimum, it is clear that an exclusive concern for well-being is not inconsistent with this sort of equality requirement; hence, such a principle of equality is not among the notions of fairness that we criticize.

There is another aspect of equality, however, that we have not discussed directly: equal treatment under the law. That is, if two individuals are identical in relevant respects, it is often suggested that they should therefore be treated in the same manner by legal rules and institutions.

It should be apparent that this notion of equality is also incorporated to a degree under welfare economics. Specifically, welfare economic assessments count each individual equally; hence, welfare economics usually requires equal treatment. Indeed, as some writers have emphasized, the requirement of equal treatment of equals is largely redundant with respect to a wide range of normative principles.[99] Suppose, for example, that social welfare is maximized by subjecting individual 1 to rule X. Then, if individual 2 is identical to individual 1 in all relevant respects, one would expect that welfare would similarly be maximized by subjecting individual 2 to rule X as well, rather than to some other rule.

We now consider how the requirement of equal treatment usually applies. When legal rules result in unequal treatment of individuals, there generally are two possibilities: Either there has been a mistake made with respect to at least one individual under the prevailing substantive principle (that is, one can identify a deficiency without the need to invoke any notion of equality) or the individuals are not equal in some relevant respect (in which case the requirement of equal treatment is inapplicable).[100] Thus, if Larry and

99. Hare argues that equal treatment, in addition to being implied by the notion of equal concern—which, as we discuss in subsection II.A.2, is ordinarily an aspect of welfare economics—

> can be established on the basis of the formal properties of the moral concepts. If it be granted . . . that moral judgments are universal or universalizable prescriptions, then in prescribing that such and such ought to be done to someone (say Tom) I am implicitly prescribing that the same be done to any other individual (me for example) in any precisely similar situation, and vice versa. (Hare 1984, 636)

See Hare (1997, 12), stating that it is inherent in any normative judgment that, "if we make one about one situation, we cannot, while admitting that the facts are the same in another situation, in the same breath make a conflicting one about the second situation." Compare Sidgwick (1907, 386–87), suggesting that "[t]he axiom of Justice or Equity as above stated— 'that similar cases ought to be treated similarly'—belongs in all its applications to Utilitarianism as much as to any system commonly called Intuitional," referring to deontological moral principles; and ibid. (441–42).

100. Disputes about the equal treatment of equals often involve different views about what counts as a relevant difference. See sources cited in note 102. For example, proponents of racial segregation, particularly in the past, argued that there are racial differences that warrant different treatment (in particular, segregated or subservient treatment), whereas opponents

Mary are similarly situated (for example, both engage in the same behavior and cause identical accidents that result in equal harm), and if the system makes Larry pay $1,000 and Mary pay $2,000, it is probably the case that: there was a mistake (Larry should have to pay $2,000, Mary should have to pay $1,000, or both should have to pay some other amount) or Larry and Mary were differently situated (perhaps Larry, unlike Mary, was only partly at fault for the accident he caused).[101] In either case, equality has no independent import: We must look to some other substantive principle to determine whether Larry and Mary are identically situated in relevant respects (that is,

---

either denied the existence of racial differences or argued that they were irrelevant—or, more strongly, that discriminatory treatment was itself injurious, beyond any loss from failing to treat one or another group in an ideal manner. This latter view also informs the argument that the government should not impose a higher minimum legal age for drinking on males based on the fact that young males are more likely than young females to be irresponsible, such as by driving while intoxicated; the idea is that such a law might reinforce sex role stereotypes and thereby reduce women's social opportunities.

As we suggest in the text, under welfare economics equal treatment is generally favored unless there are grounds—relating to welfare—for different treatment. For example, one might adopt different screening practices by race or sex for diseases whose incidence differs across races or between the sexes. This policy might be contrasted with a case in which it is proposed that members of a minority race be subject to harsher law enforcement on the ground that their crime rate is higher than that of other groups. In this latter instance, the differential treatment may be injurious to the targeted race—independently of the direct effect of the policy—and might reinforce stereotypes that lead others to treat the targeted group badly. Thus, if discrimination itself in many instances reduces individuals' well-being in the manner that most today believe that it does, there is an additional reason for equal treatment under welfare economics. Likewise, some of these examples indicate the relevance of the possibility that the law may affect preferences and of arguments about ignoring undesirable preferences, issues that we discuss in subsections B.2 and B.3. In addition, discrimination may arise when a majority is able to impose its wishes on a minority, a problem involving abuse of power, which we discuss in subsection A.2.

101. Another possibility is that it is optimal to employ some random process. Thus, Larry and Mary may both exceed the speed limit by the same amount, posing the same risk of harm, but the use of random police patrols may result in one being fined while the other goes unpunished. Although such schemes are often efficient, we do not address this possibility in the text because we believe that most do not have it in mind when considering the subject of equal treatment. (We also note that such schemes often provide equal treatment ex ante.)

Yet another complication arises when it is impossible to treat two individuals identically, such as when a life boat can only hold one of them. Here, insisting on equal treatment would require that neither individual be saved. A common resolution of such problems is for the individuals to use a random mechanism, like drawing straws, to decide who gets to use the life boat. Such an approach creates equal treatment ex ante, which would be sufficient if one were to adopt the perspective we defend in subsection 1.

to determine which respects are relevant) and to ascertain what treatment is correct if they are.[102]

Even if the requirement of equal treatment is an essentially redundant evaluative principle, it is still true that consideration of whether equal treatment is provided can serve as a useful proxy device under welfare economics: Violations of equality prompt the analyst or policymaker to probe more deeply to determine whether mistreatment is present and, if it is, how to correct it.[103] Accordingly, we affirm that the notion of equality is important in this practical manner. In fact, testing for inequality can be a powerful diagnostic technique; when inequality is observed in circumstances in which it is generally regarded to be problematic, it will often be the case that rules or institutions are flawed.[104]

It may nevertheless be asserted that unequal treatment is independently undesirable as a normative matter. If it is, then when one individual has already been treated incorrectly, it may be appropriate to treat another indi-

102. The idea that equality must be supplemented by some other principle in order to reach any conclusions has long been noted in legal discourse. See, for example, Kelsen (1957), emphasizing that Aristotle's requirement of equality before the law is insufficient to assess whatever system of law happens to exist, and Chemerinsky (1983, 575 n.6, 578 n.15), citing sources. Westen is the legal academic most associated with emphasizing and developing the idea. See Westen (1982, 1990). For criticism, see, for example, Chemerinsky (1983), and note 110, in which we discuss Greenawalt's views. For related arguments in the context of tax policy, see Kaplow (1989).

103. We note, however, that equal treatment can never be perfectly achieved: All procedures, legal and otherwise, are subject to error. Hence, it is usually not feasible, much less cost-effective, to root out all unequal treatment. In addition, explicit randomness—as in law enforcement, in which no attempt is made to solve all crimes or to audit every individual, see note 101—is often a feature of legal design. The accepted legitimacy of such procedures (as long as there is no improper conduct in selecting the targets) suggests that, on reflection, the notion of equal treatment is not a truly independent evaluative principle.

104. Compare Chemerinsky (1983, 587–90), suggesting that unequal treatment creates a burden of justification. Mistreatment may reflect a low-quality procedure, specific design defects, or misbehavior by agents (which itself might reflect laziness or ulterior motives). Whatever the reason, welfare economic analysis will call for correction, as long as the costs of correction do not exceed the gains. Compare our discussion in section A of institutional concerns. We observe that, in many of the examples offered to suggest the importance of equality in response to Westen's argument that equality is a redundant concept, see note 102, there is reason to suspect that the decisionmaker was abusing power by applying improper criteria, an issue we address in subsection A.2. See Chemerinsky (1983, 580–84). Imposing an equal treatment requirement may itself constrain abuse by government officials. See ibid. (589): "No other principle [than equality] so systematically and comprehensively restrains the abuse of political power."; and Mirrlees (1982, 82).

vidual incorrectly, in order to avoid inequality in the treatment of the two individuals.[105] The suggestion is that two wrongs make a right—or at least less of a wrong than if only one wrong had occurred.[106] In certain instances, one wrong might justify another on grounds relating to overall well-being. For example, in a sports competition, a mistake by a referee that favors one team might best be balanced by a mistake of similar magnitude that favors the other, because spectators value competitive parity and victory based on the actual comparative strengths of the teams. We suspect, however, that this argument for giving independent weight to equality is exceptional and is unlikely to be relevant in most domains of legal policy analysis.[107]

Much more broadly, many believe that unequal treatment is evil, independent of its effects on anyone's actual well-being. This notion may not conflict with individuals' well-being (and, in some instances, with the interests of all individuals, viewed ex ante) if individuals have a taste for equality.[108] To the extent that individuals do have such a taste, however, the normative economic approach would accord weight to it just as to any other taste, as we discuss in subsection B.4.[109] A welfare economic evaluation would

105. See Peters (1997). See also Greenawalt (1997), noting other possibilities. Another implication is that, if equality has independent normative force, random procedures should be less acceptable than otherwise (see note 103)—that is, less than would be warranted in light of the benefits and costs with regard to individuals' well-being of reducing randomness. An analogous statement can be made about the extent to which error should be tolerated rather than reduced (at a cost).

106. This position can easily be overapplied. Usually, error will be the exception rather than the rule, so adding a second wrong to the first would likely increase aggregate inequality, given the large numbers who are treated correctly. As a result, one must either ignore the inequality in the treatment of the few or implement full equality, which (in the absence of perfection) would require, for example, imposing traffic fines on everyone (regardless of whether they committed a violation) or on no one, for then and only then would all equals be treated equally by the legal system.

107. As one exception, inefficient favoritism for one industry may, in some instances, best be offset (if it cannot be eliminated) by similar favoritism to a closely competing industry, to avoid resource misallocation between the two industries. In many instances, though, competitive advantages and pricing decisions will reflect ex ante analysis. Thus, the possibility of favorable or unfavorable errors ex post in the treatment of a particular competitor may not induce excessive expansion or contraction by that competitor.

108. For other reasons why equal treatment may promote welfare, see note 100.

109. It may be that the evil of unequal treatment hypothesized in the text involves well-being after all. Consider the case in which a benefit is provided to Larry but not to Mary, and it is understood that the motivation for favoring Larry involves a negative view of Mary (or perhaps of women generally). This disparate treatment might directly reduce Mary's well-being by hurting her feelings. Hence, even if neither Larry nor Mary should have received favorable treatment in the first place, once Larry has been favored it might be that the benefit

not, however, accord weight to equality if doing so would make individuals worse off, and we do not find in the literature a basis for rejecting this prescription.[110]

D. Additional Concerns about the Application of Welfare Economics

In this section, we comment on a number of additional issues—ranging from problems of evaluation to problems of predicting individuals' behavior—that some believe raise difficulties for the normative economic approach. Our view is that many of these issues present practical challenges

---

to Mary from treating her favorably as well—supposing that such treatment would repair her self-esteem—will exceed the degree of harm attributable to compounding the original error. See, for example, Simons (2000, 754–55), discussing such an example, referring to the benefits of equal treatment as the elimination of "insulting and stigmatizing" effects, but not indicating whether he views such benefits as rooted in the individual's well-being. Note that the hypothesized taste for equality involves a negative taste for unequal treatment and that the experience of this distaste is assumed to be avoided or eliminated by providing equal treatment to the victim of discrimination.

110. The most recent and explicit proponent of giving normative weight to equality in this context is Greenawalt (1997). Interestingly, the two examples he offers in support of his view, ibid. (1276–77), can both be modified such that the affected individuals would unanimously prefer unequal treatment. He even notes this feature in one of his examples. See ibid. (1277 n.39). Yet he does not attempt to explain how one can normatively justify subjecting individuals to a regime under which they are all worse off.

Greenawalt does suggest that individuals may have a taste for equality. Ibid. (1283). He does not consider whether, if such a taste were to exist, it would persist if individuals understood the cost of adhering to the notion. Moreover, he suggests that the existence of the taste is evidence of an underlying deontological principle—in the absence of any reason to doubt the taste's probity in this regard. Ibid. (1284–85). Aside from ignoring the obvious objection just noted, the logic of this argument is problematic. Greenawalt begins with a taste and infers directly from it a deontological principle, a move that seems difficult to justify. (Do we infer a deontological principle favoring chocolate from the fact that most people have a taste for chocolate?) Moreover, he does not consider the source of this taste or of tastes in general. Suppose it is truly instinctive (like tastes for sugar and fat). Or suppose that it is one of those social norms that is inculcated in childhood for what we argue to be welfare-promoting reasons. See subsection II.D.1. Or suppose that the taste reflects a desire to conform to contemporary notions of political correctness. In the end, Greenawalt seems to suggest that what he is calling a deontological principle is nevertheless justified because of the principle's desirable consequences. Greenawalt (1997, 1287–88). In spite of all the attention that scholars have devoted to studying notions of equality, even sophisticated proponents have difficulty in identifying a sound basis for considering equal treatment as an independent evaluative principle.

to legal policy analysts but that these challenges do not indicate conceptual shortcomings of the welfare economic framework. The problems arise because pursuing what we argue is the proper objective—promoting individuals' well-being—is neither easy nor devoid of uncertainty, given the complexity of the world. In the end, analysts must do the best they can when attempting to determine how legal rules affect individuals' well-being. To see the difficulties that we examine here as criticisms of the welfare economic framework involves a misunderstanding. Such a view implicitly suggests that a different normative program (usually unspecified) should be pursued, but an alternative approach can avoid the identified problems only if it ignores the important issues that give rise to them.[111]

1. Difficulty in Valuing Life, Pain and Suffering, and Other Nonpecuniary Factors

Some object that the economic approach requires placing a dollar value on life, pain and suffering, and other important concerns that do not seem readily convertible into such a common denominator. But finding a common denominator is a prerequisite to coherent policy assessment. As a matter of logic, it has long been understood that, if any tradeoffs are to be made among factors of concern, implicit prices can be used to signify the tradeoffs.

To explain, we begin by observing that any complete theory that can be used for the evaluation of policy must be able to tell us whether it is desirable to spend, say, $1 on safety improvements in order to reduce the expected loss of life by one person, and also whether it is desirable to spend $1,000, $1,000,000, $1,000,000,000, or half the GDP to do so. Furthermore, we presume that any plausible theory will answer affirmatively if the cost is sufficiently low (only $1) and negatively if the cost is sufficiently high (half the GDP).[112] Under any such theory, therefore, all else being equal, there will

---

111. See also subsection VII.B.1, suggesting that the relative ease of applying many notions of fairness, which is due to their exclusion of relevant but complicating factors, may help to explain their appeal to legal academics.

112. That is, we are assuming that, even though human life is viewed as precious, or, as some might say, infinitely valuable, tradeoffs must inevitably be made. Griffin offers a similar view:

> An individual human life has no equivalent. But that is not to say that nothing can be ranked with, let alone outrank, a human life. The French government knows that each year several drivers lose their lives because of the beautiful roadside avenues of trees, yet they do not cut them down. Even aesthetic pleasure is (rightly) allowed to outrank a certain number of human lives. It is easy here to move imperceptibly from Kant to cant. We want to express our sense of the enormous value of certain

be some point—some dollar cost—below which it is deemed appropriate to make the expenditure and above which it is deemed inappropriate to do so.[113] The concept of a monetary value of life in the present context simply refers to that point, whatever it happens to be.[114]

Moreover, if we do care about saving lives and reducing pain, there is a virtue in formal policy analysis being explicit about the valuations to be used. If tradeoffs are to be made consistently—which is necessary if one wishes, for example, to save more rather than fewer lives—one must know what those tradeoffs are. The now-familiar example is that some government regulations save a statistical life at costs of a hundred thousand dollars and others at costs in the billions; if the regulations were rationalized to use a consistent implicit valuation and if they continued to require the expenditure

---

things—human standing, an individual human life—and once again we reach for strong expressions. But in real life, in concrete situations, we often do, and should, back down. We find that we did not mean literally what, in searching for strong expressions, we ended up saying. (Griffin 1986, 82)

113. To be more precise about the logic, two steps are involved. The first, stated in the text, is that a complete theory must give some answer to the question for any possible level of cost. The second, implicit in the text, is that any coherent theory, having deemed an expenditure of $X worth making to save a life, would a fortiori deem any expenditure less than $X worth making. Likewise, if an expenditure of $Y were deemed excessive, so would any expenditure greater than $Y.

114. See, for example, Viscusi (1992, chapter 2). As the text indicates, dollar valuations really are little more than indicators of how analysts or decisionmakers ultimately choose to make tradeoffs. Money is a particular social institution, and valuations of life are mere analytical constructs. The actual metric under welfare economics is individuals' well-being. What matters is life itself, pain and suffering, and so forth. The numbers assigned to measure individuals' well-being are merely constructs that the analyst uses to represent the choices that individuals would make between alternatives, as we elaborate in the text to follow and in note 118, in our discussion of how economists attempt to value life and other nonpecuniary costs and benefits. See notes 6 and 15 in chapter II.

Despite the need to employ consistent valuations of diverse things (such as saving life and facilitating recreational activity) if one is to make intelligent policy decisions, some legal academics and philosophers object to the use of a common denominator or otherwise express skepticism about commensurability. See, for example, Craswell (1998, 1419 nn.1–2), citing authors who present such views; Symposium: Law and Incommensurability (1998), offering different views on incommensurability; and Tribe (1972). We do not, however, understand how these commentators address the basic point that logically consistent choice intrinsically involves choosing between alternatives that, accordingly, are compared to each other. (In fact, as Craswell explains, many writing about commensurability do not deny the possibility of making consistent decisions; instead, they express skepticism about the ability to compare disparate types of justifications for decisions.)

of the same total amount of resources, *many* more lives would be saved.[115] The reason is that reallocating expenditures from places where they have a very low payoff in terms of saving lives to places where they have a very high payoff will greatly increase the number of lives saved. The use of seemingly cold-hearted language in academic papers and technical reports, written and read primarily by experts who analyze such problems, would have to count as a huge social detriment per se to outweigh these benefits.[116]

115. See, for example, Breyer (1993, 21–29), Viscusi (1992, 32), Tengs and Graham (1996), and Hahn (1999). See also Jones-Lee (1994, 294), describing a similar situation in the United Kingdom.

116. Some also object that the process of explicit quantification will change the values of the analyst in an undesirable manner: The analyst may become cold-hearted or adopt a narrow view of what truly matters. Compare Tribe (1972, 97–98), suggesting that the "antiseptic" language of policy analysis obscures what is really at stake. However, this outcome is hardly inevitable. In fact, explicit attention to and careful study of how people value their own lives in various situations may make the analyst more appreciative of the value of life. In any event, we are unaware of direct evidence for this objection. (There is some limited— and mixed—evidence on whether economists, either because of self-selection or training, tend to be less socially cooperative than others. See, for example, Frank, Gilovich, and Regan (1996) and Yezer, Goldfarb, and Poppen (1996).) There is some reason to believe that the economics profession as a whole is not inclined to take a limited view of what is important; indeed, some see economists as imperialists who increasingly seek to embrace all aspects of human behavior (consider, for example, the work of Becker). Moreover, prominent scholars who employ a welfare economic or utilitarian calculus have historically been associated with humanitarian reform efforts and currently include individuals concerned with the welfare of destitute people in developing countries (for example, Mirrlees and Stiglitz) and ardent proponents of humane concerns such as animal rights (for example, Singer, as well as most classical utilitarians, see, for example, Sidgwick (1907, 414), referring to Bentham, Mill, utilitarians generally, and himself as concerned with all sentient beings).

In addition, even if systematic assessment does take a toll on the analyst, it is a small price for society to pay in light of the huge benefits to be obtained from better analysis of such important matters as saving life. (By analogy, one would hardly object to all medical care because, for instance, some individuals who must build hospitals engage in hard labor that hardens their hearts, or hospital orderlies must become accustomed to suffering and thus less sensitive to it.) In this respect, note that our argument concerns the duty of legal academics, not of ordinary individuals. Sometimes, experts must make personal sacrifices for the benefit of society. (Doctors, for example, are exposed to cadavers early in their education and undergo other training that may render them psychologically less sensitive than the rest of us to the sight of blood and human suffering. This result is, of course, necessary if they are to focus on their work in an emergency room or during surgery. Alas, with doctors, becoming cold-hearted has a cost even in the daily performance of their duties because bedside manner may directly affect patient treatment and recovery. In contrast, legal academics are more like medical researchers who work in laboratories, never seeing patients.) See also subsection 3 and note 132, discussing the possible effects of using markets on individuals' attitudes.

(continued)

Under welfare economics, the method for arriving at social valuations is to use the valuations of the individuals who would be affected by the policy under consideration.[117] For example, some empirical work using this technique indicates that the valuations of life traditionally used in tort cases are too low;[118] if this finding is true, it may be that the legal system—which does, in the end, place a dollar value on lives when setting damages—is not providing adequate deterrence and thus may be unduly sacrificing lives. A

The question whether ordinary individuals in their everyday decisionmaking should be explicit about tradeoffs involving life and resources is qualitatively different, as we emphasize in subsection II.D.2 and chapter VII, and its correct resolution may be different from that for professional policy analysts. For example, rhetoric about the priceless nature of life usefully reinforces social norms about the importance of life—especially others' lives, which we may be otherwise inclined to discount. Nevertheless, individuals cannot help but make such tradeoffs (such as in deciding whether to save money by driving rather than flying to a vacation destination, given that driving poses greater risks), and they gain by making tradeoffs consistently because, as a consequence, they can both save more money overall and reduce their total exposure to risk.

117. See, for example, Schelling (1981, 44–50; 1984, chapter 5), Viscusi (1992, 1993), Jones-Lee (1994, 306–14), and Thaler and Rosen (1976). Typical presentations of the method oversimplify because they neglect externalities: Valuations ordinarily concern only the individuals directly affected, but others' well-being might be affected as well because of psychological interdependence and tangible economic effects (the latter including that individuals who die are no longer productive but also no longer consume resources). See, for example, Arthur (1981).

118. See, for example, L. Cohen (1985), stating that wrongful death awards, based largely on lost earnings, omit important factors, notably, the value of life to the victim, and accordingly are much lower than economic theory suggests is appropriate; and Viscusi (2000, 562–63), stating that typical wrongful death awards based on lost earnings may be less than $1 million, whereas appropriate economic value-of-life estimates are approximately $5 million. See also Jury Verdict Research, Inc. (1987, 4), presenting data indicating an average wrongful death award for single males age 25–35 of $526,558; Boxold (1999, 8), showing a national median jury award for wrongful death cases of $654,000; and Viscusi (1993, 1926–27 table 2, 1930–31), stating that labor market estimates of the value of a statistical life cluster in the $3 million to $7 million range. Such valuations are usually obtained from individuals' implicit valuations as evidenced by their market behavior. For example, one might measure how much of a wage increase is required to induce individuals to work in more hazardous occupations. Or one might make inferences about how much individuals value a safe neighborhood or cleaner environment by examining land valuations or housing rental prices. We do not mean to suggest that reliable estimates are easy to come by, as researchers must confront issues of potentially imperfect information by the individuals acting in the marketplace as well as alternative explanations for observed differences in wages, values, rents, and the like. Rather, we merely wish to explain conceptually how one might approach the question of valuation in such settings.

benefit of the welfare economic approach is that it makes explicit both the evaluations themselves and the process of deriving them; as a result, they are more readily subject to debate and can more intelligently be used in guiding reform.

2. Omission of "Soft" Variables

Another common objection to economic analysis is that it is inclined to omit "soft" variables, such as intangible factors. The suggestion is that analysts, who aim to be rigorous and thus to speak about tradeoffs in quantitative terms, ignore factors that are difficult to quantify.[119]

This claim may have some truth, but we see it as an argument for undertaking more comprehensive analysis, not for substituting an incorrect form of analysis that, as we have shown, does not even in principle pay attention to the correct variables. Implicit in the usual criticism of economic analysis is the supposition that another mode of analysis exists that can capture all the relevant effects, combine them in complex ways, give proper weight to each factor, and yet avoid being explicit or engaging in quantification of obviously relevant effects. This assumption is implausible.[120] Underlying this criticism is the view that analysts of, for example, government health and safety regulations should forgo the attempt to quantify what they can. But this refusal implies that regulations should be designed without explicit regard for how many lives will be saved, how much pain will be avoided, how much implementation will cost, and so forth. It is hard to imagine that such an approach would successfully identify which policies best advance individuals' well-being.

We also observe that the criticism that economists tend to omit soft variables is in tension with the previously mentioned criticism that economists quantify even those factors that seem least amenable to measurement.[121] In addition, we find it somewhat ironic that legal analysts who rely

119. See, for example, Tribe (1972, 96–97; 1973, 627).

120. And critics do not offer constructive alternatives. See, for example, Tribe (1972, 1973). Calabresi and Bobbitt, when addressing the problem of how best to proceed when some aspects of a problem can be readily quantified and others cannot, offer the following advice: "It may be better to forgo market information, even as to those elements for which it is available and accurate, than to try to monetize the whole affair. A simple, muddled, collective determination may be preferable." Calabresi and Bobbitt (1978, 109).

121. Rose, in her review of Sagoff (1988), states:

> Early in the book, one notices that Sagoff rails at economists for failing to take environmental "values" into account, and then he turns around and rails at them even more when they try to do just that. The poor economists: First everybody said

on notions of fairness criticize the incompleteness of some economic analysis. Throughout this book, we show that discourse based on notions of fairness pays little or no attention to obviously important variables—such as lives saved on account of deterrence or costs of implementation—and instead devotes almost exclusive attention to considerations that may not have any connection to individuals' well-being.

3. Possible Costs of Permitting Market Trade

Many believe that economists favor the use of largely unfettered markets across the board,[122] and critics of economic analysis contend that market trade is inappropriate in certain contexts.[123] For example, many critics would object to permitting a market for human organs[124] or a market for adopted children.[125]

We first observe that welfare economics does not automatically endorse unregulated market trade.[126] Problems of imperfect information, monopoly, public goods, and externalities are well-understood justifications for restrictions on markets.[127] Thus, even if an adoption market were beneficial to

---

they ignored nonmarket goods, like wildlife and mountainous scenery; and now here is Sagoff telling them they are imbeciles and rogues for trying to translate those nonmarket goods into a cost-benefit calculation for decisionmakers. (Rose 1989, 1635)

122. For a survey of economists' attitudes toward the use of markets, see Frey (1986).

123. Trebilcock critically reviews the literature and emphasizes that one can analyze the relevant issues as instances of market failure. See Trebilcock (1993, chapter 2). In the legal literature, the concern that excessive reliance on markets and other attempts at monetization of rights might be dangerous was noted by Calabresi and Bobbitt, who state that "there remains the offense inherent in giving money values to sacred rights." Calabresi and Bobbitt (1978, 115). More recently, the issue has been emphasized in Radin (1987, 1996). For a critique of the view that wide use of markets will have detrimental effects on how we value things that we wish to be outside of markets, see Mack (1989). We cite other work addressing particular contexts in subsequent notes.

124. For economic analyses of a market for human organs, see, for example, L. Cohen (1989) and Hansmann (1989).

125. For articles discussing the potential effects of moving to a freer market, compared to the highly regulated adoption market and black market that now exist, see, for example, E. Landes and R. Posner (1978) and Prichard (1984).

126. See, for example, Craswell (1992, 823), noting that standard economic analysis does not per se endorse a market paradigm, as some believe, but that it views the market as a means to the end of promoting a notion of social welfare and that whether markets serve this goal well is a contingent, empirical question.

127. Distributive concerns also seem to animate some arguments in favor of various sorts of rationing. From this perspective, however, one would also wish to allow secondary

adults who entered the market (because voluntary trade increases the well-being of the buyer and the seller), it would not directly account for the welfare of children (third parties who do not act in the market), so there is a presumptive argument for regulation of some sort.[128] A regime of market purchases of blood might be undesirable if it discourages voluntary donations and if voluntary donors provide more reliable information about their medical histories and thus their blood quality than paid donors do.[129]

Some critics, however, believe that there is a problem with the very existence of certain markets—a problem apart from the allocations that result.[130] In examining the potential sources of such objections, we find that those that seem plausible also relate to individuals' well-being and thus are already encompassed by welfare economics. One possibility is that a large number of individuals would find the operation of certain markets, for instance, a market for human organs, distasteful; as we have noted, such tastes would be registered under welfare economics.[131] We should, however, be cautious about condemning such markets on these grounds. If many individuals die for want of organs that a market could provide, there is a heavy burden on healthy individuals who find such markets upsetting to demonstrate that their discomfort is so great that people in need should not have access to a regime that could save their lives. Furthermore, strong antimarket attitudes might not persist if, over time, the actual use of such a market was seen to result in substantial benefits.

Another possible objection to markets is that the existence of, for exam-

---

market trading of the initial entitlements because such trading would benefit the poor, but such trading would be impermissible if a market were forbidden completely. Indeed, rationing combined with secondary market trading is, in the end, essentially the same as permitting a free market and engaging directly in some income redistribution through the tax and transfer system. (On the proper role of distributive concerns under welfare economics, see subsection II.A.3.)

128. The alternative of a legal regime that considers only the best interests of the child—as is advocated for and to an important extent governs child custody disputes—is also improper: The parents, after all, are people too. Moreover, one must account for the incentive effects of ignoring parental interests. Incentives to marry, divorce, have children, and put them up for adoption may all be affected by legal rules; these incentive effects may in turn affect the well-being of children. By taking an ex post view that ignores incentive effects, the "best interests of the child" test may fail to serve the best interests of children.

129. See Titmuss (1971); Arrow (1972), criticizing Titmuss; and Singer (1973). See also Frey and Oberholzer-Gee (1997), discussing the theory that monetary compensation reduces intrinsic motivation and presenting survey evidence involving the siting of a nuclear waste storage facility.

130. See sources cited in note 123.

131. See subsections II.A.1, II.D.2, and VIII.B.4.

ple, an adoption market might in the long run adversely affect individuals' attitudes about important aspects of their lives.[132] As we discuss in subsection B.2, if one could predict such a result and if the change in attitudes would have a detrimental effect on individuals' well-being, then welfare economics would credit this effect in assessing the merits of permitting a market.

However the matters considered in this subsection are resolved, we suggest that these sorts of questions—those posed by welfare economics, concerning how markets directly and indirectly affect individuals' well-being—are the correct ones to consider.

4. Indeterminacy

(a) Indeterminacy Due to Empirical Uncertainty. Another difficulty with welfare economics is that it often yields results in which we can have only limited confidence because policy conclusions may depend on empirical facts about which existing knowledge is sparse. The uncertainty that may accompany policy analysis is sometimes described as indeterminacy, but this is a mischaracterization. The problem is not that analysts cannot make coherent judgments when available information is meager; instead, the real concern is that conclusions may turn out to be mistaken, and subsequent revision of policy may be required.

The world is complex, and empirical research on the legal system is in its infancy, so this state of affairs is unavoidable. Implicit in the notion that this uncertainty (so-called indeterminacy) constitutes a criticism of welfare economics is that easily answered questions—which necessarily ignore relevant, although complicated, features of reality—are somehow better to con-

---

132. See, for example, sources cited in note 123. Mack offers a skeptical view of such an objection:

> If nonmarket activities and relations are so much better, so much more valuable, than their market counterparts (if any), and if market activities and relations do not preclude these internally valuable activities and ties . . . , then won't people in general continue their nonmarket, internally motivated, actions and relations— unless people in general be knaves or fools? And if the problem is that people are such knaves or fools that they cannot recognize or will not choose these components of human flourishing, then who is to be entrusted to design and enforce limitations on the market that will advance genuine personhood and community? (Mack 1989, 223)

See also note 116, discussing the effect of explicit analysis on analysts themselves. For a more general discussion of ways in which markets may affect individuals' preferences, see Bowles (1998).

sider. In fact, this supposed virtue of alternatives to economic evaluation, such as appeals to notions of fairness, is an important demerit. As we emphasize throughout this book, notions of fairness may favor one rule over another without regard to many or any of the rules' effects on behavior, the level of administrative costs, and so forth. If we seek to choose policies on the basis of their effects on individuals' well-being, this easier and superficially more attractive[133] approach is unacceptable.[134]

There remains, however, the question of how society can use welfare economics in those cases in which it yields highly uncertain conclusions. In the short run, decisions must be based on incomplete empirical data, even conjecture. The benefit of undertaking the proper analysis is that it identifies the relevant data and beliefs and how they bear on which legal rule is likely to be best. For example, analysis might indicate that, given the extent of administrative costs, behavioral effects would have to be very large for some rule to be preferable; even if the analyst or decisionmaker does not know the magnitude of the behavioral response with any confidence, it may seem implausible that any response would be high enough to justify the rule.

Moreover, proper analysis, even when it yields tentative conclusions in which we may have little confidence, is necessary to the formulation of scholarly agendas and government policy toward support of research. By identifying which factors are important, welfare economic analysis highlights what must be learned if better guidance is to be provided in the future. To date, empirical work on the legal system and the effects of legal rules has been modest in most areas, but this situation is changing. The rate of progress will presumably be faster and the usefulness of future empirical work greater, the more the work of legal academics and other policy analysts reveals the questions that most deserve study. As we emphasize in chapter VII, our primary audience is the community of legal academics and other policy analysts who are responsible for the present state of analytical and empirical work and capable of improving it in the future.

(b) Conceptual Indeterminacy. Some legal academics critical of normative economic analysis emphasize the potential indeterminacy of the Kaldor-Hicks "efficiency" test, which considers a policy change to be desirable if the winners

133. See subsection VII.B.1, discussing how legal academics who seek to have direct influence might prefer modes of analysis that yield simple, unambiguous conclusions.

134. Hare offers a similar observation regarding certain critiques of utilitarianism:

It has been thought to be a defect in utilitarianism that it is in this way at the mercy of the facts. But in truth this is a strength and not a weakness. Likewise, it shows the lack of contact with reality of a system based on moral intuitions without critical

gain by a sufficient amount that they could in principle compensate the losers.[135] Analysts have long recognized the paradox that, according to this test, it is possible that both a change from regime *A* to regime *B* and a change from *B* back to *A* could be deemed efficient.[136] The explanation for this phenomenon is that, when regimes change, the distribution of income may change as well, and individuals' valuations of what is available under each regime depend on their levels of income. In the history of economic thought, the potential internal inconsistency of the Kaldor-Hicks test was of some importance because the test was favored by many who aspired to offer policy recommendations without having to make any judgment about the income distribution. Not surprisingly, however, when a particular policy choice significantly affects the distribution of income, one cannot make a definitive policy recommendation while remaining agnostic about distributive questions.[137]

As should be clear from our discussion in subsections II.A.2 and II.A.3, the possible indeterminacy of the Kaldor-Hicks test is not a problem within the standard normative economic framework of welfare economics because welfare economics encompasses distributive judgments.[138] That is, any decision that is indeterminate under the Kaldor-Hicks criterion—which will implicitly relate to the importance of redistribution—becomes determinate under welfare economics, for under it distributive judgments are made.[139] Moreover, even when the Kaldor-Hicks test is determinate, distributive effects are possible, and, accordingly, a decision based on the Kaldor-Hicks test will not necessarily align with one under welfare economics.

---

thought, that it can go on churning out the same defences of liberty and democracy *whatever* assumptions are made about the state of the world or the preferences of its inhabitants. (Hare 1981, 167)

135. See, for example, Kelman (1987, 141–50) and Kennedy (1981).

136. That is, the winners in the change from *A* to *B* might be able to compensate the losers, and yet the winners in the change in the reverse situation, from *B* to *A*, might be able to compensate the losers as well. See, for example, Scitovszky (1941).

137. See, for example, Boadway and Bruce (1984, 96–101) and Little (1957, chapter 6).

138. By contrast, indeterminacy can be a problem with wealth maximization, which we discuss in subsection II.A.3. Indeed, wealth maximization may be viewed as another way of describing the attempt to make policy decisions in exclusive reliance on the Kaldor-Hicks efficiency test.

139. To provide a rough illustration, it may be indeterminate whether regime *A*, in which Jack gets $100 and Jill gets $50, or regime *B*, in which each gets $75, is more efficient, but a social welfare function (which expresses total welfare as a function of individuals' well-being, which in turn is a function of their respective incomes) would produce a clear choice. In this example, plausible social welfare functions would ordinarily favor the more equal distribution, as we explain in subsection II.A.3.

Even though the Kaldor-Hicks test is not appropriate as a matter of principle, the test can be quite useful because, as we explain in our discussion of distributive issues in subsection II.A.3, it often is sensible for legal policy analysis to focus on efficiency. Focusing on efficiency allows the analyst to obtain a better understanding of certain aspects of a problem, provides a nearly complete appraisal of the many legal rules that do not have significant distributive effects, and also may be the appropriate benchmark for choosing other legal rules because distributive concerns are more effectively addressed directly, through the income tax and transfer system. We note that the last reason suggests another means of addressing the indeterminacy problem with which we began: One can change legal rules and also make offsetting adjustments to the income tax and transfer system to ensure that the overall income distribution remains the same;[140] if this is done, the pure efficiency test will be determinate, and, more importantly, it will indicate which reforms raise individuals' well-being and thus increase social welfare.

Finally, some commentators suggest other sources of indeterminacy—that is, reasons other than distributive effects that may cause individuals' valuations to vary across legal regimes.[141] As we explain briefly in the margin, however, once the causes are understood, it is usually apparent how welfare economics would deal with them.[142] In essence, problems that result in inde-

---

140. See sources cited in note 38 in chapter II.

141. See, for example, Kelman (1987, 145–48). For representative empirical literature on what is usually referred to as the endowment effect, see Coursey, Hovis, and Schulze (1987), Hanemann (1991), and Kahneman, Knetsch, and Thaler (1990).

142. We sketch some of the plausible causes. (1) Real differences in value may be a result of different histories. For example, someone may value a house that he has lived in for years more than an otherwise comparable house. Likewise, he may have sentimental attachment to particular objects in his possession. In such instances, the greater valuation placed on items already in one's possession reflects a real difference between items one has and items one does not have. See, for example, Becker (1992, 337), giving this example as a source of the endowment effect. In this instance, the regime that actually corresponds to the status quo is the proper reference point for such valuations. Thus, the fact that others would have valued the house if—but only if—they instead had lived in it for the last ten years is not a reason to impute a high value to them when they did not in fact reside there. (2) Changing laws may result in changes in preferences, a possibility emphasized in Kelman (1979b). We consider how this possibility should be analyzed in subsection B.2. (3) Individuals may be confused on account of imperfect information or inadequate reflection, or they may suffer from various cognitive biases and other limitations on their decisionmaking ability, as we discuss in subsection B.1. See, for example, Baron (1994a, 4): "Status-quo bias . . . can result from overgeneralization of rules that are often useful, such as, 'If it ain't broke, don't fix it.' "; and Baron (1995, 37), suggesting that the results of "mug" experiments reflect a status quo heuristic that is often valuable but that is used even when its rationale is absent. Some of these explanations

terminacy arise because of difficulties in assessing individuals' well-being under different regimes; once individuals' well-being has been appraised, straightforward application of the welfare economic approach will yield a determinate result.[143] Thus, other sources of indeterminacy in applying the Kaldor-Hicks efficiency test do not raise any valid criticism of welfare economics. As we observe repeatedly, difficulties in measuring what we truly value should spur us to improve our methods of measurement, not to replace them with principles that, while easier to apply, do not properly account for what we value.

5. The Difficulty of Predicting the Behavior of Individuals, Who Are Not Always Rational Maximizers of Their Own Well-Being

Some commentators find economic assessment problematic because individuals do not always behave in the manner that economists usually suppose, as rational maximizers of their own well-being. Individuals may be compulsive, myopic, inconsistent, confused by uncertainty, irrational in their reactions to risk, and so forth.[144] Moreover, as we discuss in subsection II.D.1, they may be motivated in part by the desire to adhere to social norms that appear to be inconsistent with the pursuit of self-interest. Because much behavior does not comport with the assumptions of standard economic models, it is argued that policy cannot be predicated on such models.

We believe that such critiques have an important element of truth, but

---

seem consistent with the fact that modest rephrasings of opinion polls, including valuation surveys, sometimes produce very different responses. Compare Harris and Joyce (1980, 174–76), suggesting that different responses to their two experiments, which differed only in how the question was posed to participants, may have reflected an inadequate understanding of the situation and of the implications of their answers; and Kahneman and Varey (1991, 151), suggesting that endowment effects may be framing effects. Because of these problems, researchers need to develop better techniques or to find alternative means of eliciting individuals' valuations, such as observing actual market choices in contexts in which information is reasonably good (although the factors identified in subsection B.1 suggest that market behavior itself does not always accurately indicate what individuals actually value).

143. Of course, analysts can disagree about what principles should govern distribution—that is, the proper form of the social welfare function. And it is obvious that such disagreements may produce disagreements about policy when redistribution is involved. However, our analysis in subsection II.A.3 suggests that society stands to gain if such disagreements are resolved entirely in calibrating the income tax and transfer system, adopting whatever legal rules are efficient given the distribution that society ultimately selects.

144. See, for example, Baron (1994c), Hogarth and Reder (1987), Nisbett and Ross (1980), and sources cited in note 23.

their implications are not what is sometimes supposed. The valid core of the criticism is that human behavior is complex and not always easy to predict. Any set of simple behavioral assumptions will not fully capture reality and may, in some contexts, be misleading. This difficulty, as we note previously,[145] is inherent in the nature of analysis, which seeks to make problems tractable enough that some illumination is possible. The most straightforward implication of these critiques is that analysts should be sensitive to their behavioral assumptions and open-minded about exploring alternative premises. As alternative theories become more fully developed, analysts should employ the most accurate and useful understanding of behavior in predicting the effects of policies. We believe that the standard assumption of rational maximization is apt for many legal applications—notably, the study of the behavior of private enterprise—and has proved to be useful in a wide range of other settings.[146] Nevertheless, when behavioral economics, cognitive psychology, evolutionary biology, sociology, or anthropology yield valid insights, they should be incorporated in legal policy analysis.[147]

Next, we assess the implications of the behavioral critique for our analysis. The *normative* economic approach—welfare economics—is committed to determining which legal rules and institutions best promote individuals' well-being. The appropriate *positive* analysis is, by definition, that which provides the most accurate predictions of behavior, thus allowing the analyst to determine as reliably as possible which policies are best for individuals. The fundamental claim of this book concerns only the normative question. That is, whatever are the actual effects of legal rules and however they might best be determined, our argument is that legal rules should be *evaluated*

145. See page 32 and note 33 in chapter II.

146. Certain important predictions of economic theory do not depend on the assumption of rational behavior. See, for example, Becker (1962). Some scholars agree that the rationality assumption has led to important results but suggest that further advances require taking a broader view of human motivation. See Ellickson (1989) and Hirshleifer (1985, 54).

147. For useful surveys of the psychology literature on decisionmaking, see Baron (1994c), Hogarth and Reder (1987), Kahneman, Slovic, and Tversky (1982), and Nisbett and Ross (1980). For references on behavioral economics, see Arlen (1998), Camerer (1995), Jolls, Sunstein, and Thaler (1998), Kahneman and Varey (1991), M. Rabin (1998), and Sunstein (2000). For a discussion of economics and other social sciences, see Ellickson (1989). For examinations of the relationship between positive economic analysis, other social sciences, and biology, see, for example, Hirshleifer (1977, 1985) and Wilson (1977). See also Cosmides, Tooby, and Barkow (1992, 3), stating that evolutionary psychology, "by focusing on the evolved information-processing mechanisms that comprise the human mind, supplies the necessary connection between evolutionary biology and the complex, irreducible social and cultural phenomena studied by anthropologists, sociologists, economists, and historians."

based solely on the resulting levels of individuals' well-being, not based on the rules' alignment with notions of fairness.[148]

It should be clear that the strength of our argument about the proper form of normative analysis is independent of the actual techniques that are best suited to positive analysis. To illustrate, suppose that conventional positive economic analysis indicates that a given regime of medical malpractice is the best means of supplementing doctors' incentives to take proper care. We might suspect from the work of cognitive psychologists and confirm by direct inquiry, however, that the regime results in excessively defensive medical practice because doctors overreact to highly publicized jury verdicts. In that case, we might ultimately conclude that medical malpractice liability should be subject to additional limitations.

As another example, consider laws that penalize behavior such as littering or tax evasion. Sociologists might teach us that reductions in compliance by some people will reduce voluntary compliance by others because the sight of widespread violations dilutes the feelings of guilt otherwise aroused by law-breaking.[149] In this instance, greater enforcement might produce higher marginal returns in terms of deterring illegal behavior than would otherwise occur.

In both instances, the final evaluation of legal policies still depends on the effects of the policies on behavior and thus ultimately on individuals' well-being. These examples illustrate the proposition that our project of determining the proper ends of legal policy analysis does not depend on the content of future developments in positive social science research or on whether the methods that win out are "economic" or belong to some other academic field.[150]

148. Compare Hammond (1982b, 91): "Bayesian rationality has often been criticised, but mostly on the grounds that individuals' actual behaviour is not in accord with it. . . . The utilitarian welfare economist, of course, is interested in a normative criterion for choice under uncertainty, and then Bayesian rationality or expected utility maximisation becomes much more acceptable."

149. See generally Roth, Scholz, and Witte (1989, chapter 2); Wilson and Herrnstein (1985, 292–99), discussing peer group effects on criminal behavior; and Wilson and Kelling (1982, 31), discussing Zimbardo's experiment in which individuals were willing to vandalize an automobile once an initial act of vandalism had occurred.

150. Compare R. Posner (1989, 61–62): "Whether the hypotheses that legal scholars test by confronting them with data on number of cases, frequency and severity of punishments, crime rates, damage awards, judicial affirmances, settlement rates, appeals rates, and the other abundant but neglected data on the legal system come from psychology, sociology, economics, or some other social science is unimportant. The important thing is to get on with the testing."

CHAPTER IX

———□———

Conclusion

We have advanced the thesis that legal policy should be evaluated using the framework of welfare economics, under which assessments of policies depend exclusively on their effects on individuals' well-being. We stressed that the welfare economic conception of an individual's well-being is all-encompassing (and thus not limited to wealth or other tangible elements) and that welfare economic evaluation reflects concerns about the distribution of income.[1] In arguing that no evaluative importance should be given to notions of fairness, we are criticizing principles that give weight to factors that are independent of individuals' well-being or its overall distribution. These notions of fairness, such as corrective justice and retributive justice, which are employed in evaluating legal rules, depend directly on characteristics of individuals' acts (for example, whether injurers behave wrongfully) rather than on the effects of rules on individuals' well-being (such as the extent to which penalizing injurers reduces the rate of injuries). Of course, most legal policy analysts hold mixed evaluative views that accord weight both to notions of fairness and to individuals' well-being (so that an unfair rule might be chosen if the fair rule is much too costly). However, our criticism implies that mixed views should not be employed in the evaluation of legal policy; instead, such evaluation should be concerned solely with individuals' well-being, the focus of welfare economics.

We based our claim that legal policy assessment should rely exclusively on welfare economics on two arguments. First, pursuing notions of fairness comes at the expense of individuals' well-being. Indeed, giving weight to any

---

1. See section II.A.

notion of fairness entails accepting the conclusion that it may be good to adopt legal rules under which literally everyone is made worse off.[2] For example, when we examined reciprocal settings in the tort context, we saw that whenever a notion of fairness led an analyst to choose a legal rule different from the one favored under welfare economics, every individual's well-being was reduced.[3] Thus, notions of fairness are opposed in a fundamental sense to individuals' well-being.

Second, we did not find rationales for notions of fairness that justify advancing them at the expense of individuals' well-being. We examined the legal and philosophical literature, as well as experience and intuition, to identify major notions of fairness that apply in four basic legal contexts—torts, contracts, legal procedure, and law enforcement—in an attempt to determine why it might be thought that notions of fairness should be pursued. We found that proponents of notions of fairness usually do not furnish explicit grounds for the notions; nor do proponents address the conflict with individuals' well-being that we identified in basic, paradigmatic settings in which one would expect that notions of fairness would provide clear guidance. On close examination of the various notions of fairness, the actual situations under consideration, and the consequences of choosing rules based on these principles, we found it difficult to uncover sound reasons for deeming fairness principles to have independent normative force. In many instances, individuals who would seem to be the intended beneficiaries of a notion of fairness—for example, the victims of accidents or of breaches of contracts[4]— were worse off under rules that were supposed to be fair to them. And in other respects, the fair rules seemed to have little connection to the ideas underlying the notions of fairness; for instance, rules that seem to be implied by the promise-keeping theory of contracts arguably violate rather than uphold what can best be understood as the "true" promise of the parties.[5]

We also devoted substantial attention to the question of why notions of fairness possess so much appeal, if our criticism of them has the force that we claim. An important part of our answer involves social norms.[6] We

---

2. See subsection II.C.1.

3. See subsections III.C.1 and III.D.1.

4. See sections III.C and IV.C.

5. See subsection IV.C.2(e)(i).

6. Additional reasons concern the manner in which notions of fairness may serve as proxy principles that aid in the identification of welfare-promoting policies (as we discuss in the text to follow), the apparent attractiveness of the ex post perspective adopted under most notions of fairness (see, for example, subsection II.B.2(c)), and a number of factors that make the notions particularly appealing to legal academics (see subsection VII.B.1).

began by observing that most notions of fairness seem to correspond to social norms, principles that well-socialized members of society use to guide their behavior in everyday life. Then, drawing on a long tradition of scholarship, we suggested that social norms that underlie leading notions of fairness tend to have the function of promoting individuals' well-being in ordinary interactions—for example, by discouraging opportunistic behavior. Finally, we explained the implications of these points for the role of notions of fairness in policy assessment.[7] Because social norms have a powerful influence on our minds, it is not surprising that related ideas of fairness seem important. (To illustrate, our attachment to the social norm that promises should be kept naturally inclines us to favor the promise-keeping notion of fairness when we assess contract law.[8]) Nevertheless, our attachment to social norms, whether due to socialization or evolution, does not imply that analysts should elevate them to the status of independent evaluative principles when assessing legal policy. Indeed, it would be ironic to treat social norms as the basis for giving weight to notions of fairness if in fact the purpose of the social norms is to promote individuals' well-being in the contexts in which the norms have arisen—because the consequence of treating notions of fairness as independent principles for policy analysis can only be to reduce individuals' well-being.

We considered as well other implications of the correspondence between social norms and notions of fairness that may help to explain the appeal of these notions. First, when a notion of fairness is related to an underlying social norm, individuals may have direct tastes concerning legal rules and the operation of the legal system. (For example, a person may be upset if criminals guilty of horrible acts are not appropriately punished.) Under welfare economics, such a taste is treated as a component of individuals' well-being; its significance therefore rests on an empirical question, not a philosophical one, and the existence of individuals' tastes for something does not, of course, render it an independent normative principle.[9]

Second, because social norms generally are functional, pursuing associated notions of fairness may serve as a proxy device for identifying welfare-promoting policies. (For instance, the requirement of corrective justice that injurers compensate their victims will tend to deter harmful acts.) This use of a notion of fairness, however, is an instrumental one, relating to the objectives of welfare economics. Such use would not justify treating the notion

7. We developed these points in each of the contexts that we considered and discussed them in general terms in section II.D.

8. See subsection IV.C.2(g).

9. See subsections II.A.1, II.D.2, and VIII.B.4.

of fairness as an independent principle when analysis reveals that, in fact, the notion does not advance individuals' well-being in a particular situation. Furthermore, the formal legal system differs in a number of ways from the operation of social norms in everyday life. (For example, the formal legal system uses damage awards and incarceration instead of guilt and disapprobation to discourage undesirable behavior, and the administrative costs in each setting are quite different.[10]) Accordingly, there is reason to expect that the best rule for everyday life may not be the optimal rule for the legal system. Thus, the allure of notions of fairness can be deceptive. A principle may seem attractive because we implicitly appreciate that in many instances pursuing it tends to enhance individuals' well-being, but it would be a mistake to apply such a principle in settings in which it does not have this feature.

When decisions are based on notions of fairness, the decisions depend on our instincts and intuitions, our general sense of what is appropriate. This manner of decisionmaking makes sense for many of the choices that individuals confront in everyday life, because there is often little time for careful reflection and there is a need to curb natural, self-interested tendencies. But these justifications for reliance on notions of fairness have no place in the design of the research agenda of legal academics and other policy analysts, who are engaged in the long-term enterprise of analyzing and empirically investigating the legal system in order to identify which legal rules are socially best. Indeed, an important purpose of this enterprise is to determine when our instincts and intuitions lead us astray.[11] We have suggested, in the various legal contexts that we have examined, that reliance on notions of fairness sometimes results in legal policy that is inferior to that which might be chosen if welfare economics played a more central role.

It is worth reflecting on the senses in which we have demonstrated our claim that legal policy analysis should rely exclusively on welfare economics. One type of argument employed deductive logic. Notably, we showed that, if one embraces any notion of fairness, logical consistency implies that one has thereby endorsed the view that adopting a legal rule that makes everyone worse off may well be good.[12] Of course, logic alone cannot resolve disagreement about normative issues; a value judgment is involved in positing that individuals' well-being should be our sole concern. We suppose, however, that most of us do believe that individuals' well-being matters, and we sus-

---

10. There are other reasons as well, such as the fact that social norms need to be relatively simple and general.

11. See subsection VII.B.2.

12. See subsections II.C.1 and III.C.1(e)(iii).

pect that the fact that any notion of fairness may involve making everyone worse off will be seen as troubling.

Moreover, our argument that notions of fairness have implications that are opposed to the well-being of all individuals in society did not stand alone. We also contended that there do not seem to be good reasons for sacrificing individuals' well-being in the contexts that we examined. In addition, we suggested that the attraction that notions of fairness hold for all of us can best be explained in ways that do not lend support to viewing them as independent principles. We believe that these points, taken together, provide grounds for our conclusion that notions of fairness should not be given independent weight in the evaluation of legal rules.

A further argument in support of our claim that normative analysis of legal policy should be based exclusively on welfare economics involves a form of inductive generalization.[13] We have attempted to show that, on examination, there is no basis for sacrificing individuals' well-being to promote any of the identified notions of fairness in the range of basic legal contexts that we have considered. This finding, however, is insufficient to prove that there does not exist some rationale that we have failed to appreciate or that has yet to be offered, or that there does not exist some different, more defensible notion of fairness, or that in other legal contexts that we have not studied there may not be some notion of fairness that is compelling. Thus, even readers who accept much of what we have said may differ in the degree to which they are led to accept our broader proposition and the extent to which they might think it worthwhile to continue to search for notions of fairness that might survive scrutiny. Nevertheless, we have analyzed many of the most prominent notions of fairness and have considered paradigmatic settings in basic areas of law that serve as the foundations for many other legal subjects. Moreover, we have shown that quite similar criticisms are applicable across the board. These points suggest that, to the extent that our arguments have force, they also have a degree of generality.

Given the intensity with which we all believe in notions of fairness and the related difficulty of setting aside our instincts and intuitions when we find ourselves in the role of policy analysts, it is inevitable that many scholars will continue to advance notions of fairness as principles that should be given independent weight in the evaluation of legal policy. In light of the arguments that we have offered, we suggest that such views be examined

---

13. Such generalization is important in establishing our broad claim that no notion of fairness should be given independent weight in assessing any legal rule, but, of course, we did not rely on this inference to demonstrate our claims about the specific notions of fairness that we have criticized directly.

carefully before they are accepted. In particular, it seems that a number of specific issues need to be addressed if a proposed notion of fairness is to be taken seriously.

First, proponents of a notion of fairness must state the principles they are defending with some degree of precision and in a manner that is reasonably complete. Virtually all of the leading notions of fairness that we have examined fail to meet this basic test, even though the notions have long been under consideration. For example, under the retributive theory of fair punishment, which requires punishment proportional to the gravity of the offense, it is difficult to understand what criteria should be employed to ascertain which wrongs are offenses that should be punished, the relative gravity of different offenses, and the degree of punishment entailed by the proportionality requirement.[14] When theories are not well defined or adequately specified, we cannot know what they mean; hence, we cannot determine whether they are compelling. The frequent lack of completeness of the definitions of fairness principles seems to reflect a failure to identify the underlying rationales for the principles, for if the rationales were well understood, it would not be so difficult to determine the theories' basic requirements.

Second, adherence to notions of fairness often leads to consequences that seem to conflict with the underlying motivations of the notions, a tension that the notions' proponents need to resolve. Satisfying corrective or retributive justice, for instance, can lead to an increase in the number of wrongs that occur (through failure to deter); yet the view that wrongs need to be rectified, which is central to both of these notions of fairness, seems grounded in the belief that wrongful acts are unjust. Thus, there is an important sense in which pursuing justice may well entail injustice under these theories.[15]

---

14. See subsection VI.B.2.

15. We suggested that this problem and some others that we have identified with notions of fairness seem attributable to the tendency of fairness-based analysts to adopt an ex post perspective that focuses on particular, given outcomes (such as that a crime has been committed and that the criminal has been captured and convicted). Adopting an ex post view leads to a failure to consider other, often more likely outcomes (such as that the majority of criminals are not caught) as well as the effect of rules on ex ante behavior (the decision whether to commit a crime). See subsection II.B.2(c). Although one need not adopt welfare economics to avoid these limitations of fairness-based analysis, it would be necessary to embrace quite different notions of fairness that would involve approaches to legal policy that are similar in structure to the method of welfare economics. One would have to engage in ex ante, consequentialist analysis that weighs costs and benefits. The remaining difference, if any, would be that the weights on various effects of rules would not, as under welfare economics, depend on how such effects matter to individuals' well-being but instead would be based on some other considerations—raising the issues that follow in the text.

Third, because notions of fairness sometimes result in a reduction in individuals' well-being—and in certain cases lead to a reduction in everyone's well-being—when they are given weight as independent evaluative principles, the manner in which a notion of fairness sacrifices welfare should be identified clearly so that it will be possible to appreciate what is at stake in adopting the principle. Furthermore, we would argue that this is best done in simple, paradigmatic settings that go to the heart of the problems addressed in basic areas of law. Thus, retributivists, who for centuries have been substantially concerned with demonstrating the evils of assessing punishment based on its deterrent effect, should apply their principles to the most standard situations in which setting the punishment at a fair level involves a sacrifice in deterrence.[16] Many proponents instead examine their principles only abstractly, which may obscure their implications. Moreover, when they give concrete examples, commentators often pose atypical, even bizarre cases, in which our intuitions are notoriously unreliable and in which the implications for the far more important ordinary case are uncertain.[17]

Fourth, the rationale for giving weight to notions of fairness should be made clear. We know that pursuing fairness is never "free"—whenever it leads to departures from the rules that would be chosen under welfare economics, individuals are worse off. Therefore, we should insist on knowing the point of this sacrifice. One possibility is that notions of fairness are to be taken as primitive, needing no justification. Proponents adopting this view should state it explicitly. In addition, they should address the question of how we can know which of the many, often conflicting notions of fairness are the correct ones. Others undoubtedly believe that it is important to provide reasons for adhering to notions of fairness in the context of assessing legal policy. In that regard, we have suggested that commonly offered metaphors, such as the notion that providing corrective or retributive justice restores moral balance,[18] are insufficient. Metaphors may suggest reasons, but they are not reasons in themselves, and one can often suggest competing metaphors (such as the idea that the government, by imposing any punishment, is further polluting the moral order). Moreover, one must be wary of question-begging rationales, such as the argument that pursuing a principle makes the world more just or is right, when the issue at hand is precisely to determine what should be viewed as just or right in the first instance.

Fifth, it is necessary to consider possible alternative explanations of the source of the underlying attraction of notions of fairness. This demand is

---

16. See section VI.C.
17. See, for example, subsection VI.C.4(b).
18. See subsection VI.B.1.

especially important because of the existence of a set of related theories developed by philosophers, social scientists, and evolutionary biologists during the past several centuries. As we noted in connection with social norms, these theories explain the apparent psychological force of notions of fairness—the origins of our moral instincts and intuitions—in terms of their functionality in promoting individuals' well-being. Thus, the appeal of provocative examples commonly offered to support various notions of fairness, especially in philosophical discourse, has been linked to the manner in which the principles that seem to be embodied in our moral instincts and intuitions are actually grounded in human welfare. Those who advance notions of fairness, especially those who take the notions as primitive (or nearly so), must discredit this welfare-based explanation for the notions' appeal and give reasons to believe that their favored principles have different antecedents, ones that provide grounds for viewing the notions as independent evaluative principles for purposes of assessing legal policy.

Our object has been to convince legal policy analysts to pursue a research agenda focused on identifying which legal rules best promote individuals' well-being, with due regard for the breadth of factors that may be relevant to well-being and for the distribution of income. It should be clear from the foregoing that our claim concerns legal academics and other policy analysts, not ordinary individuals who must make decisions in everyday life; social norms, which we suggest correspond to many notions of fairness, were designed—or in some sense evolved—for just this setting.[19] We also devoted some attention to another important group of individuals, government decisionmakers (legislators, regulators, judges), whose task is to use the work of policy analysts in order to choose legal rules that best advance the interests of the citizens whom they serve.[20] We acknowledge that the problem of government officials is complicated by the fact that their constituents may not always be able to understand proper analyses of legal rules (or of many other government policies). Nevertheless, we believe that responsible government decisionmakers will be able to make better policy decisions if those who analyze legal policy devote themselves to identifying the effects of legal rules on individuals' well-being—that is, if they employ welfare economics rather than base their analysis on notions of fairness.

---

19. We also note that much of the philosophical literature from which legal academics draw focuses on norms that guide individuals' ordinary decisions, although writers do not usually disclaim implications for other contexts. See note 121 in chapter II.

20. See section VII.C. In our discussion of government officials, we recognize that the role of particular government decisionmakers, such as judges, may appropriately be circumscribed in various respects.

REFERENCES

INDEX

REFERENCES

Ackerman, Bruce. 1971. Regulating Slum Housing Markets on Behalf of the Poor: Of Housing Codes, Housing Subsidies and Income Redistribution Policy. *Yale Law Journal* 80:1093–1197.

Adler, Matthew D. 2000. Expressive Theories of Law: A Skeptical Overview. *University of Pennsylvania Law Review* 148:1364–74.

Adler, Matthew D., and Eric A. Posner. 1999. Rethinking Cost-Benefit Analysis. *Yale Law Journal* 109:165–247.

Aghion, Philippe, Mathias Dewatripont, and Patrick Rey. 1994. Renegotiation Design with Unverifiable Information. *Econometrica* 62:257–282.

Akerlof, George A. 1980. A Theory of Social Custom, of Which Unemployment May Be One Consequence. *Quarterly Journal of Economics* 94:749–775.

Alexander, Lawrence. 1980. The Doomsday Machine: Proportionality, Punishment and Prevention. *Monist* 63:199–227.

———. 1983. Retributivism and the Inadvertent Punishment of the Innocent. *Law and Philosophy* 2:233–246.

———. 1987a. Causation and Corrective Justice: Does Tort Law Make Sense? *Law and Philosophy* 6:1–23.

———. 1987b. The Relationship Between Procedural Due Process and Substantive Constitutional Rights. *University of Florida Law Review* 39:323–343.

———. 1998. Are Procedural Rights Derivative Substantive Rights? *Law and Philosophy* 17:19–42.

Alexander, Lawrence, and Emily Sherwin. 1994. The Deceptive Nature of Rules. *University of Pennsylvania Law Review* 142:1191–1225.

Alexander, Richard D. 1987. *The Biology of Moral Systems*. Hawthorne, N.Y.: A. de Gruyter.

Allison, John R. 1994. Ideology, Prejudgment, and Process Values. *New England Law Review* 28:657–743.

Alt, James E., and Kenneth A. Shepsle, eds. 1990. *Perspectives on Positive Political Economy*. Cambridge and New York: Cambridge University Press.

Amendments to the Federal Rules of Civil Procedure and Forms. 1993. (House Doc. 103–74.) Washington, D.C.: U.S. Government Printing Office.

American Council of Life Insurance. 1996. *1996 Life Insurance Fact Book.* New York: Institute of Life Insurance.

Andenaes, Johannes. 1966. The General Preventive Effects of Punishment. *University of Pennsylvania Law Review* 114:949–983.

———. 1974. *Punishment and Deterrence.* Ann Arbor: University of Michigan Press.

———. 1983. Deterrence. In *Encyclopedia of Crime and Justice,* edited by Sanford H. Kadish. Vol. 2. New York: Free Press.

Anderson, Jami L. 1999. Annulment Retributivism: A Hegelian Theory of Punishment. *Legal Theory* 5:363–388.

Andreoni, James, Brian Erard, and Jonathan Feinstein. 1998. Tax Compliance. *Journal of Economic Literature* 36:818–860.

Appleman, John Alan, and Jean Appleman. 1972. *Insurance Law and Practice.* Rev. ed. St. Paul: West Publishing Co.

Árdal, Páll S. 1968. "And That's a Promise." *Philosophical Quarterly* 18:225–237.

Arendt, Hannah. 1963. *On Revolution.* New York: Viking Press.

Arenella, Peter. 1983. Rethinking the Functions of Criminal Procedure: The Warren and Burger Courts' Competing Ideologies. *Georgetown Law Journal* 72:185–248.

———. 1992. Convicting the Morally Blameless: Reassessing the Relationship Between Legal and Moral Accountability. *UCLA Law Review* 39:1511–1622.

Aristotle. 1980. *The Nicomachean Ethics.* Rev. ed. Translated by David Ross and edited by J. L. Ackrill and J. O. Urmson. New York: Oxford University Press.

Arlen, Jennifer H. 1992. Should Defendants' Wealth Matter? *Journal of Legal Studies* 21:413–429.

———. 1998. Comment: The Future of Behavioral Economic Analysis of Law. *Vanderbilt Law Review* 51:1765–1788.

Armstrong, K. G. 1961. The Retributivist Hits Back. *Mind* 70:471–490.

Arrow, Kenneth J. 1951. *Social Choice and Individual Values.* New York: John Wiley and Sons.

———. 1958. The Measurement of Price Changes. In *The Relationship of Prices to Economic Stability and Growth: Compendium of Papers Submitted by Panelists Appearing Before the Joint Economic Committee.* Washington, D.C.: U.S. Government Printing Office.

———. 1972. Gifts and Exchanges. *Philosophy and Public Affairs* 1:343–362.

Arthur, W. B. 1981. The Economics of Risks to Life. *American Economic Review* 71: 54–64.

Atiyah, P. S. 1979. *The Rise and Fall of Freedom of Contract.* Oxford and New York: Oxford University Press.

———. 1981. *Promises, Morals, and Law.* Oxford and New York: Oxford University Press.

———. 1986. *Essays on Contract.* Oxford and New York: Oxford University Press.

———. 1997. *The Damages Lottery.* Oxford: Hart Publishing.

Austin, John. [1832] 1995. *The Province of Jurisprudence Determined.* Edited by Wilfrid E. Rumble. Cambridge: Cambridge University Press.

Avio, K. L. 1993. Economic, Retributive and Contractarian Conceptions of Punishment. *Law and Philosophy* 12:249–286.

Axelrod, Robert. 1984. *The Evolution of Cooperation.* New York: Basic Books.

———. 1986. An Evolutionary Approach to Norms. *American Political Science Review* 80:1095–1111.

Axelrod, Robert, and William D. Hamilton. 1981. The Evolution of Cooperation. *Science* 211:1390–1396.

Babcock, Barbara A., and Toni M. Massaro. 1997. *Civil Procedure: Cases and Problems.* Boston: Little, Brown.

Baier, K. 1955. Is Punishment Retributive? *Analysis* 16:25–32.

Baker, C. Edwin. 1975. The Ideology of the Economic Analysis of Law. *Philosophy and Public Affairs* 5:3–48.

Bardhan, Pranab. 1997. Corruption and Development: A Review of Issues. *Journal of Economic Literature* 35:1320–1346.

Barnett, Randy E. 1977. Restitution: A New Paradigm of Criminal Justice. *Ethics* 87:279–301.

———. 1986a. A Consent Theory of Contract. *Columbia Law Review* 86:269–321.

———. 1986b. Contract Remedies and Inalienable Rights. *Social Philosophy and Policy* 4:179–202.

———. 1989. Foreword: Of Chickens and Eggs—The Compatibility of Moral Rights and Consequentialist Analyses. *Harvard Journal of Law and Public Policy* 12:611–635.

———. 1992a. Some Problems with Contract as Promise. *Cornell Law Review* 77:1022–1033.

———. 1992b. The Sound of Silence: Default Rules and Contractual Consent. *Virginia Law Review* 78:821–911.

Baron, Jonathan. 1992. The Effect of Normative Beliefs on Anticipated Emotions. *Journal of Personality and Social Psychology* 63:320–330.

———. 1993. *Morality and Rational Choice.* Boston: Kluwer Academic Publishers.

———. 1994a. Nonconsequentialist Decisions. *Behavioral and Brain Sciences* 17:1–10.

———. 1994b. Normative, Descriptive and Prescriptive Responses. *Behavioral and Brain Sciences* 17:32–42.

———. 1994c. *Thinking and Deciding.* 2d ed. Cambridge and New York: Cambridge University Press.

———. 1995. A Psychological View of Moral Intuition. *Harvard Review of Philosophy* 5:36–40.

———. 1996. Norm-Endorsement Utilitarianism and the Nature of Utility. *Economics and Philosophy* 12:165–182.

———. 1997. Biases in the Quantitative Measurement of Values for Public Decisions. *Psychological Bulletin* 122:72–88.

———. 1998. *Judgment Misguided: Intuition and Error in Public Decision Making.* New York: Oxford University Press.

Baron, Jonathan, and John C. Hershey. 1988. Outcome Bias in Decision Evaluation. *Journal of Personality and Social Psychology* 54:569–579.

Baron, Jonathan, and Ilana Ritov. 1993. Intuitions About Penalties and Compensation in the Context of Tort Law. *Journal of Risk and Uncertainty* 7:17–33.

Becker, Gary S. 1962. Irrational Behavior and Economic Theory. *Journal of Political Economy* 70:1–13.

———. 1992. Habits, Addictions, and Traditions. *Kyklos* 45:327–345.

———. 1993. Nobel Lecture: The Economic Way of Looking at Behavior. *Journal of Political Economy* 101:385–409.

———. 1996. *Accounting for Tastes.* Cambridge, Mass.: Harvard University Press.

Bedau, Hugo Adam. 1977. Concessions to Retribution in Punishment. In *Justice and Punishment,* edited by J. B. Cederblom and William L. Blizek. Cambridge, Mass.: Ballinger Publishing Co.

Bell, Peter A., and Jeffrey O'Connell. 1997. *Accidental Justice: The Dilemmas of Tort Law.* New Haven: Yale University Press.

Benn, Stanley I. 1958. An Approach to the Problems of Punishment. *Philosophy* 33: 325–341.

———. 1967. Punishment. In *The Encyclopedia of Philosophy,* edited by Paul Edwards. Vol. 7. New York: Macmillan.

Ben-Ner, Avner, and Louis Putterman, eds. 1998. *Economics, Values, and Organization.* Cambridge and New York: Cambridge University Press.

Bennett, Jonathan. 1966. Whatever the Consequences. *Analysis* 26:83–102.

———. 1981. Morality and Consequences. In *The Tanner Lectures on Human Values,* Vol. 2, edited by Sterling M. McMurrin. Salt Lake City: University of Utah Press.

Benson, Bruce L., David W. Rasmussen, and Brent D. Mast. 1999. Deterring Drunk Driving Fatalities: An Economics of Crime Perspective. *International Review of Law and Economics* 19:205–225.

Benson, Peter. 1992. The Basis of Corrective Justice and Its Relation to Distributive Justice. *Iowa Law Review* 77:515–624.

Bentham, Jeremy. [1781] 1988. *The Principles of Morals and Legislation.* Amherst, N.Y.: Prometheus Books. (First published as *An Introduction to the Principles of Morals and Legislation.*)

———. [1822–23] 1990. *Securities Against Misrule and Other Constitutional Writings for Tripoli and Greece.* Edited by Philip Schofield. Oxford and New York: Oxford University Press.

Bernheim, B. Douglas, and Oded Stark. 1988. Altruism Within the Family Reconsidered: Do Nice Guys Finish Last? *American Economic Review* 78:1034–1045.

Bernstein, Lisa. 1992. Opting Out of the Legal System: Extralegal Contractual Relations in the Diamond Industry. *Journal of Legal Studies* 21:115–157.

———. 1996. Merchant Law in a Merchant Court: Rethinking the Code's Search for Immanent Business Norms. *University of Pennsylvania Law Review* 144: 1765–1821.

————. 1999. The Questionable Empirical Basis of Article 2's Incorporation Strategy: A Preliminary Study. *University of Chicago Law Review* 66:710–780.

Berridge, Kent C. 1996. Food Reward: Brain Substrates of Wanting and Liking. *Neuroscience and Biobehavioral Reviews* 20:1–25.

Bicchieri, Cristina. 1990. Norms of Cooperation. *Ethics* 100:838–861.

Binmore, Ken. 1998. *Game Theory and the Social Contract II: Just Playing.* Cambridge, Mass.: MIT Press.

Blackstone, William. 1769. *Commentaries on the Laws of England.* 3d ed. Dublin: Printed for John Exshaw, Henry Saunders, Boulter Grierson, and James Williams.

Blumstein, Alfred. 1983. Incapacitation. In *Encyclopedia of Crime and Justice,* edited by Sanford H. Kadish. Vol. 3. New York: Free Press.

Blumstein, James F., Randall R. Bovbjerg, and Frank A. Sloan. 1990. Beyond Tort Reform: Developing Better Tools for Assessing Damages for Personal Injury. *Yale Journal on Regulation* 8:171–212.

Boadway, Robin, and Neil Bruce. 1984. *Welfare Economics.* Oxford: Basil Blackwell.

Bone, Robert G. 1992. Rethinking the "Day in Court" Ideal and Nonparty Preclusion. *New York University Law Review* 67:193–293.

————. 1993. Statistical Adjudication: Rights, Justice, and Utility in a World of Process Scarcity. *Vanderbilt Law Review* 46:561–663.

Bonnie, Richard J., Anne M. Coughlin, John C. Jeffries, Jr., and Peter W. Low. 1997. *Criminal Law.* Westbury, N.Y.: Foundation Press.

Bosanquet, Bernard. [1899] 1965. *The Philosophical Theory of the State.* 4th ed. London: Macmillan & Co.

Boskin, Michael J., and Eytan Sheshinski. 1978. Optimal Redistributive Taxation When Individual Welfare Depends upon Relative Income. *Quarterly Journal of Economics* 92:589–601.

Bovbjerg, Randall R., Frank A. Sloan, and James F. Blumstein. 1989. Valuing Life and Limb in Tort: Scheduling "Pain and Suffering." *Northwestern University Law Review* 83:908–976.

Bowles, Samuel. 1998. Endogenous Preferences: The Cultural Consequences of Markets and Other Economic Institutions. *Journal of Economic Literature* 36:75–111.

Boxold, Dave, ed. 1999. *1999 Massachusetts Verdict Survey.* Horsham, Pa.: Jury Verdict Research.

Bradley, F. H. [1876] 1927. *Ethical Studies.* 2d ed. Oxford: Oxford University Press.

Braithwaite, John, and Philip Pettit. 1990. *Not Just Deserts: A Republican Theory of Criminal Justice.* Oxford and New York: Oxford University Press.

Brandt, Richard B. 1959. *Ethical Theory: The Problems of Normative and Critical Ethics.* Englewood Cliffs, N.J.: Prentice-Hall.

————. 1969. A Utilitarian Theory of Excuses. *Philosophophical Review* 78:337–361.

————. 1979. *A Theory of the Good and the Right.* Oxford and New York: Oxford University Press.

Breyer, Stephen. 1993. *Breaking the Vicious Circle: Toward Effective Risk Regulation.* Cambridge, Mass.: Harvard University Press.

Brickman, Lester. 1973. Of Arterial Passageways Through the Legal Process: The Right of Universal Access to Courts and Lawyering Services. *New York University Law Review* 48:595–668.

Brock, Dan. 1983. Paternalism and Promoting the Good. In *Paternalism,* edited by Rolf Sartorius. Minneapolis: University of Minnesota Press.

Brookings Institution. 1989. *Justice for All: Reducing Costs and Delay in Civil Litigation.* Washington, D.C.: Brookings Institution.

Broome, John. 1984. Uncertainty and Fairness. *Economic Journal* 94:624–632.

Brunet, Edward. 1991. The Triumph of Efficiency and Discretion over Competing Complex Litigation Policies. *Review of Litigation* 10:273–308.

Buchanan, James M., and Gordon Tullock. 1962. *The Calculus of Consent.* Ann Arbor: University of Michigan Press.

Buchanan, James M., Robert D. Tollison, and Gordon Tullock, eds. 1980. *Toward a Theory of the Rent-Seeking Society.* College Station: Texas A&M University Press.

Burbank, Stephen B., and Linda J. Silberman. 1997. Civil Procedure Reform in Comparative Context: The United States of America. *American Journal of Comparative Law* 45:675–704.

Burgh, Richard W. 1982. Do the Guilty Deserve Punishment? *Journal of Philosophy* 79:193–210.

Burrows, Paul. 1993. Patronising Paternalism. *Oxford Economic Papers* 45:542–572.

———. 1995. Analyzing Legal Paternalism. *International Review of Law and Economics* 15:489–508.

Byrd, B. Sharon. 1989. Kant's Theory of Punishment: Deterrence in Its Threat, Retribution in Its Execution. *Law and Philosophy* 8:151–200.

Calabresi, Guido. 1970. *The Costs of Accidents.* New Haven: Yale University Press.

Calabresi, Guido, and Philip Bobbitt. 1978. *Tragic Choices.* New York: W. W. Norton & Co.

Camerer, Colin. 1995. Individual Decision Making. In *The Handbook of Experimental Economics,* edited by John H. Kagel and Alvin E. Roth. Princeton: Princeton University Press.

Campbell, Donald T. 1975. On the Conflicts Between Biological and Social Evolution and Between Psychology and Moral Tradition. *American Psychologist* 30:1103–1126.

———. 1987. Rationality and Utility from the Standpoint of Evolutionary Biology. In *Rational Choice: The Contrast Between Economics and Psychology,* edited by Robin M. Hogarth and Melvin W. Reder. Chicago: University of Chicago Press.

Carrington, Paul D., and Barbara Allen Babcock. 1983. *Civil Procedure.* 3d ed. Boston: Little, Brown.

Carritt, E. F. 1947. *Ethical and Political Thinking.* Oxford: Oxford University Press.

Carroll, Stephen J., and James S. Kakalik. 1993. No-Fault Approaches to Compensating Auto Accident Victims. *Journal of Risk and Insurance* 60:265–287.

Carroll, Stephen J., James S. Kakalik, Nicholas M. Pace, and John L. Adams. 1991. *No-Fault Approaches to Compensating People Injured in Automobile Accidents.* Santa Monica: RAND Institute for Civil Justice.

Chang, Howard F. 2000a. A Liberal Theory of Social Welfare: Fairness, Utility, and the Pareto Principle. *Yale Law Journal* 110:173–235.

———. 2000b. The Possibility of a Fair Paretian. *Yale Law Journal* 110:251–258.

Charny, David. 1990. Nonlegal Sanctions in Commercial Relationships. *Harvard Law Review* 104:373–467.

———. 1991. Hypothetical Bargains: The Normative Structure of Contract Interpretation. *Michigan Law Review* 89:1815–1879.

Chemerinsky, Erwin. 1983. In Defense of Equality: A Reply to Professor Westen. *Michigan Law Review* 81:575–599.

Chevigny, Paul G. 1989. Fairness and Participation. *New York University Law Review* 64:1211–1223.

Coase, Ronald H. 1960. The Problem of Social Cost. *Journal of Law and Economics* 3:1–44.

Cohen, Lloyd. 1985. Toward an Economic Theory of the Measurement of Damages in a Wrongful Death Action. *Emory Law Journal* 34:295–340.

———. 1989. Increasing the Supply of Transplant Organs: The Virtues of a Futures Market. *George Washington Law Review* 58:1–51.

Cohen, Morris R. 1933. The Basis of Contract. *Harvard Law Review* 46:553–592.

———. 1940. Moral Aspects of the Criminal Law. *Yale Law Journal* 49:987–1026.

Coleman, Jules L. 1992a. The Mixed Conception of Corrective Justice. *Iowa Law Review* 77:427–444.

———. 1992b. *Risks and Wrongs.* Cambridge and New York: Cambridge University Press.

———. 1995. The Practice of Corrective Justice. *Arizona Law Review* 37:15–31.

Coleman, Jules L., and Charles Silver. 1986. Justice in Settlements. *Social Philosophy and Policy* 4:102–144.

"Common Sense" Legislation: The Birth of Neoclassical Tort Reform. 1996. *Harvard Law Review* 109:1765–1782.

Contract As Promise: A Theory of Contractual Obligation (review). 1983. *Michigan Law Review* 81:904–908.

Corbin, Arthur L. 1964. *Corbin on Contracts.* Vol. 5. St. Paul: West Publishing Co.

Cosmides, Leda, John Tooby, and Jerome H. Barkow. 1992. Introduction: Evolutionary Psychology and Conceptual Integration. In *The Adapted Mind: Evolutionary Psychology and the Generation of Culture,* edited by Jerome H. Barkow, Leda Cosmides, and John Tooby. New York: Oxford University Press.

Cottreau, Steven T. O. 1998. The Due Process Right to Opt Out of Class Actions. *New York University Law Review* 73:480–528.

Coursey, Don L., John L. Hovis, and William D. Schulze. 1987. The Disparity Between Willingness to Accept and Willingness to Pay Measures of Value. *Quarterly Journal of Economics* 102:679–690.

Craswell, Richard. 1989. Contract Law, Default Rules, and the Philosophy of Promising. *Michigan Law Review* 88:489–529.

———. 1991. Passing on the Costs of Legal Rules: Efficiency and Distribution in Buyer-Seller Relationships. *Stanford Law Review* 43:361–398.

———. 1992. Efficiency and Rational Bargaining in Contractual Settings. *Harvard Journal of Law and Public Policy* 15:805–837.

———. 1998. Incommensurability, Welfare Economics, and the Law. *University of Pennsylvania Law Review* 146:1419–1464.

———. 2000. Against Fuller and Perdue. *University of Chicago Law Review* 67:99–161.

Craswell, Richard, and John E. Calfee. 1986. Deterrence and Uncertain Legal Standards. *Journal of Law, Economics, and Organization* 2:279–303.

Crisp, Roger. 1998. Editor's Introduction to *Utilitarianism*, by J. S. Mill. New York: Oxford University Press.

Crocker, Lawrence. 1992. The Upper Limit of Just Punishment. *Emory Law Journal* 41:1059–1119.

Cummings, Ronald G., Glenn W. Harrison, and E. Elisabet Rutström. 1995. Homegrown Values and Hypothetical Surveys: Is the Dichotomous-Choice Approach Incentive-Compatible? *American Economic Review* 85:260–266.

Cyert, Richard M., and Morris H. De Groot. 1975. Adaptive Utility. In *Adaptive Economic Models,* edited by Richard H. Day and Theodore Groves. New York: Academic Press.

Daly, Martin, and Margo Wilson. 1988. *Homicide.* New York: A. de Gruyter.

Dan-Cohen, Meir. 1984. Decision Rules and Conduct Rules: On Acoustic Separation in Criminal Law. *Harvard Law Review* 97:625–677.

Darwin, Charles. [1874] 1998. *The Descent of Man.* Reprint of 2d ed. Amherst, N.Y.: Prometheus Books.

Dau-Schmidt, Kenneth G. 1990. An Economic Analysis of the Criminal Law as a Preference-Shaping Policy. *Duke Law Journal* 1990:1–38.

Davis, Nancy. 1984a. The Doctrine of Double Effect: Problems of Interpretation. *Pacific Philosophical Quarterly* 65:107–123.

———. 1984b. Using Persons and Common Sense. *Ethics* 94:387–406.

———. 1991. Contemporary Deontology. In *A Companion to Ethics,* edited by Peter Singer. Oxford: Blackwell Reference.

Derfner, Mary F., and Arthur D. Wolf. 1999. *Court Awarded Attorney Fees.* Vol. 3. Part 3, *Statutes and Rules.* New York: Matthew Bender & Co.

Dewees, Don, David Duff, and Michael Trebilcock. 1996. *Exploring the Domain of Accident Law: Taking the Facts Seriously.* New York: Oxford University Press.

Diamond, Peter A. 1967. Cardinal Welfare, Individualistic Ethics, and Interpersonal Comparison of Utility: Comment. *Journal of Political Economy* 75:765–766.

Diamond, Peter A., and Jerry A. Hausman. 1994. Contingent Valuation: Is Some Number Better than No Number? *Journal of Economic Perspectives* 8, no. 4:45–64.

Dolinko, David. 1991. Some Thoughts About Retributivism. *Ethics* 101:537–559.

———. 1992. Three Mistakes of Retributivism. *UCLA Law Review* 39:1623–1657.

————. 1997. Retributivism, Consequentialism, and the Intrinsic Goodness of Punishment. *Law and Philosophy* 16:507–528.

Downs, Anthony. 1957. *An Economic Theory of Democracy*. New York: Harper & Brothers.

Doyle, James F. 1967. Justice and Legal Punishment. *Philosophy* 42:53–67.

Drèze, Jean, and Nicholas Stern. 1987. The Theory of Cost-Benefit Analysis. In *Handbook of Public Economics*, vol. 2, edited by Alan J. Auerbach and Martin Feldstein. Amsterdam: Elsevier Science Publishers.

Duesenberry, James S. 1949. *Income, Saving and the Theory of Consumer Behavior*. Cambridge, Mass.: Harvard University Press.

Dworkin, Gerald. 1983. Paternalism. In *Paternalism*, edited by Rolf Sartorius. Minneapolis: University of Minnesota Press. Originally published in *Monist* (1972).

————. 1987. Intention, Foreseeability, and Responsibility. In *Responsibility, Character, and the Emotions: New Essays in Moral Psychology*, edited by Ferdinand Schoeman. Cambridge and New York: Cambridge University Press.

Dworkin, Ronald. 1977. *Taking Rights Seriously*. Cambridge, Mass.: Harvard University Press.

————. 1980. Is Wealth a Value? *Journal of Legal Studies* 9:191–226.

————. 1981a. What Is Equality? Part 1: Equality of Welfare. *Philosophy and Public Affairs*. 10:185–246.

————. 1981b. What Is Equality? Part 2: Equality of Resources. *Philosophy and Public Affairs* 10:283–345.

————. 1985. Principle, Policy, Procedure. In *A Matter of Principle*. Cambridge, Mass.: Harvard University Press.

Easterbrook, Frank H. 1984. The Supreme Court, 1983 Term—Foreword: The Court and the Economic System. *Harvard Law Review* 98:4–60.

Edlin, Aaron S., and Stefan Reichelstein. 1996. Holdups, Standard Breach Remedies, and Optimal Investment. *American Economic Review* 86:478–501.

Eisenberg, Melvin Aron. 1982. The Bargain Principle and Its Limits. *Harvard Law Review* 95:741–801.

Eisgruber, Christopher L. 1992. Is the Supreme Court an Educative Institution? *New York University Law Review* 67:961–1032.

Ellickson, Robert C. 1989. Bringing Culture and Human Frailty to Rational Actors: A Critique of Classical Law and Economics. *Chicago-Kent Law Review* 65:23–55.

————. 1991. *Order Without Law: How Neighbors Settle Disputes*. Cambridge, Mass.: Harvard University Press.

Elster, Jon. 1983. *Sour Grapes: Studies in the Subversion of Rationality*. Cambridge and New York: Cambridge University Press.

————. 1989. Social Norms and Economic Theory. *Journal of Economic Perspectives* 3, no. 4:99–117.

Epstein, Richard A. 1973. A Theory of Strict Liability. *Journal of Legal Studies* 2:151–204.

———. 1974. Defenses and Subsequent Pleas in a System of Strict Liability. *Journal of Legal Studies* 3:165–215.

———. 1979. Nuisance Law: Corrective Justice and Its Utilitarian Constraints. *Journal of Legal Studies* 8:49–102.

Ezorsky, Gertrude. 1972. The Ethics of Punishment. In *Philosophical Perspectives on Punishment*, edited by Gertrude Ezorsky. Albany: State University of New York Press.

———. 1974. Punishment and Excuses. In *Punishment and Human Rights*, edited by Milton Goldinger. Cambridge, Mass.: Schenkman Publishing Co.

Fallon, Richard H., Jr. 1989. What Is Republicanism, and Is It Worth Reviving? *Harvard Law Review* 102:1695–1735.

Farber, Daniel A. 1982. Book review of *Contract As Promise* (Fried). *Minnesota Law Review* 66:561–566.

Farber, Daniel A., and John H. Matheson. 1985. Beyond Promissory Estoppel: Contract Law and the "Invisible Handshake." *University of Chicago Law Review* 52:903–947.

Farnsworth, E. Allan. 1999. *Contracts.* 3d ed. New York: Aspen Law & Business.

Federal Rules of Civil Procedure. 2001. In *Federal Civil Procedure and Rules.* St. Paul: West Group.

Federal Rules of Evidence. 2001. In *Federal Civil Procedure and Rules.* St. Paul: West Group.

Feinberg, Joel. 1960. On Justifying Legal Punishment. In *Nomos III: Responsibility,* edited by Carl J. Friedrich. New York: New York University Press.

Fischer, David A. 1981. Products Liability—An Analysis of Market Share Liability. *Vanderbilt Law Review* 34:1623–1662.

Fischhoff, Baruch. 1975. Hindsight ≠ Foresight: The Effect of Outcome Knowledge on Judgment Under Uncertainty. *Journal of Experimental Psychology: Human Perception and Performance* 1:288–299.

Fischhoff, Baruch, Ned Welch, and Shane Frederick. 1999. Construal Processes in Preference Assessment. *Journal of Risk and Uncertainty* 19:139–164.

Fiss, Owen M. 1982. The Social and Political Foundations of Adjudication. *Law and Human Behavior* 6:121–128.

———. 1984. Against Settlement. *Yale Law Journal* 93:1073–1090.

———. 1993. The Allure of Individualism. *Iowa Law Review* 78:965–979.

Fletcher, George P. 1972. Fairness and Utility in Tort Theory. *Harvard Law Review* 85:537–573.

———. 1978. *Rethinking Criminal Law.* Boston: Little, Brown.

———. 1983. The Search for Synthesis in Tort Theory. *Law and Philosophy* 2:63–88.

———. 1993. Corrective Justice for Moderns. *Harvard Law Review* 106:1658–1678.

Flew, Antony. 1954. The Justification of Punishment. *Philosophy* 29:291–307.

Foot, Philippa. 1967. The Problem of Abortion and the Doctrine of Double Effect. *Oxford Review* 5:5–15.

Forcier, James R. 1994. *Judicial Excess: The Political Economy of the American Legal System.* Lanham, Md.: University Press of America.

Frank, Robert H. 1985. *Choosing the Right Pond: Human Behavior and the Quest for Status.* New York: Oxford University Press.

———. 1988. *Passions Within Reason: The Strategic Role of the Emotions.* New York: W. W. Norton & Co.

Frank, Robert H., Thomas D. Gilovich, and Dennis T. Regan. 1996. Do Economists Make Bad Citizens? *Journal of Economic Perspectives* 10, no. 1: 187–192.

Frederick, Shane, and Baruch Fischhoff. 1998. Scope (In)sensitivity in Elicited Valuations. *Risk, Decision and Policy* 3:109–123.

Frey, Bruno S. 1986. Economists Favour the Price System—Who Else Does? *Kyklos* 39:537–563.

Frey, Bruno S., and Felix Oberholzer-Gee. 1997. The Cost of Price Incentives: An Empirical Analysis of Motivation Crowding-Out. *American Economic Review* 87:746–755.

Fried, Charles. 1970. *An Anatomy of Values: Problems of Personal and Social Choice.* Cambridge, Mass.: Harvard University Press.

———. 1980. Book review of *The Rise and Fall of Freedom of Contract* (Atiyah). *Harvard Law Review* 93:1858–1868.

———. 1981. *Contract As Promise: A Theory of Contractual Obligation.* Cambridge, Mass.: Harvard University Press.

Friedmann, Daniel. 1989. The Efficient Breach Fallacy. *Journal of Legal Studies* 18: 1–24.

———. 1995. The Performance Interest in Contract Damages. *Law Quarterly Review* 111:628–654.

Fuller, Lon L. 1941. Consideration and Form. *Columbia Law Review* 41:799–824.

———. 1978. The Forms and Limits of Adjudication. *Harvard Law Review* 92:353–409.

Fuller, Lon L., and William R. Perdue, Jr. 1936. The Reliance Interest in Contract Damages: 1. *Yale Law Journal* 46:52–96.

———. 1937. The Reliance Interest in Contract Damages: 2. *Yale Law Journal* 46: 373–420.

Galanter, Marc. 1983. Reading the Landscape of Disputes: What We Know and Don't Know (and Think We Know) About Our Allegedly Contentious and Litigious Society. *UCLA Law Review* 31:4–71.

———. 1994. Predators and Parasites: Lawyer-Bashing and Civil Justice. *Georgia Law Review* 28:633–681.

Galanter, Marc, and Mia Cahill. 1994. "Most Cases Settle": Judicial Promotion and Regulation of Settlements. *Stanford Law Review* 46:1339–1391.

Garber, Steven. 1993. *Product Liability and the Economics of Pharmaceuticals and Medical Devices.* Santa Monica: RAND Institute for Civil Justice.

Gardbaum, Stephen A. 1992. Law, Politics, and the Claims of Community. *Michigan Law Review* 90:685–760.

Gendin, Sidney. 1971. A Plausible Theory of Retribution. *Journal of Value Inquiry* 5:1–16.

Gibbard, Allan. 1982a. Human Evolution and the Sense of Justice. In *Social and Political Philosophy*, edited by Peter A. French, Theodore E. Uehling, Jr., and Howard K. Wettstein. Minneapolis: University of Minnesota Press.

———. 1982b. Inchoately Utilitarian Common Sense: The Bearing of a Thesis of Sidgwick's on Moral Theory. In *The Limits of Utilitarianism*, edited by Harlan B. Miller and William H. Williams. Minneapolis: University of Minnesota Press.

Gilmore, Grant. 1974. *The Death of Contract.* Columbus: Ohio State University Press.

Gintis, Herbert. 1972. A Radical Analysis of Welfare Economics and Individual Development. *Quarterly Journal of Economics* 86:572–599.

Glaeser, Edward L., and Bruce Sacerdote. 2000. The Determinants of Punishment: Deterrence, Incapacitation and Vengeance. Working Paper No. 7676. Cambridge, Mass.: National Bureau of Economic Research.

Glover, Jonathan. 1977. Ends and Means: Double Effect. In Glover, *Causing Death and Saving Lives.* Harmondsworth: Penguin Books.

Goldman, Alan H. 1979. The Paradox of Punishment. *Philosophy and Public Affairs* 9:42–58.

Goodin, Robert E. 1995. *Utilitarianism As a Public Philosophy.* Cambridge and New York: Cambridge University Press.

Gorecki, Jan. 1983. *Capital Punishment: Criminal Law and Social Evolution.* New York: Columbia University Press.

Green, Thomas A. 1988. A Retrospective on the Criminal Trial Jury, 1200–1800. In *Twelve Good Men and True: The Criminal Trial Jury in England, 1200–1800,* edited by J. S. Cockburn and Thomas A. Green. Princeton: Princeton University Press.

Greenawalt, Kent. 1983. Punishment. *Journal of Criminal Law and Criminology* 74: 343–362.

———. 1997. "Prescriptive Equality": Two Steps Forward. *Harvard Law Review* 110: 1265–1290.

Greenwood, Peter, C. Peter Rydell, Allan F. Abrahamse, Jonathan P. Caulkins, James Chiesa, Karyn E. Model, and Stephen P. Klein. 1996. Estimated Benefits and Costs of California's New Mandatory-Sentencing Law. In *Three Strikes and You're Out: Vengeance As Public Policy,* edited by David Shichor and Dale K. Sechrest. Thousand Oaks, Cal.: Sage Publications.

Grey, Thomas C. 1977. Procedural Fairness and Substantive Rights. In *Nomos XVIII: Due Process,* edited by J. Roland Pennock and John W. Chapman. New York: New York University Press.

Griffin, James. 1986. *Well-Being: Its Meaning, Measurement, and Moral Importance.* Oxford and New York: Oxford University Press.

Gross, Samuel R. 1987. The American Advantage: The Value of Inefficient Litigation. *Michigan Law Review* 85:734–757.

Gross, Samuel R., and Kent D. Syverud. 1996. Don't Try: Civil Jury Verdicts in a System Geared to Settlement. *UCLA Law Review* 44:1–64.

Hahn, Robert W. 1999. Regulatory Reform: Assessing the Government's Numbers.

Working Paper No. 99–6. Washington, D.C.: AEI-Brookings Joint Center for Regulatory Studies.

Hall, Jerome. 1947. *General Principles of Criminal Law.* Indianapolis: Bobbs-Merrill Co.

Hammond, Peter J. 1982a. Book review: The Economics of Justice and the Criterion of Wealth Maximization. *Yale Law Journal* 91:1493–1507.

———. 1982b. Utilitarianism, Uncertainty and Information. In *Utilitarianism and Beyond,* edited by Amartya Sen and Bernard Williams. Cambridge and New York: Cambridge University Press.

———. 1983. Ex-post Optimality as a Dynamically Consistent Objective for Collective Choice Under Uncertainty. In *Social Choice and Welfare,* edited by Prasanta K. Pattanaik and Maurice Salles. Amsterdam: Elsevier Science Pub. Co.

———. 1991. Interpersonal Comparisons of Utility: Why and How They Are and Should Be Made. In *Interpersonal Comparisons of Well-Being,* edited by Jon Elster and John E. Roemer. Cambridge and New York: Cambridge University Press.

Hampton, Jean. 1984. The Moral Education Theory of Punishment. *Philosophy and Public Affairs* 13:208–238.

———. 1992. Rational Choice and the Law. *Harvard Journal of Law and Public Policy* 15:649–681.

Hanemann, W. Michael. 1991. Willingness to Pay and Willingness to Accept: How Much Can They Differ? *American Economic Review* 81:635–647.

———. 1994. Valuing the Environment Through Contingent Valuation. *Journal of Economic Perspectives* 8, no. 4:19–43.

Hansmann, Henry. 1989. The Economics and Ethics of Markets for Human Organs. *Journal of Health Politics, Policy and Law* 14:57–85.

Hanson, Jon D., and Melissa R. Hart. 1996. Law and Economics. In *A Companion to Philosophy of Law and Legal Theory,* edited by Dennis Patterson. Cambridge, Mass.: Blackwell Publishers.

Hardin, Russell. 1986. The Utilitarian Logic of Liberalism. *Ethics* 97:47–74.

Hare, R. M. 1963. *Freedom and Reason.* Oxford: Oxford University Press.

———. 1964. The Promising Game. *Revue Internationale de Philosophie* 70:398–412.

———. 1971. *Essays on Philosophical Method.* London: Macmillan.

———. 1973a. Principles. *Proceedings of the Aristotelian Society* 73:1–18.

———. 1973b. Rawls' Theory of Justice—I. *Philosophy Quarterly* 23:144–155.

———. 1981. *Moral Thinking: Its Levels, Method, and Point.* Oxford and New York: Oxford University Press.

———. 1982. Ethical Theory and Utilitarianism. In *Utilitarianism and Beyond,* edited by Amartya Sen and Bernard Williams. Cambridge and New York: Cambridge University Press. (Originally published in *Contemporary British Philosophy,* edited by H. D. Lewis. London, 1976.)

———. 1984. Arguing About Rights. *Emory Law Journal* 33:631–647.

———. 1986. Punishment and Retributive Justice. *Philosophical Topics* 14, no. 2: 211–223.

———. 1988. Comments. In *Hare and Critics: Essays on Moral Thinking.* Edited by Douglas Seanor and N. Fotion. Oxford and New York: Oxford University Press.

———. 1989a. Rights, Utility, and Universalization: Reply to J. L. Mackie. In Hare, *Essays on Political Morality.* Oxford and New York: Oxford University Press.

———. 1989b. Utilitarianism and the Vicarious Effects. In Hare, *Essays in Ethical Theory.* Oxford and New York: Oxford University Press.

———. 1997. *Sorting Out Ethics.* Oxford and New York: Oxford University Press.

Harper, Fowler V., and Fleming James, Jr. 1956. *The Law of Torts.* Boston: Little, Brown.

Harris, Richard J., and Mark A. Joyce. 1980. What's Fair? It Depends on How You Phrase the Question. *Journal of Personality and Social Psychology* 38:165–179.

Harrod, R. F. 1936. Utilitarianism Revised. *Mind* 45:137–156.

Harsanyi, John C. 1953. Cardinal Utility in Welfare Economics and in the Theory of Risk-Taking. *Journal of Political Economy* 61:434–435.

———. 1953–1954. Welfare Economics of Variable Tastes. *Review of Economic Studies* 21:204–213.

———. 1955. Cardinal Welfare, Individualistic Ethics, and Interpersonal Comparisons of Utility. *Journal of Political Economy* 63:309–321.

———. 1958. Ethics in Terms of Hypothetical Imperatives. *Mind* 67:305–316.

———. 1975. Nonlinear Social Welfare Functions: Do Welfare Economists Have a Special Exemption from Bayesian Rationality? *Theory and Decision* 6:311–332.

———. 1977. *Rational Behavior and Bargaining Equilibrium in Games and Social Situations.* Cambridge: Cambridge University Press.

———. 1982. Morality and the Theory of Rational Behavior. In *Utilitarianism and Beyond,* edited by Amartya Sen and Bernard Williams. Cambridge and New York: Cambridge University Press.

———. 1988. Problems with Act-Utilitarianism and with Malevolent Preferences. In *Hare and Critics: Essays on Moral Thinking.* Edited by Douglas Seanor and N. Fotion. Oxford and New York: Oxford University Press.

———. 1995. A Theory of Prudential Values and a Rule Utilitarian Theory of Morality. *Social Choice and Welfare* 12:319–333.

Hart, H. L. A. 1958a. Legal and Moral Obligation. In *Essays in Moral Philosophy.* Edited by A. I. Melden. Seattle: University of Washington Press.

———. 1958b. Legal Responsibility and Excuses. In *Determinism and Freedom in the Age of Modern Science,* edited by Sidney Hook. New York: New York University Press.

———. 1968a. Postscript: Responsibility and Retribution. In Hart, *Punishment and Responsibility: Essays in the Philosophy of Law.* New York: Oxford University Press.

———. 1968b. Prolegomenon to the Principles of Punishment. In Hart, *Punishment and Responsibility: Essays in the Philosophy of Law.* New York: Oxford University Press.

———. 1968c. *Punishment and Responsibility: Essays in the Philosophy of Law.* New York: Oxford University Press.

Hart, Oliver. 1987. Incomplete Contracts. In *The New Palgrave: A Dictionary of Economics,* edited by John Eatwell, Murray Milgate, and Peter Newman. Vol. 2. London: Macmillan Press.

Hart, Oliver, and John Moore. 1988. Incomplete Contracts and Renegotiation. *Econometrica* 56:755–785.

Hay, Bruce L. 1997. Procedural Justice—Ex Ante vs. Ex Post. *UCLA Law Review* 44:1803–1850.

Hay, Bruce, and David Rosenberg. 2000. The Individual Justice of Averaging. Discussion Paper Number 285, John M. Olin Center for Law, Economics, and Business, Harvard Law School, Cambridge, Mass.

Hayden, Robert M., and Jill K. Anderson. 1979. On the Evaluation of Procedural Systems in Laboratory Experiments: A Critique of Thibaut and Walker. *Law and Human Behavior* 3:21–38.

Hayek, F. A. 1973. *Law, Legislation and Liberty.* Vol. 1, *Rules and Order.* Chicago: University of Chicago Press.

Hazard, Geoffrey C., Jr., and Michele Taruffo. 1993. *American Civil Procedure: An Introduction.* New Haven: Yale University Press.

Hegel, G. W. F. [1821] 1952. *Hegel's Philosophy of Right.* Translated by T. M. Knox. Oxford and New York: Oxford University Press.

Henderson, James A., Jr. 1991. Judicial Reliance on Public Policy: An Empirical Analysis of Products Liability Decisions. *George Washington Law Review* 59: 1570–1613.

Hensler, Deborah R., Nicholas M. Pace, Bonita Dombey-Moore, Beth Giddens, Jennifer Gross, and Erik K. Moller. 2000. *Class Action Dilemmas: Pursuing Public Goals for Private Gain.* Santa Monica: RAND Institute for Civil Justice.

Hensler, Deborah R., Mary E. Vaiana, James S. Kakalik, and Mark A. Peterson. 1987. *Trends in Tort Litigation: The Story Behind the Statistics.* Santa Monica: RAND Institute for Civil Justice.

Hirshleifer, Jack. 1977. Economics from a Biological Viewpoint. *Journal of Law and Economics* 20:1–52.

———. 1978. Natural Economy Versus Political Economy. *Journal of Social and Biological Structures* 1:319–337.

———. 1985. The Expanding Domain of Economics. *American Economic Review* 75, no. 6:53–68.

———. 1987. On the Emotions as Guarantors of Threats and Promises. In *The Latest on the Best: Essays on Evolution and Optimality,* edited by John Dupré. Cambridge, Mass.: MIT Press.

Hochman, Harold M., and James D. Rodgers. 1969. Pareto Optimal Redistribution. *American Economic Review* 59:542–557.

Hogarth, Robin M., and Melvin W. Reder, eds. 1987. *Rational Choice: The Contrast Between Economics and Psychology.* Chicago: University of Chicago Press.

Holmes, Oliver W., Jr. 1881. *The Common Law.* Boston: Little, Brown.

———. 1897. The Path of the Law. *Harvard Law Review* 10:457–478.

Horwitz, Morton J. 1980. Law and Economics: Science or Politics? *Hofstra Law Review* 8:905–912.

Houlden, Pauline, Stephen LaTour, Laurens Walker, and John Thibaut. 1978. Preference for Modes of Dispute Resolution as a Function of Process and Decision Control. *Journal of Experimental Social Psychology* 14:13–30.

Hume, David. [1739] 1992. *Treatise of Human Nature.* Buffalo, N.Y.: Prometheus Books.

———. [1751] 1998. *An Enquiry Concerning the Principles of Morals.* Edited by Tom L. Beauchamp. Oxford and New York: Oxford University Press.

Husak, Douglas N. 1995. The Nature and Justifiability of Nonconsummate Offenses. *Arizona Law Review* 37:151–183.

Hutcheson, Francis. [1725–1755] 1994. *Philosophical Writings.* Edited by R. S. Downie. London: Everyman's Library.

Hyde, Alan. 1983. The Concept of Legitimation in the Sociology of Law. *Wisconsin Law Review* 1983:379–426.

Hylland, Aanund, and Richard Zeckhauser. 1979. Distributional Objectives Should Affect Taxes but Not Program Choice or Design. *Scandinavian Journal of Economics* 81:264–284.

Insurance Information Institute. 1998. No-Fault Auto Insurance. *Insurance Issues Update.* (December 1998.)

———. 2000. The Liability System. At http://www.iii.org/media/issues/liability.html (June).

Internal Revenue Service. 1996. *Federal Tax Compliance Research: Individual Income Tax Gap Estimates for 1985, 1988, and 1992.* Washington, D.C.: U.S. Department of the Treasury.

———. 2000a. Criminal Investigation Program, by Status or Disposition, FY 1998. In *1998 Data Book.* Internal Revenue Service Publication 55b. Washington, D.C.: U.S. Department of the Treasury.

———. 2000b. Examination Coverage: Returns Examined, by Type of Return and Internal Revenue Region, District, and Service Center, FY 1998. In *1998 Data Book.* Internal Revenue Service Publication 55b. Washington, D.C.: U.S. Department of the Treasury.

Jaeger, Walter H. E. 1968. *A Treatise on the Law of Contracts.* 3d ed., 1st ed. by Samuel Williston. Vol. 11. Mount Kisco, N.Y.: Baker, Voorhis & Co.

Jolls, Christine. 1998. Behavioral Economics Analysis of Redistributive Legal Rules. *Vanderbilt Law Review* 51:1653–1677.

Jolls, Christine, Cass R. Sunstein, and Richard Thaler. 1998. A Behavioral Approach to Law and Economics. *Stanford Law Review* 50:1471–1575.

Jones-Lee, M. W. 1994. Safety and the Saving of Life: The Economics of Safety and Physical Risk. In *Cost-Benefit Analysis.* 2d ed. Edited by Richard Layard and Stephen Glaister. Cambridge and New York: Cambridge University Press.

Jury Verdict Research, Inc. 1987. *Personal Injury Valuation Handbooks No. 2.97.1.* Solon, Ohio: Jury Verdict Research.

Kadish, Sanford. 1967. The Crisis of Overcriminalization. *Annals of the American Academy of Political and Social Science* 374:157–170.

Kagan, Jerome. 1984. *The Nature of the Child.* New York: Basic Books.

Kahan, Dan M. 1997. Social Influence, Social Meaning, and Deterrence. *Virginia Law Review* 83:349–395.

———. 1998. Social Meaning and the Economic Analysis of Crime. *Journal of Legal Studies* 27:609–622.

Kahneman, Daniel. 1994. New Challenges to the Rationality Assumption. *Journal of Institutional and Theoretical Economics* 150:18–36.

Kahneman, Daniel, and Jack L. Knetsch. 1992. Valuing Public Goods: The Purchase of Moral Satisfaction. *Journal of Environmental Economics and Management* 22: 57–70.

Kahneman, Daniel, and Carol Varey. 1991. Notes on the Psychology of Utility. In *Interpersonal Comparisons of Well-Being,* edited by Jon Elster and John E. Roemer. Cambridge: Cambridge University Press.

Kahneman, Daniel, Jack L. Knetsch, and Richard H. Thaler. 1987. Fairness and the Assumptions of Economics. In *Rational Choice: The Contrast Between Economics and Psychology,* edited by Robin M. Hogarth and Melvin W. Reder. Chicago: University of Chicago Press.

———. 1990. Experimental Tests of the Endowment Effect and the Coase Theorem. *Journal of Political Economy* 98:1325–1348.

Kahneman, Daniel, Paul Slovic, and Amos Tversky, eds. 1982. *Judgment Under Uncertainty: Heuristics and Biases.* Cambridge and New York: Cambridge University Press.

Kamm, F. M. 1996. *Morality, Mortality.* Vol. 2, *Rights, Duties, and Status.* New York: Oxford University Press.

Kant, Immanuel. [1775–1780] 1963. *Lectures on Ethics.* Translated by Louis Infield. New York: Harper & Row.

———. [1785] 1997. *Groundwork of the Metaphysics of Morals.* Translated and edited by Mary Gregor. Cambridge: Cambridge University Press.

———. [1796–1797] 1887. *The Philosophy of Law.* Translated by W. Hastie. New York: Scribner and Welford.

———. [1797] 1983. The Metaphysical Principles of Virtue. In *Ethical Philosophy.* Translated by J. W. Ellington. Indianapolis: Hackett Pub. Co.

———. [1797] 1996. *The Metaphysics of Morals.* Translated and edited by Mary Gregor. Cambridge: Cambridge University Press.

Kaplow, Louis. 1986. Private Versus Social Costs in Bringing Suit. *Journal of Legal Studies* 15:371–385.

———. 1989. Horizontal Equity: Measures in Search of a Principle. *National Tax Journal* 42:139–154.

———. 1994a. Optimal Insurance Contracts When Establishing the Amount of Losses Is Costly. *Geneva Papers on Risk and Insurance Theory* 19:139–152.

———. 1994b. The Value of Accuracy in Adjudication: An Economic Analysis. *Journal of Legal Studies* 23:307–401.

———. 1995. A Note on Subsidizing Gifts. *Journal of Public Economics* 58:469–477.

———. 1998. Accuracy in Adjudication. In *The New Palgrave Dictionary of Economics and the Law,* edited by Peter Newman. Vol. 1. London: Macmillan Reference Limited.

———. 2000. General Characteristics of Rules. In *Encyclopedia of Law and Economics,* edited by Boudewijn Bouckaert and Gerrit De Geest. Vol. 5. Cheltenham, U.K.: Edward Elgar.

Kaplow, Louis, and Steven Shavell. 1994a. Accuracy in the Determination of Liability. *Journal of Law and Economics* 37:1–15.

———. 1994b. Why the Legal System Is Less Efficient Than the Income Tax in Redistributing Income. *Journal of Legal Studies* 23:667–681.

———. 1996. Accuracy in the Assessment of Damages. *Journal of Law and Economics* 39:191–210.

———. 1999. The Conflict Between Notions of Fairness and the Pareto Principle. *American Law and Economics Review* 1:63–77.

———. 2000a. Notions of Fairness Versus the Pareto Principle: On the Role of Logical Consistency. *Yale Law Journal* 110:237–249.

———. 2000b. Should Legal Rules Favor the Poor? Clarifying the Role of Legal Rules and the Income Tax in Redistributing Income. *Journal of Legal Studies* 29:821–835.

———. 2001. Any Non-welfarist Method of Policy Assessment Violates the Pareto Principle. *Journal of Political Economy* 109:281–286.

Katz, Avery. 1988. Reflections on Fuller and Perdue's *The Reliance Interest in Contract Damages:* A Positive Economic Framework. *University of Michigan Journal of Law Reform* 21:541–560.

———. 1990a. The Strategic Structure of Offer and Acceptance: Game Theory and the Law of Contract Formation. *Michigan Law Review* 89:215–295.

———. 1990b. Your Terms or Mine? The Duty to Read the Fine Print in Contracts. *RAND Journal of Economics* 21:518–537.

———. 1996. Positivism and the Separation of Law and Economics. *Michigan Law Review* 94:2229–2269.

Kearns, Thomas R. 1977. On De-Moralizing Due Process. In *Nomos XVIII: Due Process,* edited by J. Roland Pennock and John W. Chapman. New York: New York University Press.

Keating, Gregory C. 1996. Reasonableness and Rationality in Negligence Theory. *Stanford Law Review* 48:311–384.

———. 1997. The Idea of Fairness in the Law of Enterprise Liability. *Michigan Law Review* 95:1266–1380.

Keeton, Robert E., and Jeffrey O'Connell. 1965. *Basic Protection for the Traffic Victim: A Blueprint for Reforming Automobile Insurance.* Boston: Little, Brown.

Keeton, W. Page, Dan B. Dobbs, Robert E. Keeton, and David G. Owen. 1984. *Prosser and Keeton on the Law of Torts.* 5th student ed. St. Paul, Minn.: West Pub. Co.

Kelman, Mark. 1979a. Choice and Utility. *Wisconsin Law Review* 1979:769–797.

————. 1979b. Consumption Theory, Production Theory, and Ideology in the Coase Theorem. *Southern California Law Review* 52:669–698.

————. 1987. *A Guide to Critical Legal Studies.* Cambridge, Mass.: Harvard University Press.

Kelsen, Hans. 1957. Aristotle's Doctrine of Justice. In *What Is Justice? Justice, Law, and Politics in the Mirror of Science: Collected Essays by Hans Kelsen.* Berkeley: University of California Press.

Kennedy, Duncan. 1981. Cost-Benefit Analysis of Entitlement Problems: A Critique. *Stanford Law Review* 33:387–445.

————. 1982. Distributive and Paternalist Motives in Contract and Tort Law, with Special Reference to Compulsory Terms and Unequal Bargaining Power. *Maryland Law Review* 41:563–658.

————. 1987. The Effect of the Warranty of Habitability on Low Income Housing: "Milking" and Class Violence. *Florida State University Law Review* 15:485–519.

Kessler, Daniel, and Steven D. Levitt. 1999. Using Sentence Enhancements to Distinguish Between Deterrence and Incapacitation. *Journal of Law and Economics* 42:343–363.

Kessler, Friedrich. 1943. Contracts of Adhesion—Some Thoughts About Freedom of Contract. *Columbia Law Review* 43:629–642.

Klitgaard, Robert. 1988. *Controlling Corruption.* Berkeley: University of California Press.

Kornhauser, Lewis A. 1989. The New Economic Analysis of Law: Legal Rules as Incentives. In *Law and Economics,* edited by Nicholas Mercuro. Boston: Kluwer Academic.

————. 1998. Wealth Maximization. In *The New Palgrave Dictionary of Economics and the Law,* edited by Peter Newman. Vol. 3. London: Macmillan Reference Limited.

————. 1999. The Normativity of Law. *American Law and Economics Review* 1:3–25.

Korsgaard, Christine M. 1996. *Creating the Kingdom of Ends.* Cambridge and New York: Cambridge University Press.

Kraakman, Reinier H. 1984. Corporate Liability Strategies and the Costs of Legal Controls. *Yale Law Journal* 93:857–898.

Kraus, Jody S. 1997. A Non-Solution to a Non-Problem: A Comment on Alan Strudler's "Mass Torts and Moral Principles." *Law and Philosophy* 16:91–100.

Kronman, Anthony T. 1980a. Contract Law and Distributive Justice. *Yale Law Journal* 89:472–511.

————. 1980b. Wealth Maximization As a Normative Principle. *Journal of Legal Studies* 9:227–242.

————. 1981. A New Champion for the Will Theory. *Yale Law Journal* 91:404–423.

————. 1983. Paternalism and the Law of Contracts. *Yale Law Journal* 92:763–798.

LaFave, Wayne R., and Austin W. Scott, Jr. 1986. *Criminal Law.* 2d ed. St. Paul, Minn.: West Pub. Co.

Landes, Elisabeth M., and Richard A. Posner. 1978. The Economics of the Baby Shortage. *Journal of Legal Studies* 7:323–348.

Landes, William M., and Richard A. Posner. 1976. Legal Precedent: A Theoretical and Empirical Analysis. *Journal of Law and Economics* 19:249–307.

Lando, Henrik. 1997. An Attempt to Incorporate Fairness into an Economic Model of Tort Law. *International Review of Law and Economics* 17:575–587.

Langbein, John H. 1985. The German Advantage in Civil Procedure. *University of Chicago Law Review* 52:823–866.

Lerner, Abba P. 1944. *The Economics of Control: Principles of Welfare Economics.* New York: Macmillan.

Leubsdorf, John. 1984. Constitutional Civil Procedure. *Texas Law Review* 63:579–637.

Lind, E. Allan, and Tom R. Tyler. 1988. *The Social Psychology of Procedural Justice.* New York: Plenum Press.

Lind, E. Allan, Robert J. Maccoun, Patricia A. Ebener, William L. F. Felstiner, Deborah R. Hensler, Judith Resnik, and Tom R. Tyler. 1990. In the Eye of the Beholder: Tort Litigants' Evaluations of Their Experiences in the Civil Justice System. *Law and Society Review* 24:953–996.

Little, I. M. D. 1957. *A Critique of Welfare Economics.* 2d ed. Oxford: Oxford University Press.

———. 1985. Robert Cooter and Peter Rappoport, "Were the Ordinalists Wrong About Welfare Economics?": A Comment. *Journal of Economic Literature* 23:1186–1188.

Little, I. M. D., and J. A. Mirrlees. 1974. *Project Appraisal and Planning for Developing Countries.* New York: Basic Books.

Locke, Don. 1972. The Object of Morality, and the Obligation to Keep a Promise. *Canadian Journal of Philosophy* 2:135–143.

Lyons, David. 1969. On Sanctioning Excuses. *Journal of Philosophy* 66:646–660.

Mabbott, J. D. 1939. Punishment. *Mind* 48:152–167.

MacCormick, Neil. 1972. Voluntary Obligations and Normative Powers I. *Proceedings of the Aristotelian Society, Annual Supplement* 46:59–78.

MacIntyre, Alasdair. 1984. *After Virtue: A Study in Moral Theory.* 2d ed. Notre Dame, Ind.: University of Notre Dame Press.

Mack, Eric. 1989. Dominos and the Fear of Commodification. In *Nomos XXXI: Markets and Justice,* edited by John W. Chapman and J. Roland Pennock. New York: New York University Press.

Mackie, J. L. 1982a. Co-operation, Competition, and Moral Philosophy. In *Cooperation and Competition in Humans and Animals,* edited by Andrew M. Colman. Workingham, U.K.: Van Nostrand Reinhold.

———. 1982b. Morality and the Retributive Emotions. *Criminal Justice Ethics* 1:3–10.

———. 1991. Retributivism: A Test Case for Ethical Objectivity. In *Philosophy of*

Law, 4th ed., edited by Joel Feinberg and Hyman Gross. Belmont, Cal.: Wadsworth Publishing Co.

Macneil, Ian R. 1982. Efficient Breach of Contract: Circles in the Sky. *Virginia Law Review* 68:947–1084.

Magat, Wesley A., and Christopher H. Schroeder. 1984. Administrative Process Reform in a Discretionary Age: The Role of Social Consequences. *Duke Law Journal* 1984:301–344.

Magat, Wesley A., and W. Kip Viscusi. 1992. *Informational Approaches to Regulation.* Cambridge, Mass.: MIT Press.

Marcus, Richard L., Martin H. Redish, and Edward F. Sherman. 2000. *Civil Procedure: A Modern Approach.* 3d ed. St. Paul, Minn.: West Group.

Mashaw, Jerry L. 1976. The Supreme Court's Due Process Calculus for Administrative Adjudication in *Mathews v. Eldridge:* Three Factors in Search of a Theory of Value. *University of Chicago Law Review* 44:28–59.

———. 1981. Administrative Due Process: The Quest for a Dignitary Theory. *Boston University Law Review* 61:885–931.

Mayhew, Leon H. 1975. Institutions of Representation: Civil Justice and the Public. *Law and Society Review* 9:401–429.

McAdams, Richard H. 1995. Cooperation and Conflict: The Economics of Group Status Production and Race Discrimination. *Harvard Law Review* 108:1003–1084.

———. 1997. The Origin, Development, and Regulation of Norms. *Michigan Law Review* 96:338–433.

McCarthy, David. 1996. Liability and Risk. *Philosophy and Public Affairs* 25:238–262.

McCloskey, H. J. 1962. The Complexity of the Concepts of Punishment. *Philosophy* 37:307–325.

———. 1965. A Non-Utilitarian Approach to Punishment. *Inquiry* 8:249–263.

———. 1967. Utilitarian and Retributive Punishment. *Journal of Philosophy* 64:91–110.

McNeilly, F. S. 1972. Promises De-Moralized. *Philosophical Review* 81:63–81.

McTaggart, J. Ellis. 1896. Hegel's Theory of Punishment. *International Journal of Ethics* 6:479–502.

Melden, A. I. 1956. On Promising. *Mind* 65:49–66.

Menkel-Meadow, Carrie. 1995. Whose Dispute Is It Anyway?: A Philosophical and Democratic Defense of Settlement (In Some Cases). *Georgetown Law Journal* 83:2663–2696.

Menninger, Karl. 1968. *The Crime of Punishment.* New York: Viking Press.

———. 1973. Therapy, Not Punishment. In *Punishment and Rehabilitation,* edited by Jeffrie G. Murphy. Belmont, Cal.: Wadsworth Publishing Co.

Michelman, Frank I. 1973. The Supreme Court and Litigation Access Fees: The Right to Protect One's Rights—Part I. *Duke Law Journal* 1973:1153–1215.

———. 1974. The Supreme Court and Litigation Access Fees: The Right to Protect One's Rights—Part II. *Duke Law Journal* 1974:527–570.

———. 1977. Formal and Associational Aims in Procedural Due Process. In *Nomos XVIII: Due Process*, edited by J. Roland Pennock and John W. Chapman. New York: New York University Press.

Mill, John Stuart. 1859. *On Liberty*. London: J. W. Parker.

———. [1861] 1998. *Utilitarianism*. Edited by Roger Crisp. Oxford: Oxford University Press.

Mirrlees, James A. 1971. An Exploration in the Theory of Optimum Income Taxation. *Review of Economic Studies* 38:175–208.

———. 1982. The Economic Uses of Utilitarianism. In *Utilitarianism and Beyond*, edited by Amartya Sen and Bernard Williams. Cambridge and New York: Cambridge University Press.

Moberly, Walter. 1968. *The Ethics of Punishment*. London: Faber & Faber.

Moore, Michael S. 1984. *Law and Psychiatry*. Cambridge and New York: Cambridge University Press.

———. 1987. The Moral Worth of Retribution. In *Responsibility, Character, and the Emotions: New Essays in Moral Psychology*, edited by Ferdinand Schoeman. Cambridge and New York: Cambridge University Press.

———. 1993a. *Act and Crime: The Philosophy of Action and Its Implications for Criminal Law*. Oxford and New York: Oxford University Press.

———. 1993b. Justifying Retributivism. *Israel Law Review* 27:15–49.

Morris, Herbert. 1968. Persons and Punishment. *Monist* 52:475–501.

Mueller, Dennis C. 1989. *Public Choice II*. Cambridge and New York: Cambridge University Press.

———, ed. 1997. *Perspectives on Public Choice: A Handbook*. Cambridge and New York: Cambridge University Press.

Mundle, C. W. K. 1954. Punishment and Desert. *Philosophical Quarterly* 4:216–228.

Munzer, Stephen R. 1979. Persons and Consequences: Observations on Fried's *Right and Wrong*. *Michigan Law Review* 77:421–445.

———. 1984. Intuition and Security in Moral Philosophy. *Michigan Law Review* 82:740–754.

Murphy, Jeffrie G. 1973. Marxism and Retribution. *Philosophy and Public Affairs* 2:217–243.

———. 1987. Does Kant Have a Theory of Punishment? *Columbia Law Review* 87:509–532.

———. 1991. Retributive Hatred: An Essay on Criminal Liability and the Emotions. In *Liability and Responsibility: Essays in Law and Morals*, edited by R. G. Frey and Christopher W. Morris. Cambridge and New York: Cambridge University Press.

Murphy, Jeffrie G., and Jules L. Coleman. 1990. *Philosophy of Law: An Introduction to Jurisprudence*. Rev. ed. Boulder: Westview Press.

Myerson, Roger B. 1981. Utilitarianism, Egalitarianism, and the Timing Effect in Social Choice Problems. *Econometrica* 49:883–897.

Nagel, Thomas. 1979. Moral Luck. In Nagel, *Mortal Questions.* Cambridge and New York: Cambridge University Press.

Narveson, Jan. 1971. Promising, Expecting, and Utility. *Canadian Journal of Philosophy* 1:207–233.

Neill, Helen R., Ronald G. Cummings, Philip T. Ganderton, Glenn W. Harrison, and Thomas McGuckin. 1994. Hypothetical Surveys and Real Economic Commitments. *Land Economics* 79:145–154.

Newman, Jon O. 1985. Rethinking Fairness: Perspectives on the Litigation Process. *Yale Law Journal* 94:1643–1659.

Ng, Yew-Kwang. 1979. *Welfare Economics: Introduction and Development of Basic Concepts.* London: Macmillan.

———. 1981a. Bentham or Nash? On the Acceptable Form of Social Welfare Functions. *Economic Record* 57:238–250.

———. 1981b. Welfarism: A Defense Against Sen's Attack. *Economic Journal* 91: 527–530.

———. 1984. Quasi-Pareto Social Improvements. *American Economic Review* 74: 1033–1050.

———. 1988. Economic Efficiency Versus Egalitarian Rights. *Kyklos* 41:215–237.

———. 1999. Utility, Informed Preference, or Happiness: Following Harsanyi's Argument to Its Logical Conclusion. *Social Choice and Welfare* 16:197–216.

———. 2000. *Efficiency, Equality and Public Policy: With a Case for Higher Public Spending.* Hampshire, U.K.: Macmillan Press Ltd.

Nisbett, Richard, and Lee Ross. 1980. *Human Inference: Strategies and Shortcomings of Social Judgment.* Englewood Cliffs, N.J.: Prentice-Hall.

Niskanen, William A., Jr. 1971. *Bureaucracy and Representative Government.* Chicago: Aldine, Atherton.

Nozick, Robert. 1974. *Anarchy, State, and Utopia.* New York: Basic Books.

———. 1981. *Philosophical Explanations.* Cambridge, Mass.: Harvard University Press.

Nussbaum, Martha, and Amartya Sen, eds. 1993. *The Quality of Life.* Oxford and New York: Oxford University Press.

O'Connell, Jeffrey, and Rita J. Simon. 1972. Payment for Pain and Suffering: Who Wants What, When and Why? *University of Illinois Law Forum* 1972:1–120.

Olson, Mancur, Jr. 1965. *The Logic of Collective Action.* Cambridge, Mass.: Harvard University Press.

O'Neill, Onora. 1989. *Constructions of Reason: Explorations of Kant's Practical Philosophy.* Cambridge and New York: Cambridge University Press.

Ordeshook, Peter C. 1986. *Game Theory and Political Theory: An Introduction.* Cambridge and New York: Cambridge University Press.

Owen, David G. 1985. Deterrence and Desert in Tort: A Comment. *California Law Review* 73:665–676.

———. 1989. The Moral Foundations of Punitive Damages. *Alabama Law Review* 40:705–739.

————. 1993. The Moral Foundations of Products Liability Law: Toward First Principles. *Notre Dame Law Review* 68:427–506.

Packer, Herbert L. 1968. *The Limits of the Criminal Sanction.* Stanford, Cal.: Stanford University Press.

Paley, William. [1785] 1825. *The Principles of Moral and Political Philosophy.* 11th American ed. Boston: Richardson and Lord.

Parisi, Francesco. 2001. The Genesis of Liability in Ancient Law. *American Law and Economics Review* 3:82–124.

Parking Enforcement District, New York City Police Department. 2000. *History of the Parking Enforcement District.* At http://www.ci.nyc.ny.us/html/nypd/html/transportation/history2.html (September 28).

Perry, Stephen R. 1992a. Comment on Coleman: Corrective Justice. *Indiana Law Journal* 67:381–409.

————. 1992b. The Moral Foundations of Tort Law. *Iowa Law Review* 77:449–514.

————. 1996. Tort Law. In *A Companion to Philosophy of Law and Legal Theory,* edited by Dennis Patterson. Cambridge, Mass.: Blackwell Publishers.

————. 1997. Libertarianism, Entitlement, and Responsibility. *Philosophy and Public Affairs* 26:351–396.

Peters, Christopher J. 1997. Equality Revisited. *Harvard Law Review* 110:1210–1264.

Pettit, Philip. 1990. *Virtus Normativa:* Rational Choice Perspectives. *Ethics* 100:725–755.

Philips, Michael. 1985. The Inevitability of Punishing the Innocent. *Philosophical Studies* 48:389–391.

Pincoffs, Edmund L. 1966. *The Rationale of Legal Punishment.* New York: Humanities Press.

Pius XII. 1960. Crime and Punishment. *Catholic Lawyer* 6:92–109, 125.

Pocock, J. G. A. 1975. *The Machiavellian Moment.* Princeton: Princeton University Press.

Polinsky, A. Mitchell. 1974. Economic Analysis As a Potentially Defective Product: A Buyer's Guide to Posner's *Economic Analysis of Law. Harvard Law Review* 87:1655–1681.

————. 1983. Risk Sharing Through Breach of Contract Remedies. *Journal of Legal Studies* 12:427–444.

Polinsky, A. Mitchell, and Steven Shavell. 1998. Punitive Damages: An Economic Analysis. *Harvard Law Review* 111:869–962.

————. 2000. The Fairness of Sanctions: Some Implications for Optimal Enforcement Policy. *American Law and Economics Review* 2:223–237.

Porter, Bruce, and Marvin Dunn. 1984. *The Miami Riot of 1980: Crossing the Bounds.* Lexington, Mass.: Lexington Books.

Posner, Eric A. 1996a. Law, Economics, and Inefficient Norms. *University of Pennsylvania Law Review* 144:1697–1744.

————. 1996b. The Regulation of Groups: The Influence of Legal and Nonlegal Sanctions on Collective Action. *University of Chicago Law Review* 63:133–197.

————. 1998. The Strategic Basis of Principled Behavior: A Critique of the Incommensurability Thesis. *University of Pennsylvania Law Review* 146:1185–1214.

————. 2000. *Law and Social Norms.* Cambridge, Mass.: Harvard University Press.

Posner, Richard A. 1972. A Theory of Negligence. *Journal of Legal Studies* 1:29–96.

————. 1979. Utilitarianism, Economics, and Legal Theory. *Journal of Legal Studies* 8:103–140.

————. 1980a. The Ethical and Political Basis of the Efficiency Norm in Common Law Adjudication. *Hofstra Law Review* 8:487–507.

————. 1980b. Retribution and Related Concepts of Punishment. *Journal of Legal Studies* 9:71–92.

————. 1980c. A Theory of Primitive Society, with Special Reference to Law. *Journal of Law and Economics* 23:1–53.

————. 1980d. The Value of Wealth: A Comment on Dworkin and Kronman. *Journal of Legal Studies* 9:243–252.

————. 1981a. The Concept of Corrective Justice in Recent Theories of Tort Law. *Journal of Legal Studies* 10:187–206.

————. 1981b. *The Economics of Justice.* Cambridge, Mass.: Harvard University Press.

————. 1981c. A Reply to Some Recent Criticisms of the Efficiency Theory of the Common Law. *Hofstra Law Review* 9:775–794.

————. 1985. An Economic Theory of the Criminal Law. *Columbia Law Review* 85: 1193–1231.

————. 1989. The Future of Law and Economics: A Comment on Ellickson. *Chicago-Kent Law Review* 65:57–62.

————. 1990. *The Problems of Jurisprudence.* Cambridge, Mass.: Harvard University Press.

————. 1995a. *Overcoming Law.* Cambridge, Mass.: Harvard University Press.

————. 1995b. Wealth Maximization and Tort Law: A Philosophical Inquiry. In *Philosophical Foundations of Tort Law,* edited by David G. Owen. Oxford and New York: Oxford University Press.

————. 1997. Social Norms and the Law: An Economic Approach. *American Economic Review* 87, no. 2, Papers and Proceedings: 365–369.

————. 1998. The Problematics of Moral and Legal Theory. *Harvard Law Review* 111:1637–1717.

————. 1999. *The Problematics of Moral and Legal Theory.* Cambridge, Mass.: Harvard University Press.

Posner, Richard A., and Eric B. Rasmusen. 1999. Creating and Enforcing Norms, with Special Reference to Sanctions. *International Review of Law and Economics* 19:369–382.

Pratt, John W., and Richard J. Zeckhauser, eds. 1985. *Principals and Agents: The Structure of Business.* Boston: Harvard Business School Press.

Prichard, J. Robert S. 1984. A Market for Babies? *University of Toronto Law Journal* 34:341–357.

Priest, George L. 1985. The Invention of Enterprise Liability: A Critical History of the Intellectual Foundations of Modern Tort Law. *Journal of Legal Studies* 14: 461–527.

———. 1987. The Current Insurance Crisis and Modern Tort Law. *Yale Law Journal* 96:1521–1590.

Quigley, William P. 1998. The Demise of Law Reform and the Triumph of Legal Aid: Congress and the Legal Services Corporation from the 1960's to the 1990's. *St. Louis University Public Law Review* 17:241–264.

Quinn, Warren. 1993. *Morality and Action.* Cambridge and New York: Cambridge University Press.

Quinton, A. M. 1954. On Punishment. *Analysis* 14:133–142.

Rabin, Matthew. 1998. Psychology and Economics. *Journal of Economic Literature* 36:11–46.

Rabin, Robert L. 1996. Law for Law's Sake. *Yale Law Journal* 105:2261–2283.

Radin, Margaret Jane. 1987. Market-Inalienability. *Harvard Law Review* 100:1849–1937.

———. 1996. *Contested Commodities.* Cambridge, Mass.: Harvard University Press.

Raiffa, Howard. 1968. *Decision Analysis: Introductory Lectures on Choices under Uncertainty.* New York: Random House.

Rakoff, Todd D. 1983. Contracts of Adhesion: An Essay in Reconstruction. *Harvard Law Review* 96:1173–1284.

———. 1991. Fuller and Perdue's *The Reliance Interest* As a Work of Legal Scholarship. *Wisconsin Law Review* 1991:203–246.

Rakowski, Eric. 1991. *Equal Justice.* Oxford and New York: Oxford University Press.

Rasmusen, Eric. 1996. Stigma and Self-Fulfilling Expectations of Criminality. *Journal of Law and Economics* 39:519–543.

Rawls, John. 1955. Two Concepts of Rules. *Philosophical Review* 64:3–32.

———. 1971. *A Theory of Justice.* Cambridge, Mass.: Harvard University Press.

———. 1980. Kantian Constructivism in Moral Theory. *Journal of Philosophy* 77: 515–572.

———. 1982. Social Unity and Primary Goods. In *Utilitarianism and Beyond,* edited by Amartya Sen and Bernard Williams. Cambridge and New York: Cambridge University Press.

———. 1988. The Priority of Right and Ideas of the Good. *Philosophy and Public Affairs* 17:251–276.

Raymond, Margaret. 1998. Rejecting Totalitarianism: Translating the Guarantees of Constitutional Criminal Procedure. *North Carolina Law Review* 76:1193–1263.

Raz, Joseph. 1972. Voluntary Obligations and Normative Powers II. *Proceedings of the Aristotelian Society, Annual Supplement* 46:79–102.

———. 1977. Promises and Obligations. In *Law, Morality, and Society: Essays in Honour of H. L. A. Hart.* Edited by P. M. S. Hacker and J. Raz. Oxford: Oxford University Press.

———. 1982. Promises in Morality and Law. *Harvard Law Review* 95:916–938.

———. 1986. Dworkin: A New Link in the Chain. *California Law Review* 74:1103–1119.

Redish, Martin H., and Lawrence C. Marshall. 1986. Adjudicatory Independence and the Values of Procedural Due Process. *Yale Law Journal* 95:455–505.

Resnik, Judith. 1984. Tiers. *Southern California Law Review* 57:837–1035.

———. 1986. Failing Faith: Adjudicatory Procedure in Decline. *University of Chicago Law Review* 53:494–560.

Resnik, Judith, Dennis E. Curtis, and Deborah R. Hensler. 1996. Individuals Within the Aggregate: Relationships, Representation, and Fees. *New York University Law Review* 71:296–401.

Restatement of the Law Second: Contracts. 1981. St. Paul, Minn.: American Law Institute.

Restatement of the Law Second: Torts. 1977. St. Paul, Minn.: American Law Institute.

Riordan, Thomas M. 1994. Copping an Attitude: Rule of Law Lessons from the Rodney King Incident. *Loyola of Los Angeles Law Review* 27:675–733.

Robbins, Lionel. 1932. *An Essay on the Nature and Significance of Economic Science.* London: Macmillan.

———. 1935. *An Essay on the Nature and Significance of Economic Science.* 2d ed. London: Macmillan.

———. 1938. Interpersonal Comparisons of Utility: A Comment. *Economic Journal* 48:635–641.

Robinson, Paul H., and John M. Darley. 1995. *Justice, Liability, and Blame: Community Views and the Criminal Law.* Boulder: Westview Press.

———. 1997. The Utility of Desert. *Northwestern University Law Review* 91:453–499.

Roemer, John E. 1996. *Theories of Distributive Justice.* Cambridge, Mass.: Harvard University Press.

Rogerson, William P. 1984. Efficient Reliance and Damage Measures for Breach of Contract. *RAND Journal of Economics* 15:39–53.

Romer, Paul M. 1996. Preferences, Promises, and the Politics of Entitlement. In *Individual and Social Responsibility: Child Care, Education, Medical Care, and Long-Term Care in America.* Edited by Victor R. Fuchs. Chicago: University of Chicago Press.

Rose, Carol M. 1989. Environmental Faust Succumbs to Temptations of Economic Mephistopheles, or, Value by Any Other Name Is Preference. *Michigan Law Review* 87:1631–1646.

Rose-Ackerman, Susan. 1978. *Corruption: A Study in Political Economy.* New York: Academic Press.

Rosenberg, David. 1984. The Causal Connection in Mass Exposure Cases: A "Public Law" Vision of the Tort System. *Harvard Law Review* 97:849–929.

———. 1987. Class Actions for Mass Torts: Doing Individual Justice by Collective Means. *Indiana Law Journal* 62:561–596.

———. 1989. Of End Games and Openings in Mass Tort Cases: Lessons From a Special Master. *Boston University Law Review* 69:695–730.

Rosenberg, Maurice, Hans Smit, and Rochelle C. Dreyfuss. 1990. *Elements of Civil Procedure: Cases and Materials.* 5th ed. Westbury, N.Y.: Foundation Press.

Ross, W. D. 1929. The Ethics of Punishment. *Journal of Philosophical Studies* 4:205–211.

———. 1930. *The Right and the Good.* Oxford: Oxford University Press.

Roth, Jeffrey A., John T. Scholz, and Ann Dryden Witte, eds. 1989. *Taxpayer Compliance, Volume 1: An Agenda for Research.* Philadelphia: University of Pennsylvania Press.

Royal Swedish Academy of Sciences. 1996. The *Sveriges Riksbank* (Bank of Sweden) Prize in Economic Sciences in Memory of Alfred Nobel. Press release, 8 October, 1996.

Rubin, Paul H. 1982. Evolved Ethics and Efficient Ethics. *Journal of Economic Behavior and Organization* 3:161–174.

Russ, Lee R., and Thomas F. Segalla. 1997. *Couch on Insurance.* 3d ed. Vol. 2. Deerfield, Ill.: Clark Boardman Callaghan.

Rutherford, Murray B., Jack L. Knetsch, and Thomas C. Brown. 1998. Assessing Environmental Losses: Judgments of Importance and Damage Schedules. *Harvard Environmental Law Review* 22:51–101.

Sagoff, Mark. 1988. *The Economy of the Earth.* Cambridge and New York: Cambridge University Press.

Saks, Michael J., and Peter David Blanck. 1992. Justice Improved: The Unrecognized Benefits of Aggregation and Sampling in the Trial of Mass Torts. *Stanford Law Review* 44:815–851.

Sanchirico, Chris W. 2000. Taxes Versus Legal Rules As Instruments for Equity: A More Equitable View. *Journal of Legal Studies* 29:797–820.

Sandel, Michael J. 1982. *Liberalism and the Limits of Justice.* Cambridge and New York: Cambridge University Press.

Sartorius, Rolf. 1969. Utilitarianism and Obligation. *Journal of Philosophy* 66:67–81.

———. 1972. Individual Conduct and Social Norms: A Utilitarian Account. *Ethics* 82:200–218.

———, ed. 1983. *Paternalism.* Minneapolis: University of Minnesota Press.

Savage, Leonard J. 1972. *The Foundations of Statistics.* 2d rev. ed. New York: Dover Publications.

Scanlon, Thomas M. 1977. Due Process. In *Nomos XVIII: Due Process,* edited by J. Roland Pennock and John W. Chapman. New York: New York University Press.

———. 1990. Promises and Practices. *Philosophy and Public Affairs* 19:199–226.

———. 1998. The Status of Well-Being. In *Tanner Lectures on Human Values.* Vol. 19. Salt Lake City: University of Utah Press.

Schauer, Frederick. 1991a. The Calculus of Distrust. *Virginia Law Review* 77:653–667.

———. 1991b. *Playing by the Rules: A Philosophical Examination of Rule-Based Decision-Making in Law and in Life.* Oxford and New York: Oxford University Press.

Schedler, George. 1980. Can Retributivists Support Legal Punishment? *Monist* 63: 185–198.

Schelling, Thomas C. 1981. Economic Reasoning and the Ethics of Policy. *Public Interest* 63:37–61.

———. 1984. The Life You Save May Be Your Own. In Schelling, *Choice and Consequence.* Cambridge, Mass.: Harvard University Press.

Schroeder, Christopher H. 1990. Corrective Justice and Liability for Increasing Risks. *UCLA Law Review* 37:439–478.

———. 1995. Causation, Compensation and Moral Responsibility. In *Philosophical Foundations of Tort Law,* edited by David G. Owen. Oxford and New York: Oxford University Press.

Schwartz, Alan, and Louis L. Wilde. 1979. Intervening in Markets on the Basis of Imperfect Information: A Legal and Economic Analysis. *University of Pennsylvania Law Review* 127:630–682.

Schwartz, Gary T. 1994. Reality in the Economic Analysis of Tort Law: Does Tort Law Really Deter? *UCLA Law Review* 42:377–444.

———. 1997. Mixed Theories of Tort Law: Affirming Both Deterrence and Corrective Justice. *Texas Law Review* 75:1801–1834.

———. 2000. Auto No-Fault and First-Party Insurance: Advantages and Problems. *Southern California Law Review* 73:611–675.

Scitovszky, Tibor de. 1941. A Note on Welfare Propositions in Economics. *Review of Economic Studies* 9:77–88.

Searle, John. 1964. How To Derive "Ought" from "Is." *Philosophical Review* 73:43–58.

Seavey, Warren A. 1931. Book Review. *Harvard Law Review* 45:209–212.

Sen, Amartya. 1970. The Impossibility of a Paretian Liberal. *Journal of Political Economy* 78:152–157.

———. 1973. *On Economic Inequality.* Oxford: Oxford University Press.

———. 1979. Utilitarianism and Welfarism. *Journal of Philosophy* 76:463–489.

———. 1982. *Choice, Welfare and Measurement.* Cambridge, Mass.: MIT Press.

———. 1985. *Commodities and Capabilities.* Amsterdam: Elsevier Science Publishers.

———. 1992. Minimal Liberty. *Economica* 59:139–159.

Sen, Amartya, and Bernard Williams, eds. 1982. *Utilitarianism and Beyond.* Cambridge and New York: Cambridge University Press.

Shapiro, David L. 1988. Courts, Legislatures, and Paternalism. *Virginia Law Review* 74:519–575.

Shavell, Steven. 1980a. Damage Measures for Breach of Contract. *Bell Journal of Economics* 11:466–490.

———. 1980b. Strict Liability Versus Negligence. *Journal of Legal Studies* 9:1–25.

———. 1981. A Note on Efficiency vs. Distributional Equity in Legal Rulemaking: Should Distributional Equity Matter Given Optimal Income Taxation? *American Economic Review* 71, no. 2, Papers and Proceedings: 414–418.

———. 1982a. On Liability and Insurance. *Bell Journal of Economics* 13:120–132.

————. 1982b. The Social Versus the Private Incentive to Bring Suit in a Costly Legal System. *Journal of Legal Studies* 11:333–339.

————. 1984. The Design of Contracts and Remedies for Breach. *Quarterly Journal of Economics* 99:121–148.

————. 1985a. Criminal Law and the Optimal Use of Nonmonetary Sanctions As a Deterrent. *Columbia Law Review* 85:1232–1262.

————. 1985b. Uncertainty over Causation and the Determination of Civil Liability. *Journal of Law and Economics* 28:587–609.

————. 1987. *Economic Analysis of Accident Law.* Cambridge, Mass.: Harvard University Press.

————. 1997. The Fundamental Divergence Between the Private and the Social Motive to Use the Legal System. *Journal of Legal Studies* 26:575–612.

————. 1999. The Level of Litigation: Private Versus Social Optimality of Suit and of Settlement. *International Review of Law and Economics* 19:99–115.

————. 2000. On the Social Function and the Regulation of Liability Insurance. *Geneva Papers on Risk and Insurance: Issues and Practice* 25:166–179.

Shleifer, Andrei, and Robert W. Vishny. 1993. Corruption. *Quarterly Journal of Economics* 108:599–617.

————. 1997. A Survey of Corporate Governance. *Journal of Finance* 52:737–783.

Sidgwick, Henry. 1907. *The Methods of Ethics.* 7th ed. London: Macmillan and Co.

Simons, Kenneth W. 1990. Corrective Justice and Liability for Risk-Creation: A Comment. *UCLA Law Review* 38:113–142.

————. 2000. The Logic of Egalitarian Norms. *Boston University Law Review* 80: 693–771.

Singer, Peter. 1972. Is Act-Utilitarianism Self-Defeating? *Philosophical Review* 81:94–104.

————. 1973. Altruism and Commerce: A Defense of Titmuss Against Arrow. *Philosophy and Public Affairs* 2:312–320.

————. 1981. *The Expanding Circle: Ethics and Sociobiology.* New York: Farrar, Straus & Giroux.

Slawson, W. David. 1971. Standard Form Contracts and Democratic Control of Lawmaking Power. *Harvard Law Review* 84:529–566.

Sloan, Frank A., Bridget A. Reilly, and Christoph M. Schenzler. 1994. Tort Liability Versus Other Approaches for Deterring Careless Driving. *International Review of Law and Economics* 14:53–71.

Smart, J. J. C. 1965. The Methods of Ethics and the Methods of Science. *Journal of Philosophy* 62:344–349.

————. 1973. An Outline of a System of Utilitarian Ethics. In *Utilitarianism: For and Against,* by J. J. C. Smart and Bernard Williams. Cambridge: Cambridge University Press.

Smith, Adam. [1790] 1976. *The Theory of Moral Sentiments.* Reprint of 6th ed. Edited by D. D. Raphael and A. L. Macfie. Oxford: Oxford University Press.

Smith, Steven K., Carol J. DeFrances, Patrick A. Langan, and John Goerdt. 1995.

Bureau of Justice Statistics, Tort Cases in Large Counties. Washington, D.C.: U.S. Department of Justice.

Speiser, Stuart M., Charles F. Krause, and Alfred W. Gans. 1983. *The American Law of Torts.* Rochester, N.Y.: Lawyers Cooperative Pub. Co.

Spence, A. Michael. 1975. Monopoly, Quality, and Regulation. *Bell Journal of Economics* 6:417–429.

———. 1977. Consumer Misperceptions, Product Failure and Producer Liability. *Review of Economic Studies* 44:561–572.

Sprigge, T. L. S. 1965. A Utilitarian Reply to Dr. McCloskey. *Inquiry* 8:264–291.

State Attorney Fee Shifting Statutes: Are We Quietly Repealing the American Rule? 1984. *Law and Contemporary Problems* 47 (Winter):321–346.

Steering Committee Report. 1989. American Law Institute Study on Paths to a "Better Way": Litigation, Alternatives, and Accommodation. *Duke Law Journal* 1989: 811–823.

Stephen, James Fitzjames. 1883. *A History of the Criminal Law of England.* London: Macmillan and Co.

Stigler, George J. 1970. The Optimum Enforcement of Laws. *Journal of Political Economy* 78:526–536.

———. 1972. The Law and Economics of Public Policy: A Plea to the Scholars. *Journal of Legal Studies* 1:1–12.

Stigler, George J., and Gary S. Becker. 1977. De Gustibus Non Est Disputandum. *American Economic Review* 67:76–90.

Stiglitz, Joseph E. 1987. Principal and Agent (II). In *The New Palgrave: A Dictionary of Economics,* edited by John Eatwell, Murray Milgate, and Peter Newman. Vol. 3. London: Macmillan Press.

Strotz, R. H. 1955–1956. Myopia and Inconsistency in Dynamic Utility Maximization. *Review of Economic Studies* 23:165–180.

———. 1958. How Income Ought To Be Distributed: A Paradox in Distributive Ethics. *Journal of Political Economy* 66:189–205.

Strudler, Alan. 1992. Mass Torts and Moral Principles. *Law and Philosophy* 11:297–330.

Subrin, Stephen N., and A. Richard Dykstra. 1974. Notice and the Right To Be Heard: The Significance of Old Friends. *Harvard Civil Rights–Civil Liberties Law Review* 9:449–480.

Sugarman, Stephen D. 1985. Doing Away with Tort Law. *California Law Review* 73: 555–664.

Summers, Robert S. 1974. Evaluating and Improving Legal Processes—A Plea for "Process Values." *Cornell Law Review* 60:1–52.

Sumner, L. W. 1996. *Welfare, Happiness, and Ethics.* Oxford and New York: Oxford University Press.

Sunstein, Cass R. 1986. Legal Interference with Private Preferences. *University of Chicago Law Review* 53:1129–1174.

———. 1996a. On the Expressive Function of Law. *University of Pennsylvania Law Review* 144:2021–2053.

———. 1996b. Social Norms and Social Roles. *Columbia Law Review* 96:903–968.

———. 1997. Bad Deaths. *Journal of Risk and Uncertainty* 14:259–282.

———, ed. 2000. *Behavioral Law and Economics*. Cambridge and New York: Cambridge University Press.

Symons, Donald. 1992. On the Use and Misuse of Darwinism in the Study of Human Behavior. In *The Adapted Mind: Evolutionary Psychology and the Generation of Culture*, edited by Jerome H. Barkow, Leda Cosmides, and John Tooby. New York: Oxford University Press.

Symposium: Law and Incommensurability. 1998. *University of Pennsylvania Law Review* 146:1169–1731.

Symposium: Law, Economics, and Norms. 1996. *University of Pennsylvania Law Review* 144:1643–2339.

Symposium on Efficiency As a Legal Concern. 1980. *Hofstra Law Review* 8:485–770.

Taylor, Charles. 1989. *Sources of the Self: The Making of the Modern Identity*. Cambridge, Mass.: Harvard University Press.

Ten, C. L. 1991. Crime and Punishment. In *A Companion to Ethics*, edited by Peter Singer. Oxford: Blackwell Reference.

Tengs, Tammy O., and John D. Graham. 1996. The Opportunity Costs of Haphazard Social Investments in Life-Saving. In *Risks, Costs, and Lives Saved: Getting Better Results from Regulation*, edited by Robert W. Hahn. New York: Oxford University Press.

Thaler, Richard, and Sherwin Rosen. 1976. The Value of Saving a Life: Evidence from the Labor Market. In *Household Production and Consumption*, edited by Nestor E. Terleckyj. New York: National Bureau of Economic Research.

Thibaut, John, and Laurens Walker. 1975. *Procedural Justice: A Psychological Analysis*. Hillsdale, N.J.: L. Erlbaum Associates.

Titmuss, Richard. 1971. *The Gift Relationship*. New York: Pantheon Books.

Tobias, Carl. 1994. Improving the 1988 and 1990 Judicial Improvements Acts. *Stanford Law Review* 46:1589–1634.

———. 1995. Common Sense and Other Legal Reforms. *Vanderbilt Law Review* 48:699–737.

———. 1998. Reforming Common Sense Legal Reforms. *Connecticut Law Review* 30:537–567.

Tonry, Michael. 1996. *Sentencing Matters*. New York: Oxford University Press.

Trangsrud, Roger H. 1985. Joinder Alternatives in Mass Tort Litigation. *Cornell Law Review* 70:779–849.

———. 1989. Mass Trials in Mass Tort Cases: A Dissent. *University of Illinois Law Review* 1989:69–88.

Trebilcock, Michael J. 1993. *The Limits of Freedom of Contract*. Cambridge, Mass.: Harvard University Press.

Tribe, Laurence H. 1972. Policy Science: Analysis or Ideology? *Philosophy and Public Affairs* 2:66–110.

———. 1973. Technology Assessment and the Fourth Discontinuity: The Limits of Instrumental Rationality. *Southern California Law Review* 46:617–660.

———. 1974. Ways Not To Think About Plastic Trees: New Foundations for Environmental Law. *Yale Law Journal* 83:1315–1348.

———. 1985. Constitutional Calculus: Equal Justice or Economic Efficiency? *Harvard Law Review* 98:592–621.

———. 1988. *American Constitutional Law*. 2d ed. Mineola, N.Y.: Foundation Press.

Trivers, Robert L. 1971. The Evolution of Reciprocal Altruism. *Quarterly Review of Biology* 46:35–57.

Trubek, David M., Austin Sarat, William L. F. Felstiner, Herbert M. Kritzer, and Joel B. Grossman. 1983. The Costs of Ordinary Litigation. *UCLA Law Review* 31:72–127.

Tuomala, Matti. 1990. *Optimal Income Tax and Redistribution*. Oxford and New York: Oxford University Press.

Tversky, Amos, and Daniel Kahneman. 1973. Availability: A Heuristic for Judging Frequency and Probability. *Cognitive Psychology* 5:207–232.

Tyler, Tom R. 1987. Procedural Justice Research. *Social Justice Research* 1:41–65.

———. 1990. *Why People Obey the Law*. New Haven: Yale University Press.

———. 1997. Citizen Discontent with Legal Procedures: A Social Science Perspective on Civil Procedure Reform. *American Journal of Comparative Law* 45:871–904.

Ullmann-Margalit, Edna. 1977. *The Emergence of Norms*. Oxford: Oxford University Press.

Urmson, J. O. 1953. The Interpretation of the Moral Philosophy of J. S. Mill. *Philosophical Quarterly* 3:33–39.

———. 1975. A Defence of Intuitionism. *Proceedings of the Aristotelian Society* 75:111–119.

U.S. Census Bureau, U.S. Department of Commerce. 1997. *Health Insurance Coverage: 1996—Table A*. At http://www.census.gov/hhes/hlthins/cover96/c96taba.html.

Van den Haag, Ernest. 1987. Punishment: Desert and Crime Control. *Michigan Law Review* 85:1250–1260.

Vanderschraaf, Peter. 1999. Game Theory, Evolution, and Justice. *Philosophy and Public Affairs* 28:325–358.

Vargo, John F. 1993. The American Rule on Attorney Fee Allocation: The Injured Person's Access to Justice. *American University Law Review* 42:1567–1636.

Vickrey, William. 1945. Measuring Marginal Utility by Reactions to Risk. *Econometrica* 13:319–333.

———. 1947. *Agenda for Progressive Taxation*. New York: Ronald Press Company.

Vidmar, Neil. 2000. Retribution and Revenge. Working Paper No. 2, Duke Law School Public Law and Legal Theory Working Paper Series.

Viscusi, W. Kip. 1992. *Fatal Tradeoffs: Public and Private Responsibilities for Risk*. New York: Oxford University Press.

———. 1993. The Value of Risks to Life and Health. *Journal of Economic Literature* 31:1912–1946.

———. 2000. Corporate Risk Analysis: A Reckless Act? *Stanford Law Review* 52:547–597.

Viscusi, W. Kip, and Wesley A. Magat. 1987. *Learning About Risk: Consumer and Worker Responses to Hazard Information.* Cambridge, Mass.: Harvard University Press.

Von Hirsch, Andrew. 1976. *Doing Justice: The Choice of Punishments.* New York: Hill and Wang.

———. 1985. *Past or Future Crimes: Deservedness and Dangerousness in the Sentencing of Criminals.* New Brunswick: Rutgers University Press.

Waal, Frans de. 1982. *Chimpanzee Politics.* New York: Harper & Row.

Waldron, Jeremy. 1992. Lex Talionis. *Arizona Law Review* 34:25–51.

Walker, Laurens, and John Monahan. 1998. Sampling Damages. *Iowa Law Review* 83:545–568.

———. 1999. Sampling Liability. *Virginia Law Review* 85:329–351.

Walker, Nigel, and Michael Argyle. 1963–1964. Does the Law Affect Moral Judgments? *British Journal of Criminology* 4:570–581.

Walzer, Michael. 1983. *Spheres of Justice: A Defense of Pluralism and Equality.* New York: Basic Books.

Wasserstrom, Richard A. 1967. H. L. A. Hart and the Doctrines of *Mens Rea* and Criminal Responsibility. *University of Chicago Law Review* 35:92–126.

———. 1977. Some Problems with Theories of Punishment. In *Justice and Punishment,* edited by J. B. Cederblom and William L. Blizek. Cambridge, Mass.: Ballinger Publishing Co.

Weber, Max. [1922] 1947. *The Theory of Social and Economic Organization.* Translated by A. M. Henderson and Talcott Parsons. New York: Oxford University Press.

Weinrib, Ernest J. 1983. Toward a Moral Theory of Negligence Law. *Law and Philosophy* 2:37–62.

———. 1989a. The Special Morality of Tort Law. *McGill Law Journal* 34:403–413.

———. 1989b. Understanding Tort Law. *Valparaiso University Law Review* 23:485–526.

———. 1992. Corrective Justice. *Iowa Law Review* 77:403–425.

———. 1994. The Gains and Losses of Corrective Justice. *Duke Law Journal* 44:277–297.

———. 1995. *The Idea of Private Law.* Cambridge, Mass.: Harvard University Press.

Weinstein, Jack B., and Eileen B. Hershenov. 1991. The Effect of Equity on Mass Tort Law. *University of Illinois Law Review* 1991:269–327.

Weisbrod, Burton A. 1977. Comparing Utility Functions in Efficiency Terms or, What Kind of Utility Functions Do We Want? *American Economic Review* 67:991–995.

Weizsäcker, Carl Christian von. 1971. Notes on Endogenous Change of Tastes. *Journal of Economic Theory* 3:345–372.

Wertheimer, Alan. 1975. Should Punishment Fit the Crime? *Social Theory and Practice* 3:403–423.

———. 1976. Deterrence and Retribution. *Ethics* 86:181–199.

———. 1977. Punishing the Innocent—Unintentionally. *Inquiry* 20:45–65.

West, Robin L. 1990. Taking Preferences Seriously. *Tulane Law Review* 64:659–703.

Westen, Peter. 1982. The Empty Idea of Equality. *Harvard Law Review* 95:537–596.

———. 1990. *Speaking of Equality: An Analysis of the Rhetorical Force of "Equality" in Moral and Legal Discourse.* Princeton: Princeton University Press.

Westermarck, Edward. 1932. *Ethical Relativity.* New York: Harcourt, Brace and Company.

White, Michelle J., and Yu-Ping Liao. 1999. No-Fault for Motor Vehicles: An Economic Analysis. University of Michigan Department of Economics, Paper No. 99–106.

Wiggins, David. 1998. Universalizability, Impartiality, Truth. In *Needs, Values, Truth: Essays in the Philosophy of Value.* 3d ed. Oxford: Oxford University Press.

Williams, Bernard. 1973. A Critique of Utilitarianism. In *Utilitarianism: For and Against,* by J. J. C. Smart and Bernard Williams. Cambridge: Cambridge University Press.

———. 1981. *Moral Luck: Philosophical Papers, 1973–1980.* Cambridge and New York: Cambridge University Press.

Wilson, Edward O. 1977. Biology and the Social Sciences. *Daedalus* 106, no. 4:127–140.

———. 1980. *Sociobiology.* Abr. ed. Cambridge, Mass.: Harvard University Press.

Wilson, James Q. 1993. *The Moral Sense.* New York: Free Press.

Wilson, James Q., and Richard J. Herrnstein. 1985. *Crime and Human Nature.* New York: Simon and Schuster.

Wilson, James Q., and George L. Kelling. 1982. Broken Windows: The Police and Neighborhood Safety. *Atlantic Monthly* (March 1982):29–38.

Wittman, Donald. 1974. Punishment as Retribution. *Theory and Decision* 4:209–237.

Wood, Ledger. 1938. Responsibility and Punishment. *Journal of the American Institute of Criminal Law and Criminology* 28:630–640.

Woolley, Patrick. 1997. Rethinking the Adequacy of Adequate Representation. *Texas Law Review* 75:571–630.

Wootton, Barbara. 1963. *Crime and the Criminal Law.* London: Stevens.

Wright, Charles Alan, and Arthur R. Miller. 1987. *Federal Practice and Procedure.* 2d ed. Vol. 4. St. Paul: West Pub. Co.

Wright, Charles Alan, Arthur R. Miller, and Edward H. Cooper. 1981. *Federal Practice and Procedure.* Vol. 18. St. Paul, Minn.: West Pub. Co.

Wright, Richard W. 1992. Substantive Corrective Justice. *Iowa Law Review* 77:625–711.

Yeazell, Stephen C. 1987. *From Medieval Group Litigation to the Modern Class Action.* New Haven: Yale University Press.

Yezer, Anthony M., Robert S. Goldfarb, and Paul J. Poppen. 1996. Does Studying Economics Discourage Cooperation? Watch What We Do, Not What We Say or How We Play. *Journal of Economic Perspectives* 10, no. 1:177–186.

Yorio, Edward, and Steve Thel. 1991. The Promissory Basis of Section 90. *Yale Law Journal* 101:111–167.

Zamir, Eyal. 1998. The Efficiency of Paternalism. *Virginia Law Review* 84:229–286.

INDEX

Abuse of power: protection against, 26n18, 39n48, 284–286, 406–407, 406n11, 407n12, 418n44, 447n104; limited by legal procedures, 26n18, 284–286, 284n153, 284n154–285n154, 285n156, 288; and well-being, 225, 384n7, 404n2, 406–407, 418n44; and welfare economics, 284–286, 384n7, 404n2, 406–407; Aristotle on, 284n154; Gross on, 284n154; Resnik on, 284n154; Scanlon on, 284n154–285n154; and notions of fairness, 384n7, 404n2, 406–407; Mill on, 404n2, 435n76; Tribe on, 404n2, 406n11; and utilitarianism, 404n2; constitutional provisions relating to, 406n11; by the majority against minority, 435n76, 446n100; and hypothetical consent, 441n93. *See also* Government decisionmakers; Paternalism, governmental

Accuracy in adjudication. *See under* Legal procedures

Act/omission distinction, 344n106–347n106, 434n72

Adjudication. *See under* Legal procedures

Administrative costs. *See* Costs, administrative

Alexander, Lawrence: on corrective justice, 152n165, 271n116; on procedural and substantive rights, 226n3; on legal costs, 251n63; on legal procedures, 251n63,

282n149; on retributive justice, 302n18, 326n70; on punishment, 302n18, 326n70, 336n91, 341nn99,101, 344n106; on punishment of the innocent, 341nn99, 101, 344n106; on ruling authorities, 401n45

Andenaes, Johannes: on deterrence, 292n2; on educative influence of criminal law, 293n6; on punishment and social norms, 370n161

Aquinas, Thomas: and the doctrine of double effect, 344n106

Árdal, Páll: on promise-keeping, 206n122

Arenella, Peter: on legal procedures, 253n66, 286n161; on right to participate, 281n145; on culpability, 370n159

Aristotle: and two-level moral analysis, 80n121; on corrective justice, 89n9, 91n12, 93n15, 94nn15,16, 95n17, 96n20, 115n76, 166n27; Posner on, 89n9, 91n12, 94n16, 95n17, 96n20; Weinrib on, 89n9, 93n15, 94n16, 96n20; Wright on, 93n15, 96n20, 115n76; Fletcher on, 96n20; Fuller and Perdue on, 166n27; on abuse of power, 284n154; on equality before the law, 447n102

Asymmetric/nonreciprocal contexts, 90n10, 113n70, 123n96; applications of notions of fairness making everyone worse off in, 52–54, 53n75–54n75, 55n76, 109n60,